VINCE

VINCE

a
Personal Biography
of
VINCE LOMBARDI

by
Michael O'Brien

William Morrow and Company, Inc.
New York

For Sally

Library of Congress Cataloging-in-Publication Data

O'Brien, Michael, 1943–
    Vince: a personal biography of Vince Lombardi.
    Bibliography: p.
    Includes index.
    1. Lombardi, Vince. 2. Football—United States—
Coaches—Biography. I. Title.
GV939.L6027   1987   796.332'092'4   87-12980
ISBN 0-688-07406-5

Printed in the United States of America

First Edition

1 2 3 4 5 6 7 8 9 10

BOOK DESIGN BY ART FOR CASH

Acknowledgments

I HAVE INCURRED MANY DEBTS FOR HELP IN PREPARING THIS BOOK AND AM delighted to express my deep gratitude. Rev. Thomas F. Brady provided important papers about Vince's training at Cathedral Preparatory Seminary; Brother Becket Ryan performed the same service for Saint Francis Preparatory School. Marie T. Capps, librarian at the U.S. Military Academy at West Point, expertly guided me through the papers at her disposal. Rev. Edward Dunn, archivist at the Fordham University Library, not only assisted my research, but fed and housed me during part of my stay at Fordham and diligently responded to all my requests. A special thanks also to Katherine O'Mahoney of Fordham for her friendly hospitality during my research in New York. Wellington Mara of the New York Giants, Tom Miller of the Green Bay Packers, and Edward Bennett Williams of the Washington Redskins made available important information about their respective teams. The *Green Bay Press-Gazette* and the *Milwaukee Journal* kindly consented to allow me to inspect their files.

Several persons graciously allowed me to use their personal papers. Among them were Tim Cohane, Roger Fay, William Fetridge, W. C. Heinz, Ruth McKloskey, Joseph McPartland, and Russell Reeder. Patrick Best provided an early and important list of persons to interview. Thanks also must go to the over two hundred persons I interviewed. With

Acknowledgments

few exceptions they were frank, informative, and patient. Only on occasion did some individuals request that they not be named in connection with certain statements.

I have placed a heavy burden on present and former secretaries at the University of Wisconsin Center–Fox Valley who have, nonetheless, responded unfailingly with good humor and patience, and, above all, with expert typing. For this I am indebted to Gail Abendroth, Audrey Herlache, Kathy Hosmer, Mary Kessler, and Connie Klister. April Kain-Breese and Patricia Warmbrunn, librarians at the UWC–Fox Valley, efficiently processed all of my interlibrary loan requests. Former Dean Rue Johnson kindly supported my project from the start and tried to accommodate all my requests for assistance. The University of Wisconsin–Fox Cities Foundation, Inc., provided two small but timely grants, and the University of Wisconsin awarded me a sabbatical during a critical stage of my writing.

This is not an authorized biography. I never met Vince Lombardi and did not seek the approval of the Lombardi family to write my study. Nonetheless, I deeply appreciate the warm hospitality and the assistance of Vince's son and daughter. Vince Lombardi, Jr., and his wife, Jill, welcomed me to their home in Bloomfield Hills, Michigan, to inspect their portion of the family's papers. Moreover, Vince, Jr., helped to secure valuable educational and medical records of his father. Susan (Lombardi) Bickham of Plantation, Florida, provided assistance and advice while I researched her portion of the family's papers. Despite the affection they hold for their father and their natural desire to influence my opinion of him, Vince, Jr., and Susan did not attempt to restrict my research in any way, and left me completely free to gather and interpret the facts. For their respect for truth, I am grateful.

Two of my colleagues, Theda McLaren and Daniel Putman, offered valuable suggestions for improving specific aspects of the biography. Len Wagner, Chuck Johnson, and Benjamin Rader read several chapters and gave valuable advice. Several friends and critics read large portions of the manuscript, offering their encouragement, insights, and painstaking critiques. For their efforts I deeply appreciate David Brunet, Paul Hass William Skelton, and Robert Zieger.

Three persons deserve special thanks. Rev. Kenneth Moore maintained an interest in my project for several years and offered intelligent insights and suggestions of persons to contact. His delightful brother, Rev. Timothy Moore, chauffeured me around New Jersey and New York, furnished food and lodging, and directed me through the valuable papers stored at St. Cecilia High School. Finally, my deep gratitude to William

N. Wallace, who with wit and intelligence served as my advisor, critic, and friend. Above all, he provided crucial encouragement, sustaining me during the darkest hours of this project.

My wife, Sally, weathered her husband's second book and again did so with patience, encouragement, and love. Also thanks to Tim, Sean, Jeremy, and Carey for many reasons.

Contents

Introduction • 13

I • *The Early Years* • 19

II • *College at Fordham (1933–37)* • 34

III • *St. Cecilia High School (1939–47)* • 51

IV • *Back to Fordham (1947–48)* • 77

V • *West Point (1949–53)* • 86

VI • *New York Giants (1954–58)* • 107

VII • *The First Year* • 129

VIII • *Drive for Championships (1960–66)* • 153

IX • *The Man and His Beliefs* • 181

X • *The Community, the Franchise, and the General Manager* • 210

XI • *The Media* • 224

XII • *Player Relations: Teaching, Preparation, and Motivation* • 236

XIII • *Leisure, Home, and Family* • 269

XIV • *The Dramatic Year (1967)* • 290

XV • *The Agony of Retirement* • 310

XVI • *Washington Redskins* • 338

XVII • *Illness and Death* • 369

Epilogue • 377

Notes • 384

Sources • 441

Index • 449

Introduction

It WAS ALMOST UNPRECEDENTED. VINCE LOMBARDI, ALWAYS PUNCTUAL, RE-nowned for insisting his players show up for meetings on Lombardi time—fifteen minutes early—was himself late to arrive at the projection room in the New York television studio. He was nervous, as anyone would be under the circumstances. He was about to watch his life unfold on the screen because on the forthcoming Sunday, September 15, 1968, CBS would preempt *The Ed Sullivan Show* to broadcast the fifty-one-minute television special titled simply, "Lombardi." Vince had come to see the preview.[1]

Stocky, strong, healthy-looking at fifty-five, with an extra crop of white in his hair the only visible change in his appearance since he arrived in Green Bay in 1959, Vince had been a fabulously successful coach. During nine years as coach of the Green Bay Packers his teams had won 141 of 184 games, five NFL championships, and the first two Super Bowls. "He is respected, admired, looked on with awe as if he were some great natural phenomenon like the Grand Canyon or the Rocky Mountains," wrote a columnist for the *Green Bay Press-Gazette* only a month earlier. "He has become, in this part of the land, an epic hero—a man who will always find a way to emerge triumphant."[2]

Thanks to television and football's popularity, Vince was a hero far beyond Green Bay and Wisconsin, and for more reasons than just his coaching prowess. He had become a symbol of the virtues needed to succeed in anything. A dynamic speaker and popular philosopher, he equated football with life and mesmerized business executives with his maxims on leadership, discipline, authority, dedication, courage, and the will to win. Earlier in 1968 rumor had circulated he would run for a major political office, and no one doubted he could have been a formidable candidate. Vince had retired from coaching after the 1967 season but had retained his duties as general manager of the Packers. He missed coaching, especially his rapport with the players and the "fire on Sunday." Restless and bored, he was quietly contemplating a way to return to the profession he knew best.

The film Vince was about to view was produced for NFL Films by Ed Sabol, one of the first persons with a camera to appreciate fully the possibility of linking football with the spectacular. A camera crew had shadowed Vince for more than a year, and had wired him for sound in several games. Vince had reserved the right to edit some material, but chose to delete only a few family scenes. He was the last to arrive in the projection room. NFL Commissioner Pete Rozelle, CBS Vice President Bill MacPhail, and over two dozen reviewers were waiting for him. He found a seat in the next-to-last row, having walked the entire length of the aisle to take the last seat up against the wall, isolating himself. Only then did the lights dim.[3]

The film was brisk and concise—a good summary of Vince's career. It opened with montage shots of the Green Bay Packers in action. Paul Hornung, Vince's great playboy halfback, had the first speaking part, a shock opener. "Coach Lombardi probably is the most hated man in football," Hornung began. Vince, watching and listening in the studio, laughed nervously. Hornung then explained that the only reason anybody hated Vince was because he was a bear for perfection. Much of the film consisted of interviews with Marie Lombardi, former players, and football teachers who praised Vince, making the film sound like a eulogy. Earl "Red" Blaik, Vince's mentor at West Point, recalled his highly volatile and enthusiastic assistant coach. Bart Starr, the Packers' quarterback, explained that Vince made a player feel that if he played less than his best he was cheating himself, his teammates, and his Maker. "You grow in stature under Vince," said Starr. Jerry Kramer, the Packers' right guard and articulate author of *Instant Replay,* said at one point: "I don't think anybody knows what he can do before he tries. He makes sure you try."[4]

The film moved quickly through Vince's life history: childhood and high school in Brooklyn, college and football at Fordham, coach and teacher at St. Cecilia High School, assistant coach at West Point and the New York Giants. The narration was just barely short of total adulation. A grim voice kept intoning, "Vincent Thomas Lombardi." In the darkened studio Vince must have winced at some of the narrator's lines: "How does such a man begin the inward search? . . . How much can a man ask of himself? . . . He thinks of everybody on the club as his child . . . with nothing at stake but their pride and dignity."[5]

There were many dramatic action shots of the Packers, and Vince on the sideline, during the tense 1967 season as he drove his team to a third consecutive world championship. The sideline scenes provided a striking contrast: The interviews were laced with statements describing Vince's kind nature and good works, but the sideline shots showed his fierce competitiveness and explosive anger. When things were going bad he looked pale, somber, incredulous. Then, suddenly, there was a change, a different insight. "What the hell's going on out here?" he hollered, his tight, dark features compressed into creases. "That's interference! Can't you see it?" When the referee remained unconvinced, Vince slammed his program down on the field. He prowled the sideline like a prison guard, bawling at his players. To linebacker Lee Roy Caffey he said, "I tell you, Lee, if you don't shape up, you're not going to have a job."[6]

On December 9, 1967, the Packers played the Rams in Los Angeles. The game was crucial for the Rams but meaningless for the Packers, who had already clinched their division. Yet Vince desperately wanted to win and had vigorously motivated his players to play for their pride. On the film Vince exults when Travis Williams runs a kickoff back for a touchdown, but then he heads quickly toward defensive coach Phil Bengtson and says sharply, "Hey, Phil, get your defense together, will you, please!" With less than a minute remaining, the Packers led, 24–20, and were ready to punt.

"Do you want [Don] Chandler to punt?" Dave Hanner, one of Vince's assistants, asks.

"No!" yells Vince angrily. "I don't want him to punt. Why the hell would I want him to punt?"

"He's a quicker kicker," says Hanner.

"[Donny] Anderson is our regular punter," snaps Vince. "The other guy hasn't been punting. Suppose he kicks a line drive and they run it back?"

Of course, Vince had his way. Anderson punted—or tried to. The Rams blocked his attempt, scored a touchdown a few plays later, and won the game, 27–24. Vince's apparent mistake was there for millions of viewers to see and hear. Sabol had earlier asked Vince if he wanted to cut out the scene, but Vince said, "Let it go."[7]

The film elicited considerable media comment and scores of touching letters praising Vince's leadership and dedication. One from a Catholic seminarian said, "You, Mr. Lombardi, have added to my view of life. You have enlarged my vision of the world we live in, and I know the words you speak, the leadership you show, the philosophy you live will help me to help others. . . . I think you looked for a man that would drive forward even though he suffered, even though he was injured. . . . Your philosophy has helped me push on."[8]

However, there were other points of view. Critics complained that the film was a one-dimensional tribute, overloaded with "clichés," "platitudes," and "mawkishness." Some reviewers had earlier covered Vince and been offended by his rude attitude toward reporters. To them he was merely a successful martinet, a gruff taskmaster, a single-dimension person with a heart of stone. "If they were gonna make a movie about a saint, how come they got that gargoyle of a football coach to play the main part?"[9]

Critics charged that Vince's philosophy was as obnoxious and dangerous as his tyrannical rule. Examples:

"To play this game, you must have that fire in you, and there is nothing that stokes that fire like hate."

"I believe a coach must be a pedagogue. He has to pound the lessons into the players by rote, the same way you teach pupils in the classroom."

"Pro football . . . is a violent, dangerous sport To play it other than violently would be imbecile."

"Winning isn't the most important thing; it's the only thing."

"I think the rights of the individual have been put above everything else. . . . The individual has to have every respect for authority regardless of what authority is."

In sum, several critics charged, Vince's rude behavior, dictatorial rule, and frightening values were hardly a model for anyone. Surely he was not a shining exemplar of sport. "Is it really so necessary to win if Lombardi's formula is the price one must pay to do it?" The film was merely a "flag-waving, apple pie, pro-establishment program"; it canonized the "saint, known as Success."[10]

Overall, Vince seemed pleased with the film, happy that it didn't reveal more about him. After the preview he met with reporters.

"Well," he told them, "that film was a little nicer than people think I am."

"You mean it was cleaned up?"

"What do you mean, 'cleaned up'?" snapped Vince

"You know, the language."

"I never used language!" Vince shouted, reverting to selective memory. "I never used language in my life!" Vince finished drinking his Scotch and water and resumed his dialogue.

"A film like that exposes you, a man shouldn't be exposed. I don't know of anyone who wants to be exposed Fortunately, too much won't be exposed."[11]

I

The Early Years

VINCE LOMBARDI'S ANCESTORS WERE AMONG THE MILLIONS OF IMMIGRANTS WHO fled southern Italy, one of the poorest, most backward regions of Europe. For centuries reactionary monarchial regimes had ignored the southerners, who lived on the worn-out parched soil. In the last decades of the nineteenth century the region experienced near economic collapse. Agriculture suffered a severe depression, and the scourges of nature— earthquakes, volcanic eruptions, floods, and disease—intensified the despair, sapping the strength of both the people and the land, and weakening the bonds that tied the peasants to their villages. The northern Italians, who were more educated, skilled, and wealthy, looked with disdain on the illiterate, unskilled, and seemingly shiftless southerners.[1]

Of the five million Italians who arrived in the United States between 1876 and 1930, 80 percent were from the south. Most of the southern arrivals were poor and illiterate and over three quarters were farm workers or laborers, meaning they had no skill of value in the urban, industrial setting of the United States. Southern Italians usually settled in large American cities where dozens of "little Italys," many of them squalid slums, dotted the city landscape. They congregated in neighborhoods with others from the same region, recreating urban villages or the Italian country town in the city environment. Because they arrived in such huge numbers over a short period of time, New York and other cities had difficulty absorbing and guiding them, and they fared poorly in terms of occupational, educational, and social mobility.[2]

The flood of southern Italians (and other immigrants from southern and eastern Europe) aroused intense opposition. "The sewer is unchoked," ranted one nativist. "Europe is vomiting. She is pouring her scum on the American shore." Bias against southern Italians could be found almost everywhere. Immigrants were abused in public, cheated of wages, pelted in the streets, cuffed at work, fined and jailed on the smallest pretense, lynched by nativist mobs, and crowded into the reeking slums. Racists condemned them for being among the "brownish" races; sometimes they were lumped together with the blacks—"the Dagoes are just as bad as the Negroes." In the American South whites often denied them their whiteness, and Louisiana barred them from white schools. Nativist sentiment led to the Immigration Restriction Act of 1924, which set up a quota system that deliberately and unashamedly discriminated against southern Italians and others from southern and eastern Europe. As late as the 1940s studies of prejudice listed Italian-Americans near the bottom of American preferences.[3]

For all the hardship and the discrimination, the southern Italians had powerful virtues. Most were sober, frugal, and hard-working. Although the poorest immigrants in New York City, they had the lowest rates of pauperism. Only a small fraction wound up on relief. They were religious and sought the protection of the Catholic Church, the symbol of permanence and security that upheld the deepest values of Italian life. Above all, they valued the family. The Italian family was a stronghold in a hostile land, a bastion of warmth and security for its members. Divorce, separation, and desertion were rare. Married sons and daughters tended to stay close to their parents. Relatives helped one another to immigrate, shared households, loaned money, and assisted in the search for jobs. Families were bound closely by the strongest cements—a little wine, much talk, and much laughter. No Italian who had a family was ever alone.[4]

Vince's grandfather and namesake, Vincent Lombardi, had lived near Salerno, Italy, where he probably worked as a silk merchant. In 1892 he and his wife came to this country, apparently in search of a thief who had stolen his silk and had fled to the United States. In New York, Vincent went into the hauling business, first using horses and wagons, then modernized and bought trucks. The couple raised four children. Enrico, the second oldest, had been born in Italy on November 26, 1890. At some point the name Enrico was dropped and the name Harry adopted instead.

Vincent died while the children were still young, leaving his widow to raise them in a tenement flat on Mott Street on Manhattan's Lower East Side, only a block from Mulberry Street, the center of America's most infamous slum. In the daytime Mulberry Street resembled the marketplace in a town in southern Italy, but the color and ebullience could not conceal the misery and the high rates of death and disease caused by the overcrowded, wretched conditions. The tenement was a small, dark, stuffy, dirty hopeless place. Harry played in filthy streets and vile alleys. Few escaped the disreputable conditions unharmed, and the experience coarsened and hardened Harry. Yet he persevered and emerged with strong character, ambition, and a deep concern for the welfare of friends and loved ones.[5]

To support his widowed mother, Harry quit school after the fifth grade to work in a butcher shop. He learned the business well, saved his money, and shortly before World War I he and his brother Eddie pooled their resources to open a wholesale meat business on West Twelfth Street in the market district. For years he strove to build the business, usually working eleven hours a day, six days a week. Although he wasn't educated, experience made him a wise manager, and the small business prospered even through the Depression.[6]

Harry's friend, Frank Izzo, introduced Harry to his sister, Matilda Izzo. Harry was twenty-one and Matilda twenty when they married on September 5, 1912. Matilda's family background was similar to Harry's, except her life had not been scorched by the slums. Her father, Anthony Izzo, came to the United States in the mid-1880s when he was about eighteen. Anthony and his wife, Loretta, had come from Vietri di Potenza, a small village forty miles east of Salerno in the province of Potenza, one of Italy's poorest provinces. Anthony became a barber in New York, a common occupation among Italians there. Seeking a more peaceful, healthy environment, he quickly guided his young family out of the slums. Around 1893 he opened a barber shop in the village of Sheepshead Bay, Brooklyn, and bought a large home with extensive property at 2519 East Sixteenth Street. He hoped to take advantage of the flourishing trade there among the summer visitors and the racetrack crowd and to raise his family in a new, middle-class residential area.[7]

Anthony and Loretta had thirteen children, eight boys and five girls, and when the children married and raised their own families, most remained in Sheepshead Bay, leaving the area heavily populated with the Izzo offspring. "We almost felt like royalty in Sheepshead Bay," said one of the clan; "we were the Izzos." Matilda, the third child, was born on January 17, 1892. After completing eight years of school, she stayed at home to help her parents take care of the large family. Following their marriage, Harry and Matilda lived briefly in an apartment, and then about 1915 they purchased a home at 2542 East Fourteenth Street, only two blocks from Matilda's parents.[8]

Sheepshead Bay had been founded by a strong-minded, independent woman, Lady Deborah Moody, who had squabbled with seventeenth-century Puritan authorities in Massachusetts, been excommunicated, and had led a small band of followers to a new home in New Amsterdam. In 1645 she received the Gravesend Patent to seven thousand acres of land, of which the southeast portion became known as Sheepshead Bay. The area's most prominent feature was a small bay connecting to the Atlantic Ocean. Coney Island in the southwestern part of Gravesend became a popular resort after 1840, but Sheepshead Bay slumbered into the nineteenth century, a small rural hamlet of fishermen and farmers and a paradise for visiting hunters and sports fishermen. In 1894 Gravesend became part of Brooklyn, which merged four years later with Greater New York.

The community changed drastically in 1880 after it was selected as the site of a huge racetrack. Promoters acquired farmland and built a track so splendid that it rivaled the Kentucky Derby and established the area as a resort center. The track attracted the sporting set, including the Vanderbilts and the Astors, and so many wealthy New Yorkers built elegant Victorian mansions that Emmons Avenue along the bay was nicknamed Millionaires Row. Fine hotels and restaurants sprang up along the water, and Brighton and Manhattan beaches attracted thousands of bathers daily. The racetrack prospered, but it lured such a motley swarm of sharpies and crooks that in 1910 the eminently respectable Governor Charles Evans Hughes outlawed racing in the city and the track was closed. Nonetheless, the seaside activities flourished.

Until World War I little development had taken place in the inland sections of Sheepshead Bay, and extensive farmland remained into the 1930s. It was inland that Harry and Matilda bought their three bedroom, two-story frame home in a neighborhood of many nationalities but mainly of hard-working Irish and Italian families.[9]

Vincent Thomas Lombardi was born on June 11, 1913, in the second-floor bedroom of the Izzo home on Sixteenth Street. Over a seventeen-year period there followed four more children—Madeline, Harold, Claire, and Joe—so that Vince was almost a generation older than his youngest brother. The Lombardis' experience resembled that of most Italian-Americans: the supportive, tight-knit family, the nearby relatives, faith in the Catholic Church, and the bitter taste of discrimination. It differed most notably in that Harry and Matilda raised their children away from the degrading slums. The Lombardis were not poor. They lived in a pleasant house in a decent neighborhood and had enough money for all the necessities. "We were never hungry," said Madeline; "we never missed anything in life."

Harry Lombardi was a short, stocky, powerfully built man who intimidated people with his brusque, stern manner and his volatile temperament. Underneath, though, Harry was kind and loving. "His heart weighed a thousand pounds," stated an Izzo relative. Constantly striving to provide his children with benefits and opportunities denied him as a youth, Harry moved his family to a better home in Flatbush in 1933, and then in 1941 to a better one in Englewood, New Jersey. "Whenever we moved, it was always up," Madeline observed. Both Harry and Matilda strongly encouraged their children's education, and their three sons received college degrees.[10]

Harry had been taught to work hard, and he saw nothing wrong with the way he was brought up. The virtues of work were obvious and required no discussion. His sons must help out so the family could maintain its toehold in the new world. At the butcher shop young Vince had the unpleasant task of lugging huge sides of meat and cutting up beef and pork carcasses. He detested the work, but it helped develop his powerful physique. When Harry decided to fix the basement under the house and tear down an old barn in the backyard, Vince had to help, and the work had to be performed exactly as Harry directed. "There was only right and wrong," Vince recalled, "and he believed that you only did the right thing all the time. He was a perfectionist. He was a perfectionist if there ever was one." When the work passed Harry's inspection, Vince was paid in cash. Harry paid no allowance; you had to earn your money with him.

Harry's volatile temper and harsh discipline scarred Vince, who, nonetheless, developed a similar temperament and a similar approach to life. Harry's word was law and he countenanced no back talk. By the time the younger children arrived he had mellowed slightly, but with Vince he was consistently stern and often verbally abusive. He also delivered physical punishment. Vince later downplayed the effects of his father's rage, observing that when "there was one of those violent scenes, . . . he was not one to remember it any more than I am when I chew out a boy and fifteen minutes later can't tell you who it was." Despite the harsh regimentation, Vince recalled fondly his father's most important advice. "Before you can do what you want to do," Harry told him, "before you can exist as an individual, the first thing you have to accept is duty, the second thing is respect for authority, and the third . . . is to develop a strong mental discipline."[11]

Vince inherited most of his softer qualities from Matilda, who was warm, gracious, and sensitive. Her family meant everything to her. Meticulous in keeping up her appearance and her house, she was also a marvelous cook, who entertained scores of friends, neighbors, and relatives. On Sunday she started serving dinner at 2:00 P.M., and Harry wouldn't allow the children to leave the table until she finished serving, usually three or four hours later. Like many Italian wives, she appeared to live in the shadow of her husband, but in subtle ways she helped direct the household. She was understanding, thought things out carefully, and acted as the family's peacemaker. "My father thought he [ruled the roost] and my mother led him to believe he did," observed Vince's brother Harold.[12]

Vince had to supervise and protect the younger children. Harry told Vince what to do and Vince told his brothers and sisters, an old custom in Italian families. At times Madeline thought Vince was a bully. "I just thought he was too tough," she said. Yet they shared friends and fun together, and Vince watched over her. "I would just follow Vince," she recalled. "Whatever he did, I did."[13]

Vince occasionally visited his grandmother, who still lived in the tenement on Mott Street. Thanks to civic reformers, living conditions had improved, but the neighborhood remained overcrowded, and the Italian atmosphere was still predominant. The neighborhood fascinated him. On his way to her flat Vince passed by sidewalk markets with their delicious green vegetables, and a pasta shop with its window filled with boxes of ravioli, spaghetti, macaroni, noodles, and loaves of bread three feet long. From his grandmother's balcony he watched the Italian women shopping and the children playing. Yet as a youngster Vince had been ambivalent about his heritage because he knew that many Americans held contempt for the southern Italians. He encountered no serious problems where he lived in Sheepshead Bay, thanks to his close-knit family, nearby relatives, insular location, and the tolerant attitude of his friendly, multiethnic neighbors, but the world beyond Sheepshead Bay degraded the southern Italians and the realization hurt. Many viewed them as poor, ignorant, uncouth, unskilled, dark-skinned strangers. Militant activists had been hysterically warning of the "Italian problem."

"Being Italian was not the thing to be in those days," mused Madeline in later years. She and her brother were "kind of ashamed." Vince showed no interest in learning his Italian language and culture, and as much as he loved Grandma Lombardi, he cringed when she visited Vince and his family in Sheepshead Bay because she spoke only Italian. Nonetheless, Vince deeply resented any anti-Italian slur. Unthinking, insensitive friends insulted both him and Madeline. "You're my favorite guinea," they would say, as Madeline and Vince bridled. Vince beat up one boy for using such an ethnic slur.[14]

St. Mark's Catholic Church, only a block away, was the center of many of the family's activities, and much of its loyalty focused on the sacred, wooden building. Harry Lombardi walked to mass daily, and Vince usually did also, particularly during Lent. Sunday mass was obligatory. "We thought we were going to be struck dead if we didn't go to church even if we were sick," said Madeline. The kind pastor, Father Daniel J. McCarthy, took an active interest in the spiritual welfare of parish youngsters. He often dined at the Lombardi home and took Vince and other boys to baseball games and to picnics at Coney Island. Vince was an altar boy at St. Mark's and an exceptionally conscientious one. If he had to serve at 7:00 A.M. mass, he arrived at 6:40 A.M. and grew indignant at a late-arriving partner. At funerals and other special church ceremonies the altar boy carrying the cross held the place of honor and marched at the head of the procession. Vince always insisted on having the place of honor. "He was determined that he would carry the cross and that I would carry the candle," recalled Paul Morris, a friend and fellow server.[15]

With over fifty young Izzo cousins and nephews living in Sheepshead Bay, Vince had no problem finding playmates. His closest friend was a neighbor, Joe Goettisheim. Both were altar boys at St. Mark's and attended school together. They played games, and went to the beach, to baseball and football games, and to cowboy movies at the two local theaters. "We never bothered with girls," said Goettisheim. Even in youthful games, Vince occasionally found defeat hard to accept. When he played the card game Hearts, he reacted furiously when a player stuck him with the queen of spades and had thirteen points charged against him.[16]

Vince and his family and friends spent much of the summer at nearby Brighton and Manhattan beaches, the summer playground for millions of New Yorkers. The streets and walkways near the beaches teemed with people strolling about or heading for the outdoor bowling alleys, golf ranges, games, amusements, refreshment stands, lounges, and restaurants. Popular bands entertained thousands nightly in a huge shell, and fireworks displays lit up the sky. Starting at about age seventeen, Vince worked five consecutive summers at Brighton Beach as a lifeguard, maintenance man, and special policeman.[17]

Vince loved sports, and although Goettisheim didn't, Vince dragged him to watch New York Yankee and Brooklyn Dodger baseball games. Vince's primary interest was football. "Come on, Joe," Vince would say, "let's go to the Polo Grounds." Watching Bo Molenda, a star fullback for the professional New York Giants, particularly fascinated him. Vince played football on the sandlots of Brooklyn, where many New York youths learned the game. Players collected their rudimentary equipment, collared friends, and played a partially organized game that Vince helped to organize. "He had leadership even then," said Madeline. "He was a perfectionist even in sandlot football. You played it right or you didn't play it at all." Harry encouraged him, but Matilda worried he would get hurt. Vince never explained how he became attracted to football as a youth. Perhaps it was the excitement of the tactics, the strategy, and the violence. He probably found release from deeply buried emotions and earned respect among his peers.[18]

At age fifteen, Vince made a vocational decision that ended sadly. He had attended grade school at P.S. 206, a sixteen-block walk from his home. (His brothers and sisters later went to St. Mark's Catholic School, but that facility hadn't opened in time for Vince to attend.) Then in the fall of 1929, he enrolled as a high-school freshman at Cathedral Prep, the abbreviated name of Cathedral College of the Immaculate Conception, Preparatory Seminary. The school was a preseminary run by the Catholic Diocese of Brooklyn for boys who intended to be priests. Vince never explained why he entered the school nor why he left three years later. Religion was always an intensely personal matter with him, and he seldom talked about it. A reporter coaxed a few thoughts from him in 1967. "I've got a great deal of faith in God," he said, "a great deal of dependency on God. I don't think I'd do anything without that dependency." As the deeply religious, eldest son in a deeply religious family, he may have thought it was expected of him. He and his parents probably talked over the decision with Father McCarthy.[19]

Located in a large, handsome building on Atlantic Avenue in Brooklyn, Cathedral Prep had opened in 1915. The school had a six-year program: four years of high school and two years of college liberal arts. Vince lived at home and had summers free, like other high-school students. Dating, while not forbidden, was discouraged, and an odd feature in the weekly schedule—the fact that students took Thursday off and attended classes on Saturday—partially curbed the future priests' contact with young women.

Vince took traditional high-school courses in history, English, math, and science. The major difference from other parochial high schools was the requirement of four years of Latin and three of Greek. Naturally, spiritual development was the primary focus of the school. Students had to attend daily Mass and have their local pastor sign a card confirming their attendance. A weekly confession was recommended, and special Masses, devotions, and retreats dotted the school calendar. Vince was a conscientious student and maintained a B+ average. He was also respected by his classmates. The school broke each class into sections of about thirty-five students. There were three sections in Vince's freshman class and two thereafter, and fellow students elected him president of his section all three years.[20]

Cathedral aimed to mold priests, not athletes, and consequently placed little emphasis on sports, but Vince took advantage of all that was available. The school had no football program but did field basketball and baseball teams, both coached by a layman, John Crane. The teams competed against New York area parochial schools and usually fared poorly. In Vince's freshman year Cathedral's intramural basketball program provided the most dramatic sports event, with Vince as one of the heroes. Each class section organized a team and played in a league divided into a Junior Division (high school freshmen and sophomores) and a Senior Division (juniors, seniors, and college students). The winner of each division played in the championship game, in which the Senior Division invariably crushed their younger, smaller schoolmates. Vince played guard on the Junior Division champions, who were matched against the college sophomores for the championship. "It did indeed seem that a veritable slaughter was in the making," said the school annual. Surprisingly, the "little fellows" won, 26–22, and Vince was awarded first-team honors on the All-Class Basketball Team.[21]

In his sophomore year he played center on the junior varsity, but his team won only four of thirteen games. Nonetheless, the school's annual tabbed him as the team's "star" for two reasons: his rugged defensive abilities—he held opposing centers to a total of two points in the opening six games—and his talent for controlling the crucial center jump at a time when the jump ball occurred after every basket. On offense, though, Vince was overly deliberate and a poor shooter, and he averaged less than three points a game. Still, his assets won him promotion to the varsity at the end of the season, but he seldom played. He remained on the varsity his entire junior year, but since Cathedral had few talented athletes and confronted a murderous schedule against the city's finest parochial-school teams, the team took a terrible beating, winding up with a 2–16 record. Students lost interest, and few attended the games. Vince was the second-string guard and forward. Because he had almost stopped growing, at 5-8 he could no longer compete at center against varsity competition. He saw little action during the season and scored only nine points.[22]

On the Cathedral baseball team Vince was a journeyman outfielder, and also became the substitute catcher after his determined performance in a game against Brooklyn Prep. When the regular catcher was injured, Coach Crane asked for a volunteer replacement, and Vince stepped forward immediately, even though he had no experience at the position. His loyalty to the team and his courage in accepting the difficult assignment won the lasting respect of Coach Crane. Vince's catching prowess in the game, while aggressive, was not particularly successful. Early in the contest Brooklyn Prep had a player on second base. As he attempted to steal third, the batter leaned in front of Vince, successfully obstructing his throw. The same situation occurred again a few innings later, only this time when the player attempted to steal third and the batter leaned forward, Vince took his left hand and knocked the batter to the dirt. Unfortunately, his throw sailed over the third baseman's head into left field.[23]

In mid-June 1932, after final exams, Vince left Cathedral Prep, having decided that the priesthood was not for him. Leaving after three years of prayer and dedicated preparation was a traumatic experience, and he probably felt he had failed in some way. Years later, even among close friends and relatives, he wouldn't discuss the subject. He deflected questions from prying reporters. Why had he changed his mind about being a priest? one asked him in 1967. "Oh, nothing," Vince answered and then waited silently for the next question. "The Greek got him," his father speculated, but that possibility seems remote, since Vince did excellent work afterward in his Greek studies. Perhaps the rule of celibacy seemed too formidable. "It was the only decision Vin made in his life," observed Madeline, "that did not have the courage of his convictions." Most likely, Vince thought he did not have the proper attributes or a strong enough desire to continue preparation for a most difficult vocation.[24]

He left with no lasting bitterness. On the contrary, he later praised the instruction he received at Cathedral, contributed large sums of money to training centers and charities managed by priests and nuns, and developed a large number of close friendships with priests. In 1964 a thirteen-year-old boy from Chicago wrote him asking the coach's advice about entering a Catholic seminary. "Trust in God," Vince responded in a touching personal note. "If you have the vocation to become a priest you will be a very fortunate young man."[25]

After he decided to leave the seminary he formed an ambitious new plan: He would play football his senior year in high school and play well enough to win a college scholarship. The plan started off much better than he could have expected. School officials at St. Francis Prep in Brooklyn, who had learned of Vince's skill on the Brooklyn sandlots, had just embarked on an ambitious program to win recognition as a gridiron power and offered Vince one of its new football scholarships, worth $150 in tuition and books. The generous offer suited Vince's goals perfectly, and in the late summer of 1932, he enrolled.

In 1858 two Franciscan brothers and three other teachers had founded St. Francis Academy, a primitive school in an old house on Baltic Street and the first private Catholic school on Long Island. By 1932 the Baltic Street site included a monastary, a grade school, and a high school in a three-story, yellow-brick building so dilapidated observers wondered how it ever could pass a building inspection. An "atmosphere of poverty" pervaded the school, a teacher recalled. Three hundred male students—mostly Irish, Polish, and Italian boys from medium- and low-income families—attended the high school.[26]

The heavy emphasis on football had begun a year or two before Vince's arrival. When Brother Jerome, the principal, asked Brooklyn Prep, its Jesuit competitor, to schedule a football game, an official at the Jesuit school rebuffed him, allegedly remarking that St. Francis was not a worthy opponent and should first establish a football reputation before asking Brooklyn Prep for a game. The insult incensed Brother Jerome. "I will make St. Francis the elite school of Brooklyn," he told a faculty meeting shortly after. To achieve his goal he started handing out football scholarships to outstanding athletes. The team quickly became a power-house in the New York area, but the new program hurt the school's academic reputation because many of the recruits were poor students. The faculty split on the wisdom of granting such scholarships, and other schools criticized St. Francis for its recruiting practices. Even the assistant football coach, Salvator "Tut" Maggio, thought the school acquired a "bad reputation" while the program lasted. Vince was not part of the problem, however, since he was both a good student and a good football player, but he gained more recognition by playing for such an outstanding team.[27]

His coach was outstanding as well. Portly, energetic Harry Kane was one of the most renowned and successful high-school coaches in New York. In the course of building the football program, Brother Jerome had lured him away from Commerce High School in New York, where he had turned out championship teams. Among his protégés was the great Lou

Gehrig, an outstanding football player before he became a baseball star of the New York Yankees. Knicknamed the "silver-thatched orator" for his premature gray hair and fiery locker-room talks, Kane insisted that his players be gentlemen, but he also emphasized winning and demanded an all-out effort. His efficient practices stressed fundamentals. "It was so many steps out and over and then in," Vince said, admiring Kane's meticulous teaching, "and he made the reasons clear."[28]

In late August 1932, Vince went to Camp Alverno in Centersport, New York, to begin practice with the St. Francis team. At Camp Alverno, away from the distractions of family and friends, the coaches could concentrate totally on molding a football team. Because Vince was a newcomer, the other boys immediately tested his mettle. "Let's get this guinea," one said at the first practice, and others agreed. But they underestimated Vince. At 168 pounds, with his muscular neck, broad, powerful shoulders, and large chest, he pulverized them with his bulldozing runs and fierce-charging blocks and won their respect. "This guinea [hits] like the Fifth Avenue el," a stunned teammate observed at the end of the first day. With his affable charm, Vince quickly won friends off the field. "You couldn't help but like Lombardi," said Coach Maggio. At camp he became close friends with teammate Pat Joyce, an all-around athlete and student leader. "You're the roughest one I ever came across," Joyce often told Vince during their year together.

After school started, buses transported the team to practice on an old storage lot dotted with stones and scrap iron but little grass. It was similar to the sandlots Vince had played on for years, so he felt comfortable. Vince quickly became a team leader because the coaches and players respected his athletic ability and admired his intelligence, rugged determination, and spirit. Kane and Maggio particularly appreciated Vince's serious attitude but worried that he took the game too seriously. "He had difficulty being loose and relaxed," recalled Maggio.[29]

Vince played guard on defense, and on offense he alternated between guard and halfback. He was an outstanding tackler. "When he hit you, you knew it," said a teammate. As an offensive lineman he was aggressive and determined, but because he had received no formal coaching, his blocking techniques needed considerable refinement. The coaches taught him different types of blocks, improved his timing, and warned him to keep his feet under him and to avoid his opponent's feints. On short-yardage situations he was pulled back to the halfback position. Kane seldom sent him around end because he lacked the flair, speed, and shiftiness to make yardage. His running talent lay exclusively in the straight-ahead, bull-like charge, an uncomplicated maneuver he performed with zest and with disdain for tacklers. He ran with a peculiar short, loping, rabbitlike stride, but with great power. "When you needed one or two yards, you gave it to Vinny, and he got it for you," said Joyce.[30]

Because St. Francis had no home field, the team played games at stadiums all over New York. Large pep rallies at school drummed up excitement, and crowds at the games ranged from thirty-five hundred to seven thousand. The team lost its opening game, 13–0, to Erasmus High School as Sid Luckman, the brilliant sophomore quarterback of Erasmus and later a star at Columbia University and with the Chicago Bears, devastated St. Francis with his running and passing. Erasmus, however, was an exceptional team, then in the midst of a seventeen-game winning streak. St. Francis won its remaining five games, against Brooklyn Prep, Xavier, Far Rockaway, Brooklyn Tech, and St. John's. St. Francis didn't overpower opponents, scoring only forty-nine points all season, but its defense, with Vince as a bulwark, allowed only twenty points and shut out four of its six opponents. Despite the loss to Erasmus, St. Francis tied for best record among private schools in New York.

Vince played almost every minute of every game. "You couldn't knock the guy out," said Joyce; "he'd never give up." Afterward Vince usually was bruised and bloodied. He cut his mouth and lips so often that Maggio convinced him to wear a primitive rubber mouthpiece, but the rubber upset his digestive system, making him sick after each game. He scored only one touchdown during the season, but his overall play earned him selection to the All-City team.[31]

Because of football and his schoolwork, Vince had little time left for social activities. Except for drumming up support for the football team, St. Francis arranged few social functions. It was a commuter school; students rushed to buses or the subway at the end of the day. Vince spent thirty-five minutes one way on the subway covering the nine miles between home and school. He had no steady girlfriend and seldom dated. He took his cousin Dorothy Izzo to the school prom, double-dating with Joe Goettisheim, who took Madeline. The girls loved the dance and so did Vince, but he was quiet and reticent.[32]

Vince was well liked by his classmates. *Sanfran,* the school annual, highlighted two features noted by his fellow students. The first, in the "As We Know Them" column, referred to his muscular physique and football prowess: "Lombardi—to be strong is to be happy." The other feature won him affection all his life. "Lombardi is famous throughout the school for his smile that only seems to become bigger under adverse circumstances," said the annual's editors, who detected nothing artificial about the smile. "Lombardi can no more help smiling than the sun can help shining. It is the natural outward reaction of his inner, happy nature. Lombardi is friendly with everyone," the annual added, "[and] charitable towards lower classmen."[33]

In the classroom Vince was quiet, seldom taking part in class discussion, but serious and conscientious. He took English, math, history, religion, and Greek, and, again, he earned about a B+ average. Brother Edmund, his English teacher, judged his work good but not exceptional. What most struck Brother Edmund was the striking contrast between Vince's student and gridiron personalities. "When I looked at him [on the football field] and realized that he was a student in my class, I said to myself, 'This is two different people! In the classroom he's silent, polite, mannerly, [but] on the football field he's a terror!' "

Strict discipline pervaded St. Francis. Students had a "holy fear" of Brother Jerome, who occasionally dealt with troublemakers by slapping them across the face. Vince, though, wasn't a troublemaker. He quietly obeyed the rules and was beginning to judge them as a necessarily important feature of life. On one remarkable occasion, in fact, when given authority himself, he displayed the kind of unrestrained rage at rule-breakers that often shocked persons unaware of his volcanic temper. Brother David, one of his teachers, had to leave the room briefly as class began and asked Vince to lead students in the opening prayer, the "Hail Mary." When the brother returned, he discovered to his horror that Vince had grabbed a student by the throat and was banging his head against the blackboard. After separating the pair, Brother David demanded an explanation. "He wouldn't say the 'Hail Mary,' " Vince responded.[34]

Vince's favorite teacher and most helpful mentor was Dan Kern, a twenty-four-year-old Fordham University graduate who agreed to tutor Vince in Greek because Vince needed one more semester to complete a two-year language requirement for graduation. Kern assigned Vince to translate the *Anabasis,* the famous narrative account by Athenian historian Xenophon of the ten thousand Greek mercenary soldiers who struggled to get out of Persia in about 400 B.C. The story concerned a humane leader who combined intelligence, discipline, and organization to rally his troops, words Vince's admirers later used to describe his own leadership.

On pleasant days Kern and Vince conducted their sessions outdoors on a bench by a gazebo near the garden exit of the prep. Normally Kern assigned students twenty lines to translate daily, but Vince was so proficient that Kern gave him sixty lines. Yet each morning Vince would "breeze right through it," Kern recalled. He earned a grade of 92 percent.

One morning in early May 1933, as they sat together by the gazebo, Vince asked Kern an important favor. At that moment, with his hands placed awkwardly between his legs, Vince seemed abnormally shy, undoubtedly worried about Kern's reaction. He asked if Kern would help him win a football scholarship to Fordham. He explained that he already had an excellent scholarship offer from Lou Little, the head coach of Columbia, but that "my mother would like me to go to a Catholic institution." Vince probably assumed that as a Fordham alumnus Kern's recommendation could be influential.

Kern agreed to help, and that evening he wrote to Jack Coffey, Fordham's athletic director, touting Vince's fine scholastic ability and football accomplishments. His letter inflated Vince's weight from 170 to 185 because, he later explained, "they wouldn't have looked at him if I said he was so low in weight." Besides, Kern rationalized, Vince was exceptionally strong at 170 pounds. Coffey responded shortly after, invited Vince to visit Fordham, and then awarded him a scholarship.[35]

II

College
at Fordham
(1933–37)

FORDHAM UNIVERSITY WAS FOUNDED IN 1841 WHEN BISHOP JOHN HUGHES OF New York, upset by the shortage of Catholic schools in the city and the intolerance against Catholics, invited three Jesuit priests from Kentucky to begin a college at the site of the old Rose Hill estate in the Bronx section of New York. Six thousand students were enrolled in 1933, making it the largest Catholic university in the country and the biggest Jesuit educational institution in the world. Vince loved the four years he spent there. He didn't excel in his academic work, but he studied diligently, and the demanding values of Scholastic philosophy molded his mind and deepened his character. Although often frustrated in trying to meet the rugged challenge of major-college football, he persevered, competed furiously, learned valuable lessons from his brilliant coaches, and in his exhilarating senior season played guard on the most famous line in college football history.[1]

At Fordham Vince also met the only woman he ever loved. He roomed with Jim Lawlor, a fellow New Yorker, who also had a football scholarship. In the fall of 1934, Lawlor met his cousin Arthur Planitz for the first time after Planitz had enrolled for his freshman year at Fordham. Planitz invited Lawlor to his apartment to meet his family, and Lawlor brought Vince along. There Vince met Arthur's sister, Marie Planitz, and the two began to date. "Suddenly [he] plopped into my life," Marie recalled, "and nothing was ever the same." Born on May 25, 1915, Marie had grown up in Red Bank, New Jersey, but recently her father had moved the family to New York so he could be closer to his job as a Wall Street broker. Tall, blond, blue-eyed, and with strikingly handsome features, Marie started nurse's training at Roosevelt Hospital until illness forced her to drop out. Her family lived in an apartment less than a mile from Vince's dorm, and by 1935 they were dating steadily. He often visited her apartment for dinners and parties, and they attended the major proms and dances sponsored by campus groups. Marie was the only girlfriend Vince ever had and one of the few women he had ever dated. Ironically, she had been brought up by her strict German father to believe there was no place in a person's life for tears, yet she was about to spend most of the rest of her life with an emotion-torn man.[2]

As freshmen and sophomores Vince and Lawlor lived above the dining hall and in their last two years in St. John's Hall, one of the oldest buildings on campus. The prefect of St. John's, Reverend Harold Mulqueen, left an indelible mark on generations of Fordham's resident students. The diminutive, cigar-smoking Irishman taught philosophy and religion and directed the band, but he was most remembered for advising, disciplining, and inspiring the students of St. John's Hall. Mulqueen exuded authority, but like other authority figures Vince admired, he combined it with intelligence, integrity, and a sense of fairness, earning the love and respect of students.

The students also feared him. The dean of discipline normally punished the infractions of students, but in St. John's Father Mulqueen preferred to handle the problems himself. Students welcomed his localized discipline but still feared his method. When the priest discovered a late-night truant, he would usually barge into the student's room at 6:45 A.M. and say, "Do you want my punishment or the dean's?" Invariably the reply was, "Your punishment, Father." "Turn over," the priest ordered, and he would whack the student on the rear end with his drumstick. Despite their fear, cooped-up students often risked punishment and sneaked out of the dorm. Vince broke few rules at Fordham, but he had the normal amount of youthful energy and devil-may-care attitude, and sneaked out a few times, too, usually to a late-night beer-and-sandwich joint in the basement of an apartment building four blocks from the dorm. Father Mulqueen occasionally caught him.

One evening, as Mulqueen entered St. John's and started toward the stairway, he spotted Vince and Lawlor, shoes in hand, creeping down the stairs. The priest reached for his drumstick and headed toward them. The pair froze in their tracks, then pivoted on the stairs and headed back to their room, still tiptoeing, still holding their shoes. Normally Mulqueen would have leaped out and tattooed them with his stick, but the sight of the two burly football players pretending not to be sneaking out struck him as hilarious. He left them alone and went chuckling back to his room.[3]

On another evening Vince and Lawlor turned out their dorm light, tiptoed down the stairs and out the building, crossed the handball courts next to the dorm, ran the length of the Fordham football field, climbed a ten-foot wall, and exited near the Bronx Park Botanical Garden. After catching his breath, Vince asked Lawlor how much money he had. "None," replied Lawlor. "I don't have anything either," Vince lamented. With no money and no plans they decided they may as well return to their room, so they retraced their difficult route and avoided detection. "We just wanted to sneak out," recalled Lawlor.[4]

Most of the time, though, Vince was a quiet, serious, rule-abiding, and deeply religious student. Fordham required resident students to attend daily Mass before breakfast each morning or be restricted to campus for the weekend. Vince resented the rule; he didn't like to be forced to go. He attended daily Mass because he wanted to be there. Unlike other students, who sat with friends, he and a few others sat alone so they could concentrate on their Mass prayers. Also, unlike many others, Vince almost always received communion. "You could tell he was a very religious young man," a classmate observed. "We all thought he was going to be a priest," said another.

For four years Vince belonged to the Parthenian Sodality, one of the oldest campus organizations, whose members usually were the most devoted Catholics. Vince was an officer in his junior year. Members met at 7:20 A.M. each Wednesday morning. One year they studied the life of Christ and another the Catholic liturgy. Sodality members were expected to attend daily Mass, to pray the rosary, and to ask for God's grace. Each May on the Fordham quadrangle the sodality organized a ceremony honoring the Blessed Virgin where members sang "praises of Our Lady" and meditated on "her numberless virtues." Fordham also conducted special religious retreats. At Vince's senior retreat the Jesuit retreatmaster asked students to consider three vital questions: "Where did I come from? Why am I here? Where am I going?" Vince spent the rest of his life coming to terms with those weighty spiritual questions.[5]

When Vince prayed, he undoubtedly asked God's assistance in meeting the rigorous academic standards of Fordham's Jesuits. The Jesuits have many enemies, but none of them have ever said that they do not know how to teach. The Jesuit system of education was thorough, organized, efficient, and exacting. Jesuits have the reputation for turning out persons of strong willpower and long vision. These were the goals of Fordham's Jesuits as well. Student life and the classroom were regulated to establish the conditions for rigorous academic work. Students must be in their rooms—and were expected to study—from 7:30 to 10:00 P.M. Sunday through Thursday. Some students wasted their time, but not Vince. He studied. From 10:00 to 10:30 P.M. they could socialize in the dormitory, but lights went out at 10:30 P.M., and room check followed. Seniors could leave the dorm on Wednesday evening until 10:30 P.M., and all students were allowed out until 10:00 P.M. on Friday and 11:00 P.M. on Saturday. Fordham didn't permit a student to enter a class late. Nor could he cut any classes without an excused absence; even excused cuts could not exceed 15 percent of the semester. Through such rules Fordham's Jesuits hoped to produce dedicated, self-sacrificing, and committed students. In Vince's case they succeeded.[6]

Yet Vince's grades were not exceptional. Later, most accounts of his college life exaggerated his academic record. He graduated *cum laude,* many said; or *magna cum laude* or even *summa cum laude,* a few assumed. He made the honor roll "all four years." Actually, seventeen seniors in Vince's class graduated *cum laude* or higher, but Vince was not among them. Nor did he make the honor roll except in the second semester of his freshman year, when his 84.5 percent average—rounded off to 85 percent—barely won him the distinction. In the other seven semesters he missed the honor roll and averaged 80 percent (B−). His grades followed a consistent pattern. He did poorly in the first quarter of the fall semester, when the rigors of the long football season took its toll on his studies, but then he improved. In four years he earned only two A's, both in introductory French. He received good marks (B's) in philosophy, physics, religion, economics, psychology, and English. His poorest grades (C's) were in public speaking, advanced French, business law, and business administration. With a 60 percent average he came within one point of flunking trigonometry. Father Edward Bunn, who gave Vince a B− in the senior psychology course, described him as a hardworking student, adding, "He was not a sophisticated person at all. He was very simple and direct. . . . He took things as they were spoken and never looked for any double meanings."[7]

The inflated accounts of his undergraduate record apparently evolved accidentally, but for the next thirty years Vince made no attempt to correct them. When he later coached at West Point, all the football programs from 1949 to 1953 described him as having "graduated *cum *laude* in 1937 after making the dean's honor list for four years." A few words to West Point's sports information director could have corrected the programs, but Vince chose not to do so. Combined with an outstanding coaching record, a reputation as a brilliant student might help him reach his primary goal: a head coaching position at a major college.[8]

Finally, in 1968, now more secure in his reputation, Vince set the record straight in the opening remarks of a speech. "I read now where I graduated from Fordham University *cum laude, magna cum laude,* yes, and even *summa cum laude*; also that I was an All-American," he said. "Of course, I was not." He didn't add, though, that he had missed the honor roll most of the time as well.[9]

Although Vince did not excel in his academic work, he was a dedicated, hardworking student. He was just as interested in his report card as he was in the Pitt game. He was good enough to rank in the top 25 percent of his class and in the upper 10 percent among football players. He studied diligently in his room every weekday evening. "Anything Vince did [at Fordham]," said Lawlor, "he did wholeheartedly." He had gone to school to learn and to win his degree, and as his friend Wellington Mara observed of his attitude, "he was darn well sure he was going to get what he went after." He competed with friends for good grades. If Mara (a *cum laude* graduate) or Leo Paquin (a good student and a football player) received a higher grade on an exam, Vince responded, "I'll get you next time!" He meant his challenge seriously, yet displayed no resentfulness or unfriendly attitude. He also tutored students with academic problems. "He was a good teacher even then," a classmate observed.[10]

Scholastic philosophy permeated the academic atmosphere at Fordham, and its principles molded Vince's moral and intellectual development. Scholasticism was the method of learning in the medieval cathedral schools. St. Thomas Aquinas, its principal formulator, brought together into a formidable synthesis the insights of classical philosophy (mainly Aristotle's) and Christian theology. The system's method relied on strict logical deduction taking the form of an intricate system; one established premises that led inexorably to a conclusion. In the Scholastic system, philosophy was directly and immediately subordinate to Catholic theology. Riches, pleasure, power, and knowledge were all goods and legitimate objects of the appetites, but perfect happiness was found not in created things but in God, the supreme good.[11]

"Scholastic philosophy was everyone's major at Fordham," reflected Mara. Courses in religion and philosophy indoctrinated students in the Scholastic method; psychology courses studied all the psychological theories, including Sigmund Freud's, but concluded that Scholasticism was paramount. Judgments tended to be either right or wrong, an approach offering less room for independent thinking than was possible at major secular universities.[12]

At Fordham intellectual virtues mattered less than character and moral development. "Men are not made better citizens by the mere accumulation of knowledge," said the *Fordham University Bulletin*. Knowledge was secondary because it had "no moral efficacy." Only religion could "purify the heart, and guide and strengthen the will." The principal faculties to be developed were the moral faculties. "Morality . . . must be the atmosphere the student breathes; it must suffuse with its light all that he reads, illuminate all that is noble, expose what is base, and give to the true and false their relative light and shade." The *Bulletin*'s philosophy was aggressively promoted by Reverend Robert I. Gannon, the Fordham president, who in 1936 condemned "the singleminded pursuit of the intellectual virtues." In contrast, said Gannon, Fordham devoted itself to the "character-building theory."[13]

Philosophy was Vince's favorite subject at Fordham, and the ideas of Reverend Ignatius Cox, his ethics professor, left an indelible impression on his mind. Father Cox, a dramatic classroom showman, taught ethics to 350 seniors in a large lecture hall, and Vince listened attentively. Because the priest had difficulty holding everyone's attention in the large class, he used tricks to keep them alert. Picking names at random was a favorite ploy:

"Is that clear to you, Mr. Mara?"

"Yes, Father," Mara responded.

"Is that clear to you, Mr. Paquin?"

"Yes, Father," Paquin answered.

"Is that clear to you, Mr. Lombardi?"

"Yes, Father," Vince said.

"What's clear to you, Mr. Lombardi?" the priest asked slyly. Unprepared students fumbled their response at this point, but Vince foiled the priest because he always knew what was clear to him.[14]

In 1936 Father Cox first published *Liberty: Its Use and Abuse* and adopted it as his class text. The book was too abstract and complex for Vince and many other students to comprehend fully, but they remembered its major themes more vividly than any other they studied at Fordham. In his dedication Father Cox urged his students to be "leaders in a world in need of their leadership against the materialism besetting man's liberty." In thunderingly authoritative definitions, deductions, and proofs—all arranged in the Scholastic method—Father Cox set forth the theoretical

Michael O'Brien

principles of ethics and their application. He stressed the importance of character, morality, perfection, will, authority, tradition, duty, God's preeminence, and the dignity of the individual. Catholic publications received the book enthusiastically. "A lucid exposition and reasonable defense of the [ethical] principles," said a reviewer. But a secular critic unmercifully panned it. "Catholic platitudes . . . engulfing conceit . . . overpowering fanaticism . . . dogmatic," he charged, mere "propaganda to reassure the faithful" who "are ever in need of such reassurance." Because he was faithful and in need of reassurance, Vince adopted Father Cox's lessons as the bedrock of his value system.[15]

Football was an exciting challenge for Vince but frustrating as well. Just as good fortune had come his way in the person of Coach Harry Kane at St. Francis Prep, so it arrived again at Fordham with Jim Crowley, one of the greatest college coaches of the 1930s. Crowley grew up in Green Bay, Wisconsin, where his high-school coach had been Earl "Curly" Lambeau, one of the founders and the longtime coach of the Green Bay Packers. Crowley went on to star under Knute Rockne at Notre Dame. In 1924 Grantland Rice, the great sports sage, coined the famous phrase the "Four Horsemen" to describe the Notre Dame backfield of Crowley, Harry Stuhldreher, Elmer Layden, and Don Miller. As the left halfback, Crowley was probably the most colorful and versatile member of that most colorful and versatile backfield. He was the head coach at Michigan State from 1929 to 1932, when Fordham recruited him to replace the Rams' ailing coach, Frank Cavanaugh.[16]

Crowley coached Fordham for nine seasons, from Vince's freshman year in 1933 through 1941. Under his leadership, Fordham upgraded its program, scheduling such national powers as Pittsburgh, Georgia, St. Mary's, Purdue, Tennessee, and Southern Methodist. Fordham played sophisticated, big-city football. It seldom played games away from home, and its "campus stadium" was the Polo Grounds. Crowley's record, 58–13–7, was the best in the East during his tenure and one of the best in the nation. A natural leader and a shrewd psychologist, Crowley knew instinctively which players needed stimulation or needling and which were self-motivated and were best left alone. (He usually left Vince alone.) Crowley was an outstanding recruiter of mostly lower-middle-class, Polish, Italian, and Irish boys from New England and the coal regions of eastern Pennsylvania. "Short, snappy, thorough drills are the key to a successful campaign," he said of his practice routine. "No loafing, no halfhearted effort, no indifference either mental or physical, but hard, aggressive, brainy work from beginning to end."[17]

Fordham's offense seldom sparkled under Crowley's direction, partly because he had few outstanding running backs but also because of his unimaginative play selection. "Try the other play now, Jim!," students chanted, ridiculing his play calling. But Crowley had exceptional ability to analyze an opponent's offense and to devise a defense against it. "I knew he was good while I played under him," Vince later said, "but I never knew how great he was until I got out."[18]

Crowley also had the capacity to instill an almost mystical sense of *esprit de corps* in his team. To win for alma mater his players must develop a temporary obsession that ended only when the game ended; then it must be renewed the following week. A masterful public speaker, his locker-room pep talks came from the go-out-and-win-one-for-the-Gipper school of oratory, and he delivered them in a resonant, dramatic voice with Rockne-like shading in his inflections and staccatos. Some players disliked his affected style and tired of hearing the same lines year after year, but most, including Vince, found his pep talks exhilarating. Before the important game with St. Mary's in 1936, Crowley reminded his players that millions would be listening to the radio broadcast, among them his own mother, sitting in her rocking chair in Green Bay and praying for a Fordham victory. He suddenly stopped. The room fell silent. He turned to the student manager and warned: "Son, you better open that door and get out of the way fast! Here comes my Fordham team!"[19]

When he left Michigan State, Crowley brought with him his excellent all-Notre Dame staff of Frank Leahy, Glen Carberry, Earl Walsh, and Hugh Devore. Vince had the most direct contact with Leahy, who coached the centers and the guards. Leahy was another Rockne protégé, who after leaving Fordham in 1939 became the brilliant and successful—some would add ruthless and fanatical—coach of Boston College and then Notre Dame. Distant and reticent socially but tough, methodical, and conscientious on the practice field, Leahy conveyed determination and a winning spirit to his linemen. He arrived at practice early to work with his players and insisted that each lineman block him personally. His uniqueness lay in the tenacity with which he concentrated on every detail that would perfect the skills of his linemen.[20]

In the 1930s football was a game that hurt, a game of pads slapped against unguarded faces, of two players charging point-blank into an opponent and driving him to the ground, of thumping blocks as a wave of interference rolled a man out of the way. There were few intricate pass plays or quick, concealed runs. The game Vince learned was a perfect expression of football's basic elements of blocking and tackling.[21]

When Vince showed up for the first practice in his freshman year, he tried out for fullback, but the coaches quickly realized that he couldn't make the grade as a college running back. "He wasn't fast enough," recalled Crowley. Yet Crowley could see that he had potential because he was such a "rugged character," so Crowley converted him to guard. Friends kidded him about the change. "A guard was a fullback with his brains knocked out," they said. But Vince never complained; he just wanted to play somewhere. "Who was I to tell Crowley I wanted to play fullback?" Vince later said matter-of-factly. "So I played guard." At an early practice, Leahy demanded that Vince block him. Each lined up in a three-point stance and Leahy smashed into Vince, knocking him to the ground. "Let's do it again," said Leahy. Prepared this time, Vince uncoiled and smashed into Leahy, creating a brief, noisy tussle. "Okay, Vinnie," said Leahy, "you pass." Vince watched attentively at practice, listened to his coaches' instructions, and subsequently taught many of the same blocking techniques himself. He later argued that playing guard made him a more effective offensive coach because he mastered the blocking assignments and techniques that made a play succeed.[22]

As a guard Vince had one serious physical limitation that made it difficult for him to break into the starting lineup and nearly impossible for him to excel. He weighed only 180 pounds and usually had to compete against players—both in practice and in games—who were much heavier and stronger. "He was a journeyman guard like the rest of us," recalled Michael Kochel, a substitute guard; "his playing got better and better each year as he became famous as a coach." Most of his teammates and coaches, though recognizing his limitations, respected his abilities and especially his attitude. "Once I saw his fight and desire," a teammate observed, "I began to appreciate him." He was quick coming out of the line, charged his opponent fiercely, improved his techniques, and mastered his assignments. "He didn't shine," Crowley conceded, "but he was a good, steady player [and] always reliable, responsible, and very dependable." Crowley was most impressed with the intangible quality Vince added to the team. "He had great spirit. He didn't like to lose. That's what [helped] him make the team."[23]

Because of intense competition from more gifted teammates and frustrating, painful injuries, Vince didn't play much until his senior year. He learned what it was like to be a bench warmer. Through it all he fortified his resolve, maintained his spirit, and learned valuable lessons on how to succeed in football. His freshman year was a major disappointment. The Fordham freshman played a three-game schedule in the fall of 1933, but Vince missed a month of practice and all the games because of an injured ankle. In his sophomore season he competed with twelve other guards for the varsity roster. "A promising prospect," the school newspaper noted of his chances. He made the team but didn't expect to play regularly because experienced upperclassmen held firm grasps on the starting line positions. Then, suddenly, three starting linemen suffered serious injuries, forcing Crowley to plan to start Vince at tackle against St. Mary's. He never realized the opportunity, however, because he sustained an injury himself, the most serious of his career. On the last play of the Wednesday scrimmage before the St. Mary's game, just as darkness fell over the Fordham practice field, Vince emerged groaning from the bottom of a heap of players. He had been kicked in the abdomen and suffered a separation of the duodenum, part of the small intestine, and the injury caused internal hemorrhaging. Trainers carried him off the field semiconscious and placed him in the infirmary. Incredibly, he showed up on the field on Thursday and attempted to practice but collapsed again. He remained in the infirmary a few more days and played little the rest of the season.[24]

"Lombardi is back, completely recovered from the injury," Crowley happily told the press at the start of spring practice in 1935. Since many outstanding linemen had graduated and he was now an experienced, healthy upperclassman, Vince expected to play more in his junior year. Crowley respected him, but the head coach respected others as well. "We . . . have some pretty good guards who have come up from the freshmen ranks," Crowley pointed out before the 1935 season. Indeed, now Vince had to face formidable competition from an outstanding sophomore class of linemen. Among them was Ed Franco, a bull of a man, soon to become one of the greatest linemen in Fordham's history. Vince was wary of Franco's challenge. When Vince and Marie met him in an ice-cream parlor, Marie said to him, "So you're Ed Franco. You're the fellow who's trying to take my boyfriend's job." In the early-season games of 1935 Vince started at right guard, but an injured shoulder forced him to miss two games, and Franco replaced him. When Vince recovered, he had lost his starting position and had to share playing time at both left and right guards with Franco, Nat Pierce, and Al Babartsky, another outstanding sophomore lineman.[25]

Another injury in 1935 cost Vince many of his teeth but not any playing time. Early in the game with St. Mary's he caught an elbow, forearm, or fist in the mouth and nose. At halftime, sitting in the dressing room of the Polo Grounds, he felt as though "every tooth in my head was loose." He had arranged to double-date that evening with Pat Joyce, his high-school friend, but when Joyce went to the locker room to pick him up and saw his swollen, mangled nose and mouth, he was shocked. "He looked like a Ubangi," recalled Joyce. "Pat, I don't think I can keep that date," Vince said. Joyce understood, and as he left, Vince shouted to him, "You ought to see what happened to the other guy!"[26]

For a while it appeared that Vince wouldn't make the starting team in his senior year either. In the spring and the early fall practices of 1936 Crowley had him listed as a reserve guard behind starters Pierce and Franco. Just before the first game, though, Crowley adjusted the lineup and placed Vince at right guard, making it possible for him to start on what turned out to be the most famous line in college football history. "In putting together the team," Crowley explained to the press, "I tried to get the best eleven men into the lineup. That's why I moved Franco from guard to tackle. We had two fine men for the guard positions, Lombardi and Pierce."[27]

Throughout his senior year Vince played steady, intelligent, aggressive football. He played both offense and defense. On defense his primary role was to stabilize the line so that his more talented teammates—particularly Franco and Alex Wojciechowicz—could gamble and make outstanding plays. "He hardly ever made a mistake," said a fellow lineman. He wasn't a star, but his spirit was infectious. "He was an inspiration to us," said Wojciechowicz. Vince had always led by quiet example, but on the bus from the campus to the Polo Grounds on the day of the game, he led the team in spirited songs. One of them, "The Fordham Ram," ended with the lines "We'll do or die," and it was with this attitude that Vince and his teammates played the game. "We would stare straight in our opponents' eyes," recalled Wojciechowicz. "We would not say it out loud, of course, but our look would say, 'We are ready to do or die. Are you?' " As for Vince, added Wojciechowicz, "He was ready to kill himself to win."[28]

Vince played his most courageous—and his finest—game in his senior year against Pittsburgh. For three consecutive seasons—1935, 1936, and 1937—Pitt and Fordham fought to scoreless ties in what one sportswriter described as a "rock-'em-sock-'em series . . . football's finest hour." Fordham could not match Pitt's striking power, but its mobile, instinctive, powerful defense hit back with devastating force. The 1936 game was played before fifty-seven thousand fans at the Polo Grounds and three days before the Roosevelt-Landon presidential election. Led by Marshall Goldberg, one of the greatest running backs of the decade, Pitt would close the season ranked third nationally by the Associated Press. It was a classic confrontation: Pitt's great offense against Fordham's great defense. Most of the time Vince had to block Pitt's All-American Tony Matisi, a fast, aggressive tackle who outweighed him by thirty pounds.

Vince's blocking helped punch holes in the huge Pitt line, but in the process he again damaged his mouth. "We had a play on which I was supposed to trap the Pitt tackle [Matisi]," Vince recalled years later. "It worked fine, so our quarterback kept calling it. But every time I trapped that guy, he jabbed me right in the teeth with his elbow."[29]

His mouth bled so badly that Crowley took him out of the game. Pierce, the other guard, was also injured and had to come out as well. "When Pitt began marching toward what looked like a score," reported the *New York Sun,* "Crowley rushed them in and stemmed the charge." With blood gushing from his mouth, Vince made a key tackle on Fordham's four-yard line, stopping Pitt's drive. One of the few accolades Vince earned during his playing days came from the *New York Post,* which praised his contribution: "Opposition scouts went away speaking most kindly and at greatest length about Lombardi." In the locker room after the game Dr. Gerry Carroll, the team physician, sewed thirty stitches inside Vince's mouth. Harry Lombardi had always admonished his son to ignore small injuries. "Hurt is in the mind!" Harry insisted. "When I got home that night," Vince later said, "I was certainly hurting in my mind."[30]

After his fine performance against Pittsburgh, the *New York Post* wrote a feature story about him. New York sportswriters had often profiled prominent Fordham players, but the *Post* article was the only feature on Vince. Much of the article was mundane. Vince enjoyed music, his philosophy classes, and the New York baseball teams, the story said, and was the only Fordham starter from New York City. More significantly, the *Post* attempted to explain why Vince had received little recognition compared to his teammates, and it offered two theories. Vince and Nat Pierce played guard, an unglamorous position, "the least conspicuous spots on the field." Plus, Vince "doesn't talk much. . . . If he did, the man probably would be a more celebrated character." In general, Vince had to be flattered by the story, since it praised his "epic battle" against Pitt's linemen and tabbed him as New York's "hero."[31]

Throughout 1936 Fordham's defense was outstanding, allowing only thirty-three points in eight games. After the team prevented any touchdowns in victories over Southern Methodist, St. Mary's, and Purdue and had played the scoreless tie with Pittsburgh, Tim Cohane, the Fordham sports information director, adopted the phrase "Seven Blocks of Granite" to describe the Rams' stone-wall qualities. Cohane had recalled a brief, long-forgotten Associated Press dispatch of 1930 that used the phrase to describe Fordham's rugged line. He resurrected it and applied the tag to the 1936 line of Leo Paquin (left end), Ed Franco (left tackle),

Nat Pierce (left guard), Alex Wojciechowicz (center), Lombardi (right guard), Al Babartsky (right tackle), and John Druze (right end). This time the phrase caught on in the press, making the Seven Blocks of Granite immortal.[32]

Fordham remained undefeated until the last game with archrival but unheralded New York University. Feverishly excited Fordham fans were already planning to go to Pasadena on New Year's Day to watch their Rams play in the Rose Bowl. But NYU upset Fordham, 7–6, dashing hopes for the Rose Bowl bid and bringing a bitter end to an otherwise exceptional season. Vince never forgot the hard lesson: Don't take an "easy" opponent lightly. After the season five of the Seven Blocks of Granite were selected to at least one major All-American team, but Vince was not among them. He did manage to win "honorable mention" on the Associated Press Eastern All-American squad. (He also earned an unusual honor: second-team "All-Italian American," sponsored by an Italian group in Des Moines, Iowa.)[33]

Reflecting on the lessons he learned about football at Fordham, Vince stressed the "fourth dimension." Three dimensions that determined success or failure were the quality of the players, the quality of the coaching, and the quality of the opposition. "The fourth," he said, "is selfless teamwork and collective pride, which accumulate until they have made positive thinking and victory habitual."[34]

Classmates liked Vince, most often describing his off-the-football-field personality as nice, quiet, kind, and serious. He played handball and intramurals, helped Lawlor run surreptitious crap games in their room, and frequented the off-campus movie theaters, restaurants, and bars. "He wasn't a prude," said classmate George Mulrey; "he'd go out and have a drink and, occasionally, he might have one too many, like all of us would."[35]

At times, though, Vince's powerful emotions erupted—sometimes violently. On one occasion he found revenge for a slight by concocting a prank on Brother Quinn, who dispensed student jobs in the cafeteria and had rejected Vince's application for a position. The brother also insulted athletes by baiting them as they entered the cafeteria. "Here they come!" Brother Quinn would say. "Here come the hogs to the trough!" "I'm going to get even with that Irish bastard," Vince told friends. As the bald brother stood by the entrance to the dining room, Vince piled heaps of butter on a piece of bread, coaxed friends to crowd around him, and as the group passed by Brother Quinn, Vince stuck out his arm and plopped the buttered bread square on top of the brother's bald head. He escaped undetected.[36]

Slurs against him and his Italian heritage sparked Vince's most violent outbursts. Only fun-loving Jim Lawlor could tease him about being Italian without incurring his wrath. "Jesus Christ," Lawlor would say on entering their dorm room, "open the window! This place smells [like] olive oil!" Vince would shoot back with an expletive and a derogatory jab at Lawlor's Irish ancestors.[37]

Normally, though, a slur set off his very short fuse and twice resulted in violent brawls. After an exhausting Wednesday afternoon scrimmage prior to the important game against St. Mary's in 1936, Vince and Leo Paquin were showering in a small shower room when a teammate, a second-string end, also entered the shower. Then a fourth person, with a dark complexion, entered the room and waited by the door. The end called out to the man at the door: "Hey, come here. Stand alongside Lombardi. I want to see which one of you looks more like a nigger." Vince's eyes blinked and then boom, he let go a left hook that caught his tormentor square on the nose. The end was tough, ten pounds heavier than Vince, and refused to back off, so a bloody fight ensued. Vince wore a class ring that cut his foe badly, but he battered Vince as well. When word of the fight reached Crowley, he suspended both of them. "Crowley wasn't dumb, though," said Paquin. "He only suspended Vinny until Friday afternoon [so] he was able to play Saturday." Crowley suspended the reserve end through the whole weekend.[38]

A second fight occurred when Marie invited Vince and Lawlor to meet her at an off-campus sorority dance at a hotel. The minute the pair walked in the door they sensed the sharp resentment from a group of fraternity brothers. Near the entrance foyer four of them formed a gauntlet, two on each side, and when Vince and Lawlor walked through, a fraternity member said, "Who's the little wop?" Lawlor described the scene: "Vince never stopped. He turned around and as he did his fist came with him and he hit the guy right in the mouth." They exchanged blows until Vince and Lawlor escaped. As they ran down the steps to the door, two policemen entered the hotel. "Where's the fight, fellows?" a policeman inquired. "Right up there," Vince answered, pointing up the stairs as he and Lawlor continued their hasty exit.[39]

Fordham football players often got into skirmishes on the practice field and in games. An elbow would fly into a face, causing a brief ruckus. Vince, though, flared up more easily and more often than others. Frank Leahy admired Vince's fortitude and determination but found his hot-headedness disturbing: "His terrible temper occasionally frightened us before he learned to control it." Leahy's assessment was only partially correct. Vince apparently never physically fought with anyone after he graduated from Fordham, but he had only sporadic success in controlling his temper. He partially compensated by learning how to apologize.[40]

Leo Paquin, a teammate, friend, and the most perceptive observer of Vince's college years, has pointed out that Vince displayed no exceptional ability in any single category at Fordham. No one anticipated that he would become the most illustrious member of his class. "Football? He was a fine player, but he wasn't one of the best," said Paquin. "Studies? He and I and Wellington Mara . . . had a running competition to see who got the highest grades, and we were all far above average, but there were smarter students than we were. The spiritual life? Vinny used to go to Mass every morning, but so did most of us. He wasn't the acolyte, so shiny that the priests fussed over him. Strong character? Certainly. Vince was always a decent person, but he wasn't a saint. He enjoyed his occasional beer and he liked a good dice game . . . he had no holier-than-thou-attitude." In any single category—athletics, academics, religion, character—Vince did not excel. Yet there was another important standard of judgment. "What you'd notice if you looked carefully," Paquin added, "was that Vinny was among the top group in every category."[41]

Vince graduated on June 16, 1937, with a B.S. degree. At the ceremonies 350 men received their diplomas, and all of them wore the traditional black shoes under their graduation gowns—all except Vince. Sticking out conspicuously from under his black gown were Vince's white shoes. When classmates asked him why he wore the white shoes, he answered laconically, "Because I like white shoes." Friends interpreted his action as a sign of his independence. More likely it displayed his lack of social sophistication—he didn't realize he was supposed to wear black shoes.[42]

Life after graduation was frustrating for Vince as he struggled to start a career in the latter part of the Depression. He continued to play football but wasn't big enough or talented enough to sustain a professional career. In the fall of 1937, he played guard for the semiprofessional Wilmington, Delaware, Clippers. The team played a few exhibitions against powerful National Football League teams, including the New York Giants and the Washington Redskins. (Vince broke his nose at one practice.) The following year he played for the Brooklyn Eagles of the American Football Association and later for a semipro team in Springfield, Massachusetts. He and a few friends usually worked out on their own during the week and played a game on the weekend. The pay was excellent: $125 to $150 a game plus travel and meals, about as much as he made per month working after graduation.[43]

Throughout college Vince had been uncertain about his career goals, and his dilemma continued after graduation. He considered business, teaching, and law. At Fordham he belonged to the Business Forum, a club that brought speakers to the campus from business and the professions; club members also toured New York area banks and industries and advised each other on the "ever-increasing difficulty of obtaining positions after graduation." But Vince wasn't able to find a position in business that was exciting and challenging. Nor had he done well in his business courses at Fordham.[44]

Because he wanted to work with young people, he considered high-school teaching with perhaps coaching as a sidelight. He couldn't conceive of coaching as a full-time career. "Not until I was well over twenty-five did I know for sure that I wanted to make coaching football my life's work," he said later. In any case, few high-school teaching positions were available, and he didn't pursue any openings.[45]

Mostly he thought of being a lawyer. A lawyer had status and respect, he reasoned, and the profession was lucrative enough to support a family. He talked with friends about the advantages a native New York lawyer with a Fordham degree had in making contacts among the many Fordham alumni in the New York area. Moreover, Vince's father vigorously urged him to go to law school.[46]

While he pondered his future, he moved in with his family at their new residence at 2808 Avenue S in Brooklyn and tried to scratch out a living. Even that limited goal proved frustratingly difficult. The Depression restricted opportunities, and, most aggravating, he sensed that doors were closed to him because he was Italian. Finally he and Lawlor accepted jobs as assistant managers at a New York finance company. The pay—$150 a month—was adequate, but the work was heartless. Their assignment was to visit the homes of people—many of whom were poor and unemployed—and pressure them to pay back their loans to the finance company. The work was so distasteful that Vince occasionally gave the pathetic victims some of his own money to help them make their payments.[47]

After a year at the finance company, Vince quit, and in September 1938 he enrolled at Fordham Law School. Unfortunately, he couldn't measure up to law school's demanding standards, and he withdrew on February 1, 1939, after completing only one semester. He averaged only 73 percent in three courses: 81 percent in domestic relations, 78 percent in contracts, and 60 percent—one point from flunking—in pleading. His performance mortified him, and he concealed it for the rest of his life. Usually he gave the impression that he had almost completed his law degree and had dropped out only to get married. Why he did so poorly is a mystery. Perhaps he lacked the aptitude for legal study, or couldn't motivate himself, or found law too dull. His eyes were bothering him at the time, and studying may have aggravated his vision problem.[48]

After the disappointment of law school, he worked briefly as a chemist for the DuPont Chemical Company in Wilmington, Delaware, but he wasn't content. Finally, two years after graduation, his luck suddenly changed. In August 1939, a former college classmate phoned and asked him to accept a teaching position at St. Cecilia High School in Englewood, New Jersey, and the invitation dramatically changed the course of his life.

III

St. Cecilia
High School
(1939–47)

Vince taught and coached at St. Cecilia for eight years, a period he later described as the happiest of his life. It was also a crucial turning point. He arrived as a bachelor, with dormant talents, no profession, and uncertain goals; he left with a young family, valuable teaching experience, an exciting new career, and a reputation for dynamic, successful coaching that won the admiration of almost everyone who met him. The world he conquered in Englewood was a small one, but the experience left him confident and with a burning desire for a larger challenge.

That Vince ever secured the St. Cecilia job was fortuitous, the result of disruptive staff changes at the school in the summer of 1939. Nat Pierce, the ''other'' guard on the Seven Blocks of Granite, had been a teacher and the head football coach at St. Cecilia, but he resigned at the beginning of the summer to become freshman football coach at Fordham under Jim Crowley. Andy Palau, Pierce's former college roommate, was hired to replace him. Then Roger Mantell, the head basketball coach, also resigned, to become athletic director at another high school. In early August, when St. Cecilia hired Rudy Pfeifer to teach, coach basketball, and assist with football, the staff finally seemed stabilized. A few weeks later, however, Pfeifer suddenly changed his mind, took a position at another high school, and left. With classes and football practice about to start, St. Cecilia desperately needed one person to teach physics, chemistry, Latin, and physical education, plus coach basketball and assist with football—all for $1,000 a year.[1]

Palau asked help from Jack Coffey, the athletic director at Fordham, and Coffey provided him with three potential candidates, including Vince. Palau was Vince's classmate at Fordham, and since he knew Vince had been an intelligent student and a hard-nosed, spirited teammate, he asked Vince to take the job. Vince jumped at the opportunity. His job at DuPont paid poorly and didn't excite him. The St. Cecilia position didn't pay much either, of course, but he could find extra work to supplement it, especially in the summer. He hadn't given up the idea of becoming a lawyer either; when he had time he hoped to resume law classes. Most important, he wanted to marry Marie and felt pressure to pursue a full-time career. "You're not going to get married until you can support yourself!" Harry Lombardi had insisted.[2]

Vince moved to Englewood in late August 1939 and bunked in with Palau at a $2-a-week room in a house on James Street only fifty feet from the steps of St. Cecilia's Church. Originally a Dutch settlement, Englewood is located in the southern part of Bergen County about three miles from the George Washington Bridge and ten miles from Times Square. With its spacious, tree-dotted lots and proximity to New York City, it had become a popular residential suburb, with a population of nineteen thousand when Vince moved there.[3]

St. Cecilia, one of the oldest churches in Englewood, had opened its grade school in 1874 and its high school in 1924. Both were administered and partially staffed by the Sisters of Charity; Carmelite fathers ran the parish and also taught. In 1939 the salary for lay teachers was minimal and included no fringe benefits—no tenure or medical insurance or pension or Social Security. Starting at $1,000 a year, Vince's salary rose to $1,700 in 1942 and to $3,500 at the time he left in 1947. Despite the meager financial rewards, the school had created an alluring, happy, caring atmosphere and infectious school spirit.[4]

Vince worked feverishly that first fall preparing his classes and learning to coach. The football team immediately fascinated him. The "Saints" practiced at Mackay Park, a seven-block walk for players through the business district, and played home games at Winton White Stadium, a five-thousand-seat facility that swelled to standing-room-only crowds during the Lombardi era. Palau and Vince quickly became a close, effective coaching duo. Palau had been a 160-pound quarterback on the Seven Blocks of Granite team and an outstanding all-around athlete. He and Vince were both intelligent and dedicated, but Palau's soft-spoken, easygoing manner contrasted sharply with Vince's aggressiveness and loud volatility. Palau directed the team overall and instructed the offensive and defensive backs; Vince coached the lines and concentrated more on details and fundamentals. The two held what Vince later described as "big meetings" to decide offensive strategy. They adopted the Notre Dame single wing (or "box"), the same offense Crowley had taught them at Fordham. "It was all we really knew," Vince later said, "and in this coaching business, as in anything else, that's where you have to start." They used mostly a balanced line, passed often, and modified Crowley's approach slightly by using flankers and men in motion. Their coaching impressed immediately. In September 1939, Merv Hyman, sportswriter for the *Englewood Press,* said they had "worked harder than most of the county's coaches in getting this St. Cecilia team in shape."[5]

Vince had difficulty adjusting his high expectations to the limited abilities of young high-school athletes. He tried to teach them more than they could absorb, and he grew impatient when they didn't learn fast enough. "This was my first experience in giving rather than receiving," he later observed. How do you motivate so many different personalities? "Some need a whip and others a pat on the back," he was beginning to learn, "and others are better off when they are ignored." Some players had a breaking point. "In the beginning, I don't think he had enough patience with the kids who couldn't perform the way he wanted them to," Hyman reflected. At practice, while Vince drilled the team on a reverse play, an end kept making the same mistake. After enduring Vince's withering criticism, the player finally broke down and cried right on the practice field. Vince was embarrassed: "I realized then that he was just a seventeen-year-old kid and we were asking the impossible." Actually, Vince would always continue to demand what many players thought impossible, and for him patience usually remained an elusive virtue, but the practice field incident apparently made him more sensitive to the degree of pressure he could put on a young man.[6]

Vince discovered a hidden talent that first autumn. When the season started, Palau assumed the customary head coach's role and delivered the pep talks to players before the game. After four games he asked Vince if he wanted to try one. "Sure, I'll be glad to," Vince said. The result was startling. "[At] that first pep talk of Lombardi the gymnasium shook," Palau marveled. "He was absolutely fantastic." Palau made sure Vince gave most of the talks from then on. "He'd get you so roused up," observed Roger Fay, a member of the 1939 squad, "you'd run through a wall for the man."[7]

Palau and Lombardi had outstanding teams in their three years together, winning twenty-one games, losing three, and tying two. All three years St. Cecilia was awarded the North Jersey Group 2 Parochial Championship. The 1940 team went undefeated—the first undefeated St. Cecilia team since 1933—and remained unscored upon until the last game. Palau always graciously credited Vince's contribution to the team's success, and so did other observers. Local reporters often referred to "Palau and Lombardi" as the coaches of St. Cecilia, a distinction they did not convey on assistants at other area schools. They knew that Vince was no ordinary assistant coach. One year Hyman went so far as to name Palau and Vince as his "Coaches of the Year" in the *Englewood Press*.[8]

Besides his new job, Vince had another primary concern: his courtship with Marie. He spent many weekends visiting her in the Bronx, where they planned their wedding. After an argument they temporarily broke off their engagement and separated for a few weeks. Late one evening, after Vince and his friends returned to his room from a night out, he found Marie asleep in a chair. They patched up their differences that evening and resumed their wedding plans. On August 31, 1940, they were married at the Church of Our Lady of Refuge in the Bronx. (Vince's childhood friend, Joe Goettisheim, was the best man.) They honeymooned in Maine, but Vince cut short the trip to return home in time for the September 3 opening of football practice, a decision symptomatic of his priority for the rest of his married life. A few years later, when Marie learned at a party that a former St. Cecilia player had decided on a coaching career, she urged the young man's fiancée to change his mind. "You're not going to see him! Don't you understand? He's married to the football team!"

The newlyweds moved into a small second-floor apartment in Sheridan Court on Grand Avenue in Englewood, and moved again briefly to a larger apartment after the birth of Vincent, Jr., on April 27, 1942. Then in 1944 they purchased a two-story home on Mountain View Road, a middle-class section of the city and a mile from St. Cecilia, where they lived for five years. A daughter, Susan, was born on February 18, 1947. Shortly after Vince's wedding, Harry Lombardi moved his family to Englewood because he wanted to get out of Brooklyn and follow more closely the coaching career of his oldest son. Harry bought a home on Kensington Court, only a block and a half from Vince's home on Mountain View Road, and generously kept Vince's refrigerator filled with meat.[9]

Vince had many friends in Englewood and led an active social life. In a crowd of mostly strangers, though, he was quiet and retiring. He blinked his eyes nervously in uncomfortable situations, a noticeable habit when he was angry as well. Around women he was particularly shy. "There were several girls in Englewood who were crazy about Vince," Merv Hyman said, "but he wouldn't give them a glance." When students asked him and Marie to chaperone a school dance, Vince implored Hyman and his new wife to come also. That evening Vince wouldn't dance with Marie or anyone else. Instead, he stood in the corner all night. "I don't know what he would've done if one of the young girls had asked him to dance," said Hyman. "He probably would've run."[10]

But with his friends Vince was outgoing and fun. He loved eating at good restaurants, spending an evening with the guys drinking beer, or attending boxing matches and basketball games at Madison Square Garden. He played cards often, especially pinochle, his favorite game. Friends loved his hearty laugh and his joking. When he told a joke, he was usually laughing boisterously before he even finished the punch line. He often invited his favorite players to his home for a meal, cards, and jokes. "He loved people; he just never wanted to be alone," a player recalled. Some of his favorites came from troubled backgrounds, and he never missed an opportunity on those informal occasions to advise them.

When he first moved to Englewood, he chummed with Palau and Hyman when all three were still bachelors. "We used to sit around and drink beer," Hyman recalled, "and when we got twenty-two cans, we'd set up an offense and a defense and run through football plays. All Vince talked about, all he thought about was football."[11]

Many of his friends were fellow high-school coaches whom he saw regularly at meetings of the Bergen County Coaches Association, an organization he directed for a while. Francis ("Red") Garrity, the respected basketball coach of Englewood High School, was a close friend. They and their wives played duplicate bridge together, went to New York shows together, and celebrated birthdays, anniversaries, and New Year's Eves. Yet during the week of the St. Cecilia-Englewood basketball game, they didn't even speak to each other in church. "We were bitter rivals and yet close friends with mutual respect," recalled Garrity.[12]

Another close friend was Father Timothy Moore, the tough but warmhearted Carmelite priest who became athletic director at St. Cecilia in July 1942. Father Tim had graduated from St. Cecilia in 1928 and had been an All-State athlete in three sports. Both shared an intense interest in the fortunes of the St. Cecilia football and basketball teams. They occupied the same school office and were so close that Vince often said, "Tim, I want to go to confession," and then he would kneel down on the office floor as Father Moore heard his confession.[13]

When World War II broke out, Vince's friends, college classmates, and even some of his older students and players enlisted in the armed services. That Vince would be accepted seemed unlikely because of his terrible eyesight. He could see little without his glasses (though he hated to wear them and took them off on many occasions, including posing for photographs). "In those days, I'd think twice before I went in a car with him," recalled Father Moore. Still, he tried to enlist. He and Red Garrity went to Church Street in New York, where the services had recruiting offices, but at each stop both kept getting rejected. Finally, while standing in line at the Navy office, their last opportunity, Vince took off his glasses to divert attention from his eyes and fool the examining doctor. Moments later an elderly Navy officer, with snow-white hair, passed by. "Look at that guy," Vince whispered to Garrity. "He must have been wounded. He's all bandaged in the head!" Garrity laughed and advised Vince that his situation was hopeless, that he may as well wear his glasses. They both flunked the Navy exam. Not serving in World War II was often a social stigma, but Vince showed no sign of regret or embarrassment.[14]

At St. Cecilia one of Vince's multiple duties was to coach basketball, and when Palau first informed him of the assignment, Vince was incredulous. "Holy Jesus! Coach basketball?" He was upset, for while he had played the sport at Cathedral Prep and St. Francis, he never paid close attention to the intricacies of the game. Nonetheless, he took his new task very seriously and soon was enjoying the challenge. He never acquired the knowledge or the easy familiarity with basketball that he developed with football, but he approached basketball with the same intensity, dedication, and sternness, and with the same dynamic ability to teach and lead. Within a few years his success earned respect and praise throughout Bergen County.

Vince had little chance to prepare for his first season coaching basketball because fall football and his new teaching assignments occupied most of his time. Palau helped him get started by instructing him in the gym on the fundamentals of the 2–1–2 zone defense. Despite his limited knowledge and his team's limited talent, he managed to sneak above the .500 mark with a 10–9 record in his first season.[15]

After Palau's hasty instructions, Vince studied the game systematically to make himself an outstanding coach. He took training to become a basketball official, passed his exam, and began officiating. He sought the advice of Red Garrity, who tutored him on the relative merits of various offensive and defensive strategies. He contacted the coaches of several New York area college teams—City College of New York, Fordham, St. John's—and his sessions with them sometimes lasted into the early-morning hours. He even acquired films of college games and analyzed them. Then there were frequent visits to Madison Square Garden to watch games. After returning from the Garden, he often excitedly announced to Father Moore, "Tim, I've got a new system!" and he would begin to install it immediately. "We'd have a new offense the next week," a player said. "He became a hell of a basketball coach," Palau observed.[16]

Vince adopted a rigid but organized and logical approach to the game. He drilled his players on fundamentals—the "give and go," the pivot, the layup, the rebound blockout, and the accurate pass. He used a sliding 2–1–2 zone defense almost exclusively and devised innovative traps within the zone. He instructed his players to break out of the zone quickly, fill the lanes, and score fast-break layups. He used a series of set plays, and he taught every player exactly what to do when he had the ball or didn't have it. Players could not experiment with new techniques and could shoot only the conventional running one-hander or the two-handed set shot. No jump shots were permitted, nor any fancy dribbling. One *never* passed the ball behind the back. "If you deviated from the system, he'd go crazy," one of his players complained. "He wanted you to play like a robot. We weren't allowed to think for ourselves." Most of Vince's players, though, disagreed with this critical assessment. They liked Vince's regimented approach, learned from it, and enjoyed playing for him.[17]

Vince often lost his temper and occasionally treated players too harshly. Repeated mistakes sent him into a rage. With his nose an inch from the player's nose, he would holler, "You've got a thick head!" During one outburst he called a non-Italian a "stupid guinea." Occasionally he would jam the ball into the stomach of a player, knocking his wind out. "When his eyes blinked, you just knew he was mad and you couldn't do anything about it," observed a player. After one lackluster first half, he repeatedly kicked a garbage can in the corner of the locker room so hard he almost cut it in half. When something went wrong during a game he occasionally threw his set of keys clear across the court. A few times he jumped up off the bench only to bash his head on a low-hanging steel beam in the St. Cecilia gym. One such blow left him sprawled on the court, semiconscious. "He was pretty excitable," Hyman said with classic understatement. Dramatic games left Vince in a state of near physical and emotional exhaustion. In 1942 the Saints snapped Lodi High School's eighteen-game winning streak by the score of 23–20, and when the game ended, the *Englewood Press* reported, "Coach Lombardi was actually shaking with excitement [and] had to remain on the bench for several minutes before he was able to act normal." Al Del Greco, sportswriter for the *Bergen Evening Record,* observed during the 1945 state parochial basketball tournament that "Lombardi is another one of the tribe who dies a million deaths before a contest." When St. Cecilia won the tournament, its fans broke into joyous celebration, but Vince remained glum. "He doesn't know the game is over," quipped a tournament official.[18]

In Vince's first year he coached in perhaps the oddest basketball game in New Jersey's history, one that illustrated his stubborn persistence and his indignation at anything that marred the integrity of a sporting contest. On February 28, 1940, St. Cecilia hosted Bogota High School which had defeated the Saints easily in an early-season contest. Everett Hebel, the fine Bogota coach, decided to conserve the energy of his players for a more important contest the following evening. He therefore adopted a very radical strategy.

St. Cecilia won the opening tip but missed the first shot. Bogota controlled the rebound and, under the rules, took the ball over the center-court line, where the Bogota guard placed the ball under his arm and stood there for the rest of the quarter while Lombardi's team remained in its zone defense. Bogota held the ball for the entire second quarter, too. Score at halftime: 0–0. Vince had stubbornly refused to alter his defense. "Get back in your zone!" he shouted at his players. He realized that he had the inferior team and that his best gamble was to turn Hebel's strategy to his own advantage. He would wait for his opportunity.

The Saints won the third quarter tap, took a shot, but missed again. The Bogota guard took the ball past center court, stuck the ball under his arm, and waited. "Stay in your zone!" Vince hollered. Score at the end of the third quarter: 0–0. It remained that way until about three minutes remained in the game, when Vince finally ordered his players to go after the ball. There was a flurry of action for those few minutes and St. Cecilia ended up winning, 6–1.

Vince was furious at Hebel afterward for what he considered unsportsmanlike strategy. The crowd, anticipating his rage, watched silently as he walked across the floor to meet Hebel. "If a cat would have walked across the rug, it would have sounded like thunder," one witness recalled. "He dressed Coach Hebel up and down for a minute and a half. . . . You could hear him all the way to Mrs. O'Malley's candy store about a good half a block away."[19]

In eight years Vince compiled an outstanding record, much better than sports observers had anticipated. He had only one losing season (his last, in 1946–47). In 1944 a new Catholic conference was formed for basketball in Passaic and Bergen counties, and St. Cecilia won the conference championship in two of the three years Vince coached. At one point his team had a twenty-three-game winning streak in conference play. The Saints went to the State Parochial Schools Tournament four times, losing in the first round on three occasions but winning the title in 1945. He had outstanding talent on that 1945 team: Charles Bollinger, a giant 6-7 center; two tall forwards; and two swift guards. Overall, his teams compiled a 111–51 record, a winning percentage of .681.

Sportswriters praised his teams and marveled at his skillful coaching despite his lack of experience. St. Cecilia was "the fightingest team in the county." As the Saints drove toward their 1945 state tournament title, Hyman credited Vince as the "driving force" behind the success and added: "Vincent Lombardi is an unusual young man. He is a hard taskmaster yet is sincerely admired and respected by all of his charges. He demands perfection and gets it because his boys are willing to work for and with him."[20]

A similar observation could have been made of Vince's classroom teaching: He was an excellent instructor and a fearsome one. He always claimed that when he took the St. Cecilia position, "I wanted to be a teacher more than a coach." He taught five classes a day, and for all eight years his primary responsibility was to teach chemistry and physics. He also taught physical education for four years and one year each of Latin and biology. At first he struggled to keep "one lesson ahead of the class." Quickly, though, he mastered the material and lectured with few notes effortlessly and with intense enthusiasm.[21]

He was always prepared, organized, lucid, and demanding. Even his appearance and demeanor suggested that he was cut out for teaching. Hyman occasionally referred to him as the "professor"; a teaching colleague thought he approached his duties like a "scholar." In his early years at the school, he upgraded his skills and worked toward state certification by taking courses at Seton Hall College. With school funds he purchased new scientific equipment and visual aids to improve his classes, and he dutifully participated in PTA meetings and Parent Club functions.

In his science classes he stressed basic concepts and reviewed them constantly. "I learned in the classroom that you can't travel faster than your slowest pupil," he argued. His approach might occasionally bore the brighter students, he realized, but in this way he knew everyone understood the material. He often told jokes to relieve the pressure on what was usually a very rigorous class.[22]

Because of his outstanding teaching, most students studied hard in his classes and admired him. "The kids liked him," said Neal Roche, an

English teacher, "and that's motivation in any classroom." Some students who later went on to careers in science or education described Vince as their finest teacher. He impressed a few of his most gifted athletes more as a teacher than as a coach. His peers winced occasionally at his volcanic temper, but in general they enjoyed his pleasant personality and admired his excellent teaching.[23]

One year the student annual commented sardonically on the other feature of Vince's teaching, noting "Mr. Lombardi's 'melodious' voice and 'sympathetic' understanding." Actually, in the view of his students, Vince didn't possess either of those qualities. He was probably the best teacher in the school, but he was certainly the most feared. Students were in school to learn, he reasoned, and shouldn't waste time or act foolish. They must use proper etiquette and never interfere with the concentration of the teacher or other students. They must follow the rules, must never be late for class, must always turn in their homework on schedule, and, of course, must never cheat on an exam. "You didn't dare read a book . . . or turn your head or look at the person next to you," commented one student. "He'd walk around that room like a tiger." If he found students inattentive or unprepared he'd throw whatever he had in his hand—usually an eraser or chalk—at their heads or would make them do extra assignments. "You could hear a pin drop in his class," a colleague observed.[24]

He directed his anger (and erasers and chalk) mainly at male students because he assumed they were tougher. "I was extremely conscientious about his class," a star football player recalled. "I wouldn't dare go to his class unprepared." Part of the reason students feared him stemmed from his intimidating demeanor. Intense, erect, he barked out his lecture in a low, booming voice. He didn't always express verbally his displeasure with a student. An icy, silent glare achieved the same effect. "He was a strong male," Roche said. At exam time he exasperated tension by repeating his favorite classroom expression: "There shall be weeping and gnashing of teeth." He petrified some female students. A few began sobbing uncontrollably when told they had been assigned to his class. When his classroom grilling became too intense and girls would begin to cry, Vince, realizing he had gone too far, would apologize in front of the class.[25]

In the summer of 1942, the focus of Vince's career changed suddenly when Andy Palau resigned from St. Cecilia to become varsity backfield coach at Fordham. Vince was the logical choice to succeed him as football coach, and Father Moore, the new athletic director, confirmed expectations and promoted him. Vince, therefore, began his five-year stint as head football coach, his only head coaching experience in football until 1959. Most observers assumed that with his many talents he would eventually match the outstanding record he and Palau achieved during the previous three years. The immediate prospect for glory, however, was less certain, a predicament alluded to by Al Del Greco when he judged the appointment "poor timing" for Vince. "You're following a fellow who turned out an unbeaten club."[26]

Vince did all he could to dampen expectations. He moaned when a reporter asked him about the team's potential and then listed all the problems: only three returning veterans, a totally inexperienced line, and a strenuous nine-game schedule. He must "make supermen out of second-team players," Hyman concurred. Soon "ear-splitting shouts" began emanating from Mackay Park as Vince and Father Moore, his main assistant, began readying the team. St. Cecilia lost the first game, to Englewood High School, but didn't lose again that year, ending up with a record of 6–1–2, including a rematch victory over Englewood. It was an impressive start because even the most ardent St. Cecilia boosters had expected the Saints to lose at least three games. After the opening loss to Englewood, Vince guided his teams to one of the longest non-losing streaks in the history of New Jersey high-school football, making him a local celebrity and spurring his desire for a larger challenge.[27]

He succeeded because he had learned to master the game sufficiently to dominate at the high-school level. He was perceptive, innovative, and exceptionally dedicated and enthusiastic. His preparation left little to chance. He carefully monitored training rules, devised strategy, directed practices, scouted opponents, and motivated his players. Although his extreme verbal abuse scared some players and worried a few observers, he won praise for his integrity, his sportsmanship, and especially his outstanding winning record.

If players wanted to play football for him, Vince insisted they follow his system completely—his rules, his practice routines, and all his instructions. He was openly authoritarian. "I'll do all the thinking," he told the players. "Just do exactly as I tell you. I'll take the responsibility. Don't improvise!" He seldom appeared puzzled or confused. He imposed only a few rules but explained them clearly and enforced strict but evenhanded punishment. Smoking, drinking, curfew violation, and missing practice or the team bus were major offenses. If he judged an offense serious, he would tell the player, "Turn in your uniform." He imposed the same punishment on star players as he did on second-stringers. Two players with outstanding potential—a quarterback and a lineman—were each ordered, "Turn in your uniform."[28]

Each fall he brought Red Garrity and his team of officials to an early practice to explain football rules to his players. Beginning in 1942, Vince experimented with motion pictures as a coaching tool. Neal Roche, the English teacher and avid supporter of the team, would film Sunday's game, develop the film quickly, and Vince would show it to the team on Monday at noon. A critical error would prompt him to stop the projector. "I always told you, Dominic, that when you tackle you don't take your eyes off the fellow you're tackling."[29]

At St. Cecilia Vince started what later became known as "Lombardi time." If he scheduled a meeting for 9:00 A.M., players learned they had better arrive fifteen minutes early or be judged late. Actually, Vince was developing a phobia about time. "Time meant so much to him," recalled his brother Joe. If he could walk to the locker room faster than usual, he discovered he could save five minutes a day, or twenty-five minutes a week, to devote to something constructive.[30]

A strange dichotomy emerged between Vince's view of conventional manners and morals and his approach to the game of football. He insisted that his players be gentlemen off the field, dress properly, maintain high moral standards, hold the chair for Mother, and even help old ladies across the street. "I don't want animals walking the street!" he said. Yet when they stepped on the football field, he expected them to be "mean, nasty, and aggressive." At halftime of one game, he angrily inquired why the opposing quarterback hadn't been knocked to the ground. When a player explained that he had simply tried to avoid a penalty for roughing, Vince exploded: "You didn't want to draw a penalty? You hit that quarterback. You hit him on every play. I'll take the penalty—I'll worry about the penalty! Hit him! Hit him! Hit him!"[31]

Vince concentrated on teaching football fundamentals. His teams were seldom fancy. "They just went out and beat the living hell out of you," commented a local sportswriter who never saw a better-coached high-school team. "They blocked and tackled you to death." St. Cecilia did not own a blocking sled, only beat-up old dummies. Like Frank Leahy had been at Fordham, Vince was the blocking sled and an incredibly strong and durable one. Some of his linemen outweighed him by twenty-five pounds; yet, without padding, Vince would make a player hit him five times in a row and then absorb similar blows from the next player and the next. He resisted or threw aside a blocker if the player used the wrong technique. "If he didn't want you to [block him], you just couldn't do it." All the while he'd be yelling, "Drive! Drive! Drive! Block! Block! Block!" If a player attacked weakly, he screamed, "Hit!

I'm telling you hit! You call that hitting?'' Only when the blocker performed the technique properly and forcefully did he retreat.[32]

He looked for evidence of aggressive blocking. On one occasion he was surprised to see that his first-string tackle had a bloody nose. "Who did that? Who made his nose bleed?" When a second-string tackle meekly admitted he had done it, Vince praised him enthusiastically. "Good. Good. I like to see that!" Even when Vince himself became the victim of aggressive blocking, his attitude didn't change. "Stand up! Hit me! Do you understand? Hit me!" Vince insisted of Frank McPartland. The young freshman took the taunt literally and hit Vince square in the nose with his elbow. Startled, with blood dripping from his nostrils, Vince still managed to praise: "That's nice. That's *really* nice."[33]

Because he worried about each opponent and wanted to ward off overconfidence on his team, Vince lavished praise on all opponents and downplayed his own team's prospects. The local media came to expect his weekly lament. "This Lincoln High team is one of the best high-school teams I've ever seen," he told the local newspapers. His comment prompted Del Greco to chide him in the *Evening Record*: "If you think Frank Leahy of Notre Dame can cry the blues, then you ain't heard nothin' yet! St. Cecilia's Vince Lombardi out-Leahyed the coach of the Irish all season long. . . . The more Vince worried . . . the higher the St. Cecilia score."[34]

Vince dissected opponents through his expert scouting. Friends and alumni also scouted for him. Most high schools played on Saturday, but since St. Cecilia usually played on Sunday, Vince spent Saturday afternoons analyzing upcoming foes from the distant stands. In his report to the team he instructed his players, in minute detail, about the tendencies of opposing players and techniques to counteract them. "It was incredible what he would find out when he'd scout," a player marveled.[35]

On the Thursday evening before a game, Vince invited a few key players and team leaders to his home for dinner and a relaxed discussion of strategy. The two quarterbacks were always invited. Vince paid special attention to his quarterbacks (or his signal caller, since the quarterback did not always call the signals on Vince's teams). They had to be expertly prepared because the rules allowed few plays to be sent in by the coach. He expected the quarterback to be an extension of himself, to be intelligent enough to know the responsibilities of every offensive player on every play. "You must have command of your plays!" he insisted. Every free moment he used to instruct his quarterbacks. In his school office he placed a three-foot miniature football field, where he devised plays and strategy in his free time and called in his quarterback for a quick skull session.

The year Ken Clare called signals, Vince would beckon him into his office and start to quiz him. "Here's the ball. It's the third quarter. The score is [14–6] in favor of the opponent. What play do you call?" The first sessions confused Clare, but Vince persisted. Finally Clare learned to analyze the situation the way Vince wanted. "Okay, Coach," Clare said, "which way is the wind blowing? What team are we playing? . . ." Vince was delighted. "Now you've got it!" On Sunday morning before the game, he added one last bit of preparation. He gathered all the players into the gym and reviewed each player's responsibilities. By the time the game started, said halfback Richard Doheny, "there was nothing we didn't know."[36]

Vince kept talent flowing by offering St. Cecilia's tuition and book scholarships to talented athletes in Englewood and nearby communities. The practice was unusual but within the rules. He scouted big, strong, athletic eighth-graders. When he found one, he visited the boy's parents and at their kitchen table sold them on the advantages of St. Cecilia: the jacket and tie to make their boy a gentleman, discipline, religious training, a sound academic program, and, with dedication on the player's part and Vince's assistance, a possible college scholarship. His approach often worked, and he attracted outstanding talent to the school.[37]

Despite his explosive temper and passionate desire to win, Vince won praise for his sportsmanship in both basketball and football. Referees seldom if ever disciplined him. Against inferior teams he substituted players early so as not to run up the score. Coaching rivals liked and respected him. "Vince was very gracious in defeat," said Tom Morgan, the football coach at Englewood High School. Although Vince wanted his players to play football aggressively, he never tolerated unsportsman-like conduct. By all accounts St. Mary's of Rutherford, New Jersey, played exceptionally dirty in a game with St. Cecilia, and fights broke out. But Vince insistently warned his players during the game that "If anyone raises a hand [to hit someone], you're coming out." At the end of the game, Vince stormed over to the St. Mary's coach and bawled him out. Hyman observed afterward in the *Englewood Press* that Vince "coached his boys to play clean, hard football." St. Cecilia subsequently discontinued the football series with St. Mary's.[38]

Vince constantly sought innovative approaches to improve his teams, and he adopted two important ones in his second year as head coach. In August 1943 he began taking his team to an early preseason camp before school opened. Later, rules standardized the starting time for high-school practice, but Vince's camp fell within them while he coached at St. Cecilia. No other teams in the area, though, and few in the entire East went away to camp or started so early because they lacked the money or did not want to overemphasize football. Vince raised the money by having each team member sell candy to pay the $10 per-person cost. And in pursuit of football excellence nothing was excessive to Vince except infringements on religion, family, school, sportsmanship, or rules—none of which he felt applied in this case.

The first two years he took his team to a Knights of Columbus camp at Culver Lake, New Jersey, about fifty miles from Englewood—far enough away, Hyman noted perceptively, "from the kibitzers and Saturday Night Quarterbacks to enable Lombardi and Father Moore to get in uninterrupted coaching." Harry Lombardi attended also and, under a shady tree, cheered on the boys who now included young Joe Lombardi as well.[39]

At Culver Lake players lived in primitive cabins with straw in the mattresses. The camp had no showers or even running water. After two years, Vince moved the team to better facilities, at St. Joseph's Villa near Hackettstown, New Jersey. The camps ran for about nine days in late August and early September. (Vince missed a few days to return home to celebrate his wedding anniversary.) Vince and Father Moore directed calisthenics, sent the boys running up and down nearby hills, and supervised the drills. There were no heavy-contact sessions or scrimmages.

A sportswriter assumed that the boys could "relax" at camp and do some "swimming." Actually, they did little of the first and none of the second. "Vince ran the camp like . . . the army," said Father Moore. Players rose at seven forty-five. After Mass and breakfast, they labored through two hours of exercises and practice. Then came lunch, followed by a skull session and a three-hour afternoon practice. After 6:00 P.M. supper the boys could relax until 10:00 P.M. curfew. The players were not allowed to swim in the nearby lake, though they craved the opportunity, because Vince believed that swimming stretched their muscles. "I want strong, tight muscles," he explained. After the last practice he permitted them to jump into the lake up to their waist, wash up with soap, and rinse off. Then he blew his whistle and ordered them out.

"The boys are thriving on the regular life they are leading," Vince said in the midst of his 1943 camp. Indeed, they did seem to enjoy it despite the rigors. "They were the greatest days of my life," one recalled. The camp gave St. Cecilia a definite advantage over its opponents. In September 1943, the *Englewood Press* observed that the St. Cecilia team was "at least a week ahead of any other squad in Bergen County," exactly the situation Vince had anticipated.[40]

The other major innovation Vince adopted was the T formation, the dynamic new offensive system that became the rage in college and professional football in the early 1940s. The modern T was brought to perfection by George Halas, coach of the Chicago Bears, and by Clark Shaughnessy, who worked closely with the Bears' coach. Prior to World War II, Shaughnessy used the new offense to build powerhouse teams at Stanford. Halas and his great T quarterback, Sid Luckman, demonstrated the power of the T in a 73–0 massacre of the Washington Redskins in the 1940 NFL playoff game. In 1942, Frank Leahy, then in his second year as head coach at Notre Dame, learned the system during long sessions with Halas, Luckman, and Shaughnessy, after which Leahy scrapped the old Notre Dame single wing and also adopted the T.[41]

There were many advantages in the new offense, the principal ones being its balanced attack, deception, speed, and more effective blocking. The quarterback took the snap from directly behind the center, who could now feel his target and didn't have to tip off the snap by looking through his legs. Deception improved because at the snap of the ball the center partially obstructed the defense's view of the quarterback, and the quarterback could fake close to the line of scrimmage. The T utilized quick-hitting plays in which the back slashed through the hole before the defense could react. The hole did not have to remain open for long, either, allowing more man-for-man blocking rather than the inefficient double-team block. Linemen away from the hole brush-blocked their men and headed off to remove linebackers and the safetymen from the play, providing more effective blocking downfield. "On the signal caller," Leahy said, "rest all of your hopes of success." The quarterback became the crucial player in the T and was the major reason that Vince always developed close working relationships with his quarterbacks.[42]

By 1942 Vince had become convinced of the potential in the new offense, but so had other coaches. Many simply viewed the system as a magic formula. You installed it and you won. Vince knew better and marched one giant step ahead of his peers. "In order for him to have confidence in the T, he went to school," observed Leo Paquin, Vince's friend and fellow coach at Xavier High School in New York. "He picked the brains of anyone he knew who had anything to do with the T." The difference between Vince and his peers was the degree to which he learned the intricacies of the new system and then carefully prepared his teams to use it. He wrote Shaughnessy for detailed information. He sat down for lengthy discussions with Leahy at coaches' conventions. Leahy gave Vince a copy of his T formation playbook, which became Vince's football bible. During Holy Week of 1942, Vince brought in Eddie Doherty, the quarterback at Boston College, to demonstrate the T to his team in the St. Cecilia gym.[43]

During the 1942 season Vince used both the T and the single wing, and then in 1943 he converted almost exclusively to the new system. Because St. Cecilia was one of the first high schools in the East to master the T, the team overwhelmed opponents who hadn't learned how to adjust their defense. At meetings of the Bergen County Coaches' Association Vince shared his knowledge with his colleagues and argued the system's merits. "It's the only way!" he exclaimed, ending one discussion.[44]

An additional factor aided Vince in his quest for football victories: the nation's attitude in World War II toward competitive sports. An ideology emerged during the conflict that insisted national morale and fervency could best be achieved by those with athletic backgrounds. Sportswriter John Kieran of *The New York Times* argued that "war is competition and the boys in this country grew up on a background of competition. . . . We're not content to play a game, we want to win that game. . . . To lose is intolerable." The war was a considerable stimulant to football. Writers fostered the image of war as a gigantic football game in which a "unified command"—the head coach—was the "best way of winning the big game." All rigorous contact sports were glorified because they forced a psychological orientation toward the denial of physical comforts. Coaches were urged to make their physical conditioning as demanding as possible. Many parents who earlier had discouraged their sons from playing football for fear of injury now more willingly let them play.[45]

Bergen County, New Jersey, mirrored the national ideology. The *Bergen Evening Record* thought football was the "ideal conditioner" and reported that the government wanted its youth "rough and tough and ready for action, and football is one of the best means of learning how to take it and dish it out." Thus when Vince stressed stamina, courage, resourcefulness, self-discipline, loyalty, the will to win, and the host of other virtues he saw in football, he met with a receptive audience among those who expected the virtues to benefit young men as soldiers, sailors, and marines.[46]

Vince concentrated so intensely on the problems and prospects of his team that at times he seemed oblivious to ordinary daily activities. More than once after practice he drove home, exhausted, still contemplating the team's progress, parked his car three driveways down from his own, and marched into a strange house. During a game he was a bundle of nerves, pacing up and down the sideline, blinking and smoking incessantly.[47]

In order to express himself on the field Vince had to shout, and it didn't take much to irritate him. "He felt that he had to bawl out the kids to make them better players," Hyman observed, "but I know, from our conversations, that it hurt him to do it." Some players never forgave his abusiveness. "I could never agree with him flying off," said one. Vince became most upset when a player made a mistake Vince thought he shouldn't have made because Vince had prepared him not to make it. Sometimes he got upset with himself because he thought he had failed to make himself clear. He swore often. "Goddamnit, run that play right!" was a typical outburst. While dealing with his players, he often reversed the recommended method of personal relations: He bawled a player out in public and praised him in private. When he saw a mistake on the practice field, he felt compelled to correct it immediately; later, realizing he had been too abusive, he felt equally compelled to apologize or praise in private, as if doing penance for his sin.[48]

Vince apparently never apologized, though, to the person who most deserved an apology: his own brother Joe. His callous mistreatment of his youngest brother illustrates what happened when the well-meaning teacher and coach chose to enforce rigidly his ideas on fairness, perfection, and manliness. Joe Lombardi was seventeen years younger than Vince and idolized his brother. When Harry and Matilda moved the family to Englewood, Joe was in elementary school, and in the fall of 1943, he entered St. Cecilia as a 5-8, 165-pound, thirteen-year-old freshman. He joined the football squad and played guard, Vince's position at Fordham.

Joe's presence was both a challenge and an opportunity for Vince, one he handled poorly. In Vince's view he had to be fair and demanding with Joe. Any sign of favoritism could seriously undermine team morale and unity. He must insist that Joe develop as an athlete, as a student, and as a man—in short, he must become like Vince himself. As a result Joe had to endure four years of unrelenting pressure and harassment. "He never let up," Joe reflected later. "I was his brother. . . . I don't think Vince ever praised me once."[49]

When practice started each day, Joe always had to be the first player to block Vince one-on-one. "Hit me on three," Vince would say, and he would count, but on two he would smack Joe. This routine continued for four years until Joe finally wised up and hit Vince on one and a half. "It's about time," Vince said as he ended that particular torture. But there were other confrontations on the field. "It was brutal," one player observed. "Joe took a hell of a beating," said another; "there was blood all over the place." Players tried to concentrate on their practice assignments but were distracted by the violence as the Lombardi brothers warred with each other. Vince taunted Joe to make him improve: "You stink, Joe! You stink!" Or he would appeal to family pride: "I want you to be proud of that name Lombardi!"[50]

Joe had to play with injuries and follow training rules just as other players. In one game Joe broke what later was identified as a metatarsal bone. Initially Vince insisted the injury wasn't serious. "There's nothing wrong with your foot," he told his brother. Joe continued to play, and after the game Vince rewarded him with the game ball for his valor. On the evening before another game, Joe was scrubbing and waxing floors at home when Vince stopped by at 10:30 P.M., a half hour past curfew. He bawled Joe out and benched him for the game. "It didn't make any difference what I was doing or why I was doing it," Joe recalled; "I'd broken the rule."[51]

Vince was equally insistent that Joe reach his potential in the classroom. In his sophomore year Joe did poorly in some classes, prompting a bizarre public encounter with his demanding brother. At the close of the school year, St. Cecilia held an academic convocation attended by students and faculty. As the moderator, Vince summoned students up to the stage to receive their report cards, but he skipped Joe's name and saved it for the end. When he finally called his brother, Joe walked up innocently, only to have Vince hit him and knock him clear off the stage. The audience was stunned. "Joe ran like hell," a witness observed, with Vince in hot pursuit down the aisle. A student who happened to be standing at the exit opened the door for Joe's escape but slammed it in Vince's face. "When I did get home," Joe recalled, "my father hit me again." Joe's schoolwork improved afterward.[52]

Joe received small but satisfying recognition from his brother at the end of his senior season. After Joe was selected to the All-Metropolitan team, Vince accompanied his proud brother to the award dinner. "I think that was my greatest thrill," Joe said of Vince's presence. Much of the time Joe had resented his brother's treatment, but he thought years later that he had benefited overall. "He was bringing something out of me. . . . He was making me into a man." Would not a less humiliating approach have achieved the same result?[53]

Vince's mistreatment of his brother was an exceptional case. Most players learned to adjust or to tolerate his tantrums. They realized they had made a mistake and deserved correction. They also understood that Vince's outbursts stemmed from his desire to improve their performance, a goal they also shared. Finally, they knew his anger subsided quickly, that he never carried a grudge, and that deep down, as one player put it, he was a "loving, gentle person."[54]

Vince used various psychological ploys to motivate his team, and although their transparent nature later became evident—and even laughable—their immediate effect overwhelmed. Before an important encounter with archrival Englewood High School, Vince announced that he would hold a "secret" evening practice. Players became caught up in the drama. Parents drove their cars to the Mackay Park practice field and turned on their headlights to illuminate the field for what turned out to be a routine practice. Vince didn't install any new plays or devise a new strategy. Nor had the evening session been secret; anyone could have stopped by to watch. Yet the practice did focus attention on the Englewood game, which the Saints won.[55]

A blatant deception helped defeat Brooklyn Prep, another major rival. During the week before the game, each St. Cecilia player received a "postcard" in the mail from a Brooklyn Prep counterpart filled with insulting comments about the St. Cecilia player and the team. This was like waving a red flag in front of a bull; no coach in his right mind would allow his players to enrage an opponent. But the naïve St. Cecilia players assumed the cards were legitimate. "Naturally, we got all fired up and went out and beat Brooklyn Prep," said one. They discovered later that Vince had written the cards himself and had gone to Brooklyn to mail them. He laughed heartily about it afterward.[56]

Another stratagem, his "pill story," became a legend at St. Cecilia. Again the upcoming opponent was Brooklyn Prep, whose team averaged about fifteen pounds heavier per man than the Saints. To counter the advantage, Vince sought to make his players *feel* larger and more powerful. In the locker room before the game he told his charges in slow, measured tones the story of how Fordham had defeated a huge, powerful St. Mary's team during Vince's playing days. Crowley had given each Fordham player a pill before the game, he said, that actually made them bigger and stronger. He showed his bug-eyed Saints' players how his chest had expanded and muscles had hardened after taking the mysterious concoction. Luckily, Vince dramatically announced, he had been able to secure some of the potent pills for his own players for the Brooklyn Prep game. He then took out a tweezer and a bottle of pills and, like a religious ritual, carefully gave each player one pill. The pill was a placebo, of course, and the Crowley-Fordham-St. Mary's story pure hokum, but the ploy worked. "We believed him," a player recalled. "We went out feeling bigger and stronger and beat Brooklyn Prep." Students later caught on to the ruse, but the knowledge did not lessen the joy of hearing

Lombardi retell it. "Tell us the pill story!" students chanted at later pep assemblies and banquets, and Vince would have to tell it again, year after year.[57]

The clever, manipulative tricks Vince used to motivate his players effectively served his immediate goal, but they were not the most sustained source of player motivation. That source was Vince himself—his character, personality, enthusiasm, and example. Most of the players held him in awe and admired his integrity. They saw him at Mass daily and knew he didn't chase around with women or drink heavily. He taught them about life as well as sports. When a few players sneaked into the school cafeteria after practice to steal small containers of ice cream, and school officials caught them, Vince lectured the group about the lesson to be learned. "Your moral integrity is the most priceless thing you possess," he said. He improved the lives of many of his players. "He changed my life," said one. "His moral values were great," said another. "He had the will of a perfectionist, the mind of a fundamentalist, and the heart of a father," recalled Father Guy McPartland.

He made his players work hard in practice, but they responded to his tough regimen and came to appreciate, as one player said, that through "work, progress, and development we became winners and there is no greater motivation than that." His players loved the sport, and he made sure they had fun. "And when you're winning," a player said, "it sure is a lot of fun." Vince's smile and teasing made players feel that he had a deep, personal interest in and affection for them. On occasion he went out of his way to show how much he cared about a player. Al Quilici, a star end, had to miss a game because of a high fever. After St. Cecilia won the game, Vince routed the team bus to Quilici's apartment, walked up to the door, gave Quilici a big hug and a kiss and said warmly, "Al, we won, but we really missed you."[58]

Players could see that Vince was so dedicated to the team's success, so intense and enthusiastic, that they absorbed those traits themselves. "I felt I was winning the game for him," recalled John DeGasperis, "because if you lost he would take it the hardest, and if you won he would be so happy." Vince encouraged his seniors to lead by example, and they did. As soon as he issued instructions, the seniors responded immediately. He usually arrived late for practice after school because he had to gather all the equipment in his car, but the seniors would round up the team in his absence and begin practice on their own. "We'd be blocking one-on-one [and] he wasn't even there yet," one player marveled; "that's the kind of dedication he instilled." He was so enthusiastic that even during the school day he devised new plays and would break the news to players in the school corridor. "Wait till we get out to practice!" he would say, wringing his hands and grimacing gleefully. "I dreamed up a new play. I woke up at three in the morning!" He would even assign a number to it right on the spot.[59]

He gave special attention to key players, especially if he thought they lacked concentration or a good attitude. He constantly berated one outstanding, swivel-hipped halfback at practice, but on the Sunday morning before the game he brought him into his office for private encouragement and the player walked out "ten feet tall." Vince carefully bolstered the morale of all his players, not just outstanding ones. If a halfback scored on a dramatic long run, Vince praised his supporting cast when the offense returned to the sideline. "That was a super block, Billy!" he'd say to the tackle. "We went for a touchdown because you faked all the way!" he'd yell to the other halfback.

His dynamic pep talks aroused students, faculty, and players. The students clapped long and loud as Vince rose to speak at the Friday afternoon pep rally. In the locker room before the game he appealed to the players' pride: "Your mother and father are out there. They're looking at you! Five thousand people will be looking at you!" Then he'd walk up to some of the starting players and, nose to nose, urge them to perform vigorously. To an offensive lineman: "They'll be watching that block!" To a halfback: "They'll be watching you run!" The effect was overwhelming. "He got more out of a kid who didn't show any sign of ability than anybody I ever knew," observed Father Moore.[60]

During World War II Vince's coaching brought spectacular results. After the loss to Englewood in 1942, St. Cecilia didn't lose again until the third game of the 1945 season. Of the thirty-two games in that period, St. Cecilia won twenty-eight and tied four. The non–losing streak also included twenty-five wins in a row. His great, undefeated 1943 team outscored opponents 267–19, shutting out eight of its eleven foes.

When a New Jersey chapter of the American Legion started the "Legion Bowl," it invited St. Cecilia to play in its 1943 and 1944 games. On December 5, 1943, twelve thousand spectators watched St. Cecilia defeat Lincoln High School of Jersey City, 6–0. The following year the Saints played a 0–0 tie with Union City, New Jersey, before another large crowd. After the game a diehard St. Cecilia nun was crying in the locker room because the tie snapped the Saints' twenty-five game winning streak. Vince's mother tried to console her. "You didn't lose," Matilda Lombardi said to the nun. "But we didn't win," Vince emphasized.[61]

During the non-losing streak Vince remained modest and fatalistic. "We've been lucky," he told a reporter; "our number is coming up someday." His team's number finally came up in the fall of 1945, when the Saints lost, 12–0, to the powerful, veteran squad of Seton Hall High School. The weather that day reflected Vince's mood. The sky was dark and the rain heavy. Up in the stands Marie's friends suggested she leave early to avoid the crowd and the weather, but she insisted on staying. "He was standing in the rain in the middle of a puddle and he looked like he was getting smaller and smaller," she recalled. "I told [my friends] that if he can stand there and take it, then I can take it, too. I walk beside him."[62]

After the loss to Seton Hall, Vince's record for the rest of his coaching career at St. Cecilia was 11–5–1, still impressive but not exceptional. He had enjoyed an advantage from 1942–45 because so many outstanding high-school coaches had gone to war. Now they were back, and their teams provided more challenging competition than he had faced earlier. Moreover, aggressive coaches quickly adopted the new innovations that he used so successfully. In 1945 Englewood High School began taking its team to a Lombardi-style early-season camp, and Englewood defeated St. Cecilia in 1945 and 1946. When Memorial High School smashed the Saints, 43–6, in 1946, Memorial used a powerful T formation offense.

Although his glowing record diminished somewhat at the end, on the whole the Lombardi era at St. Cecilia had created abundant joy among the school's partisans. Crowds of ten thousand persons often filled Winton White Stadium. Local newspapers constantly praised the "glorious spirit" at the school. During a speech to Rotarians, an Englewood High School official bemoaned the lack of spirit at his school compared to its parochial-school rival. At pep rallies on Friday afternoon and at year-end football banquets "school songs and team cheers . . . filled the spacious gym." After a game hundreds of players and students paraded through city streets, stopping for a while to serenade the Lombardi family at Harry's home. Harry opened his house to the roving bands and served them cases of soda. "There was fun in coaching then," Vince reminisced of his St. Cecilia years.[63]

As Vince's teams kept winning, his reputation grew, and from 1944 to 1946 rumors circulated in the press that he was under consideration for coaching jobs at high schools and a few colleges. To those who observed him closely he was a diamond in the rough. "You knew even then," recalled Hyman, "that one day he was going to be the best damn football coach in the country." A pattern emerged: Some area high schools offered him jobs he rejected, and he applied for college vacancies but was turned down. Sometime after 1939 he abandoned the idea of becoming a lawyer. He told friends many times his primary goal: "I dreamed of someday being head coach at Fordham." However, when Fordham resumed football after the war, the head coaching job went to Ed Danowski, a former All-American quarterback at Fordham and later a star with the New York Giants. Vince was disappointed, but in the meanwhile he applied for assistant coaching jobs at Holy Cross and the University of San Francisco, and probably for the head coaching position at City College of New York. But nothing materialized. Tenafly High School in New Jersey and Horace Mann Prep School in New York offered him head coaching positions, but their inducements were not enough for him to uproot his family and leave the school he loved.[64]

Finally, in May 1945, he accepted the best noncollege job he could find. Officials at nearby Hackensack High School had been impressed with Vince's record (then 27–1–3) and asked him to become the school's new coach. He mulled the offer over quietly for a few days and then accepted the job. "I'll be making less at Hackensack," he told the press, "but it's a move I must make when I consider my family. I'll be protected by tenure after three years. That counts a lot with teachers." Vince seldom lied, but he did on this occasion. It wasn't tenure that attracted him. He had no fear of losing his job at St. Cecilia. He was so highly respected that he wouldn't lose his job unless the school closed, an unlikely prospect. He needed to support his family, and money lured him away. Hackensack had offered him $6,000 a year, almost double his current salary. Why he tried to deceive the press is unclear. Perhaps he simply didn't want people to think he was leaving for monetary reasons. In any case, the new job excited him, and he began making plans to move his family to Hackensack. "Funny thing," he said; "I just bought a home in Englewood. Guess there won't be too much trouble selling it." "They have good material, haven't they?" he asked a reporter about the players on the Hackensack team.[65]

When questioned by the press about Vince's new job, Father Moore tried to be diplomatic. Yes, St. Cecilia had consented to accept Vince's resignation on May 14. "He's going against my will. Lombardi did a fine job here and we tried to give him everything. There were no complaints with the way he handled his job. It puts us on the spot about getting another coach, but we're working on that now." Privately, Father Moore was enraged. How could St. Cecilia find a wartime replacement for Vince's multifaceted position? What new coach could possibly bring the glory, the joy, and the money to St. Cecilia that Vince's teams had? And, most galling to the priest and many students, how could Vince accept a job at a rival, public high school? Those who expected him to leave someday assumed he would move up to Fordham or some other college.

But Hackensack High School? That was treason. "If that's your ambition in life, to make six thousand dollars, then go ahead," Father Moore angrily told him. Why hadn't he waited for a college offer to come his way? Father Moore inquired. Vince replied that he had waited patiently long enough. "When is it going to happen?" Vince half pleaded with his friend.

Vince's response didn't satisfy Father Moore, who organized a campaign to convince him to stay. The priest shocked students in his religion class when he lashed out at Vince, telling the students how "lousy" Lombardi had been to leave St. Cecilia in the lurch. He encouraged Vince's family and friends not to speak to him. The silent treatment partially succeeded, and the withdrawal of affection deeply hurt Vince.[66]

In late May the *Englewood Press* discovered that a "peculiar situation" had emerged at St. Cecilia. "Letters and petitions have been drawn up, signed by the students, and sent to Lombardi, imploring him to reconsider. . . . The boys and girls have cornered him at every opportunity, attempting to prevail upon him to change his mind." A delegation of athletes met with him and begged him to stay. During the session some of the underclassmen began crying, causing Vince to choke up and tear himself.[67]

After ten days of enduring the pleas and petitions of students, the icy silence of loved ones, and the hostility of his priest friend, Vince had had enough. The evening before he was to sign his Hackensack contract, he phoned Father Moore. "Tim, you've got to get me out of it," he said. After a few drinks together, they agreed on a face-saving way out. The explanation given to the Hackensack Board of Education and the press in late May made no mention of Vince's change of heart. When St. Cecilia released Vince from his contract on May 14, so the story went, it had been only an informal, verbal release. Since St. Cecilia could not find a replacement to teach science and to coach, the school had to invoke the five-year contract Vince had signed in 1943 and refuse to release him. Vince apologized to Hackensack officials but stated his hands were tied. Hackensack then reluctantly released him from their agreement. Press reports made it appear that Vince had been an ambitious contract-breaker. Yet no one criticized him publicly, no hard feelings lingered, and the incident was soon forgotten. With the ordeal finally over, Vince's peace of mind returned, especially after everyone started talking to him again. Still, Hyman observed after Vince had returned to the St. Cecilia fold that "of course, it's inevitable that Lombardi will one day leave St. Cecilia" because his future "lies in the college coaching ranks."[68]

Michael O'Brien

Hyman's observation proved prophetic. Less than two years later, in January 1947, Vince announced he had accepted a position at Fordham as assistant football coach and assistant director of physical education. This time no one tried to persuade him to stay because they knew he was on the road to fulfilling his dream. Although he wouldn't be head coach and his salary remained the same, he was returning to his alma mater and, with luck, he might take full charge of Fordham's team someday and restore it to glory.

Three hundred fifty well-wishers toasted Vince at a farewell dinner on April 10. Friends and athletic officials from throughout New Jersey presented laudatory tributes, including one from the New Jersey State Interscholastic Athletic Association, which praised his "moral qualities." The praise from friends, recollections of past glory at St. Cecilia, the prospect of leaving—all overwhelmed Vince that evening. "Coach Lombardi spoke, but he was all choked up," reported the *Bergen Evening Record*. "He put in a plug for his mother and father before he was led away by his missus."[69]

IV

Back to
Fordham
(1947–48)

VINCE CONTINUED TEACHING AT ST. CECILIA FOR THE REST OF THE 1947 SCHOOL year but drove to Rose Hill to coach spring practice. Fordham's 1946 team had been awful. "My St. Cecilia club can knock off what I've seen at Fordham," he said. But, as always, he welcomed the challenge and was pleased with the prospect of working under Ed Danowski. "Eddie is a great guy," he told the press, "and I guess what he doesn't know about forward passing isn't in the book."[1]

Actually, Vince would learn little about forward passing or anything else from Danowski. What Vince learned he picked up on his own. He worked diligently, refined some of his coaching skills, and generally acquired a better understanding of the college game, but he had wanted and expected more. He accepted the position partly because he hoped the circumstances might arise that would allow him to become the head coach. Maybe Danowski would quit after a few years. Vince's excellent coaching did indeed impress many people, including key Fordham officials who tried to maneuver him into the top spot, but they did so in such a way as to incur intense public wrath. Consequently, in the fall of 1948, Vince became embroiled in a most embarrassing and depressing controversy, one that forced him to look elsewhere for a new coaching position.

Michael O'Brien

The Fordham football program in 1947 did not have the same stature as the one Vince had left ten years earlier. Since 1936, when he became president of Fordham, Reverend Robert I. Gannon had been skeptical about the virtues of college football. He didn't enjoy the game and thought it out of control almost everywhere. At first, though, he saw no major problem at Fordham. Athletic officials followed the rules, attendance and profits soared, and Crowley's teams won. But beginning in 1938, profits began to fall precipitously even though the team continued to win. At the start of World War II Crowley enlisted in the Navy and was commissioned a lieutenant commander. Before he left he apparently squabbled with Father Gannon and entered service with the clear understanding that he would not return to Fordham after the war. Like many other colleges, Fordham dropped football for the duration and mothballed its equipment.[2]

When the war ended, many alumni desired the return to past gridiron glory, but Father Gannon had become even more concerned with the financial problems and more convinced that overemphasis on football hindered academic excellence. In October 1947, in a speech to a New Jersey alumni group, Father Gannon expressed the hope that Fordham would "never again have an outstanding team—we may, but I certainly hope not. . . . One of the things I have learned during the last decade was that a top team doesn't do us any good financially, scholastically, socially, or athletically." His next remarks alienated many alumni and friends of Fordham. In what he thought were off-the-record comments, he charged that football merely drummed up "business for the gambling fraternity," labeled the owners of the Polo Grounds "extortionists" for charging Fordham excessive rent, and described sportswriters as "tyrants of tyrants" who "think a university's sole purpose should be to provide them with an income." Predictably, New York sportswriters chastised him for his extreme views. Red Smith thought he had been "caught with his judgment down."[3]

When Fordham resumed football in 1946 the program was so confused and so meagerly funded that chaos resulted. The university hired Danowski in February 1946 at a salary of $5,000—one third the amount of Crowley's pre-war salary—and provided Danowski with only one assistant. Recruiting started late; then athletic officials muddled their way toward a disastrous middle-of-the-road policy: a big-time college schedule played with small-time resources. Danowski had accepted the position with the understanding that he would have few scholarships and few other resources, but he was told not to worry because Fordham would play small schools like Hofstra and King's Point. Yet when the schedule came out it included games against Penn State, Louisiana State University, and other powerhouses. "It was murder," said Danowski of the 1946 season. "I signed for five grand because I thought we were playing small schools." As a result, Fordham lost all of its seven games.[4]

Thirty-two years old when he took the Fordham job, Danowski had been one of Fordham's greatest players. He captained the 1933 team and won All-American honors as a triple-threat halfback on Crowley's first Ram team. He earned further acclaim as a brilliant, versatile performer for the professional New York Giants from 1934 to 1939. After coaching briefly at Haverstraw High School in New York, he enlisted in the Navy in 1942. He was quiet, shy, sincere, extremely likable, and had a blond cowlick forever falling down over his forehead.

Danowski took a lackadaisical attitude toward coaching—the opposite of Vince's approach. Football, Danowski thought, should not be "life or death." He was easygoing, nice to everyone, and accepted suggestions from his assistant coaches, but otherwise he possessed few attributes for coaching at a major college level. He couldn't project his knowledge of football, had no zeal for teaching young athletes, and was so quiet that players often didn't know what he wanted or expected. He didn't work them hard in practice and couldn't effectively motivate them. His brief high-school coaching experience had not prepared him for his difficult assignment, and the only offensive system he understood was the outdated single wing. Despite their vastly different temperaments and approaches to the game, though, Vince and Danowski were the picture of harmony until events of the late fall of 1948 ruptured their relationship.[5]

Fordham increased the number of Danowski's assistant coaches in 1947, allowing him to hire Vince. He specifically hoped that Vince could teach the team—and Danowski himself—the intricacies of the T formation. Also, the Fordham Athletic Association raised funds from alumni to support over thirty football scholarships for incoming freshmen, a major improvement in the program. Vince's assignment included coaching the freshmen recruits, assisting with the varsity, and teaching physical education classes—all for $3,500 a year. He dove into his new work so enthusiastically that he seemed oblivious to normal courtesy. When Jim Lansing, another new assistant coach, first walked into the coaches' office in the spring of 1947, Vince was standing at the blackboard diagraming a formation. Danowski introduced Lansing to Vince, but instead of extending his greeting, Vince asked Lansing insistently: "Jim, I've got this offense on the blackboard. What would you do against that defense?" Noted Lansing: "He didn't even say 'hello' "[6]

Vince taught three physical education classes a day, primarily volleyball, basketball, badminton, and conditioning. "He was a real good worker," Danowski observed of his teaching. Coaching the outstanding freshmen recruits was his primary task. As soon as he took the Fordham job, he began recruiting players in New York and New Jersey. Fordham was "reemphasizing" football, he told them, and was a "good, solid Jesuit school" whose many alumni in the New York area guaranteed career opportunities after graduation. His efforts lured a few outstanding athletes to Fordham, most notably five of his former St. Cecilia players.[7]

While Danowski continued to use the single wing with the varsity, Vince taught the freshmen the T formation. The experience of the former St. Cecilia players with both Vince and the T speeded up the learning process. Vince concentrated on quickness. "It seemed that was all he was interested in," recalled William Landmark, a freshman lineman. "You brush-blocked your opponent and then got downfield. Everything was 'downfield! downfield!' "[8]

With prospects for the varsity so dismal in 1947, many Fordham fans focused their attention on the two freshman games. Before the first one, with the Rutgers frosh, Vince gave his team an emotional send-off. They were the "white hope" who had the opportunity to re-create the "glory days" of Fordham football, he told them intently. "How you do will determine if Fordham can come back." Fordham won the game, 12–0, and Vince was ecstatic; yet afterward he played coy with the press. His team had played "fair," he told a reporter, and then provided evidence that they had played much better. They completed "twelve out of seventeen passes," he continued, "and gained over four hundred yards on the ground." "His yearlings looked like a million dollars," gushed one New York sportswriter, and "are expected to lift the Rams to the prestige they knew on the gridiron before the war." The team impressed even more in their second outing, against archrival NYU. Thirty-five hundred spectators turned out—an exceptionally large crowd for a freshman game—as Fordham exploded for three touchdowns in the opening ten minutes and coasted to an easy 33–0 victory.[9]

Reporters started to beseech Vince to confirm the flattering rumor that his freshmen ran "roughshod" over the varsity in practice. Vince answered modestly: "My kids are good but not that good." (Vince responded accurately: In scrimmages his freshmen played the varsity competitively but did not quite dominate them.) Vince also coached the varsity backfield, but that work was not nearly as successful. The varsity continued to flounder badly. Its record in 1947 (1–6–1) was not much better than the year before. Opponents outscored Fordham, 245–44. Penn State embarrassed the Rams, 75–0.[10]

Vince almost gave up coaching entirely after his first year at Fordham, when he was offered a job at a salary more than four times larger than his Fordham pay. Beginning in 1947, for two consecutive summers he worked as a foreman for the Brewster Construction Company, one of the largest construction firms in New Jersey. Ray Moore, Father Tim Moore's brother, was a project manager for Brewster and had hired Vince at $100 a week. Vince supervised a gang of fifteen workers, mostly Italians, and worked on large highway projects, including one section of a state highway near Lyndhurst, New Jersey. Some of the Brewster workers hated their slave-driving foreman, but Vince's gang loved him. "He was a real leader of men," said one Brewster worker. Because he was so efficient and dedicated and yet had such excellent rapport with his crew, in the summer of 1948 Ray Moore offered him $15,000 a year (and perhaps more) to work full time for the company. The large salary sorely tempted Vince, but he rejected it. He had fallen in love with coaching and still hoped that the head job at Fordham might open up.[11]

In 1948 Vince worked exclusively with the varsity. Many of his outstanding freshmen players had moved up with him, raising hopes for a successful season, but they turned out to be too inexperienced. In the first game Lafayette shattered the high expectations by embarrassing the Rams, 53–14. No one was more shocked and disappointed than Vince. He had started the season by teaching the T formation to the offensive backfield, but the offensive line performed so poorly that he began coaching them as well. Essentially, he became the offensive coach.[12]

During his two years at Fordham, Vince sharpened his coaching skills by constantly communicating with the nation's best football minds. He corresponded with Notre Dame's Frank Leahy and huddled with him at football conventions. Once a week in 1948 he drove to West Point to consult with Sid Gillman, Army's offensive genius. In July 1948 Vince drove to Superior, Wisconsin, to observe the training camp of the New York Giants. He also began to express publicly his thoughts on the value of football, thoughts garnered from his own experience and from Fordham's Jesuits. "How does a man meet his failures?" Vince asked on October 1, 1947, in his opening remarks to the Lions Club of Hackensack, New Jersey. "That is the measure of the man. If he does not quit or curl up he has the right stuff in him. Be a hard loser," he urged. "There is no such thing as a good loser, but in losing one can still be a good sport." The athlete was a leader in school and later in life, he contended, and was usually more alert, responsible, and healthy. "You seldom, if ever, find an athlete who is a criminal. He is essentially a good boy, a good sport, and a gentleman. He adheres to the word of God, call it the Golden Rule if you will, both on the field and off. . . . I am going to try to raise my son to be an athlete."[13]

A few players disliked Vince because they thought he didn't play them enough or because they bridled at his demands and abuse. Sometimes he hollered right into a player's ear. "It really shook you up," said one victim. Yet his fellow coaches and most players deeply respected him for his leadership, his teaching and organizing skills, and his knowledge of the game. "He did a good job for me," conceded Danowski. "He was strong in every area," said Lou DeFilippo, an assistant coach. Most of the players concurred, but more emphatically. "Of the coaching that was done, Lombardi was the only one who imparted a message [and] worked with people to build up their basic skills," observed center Herbert Seidell, who had captained the 1947 freshman team. "For all practical purposes, Lombardi ran the team," said Larry Higgins, a running back and a recruit from St. Cecilia. "He was so far ahead of Danowski and the other coaches [that] I felt sorry for [Vince]," recalled John Langan. "He had every position down in his head," said another player, and had "more zest for the game than anyone else at Fordham—that's for sure." Vince presented the blackboard lectures and the pep talks, effectively answered questions, conducted rigorous practices, and motivated the players. Unlike the other coaches, Vince could immediately see the need to alter a play. Yet he was not the head coach and could not make the crucial decisions he thought necessary. Tim Cohane, a close observer of the Fordham football situation and a staunch Lombardi supporter, pinpointed Vince's awkward predicament: "It was not a happy arrangement, for responsibility must be matched by authority."[14]

In the middle of the 1948 season Vince's enthusiastic admirers at Fordham planned to match his responsibility with authority. A three-man Athletic Council composed of Reverend Kevin O'Brien, Reverend Lawrence Walsh, and Jack Coffey, the graduate manager of athletics, supervised athletic programs and usually conducted most business quietly and without interference. A seven-member Alumni Advisory Committee composed of prominent Fordham graduates (including Wellington Mara, Vince's friend and classmate) advised the council. Father Gannon had the ultimate authority but was too busy to supervise day-to-day operations. Father O'Brien and Coffey, the most aggressive council members and the two most interested in returning Fordham to its prewar glory, had become disenchanted with Danowski and impressed with Vince, particularly after the sparkling performance of Vince's 1947 freshman team. Many ardent alumni fans agreed with their assessment. To them Danowski was ineffective, as evidenced by his two-year record of 1–13–1. They also thought he was colorless. "Lombardi . . . is rated just the opposite," argued a New York sportswriter, and is "one who will make personal appearances and is a good mixer." Danowski's three-year contract ran out at the end of the 1948 season, and Father O'Brien and Coffey secretly maneuvered to fire him and replace him with Vince.[15]

After Boston College defeated the Rams, 33–7, lowering the team's record to 2–4, Joe Williams of the *New York World-Telegram* broke the news that Fordham intended to fire Danowski at the end of the season. Other New York papers quickly picked up the story and for the next four weeks publicized the ensuing controversy. All the stories assumed that Vince would be the next head coach. "Lombardi Leads; Fordham Expected to Pick New Coach," screamed one headline. Coffey, caught off guard by the publicity, initially refused comment, which merely fueled speculation that a change would indeed occur. Then he announced that the Athletic Council would meet after the NYU game, the last game of the season. "We'll know then who it's going to be," he said, again fueling speculation.

At first Danowski was mystified by the publicity. "I suppose I could always find a job as a high-school coach," he said blandly. New York writers rushed to his defense, even though they had previously never been close to him, and their efforts rallied others to his cause. "Disgraceful," "cruel," "high-pressure tactics," they angrily charged; Danowski had performed solid work and deserved another chance. Critics directed many of their volleys at Father Gannon, who they charged had provided Danowski with such meager resources that it was impossible for him to succeed and yet was now acquiescing in the conspiracy to fire him. "[Father Gannon's] policies, rather than Danowski's coaching, popularly are deemed responsible for Fordham's lack of grid success," charged one critic.[16]

Prior to the NYU game additional support emerged for Danowski. The Alumni Advisory Committee met with Father O'Brien and strongly condemned the secret maneuvering. (Mara also agreed that Danowski had been mistreated.) Some football players publicly came to their coach's defense. "I know a lot of the boys wouldn't want to play if Danowski got fired," said center Jimmy Murphy; "he's a great guy and a good coach." Langdon Viracola, a star running back, echoed Murphy: "All the boys like Danowski, and we're going to win Saturday's game for him." The *New York Daily News* reported that the players had voted 45–1 to keep Danowski and had submitted the voting results to the Athletic Council. (No such vote actually took place, and many players privately hoped that in some humane manner Vince could move up to the head coaching position.)[17]

Meanwhile, the embarrassing public controversy mortified Vince. He had long wanted the head coaching job but not in this awkward way. He refused to answer reporters' questions on the subject. "I don't know anything about it!" he half pleaded in a conversation with his friend Leo Paquin when the stories first appeared. Paquin, who had close contact with Fordham athletic officials, agreed that Vince knew nothing about the Athletic Council's maneuvering: "Lombardi didn't start it [or] make one single move to usurp the power of Danowski. Lombardi was hurt by his best friends."[18]

After practice on Friday before the NYU game, Vince gathered the team around him and, with tears in his eyes, pointed to Danowski and said, "He is going to be your coach next year, not me." During the same week he told Paquin privately, "I just can't stay here. I'm not going to do anything to further what these people are thinking about me—that I cut Ed Danowski's throat."[19]

The team's fortunes in the last three games helped to secure Danowski's position. After the loss to Boston College, Fordham played two strong games in losing to Holy Cross and Rutgers, and then defeated NYU, 26–0. "We did it for Danowski," declared Viracola afterward in the jubilant dressing room. The alumni, reported one newspaper, were "unstinting in admiration" for how well "Ed's charges" performed in their season-ending victory.

After the NYU game, bolstered by expressions of support from the alumni, the players, and the press, Danowski seethed with anger at Father O'Brien and Coffey. He also assumed that Vince had been part of the cabal. At one meeting Danowski issued an ultimatum. "We had a showdown," he recalled; "I said, '[Lombardi] goes or I go.' " Father Gannon finally intervened and insisted on retaining the current coach. As Danowski later observed, they "decided to keep me and the kind of football they had." On December 6, 1948, Jack Coffey, speaking for the humbled Athletic Council, announced that Danowski had signed a new one-year contract. The press was jubilant. "It was an extraordinary tribute," said *The New York Times*' Arthur Daley of the outpouring of support. "It hardly would have been fair to let him go just as he had begun to see daylight."[20]

What Fordham almost did to Danowski had indeed been unfair. Although Vince lusted after the head coaching job, he had not been directly involved in the plan to fire Danowski. Moreover, Vince had performed the lion's share of the effective coaching. Most of the players realized Vince's dominant contribution but were unwilling to say anything publicly for fear of losing their scholarships or because they didn't want to hurt their likable coach. "Lombardi had so much on the ball," observed Ed Franco, another assistant coach, "that . . . it was a mistake to not give [him] the head coaching job."[21]

Vince's two years at Fordham ended sadly, but, as he did at each stop in his coaching career, he left a lasting—and mostly favorable— impression on people, particularly on his players. "His knowledge and ability to coach football will pay big dividends," predicted a sportswriter, "and that day may come sooner than a lot of people think." Herbert Seidell, who played for him both years, developed a "deep love" for him. Coaching consumed so much of his time, though, that only occasionally did he focus his attention on a single, troubled athlete. One player he did focus attention on was Langdon Viracola. Viracola's father had befriended Vince, partly because he hoped Vince could help reform his son. Langdon's terrible temper and violent brawls had repeatedly gotten him in trouble with the law. In the late fall of 1948, as the controversy raged over Danowski's job status, Vince and Viracola's father agreed that Langdon should be restricted to the Fordham campus for all but one weekend a month or else Vince would forbid him from playing. Viracola deeply resented Vince's intrusion, and, in revenge, had publicly endorsed the rehiring of Danowski.

After Vince left Fordham to coach at West Point, Viracola assaulted a police officer, resulting in a conviction for assault and battery. After he became embroiled in another fight, violating the terms of his probation in June 1951, a judge sentenced him to reform school in New Jersey, and Fordham suspended him from school. He spent fourteen months in depressed, lonely confinement. After he had been there a month, Vince came to visit him. "You still mad at me?" Vince asked the grateful inmate. From then on Vince drove forty miles to the reform school once a month to cheer him up. "It made time [go by] more easily," recalled Viracola. In August 1952, Vince intervened and helped to secure his release and his reentry into Fordham, from which he eventually graduated. "He played one of the biggest parts in my life," said Viracola.[22]

V

West Point (1949–53)

Despite Ed Danowski's insistence that Vince no longer be part of his football staff, at the close of 1948 Fordham's Athletic Council announced that Vince would be retained as assistant coach. Nonetheless, because of the embarrassing publicity and Danowski's venomous attitude toward him, Vince realized his position was untenable, and he told friends of his desire to leave. Fortunately, an assistant coaching position had recently opened at the U.S. Military Academy at West Point, and a friend who knew of his unhappiness provided him the crucial recommendation for one of the most sought-after assistant coaching jobs in the country.

After the 1948 season, Sid Gillman, West Point's extremely able offensive line coach, left to become head coach at Cincinnati University, and Colonel Earl "Red" Blaik, Army's head coach, needed to replace him. So many assistant coaches left Blaik's staff for head coaching jobs elsewhere that selecting new ones had become an annual affair. Blaik had also discovered that with two-platoon football he needed both an offensive and a defensive coach and had already hired Murray Warmath to fill the defensive slot. Blaik received about twenty-five applications to replace Gillman, but he disliked written applications and relied heavily on the advice of trusted friends.

In early December 1948, at the Eastern College Athletic Association meeting in the Biltmore Hotel in New York, Blaik ran into one of those trusted friends, Tim Cohane, then the sports editor of *Look* and the former sports information director at Fordham. Cohane was also a friend of Vince, so when Blaik asked him if he knew of anyone to replace Gillman, Cohane recommended Vince. "Send him up to see me," Blaik told Cohane.

Blaik knew nothing about Vince—not even that he had been one of the Seven Blocks of Granite—and had a few reservations about hiring him. If Vince had ability, Blaik reasoned, why hadn't Fordham utilized his talents more effectively, especially since its staff was so "woefully weak"? Vince did not seem to have the background in coaching, Blaik thought, "that would indicate he was ready for the quality of football we played at West Point."

Not an impetuous man, Blaik required Vince to undergo three interviews with himself and his staff. Nervous and desperate for the job, Vince sweated profusely during one interview, and when asked a question he jumped to the blackboard to diagram his thoughts. He kept calling Cohane to inquire if he had heard anything. After the second interview Cohane phoned Blaik to inquire about Vince's status. "He is all right," said Blaik; "he's a rough soul," meaning Blaik thought that Vince would be sufficiently stern and demanding.

Actually, Vince impressed Blaik almost immediately with his knowledge of the game and his imagination. "I knew he was ready," Blaik later recalled. "I saw the sparkle in his eyes. Right then as a young fellow, he had that special quality of being able to electrify a room." Blaik told Joe Cahill, West Point's sports information director, to phone Vince and offer him the job. "This is Joe Cahill up at West Point," he began his call, at which point Vince interrupted and yelled, "I'll take it!"[1]

Vince's starting salary was $7,000 a year, about average for an assistant coach at a college with a major football program, but coaching at West Point also included exceptional fringe benefits. Vince had the same privileges as officers: free housing on the grounds, free medical care, a grade school for the children, and a large discount at the commissary. Friends of West Point provided the coaches with additional, informal benefits. For example, Gene Leone, the celebrated New York owner of Mama Leone's restaurant, an avid Army football supporter, and Blaik's friend, rolled out the red carpet for all the coaches at his restaurant. "You have standing reservations," Leone told the coaches.

He even gave them special instructions on how to secure a table while other customers waited, and he made his parking lot available for shopping trips, movies, and the theater.[2]

The greatest advantage of coaching at West Point, though, was the opportunity to work for one of the nation's finest football programs directed by one of the game's greatest coaches. Vince was beginning his important five-year association with the man he came to admire most in the coaching profession. "I cannot conceive of a greater coach than Blaik," Vince would state often after leaving the Academy. "Only those of us who coached and played under him at the Point fully appreciate what he did. . . . He worked on me and molded me and fashioned my entire approach to the game." In selecting Blaik as his primary mentor, Vince chose wisely, because Blaik had an excellent mind, outstanding leadership qualities, and exceptional character.

Sixteen years older than Vince and of Scotch-Presbyterian heritage, Blaik grew up in Dayton, Ohio, and attended West Point during World War I. The Academy superintendent during part of his cadet days was Brigadier General Douglas MacArthur, and the two later developed a close relationship that on Blaik's part bordered on adoration. He graduated in 1920 and won the athletic saber as the best all-around athlete in his class. After resigning from the Army in 1922, he served as assistant football coach at West Point from 1927 to 1933 and then became the successful head coach at Dartmouth from 1933 to 1940. Meanwhile, West Point's teams in the late 1930s found it increasingly difficult to compete in major college football. The problem reached a climax in 1940, when the Cadets were thumped by Cornell, 45–0; Pennsylvania, 48–0; and also lost to Navy. After the season, General Robert Eichelberger, then the Academy superintendent, recruited Blaik to revive the team's sagging fortunes, and Blaik directed the team until he retired after the 1958 season.[3]

By 1944 Blaik had rebuilt the West Point program into one of the nation's finest, a task made easier during World War II. Facing less recruitment competition from other colleges, many of whose football programs shut down during the war, West Point attracted outstanding high-school athletes. Some college football stars also transferred there because the Academy was one of the few ways a college student could complete his career uninterrupted. Glenn Davis and Felix "Doc" Blanchard, the star backs of the 1944–46 teams, became so famous as Mr. Outside and Mr. Inside, respectively, that Hollywood made a movie about them. From 1944 through 1950 Army enjoyed five out of seven undefeated seasons and won two national championships, and five

Eastern titles. Blaik's record during the period was a sparkling 57–3–4 (including defeatless streaks of thirty-two and twenty-eight games).[4]

Critics portrayed Blaik as a martinet, a dictator, and a tyrant who was unapproachable, cold, and even mean. He was a distant, reserved, stern man with a commanding presence and was the unquestioned leader of the team, but otherwise the critics' assessment badly missed the mark. "He is not an easy man to know," observed sportswriter Red Smith, but "those who do know him are utterly devoted to him." Smith could have gone farther—most of Blaik's players and staff held him in awe. "Colonel Blaik is living proof that the game of football has socially redeeming value in our lifestyle," insisted Glenn Davis. "He was the most dedicated man I ever knew," said Murray Warmath; "he was the hardest-working man I ever knew."[5]

For Blaik coaching was an all-consuming passion, one he concentrated on for long hours each week all year long. During his thirty-two years in coaching he seldom took a vacation and then only after his doctor warned him that some relaxation was necessary. He had no hobbies except golf. He seldom drank and displayed a sense of humor only among friends.

On the practice field Blaik was a demanding taskmaster who insisted that his players work hard, sacrifice, and live up to his favorite slogan: "You have to pay the price." He seemed to know instinctively the ceiling of each player, demanded that he reach it, and graded him on his performance. Though a taskmaster, he was fair and never abusive or profane. He was an inexorable teacher whose players responded quickly to his direction. His mere presence intimidated. "When he looked at you," remarked one player, "you had the feeling he was looking right through you."

Blaik's natural instincts and Army training had molded him into a polished leader. Always cool and calm, the soldierly colonel had schooled himself in self-restraint such that Vince never mastered. Even with his assistants Blaik was stern and strict, like a general with his aides. He seldom praised his assistants to their face, yet praised them to others. His extreme dedication to winning was also contagious; one could not play for him or coach with him without feeling the same urge to overcome all obstacles on the path to victory. He disliked making public appearances and speeches, yet when he did speak publicly or to the team, he was an outstanding orator. "Colonel Blaik could say more in a few words than anyone I ever knew," marveled Warmath. Above all, Blaik was a perfectionist who considered superior performance normal.[6]

Despite his innate reticence and his inclination to duck the spotlight, Blaik had the capacity to make the sports headlines by provoking controversy and snubbing the status quo. He sparked a storm of protest when he criticized the poor quality of play in professional football; fought for the two-platoon system; dramatically ended the series with Notre Dame after the games became too bitter; and clashed publicly with the Army brass over the 1951 cribbing incident.[7]

Football was a "thinking job," said Blaik, one that required diligent analysis of films and constant adaptation to changes. Football captivated him. How do you approach a game and a season? How do you motivate players to play beyond their abilities? How do you adjust your personnel to the opponents? How do you make the decisive, intelligent move always under intense pressure? These perplexing questions fascinated him, and by the time Vince left Blaik's tutelage, if they hadn't already done so, they captivated Vince as well. "The possibilities are endless," Blaik observed, "and a man with an inquisitive, searching mind, like Vince's, could see those possibilities and could devote a lifetime to coping with them."[8]

Football was like "violent chess," Blaik argued, but more often he used another metaphor to describe the game: "In its steep physical, mental, and moral challenges, in its sacrifices, selflessness, and courage, football, beyond any game invented by man, is closest to war." Therefore, what schools should be more proficient at it than the service academies? Football also prepared players for the "battle of life," teaching young men that work, sacrifice, courage, perseverance, and selflessness were the price you have to pay to achieve anything worthwhile. "It is a game in which the violent body contact it is natural to shy from in everyday living teaches a most important lesson of life—the ability to walk through a storm and keep your head high."

At the Academy or anyplace else, Blaik argued, as long as academic standards were not compromised, the aim of the game is to win. "You can't tell the youngsters, 'Now, this game isn't as important as you have been led to believe, and winning isn't everything, you know.' When you do that you strip football of its essential ingredients—the importance of the game and the will to win." "Lord, oh, Lord, how this country needs this game of football," Blaik said in an interview in 1953. "This country needs anything that is vigorous." Instead, he observed with disgust, football had been replaced by the "cocktail hour and the hot rod hour."[9]

During the years Vince coached at West Point, he worked with an exceptional corps of assistants. Murray Warmath, Paul Amen, Doug Kenna, and John Green all coached during most of Vince's stay. John Sauer coached with him in 1949, and Paul Dietzel joined the staff in 1953. Five of the six later moved on to head coaching positions in colleges. There were advantages and disadvantages to coaching the cadets. The advantages were automatic discipline, natural spirit and dedication, absence of scholarship problems, and intelligent athletes who responded quickly to coaching. However, not many good football players also desired a service career, and the rigorous regimen of cadet life left less time for coaching than at other colleges.[10]

Army tried to keep its football schedule on a scale suitable to the school's national stature, yet it was substantially less ambitious than that of Big Ten schools and Notre Dame. Critics ridiculed West Point for playing teams like Davidson. "Our type of schedule," said Blaik in defense, "is sufficiently exacting for the cadets, who put in a much more rigorous day off the field than any civilian college student." Blaik usually arranged the nine-game schedule so that Army had a tough opponent about every third game. Archrival Navy was always the last and most important foe. He underrated tough opponents (to instill confidence) and overrated easy ones (to ward off overconfidence). "You knew when you had an easier opponent," observed John Sauer, because "you worked harder on that practice field than you ever worked for a tough one."[11]

Although Blaik always remained wary of Vince's "vile temper," the colonel grew to appreciate his coaching prowess—particularly his ability to teach fundamentals. "He was certainly the most able of my assistants by 1954," Blaik said; "no assistant could have been more . . . conscientious." The joy and—especially after the traumatic cribbing scandal—the deep despair they shared together cemented a warm and lasting friendship. When Vince joined the staff in January 1949, he quickly immersed himself in films and team procedures so he could arrive at spring practice informed and confident. Initially, though, it was Vince's vile temper that caught Blaik's attention. Moreover, despite his preparation, Vince acted insecure through most of 1949, and the manifestations of his insecurity—plus his loud volatility—disturbed many West Point observers that first season.

During the first practice in the spring of 1949, Blaik summoned Vince away from his linemen to discuss a technical point. As they chatted, Vince glanced down the field seventy-five feet away and spotted one of his players fooling around. He pivoted away from Blaik and bolted toward the offender, yelling and swearing in a manner that reminded Blaik of a "first sergeant of the old Army." "Vince! Vince!" Blaik called to him, and Vince abruptly turned around and came back. "Vince, we don't coach that way at West Point," Blaik told him firmly. "Yes, sir," Vince answered and rejoined his linemen. Blaik remembered this incident as the only occasion in which he had to correct Vince (though

Vince recalled being rebuked inside Blaik's office as well). "Never again," said Blaik, "did I need to challenge his method of coaching."[12]

Blaik may not have challenged Vince's method of coaching a second time, but he and others remained skeptical of him for a while. "He didn't quite have control of his emotions that first season," Blaik conceded. "The cadet players didn't really understand him, his tremendous drive and pursuit of perfection." Blaik did see some advantage in Vince's temper: "It was so extreme that it would awaken the participants [and] created a certain amount of fear in the individual."

Blaik and the other assistants were calm and controlled—more in keeping with the dignified atmosphere of West Point—and when they corrected a player they usually pulled him aside and talked to him privately. Vince loudly criticized a player in front of the others. Arnold Galiffa, the star quarterback of the 1949 team, who was also volatile, engaged in loud shouting matches with Vince in front of the team. "You'd think [Vince's] cap was going to come off and go ten feet high when he'd blow up with somebody," recalled Sauer; yet within a few minutes he calmed down and resumed his instruction. Some players noted (with disgust) that he tended to be more abusive when Blaik wasn't around and would resume a more polite demeanor with Blaik nearby.

Vince's obvious attempt to butter up to Blaik—to tell Blaik what he thought the Colonel wanted to hear—also disturbed people in 1949. "That's right, Colonel!" seemed to be his favorite expression. Some players even mimicked him. "When [Blaik] asked for his opinion," said one member of the staff, "he was ready with an answer that Red Blaik wanted to hear. This was sickening. Some of [Vince's] players, especially those on the teams of 1947 and 1948, picked this up and felt disgusted."[13]

After the first year Blaik placed Vince in charge of the offensive backfield, making Vince happier because it allowed him to work with all phases of the offense. After 1949, his relations with players improved substantially. He remained vociferous and public in his criticism, and drove the players toward perfection, and therefore alienated a few, but most grew to appreciate his natural leadership, high principles, dedication, and kindness. "He had a remarkable way, especially one-on-one, with the players," said Dietzel. All the coaches had to learn to be more careful in player relations because of the unique situation at the service academies: Players were so accustomed to their disciplined and regimented lifestyle that they had difficulty relaxing. "You'd start to correct a cadet," observed Warmath, "and he'd stand at attention and brace." The coaches constantly sought ways to loosen them up and even encouraged players to call the coaches by their first names.[14]

Vince's usual approach was to drive his players to work hard. "He was a hell of a taskmaster, a real fundamentalist," observed Harry Loehlein, whom Vince converted from a defensive end to an offensive guard; "I never worked so hard in all my life." Though quick to criticize, Vince was also quick to praise. His relations with lineman Robert Haas were typical. At one practice Vince made Haas execute a trap block ten times in a row until he improved significantly, and all the time he yelled at him. Yet, Haas insisted, "there was a love involved in that teaching." Vince often smiled after he hollered, taking some of the sting out of the abuse, and when Haas did execute properly in a scrimmage, Vince would stop the action and run down the field to praise him—"Great block!" Haas observed, "When Vince saw a spark in someone and thought [it] could be developed, he was the first to be harsh with him and the first to praise him when he came through."[15]

Vince developed a particularly close relationship with Col. Blaik's son Robert, who had entered West Point in the fall of 1948. Young Blaik had always longed to play football for his father and was a talented quarterback, but the prospect of playing high-powered football at the Academy for his own demanding father caused him extreme mental pressure. Colonel Blaik, sensitive to possible charges of favoritism, was almost equally wary of coaching his son. Happily for both, Vince intervened and took Bob under his wing. In 1949, his sophomore year, Bob played adequately, backing up Arnold Galiffa, the senior quarterback, but remained very tense. On any play that required him to fake, his execution was so stiff and hurried that he didn't fool anyone.

Vince became Bob's constant companion, spending many hours with him talking football, watching films, practicing techniques, kibitzing, and all the while trying to teach Bob to relax. "He tried to keep me relaxed all the time," said Bob. Vince touted Bob's ability to sportswriters: "I regard him as an exceptionally intelligent football player. He knows the assignment of every man on every play." As part of Bob's relaxation therapy, Vince often played golf with him in the summer. "Golf taught him the value of proper relaxation," Vince claimed; "now when he fakes a pass, he carries it out just as if he had the ball." For whatever reason, Bob enjoyed a fine season in 1950, but tragically for Vince and especially for the two Blaiks, circumstances later prevented Bob from fulfilling his potential at West Point in his senior year. Vince's warm concern, advice, and humor won Bob's lasting gratitude. "There never was a deeper and better heart than Vince's," said young Blaik. Many years afterward Colonel Blaik observed, "Bob worships Vince. [He] gets emotional about very few people, but he does about him."[16]

Michael O'Brien

Vince reveled in his job. "Lombardi was a hog for hard work," said Warmath, who shared an office with him for three years; "I honestly don't remember that we ever talked about anything besides football." The coaches arrived at their desks in the South Gym around 8:00 A.M.; staff meetings began at 9:00 A.M. and lasted, except for lunch, until midafternoon. During the day the coaches worked on plays, diagramed at the blackboard, and studied playbooks, scouting reports, and films. The specific goal was to plan the daily practice assignments—the individual, unit, and team drills. Practice lasted from 4:00 P.M. to 5:30 P.M., and after supper the coaches returned to their offices for long film sessions. "I always drove my assistants as hard as I drove myself," said Blaik. "Our families saw little of us, [which was] part of the price of our mission and the steepest part of all."

Blaik insisted that his coaches plan precisely for the late-afternoon hour-and-a-half practice to relieve some of the enormous pressure already burdening the cadets. Players had to endure the same 5:50 A.M. to 10:30 P.M. day as the rest of the corps, and faced the same over sixteen hours of concentrated effort. Other college football powers did not have their whole team engaged in rigorous training, drills, and the study of differential equations, mechanics of fluids, and electrical engineering. Football practice, then, must be perfectly organized, efficient, and precise so as not to interfere unduly with the players' other responsibilities.

Vince initially had difficulty adjusting to the demanding routine. Blaik would not permit his coaches to bring any notes to practice; they had to commit to memory every assignment for every lineman on every play. At a spring practice in 1949 Vince had only fifteen minutes to teach five plays. "Run number ten," Blaik ordered. "I'm sorry, Colonel," Vince answered sheepishly, "but I didn't have time to put it in." Blaik gave him his bland Scots stare and said, "Run number 11."[17]

By 1949 many college and professional coaches analyzed films to improve their team's performance, and Vince had studied them occasionally at St. Cecilia and as an assistant at Fordham. Few teams, however, used films as systematically or studied them as meticulously as West Point. From a thirty-foot steel tower staff members filmed the afternoon scrimmages, and, since West Point had its own film processing equipment, during spring and fall practices the coaches returned to the offices after supper, where the afternoon film would be developed and waiting. Blaik acquired films of future opponents; he even took films of opponents' games played on television. The coaches then diagramed all the formations, recorded the circumstances of each play, and kept a file on the strengths and weaknesses of all opponents, their habits collectively and

94

individually in any situation. The staff pooled the film information with scouting reports, boiled it down to essentials, and parceled it out to the cadets within the restricted time available. They prepared exceptional intelligence on key opponents. One Army scout watched Navy play seven times in 1949. For nine months the staff prepared for a game against powerful Michigan. "We sent the cadets into [every] game thoroughly briefed," said Blaik.

"Blaik's idea of fun in the summertime was to study films," Warmath stated. The colonel grew obsessed with the film of Navy's 14–2 upset of Army in 1950, a defeat that broke West Point's record of twenty-eight games without a loss. "All right," he would say whenever there was a lull, "let's get out that Navy film." One summer day Vince and the other coaches had just finished studying an upcoming fall opponent and had made plans to golf, but Blaik had other plans for them and ordered the reshowing of the old Navy film. "You could see the other coaches sneak looks at one another," Vince recalled, "and although you couldn't hear the groans, you could feel them in the room." A few moments later in the projection room, Blaik was again intently analyzing the reasons for the defeat: "Look at that. The fullback missed the block on that end. . . ." In their five years together, Vince and Blaik watched about thirty-five hundred hours of films, watched them, Blaik said, until "our brain lobes felt as worn as the film sprocket holes looked."[18]

An important innovation Vince learned at West Point was the concept of rule blocking, which Sid Gillman had instituted there in 1948. Under the old system, linemen had a different assignment for each defense they faced. Since the defense dictated who the linemen blocked, the old method was a defensive approach to offensive football. Rule blocking allowed the linemen to know who to block no matter how the defense aligned. Vince later explained: "For instance, if there is a man over the center, he'll drive—block him or cut him off. If no man is over the center, then he becomes a seal man and cuts off pursuit. Same thing for the guard No man over you—seal for the first inside linebacker; man over you— take him in the direction he wants to go." Rule blocking not only allowed the offensive line to adjust to all defenses, it also simplified line play and was no more difficult to teach.[19]

Vince's servile behavior toward Blaik ended by 1950 as he grew more confident and comfortable. Blaik welcomed innovative approaches from his coaches. After 1949 Vince took advantage of the freedom and sold his suggestions vigorously at staff meetings, though he easily became downhearted when Blaik or the staff rejected his ideas. "In a meeting he was almost like a zealot," observed Dietzel; "the side of the room could have fallen in, and he wouldn't have noticed." At one meeting the coaches engaged in spirited debate about Vince's suggestion of a new way for the quarterback to take the center's snap. Blaik argued that the quarterback could not execute the maneuver; Vince adamantly insisted that he could and stood up to demonstrate. "Look, Colonel, I can do it!" Blaik studied Vince's short, stocky build and long arms and said: "Yes, Vince, but not everyone [is] built like an ape like you are." The unintended insult stunned Vince, and he immediately grew quiet and sullen. "He thought he was being put down," said Dietzel. Yet Vince was usually convincing and often presented new ideas and approaches that Blaik and the staff later refined and adopted.

Vince was intense almost all the time at work. On game day be became so wound up that Dietzel thought "he'd explode." Coaching had always made him tense, but at West Point his emotional peaks and valleys first became evident even though his colleagues couldn't pinpoint the cause. "There were days when Vince . . . would be at the top of the world," said Paul Amen, "and the next morning when he came to work, he seemed to be in a low trough." "I wonder how Vince is going to feel today," the coaches occasionally asked each other as they waited for him to arrive at the office in the morning.[20]

Between the fall season and spring practice, Vince had more free time, and during one interlude was inspired to write a book, *How to Play Football*. Assisted by his friend Colonel Russell "Red" Reeder of the athletic department, he composed several chapters. He abandoned the project after a literary agent told him that publishers weren't interested in another football book, especially by an unknown assistant coach.[21]

In the off-season months of January and February, Vince and the other coaches usually continued their film study and also recruited players. The athletic department's staff kept files on outstanding high-school athletes who might want to attend the Academy and who could meet the rigorous entrance requirements. Vince concentrated mainly on New York and New Jersey, where his many contacts among high-school coaches helped him recruit effectively. He and Doug Kenna recruited in Wisconsin in 1950, but when they arrived in Green Bay, a snowstorm stranded them in a hotel room for three days. Frustrated by the hostile environment and the wasted time, Vince stared out his hotel window and remarked to Kenna: "Can you imagine anybody living in a place like this? This is just the end of the world."[22]

In 1951, during the Korean War, the Army's Special Services unit asked Blaik to send a delegation of his coaches to Korea to conduct football clinics on coaching and officiating to improve the morale of U.S. troops. They were also sent to Japan to teach the game to the Japanese. Vince and four other assistants went for three weeks in late June and early July 1951. They traveled near the battle lines of Korea but predominantly worked in secure areas and conducted many clinics.[23]

"Vince and I were both so absorbed in our work," said Blaik, "that we didn't have much time for hobbies or recreation." Rarely did the coaches take a vacation, partly because they knew that Blaik would still be riveted to his desk. Vince, however, managed to find more time for relaxation than the workaholic Blaik. Most Sundays Vince drove his family to Englewood for dinner at his parents'. He and the assistant coaches and a few other friends took turns hosting bridge games, cocktail parties, and cookouts. The Academy provided him with a fine Tudor-style home alongside a running brook on the West Point grounds, and after a Saturday football game at Michie Stadium, friends from Brooklyn and Englewood, friends of Marie, and friends of his parents gathered there to replay the game and to talk. With a face-splitting grin on his face, he moved from guest to guest. He never seemed happier than when he played host. His friends enjoyed him, especially his humor and loud laugh. "I don't know anybody who didn't like him," recalled Warmath. "I always thought Vince was about the warmest person I ever knew," said Kenna.

Vince played handball regularly with the other coaches and the priests who served at the Catholic chapel on the grounds (where Vince attended daily Mass). "Nobody ever outhustled him," insisted a fellow player; "nobody wanted to win more." The group tried racquetball for a while until a player accidentally smashed Vince with his racquet, causing a bloody gash on the bridge of the nose that required five stitches. "It scared us all to death," said Dietzel, and the group returned to playing handball.[24]

Vince's favorite summer recreation was golf. Blaik often played with him, but not enough. A few times Vince and Kenna sneaked off to play a late-afternoon round away from West Point so Blaik wouldn't find out. Once, when Blaik did learn about it, he inquired matter-of-factly if they had enjoyed their "vacation." West Point had a small golf course, where Vince usually played. He was a good golfer and very competitive. "He never could understand why any ball he hit didn't go straight into the hole," recalled Blaik. His playing partners laughed uproariously at his frustration and failure on the same hole on almost every round. When he teed off on a par 3, 130-yard hole, he almost always shanked his ball into the woods. As they came to the tee, Vince's golfing partners would start chuckling at his anxiety and the predictable result of his shot. The harder he tried, the worse he shanked, and the more frustrated he became. His friends even erected in the woods a sign on which they inscribed, "Lombardi's Garden."[25]

Each summer for about a week in late July and early August, before practice started, all the coaches and some of Blaik's friends vacationed in cabins on Bull Pond, a five-acre lake that lay atop a mountain eleven hundred feet above sea level near Central Valley on West Point property, eight miles southwest of the Academy. The lake provided only fair fishing but good boating and excellent swimming. The men swam, fished, ate, joked, and talked football.

Among the regular guests were three of Blaik's nonmilitary friends: Tim Cohane, Willard Mullin, sports cartoonist of the *New York World-Telegram and Sun,* and Stanley Woodward, sports editor of the *New York Herald Tribune.* Normally an Army mess sergeant cooked, but one year Blaik decreed that everyone share the duties. "The first day went excellent," Blaik said, "as Mullin and Vince Lombardi fed us like good Eagle scouts." Saturday night was always Gene Leone night. The New York restaurant owner arrived with a station wagon full of food and put on a "Lucullan feast." It was "Shangri-la," said Cohane. For Blaik and usually for Vince, the week at Bull Pond provided the only vacation each year. "We needed lightness, silliness, or madness in those days," Blaik recalled. "It was our only respite from an inexorable grind."[26]

In July 1952, Vince took a camping and canoeing trip with two friends from West Point's athletic department, Colonel Reeder and Colonel Philip Draper. Vince brought along ten-year-old Vince, Jr.; Draper came with his son; and Reeder brought his son and a nephew. All the boys were about the same age. Vince's background had not included the opportunity to canoe or camp, and his adjustment caused him some trepidation. He finally did adjust, though, and his companions—as his friends invariably did—appreciated his off-the-field, fun-loving charm.

The group's destination was LaVerendrye Park in Canada, a wild, unsettled area three hundred miles northwest of Montreal. Before departing, the adults agreed to switch the children around in the three cars so they wouldn't be nagging their own sons. Russell Reeder III, age twelve, rode with Vince and kept a diary of the early part of the journey:

> 6:30 a.m. Still raining. Mr. Lombardi almost hit a cow. We are number 3 in line. Mr. Lombardi will be first as soon as the road gets wider.

8:25 a.m. Coke stop in restaurant. When Mr. Lombardi laughs, everybody laughs. He lets out kind of a roar. He bought me some candy. I am glad that I am riding with him. I feel like I knew him forever.

Vince had been apprehensive the first day when the party drove past hotels and tourist cabins and hadn't stopped; instead, they pitched their tents in an open field off the highway. At daybreak the next morning he crawled out of his pup tent and grinned. "The best sleep of my life," he told his friends; "I never slept out before. I didn't have a chance to be a Cub Scout or a Boy Scout. This is wonderful." Red Reeder recalled: "Every day in Canada was a new experience to him."

When they put their canoes in the river at the park, Vince loaded his wrong, piling his share of the camping gear and provisions in the stern, near his feet. He set off with Draper's son Stephen, but with so much weight in the back, the youngster sat up so high in the bow that his paddle didn't even reach the water. Vince didn't know how to paddle properly, and his heavy, bull-like, muscle-bound shoulders soon tired out. Within a short time Vince's canoe was far behind. "Vince was laughing," said Red Reeder, "but it was mirth laced with embarrassment. One of the renowned Seven Blocks of Granite could paddle only fifty yards at a time." That evening Vince's canoe arrived at the campsite forty minutes behind the others. He waded ashore in a foot of water and collapsed on the bank.

On the second day, the three canoes turned a bend in the river and met a stiff west wind that churned up whitecaps. The two lead canoes inched upstream, but Vince and Stephen—again with all their supplies in the stern—spun dangerously in circles out of control until Vince managed to beach his canoe. Colonel Reeder observed of Vince's mood: "He wasn't very happy. Defeat." After reloading the gear and changing young partners, Vince was able to make steady progress the rest of the journey.

Throughout the trip Vince had growled good-naturedly about the meager provisions commissioned by the Army officers. "I can do something about this," he finally declared. He paddled his canoe back to the nearest store and returned with his craft nearly sinking under the load of beer, pop, candy, fresh fruit, Italian bread, and fancy groceries. "Hello, the camp!" he bellowed on landing. "I brought us a plastic icebox with ice for drinks, and a snort. For supper—prime sirloins. I love camping."[27]

The trip to Canada had turned out to be delightful, and Vince needed the vacation to divert his mind from the awful tragedy that had earlier befallen West Point's football program. Although Blaik's teams had enjoyed outstanding success up to 1951, his personality and the team's success sparked resentment and criticism. Then, suddenly, a scandal ruined his team, demoralized the coaching staff, and started West Point on the road to deemphasizing football. Blaik's forte was not public relations. When he dealt with military authorities or spoke out on issues, he did so with more frankness than diplomacy. He claimed that when his team's hard blocking and tackling injured opponents, critics accused him of teaching dirty football; when his teams won most games by conclusive scores, they lampooned his schedule. In his history of the Academy, Thomas Fleming noted that "the latent hostility to West Point that runs like an ominous thread through the emotions of so many Americans began to focus on the football team." The undercurrents of privilege in the status of football players upset the anti-Army, anti-Blaik cliques. Because of practice, the players arrived late for supper; they ate together at a training table during the season and inevitably formed friendships within the football circle, leading critics to label them the "Blaik boys" and "the chosen cadets." Blaik's athletes also differed from the rest of the corps "through the aura conferred on them by a sports-mad American public."[28]

Despite the criticism, Blaik's fortunes continued to soar until the news broke on Friday, August 3, 1951, that the Academy had expelled ninety cadets for violating the honor code and that among them were thirty-seven members of the football team (and a total of sixty varsity athletes). In the space of twenty-four hours the coaches learned that their football team had been ruined. The final agony for Blaik was the discovery that his son Bob, who would have been the starting senior quarterback in the fall, was among those dismissed.

The tragedy grew out of the West Point academic practice of routinely giving the identical exam to different sections of the same class on different days. Beginning with a small group in 1949, cadets who had taken the test tipped off friends, particularly fellow athletes, who were having problems with the courses. Gradually a complete intelligence system emerged. The cribbing was a violation of the West Point honor code, the principles of gentlemanly conduct that generations of military men had lived by. A cadet shall not lie, cheat, or steal, and was honor-bound to report any breach of the code. In April 1951, two cadets reported the cheating. The Academy appointed a three-man board of tactical officers to investigate, and they uncovered the infractions. By June 1951, rumor spread that the corps had been touched by scandal and that inquiries were under way behind closed doors. None of the coaches knew exactly what punishment to expect; Vince apparently thought it would be minor. A special board chaired by Judge Learned Hand reviewed the recommendations of the tactical officers, concurred with them, and the Academy expelled the ninety cadets.

The August 3 announcement immediately stirred the wrath of politicians and newspaper editors against West Point and especially against its football program. It also touched off a nationwide discussion of honesty in American life. "The profiteering of the Korean War, bribery in college basketball, the fur coats and deep-freezes of the Truman administration had shaken the nation," observed Stephen Ambrose in his history of West Point, "but they all paled beside the cheating at the Military Academy." People had placed West Point on a pedestal.[29]

Early news accounts cast the worst possible light on the football players. Gen. J. Lawton Collins, chief of staff of the Army, told a group of U.S. senators that the infractions had started with the football team and spread to others in the cadet corps of twenty-five hundred. The Academy superintendent, General Frederick A. Irving, said the scandal was "due primarily to spread among football players, their roommates, and close associates," and that the football players had come to think of themselves as a "group apart." Senator J. William Fulbright (Dem., Arkansas) angrily charged that football should be abolished at the service academies: "Intercollegiate athletics have become so perverted that it's a corrupting influence on all the youngsters in the big universities." Congressman Charles Potter (Rep., Michigan) accused the Academy of "athletic commercialism," and a New Jersey congressman urged that the Academy fire Blaik for being the "focal point" of the "infection." *The New York Times* agreed that big-time athletics played a "sinister" part in the tragic situation and that the Academy had been "guilty—along with most other American colleges—of a gross overemphasis on intercollegiate football."

Two additional criticisms of the athletic program surfaced in the aftermath of the expulsions. Army officers allegedly had lobbied congressmen for appointments of "unqualified applicants" because of their athletic prowess. Also, an informal "tutoring school" that enabled promising high-school athletes—particularly football players—to enter West Point was also condemned. (Each spring civilian alumni had paid the salaries of instructors in the cram course on the post so that aspirants could pass the entrance exams in June.)

A few months after the expulsions, the situation became clearer, the discussion more detached, and sympathy increased for the discharged cadets. Blaik never condoned what the cadets had done, but he defended them fiercely as men of good character and resented bitterly the slur upon them. Many of the dismissed cadets had not cheated, he pointed out, but merely admitted knowing about it and had condemned themselves by telling the truth. "All they had to do was refuse to answer or to plead innocence. To them this would have been dishonorable," said Blaik. He defended the tutoring school as perfectly proper and correct: "We would not be able to field a varsity team of reasonable caliber without this special tutoring."[30]

To some degree the expelled cadets were victims of McCarthyism, the raging plague of the time. They didn't learn of their expulsion until they read it in the newspapers. In deliberations they had not been represented by counsel, often did not know the charges against them or who accused them, and never had a chance to explain themselves. They were branded as cheaters without having their day in court. So many cadets were involved that the administration should have questioned the whole academic program. The honor system was too tempting at West Point; Annapolis gave different exams to midshipmen in different sections of the same class. The "special privileges" enjoyed by the players were minor. The privilege of reporting twenty minutes late to supper, noted Red Smith sarcastically, occurred because "a kid who'd been batting his brains out on the practice field needed time to shower and dress." Smith branded the whole incident a "carnival of brassbound stupidity, military buckpassing, and bureaucratic bungling."

In the final analysis the cadets who cheated were undeniably guilty. No one forced them to cheat. Others violated a time-honored code in not reporting the cheating. That so many were members of the football team indicates that the players had indeed come to regard themselves as special. Yet there were extenuating circumstances, the cadets received inadequate due process, and finally, the administration probably punished them too severely and mishandled the whole affair.[31]

For a year after the scandal a small group of Pentagon officials and a few Academy administrators attempted to nudge Blaik into retirement. In January 1952, General Irving publicly urged the separation of Blaik's duties as both director of athletics and head coach because he claimed they were too much responsibility for one person. Irving also criticized "long winning streaks" and long football trips away from the Academy because of the intense pressure they placed on cadet players. Football players should meet every cadet routine, Irving insisted, and should no longer be "privileged" or "segregated." The Academy took no action, however, and Blaik retained both positions. Nonetheless, the continuing controversy irritated the staff and indicated the administration's continued opposition to the football program. Blaik did consider resigning, but friends—most notably General MacArthur—convinced him to stay. He felt a sense of duty to the remaining players. If there was to be a congressional investigation, he probably wanted to testify in his official capacity as head coach rather than as a retired, disgruntled, former employee.[32]

"We will try to make up in fight what we lack in talent," General Irving had said a few days after the dismissal of the thirty-seven football players. For the coaching staff, however, the adjustment wasn't that simple. The aftermath left them depressed and emotionally exhausted the entire fall. They bitterly resented what had happened. They had spent thousands of hours recruiting, preparing, and coaching the outstanding athletes, had developed intense emotional rapport with them, and now the players were scattering across the country. Coaches were now consigned to using inexperienced plebes—freshmen—and untalented members of the junior varsity. "I could not, try as I would, coach with my normal enthusiasm, drive, and patience," Blaik observed sadly. Nor could Vince. "Next to me," Blaik said, "Vince was probably the most deeply affected person. He was terribly, terribly broken up. Everything we'd built up and everything we'd stood for went right out the window in twenty-four hours."[33]

Despite their demoralization, the staff returned to their customary routine of rigorous preparation and coaching, but the Army teams struggled for the next two years. In 1951 the team was a sentimental favorite. It scored in every game and was never disgraced, but defeated only Columbia and The Citadel and lost the other seven games. In the second game, against Northwestern, a three-touchdown favorite, Army led, 14–7, at one point, but finally lost, 20–14, when Northwestern scored on a long pass with less than two minutes remaining. Afterward, Vince was distraught and stood in the locker room with tears running down his face. "This was the Lombardi I knew," said Blaik. "His [subsequent] professional reputation gave no clue to the emotion that was so strong a part of his makeup."

In 1952 Army improved its record to 4–4–1, and the following year won the Eastern championship with a 7–1–1 record. Vince deeply admired the perseverance and the determination Blaik displayed during the three years after the cribbing incident. Blaik had been forced to take it on the chin, Saturday after Saturday, Vince asserted, "from teams that couldn't have given us a good workout a few years before. Yet he stuck to his job, and much sooner than anyone believed possible, he had Army back on top again." Although Blaik and his staff did rebuild the team's fortunes, Army's football program never approached the glory of the

Michael O'Brien

prescandal era. After 1951, like many other Eastern colleges and universities, West Point deemphasized football.[34]

During most of the time he coached at the Academy, Vince aspired to a head coaching position at a major college. "Like me, there was nothing else on his mind except being a head coach somewhere," said Warmath. The cribbing incident intensified the scramble to find something better because the Army brass had made it clear they no longer wanted to emphasize football. "We were all looking [after the scandal]," recalled Amen.

Vince wanted to be selective because he already had a better job than most coaches. Yet he also wanted a bigger challenge. At a party at Vince's home on a Saturday in 1953 after an Army football game, a friend, noting the outstanding fringe benefits Vince enjoyed at the Academy, told him, "You've got it made here, pal." Vince disagreed. "I'm glad you think so," he quickly responded, "but I'm thinking of making a change." The friend then catalogued Vince's many advantages. "There's more to life than just being contented," Vince answered. "I'd like to see what I can do on my own. . . . Maybe I wouldn't be successful as a head coach, but I'll never know unless I try." Unfortunately, the only offers he received were from small colleges or from larger ones then in the process of deemphasizing football. He watched carefully the situation at Fordham—and even discussed with Jack Coffey and Tim Cohane his ambitious plans to rebuild Fordham's football fortunes—but his alma mater continued to deemphasize football.

What intensified his frustration was his awareness that, for many coaches, working under Blaik provided an excellent springboard to a better job. Nineteen of Blaik's former assistants later became head coaches in colleges or professional football. Just before Vince came to West Point, Sid Gillman had gone to Cincinnati University, Herman Hickman became head coach at Yale, and Andy Gustafson moved on to the University of Miami. While Vince worked at the Academy, three assistants moved up to head coaching jobs: John Sauer went to The Citadel, Murray Warmath to Mississippi State, and John Green to Vanderbilt. Shortly after Vince left the Academy, Paul Amen became head coach at Wake Forest, and Louisiana State University hired Paul Dietzel.

Vince watched these promotions with frustration and envy and wondered why a good opportunity had been denied him. "I know I lost some jobs because of my Italian heritage," he later observed, an assessment that particularly applied to openings at Southern colleges. Blaik, who wrote scores of recommendations for him, thought that college officials

104

judged Vince as too unsophisticated. "Some fellows have that Madison Avenue smoothness," Blaik observed. "They get a coaching job and then they rattle around. Vince [wasn't] that type of man." Vince's reputation for vitriolic behavior on the field may also have frightened potential employers.[35]

When he did decide to leave West Point, the offer that lured him away did not come from a major college, nor was it the head coaching position he so desired. After the 1953 season, the professional New York Giants fired Steve Owen, their long time head coach, and in early December 1953, Wellington Mara and his brother Jack, two top executives with the Giants, tried to entice Blaik to accept the head coaching position. They met together on three occasions, and each time the Maras offered him a bigger salary. Blaik mulled over the offers but decided to remain at the Academy. The Giants then elected to promote from within their organization and tabbed Assistant Coach Jim Lee Howell to replace Owen.

The Giants, however, needed to fill a second vacancy as well. When they fired Owen, the backfield coach, Allie Sherman, left also, to coach in Canada. When the Maras met with Blaik for the last time and it became apparent that he would reject their offer, they asked him if they could talk with Vince about joining the Giants as assistant coach. Blaik agreed. Vince, though, had strong reservations about leaving his beloved West Point for another assistant's job and had never envisioned himself coaching in professional football. But Wellington Mara was a longtime friend and a persistent, convincing recruiter. The financial inducement— probably a $5,000 raise to a salary of about $14,000—seems to have been the deciding factor, and Vince signed a contract with the Giants in late December 1953.

On December 30, after Vince agreed to terms, the Giants flew him down to Lonoke, Arkansas, to talk with Howell at his farm, where the new head coach treated him to a meal of wild duck. Howell already knew and admired him from the time they had both lived in Englewood, New Jersey. Vince had visited the Giants' practices many times. Howell welcomed him as his new assistant. "Lombardi teaches the style of football I like," he told reporters; "Vinny is daring and he's brainy." The New York press also welcomed him. "An outstanding handler and tutor of backs," said the *Daily News.* Vince had been "tremendously popular" at West Point, observed the *World-Telegram and Sun,* and "is regarded by associates as one of the smartest strategists in junior coaching ranks."[36]

Vince was embarking on another new challenge and a new path to success in his profession. His five years at West Point, though, had left an indelible mark. His apprenticeship had broadened his knowledge, refined his approaches, and, most important, in Earl Blaik he had found a sterling model of character and leadership. He learned the concept of rule blocking, the techniques and advantages of systematic film study, the importance of conducting drills with military precision, and the value of practicing a few key plays to perfection. By observing Blaik, Vince improved his ability to organize, discipline, and inspire a team. "My 'football' is your 'football,' " he later told Blaik. "My approach to a problem is the way I think you would approach it." Although Vince's West Point experience molded him in important ways, the critical ingredient of his success hadn't changed. "He may have learned a few things during our years together," recalled Blaik, "but he didn't learn that magnetism at West Point. It was always in him. You don't put magnetism into people."[37]

VI

New York Giants (1954–58)

PROFESSIONAL FOOTBALL UNDERWENT A MAJOR TRANSFORMATION DURING VINCE'S five years with the Giants, but the game's origins were modest. The mine and mill towns in western Pennsylvania and Ohio were the cradles for the infant sport. By the 1890s community athletic clubs, YMCA's, and local businesses had organized football teams and paid the players a small sum for each game. Soon they began to charge gate receipts. Throughout its early years, however, professional football lacked the aura of respect ability. Unlike college football, with its origins among upper-class, old-stock Americans, pro football's rosters included a broad spectrum of racial and ethnic groups. Playing for pay carried the stigma of ungentle manly behavior, and many frowned on former collegians who joined the pro ranks or became fans of the professional game.

The American Professional Football Association was founded in 1920 and was renamed the National Football League (NFL) two years later. In the 1920s more than thirty cities dropped in and out of the league, and the NFL gradually shed its small-town image. In 1921 George Halas transferred his franchise from Decatur, Illinois, to Chicago, and the following year the Chicago Cardinals joined the NFL. The Depression in the 1930s wiped out the remaining franchises in smaller cities with the exception of the Packers in Green Bay, Wisconsin, the sole survivor of the small-town era. In the 1920s and 1930s NFL teams rarely attracted large crowds. Professional teams competed with colleges, but, unlike the collegians, lacked a built-in constituency.

By the time Vince joined the New York Giants, the franchise had weathered a storm of problems but, like other NFL teams, was on the verge of success. Vince's career paralleled the Giants' progress. His success also emerged from the close rapport he developed with the Mara family, who owned and managed the Giants; Jim Lee Howell, the head coach; and key players. The Maras were a kind, decent, close-knit family. Tim Mara, the sixty-six-year-old patriarch, was an energetic, plucky Irishman with a sure promotional touch. He had been a legal bookmaker at the New York tracks prior to the introduction of parimutuel betting and was also in the coal business. In 1925 he purchased an NFL franchise for $500 and brought pro football to New York. In the late 1930s he retired from active leadership of the Giants and turned over front-office duties to his two sons, Jack and Wellington, both friends of Vince and graduates of Fordham. Jack, the elder, was the president and ran the business side of the operations; Wellington, Vince's Fordham classmate, was the secretary and handled trades and player personnel. Complete harmony reigned in the Giants' front office, accounting for much of the team's success. Tim was a smart businessman; Jack was an excellent executive; and Wellington seemed to know everything about every player in the country. Vince became like another brother to Jack and Wellington and another son to Tim. In the off-season they dined together almost daily. "He discussed a lot of his family problems with my father," observed Wellington. "My father was very sympathetic to him and gave him good counsel."[1]

Steve Owen, the coach of the Giants since 1931, had directed many great teams, but the game had passed him by. The 1953 Giants' season had been a disaster, with the team winning only three of twelve games, the worst record in its history. The Giants scored only 179 points, the fewest in the league. Pro football had grown complex and specialized, leaving Owen in its wake. He hadn't kept up with innovations and ran virtually a one-man operation. Because of the need to study film, to scout, and to devise new offensive and defensive strategies, the modern coach had to be at least partly an organization man, like Paul Brown, the young, imaginative, and successful coach of the Cleveland Browns, whom almost everyone in football held in awe. Had the Giants been able to hire Earl Blaik, he would have fit the mold perfectly. Jim Lee Howell, the man the Giants finally settled on, didn't appear to fit the mold at all. Yet Howell's unique approach succeeded beyond anyone's expectations.

Moreover, his style allowed Vince the widest possible latitude to grow professionally, to impress his peers, and, after several more frustrating disappointments, to secure the major head-coaching position he so intensely desired.

Howell, a long-legged, 6-4 end from the University of Arkansas, had joined the Giants in 1938 and played eight seasons. In 1948 he became the assistant coach in charge of the ends. He was thirty-nine years old when the Giants promoted him to head coach in December 1953, and his appointment came as a complete surprise. Sportswriters barely knew him; eyebrows were raised, then voices in protest. Although affable, patient, and gentlemanly, he had weak coaching credentials. He lacked the prominence to attract crowds and the detailed knowledge of the T formation to help on the field. The Giants didn't have a head coach, sneered sportswriter Jerry Izenberg; "they had a head smile." Some assumed that the Mara family had settled on Howell because he could be had for less money than a prominent coach.[2]

Despite his obvious limitations, Howell was a wise choice. His outstanding capacity for public relations soon won him popularity with fans and much of the press. Easygoing and relaxed as a player and as an assistant coach, Howell became strict and serious in his new relationship with players. That he clearly recognized his limitations and willingly delegated most coaching responsibilities proved to be his major assets. Early in his career, while coaching briefly at Arkansas, he had resented the dictatorial head coach who squelched freedom of expression among the assistants. Howell's experience in World War II as a Marine captain reinforced his belief in organization, teamwork, and delegated authority; he would run the Giants like his military command, allowing each coach responsibility for his particular job. Such an arrangement works effectively, though, only if those delegated responsibility are competent. Fortunately, Howell's two chief assistants, Vince and Tom Landry, proved exceptionally competent.[3]

Tom Landry had played quarterback and fullback for the University of Texas. His fine intellect enabled him to earn college degrees in both business administration and mechanical engineering. In 1949 he played for the New York Yankees of the All-America Football Conference, and after the season, when the Yankees merged with the Giants of the NFL, he played defensive halfback and assumed increasing responsibility for coaching the Giants' defense. In 1956 he became the full-time defensive coach and refined the 4-3-4 defensive alignment, bringing it to a new level of efficiency.[4]

Both Vince and Landry were dominating, aggressive personalities, precise organizers, and fierce competitors, with exceptional knowledge of football and outstanding coaching skills. Both brilliantly dissected films and shrewdly evaluated talent. Landry was more innovative; Vince was a better teacher. Each won the other's respect. They differed most noticeably in their temperaments. "You could hear Vince laughing or shouting for five blocks," quipped Wellington Mara. "You couldn't hear Landry from the next chair." Sportswriter Gary Cartwright observed that while Vince was a "gurgling volcano, blistering everyone in his path, Landry was placid as a mountain lake." Though quiet, Landry's leadership went unquestioned. "It was a lineal strength that ran through the team," said Cartwright, "a central nervous system."[5]

With two brilliant assistants, the self-effacing Howell never pretended to be anything but the administrative overseer and disciplinarian. He joked about his role: "A famous coach told me once that the job of a head coach is to keep order and see that the footballs are pumped up. I try to do both." He bragged around the league that he had the "two smartest assistant coaches in football." As flanker Kyle Rote walked down the hall of the dormitory at training camp, what he saw symbolized the Giants' coaching arrangement: "I'd look to the left and see Lombardi in a room running the projector for his plays, and I'd look to the right and I'd see Landry running *his* plays, and then on down the hall I'd look in Jim Lee's room and see him reading the newspaper." Vince ran the offense, Landry directed the defense, and on the day of the game each ran their own units. "It probably never would [work] again," said Landry of the special chemistry among the three, "but it worked out well then."[6]

In the winter of 1954, Vince moved his family from West Point to a split-level brick home in Oradell, New Jersey, and immediately started preparing for training camp in July. He hung a sheet in the den, set up a projector, and watched films of the Giants' offense, running the projector back and forth, night and day, "until it began to drive Marie and the kids crazy, and I had to take it down to the basement." Because he never played pro football and had seldom watched it, he needed to understand not only the Giants but also other teams around the league. "On each play in every game I'd run the projector back and forth three or four times with seven or eight people in mind and then I'd run it back again to see what the three or four others were doing." He charted every play and every defense on yellow legal pads and then indexed the pads. The films revealed that the Giants had some talented offensive players, but not until training camp opened in July at Salem, Oregon, did Vince fully appreciate the exceptional ability of key players. "I can still see the fluid motion Frank Gifford had while running the ball," he later observed, "the great hands Kyle Rote exhibited in catching it, and the anticipation Charlie Conerly had in releasing the ball." The three formed the backbone of the Giants' offense and reached their full potential under Vince's direction.[7]

Four-year veteran Kyle Rote had earned All-American honors as a versatile halfback at Southern Methodist in 1950. Before Vince arrived, however, serious injuries to both knees had dimmed his professional prospects, making it necessary to move him from halfback to flanker. Rote was a perfectionist whose crafty pass routes, ingenious feints, and exceptional catching ability compensated for his loss of speed.[8]

Charlie Conerly, a seven-year veteran, didn't impress anyone on first sight. Thirty-three years old, prematurely gray, with a leathery face, he was unemotional, almost stoic. Yet in 1948 he had been the NFL's choice for Rookie of the Year. He was a good passer, a wily, intelligent signal caller with exceptional poise and courage. His teammates admired him. Unfortunately, fans hadn't perceived Conerly's attributes in 1952 and 1953 as the Giants' fortunes sagged, and he had come to symbolize the team's failure. He suffered from a dearth of speedy ends who could catch the ball and from a porous line that gave him little pass protection. Yet he never complained or alibied. When the defense covered his receivers, he had the knack for throwing the ball slightly off target so it wouldn't be intercepted or ruled intentional grounding, but fans, thinking he had simply missed his receiver again, booed him unmercifully. Because he appeared so unemotional, fans thought he didn't care. But he did care. Discouraged, he decided to retire after the 1953 season. Howell's first achievement was to lure him out of retirement by promising to defend him with effective linemen.[9]

Handsome Frank Gifford, a fluid-running, All-American offensive and defensive back at the University of Southern California, was also discouraged. During Gifford's two years with the Giants, Steve Owen couldn't decide where to play him, so he used him both as an offensive and a defensive back. He ran, passed, caught passes, defended against passes, tackled, kicked off, ran back punts, and kicked field goals. He was exhausted. In several games in 1953 he played the entire sixty minutes, causing him to lose twenty pounds. Demoralized, Gifford also contemplated retirement. After watching the films and consulting with Howell, Vince decided where to play him. When Gifford arrived at training camp, Vince greeted him: "Hi, I'm Vince Lombardi, and you're my halfback." Gifford was relieved. "They were the most important words anybody ever said to me in football. I had never been anyone's halfback."[10]

Michael O'Brien

At the 1954 training camp players immediately sensed the efficient, more professional atmosphere. Practice started precisely on time—not fifteen minutes late, as they often had under Owen—and the coaches planned every drill with purpose. For a few months, though, Vince had difficulty adjusting to the players and the professional game. "He came out of college as a good football coach," Tom Landry recalled. "He was competent but he wasn't sure." He wasn't sure he knew enough about pro football, which occasionally made him appear shy and cautious. "He was searching for a relationship with us," said Rote. At times he engaged in a cold war with the offense, and initially many players didn't like him. Few had ever heard of him. He was just another successful college coach, only noisier. They resented his running and exercise program because it was more rigorous than they had experienced under Owen. At the first meeting he looked peculiar standing before them with his stern expression, stocky build, and gold-capped inlay teeth. He failed to awe veteran players with his repeated references to what worked successfully for him in the past, his Here's-how-we-did-it-at-St.-Cecilia-High-or-at-Army attitude. They knew that the professional game was different and more difficult. Unlike the cloistered, deferential cadets at West Point, the free-spirited Giant players outspokenly challenged him. "Why are you doing this?" a player asked insistently. "That isn't going to work," argued another.

At an early meeting, angered by the players' surly attitude, Vince lost patience with them. He sought to teach them his version of "automatics," the system that allowed the quarterback to change the play at the line of scrimmage. The Giants had been using a color system to implement an automatic. If the quarterback called a running play up the middle and sought to change it at the line of scrimmage, he hollered "blue," signaling an end run instead. The color system restricted the audible to only a few plays; Vince wanted to change to almost any play. He explained his system to the skeptical players: If the play called in the huddle was 41, a run up the middle, but the defense had positioned themselves in the middle, the quarterback would holler "8," indicating that 8 be added to the play, making the new one 49, an end sweep. When a frustrated player yelled from the back of the room, "Jesus Christ! Do I have to carry an adding machine with me?" Vince threw down his chalk in disgust, turned to the players, and yelled: "You are without doubt the dumbest bunch of supposed college graduates I've ever had the misfortune to be associated with in my life!" Then he stormed out of the room. Players chuckled at his uncontrolled rage. "We've got him now!" one said with delight. "We'll run him off if he's going to be this way." The players waited for him to return, but he didn't come back. Finally, a perplexed-looking Howell entered and dismissed the players.

The next day, more determined, Vince reconvened the meeting. He had revised his system. "All right," he told them, "for you dummies who can't add or subtract, we're going to make it easier for you." When the quarterback called a play in the huddle and gave a snap signal—for example, 2—if he wanted to automatic at the line of scrimmage, he first hollered the snap signal, "2," and the next number he called—"49"— was the new play. The defense still could not detect the change, and Vince had simplified his system. This time the players were impressed.[11]

Some players resented Vince's caustic abuse. Eddie Price's bold rebellion created a comic scene at one of the first practices. Price, a hardworking fullback, had repeatedly incurred Vince's wrath during a drill. Fed up, Price abruptly announced: "Enough of this, boy. I'm quitting the game." He ran off the field, into the locker room, and started packing his bags. Vince was shocked. He never imagined a player might respond that way to him. Army cadets never had. As Price raced off the field, Vince raced after him—"like a little puppy dog," said a witness— and pleaded with him, "Eddie, Eddie, come back, come back." "Go to hell!" yelled Price. The fullback later did return to the team, but for many years afterward Vince's friends kidded him about the way he had chased after Price.[12]

Vince and Conerly approached each other warily during training camp and the preseason. In Conerly's view Vince was a rookie coach, and Conerly generally ignored rookies until they proved themselves. Conerly disappointed Vince because of his lackadaisical attitude in camp, an aspect of football he detested. Vince wanted fire, excitement, hard work, perfection; Conerly judged those qualities unnecessary and refused to work up a sweat. At West Point Vince had used the quarterback option-run play and tried to teach it to Conerly. On the play the quarterback sent the fullback off-tackle and, depending on how the defensive end reacted, he either gave the ball to the fullback, ran it himself, or pitched it back to the halfback. Vince didn't appreciate the degree to which the play risked serious injury to the quarterback, a valuable and sparse commodity in professional football. Because of his age, his poor running ability, and his keen sense of danger, Conerly scuttled the play with passive resistance. At an early practice the defensive end kept smashing Conerly to the dirt. In frustration he finally hurled the ball at Vince and exclaimed: "You want to run the goddamn play? You run it!" In dummy drills Conerly continued to run the play, but when Vince ordered it in a scrimmage or a game, Conerly always found an excuse not to call it. Finally Vince dropped the play from the Giants' repertoire.[13]

Vince's uncertainty and the players' doubts about him mostly disappeared by the middle of the 1954 season. Sensing that players were wary of him, Vince made determined efforts to win their confidence. He realized that he needed to learn more about professional football and that players sometimes contributed valuable suggestions. "We taught each other," said Gifford. Most players soon grew to appreciate Vince's warmth, intelligence, dedication, and exceptional teaching skills. His enthusiasm and spirit inspired them.

To build rapport with players at camp Vince visited their dormitory room in the evening. He specifically sought to win the affection and confidence of Conerly, Rote, and Gifford. He joked with them and played a few hands of cards but soon got around to the primary purpose of his visit: to ask their opinion of a new play or strategy. "What do you think?" he inquired. "Will it work?" Suddenly players saw another side of him. "We began to see a different person," said Gifford, "somebody you could respect . . . somebody you could have fun with, somebody you could enjoy talking with." After training camp ended and the team returned to New York, Vince invited a few players to his home in Oradell, where Marie prepared a spaghetti supper. The men engaged in friendly banter, but Vince always made the sessions at least partly business by showing films of opponents. "We learned a lot more about offense," observed Conerly of Vince's informal film sessions.[14]

Although Vince succeeded in building better rapport, he never allowed the improved relations to erode his authority. Because he was awed by their athletic ability, Vince initially acted deferentially toward Conerly, Rote, and Gifford. Sensing his attitude and his uncertainty, Rote and Conerly took advantage of him in the early preseason contests. Conerly particularly hated the meaningless games because they might cause him injury. In early games Vince started both of them and then substituted second-stringers. "Are you ready to go back in?" he asked them. "Not quite," they answered, adding that they would benefit more if they stayed on the sideline and continued to study the reactions of a rookie defensive cornerback. Vince naïvely accepted their explanation. Both gleefully relished their deception, for they knew they could easily outmaneuver a rookie. By the end of preseason, however, Vince had figured out their ploy and asserted his authority. Instead of asking them, he ordered them in. "We realized he'd caught up with us," recalled Rote.[15]

When he started with the Giants, Vince had a poor understanding of the professional passing attack. "He was far more knowledgeable about the running game," said Rote. Vince had difficulty adjusting to a quarterback who passed as effectively as Conerly or a receiver as skilled as Rote. At training camp in 1954, Emlen Tunnell, a wily defensive back, easily diagnosed Vince's unsophisticated pass patterns and broke up plays. But Vince learned quickly and adjusted. He accepted the advice of players more readily on passing plays. Bill Swiacki, the Giants' offensive end coach in 1954 and who had been a fine receiver at Columbia, taught him important lessons about the passing game—the pass routes, the faking, and how to coach them. Swiacki, though, wanted the Giants to pass more often than Vince did. "We had some violent arguments over that," Vince later observed, "but I respected him."

In the 1954 season the Giants bolted to a 6–3 record and contended for the championship, but when Gifford and Conerly were injured at the end of the season, the team slipped and finished with seven wins and five losses. "It was a start," Howell declared happily; "we're headed in the right direction." After the season, though, Vince was unhappy and wondered if he was headed in the right direction. Depressed, nostalgic, and insecure, he decided to give up on both the Giants and his head-coaching dreams to work once more for his inspiring mentor, Earl Blaik.[16]

On a Saturday morning in January, 1955 Vince phoned Blaik and asked to meet with him. Over lunch at the West Point Officers' Club, he told Blaik that his one-year contract with the Giants had expired and that he knew Blaik had recently lost two assistants. Because he thought he would be happier working again for Blaik, he asked the colonel to hire him as an assistant coach. Blaik was surprised but happily welcomed him back to his staff. They didn't attempt to negotiate a salary, although Vince understood he would have to take a cut in pay. They made an oral agreement. Vince would start work the following Monday morning. Vince left the dinner elated.

In deference to the Mara family, Blaik phoned Wellington Mara to inform him of Vince's decision. Wellington was shocked and responded angrily, "You can't talk to Lombardi!" Now Blaik was angry. He pointed out that Vince's contract with the Giants had expired, that Vince had solicited the West Point position, and he reminded Wellington that he had cooperated with the Maras in 1953 when they lured Vince from West Point. "I've hired him," Blaik said adamantly, "and that's all there is to it."

Over the weekend Giants' officials made feverish efforts to change Vince's mind. At a "farewell" luncheon, Ray Walsh, the team's general manager, told him he was "foolish" to return to West Point, but Vince remained unconvinced. Appeals by the Maras proved more successful. On Monday morning Vince arrived at Blaik's office wearing a long, troubled face. "I could read him like a book," Blaik recalled; "the effervescence and enthusiasm were gone." Vince explained his dilemma: "I have never gone back on my word in my life, and I don't intend to now, but I do think you should know that the Maras were at my house over the weekend and offered a six-thousand-dollar increase in my salary. This is a big sum of money, and I promised my wife to tell you that she is terribly upset because I'm coming back to West Point."

Without hesitation Blaik told him to forget their agreement. "Go back to the Giants as though we had never talked about you returning to West Point," said Blaik. Vince was relieved. Had Blaik insisted on upholding their oral agreement, Blaik believed Vince would have taken the West Point job. Blaik rejected the possibility that Vince had used the West Point position as leverage to secure a higher salary with the Giants. "He actually wanted to come back," said Blaik.[17]

The Giants continued to improve, thanks largely to better personnel. Except for Conerly, Gifford, Rote, and defensive back Emlen Tunnell, the Giants had few exceptional players when Vince arrived. Roosevelt Brown, Jack Stroud, Bill Austin, and Ray Wietecha had been impressive offensive linemen, but they needed help. From the 1954 draft the Giants acquired fullback Bobby Epps, defensive back Dick Nolan, and quarterback Don Heinrich. In trades came ends Bob Schnelker and Barney Poole, defensive back Herb Rich, linebacker Bill Svoboda, and tackle Ray Collins. Linebacker Cliff Livingston and end Ken MacAfee returned from military service. In its successful 1955 draft, the Giants picked up fullback Mel Triplett, defensive back Jim Patton, and defensive tackle Roosevelt Grier. They lured fullback Alex Webster from the Canadian Football League, traded for linebacker Harland Svare and defensive end Walt Yowarski, and picked up guard Ray Beck from the service. In masterful trades in 1956, Wellington Mara acquired defensive end Andy Robustelli and defensive tackle Dick Modzelewski.[18]

In 1955 the Giants started miserably and after seven games had only managed a record of 2–5. Frustrated, Howell asked his coaches for suggestions. Vince responded that he and Ed Kolman, the line coach, had one. "Let's have it, then," responded Howell. The suggestion was simple but effective: Use T formation rushing with single-wing blocking. Plays would be run from the quick-hitting T formation, except the defense would be double-blocked at the point of attack. "Everyone is brush-blocking with the T these days," Vince explained. "Ed and I thought if we put double-team blocking into our running game, we'd catch a lot of teams by surprise. I don't think there's a lineman in the game today who can handle a double-team block.'' Howell liked the idea. The results were two running plays, 47 power and 26 power. On the 47 power play Gifford, the number 4 back, took the ball on a quick opener through the number 7 hole, between tackle and end, with Ken MacAfee and Dick Yelvington double-teaming the end and Mel Triplett and Bill Austin double-teaming the outside linebacker. On the 26 power play Alex Webster, the number 2 back, hit through the number 6 hole on the opposite side of the line with double-team blocking ahead of him.

The plays lacked deception and rarely gained more than four yards, but that was enough to allow the offense to control the ball effectively. When the defense adjusted, it became more vulnerable to passes and sweeps. The new plays contributed to the team's dramatic turnabout, and the Giants finished the season with a 6–5–1 record. ''What a difference it made,'' said Howell of Vince's suggestion. The 1955 season was to be the Giants' pivotal one.[19]

The 1955 and 1956 seasons were also pivotal in another important way: They were the points at which the Giants and professional football underwent major transformation. In the early 1950s the game was still unsophisticated, lacking in prestige, media exposure, and wide popularity. It filled a few Sunday afternoons until the collegians played again. When Gifford started with the Giants, ''no one knew who you were—or cared,'' he said. ''That goes for jobs, too—off-season jobs, endorsements.'' The New York press mostly ignored the team, and few New Yorkers seemed to care. ''Sportswriters barely tolerated us,'' recalled Wellington Mara, ''and attendance was sparse and uncertain, even in nice weather.'' The team always opened on the road, which usually meant it returned home with a losing record. Baseball pushed football off the sports pages. Pro football competed for coverage with the three New York baseball teams, and because the Dodgers, Giants, and Yankees usually at least contended for a pennant each fall, the football Giants played in obscurity.

For the Giants and pro football generally, the years 1955 and 1956 brought major change. In a first for television, CBS signed a contract with the NFL in 1955 to televise selected games on a national basis beginning the following year. The contract increased team revenues and brought the game to huge audiences in a few years. Symbolic of the game's growing acceptance was the decision of *Sports Illustrated,* a popular weekly sports magazine, to begin covering pro football regularly in 1956. Attendance at NFL games jumped from an average of 25,353 in 1950 to 40,106 in 1960.

In January 1956, the Giants decided to abandon the dreary confines of the Polo Grounds and signed a twenty-year agreement with the Yankee baseball team to use the more modern and spacious (67,206 seats) Yankee Stadium. The Giants flourished there immediately. Six games at the Polo Grounds in 1955 had attracted 163,787; six games at Yankee Stadium in 1956—with a better team on display—drew 280,727. Thereafter the Giants' home attendance soared.[20]

After the Giants won four of their opening five games in 1956, Vince gathered the offense around him at a Wednesday practice. "By God, we've really got something going," he told them, his eyes sparkling and pride bursting. The Giants easily won the 1956 Eastern Conference championship—the first time since 1950 that Cleveland didn't capture that title—and smashed the Chicago Bears, 47–7, to claim the NFL championship. "One year you're nobody and then all of a sudden your phone's ringing all the time and everyone wants you for something," recalled Gifford of his own and the Giants' changing fortunes in 1956. "None of us had ever seen anything like it before. It was a ball."[21]

His apprenticeship ended, by 1956 Vince had earned the reputation within pro football circles as one of the game's finest offensive coaches. "Every single thing I learned in the 1930s has gone out the window," he explained in a 1956 interview. "Even in the last five years, football has changed tremendously." To compensate, studying the game became his obsession. "When the other coaches . . . would leave the Giant offices," said Howell, "there always was one light still burning, the one in Vince Lombardi's office." Often he worked from mid-July to early December without a day off. He carried reels of film around like a lawyer with a briefcase, or a fat notebook crammed with diagrams of offensive and defensive formations. At home he maintained a file cabinet stacked with diagrams of every offensive and defensive situation he ever encountered and notes on all phases of coaching. He studied the next opponent from movies he projected on a screen in his study at home. On trains or planes he diagramed plays on the back of an envelope, a matchbox cover, or a paper napkin. While diagraming, he was completely engrossed, oblivious to anything else. During a game he prowled the sideline like a caged tiger. With a sheaf of charts in one hand, a cigarette in the other, he busied himself buttonholing players for information, keeping his eyes glued to the field and his charts, or phoning the spotters in the upper stand.

Vince's eight years in the classroom and his seventeen years teaching football players had molded him into a masterful teacher. "People listened when he talked," observed Bob Schnelker. His West Point apprenticeship reinforced his belief that players needed condensed, uncomplicated information. "It was as if he were teaching the bottom 10 percent of the class," said Wellington Mara. Although repetitious and simple, his message was so exact that the players clearly understood, and he convinced them the plays would work. Whether he taught on the field or at the blackboard, he focused on his lesson and expressed himself articulately in a booming voice. When he enthusiastically drew a zero on the blackboard with his strong, punching, circular motion, he often crumbled the chalk.[22]

"All right," he instructed, "this is the 26 power play, 26 power play, do you have that, Eddie? 2-6-26 power play. Now, the right guard *must* pull back, must pull back, the right guard *must* pull back, and he *has to pull back* to avoid the center, who will be stepping to the onside. So the first step is back. Got that, Bill? The first step is back." "He drove us mad," said Gifford; yet the players learned and the plays worked. "Boy, this guy knows what he's talking about!" thought fullback Bobby Epps as he watched Vince diagram. The "big lane" Vince wedged on the board for the fullback made Epps so confident he could envision himself running through it for a touchdown. Out on the practice field, Vince carefully walked players through their assignments to reinforce the classroom lesson. At halftime of a game, the tone of his voice, rather than Rockne-like rhetoric, usually conveyed his message. He quickly analyzed a problem, made adjustments, and told players to go "do it."[23]

In all phases of coaching, Vince intently concentrated, resisting all distractions, focusing on the specific play or drill. "It was tunnel vision," stated center Ray Wietecha. "He was just tunneled in on that block [or] that one particular player. . . . It always worked. That's why he was so great." He inspired confidence because he was so positive his approach would work, and, as Jack Stroud insisted, "he was usually right." When the Giants started to win, the players' confidence in Vince increased. Though confident in his approach, Vince remained open to suggestions. Conerly, Rote, and Gifford recommended changes he accepted. "He was not easy to convince," said Stroud, "but if you proved that you were right . . . he'd change."[24]

Although Vince stressed fundamentals, he also relished deception. He always inserted a trick or two. "I don't like to use the term 'gambler's instinct,' but I'm willing to take a chance," he explained. He became so perceptive that he usually knew which plays would succeed. He would put in a play for a team on one Sunday and then change it slightly so it started off looking exactly the same in the next game. In one game Conerly would hand off to Triplett up the middle and gain yardage. The next week the play started the same except Conerly kept the ball and threw a quick pass to Gifford on the outside. Such tactics later became common, but they were unique and effective in the 1950s. "Defenses were a lot easier to fool," observed Gifford, "and we fooled them."[25]

Vince instituted many innovations to make film analysis more effective. Wide-angle projection allowed him to view the entire playing area and to analyze how each player lined up and reacted on each play. It was a "tremendous advantage" over the old method, he explained, "when your cameraman was often fooled by the play and you couldn't get the whole picture anyway." He stationed a coach—or sometimes Wellington Mara—in the scout's box directly above the Giants' bench in Yankee Stadium and had him snap still pictures of the opponent's defense with a quick-developing Polaroid camera. Wrapped inside an old sock, the photo was then lowered to the bench in full view of perplexed fans. "Visual education is much better than telling the quarterback the defenses," stated Vince of his unusual approach.

For a while the NFL placed an embargo on the exchange of films by teams for use in preparation for games, but the rule was continually broken by the more progressive coaches who had used films for many years and found them much better than paper-and-pencil reports by scouts. The prohibition apparently originated with older, conservative, and probably lazy coaches who worked at their jobs only half the year and did not wish to take on the additional load of film study. For Vince and a few other coaches, like Sid Gillman, the head coach of the Los Angeles Rams, coaching was increasingly becoming a year-round profession. "They aspired to excellence," noted sportswriter William Wallace, "and they were willing to work hard at film study or any other element that would help their teams to win." The Rams and the Giants, therefore, agreed to bootleg films. The Rams had a film of their recent game with the Chicago Bears. The Giants were soon to play the Bears. Gillman air-mailed the film of the Rams-Bears game to the Giants. A few weeks later a Giants-Philadelphia Eagles film would be dispatched to Los Angeles to aid the Rams in their upcoming game with the Eagles.[26]

Though usually serious, intense, and studious, Vince loved a joke and relished moments of spontaneous humor. He insisted that the dummy scrimmage be run perfectly. But while an offensive group ran against the defense, the rest of the players stood around waiting their turn. Players had to run ten yards when their turn came, and as practice wore on, they got tired of standing. Frank Gifford described their humorous mischief:

"We gradually moved closer and closer to the two teams working out until we were almost on top of them. This infuriated Vince, so we began to do it purposely. We'd keep inching up and he'd . . . scream, 'Get back, get back, stop crowding the offense!'

"One day," Gifford continued, "he saw an old beat-up orange peel that had been lying on the field for Lord knows how long. He said, 'Everyone behind the orange peel. Anyone who passes the orange peel gets a lap around the field.' This sounded so silly that we lined up single file behind the orange peel. He turned around and saw that and roared. Then we all scattered, and every time he turned to watch the play, we'd push the orange peel closer and pretty soon we were right back on top of him. He turned around, began to shout, 'I told you guys to get behind the orange' . . . looked down, and here was the orange peel. These were the things that would delight him and crack him up."[27]

Vince refused to tolerate mistakes and often raged at players to improve. "He *demanded* they play to the best of their ability *all* the time," marveled Assistant Coach Ken Kavanaugh of Vince's drive for perfection. On most occasions he accurately directed his anger at their mistakes. "I can't recall . . . many errors in judgment in that respect," observed Gifford. He was particularly abusive at the Tuesday morning film session—or, as one player described it, the "name-calling film." He "shouted, screamed, kicked, ranted, jumped up and down," said Howell of his tantrums, yet he usually remained enough in control to satisfy his head coach. "He knew how far he could go," said Howell. A few players loved to arouse him intentionally by hiding his baseball cap or baiting him during film sessions. They occasionally led him to the point where he would smash a table or throw an eraser at the blackboard.[28]

Like the incident with Eddie Price, Vince's criticism sometimes backfired. Fullback Mel Triplett, a smashing runner and a vicious blocker, exasperated Vince and the other coaches because he seemed unmotivated and often missed his assignments. Triplett thought Vince was persecuting him. At a Tuesday film session Vince criticized him for missing an important block. "What kind of an excuse for a block is that?" Vince bellowed, as he repeatedly ran the same film sequence, each time pointing out Triplett's error. "Look at yourself, Triplett! Triplett. Hear me? Triplett. Triplett." Finally Triplett, who looked frightening when angry, spoke back sharply, "Get off my back or get yourself another fullback!" The room fell silent. No one had talked back to Vince in such a menacing tone. Vince didn't respond. He pushed the forward button on the projector and continued the film. As the meeting ended and players filed out, Vince whispered to Jack Stroud, "I meant to make him mad, but I didn't mean to make him *that* mad." From then on Vince dealt more cautiously with Triplett. The two never did have a confrontation, but, said Gifford, "Vinnie walked a very dangerous line at times."[29]

Robert Mischak, a guard who played under Vince at West Point and briefly with the Giants, recalled a meeting Vince held with rookie players. "He seemed to expect us to have the same knowledge he possessed. We didn't. He got furious. He ranted and raved and screamed, and we couldn't follow his point, and for a while, he just wasn't teaching." Soon Vince calmed down, however, and started a new attack on the problem until the rookies began to understand. Mischak intensely disliked Vince's approach. "He [was] not that sensitive to people," he complained; "he tried to make me as intense as he was, and I just wasn't that type. . . . To an extent, you had to completely conform your own personality to his, or you were wiped out." Although quarterback Don Heinrich respected and liked Vince, he also found Vince's abuse distasteful. "His style of handling me was wrong. His browbeating was not the [approach] I responded to. Some players do." Nonetheless, Heinrich observed, Vince's loud criticism "did get your attention."[30]

At some point Vince criticized almost everyone on the offensive team, usually in front of the other players. The major exception was Conerly. Vince never spoke harshly to him. Vince seldom criticized his quarterbacks in front of team members anyway, but another reason explained his attitude toward Conerly. "I've never coached a football player who had more courage," Vince later observed. Conerly broke his nose in a game, causing a bloody mess, but instead of coming off the field, he remained in the game, called two consecutive time-outs, and had the trainers push his nose back into place. He continued to play. "Vinnie loved it when a man [would] show courage like that," said Gifford.

Most of the players admired Vince and minimized the importance of his caustic abuse. They adjusted to him and understood his desire to improve the team. According to Ray Wietecha, players sensed that whether Vince praised or criticized, it "came from the heart." Jack Stroud agreed: "Lombardi had heart . . . which is why I had such respect for him." "Count me among those who personally liked Vince," said Rote. "A great coach and man," echoed Conerly. "I think everyone loved the man," said Alex Webster.[31]

Vince seems to have had the most dramatic effect on Frank Gifford, who despite his outstanding success in college and professional football, felt insecure. Vince learned to motivate him and bolster his confidence, and Gifford depended on Vince's approval. "All I wanted was to be able to walk into the meeting Tuesday morning and have Vinnie give me that big grin and pat me on the fanny and let me know that I was doing what he wanted me to do," said Gifford. Under Vince's direction, Gifford became an exceptionally versatile star. He never ran the ball enough to lead the league in rushing or caught the ball enough to lead in receiving. He didn't pass often from his halfback position but was enormously effective when he did, averaging a touchdown about once in every four throws. In 1956 he was named "Player of the Year" in the NFL. He scored sixty-five points, ranked third in pass receptions with fifty-five, and was fifth in rushing with 819 yards. "I loved him," Gifford observed of Vince. "He taught me to dedicate myself. . . . Vinnie [was] probably the biggest influence of my life, even more than my own father."[32]

Vince earned mixed reviews from New York sportswriters. All applauded his coaching, many enjoyed his personality, but some objected to his rude disposition. "He is straight football, dead on the level," praised one writer, who thought his coaching showed "profundity, clarity, and imagination." "Lombardi . . . is one of the nicest guys we know in the sports world," said another. Reporters who caught him in one of his depressed or surly moods, though, or who asked him a "stupid question," found him abrasive and discourteous. Jerry Izenberg, who covered the Giants for the *New York Herald Tribune,* thought Vince was "a horrible, dreadful man in the dressing room." If Izenberg asked him a technical question about football, Vince obliged graciously, provided a straightforward answer and would even diagram a play for Izenberg's readers. But if Izenberg asked him, "Why did you decide to pass on third down?" Vince would give him a "horrible look" and "an answer that you could not print." Harold Rosenthal, another *Herald Tribune* reporter, described Vince as a "first-class pain in the ass." Rosenthal's first contact with Vince occurred when he tried to interview Jim Lee Howell in the locker room. Vince occupied a nearby locker. "There was a great deal of slamming around of equipment and things like banging the caked mud out of cleats and shouting across the room (and across our heads)," observed Rosenthal. "Vince Lombardi? Sure. Big Japanese smile. Big spacing between the two front teeth. Big noise. This guy's a goddamn nuisance."[33]

Joe King, another New York sportswriter, expertly captured Vince's contradictions. Vince might be mistaken for a "teacher of romance languages who was about ready to earn his full professorship," King wrote. "The book under Lombardi's arm would heighten the impression. So would his sober dress, his kindly, almost benign smile, his self-effacing manners . . . and if Vince were in one of his introspective fogs, the courteous [observer] no doubt would see the absent-minded 'professor' safely across the street." In Vince's case, impressions were deceiving. "Lombardi is an educated man," King continued, "but the book he carries is a football playbook. The fog he sometimes carries with him hides a Machiavellian plot for the next game, or the next hundred games. He is a professor, but only of football." Vince was "moody, Latinish, depressed, [and] explosive from time to time," said King. "He can throw that playbook into a bottomless abyss in one frustrating moment and in the next seize with the enthusiasm, tenacity, and perseverance of a terrier the roots of an idea that will become a touchdown."[34]

More than at West Point, Vince displayed periodic mood swings. "We always could tell what his mood was on a day because he couldn't hide it," observed Wellington Mara. His emotions often showed in his face. "He was either smiling or he was frowning," said Jack Stroud. Players had difficulty anticipating his disposition. At practice they wondered whether they should have a "game face on" or whether they could afford a "little luxury of laughter." The recent performance of his offense partly determined his mood. If his offense played well, he was outgoing, friendly, and excited; but if it performed poorly, he sometimes wouldn't even talk to his fellow coaches for two days. During Vince's gloomy moods Howell received only a "yes" or a "no" response from him. "He really hated to look bad," said Landry. But the coaches adjusted. "That was just Vince and we understood him," Landry said. "Most of the time he was high," stated Howell; "he wasn't low very much."[35]

Another reason for his bouts with depression stemmed from his frustrating search for a head coaching position. Depression set in most severely during the winter months. "At the end of every season," observed Wellington Mara, "after the total absorption with football subsided, he had a winter crisis. We called it 'Vinnie's winter crisis.' " Howell pinpointed the problem: "Mostly, he thought he should have been somewhere else." Howell wrote scores of recommendations for him. "Every year he would come up with about six teams that he wanted to go coach right then."

After Fordham gave up football in December 1954, for a few years Vince switched his primary attention to coaching at the University of Notre Dame. It was a great Catholic university, he thought, with a successful national recruiting program. After a poor season in 1956, pressure mounted to dismiss Terry Brennan as head coach of the Irish, and Vince closely followed the developments. "He told me several times he'd like to have that [Notre Dame] job," said Howell. Notre Dame dismissed Brennan in December 1958, but the university never seriously considered hiring Vince. Vince claimed they never even acknowledged his letter.[36]

Each job opportunity created a crisis. Should he apply? Will he get the job? When he didn't, his depression deepened. He applied for openings at Southern California, Washington, Stanford, and the Air Force Academy, but, as he later conceded, "nothing ever happened." He lacked a famous name that would impress college officials. He remained convinced that the root of the problem was prejudice against Italians. "They looked at his leathery face," said Tim Cohane, who recommended him for a few jobs, and thought he looked "like a shoemaker's son." Marie's attitude also hurt his chances and increased his anxiety. She insisted that he remain in the New York–New Jersey area and urged him to be more patient and wait until the head coaching position opened with the Giants. "She was the one who kept him there," Howell claimed; "she had a lot of influence [over] Vinnie. . . . They had some pretty [heated] talks."

Vince occasionally lost hope. "I'm wondering whether the right head coaching job ever will open up for me," he told Cohane early in 1956. "I know I can coach, but the right people never seem to know it." Cohane held little hope for Vince either but tried to cheer him up. "You'll get your chance. It's bound to come." "I hope you're right," Vince responded. "But I'll be forty-three in June, and I'm not getting any younger. I've got to make a move soon." The disappointment had one positive effect on his attitude. "Whatever the reasons," he later said, "the fact that I did not get the opportunities I felt I deserved motivated me greatly."[37]

At the start of the 1957 season Vince suddenly did become a desirable coaching commodity within the professional football fraternity. He now had three years of experience in the NFL, and the Giants' 1956 championship greatly increased his stature. After the 1957 season the Philadelphia Eagles approached him about becoming their new head coach. Hugh Devore had just completed two miserable years directing the Eagles, during which he compiled a record of 7–16–1. On January 11, 1958, the Eagles fired Devore. While searching for a successor, Vince McNally, general manager of the Eagles, heard enthusiastic reports about Vince. Frank McNamee, president of the Eagles, agreed with McNally that Vince should be approached but urged him to contact Vince directly because McNamee thought the Maras probably would not grant the Eagles permission to talk to him.

In late January 1958, McNally phoned Vince and asked to interview him about the vacant position. Vince was thrilled. "This is the first chance I've ever received to be a head coach," he told McNally. They met for a few hours at the Philadelphia train depot, and McNally offered him the job at $22,500 a year. McNally explained vaguely that the contract would extend for one or two years with the possibility of an extension if the team performed well. (McNally could not offer a longer contract because the stockholders who owned the Eagles were upset that they were obligated to pay Devore for the third year of his contract.) Vince was too excited to quibble about contract details. "He was just like a little kid," McNally recalled; "he was so happy to get a head coaching job." The prospect of coaching Norm Van Brocklin, the Eagles' great quarterback, particularly excited him. "Every time I see that guy coming on the field, I start shivering," Vince said. Concerned that Marie would resist moving, Vince requested that he be allowed to continue living in New Jersey and commute to Philadelphia. McNally agreed. "There is only one thing I have to do," Vince cautioned as they parted. "I have to go back and talk with the Maras because they have been very good to me." McNally agreed to wait.

When Vince met with Wellington Mara, his friend urged him not to accept the job. The Eagles had an unsettled situation, Wellington argued, caused by the meddling of some of the team's many stockholders. Vince would not be the general manager and therefore would have insufficient power and control. The one- or two-year contract the Eagles offered wouldn't allow Vince enough time to improve the team. He might be fired before the team succeeded. Wellington also apparently offered financial inducements to encourage Vince to stay with the Giants. Now Vince was confused. Ecstasy had turned into tormenting indecision. He was so obviously distraught after the meeting that Marie urged him to visit their parish church. "Sit in a pew and just think for a while," she advised. "Don't pray. Think." The next day Vince met again with Wellington. "I went and sat in church all yesterday afternoon and reasoned this whole thing out," Vince told him. "I think you're right." Vince called McNally and declined the offer. "I'm sorry. I talked to the Maras, and they raised my salary and my insurance policy," Vince told McNally. "I'll have to stay here. I owe it to them." Had McNally offered him a longer contract and the position of general manager, Vince probably would have accepted the job.[38]

The 1958 season was one of the most memorable in the Giants' history. On Sunday, December 28, 1958, at Yankee Stadium, the Giants played the Baltimore Colts for the NFL championship. How the Giants ever got to the playoff was almost a miracle. They lost five of six exhibition games and split the first four in the regular season. Arthur Daley of *The New York Times* thought the Giants looked "absolutely dreadful." Then in mid-October the team meshed magnificently and won eight of its last nine games. "It's possible," wrote Daley, "that no team went farther on less than the Giants. They had no speed and no one who could score a touchdown in one blazing burst.'' Great defense carried the Giants into the championship, but the offense, said Daley, was ''consumed by desire.'' ''Everyplace you went in New York, people were talking about us,'' recalled Wellington Mara. During the season New Yorkers began to drive to eastern Long Island and New Haven to spend Sunday afternoons in motel rooms watching the Giants on TV because home games were blacked out within seventy-five miles of New York City. On the morning of the championship game Vince briefed his quarterbacks, walked to the center of the clubhouse at Yankee Stadium, looked around, and said, ''If anyone had told me two months ago that we'd be here today in the playoff I'd have asked him to give me a whiff of the opium pipe he was smoking. Us in the playoff?''

The Colts-Giants game was one of the most dramatic in the history of pro football. With two minutes to play and leading, 17–14, the Giants missed a first down by inches and punted to the Colts. After Baltimore's quarterback, John Unitas, engineered a stirring drive, the Colts kicked a field goal with seven seconds remaining to knot the score at 17–17. In overtime the Colts scored an Alan Ameche's one-yard run, winning, 23–17. Many fans and sports observers judged the game the greatest ever played. ''I'm not sure whether it was the greatest game ever played,'' reflected Tom Landry, ''but there's no question . . . that it marked the time, the game, and the place where pro football really caught on, where the public attention was aroused and brought the game into the spotlight.'' At a dinner that evening Vince observed that it had been an exciting season. ''I have only two complaints about it. It was a couple inches too short and seven seconds too long.''[39]

After living in Oradell for two years, Vince moved his family to a four-bedroom home in Fair Haven, New Jersey, near the North Jersey shore. Marie loved Fair Haven because it was so close to Red Bank, where she had been raised and where her older relatives still lived. Susan and Vince, Jr., attended the Red Bank schools. Each morning Vince caught the 7:19 A.M. train from Red Bank for the fifty-mile ride to his Yankee Stadium office. When he wasn't diagraming plays, friends on the train lured him into a gin rummy game. In the summer he golfed with friends at various courses near his home. Throughout his years with the Giants, Vince used most of his off-season free time to supplement his income. He and his brother Joe opened a sporting goods store in Englewood. For a few years Vince sold insurance for the Equitable Insurance Company of Iowa. In 1958 he asked a friend, John Ryan, to teach him the municipal bond business. ''Of all the guys I've taught that to over the years," recalled Ryan, "I never met anybody that absorbed [it faster]." Vince never completed his training in bonds because banking attracted his interest. In December 1958, after the football season, he solicited a banking position from another friend, Edward Breslin, who worked for the Federation Bank and Trust Company at Columbus Circle in New York. Federation hired Vince at $200 a week as a public-relations executive. "He wasn't afraid to work," said Breslin. Vince quickly attempted to learn all the operations of the bank; within a few days Breslin found him behind a teller's cage trying to figure out how "this works." However, Vince stayed with Federation only three weeks before an attractive head coaching position lured him away from the Giants and New York.[40]

After the 1958 season two promising head coaching possibilities opened for Vince. Earl Blaik had resigned at West Point, and initially observers gave Vince an excellent chance for the job. But when Army's athletic board followed tradition and restricted candidates to former West Point graduates, the decision dashed Vince's hopes. Blaik's stamp of approval was probably crucial. Had he strongly lobbied for Vince, he may have swayed the athletic board. "Blaik didn't favor Lombardi over the rest of the field," noted one sportswriter. "If he did, it was kept a deep, dark secret." Though Vince was a friend and Blaik respected his coaching ability, Blaik may have worried about Vince's emotional stability and judged him too great a risk. Blaik favored Dale Hall, a member of his staff and a former Army backfield mate of Doc Blanchard and Glenn Davis. West Point hired Hall in January 1959.

Vince was a guest at the home of Dr. Anthony Pisani, the Giants' team physician, when he received the phone call from West Point informing him that he was no longer in contention for the Army job. Vince's face expressed his pain. "Do you mind if I call Green Bay?" he asked Pisani. The Green Bay Packers had expressed serious interest in him, and he could now focus his attention on their proposal.[41]

VII

The First Year

ON NOVEMBER 2, 1958, THE GREEN BAY PACKERS PLAYED THE COLTS IN Baltimore, and before 51,333 spectators and a midwestern television audience were humiliated, 56–0. It was the nadir of the Packers' fall from grace, the darkest two and a half hours in the team's proud, forty-year history. Fifty-six points were the most ever scored in a game against the Green Bay team. The Packers couldn't block, tackle, or run; they couldn't catch the football or stop the Colts from catching it. Leading, 28–0, at the half, the Colts inserted their reserves, who were made to look like All-Pros by the inept Packers. Green Bay completed only five of twenty-six passes and had five intercepted. Babe Parilli started at quarterback and completed one of eleven. In the second quarter Bart Starr relieved him, but he was not much better and had to run for his life from the Colts' pass rushers. In the fourth quarter Joe Francis, a rookie from Oregon State, took over for Starr, but the Packers' offense still went nowhere. A few Colts were injured, some because a Packer defensive back jumped on their runners after the players were clearly down. The Packers suffered no serious injuries, except to their feelings.

Clearly, the Packers had fallen on hard times. Yet they had a glorious past. The team was a major institution in Green Bay, Wisconsin (1960 population, 62,888), a community otherwise known for its cheesemaking and paper mills. The city is on the west side of Lake Michigan, 110 miles north of Milwaukee and where the mouth of the Fox River joins Green Bay. For most of the Packers' history, Earl "Curly" Lambeau embodied the team. Lambeau, a Green Bay native and high-school football star, had played in 1918 at Notre Dame under Knute Rockne until illness forced him to quit school. He returned home, and on August 11, 1919, formed a football team from among former high-school and college players. Lambeau worked for the Indian Packing Company, and when his boss agreed to put up $500 for the team's sweaters and stockings in return for inscribing "Indian Packing Co" on the sweaters, the Packers were born.

Two years later the Packers acquired a franchise in the American Football Association. Thirteen teams competed in the fall of 1921 in what the National Football League considers its first season, and of the original league members only the Packers still play where they started and remain in the league. When bad weather and poor attendance caused financial hardship, city merchants raised funds and in 1922 formed a public, nonprofit corporation to operate the club, with Lambeau as manager and coach.

Lambeau directed the team for thirty-one years and won six league championships, including an unprecedented three in a row in 1929, 1930, and 1931. He was one of the first pro coaches to exploit successfully the forward pass and was ruthlessly demanding of his players. He had uncanny ability to discover inexpensive players and turn them into stars. Among the NFL immortals he coached were Johnny (Blood) McNally, Arnie Herber, Clarke Hinkle, Cecil Isbell, and Don Hutson.

After the sixth championship, in 1944, things turned sour. Caught in a price war with the new All-America Football Conference, formed in 1946, and with no cash reserves, the Packers were outbid for talented players. Earlier Lambeau had been an innovative pioneer, but the new T formation offense developed by the Chicago Bears made his single wing obsolete. He converted to the T, but his offense sputtered. Lambeau's leadership qualities seemed to diminish, and players increasingly resented his arbitrary discipline.

Lambeau's primary difficulties grew out of his battles with the front office. The team's executive committee, an unwieldly group of thirteen men, sought power for itself by taking over many of Lambeau's duties. In 1947 it revamped the organization, instituting subcommittees on finance, grounds, contracts, publicity, league representation, and the draft. Lambeau resented the change. "You can't run a football team if you have to go to this committee for that and that committee for this."

Moreover, his personal life scandalized the front office and the community. He had divorced twice, married three times, and spent the winter in Malibu Beach, California, leading some to tag him "the Earl of Hollywood."

In 1947 the Packers finished with a 6–5–1 record, the team's last winning season for twelve years. Tired of the hassling, Lambeau resigned in 1950 to become vice president and coach of the Chicago Cardinals. Gene Ronzani replaced him, but the team fared poorly and Ronzani was fired near the end of the 1953 season. His replacement, Lisle Blackbourn, experienced brief success, but when his teams also floundered, he was fired after the 1957 season. Almost immediately the front office elevated Ray "Scooter" McLean, the team's backfield coach, to replace him.[1]

Whether the Packers won or lost, Green Bay was still America's most improbable football community. With pro football becoming major national entertainment, the game put the city on the map in a fashion that explorer Jean Nicolet never could. After World War II many larger communities lost one pro football franchise or another, and many thought it was only a matter of time before Green Bay's Packers would join them as merely an historical apostrophe. But the Packers survived, the only team still trying to reassert the small town's preeminence over the big city. In Green Bay the games were more than just one of many mildly amusing diversions offered by big cities. Lambeau described the Packers as a "community project and a regional religion." The players couldn't lose themselves in the impersonal whirl of a big city. Fans knew members of the team and saw them everywhere. "If you're a goof-off," said one Packer, "the people of this town find out about it faster than in any other town in the league." In 1934 the Packers began playing some home games in Milwaukee and have divided home games between Green Bay and Milwaukee ever since.[2]

Just as Green Bay's size made it unique in the NFL, so did the team's corporation. The Packers were organized under Wisconsin law as a nonprofit stock corporation. A total of 1,698 stockholders had purchased shares of stock at $25 a share. No one could own more than two hundred shares, and no dividends were declared. Their purchase amounted to a contribution to the Packers. The only privilege shareholders had was to attend the annual meeting. The forty-five members of the board of directors, selected for their devotion to the Packers and their community stature, met four times a year, listened to financial reports, and filled board vacancies. They also elected a president and an executive committee, which functioned as the administrative body of the corporation. The chief difference between the Green Bay club and other teams was that the Packer corporation could use all its profit to improve the team and protect the future of professional football in the city.[3]

The 1958 Packer season had started with an air of optimism. "Morale is high," said Art Daley, sportswriter for the *Green Bay Press-Gazette,* before the first game. "We're not shooting for just a good season," crowed Scooter McLean; "we're going after the championship." Soon the attitude changed to bitterness and despair. The Packers lost the first game, tied the second, and then lost nine of their last ten games. In columnist Red Smith's pithy words, the Packers had "overwhelmed one opponent, underwhelmed ten, and whelmed one." The 1–10–1 record was the worst in the history of the franchise.

When the Colts crushed the Packers in Baltimore in the sixth game, the embarrassing defeat unleashed withering abuse from fans and the Wisconsin media lasting the rest of the season. "Packerland is sizzling," said Daley. Critics found fault with almost all aspects of the team—poor quarterbacking, porous defense—but focused on the ineffective coaching, the attitude of the players, and the incompetence of the Packers' executive committee.

McLean had been an assistant coach with the Packers for seven years before becoming head coach but had few attributes for his new position. "We all loved the guy," said a player of the friendly, mild-mannered exceptionally forgiving coach. Nonetheless, the team failed to respond to his direction. He made little effort to work the team into proper physical condition; players often fooled around during his undemanding practices. The coaching staff showed films to the team but never used them effectively as a teaching tool. "I can't remember a thing about them," observed one player of the useless sessions. McLean adopted Blackbourn's complicated offensive system that required players to learn different blocking assignments on every play, and since the coaches often changed the assignments from week to week, the befuddled players often made mistakes.

McLean had no capacity to discipline. He was the players' friend— "like one of the guys"—and even played poker with them the night before a game. He allowed them to establish and supervise training rules and placed them on their honor to abide by them, but since some players were not honorable, his system didn't work. He appointed a committee of players to advise him of problems, and when the season turned sour, he asked the committee's advice, oblivious to the fact that some committee members were the ones "staying out late and raising hell." Observed guard Jerry Kramer: "I think every man on the club took advantage of him." There was no dress code, and when some players wore T-shirts to out-of-town games, they looked as sloppy as they played.

The Packers had accumulated talented players, mainly because Jack Vainisi, the Packers' highly respected personnel director, had selected wisely in the college draft. The fans, the media, and the players themselves knew the raw talent was there, but the realization only increased their despair and confusion. The Packers hadn't had a winning season since 1947, and defeatism infected the club. There came a point when chronic losers, with no reason for hope, played only for their paychecks and prayed for the season to end. Nor was there any sign of leadership on the team. As losers they assembled in little cliques to share their misery and to complain about the coaches and about the players in the other cliques.[4]

The fans complained about the players, too, not only for their obvious ineptitude on Sunday afternoons but also for their late-night shenanigans. The evening following the Packers' season-opening loss to the Chicago Bears, a group of players and their wives or girlfriends went to the Piccadilly, a bar on the East Side of Green Bay, where they danced to a band and drank. A week later, in a widely read letter to the *Green Bay Press-Gazette,* an anonymous writer accused the players of "putting on tavern shows" when they should have been reflecting on Sunday's loss. Why pay for a ticket, said the writer, "when for the price of a drink you can see them practically any night on the town?" For example, the letter continued, "perhaps our 'Golden Boy' should leave for Hollywood in order to enhance his career as a night-club entertainer, leaving a spot for someone who really wants to play football." Golden Boy was the nickname given Paul Hornung at Notre Dame, where he had been a versatile All-American back and winner in 1956 of the Heisman Trophy as the year's top college player. The Packers had used their bonus pick to make him the first player selected in the 1957 college draft. With the Packers Hornung had been shunted among quarterback, fullback, and halfback, and his overall play had been disappointing.

The sarcastic letter to the newspaper only vaguely suggested what the Green Bay rumor mill widely believed: that some players had engaged in public rowdyism at bars and restaurants, a few had acted scandalously, and the prime offender was Paul Hornung. As Hornung himself recalled of the incident at the Piccadilly, "It was around town that I had done a striptease and that my date had stopped at panties and bra." In the eyes of many fans, "I was a bum." Hornung denied he had done anything wrong, claiming he had only clowned around at the drums and the microphone. "We sang, and the crowd joined in. It was kind of warm, so I took off my coat and tie and loosened my shirt collar." What Hornung and other players discovered was that the public eye was especially searching in Green Bay, and, whatever the truth, the stories contributed to the widespread disgust with the team.[5]

Green Bay's fans were also disgusted with the team's executive committee and blamed it for the many years of futility. Including McLean's disastrous season, in eleven years the Packers had won only thirty-seven games, lost ninety-three, and tied two. Something was obviously wrong with the management of the team. The executive committee met weekly, and on Monday after a game the coach attended a luncheon where some committee members and guests questioned and second-guessed him. Besides meddling with the coach, the committee was plagued by petty jealousies, archaic methods of administration through subcommittees, and reluctance to relinquish authority. "Like everything else . . . that is run by a committee," recalled a Packers' front-office official, Tom Miller, "the Packers were screwed up." Oliver Kuechle, sports editor of the *Milwaukee Journal*, Wisconsin's largest newspaper, levied withering abuse on the thirteen-member "soviet." He argued that the Packers needed a general manager with "real authority," a streamlined, compact executive committee, and a great coach with the security of a long-term contract.[6]

A few disgruntled fans vented their frustration on Packer officials and players. On December 9, a five-foot dummy representing the Packers' president, Dominic Olejniczak, was found hanging from a lamp in front of the Packers' ticket office. Center Jim Ringo's daughter, who attended St. Willebrord's Catholic Grade School, was heckled by fellow classmates. One day she came home from school and asked, "Daddy, are you a bum?" When her classmates kept insisting that all Packers were bums, midway through the season Ringo took her out of school and sent her back home to Pennsylvania. Vandals spray-painted the top of Ringo's car. Anonymous phone callers needled him at all hours of the night. "If you can't play," said one, "why stay?" Ringo and other players despaired of their hopeless situation. "I just wanted one thing," said Hornung, "to get the hell out of Green Bay."[7]

Amid the pervasive gloom were a few encouraging developments. In 1957 the city completed construction of a new football stadium with a seating capacity of 32,150. The club's financial situation was improving as deficits in the early part of the decade turned to small profits at the end. Despite the poor record of 1958, attendance improved slightly over the previous year. Moreover, a change in the corporate structure of the

Packers, which seemed trifling at the time, proved the key reform that paved the way for effective leadership.

Reacting to critics, the executive committee studied reforms in the administration of the Packers and arrived at recommendations similar to those urged by Kuechle. On December 16, 1958, Olejniczak announced that the executive committee would be reduced from thirteen to seven, and instead of weekly meetings the committee would meet monthly, reducing the temptation to meddle. Most important, the new committee would confine itself only to making policy; administrative responsibilities shifted to a general manager, who previously had acted as the business manager. Executive committee member Jerry Atkinson explained the major reason for the changes: "We felt that no group, even a group of successful businessmen, can run anything. Somebody has to be in charge." Among the qualifications Olejniczak outlined for the new general manager was someone with a "dominant personality." When McLean resigned on December 17, 1958, the Packers were in the market for a new general manager and a new head coach, their fourth coach in nine years. This time they were patient. President Olejniczak asked seven other board members to act as a screening committee, and they commenced a diligent, systematic, confidential search. They contacted scores of persons, asking for recommendations of excellent candidates. Many assumed that the Packers would fill the two vacancies with different persons. Lambeau returned from California and lobbied for the general manager's position, but he had ruffled too many feathers to be seriously considered.[8]

The search committee's model was Paul Brown of the Cleveland Browns. Some members even said they wanted a "Paul Brown of Green Bay." Coincidentally, Brown was the only head coach in the NFL who was also the general manager. The Packers contacted many potential candidates but only seriously considered a few: Blanton Collier, head coach at the University of Kentucky; Otto Graham, former great quarterback of the Cleveland Browns; and Forrest Evashevski, head coach at the University of Iowa. For a while the popular and successful Evashevski was the leading candidate. Packers' officials interviewed him at the NCAA convention in early January 1959, phoned him often, and in mid-January quietly slipped him into Green Bay for a tour and another interview. But Evashevski never wanted the job. He preferred college coaching and had excellent financial arrangements at Iowa. After the Green Bay trip, he took himself out of consideration.

Vince was also a leading prospect, thanks to Jack Vainisi, who first suggested him. On December 17, 1958, Olejniczak phoned Wellington

Michael O'Brien

Mara to ask permission to talk with Vince. Mara apparently was reluctant to grant it and suggested that the Packers talk to Tom Landry instead. Mara finally consented, but in a conversation with Olejniczak and Fred Trowbridge, Sr., a member of the executive committee, he added a qualifying statement that later led to a serious misunderstanding. Mara told them that if Jim Lee Howell resigned, "I'd like your permission to bring Vince back." The two Packers' officials agreed, but in the confusion they probably hadn't fully appreciated or understood Mara's qualification.[9]

Vince's major liability was that he was an assistant coach of whom the Packers knew little. His dynamic personality, though, impressed them in the first interview. Later, when they asked for more information about him, they heard rave reviews from respected sources. Colonel Earl Blaik recommended him enthusiastically. "I shouldn't tell you this," George Halas of the Chicago Bears advised Olejniczak, "but he'll be a good one. I shouldn't tell you because you're liable to kick the crap out of us!" Of all the persons contacted, the search committee weighed most heavily the opinions of Paul Brown and Bert Bell, commissioner of the NFL and longtime friend of the Packers. Bell told them that Vince understood the business side of pro football and was an excellent coach and student of the game. "Lombardi's a real disciplinarian and a gentleman," said Bell. "He's a great believer in desire and proper conduct. You'll like him." Paul Brown recommended both Vince and Collier. "They wanted to know more about Lombardi," recalled Brown, "and the more I talked, the more interested they became." Brown pushed hard for Vince "because I really believed he would make a good coach." Yet Brown added a cautionary note: "You'll never get him . . . because he's married to the Maras. . . . He's a New Yorker and you just don't take New Yorkers out of New York."

With Evashevski unavailable, the Packers focused their attention on Vince. On January 26 they secretly flew him into Green Bay and interviewed him at Prange's Department Store. Vince insisted on the dual role of coach and general manager, and the Packers agreed to consider him for both positions. Though confident of his coaching prowess, they asked probing questions of his administrative abilities. "At no time did I ever think of Vince as the coach alone," Olejniczak later said, "but only on a combined deal so that he would be the boss. We needed a boss." After the interview on the twenty-sixth, the Packers offered him the dual position with a five-year contract at $36,000 a year. There were also bonus clauses on a sliding scale depending on whether the team finished first, second, or third. Vince asked to have the third-place money ($5,000) included in the first-place figure. The Packers agreed. Two days later the Packers' executive committee and the board of directors approved the selection, and Olejniczak announced the appointment.[10]

Vince was elated. The position was perfect for him. The five-year contract offered security and an excellent salary. The Packers wanted a strong leader and a coaching expert, one who would discipline players and keep the meddlers at bay. Those were Vince's goals exactly. Fans were desperate for a winning team; Vince thought of nothing else. Though reluctant to lose his valuable services, Wellington Mara urged him to accept the Packers' position because it was such a vast improvement over the one the Philadelphia Eagles offered a year earlier. Mara assumed that Howell would continue to coach indefinitely. "That's really why we agreed to let Vinnie go to Green Bay," said Mara, "and why a five-year contract for him didn't seem constricting."[11]

"Who the hell is Vincent Lombardi?" asked a member of the executive committee when informed of the screening committee's choice. Many Wisconsinites asked the same question when Olejniczak announced the selection on January 28. Reporters immediately supplied biographical data, commencing ten years of stories that exaggerated Vince's academic accomplishments at Fordham and his coaching record at St. Cecilia. They quoted glowing endorsements from George Halas, Paul Brown, and Bert Bell. "He's a terrific selection," said Bell. The *Green Bay Press-Gazette* praised the good judgment of the selection committee, citing Vince's dedication and success. "Over and beyond his coaching record is his scholastic record in college. He was a brilliant student . . . *cum laude*." The only skeptic among the press was Oliver Kuechle, who pointed out that except for high school Vince had "never [been] a head coach," and in "none of his assignments was he charged with administrative duties." Kuechle hoped Vince would be strong enough to stand up to the "meddling little men" on the Packers' executive committee.[12]

Actually, Vince's relationship with the new executive committee proved excellent. He quickly struck up a close, lasting friendship with two members, Richard Bourguignon, a Green Bay realtor, and Tony Canadeo, a former star halfback for the Packers. On his first visit to town, Vince explained to them that he had gone to Jesuit Fordham, where he acquired good judgment and training. Bourguignon observed that he had gone to Jesuit Marquette, where he acquired his "good judgment and training." "I graduated from [Jesuit] Gonzaga," said Canadeo, "and I've got that good judgment and training, too." They all roared.

"Between the three of us Jesuits here," said Vince, "we could kick the shit out of these non-Catholics!" Said Bourguignon: "It was as if we had been friends for a long time."[13]

When Vince returned to New York on January 27, he spent part of the day praying in church and meditating on his good fortune. He discussed the Packers' offer with Wellington Mara before he broke the news to Marie. She was distraught at the prospect of leaving Fair Haven. At a Fordham banquet on the evening of the twenty-seventh, she begged Mara to prevent Vince from leaving the Giants. "She pleaded with me to enforce the [two remaining years of his Giants'] contract and not to let him go." Mara told her the Green Bay position was perfect for Vince; that she would be unhappy if Vince was unhappy. She appeared partially convinced by his argument. "I'm still numb with excitement," she told the press bravely two days later. "The best thing would be to pack up the kids and get to Green Bay right away."

On January 29, Vince was honored by the Holy Name Society of St. Joseph's Church in Demarest, New Jersey. He told the gathering he wasn't worried about his future in Green Bay because, "After all, I need to win only two games next season and Green Bay will have improved 100 percent." Friends also hosted a luncheon for him in Rumson, New Jersey, and gave him earmuffs and "long johns" to smooth his transition.[14]

On February 2, Vince and Marie flew to Green Bay, where Vince signed his contract and met with the press. No reporter would break the ice to ask the first question until someone said, "What high school will your son enroll in?" alluding to young Vince, a seventeen-year-old high-school junior reputed to have outstanding football ability. Everyone laughed. "Sounds like somebody around here has been building him up," said Vince. He told reporters he would make strenuous efforts to shore up the Packers' defense. "A good defense is a great morale factor. It hurts the bench and the offense when a team is getting run over and scored on." When asked about his style of coaching, he indicated he would be a more "active" coach than Jim Lee Howell. "I'll work more with my assistants than Jim did with us."

"Coach Lombardi Takes Full Command of Packers," declared a *Milwaukee Journal* caption after Vince's first full day of work on February 3. He rented a house, hired two assistant coaches, reappointed the front-office personnel, ordered remodeling of the South Washington Street offices, addressed the board of directors, met with the press, and attended several meetings. At a noon luncheon at the Northland Hotel he startled the board of directors by bluntly asserting his authority. "I want it understood that I'm in complete command," he began his talk. "I expect full cooperation from you people, and you will get full cooperation from me in return. You have my confidence, and I want yours." Though startled, board members were pleased with his take-charge attitude. At a press conference he repeated his remarks and added, "I am responsible only to the executive board of six men through President Olejniczak." As Vince spoke, Olejniczak watched with obvious pride, smiling often, seemingly relieved to have a forceful, competent leader. "I've never been associated with a loser," Vince said firmly, "and I don't expect to be now." It had been a very busy day but an impressive beginning. He "minced no words," admired Art Daley, and his talk had been "warmly accepted." "He is calmly confident and efficient," concluded Chuck Johnson of the *Milwaukee Journal*. "He knows what he wants and he has no doubt that he will get it."[15]

In late February, Vince drove the family to Green Bay in their pink Chevrolet. It was a miserable journey. Vince, Jr., Susan, and Marie cried much of the way. Vince tried to paint a rosy picture but failed dismally. "It's cold, but it's a dry cold," he insisted. "Already he sounded like a chamber of commerce," observed Vince, Jr. North of Milwaukee they ran into a blizzard and completed the trip in silence.[16]

Throughout the winter and spring of 1959, Vince spoke at dozens of luncheons and banquets in eastern Wisconsin, explaining his philosophy and answering questions, in the hope of winning the support of fans and selling season tickets. Giving speeches in the Green Bay area, he discovered, was less taxing than in metropolitan New York. "When . . . I'd speak at a banquet [in New York] I'd never get home until two or three in the morning," he observed, laughing; "here sometimes I'm home at nine-thirty." At the Packers' stockholders' meeting on March 2, he reiterated that he would tolerate no meddling. "I have been hired to do a job without interference, and I don't expect to have any. If you don't like me . . ." and his voice trailed off. "Well, I don't believe that will happen. . . . You will be proud of the team because I will be proud of the team." At the conclusion, the stockholders gave him rousing applause. Often he stirred his audience with his intense determination to win. Sometimes he quoted General Douglas MacArthur's dictum that there was "no substitute for victory." "We . . . shall play every game to the hilt with every ounce of fiber we have in our bodies," he told a banquet on March 10, and the audience of four hundred sprang to their feet and gave him another rousing ovation.

Listeners asked him similar questions at each gathering. What was his major priority? "Our number one problem is defeating the defeatist attitude," Vince said. "I know it's there. You can't lose that much and still not have it." What about the quarterback situation? Quarterback was a "puzzle," but he blamed the passing woes partly on the poor offensive line. "Sammy Baugh couldn't have thrown behind last year's line." Will he trade for better players? Yes, but he wouldn't give up "my arm, your leg, and half the Packer franchise." What did he intend to do about the players' late-night shenanigans? Questioners sometimes specifically mentioned Hornung. Vince answered calmly that he would discipline the players; yet he didn't anticipate a major problem. There was, however, one obvious difference between New York and Green Bay: "In New York, a player can get 'lost' if he wants to. He can't in Green Bay." As for the Hornung stories, Vince told a YMCA banquet, such gossip was "not Christian." Vince had investigated the rumors and found them exaggerated. "Let's make molehills out of mountains and not mountains out of molehills."[17]

Besides his public appearances Vince worked diligently with his staff to prepare for the 1959 season. On his first day he appointed two coaches, John Phillip (Phil) Bengtson and John (Red) Cochran. Bengtson, forty-five, the same age as Vince, was selected to coach the defense, the same position he held for eight years with the San Francisco 49ers. He had recently lost out to Howard (Red) Hickey for the head coaching job with the 49ers. Bengtson quickly became Vince's chief lieutenant. Cochran, thirty-six, a former defensive back with the Chicago Cardinals, was named offensive backfield coach, the same position he held for three years with the Detroit Lions. For the other coaching positions Vince chose two young, former pro players, Bill Austin for the offensive line and Norb Hecker for the defensive backfield. Austin, twenty-nine, had played guard under Vince with the Giants. Hecker, thirty-one, had been a player-coach in Canada. The average age of the staff was a youthful thirty-seven. Together they mapped plans, and Vince taught them his system so they could teach the players. "It wasn't all new," said Cochran, "but the [effective] way he taught it was."

Because the Giants played in the Eastern Conference and the Packers in the Western Conference, Vince was unfamiliar with the Packers' personnel. He and the staff watched films of the team almost every day. He found the talent impressive, but the defeatism and the lackadaisical effort dismayed him. After a film session, he walked out of the room, put his hands over his face, and said dejectedly to his secretary, Ruth McCloskey, "I think I have taken on more than I can handle. Will you pray for me and help me?" Besides the poor attitude, Vince found weaknesses in the slow halfbacks, the defensive line, defensive backfield, offensive guard, depth, and the "puzzle" at quarterback. Strengths included linebacker, offensive end, tackle, center, and fullback. By April, the staff had completed their analysis of the Packers and turned their attention to the opposition. They made complete charts on the opponents' offense and defense and used them to plan strategy. In the first three and a half months Vince watched twenty thousand feet of film.[18]

Vince's shrewd trades and acquisitions improved the team, and one surprising transaction served notice on the veteran players. From the New York Giants he purchased Emlen Tunnell, the aging but still effective defensive back. To solve the quarterback problem he traded a draft choice for Lamar McHan, the veteran St. Louis Cardinals' signal caller. Guard Fred (Fuzzy) Thurston was obtained from the Baltimore Colts. His most important dealings, though, were with generous Paul Brown of the Cleveland Browns.

After the Packers hired Vince, Brown felt some responsibility for seeing him succeed and made available a list of players whom Brown was willing to trade because they would have problems making his team. Vince traded for defensive tackle Henry Jordan, defensive end Bill Quinlan, and offensive back Lew Carpenter. In acquiring Quinlan and Carpenter, both valuable additions, Vince gave up Billy Howton, a two-time All-Pro selection and the second leading pass receiver in the Packers' history behind the immortal Don Hutson. Howton, an All-American at Rice and who had been with the Packers since 1952, had the reputation as a discipline problem—a "smart ass," said a local sports-writer. That Howton was a founder and the current president of the NFL Players' Association and had chastised team owners and NFL Commissioner Bert Bell also did not endear him to Vince. Moreover, Howton's pass receptions the past two seasons had fallen below expectations. Convinced Howton was a troublemaker and insufficiently dedicated, yet excellent trade bait, Vince traded him to Cleveland on April 24. Howton performed unspectacularly for the rest of his career, and the Packers didn't miss him. Vince had Howton primarily in mind when he later explained that he cut or traded players in 1959 because they would "not make the sacrifices . . . [and] we felt we had to make an example of them."[19]

Before training camp opened Vince persuaded, cajoled, or flattered key players to accept his new regime. Jim Ringo, veteran All-Pro center, visited Vince and asked to be traded because he was discouraged with losing. Vince responded forcefully, "This *is* going to be a winning team." Unconvinced, Ringo said he had heard such rhetoric from previous Green Bay coaches. Vince grew angry. "If it costs you your job, we're going to have a winner here!" Ringo left the meeting impressed with Vince's determination. Bill Quinlan balked at being traded to Green Bay. "Not that place," he said when he heard the news. "I'll quit first." Vince, who needed Quinlan to fill a big gap at defensive end, shrewdly complimented his fine play with Cleveland and told him the Packers badly needed him. "He acted like a Quinlan fan," said the big lineman, "so I sign." Quarterback Bart Starr first met Vince at the June minicamp for quarterbacks. "His whole approach," said Starr, "the forcefulness of his voice, his carriage, his very presence—oozed confidence."[20]

The player Vince most needed was Paul Hornung. "Let's face it," Vince said on April 2, "Hornung is the guy who can make us go. He's a key player." Hornung was starting his third season, under his third coach, and had played three different positions. Soon after Vince arrived, he talked with him. "I know your reputation here," Vince said. "I've investigated you very carefully. You have done things you shouldn't have done, but I don't think you've done as many things as people say you've done." Hornung responded, "If that's the way they want to think, that's the way they'll think." Vince grinned. "I trust you. I just don't want you to let me down. If you do, it'll be your [ass]." After watching films, Vince told his staff that Hornung's versatile ability to run, pass, and catch reminded him of Frank Gifford. Vince called Hornung and told him he was going to be a halfback.[21]

By the time training camp opened in late July, Vince was thoroughly prepared and was determined to succeed. He aimed to conduct a rigorous camp, to root out the defeatest attitude, and to build a winning team. He had to establish his authority immediately with strict rules. In fact, two veterans incurred his wrath for breaking training rules before they even knew the rules. End Max McGee and fullback Howard Ferguson arrived at the St. Norbert College dormitory a few days before the reporting date for veterans. They ate dinner with the rookies in the team dining room; then went out for a night of drinking. The next morning they returned for another meal, but as they entered the dining room, Vince grabbed them and pulled them into his office. "You start working today," Vince shouted, "and you start keeping curfew today! As far as I'm concerned, when you ate a meal here yesterday, you became a part of this camp. Therefore, you abide by all my rules." "What the hell [are] you talking about?" said Ferguson angrily. "We don't have to report for two more days." Vince flew into a rage. "Listen, mister, you get your ass out there on the field—or you get your ass out of here!" The two continued screaming at each other. Mystified by the chaotic scene, McGee didn't get a word in and simply watched. "You meet a guy for the first time," McGee reflected, "and he starts chewing your ass out. . . . I was thinking maybe I ought to go somewhere else."[22]

On the evening of July 23, before the first practice, Vince explained his approach to squeamish veterans in a dynamic, uncompromising speech. He spoke slowly, easily, in a deep gruff voice that sounded like authority itself. "Gentlemen," he said, "we're going to have a football team. We are going to win some games. Do you know why? Because you are going to have confidence in me and my system. By being alert you are going to make fewer mistakes than your opponents. By working harder you are going to outexecute outblock, outtackle every team that comes your way." As he talked, players straightened up in the chairs to take a closer look at their intense coach. "I've never been a losing coach, and I don't intend to start here. There is nobody big enough to think he's got the team made or can do what he wants. Trains and planes are going in and coming out of Green Bay every day, and he'll be on one of them. I won't. I'm going to find thirty-six men who have the pride to make any sacrifice to win. There are such men. If they're not here, I'll get them. If you are not one, if you don't want to play, you might as well leave right now. . . . I've been up here all year and I've learned a lot. I know how the townspeople are and what they think of you men and I know that in a small town you need definite rules and regulations. And anybody who breaks the rules will be taken care of in my own way. . . . You may not be a tackle. You may not be a guard. You may not be a back. But you *will* be a professional."

The speech galvanized the players. As linebacker Bill Forester listened, his hands became sweaty, and chills ran up and down his spine. "He got me so keyed up, I could hardly sleep that night." "Holy cow," Bart Starr thought, "where have you been all my life?" Offensive lineman Bob Skoronski thought the speech did more to influence the team than anything Vince did as the Packers' coach. Though Vince hadn't shown it, he worried that players might take him literally and leave the team. The next day he told Max McGee that if nobody walked out on him, he knew "he had them." "Of course, everybody did stay," said McGee, "and from then on, he had us."[23]

Vince explained clearly his short list of rules and the fines for each offense. He ordered the Piccadilly and a few other bars off limits. He also placed a ban on standing at any bar. "One thing I won't stand for," he said, "is a player standing at a public bar. I don't care if he's drinking ginger ale and talking to a friend, it just doesn't look good if a fan sees him in the place." Instead, players must drink at a table or a booth.

Players must also be on time for meals, meetings, and workouts, and they quickly learned that "on time" meant fifteen minutes earlier than scheduled. Fifteen minutes early soon became known as "Lombardi time." "I believe a man should be on time," Vince said, "not a minute late, not ten seconds late. . . . I believe that a man who's late for meetings or for the bus won't run his pass routes right. He'll be sloppy."

There were other kinds of rules as well. He layed down ultimatums that players should stay off the rubbing table and play with "small hurts." Fat players must lose weight. To improve their public appearance, he bought green sport coats, with a gold Packer emblem on the breast pocket, and ordered them worn with dress shirts and ties on trips, in hotels, and at meals. They were professionals and should dress like professionals.

More important than the rules was Vince's evenhanded, strict enforcement. In motivating players Vince treated them differently, but when it came to demanding 100 percent effort and following his rules, he treated them the same. "This is more like it," said one player after a week in camp. "No prima donnas. No special treatment. No pets." Vince used his 11:00 P.M. curfew to impress upon players that the Lombardi regime meant business. The first to break it was Emlen Tunnell, who arrived back at the dorm at 11:05 P.M. "That'll be fifty dollars, Tunnell," said Vince. Tunnell thought: "Okay, Vince, I understand you." Word of Tunnell's fine passed quickly through the dorm, but in the next few days others still needed to appreciate the new order. At 11:00 P.M. Vince entered the room of fullback Jim Taylor, who was sitting on the edge of his bed with his socks and shorts on.

"Jimmy, what time you got?" said Vince.

"I've got eleven o'clock, sir," answered Taylor.

"Jimmy, you're supposed to be in bed at eleven, aren't you?"

"Yes, sir."

"Jimmy, that'll cost you twenty-five dollars."

Vince permitted only a small amount of democracy in running the team. He formed an executive committee of six players to collect fines, to arrange squad entertainment, and to handle minor problems. The one important task he assigned them was to break up the divisive cliques. Soon they disappeared. "We were a team," said Tunnell, a committee member, "and we were determined that we'd all be winners."[24]

"I've never taught so much football in my life," Vince said with a weary sigh to Marie shortly after training camp opened. At the blackboard, in film sessions, and on the field, he painstakingly explained his football system, and he won the confidence of players because he not only pointed out the proper method of execution but also the reasons for a play and its potential success. He simplified the terminology of plays and the signal calling. He used edited films to teach blocking and tackling techniques and specific plays. Everything had a purpose. In the past a player often performed a blocking assignment without understanding the reason, but Vince explained why a halfback had to block an end with his right shoulder against a particular defense. "All of a sudden it was like a road map that was clear," said quarterback Lamar McHan. "I felt when I went on the field I had some solid ideas to work with."[25]

Practice lasted about seventy-five minutes, shorter than under Blackbourn or McLean, but its intensity made it more demanding. There was no lost time, little wasted effort. Practice had a flow, a crispness that guaranteed maximum results. No meddlers interfered with Vince, either. "From the very first practice," Hornung observed, "there was no more of the board of directors and people all hanging around . . . telling the coaches what to do."

Vince drilled and drilled to polish every facet of the team's performance. He reminded them often that one play might be the crucial one, and since they could never anticipate which one it would be, players must prepare for every eventuality, must always exert themselves to the fullest. On the first day he ordered two players to run around the field twice, the awful drudgery known as laps. When they ran with disinterested lethargy, he said with a snarl: "If you fellows don't want to give me 100 percent, get on up to the clubhouse and turn in your equipment." Players soon realized they were better off putting out every ounce of energy during the drills than running laps during or after practice. When a receiver dropped an easy pass in a morning drill, Vince quickly ordered the penalty: "Take a lap." Observed Art Daley: "There wasn't a dropped pass the rest of the morning."

Most players had never experienced such rigorous practices nor been under more pressure from such a demanding, abusive coach. "Compared to Vince," said a sportswriter, "Simon Legree was a gentle humanitarian." He lashed and drove the squad relentlessly, hammering them with the persistent theme that hard work would bring success. The hardest work was the exhausting combination of wind sprints and the grass and nutcracker drills. "Run! Run! Run!" he shouted at them during the daily grind of sprints. "We may not have the best team in the league," he joked to reporters after the second day, "but we'll sure have the best legs."[26]

The grass drill was exquisite torture. The player ran in place, lifting his knees high, for as long as thirty seconds. When Vince yelled, "Down!" the player had to throw himself forward on his face. When Vince yelled,

"Up!" he got up quickly and started running in place again. If Vince was in a good mood, he gave them only three to five minutes of them. When he was angry, he kept barking at them until players reached the brink of exhaustion.

The violent nutcracker drill pitted an offensive man against a defensive man. The defensive man positioned himself between two bags that formed a chute; the offensive player, leading a ballcarrier, tried to drive the defensive man out of the chute to open a path for the ballcarrier. "Fire out!" Vince hollered at the offensive lineman on the second day of practice. "Very good block and stinking running. Move those feet behind you, don't extend them. Put your head in there. He ate you up, mister. . . . That's the way to uncoil, just like a steel spring."[27]

His voice could be heard all across the vast practice field next to the stadium. He instructed his quarterbacks to holler out the signals. "Hut! Hut! Hut! Bark it. Make it sharp so everyone takes off together." Seven blockers pushed a large sled on which Vince and another coach stood. "Let's hit it together. Who's that 64? Kramer, huh. That's the way. Hey, Jerry, that's the way to hit it." "Hot dog!" his voice cracked when he saw a good play. Within a week he was hoarse.

Exhausted players worked till their muscles barely functioned. Weights dropped dramatically in a few weeks—Tom Bettis from 245 to 220, Bill Forester from 240 to 230, Dave Hanner from 270 to 250. Hanner had to be hospitalized for sunstroke. "Nobody vomited after a couple days," Bengtson observed blandly. "He almost killed us," said Starr. When offensive end Gary Knafelc complained to Marie about Vince's demands and abuse, Marie offered little sympathy: "How would you like to live with him?"[28]

Vince partially compensated for his harsh regime with acts of kindness. When camp opened he graciously met the incoming players and made them feel welcome and comfortable. After the intrasquad game on August 8, he hosted a buffet supper for the players, their wives, and guests. "This will be a regular thing after every exhibition game," he announced. "We think it's a good thing for team spirit." He offered little praise the first year, but when he did compliment, said offensive tackle Forrest Gregg, "it made your day or week because it so seldom happened." When he praised players, though, they detected a genuine warmth and enthusiasm in his appreciation of a fine play or effort. Vince called guard Jerry Kramer a "cow" at practice and said he was the worst guard he had ever seen. Kramer, who had lost weight and had labored hard, returned dejected to the locker room. As he sat by his locker with his head down, Vince came over to him and said, "Son, one of these days you're going to be the greatest guard in the league." Kramer's mood instantly turned to elation. "I was ready to go back out to practice for another four hours." Kramer brought sixteen relatives to a preseason contest in Portland, Oregon, and after the game Vince put on another large buffet supper and graciously welcomed all of Kramer's relatives. "Bring 'em all in," he said, and he guided them through the line and offered them champagne. "He made them feel like a million dollars," said Kramer.[29]

During training camp Vince talked mostly in bland generalities with the press, but sportswriters were impressed with his coaching. Oliver Kuechle thought the squad showed "excellent spirit and desire" and was acquiring both physical and mental toughness. Vince's spirit was "infectious," said Chuck Johnson; he was reviving the Packers in "methodical fashion."

Although Vince exhibited an unswerving confidence to his players, his own mood fluctuated throughout camp. He worried constantly about all the problems, especially overcoming the defeatist attitude of the players. "I found the setup so much worse than I had expected," he said in mid-August, "that I probably wouldn't have taken the job if I had known the facts." At other times, he was optimistic. The personnel was better than he anticipated. "One of these days, the whole thing will probably catch on."[30]

The team's 4–2 record in preseason games helped create a winning attitude. Rival coaches raved about the Packers' improvement. "That's the best Packer offensive line I've seen in years," observed Red Hickey after the Packers defeated his San Francisco 49ers. The Packers were much better already, said George Halas, "because they have Vince Lombardi for a coach."

At the first meeting after the Packers defeated the Washington Redskins, 20–13, players were shocked to learn that Vince's mood could be worse following a victory than a defeat. They had played poorly, he began softly, using simple words. Soon he worked himself into a frenzy and his vocabulary became more explicit and sophisticated. By the end of the session the players were cringing. For defensive end Jim Temp, it had been the "most eloquent ass-chewing I ever heard in my life."[31]

Through most of the preseason, Vince still hadn't solved the puzzle at the critical quarterback position. He inspected the situation closely but found no one he admired as much as Charlie Conerly. At the start of training camp, three players competed for the starting berth: Bart Starr, Lamar McHan, and Joe Francis. Francis was an outstanding athlete but inexperienced and a poor passer.

The biggest puzzle was Starr. No one in the league expected him to succeed in professional football. Although he had played well in his freshman and sophomore years at the University of Alabama, he was injured in his junior year and benched as a senior. In 1956 the Packers selected him in the seventeenth round of the draft, and in his first year he was the understudy to Tobin Rote. While alternating with Babe Parilli in 1957 and 1958, Starr flashed occasional brilliance but was inconsistent and did not engineer a single victory. Physically he was not imposing. Critics said he wasn't tough enough, that his arm wasn't strong enough to throw the long pass. His background as a seventeenth-round draft choice was unimpressive. He was quiet, almost bashful, and his fellow players judged him indecisive. What intelligence he had was hidden. After studying films, Vince concluded that Starr possessed adequate arm strength and ball-handling techniques. "When I met him," Vince said later, "I found that he also had a fine analytic mind and a retentive memory, but at the same time, I found him so polite and so self-effacing that I wondered if he wasn't too nice a young man to be the authoritarian leader your quarterback must be." Vince believed that Starr's fundamental problem was lack of confidence. As a result, he didn't inspire confidence in his new coach or teammates. Starr agreed. "I wasn't a good leader," he later admitted. "I had no faith in my ability to get the job done, and consequently I didn't get it done." Ironically, in the past two years Starr had performed impressively in three games against the New York Giants. "He did an outstanding job each time," Vince conceded.

Starr came from a military background and had absorbed well the lessons taught by his father, a career U.S. Army Air Corps master sergeant. "I learned the values of discipline, dedication, and patience early." He thrived under Vince's direction. "I feel like a new quarterback under Coach Lombardi," he said during training camp, "and I'm actually comfortable in the system." He practiced hard and studied diligently to overcome his weaknesses, and Vince, who saw the spark in him, nursed him along.[32]

Lamar McHan was a moody but talented veteran, bigger and stronger than Starr. He and Starr competed evenly through most of the preseason. "The trouble is," said Vince, "no one is head and shoulders above the rest. It's a poor situation." In the last preseason game, McHan performed most impressively, and Vince chose him to start the regular season against the Chicago Bears. Moreover, Starr symbolized too much of the losing past; McHan offered a fresh beginning. "We needed somebody different for the fans and the opposition," said Vince.[33]

With the regular season about to commence, the *Press-Gazette* urged fans to be patient and not expect miracles. The Packers should win "three or four" games. Vince told friends privately that he hoped to win four. Before the opening game, against the Bears on September 27, Vince concluded a stirring pregame pep talk with the admonition, "Now go through that door and bring back a victory!" Bill Forester jumped up enthusiastically and bashed his arm against his locker. "It was the worst injury I had all year," said Forester. The Packers scored nine points in the fourth quarter to pull out a thrilling 9–6 victory. When the game ended, the players swept Vince to their shoulders and, on the run, bore him triumphantly off the field. "We're on our way now!" he shouted in the locker room.[34]

In their next two games the Packers upset the Detroit Lions and the San Francisco 49ers to lead the league with a 3–0 record. Packer fans were ecstatic. Most credited Vince's decisive leadership and discipline. "We have one boss now," stated a local cabdriver, "instead of a dozen and it makes a helluva difference." A room clerk told a New York sportswriter admiringly: "You know what he told those players? He says you're not trying out for the team once, you're trying out every game." Tom Miller, the Packers' public-relations director, threw all publicity into reverse gear. "Don't raise your hopes. This can't continue indefinitely."

It didn't. The Los Angeles Rams crushed the Packers, 45–6, commencing a five-game losing streak. Vince surprised the players, however, by handling them gently during the dark weeks. He did lose his temper after the offensive team played sloppily in losing to the Bears. He slammed lockers, threw helmets, and yelled at the cowering players. Most of the time he urged them not to be discouraged. If they gave 100 percent, blocked, tackled, and avoided mental errors, they would win. "It seemed," said Hornung, "that sometimes he was a lot easier to live with when he was losing."

In three of the five defeats the Packers played admirably, leading most observers to praise their effort. "They're beginning to ask questions about the Green Bay Packers," noted Kuechle, but he urged patience. The Packers needed better personnel, but "the coaching is superb; the spirit is fine." After the fifth loss, a close 28–24 contest with the Baltimore Colts, a reporter asked Vince when the team would win again. "I don't know," he replied, not allowing his temper to rise. "The way it's going, I don't know. We'll have to . . ." He didn't finish the sentence. Then he brightened. "I'll say this much. This club hasn't quit. They've stayed right in there."[35]

For most of the season, the quarterback situation remained unsettled. McHan directed the opening three victories but was inconsistent. When he was injured in the sixth game, Joe Francis replaced him but was ineffective and the Packers lost, 20–3, to the Giants. In the next game, with McHan reinjured, Starr replaced him and played well in a losing effort against the Chicago Bears. Starr played well again the following week in the loss to Baltimore. With McHan healthy again for the ninth game, Vince hated to choose between him and Starr. "Whenever I pick one over the other I have a fifty-fifty chance of guessing wrong." Intuition led him to select Starr. "You are going to be our quarterback from here on out," Vince told him. "I want you to relax, be calm, and continue studying like you are doing. . . . Don't be concerned about the play of anybody else. Everything else will take care of itself and we'll win these ball games."[36]

The Packers defeated the Washington Redskins, 21–0, ending their losing streak. Five days later they beat the Detroit Lions, 24–17, and evened their record at 5–5. After the Detroit victory, three thousand fans cheered the team's arrival home. "I wonder," someone remarked, "what would happen if they ever won the championship?" On December 6, the Packers avenged the earlier slaughter by the Los Angeles Rams, winning the rematch, 38–20. Vince remarked afterward, "I never dreamed we would do anything like this—six wins."[37]

On December 13, the Packers defeated the 49ers, 36–14. Starr played his finest game, completing twenty of twenty-five passes for 249 yards and two touchdowns; Hornung won the league scoring title. The victory gave the Packers a 7–5 record, their best since 1944. The *Press-Gazette* featured tributes to Vince from the mayor, businessmen, labor leaders, and former Green Bay coaches. The Packers, said Oliver Kuechle, "came up by their bootstraps—and by Lombardi." By "hard work, by keen analysis . . . by inspiration, by good trading, by forceful adminis-tration off the field and on and certainly by sound technical coaching, he led the way up." It was quite a contrast from a year earlier, when the players returned to Green Bay only if they couldn't avoid it, when coaches were resigning and fans penned angry letters to the newspapers. "Today Packerland is bright and cheery," gloated the *Press-Gazette*.[38]

The players offered many explanations for the team's dramatic turn-about; each stressed different factors, but all traced them back to Vince's leadership. "It's really Lombardi," stated halfback Don McIlhenny. "I've never seen a man with such tremendous knowledge of football," marveled McHan. "We went into games as well prepared and well organized as it was possible to be," said Starr. "Nothing was left to chance." Vince had insisted that players learn facets of the game they thought they couldn't master. "I didn't know I could block," said Gary

Knafelc; "I'd never done it." Sophisticated veteran Emlen Tunnell thought his many years of experience made him immune to inspiration by any coach. Yet when Vince gave a pep talk, "I'd cry and go out and try to kill people. Nobody else could ever do that to me." In previous years the Packers had run out of gas in the second half; in most games in 1959, they became stronger. Vince worked veteran linebacker Tom Bettis into the best physical condition of his career. "Most of us were ready to play another quarter when the game was over," said Bettis, exaggerating slightly. "We were hardly breathing hard." Linebacker Dan Currie had another explanation. "Sure, we were trained fine, but . . . the big thing was psychology." Players hadn't expected to win in 1958. "It was sort of understood we'd try to do our best, but we'd likely lose. The main thing was to come close. Not with Vince. We were trained to win. The whole psychology was aimed that way. We got confidence and spirit and we did win."[39]

On December 14, seventy-five hundred fans turned out at Green Bay's Austin Straubel Airport in freezing rain to welcome the team home from the West Coast. As the plane carrying the Packers' entourage circled Green Bay in dense fog, it appeared the plane might be detoured to a Milwaukee airport, causing Vince to remark, "It would be a shame if we couldn't land [with] all those people waiting." The plane managed to land at Austin Straubel, and fans gave each disembarking player an ovation. Vince's appearance triggered a deafening roar, surpassing all the others. He praised his staff and players. The team had never quit, he said, but "kept coming back when things got tough in the middle of the season."[40]

Shortly after the season ended, Vince's successful coaching debut plus sudden turmoil within the New York Giants' organization prompted Wellington Mara to approach Vince about returning to the Giants. Worn out, fed up with the constant pressure, Jim Lee Howell told the Mara family he wanted to quit coaching. The Maras secretly arranged for Howell to become director of player personnel, and, without consulting Packers' officials, Wellington Mara asked Vince to become the new head coach. When he left the Giants, Vince had told Wellington that the "only job in the world" he really wanted was the Giants' head coaching position. After the Packers' executive committee learned of the negotiations, some members were livid because Wellington had not followed protocol and sought permission to talk to Vince, permission Wellington thought he had secured a year earlier in his conversation with Olejniczak and Trowbridge. Vince was unaware of the permission rule or had chosen to ignore it.

Michael O'Brien

The Packers reluctantly granted Vince permission to continue his discussions, but Olejniczak warned him that "just because we're letting you talk to him doesn't mean we'll let you go. I doubt like hell we will " Vince's decision was painful, partly because the negotiations occurred during the Christmas season, when he and Marie longed to return to New York. But since the Packers might not release him from his contract, and since he had made a commitment, he asked Wellington to hold the job open for him until after the 1960 season. Mara agreed and convinced Howell to stay on for another year. "If we'd given our blessing," Olejniczak later stated, "he'd have gone to New York. I'm sure of it." As compensation for his great season and his decision to remain, the Packers gave him a $10,000 bonus. Delighted, he rushed out and bought Marie a mink coat.[41]

Vince won many awards after the season, including landslide selection as professional Coach of the Year. The banquet circuit kept him busy. In Racine, Wisconsin, the Roma League saluted him as the American of Italian extraction who had done the most for sports in Wisconsin. "They made me Italian of the Year," Vince joked. "Where do you figure that leaves Pope John?"[42]

VIII

Drive for
Championships
(1960–66)

FROM 1960 TO 1966, VINCE'S PACKERS WON 103 REGULAR-SEASON GAMES, lost only twenty, and tied three. In postseason games—to determine conference, league, and world championships—they were even more impressive, winning six of seven games. They became the standard of excellence in professional football at a time when pro football rose to the pinnacle of American spectator sports. In 1950 pro football had not yet attained the popularity of baseball and college football, but in the 1960s pushed well ahead of its rivals.[1]

A single technological marvel had a direct and profound impact on Vince's notoriety and on pro football's surge in popularity. Coinciding with Vince's arrival on the professional scene, television permitted viewers who had never seen a pro football game to watch the spectacle in the comfort of their homes. Football was ideal for telecasting. Unlike baseball's diamond, football's rectangular field fit television's rectangular box. Recurring crisis points riveted the viewers' attention to the silver screen. The pause between plays permitted them to savor the drama and second-guess the coach and the quarterback. Instant replays and slow motion often allowed the TV viewer to appreciate the game more than the spectator in the stands. In 1960 a small Wisconsin television audience watched the Packers, and a handful of state reporters covered the team;

seven years later, at Super Bowl I, television viewers had swollen to sixty-five million and the national media to over a thousand.[2]

During the period Vince won lavish praise for his intelligence, character, success, and especially for his excellent coaching. But because he was often blunt, rude, and tactless, and because he reputedly exercised ruthless, dictatorial power, he increasingly aroused criticism as well. He continued to demand excellence in himself and his players. "His wants are simple," said Red Smith near the end of Vince's seven-year odyssey, "merely to win every preseason exhibition, every game during the season, every postseason game, and every title. Give him that, and he'll ask for nothing else. . . ." Although Vince realized no one could achieve perfection in his exceptionally competitive profession, he could not entirely resign himself to the fact and especially could not resign himself to stop trying. His unrelenting quest took its toll on his physical and emotional well-being and led him to consider retiring from coaching after the 1966 season, only to have him postpone his decision for one more quest.[3]

"What a difference a year and a man can make," said the *Press-Gazette*'s Lee Remmel as training camp opened in mid-July 1960. The defeatism that had infected the team a year earlier had vanished. More veterans arrived early for camp than anyone could remember, and they arrived in better physical condition. "We know what to expect now," said Dave Hanner, "and we came prepared. I feel great right now and this is only the first day." Vince was ready, too. "I can't even concentrate on my golf," he said.[4]

Vince's training regimen remained harsh and demanding. He hustled the players through their drills and sprinted them at the end of practice. The Packers sailed through the exhibition season with a 6–0 record, extending their winning streak to ten games. "It's nice," Vince said of the fine preseason, "but it doesn't count a thing." He was right. In the league opener, the Chicago Bears shocked the Packers, 17–14. But the team rebounded, winning their next three. The week of preparation for the fifth game, against Pittsburgh, was hell as Vince yelled at reporters and players and wore a dark shadow at practices. Almost every player felt his lash. Even aging veteran Emlen Tunnell received five laps at practice for his lackadaisical effort. Later Vince explained that he had not wanted the team to slip into a long losing streak like the one experienced in midseason a year earlier.

During the Pittsburgh game Vince made a crucial decision on the lingering problem at quarterback. Despite Starr's success at the end of 1959, Vince still questioned his leadership and effectiveness. He had again alternated Starr and McHan in the exhibition season and selected Starr to direct the league opener, the loss to the Bears. Then McHan, who was brash and assertive, apparently convinced Vince to start him in the next game. Although the Packers won three consecutive games under McHan's control, his passing was unimpressive. During the Pittsburgh game Starr replaced McHan and rallied the team to a 19–13 victory, leading Vince to resolve his dilemma once and for all. "I made a mistake," he told Starr afterward. "We've been drifting back and forth. . . . I want to tell you right now, though, that there aren't going to be any more changes. You are going to be my quarterback." Five months later, McHan was traded; Starr developed into one of the most outstanding quarterbacks in the history of pro football.[5]

After the Pittsburgh game the Packers did suffer a midseason slump, losing three of their next four, and started down the homestretch with a 5–4 record, trailing the conference-leading Baltimore Colts. But Baltimore also faltered. When the Colts lost the next game and the Packers won, the teams were tied for the conference lead. The Packers' fate would be determined in two West Coast games, against the 49ers and the Rams. For the 49ers' game the team worked out at Stanford University in Palo Alto under unusually tight security. "It was like a concentration camp," said Paul Hornung. When Vince spotted a UPI photographer snapping photos through a knothole of the fence, he confiscated the film and refused to return it. Reporting from Green Bay, Red Smith described the scene as Packer fans watched the television broadcast of the 49ers' game on Saturday, December 10: "Promptly at 3:25 P.M., the town of Green Bay, Wis., shrank under its roof like a terrified turtle. Not a car moved in the streets. In the stores along Washington and Adams Sts., usually teeming on a Saturday when the farmers came in to shop, clerks slouched behind counters and gossiped or just stared at one another." The Packers won, 13–0, and when the Colts lost, the Packers vaulted into first place by one game, clinching at least a tie for the conference championship.[6]

A week later the Packers defeated the Rams, 35–21, but the Rams had outgained the Packers and had held Vince's proud running game to only fifty-eight yards. Vince concluded that his players had been affected by the "emotional strain" of the game. Though they hadn't played well and their celebration was subdued, the Packers had still won their conference and would settle the world championship in Philadelphia against the Eagles the day after Christmas. Meanwhile, Green Bay fans were exuberant. "This is the most wonderful thing that has happened to Green Bay in a long time," said Mayor Roman Denissen. The *Press-Gazette* put out the newspaper's first "extra" in twenty-one years, selling it out almost immediately. On Sunday, December 18, eleven thousand fans greeted the team's arrival at Austin Straubel Airport in a numbing twelve-degree temperature. Vince was to be the final speaker, but when the crowd chanted, "We want Vince! We want Vince" he stepped to the microphone to express his appreciation to the coaches, players, and "fine people" of Green Bay. "It's a very, very happy day for me."

In assessing the Packers' title, *Time* thought the team lacked the standard prerequisite for success: no great passer, no great receiver, no breakaway back. What the Packers did have, said *Time*, was "rugged, old-fashioned blocking to open holes for rugged, old-fashioned ballcarriers." Paul Hornung credited Vince's leadership. "He's the greatest coach I ever played under," Hornung told the *Press-Gazette*. "He's a master at handling and inspiring us. On strategy and game preparation, he's flawless. He's the kind of man you just have to win for." For *Time*, Hornung had stressed a different factor: "Lombardi raises hell."[7]

Because of the hectic preparations for the championship game in Philadelphia, Vince and Marie enjoyed none of the Christmas festivities, not even a tree. At practice on Christmas Day, the team lacked its usual zip. Young and inexperienced, they showed signs of homesickness on the holiday. Yet the Packers dominated play in the championship game. Unfortunately, they had difficulty finishing what they started, and their two first-half drives ended with field goals, not touchdowns. With less than a quarter remaining and the Packers leading, 13–10, the Eagles' Ted Dean returned a kickoff fifty-eight yards. The Eagles scored eight plays later to lead, 17–13. The Packers charged back, but Philadelphia's Chuck Bednarik stopped Jim Taylor nine yards short of the winning touchdown as time expired. The Packers had many reasons to be proud. They had won an overwhelming dominance in first downs (22–13), total yardage (401–206), passes completed (21–9), plays from scrimmage (77–48), and turnovers (1–3). Still, they had lost, and there were many tears in the locker room. In addressing them, Vince was very deliberate. He didn't raise his voice or criticize. "Perhaps you didn't realize that you could have won this game," he said. "We are men and we will never let this happen again. . . . Now we can start preparing for next year."

Vince answered the reporters' questions graciously, hiding his obvious disappointment. Yes, Dean's run back had been the turning point. His team should have made more of its early chances. The Eagles' Norm Van Brocklin was a great quarterback. "We have no excuses. They outscored us. That's all that matters." But, he added, "I'm very proud of our ball club." While the team flew back to Green Bay, Vince remained in

Philadelphia to attend the NFL draft. The day after the game he was jovial, telling reporters, "It takes about twelve hours for me to get over [a loss]."[8]

While the Packers prepared for the championship game, rumor spread that Vince would be leaving Green Bay. Beginning in the spring of 1960, reports had circulated that Vince would return to the Giants to replace Jim Lee Howell, who was retiring, and each time Vince and the Maras were seen socializing or huddling at league meetings, the rumor spread. "The word here is that . . . the Maras may prevail upon Lombardi to take the position," said Red Smith from New York in early December 1960. Vince enjoyed being the boss in Green Bay, argued Smith, but had never concealed his homesickness. "They love Vincent in Green Bay," he concluded. "They'd love him in New York." The Packers' executive committee bristled indignantly at the suggestion Vince might leave. The Giants' front office maintained a discreet and impenetrable wall of silence. Finally, in late December Vince phoned Wellington Mara and said he would stay in Green Bay. "I think I'd be leaving in bad taste out here," he told his friend. "And as much as I'd like to come to the Giants, I've made a commitment out here, and I think you're just going to have to forget about me." Though Vince had been their first choice, the Maras had an alternative and later selected Allie Sherman, Howell's offensive coach.[9]

After the 1960 season, on the heels of his nonstop, six-month, nineteen-game grind, without an extended vacation since 1958, Vince continued his hectic pace into early 1961. In January he coached the Western Conference squad in the Pro Bowl; accepted an award in Columbus, Ohio; and attended the annual NFL meeting. A joyous event occurred on April 5, when the Board of Trade of Sheepshead Bay, New York, honored its native son at a testimonial dinner in Brooklyn. "To come home and not be forgotten," Vince told the five hundred guests, "is the greatest thrill a man can experience." After the dinner, he and Marie flew to Bermuda for Vince's first work-free vacation in over two years.[10]

Before leaving for vacation Vince had issued a harsh, public warning to his players, one he would repeat with minor changes after every successful season. Football coaches were usually reluctant to change a successful team, he said, but he rejected that naïve approach. "There's no room for that emotion. Football is a hardheaded, cold business. If a player isn't as good as he was last year when he won the championship for you, he's got to go." Success tended to make players "fatheaded"; their egos overwhelmed them; they were no longer willing to "pay the price." His players must pay the price. They must have a "singleness of purpose, a complete dedication to victory. I can assure you that our staff and players will have that again in 1961."[11]

The Packers sailed through the 1961 preseason undefeated, outscoring opponents, 146–69, but again they lost the regular-season opener, this time to Detroit, 17–13. However, they won their next six games and nine of their next ten. They overcame many problems—a broken leg suffered by guard Jerry Kramer and a rash of other injuries—but the biggest problem was U.S. foreign policy. In the fall of 1961, because of the increasing tension with the Soviet Union over access to West Berlin, President John F. Kennedy ordered a buildup of the U.S. armed forces. The call-up of reserve and National Guard units affected all pro sports, including football. More than two dozen NFL and AFL players were called, but the Packers were hurt worse than any other team. Three starters—Paul Hornung, Boyd Dowler, and Ray Nitschke—were among those summoned. Vince was upset and for more than a week was quoted in a manner that suggested he found the Packers' crisis more important. "They are doing a good job on us!" he said. "You can't lose three frontliners and keep winning."

Suddenly it was revealed that Hornung had long been suffering from a pinched nerve in his neck, an injury that did not prevent him from playing football but allegedly cast in doubt his ability to perform his Army duties. His call-up was deferred until the pinched nerve could be examined, weeks in which he continued to play for the Packers. Hornung appeared to be receiving special treatment. In late October 1961, when Wisconsin's U.S. Senator Alexander Wiley publicly requested that the Department of Defense defer Hornung and Nitschke until after the season, he unleashed a storm of protest from citizens, newspapers, and fellow politicians. At a time when hundreds of other patriotic state residents were reporting to active duty, charged the *Press-Gazette*, Wiley's request was a shameful, "new low." With the strong climate of opinion against favoritism, Vince's protests fell mute. Hornung hurried through his physical, passed it, and reported to duty as a jeep driver and radio operator at Fort Riley, Kansas. Dowler and Nitschke reported to Fort Lewis, Washington.

Still, pro football players did receive special treatment. The Pentagon cooperated by granting many players weekend passes to rejoin their teams with the understanding that they would return to their military units in an emergency. Dowler and Nitschke played in every game, and Hornung missed only two. To ensure that his three players were available for games, Vince contacted a friend in the U.S. defense establishment in

Washington, D.C., who had access to President Kennedy's military adviser. "Through an arrangement," recalled the friend, "we were able to get those three players released for playing on Sunday. The Kennedy Administration cooperated unbelievably with us."

"The Green Bay Packers may be the first team ever to win the Cold War and the National Football League championship the same year," joked Los Angeles sports columnist Jim Murray. In an emergency, though, "the Packers run the risk of losing good soldier Hornung. If there's an alert, he'll have to get back to that jeep in Kansas and turn the radio off." For Vince, though, the call-up was no joking matter. That his three players couldn't practice with the team disrupted coordination, and he never knew for certain if they would be available on the weekend. Privately, he fretted about the problem most of the season.[12]

The Packers could clinch the conference title on December 3 in Milwaukee with a victory over the powerful New York Giants. "We've been moving on 'guts'," Vince passionately told an interviewer the morning of the game. "We're going to move on 'guts' today—and we're going to win." The Packers did win, 20–17. Afterward, Oliver Kuechle credited the victory to the Packers' "unbeatable aura." They had "refused to be licked. . . . This was a toss-up ball game. The little extra something, though, was Green Bay's—Lombardi's."

In early December Green Bay businessmen proclaimed the city "Titletown, U.S.A." and vigorously promoted the theme as the Packers prepared for the NFL title game against the New York Giants in Green Bay on December 31, 1961. Most observers predicted the contest would be close. The Packers had led the Western Conference with a 11–3 record; at 10–3–1 the Giants were almost as outstanding in the Eastern Conference. The Packers had scored the most points in the NFL (391), with the Giants second (368); the Giants' defense had permitted the least points in the league (220), with the Packers close behind (223).[13]

Before the championship game a year earlier Vince had practiced his team indoors for a few days to protect them from the harsh weather. Later he thought he had made a mistake. Before the game with the Giants, therefore, he ordered snowplows and jeeps to push the snow off the Packers' practice field. The temperature was minus ten degrees one day, yet Vince, wrapped in a big coat, a red stocking cap pulled down over his face with holes for the eyes, nose, and mouth, stood on the blocking sled and prodded his players to block and to stop feeling sorry for themselves. "It made us realize," Forrest Gregg later observed, "that if the mind is willing, the body can go."

Nitschke and Dowler were given passes to practice, but Hornung's release became snarled in the Army's bureaucracy. Vince made frantic phone calls to the Pentagon and, apparently, to the White House. As he awaited a return call from the Pentagon, he paced the training room like a caged tiger, chain-smoking and fussing about Hornung. After finally securing his release, Vince exclaimed, "I sure will be glad to see him. We need him to run that 49 option."[14]

The evening before the game, Vince met Wellington Mara at Austin Straubel Airport and took him to a restaurant in a small town outside Green Bay. The two longtime friends and next-day rivals enjoyed a convivial evening, and Mara thought Vince looked relaxed. Suddenly Vince stood up, signed the check he had called for, and announced, "You can find your own way back to town." Then he left. Mara was shocked. "It was like he was saying that the game officially began then," reflected Mara. "It was a helluva long cab ride."

In his office before the game, Vince was chatting with his New York friend Dr. Anthony Pisani when Bart Starr arrived. Starr, recalled Pisani, was as "nervous as a hen on a hot quilt." To settle him down, Vince placed a reassuring arm around his quarterback and said, "I don't want you to do anything else today except what you've been doing all year. And I *know* you can do it." The tortured expression immediately left Starr's face, said Pisani, and the quarterback left the room a "different person."[15]

Overall, the Packers were more poised and confident than the year before, and their composure reflected on the field. They played an almost flawless game. The Packers' offensive and defensive lines dominated the Giants; Hornung scored nineteen points; Starr averaged over sixteen yards on ten completions, including three touchdowns; Ray Nitschke hounded quarterback Y. A. Tittle, who threw four interceptions; defensive halfback Jesse Whittenton blanketed Del Shofner, the Giants' deep pass-receiving threat; and the Packers won, 37–0. Before allowing reporters into the locker room, while wiping tears from beneath his glasses, Vince told his players, "Today, you were the greatest team in the history of the National Football League." Later he reiterated the statement to reporters, adding hoarsely, "And I mean it." Had this been his biggest thrill in football? a reporter asked. Vince paused to exhale a cloud of cigarette smoke, grinned, and replied, "I would say so."

After the victory Green Bay's fans had torn down the goalposts, and the city's downtown became a sea of turmoil, cars bumper to bumper, horns blaring, headlights flickering, and fans waving "Titletown, U.S.A." banners. The next day Vince proudly displayed President Kennedy's telegraphed message: "Congratulations on a great game today. It was a fine victory for a great coach, a great team, and a great town."[16]

Because of Vince's success, mulling over new job offers (or being approached about coaching positions) was becoming an almost annual event, expected at the close of each season. In December 1961, one offer (or serious approach) came from West Point, where Dale Hall had been dismissed after the season, and the initial contact with Vince came in an exceptionally flattering, unexpected manner. On December 5, 1961, Vince had received an award at the *Sports Illustrated* Silver Anniversary banquet in New York. President Kennedy also attended, and during the evening—probably spurred on by the Army's brass—the President asked Vince if he would consider returning to West Point as head football coach. Vince was so startled he used the ruse of laughing instead of giving a direct response. "To tell the truth," he said later, "I did not have the nerve to say no." West Point officials apparently followed up with phone calls to Vince. The offer had powerful nostalgic appeal. What exquisite justice, Vince must have thought, after the many frustrating years of being overlooked for major college jobs, including the disappointment of not having been chosen to succeed Earl Blaik. One morning in December Vince walked into the Packers' office and said to some of his assistants, "How would you all like to go to West Point and coach? You won't make much money," he added, "but it's a great life. It's a great place to coach." Vince, though, was not seriously tempted. The offer was ill-timed. His success in Green Bay, his large salary, and the growing popularity and glamor of pro football made impractical any serious consideration of returning to the plains on the Hudson. Nonetheless, he delighted in telling friends afterward that he was the first person ever offered a coaching position by the President of the United States.[17]

The off-season banquet circuit kept Vince busy again. On April 30, 1962, seven hundred persons honored him at a testimonial in Green Bay. It was a well-paced affair, laced with humor and compassion. Obviously moved by the kind words and gifts, Vince did not have his normal control over his booming, foghorn voice. Starting in a hoarse whisper, he extended his appreciation, praised his "hometown," and thanked the "good Lord for His help and His understanding. And I pray to Him each day to give me enough sense of humor to be serious but never allow me to take myself too seriously."[18]

Before the 1962 exhibition season Vince was unusually candid with reporters about his team's prospects. "I have to be truthful and say that we've got a pretty solid football team. I also have to say that we're the team to beat." Nonetheless, unlike the confident commander of the ancient bastion of Troy, Vince remained watchful of wooden horses in the form of age, complacency, staleness, and poor execution. Before the season he again publicly warned his players against "fatheadedness," and as the Packers rolled to sixteen consecutive victories in the exhibition and regular seasons, he praised their performances but always found deficiencies. The team was "spotty," "inconsistent," "listless," "sputtering"—in sum, imperfect. At one practice, unhappy with their sloppiness, he said: "I don't want to seem ungrateful. I'm awfully proud of you guys, really, you've done a hell of a job. But sometimes you just disgust me."

Opponents found few imperfections in the Packers' performance. After the team had slaughtered the Philadelphia Eagles, 49–0, Eagles' veteran Chuck Bednarik described the Packers as "one of the greatest teams in the history of the league. They're superb." Another Eagles' player credited Vince: "He's a brilliant coach and that gives a team a touchdown or two at the start. Sure, he has the horses, but man, he sure knows the right way to gallop them."[19]

As the reigning champion, the Packers attracted special fan and media attention throughout 1962. On the road they were a major attraction. In August, while the team practiced for an exhibition game in Dallas, young women attending a majorette school stopped to gaze and gape. Businessmen in their suits gathered on the sidelines. Mothers with their children in buggies stood in the shade. "Is that really Paul Hornung?" a young boy asked his father. Wisconsin sportswriters lavished praise on Vince and the team. Vince was a "miracle worker," said Art Daley. Vince's arrival in Wisconsin, said Oliver Kuechle, was as significant as when "Jean Nicolet sat down with the Winnebagos three hundred years before."

"The Packers have become news since the Lombardi era," observed Cooper Rollow, explaining why the *Chicago Tribune* had assigned him to cover the Packers. "Now they're big time and as newsworthy as the hometown team in Chicago." During the year articles on Vince, Green Bay, or star Packer players—particularly Hornung and Taylor—appeared in *Time, Life, Look, The Saturday Evening Post, The New Yorker, The New York Times Magazine, Esquire, Sport, Sports Illustrated,* and *Holiday Magazine.* CBS did a prime-time, half-hour special on Vince, the team, and the city. The stories varied in quality, but as the *Press-Gazette*'s Len Wagner noted, it "wasn't so long ago that comparisons couldn't even be made."[20]

On Thanksgiving, November 22, 1962, the Packers' long winning streak—eighteen victories in all contests extending back to the previous year—was snapped by Detroit. The Lions' Joe Schmidt, Alex Karras, and Roger Brown took turns smothering Starr, and the Lions won, 26–14. The loss was embarrassing because millions had watched on national television. "The real glory is being knocked to your knees and then coming back," Vince calmly advised his players in the dressing room. "This is one game. *One* game." He encouraged Willie Davis: "Willie, we're going to come back. I know we are. We just have to button up our pride and we will come back." The following Tuesday, though, Vince began yelling at his players the moment he started the film projector, and he continued yelling at them as they dressed and practiced. He yelled at them for four straight hours. "I hated him that day," recalled Fuzzy Thurston, a target of Vince's abuse. "I hated him right up till the next Sunday," when the Packers slaughtered the Los Angeles Rams, 41–10.[21]

The Packers remained undefeated after the Lions' debacle, finished the season with a 13–1–0 record, and earned the Western Conference title for the third consecutive year. They had outscored their opponents, 415–148. Jim Taylor earned the NFL rushing title with 1,474 yards and scored nineteen touchdowns. In the ranking of quarterbacks, Starr had finished ninth in 1959, sixth in 1960, and third in 1961. In 1962 he ranked first and had a 62.5 percent completion mark.[22]

The NFL championship game would be a rematch with the New York Giants, at Yankee Stadium on December 30, 1962. After the last regular-season game, Vince cured any complacency among his players by putting them through four workouts with full pads in subzero weather. The evening before the game he had dinner with Earl Blaik at the Metropolitan Club in New York. Vince appeared to be filled with self-doubt, Blaik thought, anxious about playing for the title in his native New York, but Blaik underestimated the degree of Vince's anxiety. Suddenly, to Blaik's astonishment, Vince shouted, "We're going to win!" Then he stood up and almost bolted out of the club, not even pausing to say good-bye.

On the day of the game the temperature was fifteen degrees, but the wind, out of the north at forty miles an hour, made playing conditions atrocious. It was so cold that Vince, who normally chain-smoked on the sideline, went through his sideline stint without smoking. "Couldn't get 'em out of my pocket," he later said with a laugh. Because of their powerful running attack, conditions favored the Packers. The Giants were a passing team—specializing in the complex pass pattern and the "big bomb"—and the cold and wind wreaked havoc on their aerials. The game was a primitive slugging match, a raw, physical brawl, one of the most brutal in the history of NFL championships. Jim Taylor had violent confrontations with the Giants' defense. In an early collision with linebacker Sam Huff, Taylor bit his tongue and swallowed blood for the rest of the game. By the end, Taylor's arms, elbows, and knees were raw where flesh had been skinned off. "No one knows until they are faced with it just how much pain they can endure, how much suffering, how much effort they have left," Taylor later said of his painful afternoon. "The coach stepped in and pushed a player beyond that point. That's the way it was that day."

It was an unspectacular game, preserved from dullness only because the outcome remained in doubt until the last two minutes. But the Packers defeated the Giants, 16–7. Afterward, Vince was relieved and relaxed as he was hemmed in by an army of reporters in a small cubicle in the catacombs of Yankee Stadium. The game, though, had drained him emotionally; he had difficulty recalling crucial situations or even the final score.[23]

At the postgame press conference someone asked, "Vince, now you can go for three," a reference to a third consecutive NFL championship, a record not attained by any NFL team. (Green Bay's 1929–31 teams had won three consecutive titles, but that achievement, recorded in the premodern era and prior to the NFL division into two conferences, was considered passé.) "A third championship?," Vince replied. "I'm not going to think about that for a while." But the question had planted a seed, and "for a while" turned out to be less than twenty-four hours. After the team returned to Green Bay, linebacker Bill Forester made a brief courtesy call at Vince's home before he departed the next morning for his home in Dallas. When he arrived, Vince was hosting a party but welcomed him warmly. As Forester was leaving, Vince said, "Bubba, it's never been done three years in a row." Initially the remark confused Forester, but later he realized Vince was already thinking of a third consecutive title. "I thought," recalled Forester, "can't this man have just one night to enjoy winning before thinking about next year?"[24]

During the 1962 season, Vince was also coauthoring a book, and the result, *Run to Daylight,* was an enormous success, earning him wide acclaim. Putting the project together, however, was often confusing and frustrating, particularly for the other coauthor. The book grew out of the desire of the publisher, Prentice-Hall, to create a new series of books on sports, linking as coauthors an exceptional person in a sport and an excellent writer. Red Smith, the prominent sports columnist, was named general editor, and Smith urged Vince to be the subject of the book on football. Vince liked the idea but said he would feel most comfortable if his friend Tim Cohane was appointed coauthor. Cohane declined; instead he suggested Wilfred Charles (W. C.) Heinz. Smith agreed that Heinz would be excellent, and, although Vince didn't know Heinz, he accepted the recommendations of his friends. Heinz agreed, contracts were signed, and the book was set in motion. The Prentice-Hall series produced only two books, but the one by Heinz and Lombardi became a sports classic and a model for others, including one five years later, which also focused on Vince and the Packers: Jerry Kramer's *Instant Replay.*[25]

W. C. Heinz had been a reporter, war correspondent, and sports columnist for the *New York Sun,* and in 1950 he had begun a career as a free-lance writer. He wrote hundreds of articles and short stories, a fine novel on professional boxing (*The Professional,* 1958) and was completing his second novel (*The Surgeon,* 1963). After a few preliminary meetings, Vince remained enthusiastic, though the coauthors could not settle on the book's format. On July 1, 1962, Heinz arrived in Green Bay to commence serious work, and Vince and Marie graciously insisted he live with them. Vince cooperated for three days and the authors worked diligently. After Vince returned from early morning Mass at St. Willebrord's and the two ate breakfast, they retired to Vince's basement recreation room. With Heinz taking notes, they put in three hours, and after lunch would work for two or three more. But after three days, Vince's romance with book-writing began to wear off.[26]

"How are we doing?" Vince asked at the end of the third afternoon.

"We're doing all right," Heinz replied, because he hoped never to have to tell Vince that they were doing otherwise.

"Are we almost done?"

"Almost done?" Heinz said. "I'm only on my second notebook."

"The second notebook?" said Vince. "How many notebooks are there going to be?"

"Oh, I don't know," Heinz responded. "That's hard to say."

"Three? Or four?"

"Five or six."

"Six notebooks?" Vince said, his eyes burning, his voice thrown like a spear. "Six notebooks? How am I gonna do six notebooks? Six notebooks? I've got paperwork to do at the office! I've got players I haven't even signed yet! I've gotta play golf! Once training camp starts I can't play again until the end of the season! Six notebooks? How are we ever gonna do six notebooks?"

"I don't know, Coach," Heinz said, "but we'll find a way."

"You guys didn't tell me it was going to be this much work," he said.

"You didn't ask."

"Well, we'll have to do some of it in camp," Vince declared. "We'll

Michael O'Brien

be living in the dean's suite, and we can get in an hour or two a day there.''

Trying to work around Vince's busy schedule and coaxing him to reveal nuggets of insight caused Heinz increasing frustration. As coach, Vince was meticulous about details, but when it came to recalling details about his past life, he had a poor memory. Although he coached football at St. Cecilia for eight years, he was unable to tell Heinz the color of the Saints' uniforms. For this detail—and others—Heinz had to do the research himself. Vince had no "audio-video" recall, Heinz told him. Vince didn't understand. "It means," explained Heinz, "that you don't remember what things sounded like, who said what, or what things looked like in your youth, your adolescence, or two days ago." Vince agreed: "You're right." Because Vince had tried to eliminate all nonessentials from his life, he was mystified by Heinz's repeated requests for anecdotes. "Anecdotes, anecdotes. You always want anecdotes! Why?" Vince asked. "For the same reason," Heinz pointed out, "that when you put in a play with the Packers you don't just tell them to play. You walk to the blackboard and you diagram it. The anecdote is the illustration of the point we're trying to make." "All right, all right, I understand," Vince said. "What anecdotes do you want?"

When Vince was unavailable, Heinz interviewed players and Marie. She had time to talk, and her astute perceptions of Vince and players provided valuable insight and background. Heinz continued to shadow Vince at home, the golf course, restaurants, and the office, but by mid-July he was discouraged and ready to quit. Vince was too busy, had revealed few scintillating thoughts, and Heinz still hadn't settled on the book's format. Suddenly Heinz hit upon an imaginative plan. Spliced with flashbacks to Vince's early life, Heinz would write a detailed narrative about one week—Monday through Sunday—during the 1962 season. Soon after, almost by accident, he also discovered a simple method of bringing out the essence of Vince's brilliant coaching.

"I think I've found a way to simplify this," Heinz said to him late one morning sitting across from him at his desk, "and it'll save some time."

"Good," Vince said.

"I'm going to start naming players. When I give you a name, you tell me the first thing that comes to your mind about him, not as a player— we'll get to that another time—but as a person. Do you understand what I mean?"

"Of course I understand," he said. "Let's get started."

"Right, coach," Heinz said. "Bart Starr."

"Tense by nature, because he's a perfectionist. I've never seen him

166

display emotion outside of nervousness. Modest. Tends to be self-effacing, which is usually a sign of lack of ego. You never hear him in the locker room telling 'I' stories. He calls me 'sir.' Seems shy, but he's not. He's just a gentleman. You don't criticize him in front of others. When I came here he lacked confidence and support. He still lacks daring, and he's not as creative as I'd like him to be, but a great student of the game.''

"Paul Hornung.''

"Can take criticism in public or anywhere. You have to whip him a little. He had a hell-with-you attitude, a defensive perimeter he built around himself when he didn't start out well here. As soon as he had success, he changed. He's still exuberant, likes to play around, but serious on the field. Always looks you straight in the eye. Great competitor who rises to heights.''

"Jerry Kramer.''

"Nothing upsets him, so you can bawl him out anytime. He's been near death, but he's happy-go-lucky, like a big kid. Takes a loss quite badly, though. . . .''

"Forrest Gregg.''

"Intelligent and, like Marie says, a picture-perfect player. Gives you a 100 percent effort, a team player. Quick temper. I've seen him go at teammates in practice. Has all the emotions, from laughter to tears. Can take criticism anywhere, if it's constructive.''

"Jimmy Taylor.''

"Uses jive talk that I can't understand. Has a lot of desire because he wants to be the best football player the NFL has ever seen. He likes to knock people down and he'll go out of his way to do it. You have to keep after him, though.''

"Henry Jordan.''

"All-Pro, all-everything, but don't ever flatter him. He needs public criticism. He thinks he's the greatest and tends to be satisfied. Strangely, he's easily upset, but he needs to be upset to perform. In reviewing pictures I'll make him a target, not to impress somebody else, as you do with some of them, but to help him.''

"Willie Davis.''

"Traded to Cleveland for him,'' Vince said. "A hell of a young man. Very excitable under game conditions. A worrier. Before a game he's got that worried look, so I try to bolster his confidence. He's not worried about the team losing—he's got confidence in the team—but he's worried about how Willie Davis will perform . . . about not letting the team down. Fine brain, too. In Willie Davis we got a great one.''

In about an hour Heinz had named all thirty-six Packers, and out of their instant personality profiles emerged the heart of the book: a profile of Vince as a leader of men. "He knew them not just as football players," marveled Heinz years afterward, "but as distinct individuals each of whom he was determined to make into a better player than that man had ever thought he could be."[27]

The week before the game against the Detroit Lions on October 7, 1962, Heinz again moved into the Lombardi home and took notes as he watched practice, listened at staff meetings, attended skull sessions, and sat on the team's bench. The book's last chapter, focusing on the tense, dramatic, last-minute 9–7 victory over the Lions, was completed after Vince had come to New York, viewed films of the contest, and recalled his thoughts during the game.

Run to Daylight was profusely illustrated with Robert Riger's photos and drawings. Heinz furnished the imaginative plan, his subtle, informal style, and, while painting the scene, allowed Vince to speak directly to the reader. Vince contributed his remarkable perceptions, and, said Heinz, "his integrity—because he was always true to what he was."

However, the book did gloss over Vince's fiercer side. His anger and abuse were toned down and abstracted, his swearing ignored, simply because Vince did not want to expose those facets of his personality. The name of the opponent and individual players on the Detroit Lions were never mentioned because Vince wanted to avoid antagonizing the Lions. Vince spoke highly of his assistants and players, but at the same time his analysis of their personalities and weaknesses were often startlingly frank. The book crackled with sharp, incisive comment. It captured Vince's intense concentration and devotion to his work and provided minute-by-minute accounts of his thoughts and actions. Readers witnessed his pregame pep talk: "I want you, all of you, to know this: Regardless of what happens today, this is a team of which I am proud. Regardless of the outcome today, I'll still be proud of you."

The book was published in the fall of 1963, and because of its lucid style and mounting tension and because it presented a new, intimate view of sports—not platitudes and sportsmanship, cleats and sweaty T-shirts—reviewers were lavish with praise. "Exciting," "a gold mine of inside football information," "a work of art," "whale of an adventure story" were typical. "If a Pulitzer Prize were given for a sports book," wrote Kuechle in the *Milwaukee Journal*, "this would be my nomination." In the *Newark Star Ledger*, Jerry Izenberg simply observed: "It happens to be the best book ever written on professional football." Until criticism began to muddle Vince's reputation, *Run to Daylight* elevated him to the lofty status of statesman of modern sports.[28]

Vince was delighted with the reviews and the sales. Within three months thirty-five thousand copies were sold, and total hardbound sales eventually reached about two hundred thousand. Various paperback editions also sold briskly. It became the best-selling sports book of its time. Vince was unhappy, though, with his financial return. He had agreed to 40 percent of the royalties; Heinz and Riger each received 30 percent. Twenty years after publication, Vince's share was $21,000. After the book appeared, Vince hired an agent to handle all his "extracurricular" activities. "I contacted [the agent]," he explained to Tim Cohane, "after the hosing I received from Prentice-Hall with *Run to Daylight.*"[29]

The third consecutive title Vince hoped for was not to be—at least not in 1963—and the new year began with depressing news. On January 7, 1963, Paul Hornung's name was mentioned amid rumors swirling of a betting scandal in the NFL. Vince, who was busy preparing the Western Conference squad for the Pro Bowl in Los Angeles, apparently discounted the reports. After the game, on January 13, he and Dr. James Nellen, the Packers' team physician, stopped in Las Vegas for a brief vacation. Vince was enjoying himself until NFL Commissioner Pete Rozelle phoned and informed him of the impending suspension of Hornung for his involvement in a betting scandal. Vince was devastated, not so much for the suspension's impact on the team but for its effect on Hornung. "Isn't that an awful thing to happen to Paul?" he said to Nellen. Vince quickly became despondent, ended his vacation, and returned to Green Bay.[30]

Sometime in the next three months Vince talked to Hornung about the gambling allegations, and Hornung denied them. Vince then intended to defend his star halfback until Rozelle confronted him with overwhelming evidence. Vince was very disappointed. "His biggest disappointment," said Richard Bourguignon, "was when Hornung let him down. . . . Paul had lied to him." Hornung later conceded that Vince was "very hurt and embarrassed and disappointed that I hadn't talked to him about it."

Vince had repeatedly and explicitly warned his players to avoid any association with gamblers and had placed off-limits establishments with unsavory reputations. Yet his warnings hadn't sunken in with many players. "We couldn't see what he was referring to," one said later. That something so terrible could happen to one of his favorite players led Vince to feel he failed in some way. Briefly, he thought of quitting.

On April 17, 1963, when Rozelle publicly announced his decision, Vince made himself unavailable to reporters. Rozelle indefinitely suspended Hornung and Detroit defensive tackle Alex Karras. Hornung had placed bets on NFL and college games from 1959 to 1961 and had transmitted specific information about NFL games for betting purposes, actions that violated his contract, the league bylaws, and the league constitution. Vince accepted Rozelle's ruling without complaint. "The commissioner had no other alternative," he said the following day, "because, if allowed to continue, it could lead to more serious consequences." Vince admitted he was shocked and hurt. "I thought a great deal of Paul. He always gave me 100 percent in football." Hornung had done nothing morally or criminally wrong, Vince reminded everyone during the next few months; he had not shaved points or altered the caliber of his play. "The mistake Paul made was thinking that the rules were made for everyone but him."

"I don't think any one man is indispensable," Vince said, assessing the suspension's impact on his team, "but I'd be lying if I didn't say the loss of Hornung will hurt us." Vince did see a silver lining. "Sometimes it is good to have an obstacle to overcome, whether in football or anything. When things go bad we usually rise to the occasion." Despite the problems with his halfback, Vince stuck with Hornung amid persistent rumors he would be traded. Rozelle lifted Hornung's suspension after one year, and the halfback returned to the team, but—partly because of injuries—not with the skills and the success he had had from 1959 to 1961.[31]

Winning a third straight title, Vince said before training camp, "is at once our greatest incentive and our biggest stumbling block." Each of his players must play "great" because the "person opposite him will be playing great." The preseason, however, started disastrously as the College All-Stars ambushed the Packers, 20–17. With reporters afterward Vince tried to appear upbeat, even jovial, but privately he was embarrassed. "I'll always remember that game," he said a few weeks later, "and I suppose everybody else will remember it, too."

The Packers won their five remaining exhibition games but opened the regular season by losing a close 10–3 decision to the Chicago Bears. Later in the season, with the Bears and the Packers tied for the conference lead with identical 8–1 records, the Bears won the crucial rematch more decisively, 26–7. "I'm real happy for Papa George [Halas]," Vince said after the second loss. "He's a helluva man." Informed of Vince's remark, Halas returned the compliment. "He's a great man. . . . That's characteristic of him. I'm not at all surprised."

Unless the Bears lost, the Packers could not catch them. "Big game?" Vince said, repeating a reporter's question after the Packers had defeated the Rams in the next-to-last contest of the regular season. "The only big game left for us is the one the Bears lose." But the Bears kept winning, completing the season with an exceptional 11–1–2 record. The Packers finished 11–2–1, the second-best record in the NFL. While flying home after the team's victory over the 49ers in the season's final, Vince was informed that the Bears had also won, clinching the conference championship. He declined comment and sat quietly with Marie for the rest of the trip.[32]

Vince would later describe his 1963 team as his "best" even though it hadn't won the title. Injuries to key players had hampered the team, but all teams suffered injuries, and the Packers' list of wounded was unexceptional. Hornung's absence hurt, though Tom Moore adequately replaced him. What did he miss about Hornung? Vince was often asked after the season. "His blocking, his leadership, his 'devil-may-care attitude,' his field-goal kicking, his intelligence on the field," replied Vince. Still, probably nothing could have overcome the great Chicago Bear team of 1963.[33]

Not winning the championship in 1963 noticeably affected Vince's off-season: He received fewer speaking invitations and no awards. Fame, he discovered, was fleeting. As the 1964 season approached, though, many football prognosticators selected the Packers to win their conference. They were the "toughest, slickest, and deepest" team in the league, said one. But the Packers experienced their most disappointing and frustrating season since Vince's arrival. They won the league opener, but in the next game, after Starr was intercepted twice at crucial points in the second half, they lost to the Colts, 21–20, setting the tone for the season. Vince was deeply chagrined. Grim and tight-lipped with reporters, he barked responses, his eyes flashing sparks of indignation.

By midseason the Packers were 3–4, putting them hopelessly behind the conference-leading Colts. Assessing his team's disappointing performance, Vince targeted the widespread infection of complacency. "We're all to blame," he said on October 27, "the newspapers, the team, the coaches, and the people. Nobody got a kick out of winning anymore, or even scoring a touchdown. When we won a close game, people would wonder why we didn't win by a bigger score—or get more touchdowns. Gradually, there was less emotion, less elation with winning."

There were more concrete problems as well. Two in particular plagued the team most of the season. The offensive line was in a shambles. Guard Jerry Kramer missed the entire season with a serious illness; guard Fuzzy Thurston suffered two separated shoulders; tackle Forrest Gregg had to play guard; Bob Skoronski, who moved to center after Jim Ringo was traded, went back to tackle, and rookie Ken Bowman played center. In addition, Hornung's place-kicking was terrible. He made only twelve of thirty-eight field-goal tries all year. Missed extra points caused one-point losses to the Colts and the Vikings, and then in a rematch with Baltimore, Hornung missed five field-goal attempts in a 24–21 loss.[34]

The Packers improved in the last half of the season to finish 8–5–1, tied for second place with the Vikings but far behind the 12–2–0 record of the conference champion Colts. There had been bright spots. The 5–1–1 record in the second half was encouraging. Only the Colts' defense allowed fewer points than Bengtson's unit. Three of the five defeats had been by three points or less. There were also stellar individual performances. Jim Taylor rushed for 1,169 yards, second only to Jim Brown of the Cleveland Browns. With a completion percentage of almost 60 percent, fifteen touchdowns, and only four interceptions, Starr led the NFL in passing for the second time in three years. (In the last eleven games, Starr threw 225 passes without an interception.) "I feel it was a good season," Vince said, forgetting momentarily his oft-spoken deprecation of second place; "we all like to finish first, but as long as we couldn't finish first we did the next best thing and finished second."

Overall, though, the Packers had disappointed, and Vince shared the gloom. And the embarrassment. He couldn't help but notice the critical reports, such as the year-end summary of Wisconsin's top sports stories compiled by the Associated Press, which listed the Packers' "failure" as the second most noteworthy story of 1964. Though the preseason favorite to regain the NFL title, the AP said, the Packers had been a "bust." As if to confirm the view, on January 3, 1965, the Packers capped off their less-than-glorious season with a 24–17 loss to the St. Louis Cardinals in the Runner-up Bowl. "We played the game like we were still in our sleep," Vince bristled afterward. "Sure it doesn't mean a thing, but we're out there to win."[35]

As the 1965 season approached, many starters from the 1962 championship team had either retired or been traded, leading one sportswriter to conclude that the Packers were "gradually going to seed" and would probably soon be a "soft touch again." Vince admitted that for the past few years the college draft had not effectively replenished the Packers, but he hoped the "drop-off has gone as far as it can go." He did make two excellent trades, dealing for Don Chandler from the Giants, who solved the team's place-kicking woes, and Carroll Dale, who shored up the receiver corps. As training camp opened, Vince expressed unusually firm optimism. "We'll win it," he declared flatly on July 12. Unequivocally? he was asked. "Yes." Two weeks into the training camp he saw no reason to change his mind. His players had displayed "more spirit, more determination, more of everything than I have seen since I have been with the Packers." So far they had shown "pride," but their pride "must be there *every* day of the week."[36]

In 1965 Vince was meticulous in his motivation, mixing timely doses of pride and confidence with anger so explosive the fallout blistered the media corps. The regular season started well as the team sailed through the opening four games undefeated. In the first half of the next game, however, the Detroit Lions smashed the Packers, 21–3. As the team walked to the dressing room at halftime, players overheard the Lions' Alex Karras angrily taunt Vince. "Hey! How ya like that, ya fat wop?" Some players were "terrified" of Vince's mood and his reaction to their shoddy performance. Instead, his response surprised and reinvigorated them. Calm and businesslike, for twenty minutes he conferred with his quarterbacks and handled miscellaneous matters. He said nothing to the team until it was time to return for the second half. Then he gathered his discouraged players and said simply but dramatically, "Men, we are the Green Bay Packers. . . . The Packers have pride." In the second half, the Packers stormed back with twenty-eight points and won, 31–21. Starr later cited the halftime pep talk as a prime illustration of Vince's "remarkable sense of timing."[37]

No team in the NFL in 1965 came close to matching the Packers' outstanding defense, which allowed only 224 points all year. But in midseason came a baffling stretch when the offense averaged only nine points in four consecutive games, with the Packers losing two of them. Vince had gradually worked Kramer and Thurston back into the offensive line, and Bowman improved at center, but the line remained in flux and permitted forty-three quarterback sacks through nine games. Taylor and Starr were injured part of the time, and Hornung was usually ineffective. Since Vince concentrated on the offense, he was probably embarrassed. He was definitely angry. After the team could only squeak by the Rams in the ninth game, 6–3, and, two weeks later, lost to the Rams, 21–10, the air was blue from Vince's abuse. Each verbal pasting, though, was followed by an impressive victory.[38]

Vince had often been testy with the press, but during the 1965 slump, he was particularly bad-tempered. On October 24, the Packers defeated the Dallas Cowboys, 13–3, to remain undefeated, but the offense had played pitifully. When a reporter pointed out that the Cowboys had outgained his team, Vince snapped, "I don't give a damn about statistics as long as we win." Someone asked if the Packers had been lucky. "I don't think we were lucky," Vince shot back. "How can you say we were lucky? Our special teams caused them to fumble." A few minutes later he abruptly terminated the press conference. "That's all the questions," he said. "I don't have any more answers." A week later, after the Packers lost to the Bears, 31–10, Vince grew angry at repeated questions about why the Packers lost. He had responded vaguely until he finally exploded: "The Bears blocked better, ran better, and they passed better—and they defensed us better. That's all there was to it. What the hell do you want me to say? You're trying to make a mountain out of a molehill." On November 14, after losing two in a row, the Packers barely squeezed by the Rams in Milwaukee, 6–3. At the postgame press conference, while Vince was trying to point out that an official had erred in not awarding Jim Taylor a touchdown, a Los Angeles reporter interjected, "Depending whether the ball was up here or down at the waist." Vince's brow darkened. "Are you trying to be funny?" he said. "Are you trying to be a comedian? I don't like comedians. . . . This isn't a funny game." Indeed, for Vince midseason hadn't been the least bit funny.[39]

The Packers remained locked in a tight race with the Colts for the conference title as the two teams met in Baltimore in the next-to-last game. Vince's approach was "sweet [and] confident" again, and the Packers won, 42–27, with Hornung scoring five touchdowns. On Saturday, December 18, with their two quarterbacks, John Unitas and Gary Cuozzo, both injured, halfback Tom Matte directed the Colts to victory over the Rams. If the Packers won on Sunday, they could earn the title, but they tied the 49ers, 24–24, leaving them deadlocked with the Colts and forcing a conference playoff in Green Bay on December 26. In the tense, sudden-death overtime, the Packers won, 13–10.

On January 2, 1966, a chilled, wet crowd in Green Bay watched the Packers play the Cleveland Browns for the NFL title. Don Chandler kicked three field goals, Hornung ran for 105 yards, Taylor for ninety-six, and Ray Nitschke controlled the Browns' great fullback, Jim Brown. After Hornung scored a crucial touchdown and was returning to the bench, he hollered, "It's just like the good old days!" Vince jubilantly took up the cry. "Did you hear that?" he yelled. "It's just like the good old days! Just like the good old days!" The Packers defeated the Browns, 23–12. After the game, encircled by a crush of newsmen, Vince was a picture of restrained jubilation. "This team has more character than any other team I've had," he said. Addressing the setbacks and the midseason slump, he added, "A lot of things happened to us this season, but the players closed their mouths and never said a word to the press or anyone. They kept their mouths shut. Everything that was said was said [in the dressing room]. I'm talking about injuries and a number of things."[40]

It had been an outstanding season, leading many commentators to praise Vince. The Packers had reached a "peak of excellence" against the Browns, said *The New York Times'* Arthur Daley. The season had been Vince's "best coaching job," concluded the *Press-Gazette's* Art Daley. Red Smith agreed: "Nothing Lombardi accomplished in other years could match the job he has done in 1965." But for the first time, Vince's coaching came under scorching criticism as well. Vince had always had his critics, but up to 1965 their voices had been muted and isolated. "I'm a pretty nice fellow usually," Vince told an interviewer in late December 1965. "They build me up as a hard man, but I'm not." Ironically, critics were just beginning to question seriously Vince's self-appraisal. After two years in relative obscurity, success had brought him back into the national limelight, and his authoritarian control over the Packers, his abusiveness, his testy encounters with the media, and his evangelical passion for victory produced a spate of articles portraying him as a repugnant, harsh martinet who was seldom nice.[41]

Three articles at the close of the 1965 season illustrate the new, critical tone. "Whatever softness is in Lombardi . . . doesn't show," wrote Ken Hartnett of Wisconsin's AP. "In Green Bay his authority is absolute and unchallenged." Hartnett asked an unnamed Packer player if he understood his coach. "Of course not," came the reply. "Who does?" Sportswriter Milton Gross of the *New York Post* related a story that Vince had been seen in the locker room having the trainer shave calluses from the bottom of his feet with a razor blade. "That," said somebody watching from the doorway, "is the only place where the coach is bothered by callus. The rest of him is harder and crustier and goes so deep nobody could slice through it." Gross discovered a little tenderness in Vince, but not much. Vince decorated his Packer office in "dictator modern" and used every torturous method to prod his squad short of "thumbscrews." Vince's glare was "sterner than Green Bay's weather." He could "freeze a man with a stare faster than the icy wind coming off the Fox River." The "Man in the News" column in *The New York Times* echoed Gross's theme. Vince "bullied," "harassed," and "ragged" his team, and beneath his "gruff exterior" was a "soul of solid rocks." The *Times* continued: "Men as stout as oaken doors cringe when he enters the room, an entire American city basks in his infrequent, crooked-toothed smiles, and his wife tolerates being tuned out at least six months a year." In a few years the criticism grew sharper and the praise more lavish.[42]

As the 1966 season approached, some observers noted again that age was creeping up—perhaps overwhelming—on the Packers. Max McGee was thirty-four, Starr thirty-two, Taylor thirty-one, Hornung thirty. But Vince rejected the view. For a total of $1 million he had just signed two prized draft choices, running backs Donny Anderson and Jim Grabowski. "I say emphatically—we are not an old football team. We have experience—and that's what you need to win in this league. Youth is important, certainly, but what you must have is a blend of youth and experience."

The Packers used their experience effectively in 1966. Going into the tenth game they were 7–2 but still remained tied with the Baltimore Colts. When the Packers defeated the Bears and the Colts lost, Vince could breathe easier. In the next-to-last game, the Packers defeated the Colts, 14–10, clinching their second consecutive Western Conference title.

On the flight home from Baltimore, the team celebrated, having opened the champagne before the huge 727 had left the airport. As usual, there was no boisterous escapade, no dousing each other with champagne, only glass-clicking, talking, smiling, and singing. Players mingled in the aisles, Forrest Gregg with his arm around Willie Davis. "We've been through a lot together," one player said to a teammate. "You're the greatest," said another. Forty voices began singing, "He's got the whole world in his hands. . . ." The words changed, the singing became louder. "We've got the best team in the world. . . ." Then, "We've got the best coach in the world. . . ." Vince, sitting in the front and hearing the word "coach," rose and sang, "We've got the best players in the world. . . ." Art Daley, who witnessed the team's joy aboard the plane, observed: "You could . . . call it love. . . . This is the secret to the Pack's success, and it goes right back to . . . Lombardi, who molds men into more than football players."[43]

After defeating Baltimore, the Packers had one more—seemingly meaningless—regular-season contest, on the West Coast against the Rams on December 18. Since a victory would ensure the Rams the highest finish in their division in years, and because the Packers presumably would not be emotionally ready, oddsmakers installed the Rams as the favorite. For Vince, though, the game took on the dimensions of a crusade. He made certain his team was ready. A sloppy performance would embarrass; a letdown would hamper postseason preparations; his own and his players' honor and the reputation of professional football were at stake. The game meant nothing; yet it meant everything.

Vince was in an angry mood all week, driving his team relentlessly. He kept them at one practice an hour longer than usual. At another, exasperated by missed assignments and lackadaisical effort in an offensive drill, he called a halt and addressed the entire squad in the center of the field. "You fellows don't have any pride. All you have is shame. You're a disgrace to the National Football League. I don't know who you guys think you are. If the Rams beat you, you'll never come back. You fellows are supposed to be a championship team, but you must have been lucky to get where you are. Let's get back at it and do it right." The team then whipped through the last half hour of practice with fewer mistakes.

Later *Time* reported on the Packers' preparations for the Rams and portrayed Vince as a sadistic dictator. The Packers were already champs, *Time* said dumbfounded, "So why were they doing push-ups, and running wind sprints? Could it really have been because a chubby pip-squeak with glasses was screaming at them? . . ." When Vince "chews out" his players, *Time* said, they responded like robots. " 'Yes, sir, Coach Lombardi—sir!' and they mean it."

In the dressing room before the game, Vince was so emotional he could barely talk. He finally blurted out that if his players gave less than their best they would be "cheating" themselves, their coaches, their team-mates, "everybody in Green Bay, and everything pro football stands for." They'd be "cheating the Maker who gave you that talent." Staring directly at them, he concluded: "I know we don't have cheaters on this ball club." The Packers charged out and defeated the Rams, 27–23. Recalling the game, Bart Starr observed: "Sometimes I think no game we ever played for Coach Lombardi gave him as much satisfaction as the one we didn't have to win but did." To reporters Vince explained, "Anytime you've got a God-given talent you should use it at all times and that's the way it turned out today." Despite the testimony of numerous witnesses, he denied having called his players a "disgrace" at practice. "Never," he said. "I'd have to be out of my mind to say a thing like that about a championship team."[44]

During the season Hornung had been ailing and ineffective. Jim Taylor led the team in rushing with 705 yards, but he was declining noticeably. The Packers had no player as exciting as the Vikings' Fran Tarkenton, as theatrical as the Colts' John Unitas, as electrifying as the Bears' Gale Sayers, yet they had earned their fifth conference title in seven years. The team's 12–2–0 record was the best in the NFL. Its defense was again outstanding, allowing only 163 points, by far the fewest in the NFL. The Packers also had balance, bench strength, experience, pride, and a winning attitude and habit that grew stronger with each championship. Starr led the NFL in passing, yet the Packers had no one among the league's leading receivers. Five Packer receivers had caught more than twenty-five passes each, an indication of the team's balance. The Packers' depth allowed them to replace Hornung with Elijah Pitts and Taylor with rookie Jim Grabowski. When Starr was injured, Zeke

Bratkowski filled in capably. The Packers occasionally struck for sudden touchdowns, but usually they did their opponents in by degrees, a few yards at a time, sacrificing excitement to efficiency, the big play to a series of little ones. "You don't have to win 'em aesthetically," Vince said. "You win 'em the best you can."[45]

The day after Christmas 1966, Vince flew his team to Tulsa, Oklahoma, to practice in warm weather for the New Year's Day showdown against the Cowboys, the Eastern Conference champions, in the Cotton Bowl at Dallas, for the NFL title. Temperatures in the low twenties, however, had turned the rain-soaked turf at Skelly Stadium into a sheet of ice. Players laughed at the irony of leaving cold, snowy Green Bay to practice in "warm, dry" Tulsa, but Vince failed to see the humor. When the Packers' equipment arrived late, delaying the first practice, he fumed, "This is one fouled-up operation." For forty minutes the players slid and fell on the ice until Vince gave up in disgust and ordered them to a local indoor facility. Vince's nervousness and foul mood carried over to his relations with the media. He was rude with reporters and sparse with his comments in most interviews. "You're going to interview Lombardi?" one reporter asked another. "Lots of luck." A sportswriter for a Tulsa newspaper, a victim of Vince's rudeness, wrote that "The intelligence which Lombardi exhibits with his maneuvering on the field is not evident in his rapport with the press and the public." In a tense duel the Packers defeated Dallas, 34–27, to earn a berth in the first Super Bowl in Los Angeles, against the AFL champs, the Kansas City Chiefs. "These men have something more than respect for each other," Vince said afterward. "There is love on this ball club."[46]

The pressure of the first Super Bowl made Vince exceptionally anxious. It was to be the first encounter with the rival American Football League, which had recently merged with the NFL, and every NFL owner either called or wrote to impress upon Vince the importance of the game. "It wasn't only Packer prestige," Vince said later, "but the whole NFL [that] was on the line. We had everything to lose and nothing to gain." A few days before the game Vince trembled as he read his team a telegram from George Halas spurring them on to victory. Compounding the pressure was the media corps of over a thousand and the sixty-five million television viewers who would watch the coverage on both NBC and CBS. At the press conference the Friday before the game, Vince was grumpy and abrasive. "It was the worst I ever saw him in a mass gathering," said Jim Kensil, executive director of the NFL.

Oddsmakers picked the Packers by thirteen points because the team was vastly more experienced than the Chiefs, had faced more clutch games, and played in the league with superior personnel. Vince knew there was only a small chance his team would lose, yet he lived with the fear that the small chance would occur—on a crucial play his defensive back might fall down or his receiver might drop the ball. His preparation was serious and businesslike. Curfew at 11:00 P.M. and stiff fines for violators. The team's comfortable quarters in Santa Barbara made Vince uncomfortable. When a reporter remarked about the swimming pool and beautiful surroundings, Vince replied, "That's the trouble. It's too goddamn beautiful to train for a football game!"

To counter any complacency in his players, Vince kept emphasizing the Chiefs' great physical size and solid reputation. "He scared us to death," said Forrest Gregg. He planned to keep his running attack simple and to exploit Kansas City's inadequate pass defense. The Chiefs had weak cornerbacks, he thought, and because their defensive alignment rotated toward the strength of the offensive formation, they were vulnerable to the pass. Anytime a team tried to play the Packers with two or more linebackers inside of their defensive ends, Vince had instructed his quarterbacks to throw the ball because the opponent couldn't adequately cover an outside pattern. "Throw the ball!" he said emphatically. "He didn't care if it was third and one," said Zeke Bratkowski. "Just throw the ball because he knew your percentage was going to be high." The receivers were also well schooled. When they saw the linebackers inside, they expected the automatic from the quarterback.[47]

Before the game on January 15, 1967, television announcer Frank Gifford interviewed Vince on the field. "During the five minutes or so I talked to him," recalled Gifford, "he held on to me and he was shaking like hell." The game was close for two quarters, but no contest in the second half as the unflappable Packers pulled away to win, 35–10. They gained 250 yards passing. Max McGee, nearing his thirty-fifth birthday and retirement, seldom used during the season, enjoyed one of the most productive days of his career. Summoned to replace the injured Boyd Dowler, he caught seven passes for 138 yards and two touchdowns.

In the wake of the triumph there was incredible chaos as the record crush of newsmen, television lights, microphones, cameras, and photographers hemmed Vince in his office. He gingerly held the game ball and fielded questions. He complimented Kansas City's offense, but, as he had carefully done for two weeks, avoided any comparison of the NFL with the AFL. "I have nothing to say about it," he said. As wave after wave of reporters crowded around him, the comparison question was asked again and again until Vince relented and answered. "That's a good football team, but it is not as good as the top teams in our league." He grinned and added, "That's what you want me to say, and now I've said it. It took me a long time," he said with a laugh, "to get that out." Immediately after the press conference Vince regretted his candid response. "I came off as an ungracious winner," he said sadly to a friend, "and it was lousy." No one accused him of being an ungracious winner, and probably few thought it. Yet he always regretted the remark.[48]

Throughout 1966 there had been reports that Vince might retire. He occasionally admitted that his dual role as coach and general manager was becoming too burdensome, but he had not publicly mentioned retirement. On December 27, however, when a reporter for the *Dallas Times-Herald* asked him if he would retire, Vince said, "It's not definite, but I might make this my last season. The job has become too much to handle. I think it's time I gave somebody else a chance. There used to be an off-season," he explained. "For that matter, there used to be some time off during the season. I remember when I was in college I used to drop in on the Giants' meetings. They had one reel of film and they'd show it to the team one time and that was it." If he retired, Vince added, he would retain his role of general manager. The following day reporters met him after practice in Tulsa to quiz him about his "retirement." Vince denied he had any intention of quitting. Yes, the Dallas reporter had quoted him correctly, he said awkwardly; "the reporter just misunderstood me." He reiterated that his dual role was "getting too big" but said he would try to "cut down." He wouldn't elaborate.

The retirement story fueled speculation on Vince's future plans. The *Press-Gazette*'s Len Wagner thought he might, indeed, retire from coaching after the season. "Lombardi has become more complex than ever this year and strain is beginning to tell," he said. Red Smith wondered where Vince Lombardi the general manager would find a successor for Vince Lombardi the coach. Who would want to follow Vince's act, especially with Vince looking over his shoulder? "Vince is a scrupulous man," said Smith. "As a coach he tolerates no interference, and as general manager he would slash his wrists before interfering. And that's just it; he might very well wind up slashing his wrists."

During the two weeks before the Super Bowl, Vince smothered the retirement stories by repeatedly declaring his intention to continue in his current duties. Shortly after defeating Kansas City, though, mentally tired and emotionally depleted, he entered a Green Bay hospital for a complete physical examination. To reporters he downplayed any serious problem. "I feel a little tired," he said, adding lamely, "but fine."[49]

IX

The Man and His Beliefs

To many Vince was an enigma. "I wish I could figure him out," Jerry Kramer lamented. Even close personal friends had difficulty understanding him. Colonel Earl Blaik described him as a man of "contradictions." There did seem to be many contradictions. He was dedicated and narrow, intelligent and dogmatic, self-restrained and emotional, and abusive but apologetic. His mood could swing from deep gloom to soaring exuberance in a matter of minutes. Compassionate, kind, and charitable, he could nonetheless do unlovely things in the grip of his temper. Shy and insecure in some situations, he was loud and gregarious in others. He preached hate and love; appeared both egotistical and humble; and sought fame and success, yet often antagonized the media and guarded his privacy. Although he touted the virtues of family life, he was himself mostly a negligent father. No wonder even Marie was sometimes confused. "He's kind of a mystery," she said. "He eludes you." Despite the contradictions, Vince was essentially a simple man, a fundamentalist in his football, his character, his religion, and his values.[1]

Because Vince was a former teacher who was presumed to have graduated *cum laude* from Fordham and to have studied law for a few years, many inflated his intelligence. "He's a brilliant man," a Green Bay fan told a reporter. "He has degrees in philosophy and psychol-

Michael O'Brien

ogy. . . . He reads Plato and Aristotle and applies it to football. A genius." He wasn't a genius, but he was intelligent and was smarter than most—perhaps all—of his coaching peers. When he discussed the psychological and philosophical dimensions of football, he appeared scholarly, leading many sportswriters to refer to him as the "professor." Basically he was intelligent without being intellectual, using his penetrating, logical mind like a tool to isolate football problems and to solve them. His speeches were the antitheses of the mashed-potato-circuit orator, with the ready anecdote to illustrate each point.[2]

He was curious. When he purchased modern equipment for the office or the stadium, the technical innovations fascinated him. A stimulating conversationalist, he kept sufficiently abreast of current events to speak articulately with friends on political and social issues. He dabbled in books on poetry, philosophy, management, and quotations, mainly searching for ideas for his speeches, and read some Civil War history and a few best-selling novels (Morris West's *Shoes of the Fisherman* and Irving Stone's *The Agony and the Ecstasy*). His ability to master the study guide for the Scholastic Aptitude Test (SAT), the difficult exam for college-bound students, astonished his son. He quickly breezed through the sections on chemistry, physics, and language, correctly answering a high percentage of the questions. Retaining an impressive knowledge of Greek and Latin, he occasionally read books in the two languages. In general, on subjects unrelated to football and coaching, his mind was less impressive though still formidable. Coaching prevented him from acquiring breadth and depth of knowledge, and he preferred to spend his precious free time on entertainment and leisure—golf, dining, parties, and television—not on serious reading or intellectual pursuits.[3]

The only persons who humbled Vince, observed a sportswriter, were "God the Father, God the Son, God the Holy Ghost, and Mrs. Lombardi." Sometimes Vince seemed an egomaniac. "I won," he would say. He told the players, "I've never had a losing season. . . . I made you." Max McGee thought Vince loved the players but was primarily interested in personal glory and acclaim. "He's got to be the most egotistical man I ever met," said McGee. "I swear he preached humility to enhance his own ego."

Publicity Director Chuck Lane wrote a press release praising "Phil Bengtson's defense," noting that under Bengtson's direction the Packers' defense had never finished below second in league statistics. "The minute after that release was on his desk," said Lane, "Lombardi came through that door full speed. He reminded me—in no uncertain terms—that it wasn't *Phil Bengtson's* defenses, it was *his* defenses, and that Phil

Bengtson was merely implementing or installing them." David Carley, Vince's business partner, liked Vince but added, "If there was anything that bothered me about Lombardi . . . [it] was that he tolerated the obsequiousness around him—the people willing to kiss his ass." Once when Carley and Vince walked into a restaurant, everyone stood up and applauded. Carley was embarrassed—and thought Vince should have been—but Vince seemed to enjoy it.[4]

Yet Vince tried to be humble, though some of his attempts were transparently artificial. When reporters asked him to autograph their copy of *Run to Daylight,* he wrote in the book jacket, "With fondest memories. From a pauper in my field to a prince in his." For the most part, his friends and acquaintances thought he was sincerely humble. He didn't seem to view himself as a great person and was often apologetic about his coaching craft. He preached humility to his players and in his speeches. When friends in Bergen County, New Jersey, tried to arrange a "Vince Lombardi Day," they won enthusiastic support from everyone, including the governor, but the organizers received one letter of opposition. "I don't think Vince Lombardi is important enough to have a day set aside for him," signed Vince Lombardi. When Fordham inducted him into its Football Hall of Fame, he felt uncomfortable because he was one of the first inductees, and outstanding Fordham players—including some of his former teammates—had not yet been inducted. He privately told his son that "as far as I'm concerned they're just cheapening this award." After he was honored and praised at a major banquet, Vince usually told his audience the joke about the death of a mean, wife-beating Irishman. At his funeral the preacher lavished praise on the dead man until the wife of the deceased asked to peek into the coffin to make sure she was at the right funeral. Vince concluded: "I can't believe you're talking about me."[5]

What most impressed people about Vince was his intensity, exemplified in his concentration, his emotions, and his dedication. When he concentrated at practice, the meeting room, or in an interview, he seemed constantly to be willfully exerting the force of his personality on himself and anyone near him. "It is almost like a religious act of Zen discipline," said a *Sports Illustrated* reporter of Vince's concentration during an interview. "He exerts his personality not so much to control things as to keep himself taut, conditioned, perfectly disciplined. It is a kind of isometric exercise of the will—or perhaps of the soul. But the awareness of Lombardi's will, of the nearly physical intensity of his ego, never quite disappears when one is in his presence."

The range of emotions open to Italian males was considerably wider than that allowed upper-class Anglo-Saxon males, and Vince's ran the gamut. When he coached for the New York Giants, he had so many peaks and valleys some players nicknamed him "Hi-Low." While asking a reporter's understanding of his moodiness, he observed that for him, "Things are either just wonderful or just terrible." He often cried. "If you said good morning to him in the right way," said Wellington Mara, "you could bring tears to his eyes." Although he usually fought back his tears, he also accepted them as natural to him and natural for his profession. "Hell, I'm an emotional man. I cry. . . . I'm not ashamed of crying. Football's an emotional game. You can't be a cold fish and go out and coach. If you're going to be involved in it, you gotta take your emotions with you."[6]

"Vin had such a temper," said Marie, "that I just *knew* he was going to die of a massive heart attack." When he flew into a rage on the sideline, Marie trained herself not to look at him. "Like my father before me," Vince said, "I have a violent temper with which I have been struggling all my life." Besides being inherited, Vince's temper grew out of his frustrated ambition and his insistence on perfection. Noting the doors closed to Vince because of his Italian-Catholic heritage, columnist Jim Murray observed that "Nothing makes a man more splenetic than to be discriminated against for something other than his own failures." When Vince finally secured his position with the Packers, he attacked the job with intense drive and repressed fury to prove to himself and others that he could succeed and instill values as well as any man. At times Vince's outbursts embarrassed him. He often said he wished for "more patience and understanding"; yet, ironically, his impatience with failure, his lack of understanding of anything but complete dedication to the task of winning games, explained much of his success. "I have had to effect a compromise," he said. "[My temper] is ineradicable, but it must not be irrational. I coach with everything that is within me, and I employ that temper for a purpose."[7]

Naturally, his rudeness and tantrums caused confusion and resentment. Even friends were not exempt. Jim Manci, the owner of one of Vince's favorite Green Bay restaurants and a friend, wanted to give Vince a case of Scotch whiskey but made the mistake of bringing the gift to the practice field. "What are you doing here on the field?" Vince screamed. "I've got some stuff for you," Manci replied hesitantly. "Give it to somebody else!" Vince shot back. "Don't bother me now!" After practice, Vince was friendly again. Manci was deeply hurt but had learned a lesson. "When [Vince] was busy with football, you could not get close to him," he said. "[Vince] was really awful in his treatment of people," said the *Chicago Tribune*'s Cooper Rollow, who otherwise admired Vince. "We always used to say that Lombardi can get [away] with his high-handed, arrogant tactics as long as he keeps winning, but if he ever starts losing, God help him, he's really going to be in trouble with the media, the fans, the players—with everybody."[8]

Vince was asked if it bothered him to have to wait a "fair length of time" to become a head coach beyond high school. *"That was a long time, not a fair length of time,"* he muttered, stretching out the sentence. To sustain his ambition he disciplined and dedicated himself. "I don't think Vince was ever a child," said Marie. "I think he was born conscientious." The *Milwaukee Journal*'s Oliver Kuechle agreed: "The easy thing to say is that Lombardi is a dedicated man. Of course he is. The real meaning, though, may be lost in this simplicity. He is a completely dedicated man. There are degrees of dedication." Vince hoped his own dedication would also serve as an example. To win football games and build character in his players, he said, the team "must somehow get the feeling that there is a dedication coming from the top and it must be worth something."

The long delay in securing a head coaching job taught him a valuable lesson. "I think in the long run, the time I had to wait helped me more than anything else," he said. "It's easy to have faith in yourself and have discipline when you're a winner, when you're number one. What you got to have is faith and discipline when you're not yet a winner."[9]

A key to Vince's success and inner power stemmed from the constant reinforcement throughout his life of a narrow—yet important—set of values, which he cherished and preached with the passion of a crusader. His indomitable spirit was influenced by a lifetime of exposure to a host of values aimed at excellence, which in professional football meant winning. His whole preparation for Green Bay had been ordered and purposeful. His father, his coaching mentors, his seminary training, St. Francis Prep, the Jesuits of Fordham, St. Cecilia High School, and West Point had given him a similar vision of what life should be, and he never betrayed it. When he left West Point, he joined the New York Giants, the perfect organization for his personality. Directed by the hardworking, close-knit, Fordham-trained, and Catholic Mara family, the Giants allowed him freedom to develop his talents. He questioned the value of his vocation, and his weaknesses tormented him, but his goals were clear and unquestioned, the ordered life comfortable. There was the wrong way to do things and his father's way, the Church's way, the Army's way. There were no shadings of gray. It was all black and white.[10]

"I don't think he ever taught me any football," said Henry Jordan.

"What he'd do three times a week was preach on life." By title Vince was only a football coach, an expert in a game played by schoolboys and young men. As he himself often said, football was a simple game of blocking and tackling. Yet he also tried to make it more than a game. "Football is a way of life," he insisted. He presented himself—and others presented him—as a man of the spirit rather than just a coach. His passion to link football with life resembled a noble crusade to improve mankind. Some people judged him a primitive for his outlook, but he unabashedly taught his players to set an almost impossibly high standard of excellence for themselves and then drove them unmercifully to achieve it.

He wanted his players to mature, and a major part of maturing was to acquire character. Everyone was different in "magnitude," he said, but the capacity to achieve character was the same. "In my own life I have found that a vital dimension of this deeper life is spiritual." Indeed, his religious faith underscored both his personality and his beliefs.[11]

"It was religion in the morning and the language of the longshoreman in the afternoon," a Packer assistant coach observed of Vince. Others also noted his incongruous behavior, leading some to judge his religious convictions shallow and his behavior hypocritical. To Vince, though, the inconsistency was merely a confirmation of original sin. He was exceptionally religious. He cultivated his spiritual life, disciplining himself to stay close to God just as he disciplined himself in his work. "He never did anything without prayer," said Susan. Each morning he prayed to St. Jude or the Sacred Heart. On the wheel of his car he clipped a plastic, fluorescent rosary, which he often prayed as he drove Susan to school. After Sunday Mass on the day of a game, he secluded himself in his bedroom or hotel room, knelt down by the bed, and prayed the rosary.

When the team played a game out of town, one of his first concerns was to locate the nearest church. Early in the morning, Monday through Saturday, he attended Mass and received communion at St. Willebrord's Church in Green Bay's downtown, near his original Washington Street office. Mass settled into a comfortable routine. In the churches he attended, he always sought the same pew. At Resurrection Church on Sunday, it was the middle aisle, ten rows back. Mass also allowed him to renew warm contact with Marie, who usually accompanied him. "I'd get into church and I'd get that nice feeling," Marie said. "If I didn't go and I fought him, then I'd be unhappy with myself all day." Every year he made a retreat with friends, usually at St. Norbert College from Holy Thursday to the Saturday before Easter. Active intellectually in retreat discussions, he enjoyed playing the devil's advocate by questioning

God's existence and the Church's tenets to stimulate fellow retreatants to think deeply about their convictions. During training camp he usually served Mass at St. Norbert. He told Father Dennis Burke, president of the college, that serving made him feel "closest to God."[12]

Unlike his efforts for charities, schools, and public service, for which he lent mainly his endorsement, Vince actively took part in parish work, indicating where his priorities lay. When the family moved to Green Bay, he joined St. Matthew's Parish near his home. In 1963, when the boundaries of St. Matthew's changed, making room for new Resurrection Church, Vince joined the new congregation. He took part in Resurrection's Holy Name Society, and Marie assisted the Women's Guild. Father William Spalding, founding pastor of Resurrection, appointed him to the parish planning committee, charged with responsibility for raising $750,000 to help build and furnish the church. Vince attended every meeting, aggressively asserting himself when he had intelligent suggestions, backing off when it was time to listen and follow. "Vince used his brilliance and activity to help us get that extra funding," said a fellow committee member; he "wanted the best for the church and was willing to work for it."[13]

During Mass and prayer Vince often thought about his work and his team, but he claimed he never prayed for victory, only God's will. Nor did he attempt to impress his faith on his players, except to urge them to be religious. Before and after the game, the team prayed together, but Vince insisted his players started this practice. "We don't pray to win," he said. "We pray to play the best we can and to keep us free from injury. And the prayer we say after the game is one of thanksgiving." Most players felt that praying together fostered team unity and helped them deal with the problems and pressures that built up over a season. Players knew that Vince was a daily communicant, which intensified their respect for his dedication and deep convictions. Usually Vince kept his religious life private. Before Super Bowl I, when a photographer for a national magazine sought to photograph him praying in church, he adamantly refused. "No way!" he yelled over the phone at the man. Even the religious influence he had on Vince, Jr., and Susan he imparted mostly by example. He never insisted they attend daily Mass or pray the rosary; nor did he reveal his deepest religious convictions.[14]

Vince always extended his greetings to priests and nuns and gave them free tickets to games. While he dined at a Green Bay restaurant, television sports announcer Bob Schulze approached his table to introduce him to a priest who was dining with Schulze. In his haste to jump to attention, Vince almost knocked over his chair. "He would never have

Michael O'Brien

jumped to attention for me," said Schulze. "It was fun to make him jump when I walked over with a person with a collar on."

His faith humbled him. Few Catholics could express themselves openly to the priest in confession without the seclusion of the confessional and the screen concealing their identity, but Vince, as he had done twenty years earlier with Father Timothy Moore in their St. Cecilia office, would kneel down in the sacristy before Mass at St. Norbert and make his confession to Father Burke. "He was not embarrassed," the priest recalled; "it shows the humility of the man." In order to plan the annual preseason game for the Bishop's Charities, Vince met with Bishop Aloysius Wycislo, who presided over the Green Bay Diocese. On each occasion Vince knelt down and kissed the bishop's ring—"to my embarrassment," said Wycislo. The bishop tried to dissuade him by joking, "It'll only get you ninety days' indulgence, and football season won't even have begun by then." But Vince insisted on performing the ritual. "No," he said seriously, "I still want to do it."[15]

Vince's spiritual life both mirrored and strongly influenced his coaching philosophy, both caused and relieved intense inner anxiety. Religion reminded him of his vocation, not the restricted vocation as football coach, but his vocation as a man, the strong sense that one's life and responsibilities must tend toward evoking a sense of God's presence. Man was accountable to himself, to others, and to God for the way he cultivated or mutilated his human talents. In the 1960s the Scholastic values still served as Vince's compass, guiding him to God's will. The dignity of the individual, respect for authority, character, tradition, duty, morality, perfection, God's preeminence—plus the disciplined will to sustain those values—were still the foundation of his personal philosophy thirty years after he graduated from Fordham. Father Ignatius Cox and his other Jesuit instructors would have praised his perseverance for trying to radiate the lofty, demanding principles they had taught him.

God demanded that he discipline himself to strive for the ideal: perfection. So did Scholastic philosophy. So did the requirements of his intensely competitive profession. His father and Earl Blaik, the men he admired most and who most influenced him, were both authoritarian perfectionists. Consequently, Vince placed tremendous inner pressure on himself to be exemplary. Not living up to one's potential was the supreme tragedy. Yet he knew he was weak, limited, and sinful. That he was often restless, nervous, and angry and slipped easily into moodiness and depression were symptoms of a deeply troubled soul. "There was a tension about his faith," observed Bishop Wycislo. "I think he wanted to be as perfect a Catholic as he was a coach." Vince, Jr., thought his father's faith grew out of his need to overcome "painful inner conflict." The fame he achieved in Green Bay made him uncomfortable. "I think my father knew that he wasn't as great as people made him out to be."[16]

Vince admitted privately to friends that one reason he attended daily Mass was because "I have such a terrible temper. It's the only way I can keep it under control." He wrestled with his temper but seldom won, partly because his anger overwhelmed him, but also because he knew it usually motivated his players. Anger was only one of the problems he wrestled with. At one time or other he was rude and inconsiderate to his family, his staff, his players, the media—almost everyone he met. Success and fame swelled his ego. He swore. He almost despaired of acquiring patience. Moreover, he doubted the ultimate worth of his profession. Did God really want him to devote his life to coaching a frenzied, violent, inconsequential game that even children played? He wondered publicly whether his was a profession of "madmen." Should he have been a lawyer, as his father desired? Should he have completed his seminary studies, taken his vows, and more directly served God's will?

Fortunately, Vince's deep faith in God helped him cope with his torment. If he faithfully followed the canons of the Church, received the sacraments, and prayed, he could find union with a loving, forgiving God. "I derive my strength from daily Mass and communion," he told Father Burke. In communion he found union with Christ—a union of love—and the act, performed daily, gave him the strength and confidence to carry out his responsibilities. Marie envied the nature of her husband's faith. She had been reared to fear God. "His was divine love of God," she said. "God was down there on the field with him." Susan agreed: "I believe he really understood God. He had an intimate, personal rapport with God. Of everybody on this earth [God] was his best friend."

His sins required constant reconciliation with God and the persons he offended, an impulse that largely explained his absence of malice and his awkward, private attempts to apologize. Guilt at being merely a football coach was the primary reason for the powerful speeches he delivered in the late 1960s that attempted to relate the values of football to broader, more important themes. In prayer and the sacraments he arrived at tenuous understanding. Man was born into a world of original sin, a world of imperfect men, a predicament he must endure on earth. If he tried to perfect himself and others, God would love and forgive and raise him on the last day to everlasting life.[17]

Many of the values Vince cherished also grew out of the nature of sports and the values society attributed to them. Sports had grown in popularity in the twentieth century partly because Americans had more leisure and affluence and because they recognized the benefits of exercise. Sports were also wrapped in the mantle of virtuousness. They were the province of youth; nothing characterized young people more than the regular, enthusiastic involvement in vigorous sports. Millions of people believed with Vince that sports helped youths develop their character, improve their citizenship, and ward off the evil influences of gambling, drinking, and sex. In communities throughout the nation, young athletes were revered as "paragons of virtue and symbols of the American way." They were—or were supposed to be—clean-living, dutiful, loyal, upright, and at the same time strong, virile, and competitive.

Sports provided Vince occasion to be perfected and to perfect his players, an opportunity few occupations afforded. Sports offered clarity, self-completion, autonomy, and potency often denied others in the dreary, routinized work world. There was an absence of fakery and fraudulence. One either succeeds or he doesn't. One is alone and naked but for his ability, which counts for everything.[18]

Vince accepted the values of sports as gospel. Furthermore, his personality and approach, conditioned by over two decades of experience and exposure to great coaches, closely fit the profile sports authorities have drawn of the coach. The coach was a special kind of athlete. "If you take the salient characteristics of the athlete," said one authority, "and cube them, forcing them all into the mold of one hypertensive man, you have the foundation for a coach." The coach tends to be authoritarian because of the stress on winning and the threat of firing upon losing. He is usually aggressive, self-assertive, persistent, organized, and displays a high degree of psychological endurance. With his strength, toughness, and demand for firm discipline, the coach assumes many of the roles of the father, acting like the overlord of a large family. There is considerable pressure because he is expected to control events that are ultimately uncontrollable; display confidence and certainty while often operating on hunches and probabilities; and ensure success when the outcome depends partly on luck, officiating, human error, injuries, exhaustion, and personal problems. He is a teacher, and as he teaches, he understands better, bolstering his ego and increasing his self-confidence.

Professional football, more than other sports, is dominated by the coach. The football coach must be an inspirational leader. He must spend thousands of hours dissecting films and scouting reports to find weaknesses in the opponent, unlike baseball, which has so many games that detailed, time-consuming analysis of each opponent is impossible. Coaches of basketball and baseball have fewer players to direct, far more limited strategies available, and nothing like the football coach's problem of mentally preparing and psyching the players.[19]

Football's similarity to war is unmistakable, and the military's imprint on Vince was noticeable. The game's main objective is to conquer territory. Each game is a battle requiring its own plan; each season, a campaign. There are feints, envelopments, and strategic designs. Defenders guard the goal with the same determination as soldiers guarding their homeland. Like the branches of the armed services, football has its different positions, each with its unique function but coordinated with the rest of the team.

Because Vince never served in the armed forces, the military influence on him was less direct and pervasive than on his mentor, Colonel Earl Blaik. Still, Vince used some military maxims to inspire the players and, in his coaching office, played records of General Douglas MacArthur's speeches. Bart Starr and Phil Bengtson, two persons largely responsible for the Packers' success, were both products of military influence. Starr, the son of a career soldier, ran the team with military precision. Bengtson, a former naval officer whose college coach viewed football as a war, thought the military metaphor the most apt one for Vince's Packers. Vince was the general; the assistants were his lieutenants; the players were his soldiers.[20]

His football players were professionals, Vince believed, and required the same standards as any profession. Football was like medicine, the law, the military, and the clergy. Consequently, he made certain that meals, motels, and travel met professional standards—not like the 1950s, when, for games out of town, the Packers sometimes ate box lunches and stayed at sleazy hotels. "Everything was first-class, professional, and organized right down to the smallest detail," marveled one player. He also insisted that his players look and act like professionals. His dress code was one of the first established in professional football; he even required the media who traveled with the team to abide by it. Except for games in sweltering heat, Vince always wore a jacket, shirt, and tie. "A game day is a business day," he explained. He wanted the Packers to have "class," like baseball's New York Yankees in their heyday. "We're going to be the Yankees of football!" he often told the team. Players should take pride in being a Green Bay Packer, an attitude players appreciated in proportion to the team's growing success and fame. The manner in which he said the simple phrase "You were chosen to be a Green Bay Packer" sounded dramatic. He convinced players that being a Packer was something unique and wonderful.

Players should approach their assignments in a mature, professional manner. "You are men, not kids playing ball," he told them. "Someday you'll go out there and earn your living some other way. Approach football that way today. Make it *work* at which you become professional, not a game that you play." However, he discouraged outside business interests that interfered with the player's current responsibilities. He correctly felt that his own outside interests did not interfere with his coaching, but he increasingly worried that his players—with their endorsements, restaurants, and other business activities—allowed other interests to distract them from their primary professional duties.

When Vince demeaned and embarrassed players during his emotional tirades, he was treating them less than professionally. Although his methods didn't always live up to his own standards, he demanded that others treat football players as professionals. At a labor negotiation meeting, he exploded when a speaker demeaned the players. Leaping to his feet, he said, "Good God, man! Don't you realize that these men are artists? You aren't dealing with a bunch of hodcarriers or truck drivers. These men are artists, skilled artists, damnit!"[21]

Many athletes are unformed and undirected, no longer boys but not yet men. Vince understood because he himself had been that way at Fordham. Some players were in football because they had neither the intelligence, the control, nor experience to do anything else effectively. They were impulsive, easily impressed and swayed, tempted by praise, lured by the prospects of glory, and not much given to reflection. The Packers' success had made them sports page heroes, but there was still an "adolescent impulsiveness" in many of them. "They're like children," Vince said in a moment of disgust. Consequently, he sought to instill in them the values he cherished, both to improve their performance and their life after football.

The values Vince preached critics dismissed as platitudes and clichés. Although correct in their assessment, the critics were wrong in their dismissal. Despite his limited insight and sometimes unimaginative expression, the virtues themselves were important. "In coaching you speak in clichés," he insisted. "But I mean every one of them." Indeed, the remarkable feature of Vince's leadership and teaching was the passion, persistence, and skill with which he *successfully* transmitted virtues necessary to succeed in football. His players knew that he deeply believed every platitude, that he tried to embody every cliché.[22]

The players' improvement, Vince insisted, depended on their acceptance of his authority and his discipline. There was only one kind of discipline—perfect discipline—not only in football, but also in everything. Without "perfect discipline," he said, football "is nothing, absolutely nothing." The funny stories and jokes told about Vince reflected his remarkable success, his staunch religiosity, but especially his imperious, authoritarian manner. He was playing cards with friends after a golf match, said one tale; he was losing and the dealer at his table, who was winning, was slow to deal and started to tell a story. "Deal!" Vince yelled, and the dealers at four tables around him immediately began handing out cards. "God, your feet are cold," Marie says to Vince as he climbs into bed. The coach answers, "Dear, in the privacy of the house, you may call me Vince." When a stranger asks directions to Vince's home, the guide says, "Just go up to the end of this street and St. Peter will direct you from there."

Tackle Henry Jordan, who told a host of funny Lombardi stories, remembered only two players who ever called Vince by his first name. "One went to Pittsburgh and the other is in Cleveland, I think," Jordan explained. Even God jumped when Vince commanded. Jordan described a rainy morning at the stadium: "We had a longer meeting than usual, figuring we'd never get out to the field to practice, and Lombardi was pretty unhappy, walking around, wringing his hands, looking disgusted with the weather. Finally he cut out pacing and looked up at the heavens and shouted, 'Stop raining! Stop raining!' And there was a huge clap of thunder and flash of lightning and the rain stopped." Added Jordan: "I'm a hard-shelled Methodist, but I've been eating fish every Friday since then."[23]

Vince believed in natural law and natural order, in God-given authority that presupposed obedience. For him there were two kinds of people, leaders and followers, which in football meant coaches and players. The world would be a better place if people simply obeyed their leaders. If they did, the chaos caused by freedom would disappear and life would be orderly and understandable. People could then concentrate on doing what was right, bringing progress for both the individual and the organization. Respect for authority was not a one-way street for him. He also gave it— to the Catholic Church, his father, Earl Blaik, and Jim Lee Howell. "He gave it to me," said NFL Commissioner Pete Rozelle.

In 1959, Vince's approach meshed perfectly with the needs of the Packers, whose directors had despaired of control in a democratic manner. Under Vince the players had no power and were allowed no major decisions. Vince was the final authority. "He was the absolute dictator," said one player. "He rules," said Ron Kramer. "You do it his way or you don't do it at all." Vince was unique in the willfulness that infused his leadership. The difference between the group and the leader, he argued, was not so much lack of strength or knowledge, but lack of will.[24]

Part of his philosophy he instilled through maxims he borrowed from other coaches and rephrased. Many were similar to those used by Jim Crowley, Frank Leahy, and Colonel Earl Blaik. Vince pasted them in the locker room and explained them at meetings with players. They were practical and important:

"Confidence is contagious. So is lack of confidence."

"You need fear nothing as long as you are aggressive and keep going."

"Anything is ours providing we are willing to pay the price."

"You will find the extent of a man's determination on the goal line."

"Fatigue makes cowards of us all."

"The harder you work, the harder it is to surrender."

"Physical toughness will make the opponent weaken and mental toughness will make him crack."

Football was a "spartan" game. "I like that word," he often said. It took spartanlike qualities to play. "It takes sacrifice to play it, and it takes self-denial, which are two of the great spartan qualities." Courage, that "indefinable" quality that made a person "put out that extra something," was also crucial. For Vince courage meant the willingness to suffer, to sacrifice, to work harder than the next person. "It means you got home a little later, a little wearier, a little hungrier, and with a few more aches and pains." He especially admired courage that transcended the ordinary, the person who overcame "tremendous handicaps" to excel.[25]

Vince looked for evidence in his players of dedication, spirit, and desire—terms he used interchangeably. With teams so evenly matched, intensity of execution often made the crucial difference. Pain, weariness, and exhaustion discouraged everyone. Players might be afraid of failure, or be unsure of themselves, or be driven by strong, uncontrolled impulses. Individual and team morale were crucial. A reversal of fortunes, weariness of a key player, self-doubt, an opponent's brilliant play could take the edge off one's certainty and bring defeat. Dedication could compensate because the dedicated player performed despite exhaustion and setbacks.

A talented athlete had a special obligation to dedicate himself, Vince believed. Talent was not only a blessing, it was also a burden. Vince pointed to Frank Gifford as an illustration of a talented athlete who cultivated gifts "that a lesser man, and a lesser athlete, might have taken for granted." Gifford accepted the "moral responsibility" to perfect his talent. "He had to be better," Vince said, "and all of us who were a part of those Giant teams with him were better for that resolution, that determination."[26]

Closely allied to dedication, spirit, and desire was "mental toughness," a virtue whose definition Vince wrestled with awkwardly. "I have difficulty explaining it," but it was the "most important phase of the game to me." Sometimes he described it as a combination of the other virtues he cherished—spartanism, humility, disciplined will. Usually he meant a singleness of purpose that allowed his players to overcome mistakes and problems. "Once you have agreed upon the price that you and your family must pay for success, it enables you to forget that price. It enables you to ignore the minor hurts, the opponent's pressure, and the temporary failures."[27]

Vince believed passionately in the virtues of competition. Few aspects of life are free from competitive struggle. Business, politics, and law are all intensely competitive. Competition often leads to a host of destructive consequences, including the moral evils of deceit, lying, and hypocrisy. Though serious problems can follow in its wake, competition also provides a mechanism for assigning position, place, power, productive ability, and physical excellence. Without the powerful stimulant of competition, potentialities fail to develop. Athletics often provides the purest form of competitive struggle.

Excellence that emerged from intense competition awed Vince. At a New York restaurant sports announcer Howard Cosell introduced him to Bill Toomey, and Vince bubbled with praise for the 1968 Olympic decathlon champion. "Young man," he told Toomey, "I watched you in Mexico City. You have no idea how thrilled I was. You are the world's greatest athlete. . . . Every one of us is proud of you." When Cosell joked that Toomey couldn't be that great because he wasn't a football player, Vince responded, "Football player? What the hell's a football player? This man did it in ten events. In two days. A football player plays once a week!"

Sports were relatively unaffected by the general erosion of standards in the culture at large, and Vince was vigilant about standards. He wanted no erosion of standards. In his early years in Green Bay, his speeches often indicted high schools and colleges for emphasizing physical fitness over competition. Physical fitness was fine, but minimizing competitive sports was tragic. "Competition builds stamina in an individual, character, aggressiveness," he said in 1962, and "there is no more competitive game than football." His alma mater, Fordham, had been shortsighted when it dropped football in 1954, he said, because "A university without football is in danger of deteriorating into a medieval study hall."[28]

Michael O'Brien

With Vince competition never stopped, even off the football field. Many of his friends judged him the most intensely competitive person they had ever met. He acted childish at times, but he recovered his senses quickly, and his friends understood and teased him. One evening, as he and his party prepared to dine out, he and Tony Canadeo argued amiably about the fastest route to a restaurant in Appleton, thirty miles southwest of Green Bay. To prove their point, each decided to take his favorite route. Vince drove ninety miles an hour to win the competition. He would risk death on the highway before he would allow Canadeo to win. "I'm glad we beat them," said a passenger in Vince's car with a sigh, "because if we didn't, it was going to be a dreadful dinner!"

Golf was fun and diverting for him, but also serious competition. He was happy and jovial when he played well, sullen and moody when he did poorly. He enjoyed competitive matches, especially with fellow coach Paul Brown. "They always played *against* each other," said an observer. Shortly after he moved to Green Bay, Vince played golf with new friends at Oneida Golf and Riding Club. On the first hole he missed a short putt; on the second, he missed another. When he also failed to sink a short putt on the third hole, he hurled his putter across the creek to the fourth tee and for the next two holes was sullen. On the sixth he announced to his playing partners, "Boys, I want to apologize for acting like a damn fool."[29]

On July 24, 1961, at Oneida, Vince addressed one hundred golfers at the annual banquet of the Wisconsin Amateur Golf Association. Instead of viewing golf as an opportunity to relax, to enjoy companionship, to bask in beautiful surroundings, and to put aside for a while the demands of competition and the goal of winning, Vince chose to focus on the sport's competitive virtues. He even drew an awkward parallel between golf and football. Golf was "more than a game," he told the amateurs; "I liken it to football because it makes many of the same demands football does. For example, it takes courage—it takes a lot of guts to play golf. And it takes a lot of stamina. It also takes coordinated efficiency— and you must be dedicated to win." Golf also taught leadership qualities. It taught the "strong to know their weaknesses and, most important, it teaches you to master yourself before you can master others." He added that the game forced the golfer to have a sense of humor, to be serious but not to the point that "you take yourself seriously." It was a great game, he concluded: "If you have sons and if you want them to grow up to be men, have them play the game of golf."[30]

Vince had a keen awareness of the way success was measured in his profession. Grantland Rice's famous dictum that people remember "how

196

you played the game" was naïve when applied to modern professional sports. The goal was to win. Inequality of result is the essence of sports. The heroes are those who achieved, conquered, excelled—the baseball player who hit sixty-one home runs, the sprinter who recorded 9.1 seconds in the hundred-yard dash, the long-distance runner who first broke the four-minute mile, and the NFL football team that won three consecutive championships. Winning meant showing superiority in the outcome of the game and conferred on winners, like Vince and his Packers, the aura of superiority in general, as indicated by the swarm of autograph-seekers and the crush of media attention. Winners won more than a game. They won money, honor, esteem, glory. Winning was a uniquely modern form of immortality.[31]

Vince had heard maxims on winning—and trying to win—from all the coaches he knew since 1932. Harry Kane, Jim Crowley, Frank Leahy, and Earl Blaik had all fervently preached winning. Vince expressed his own philosophy in slightly different ways. The expression he used many times with his players—though seldom in public—was "Winning is not the most important thing; it's the only thing" (or "Winning isn't everything; it's the only thing"). He may have picked up the maxim from Henry R. (Red) Sanders, head football coach at Vanderbilt and later UCLA, who used the same expression in 1940. Actor John Wayne also said it in the 1953 movie *Trouble Along the Way*. At other times Vince stressed the importance of a winning attitude. On April 8, 1962, in a speech in Milwaukee, he touted the importance of attitude in sports, saying "Winning isn't everything. Trying to win is."[32]

"Winning . . . is the only thing" was the version the media selected to capsulize Vince's hard-nosed, uncompromising approach to sports. Most critics of the phrase lashed out at Vince later, but by 1967 a few detractors were beginning to chastise him for unhinging the platitude file on good sportsmanship. The criticism stung, and occasionally Vince expressed regret at using the phrase. Sometimes he judged it appropriate for professional sports. "What am I supposed to do, lose?" he told Jim Lawlor, his college roommate; "they hired me out here to win games." To others he said his philosophy should apply only to professional sports, not to children or youths in high school and college sports. In 1968, when sportswriter Jerry Izenberg questioned him about the quote, he claimed he had been misunderstood. "I wish to hell I'd never said the damned thing. I meant the effort. . . . I meant having a goal. . . . I sure as hell didn't mean for people to crush human values and morality."[33]

Actually, Vince insisted on both a winning attitude *and* winning. The proper winning attitude was to struggle constantly to improve, to work to the maximum of one's ability, and then to push beyond it toward perfection. The spirit, the will to win, and the will to excel were the important things that transcended the game itself. However, a winning attitude wasn't measurable. It was impossible to have a perfect attitude and yet have a consistently losing record (unless, of course, the competition was intrinsically unequal, as it had been for Fordham after World War II and for West Point after the cribbing scandal). Losing was evidence of poor leadership, organization, preparation, strategy, and attitude. Only a winning record could be measured. "There is only one yardstick in our business, and that is winning." Second place was meaningless, he said, but probably didn't believe. (Second was better than last.) You couldn't always be first, but you had to believe that you should have been. You were never beaten, he said, "time just runs out on you."

He not only tried to motivate his players to adopt a winning attitude, he also demanded that they have it. Otherwise they would get a "one-way ticket" out of Green Bay no matter who they were. "Winning is not a sometime thing here," he told them. "It is an all-the-time thing. You don't win once in a while, you don't do things right once in a while, you do them right all the time." After a poor performance in winning an exhibition game, he chastised them. "I'm going to tell you the facts, gentlemen, and the facts are these: At Green Bay, we have winners. We do not have losers. If you're a loser, mister, you're going to get your ass out of here and you're going to get your ass out of here right now. Gentlemen, we are paid to win. Gentlemen, we will win."[34]

In 1967 Vince caused a furor by describing for *Look* magazine the role of "hate" in professional football, a view that critics used—along with his maxim on "winning"—to indict his entire approach to sports. Vince described an incident at practice in which he became so enraged at offensive tackle Steve Wright that he beat on Wright's chest. Wright had the irritating habit of laughing when Vince corrected him. "I guess I was trying to get him to hate me enough to take it out on the opposition, because to play this game, you must have that fire in you, and there is nothing that stokes that fire like hate. I'm sorry, but that is the truth."

The remark unleashed criticism that partially undermined Vince's simultaneous effort to link the values of football to broader contemporary issues. He sounded like "Mussolini," charged one angry critic, who added sharply, "We would like to think football has not reached the point where a Lombardi scout is likely to turn in a report saying: 'This kid has size, strength, speed, and courage, but I don't think he'll ever be a great hater.' " There was enough hatred around without having Vince give courses in it, critics said. Young athletes were likely to take Vince's advice literally. To suggest that a player despise an opponent even for one game was "un-Christian, irrational, and out of order."

On occasion Vince did urge his players to hate opponents, particularly the Packers' traditional rivals the Detroit Lions and the Chicago Bears. (Significantly, although he desperately wanted to defeat the New York Giants, strong emotional ties prevented him from urging players to hate his old team.) The words "enthusiasm," "incentive," and "desire" did not convey the intensity of feeling Vince wanted to create in his players. Football required such hard hitting that only anger could make players more energetic. It was important to make one's hatred and rage conscious, to draw energy from it, to channel it, and to focus it on the opponent. Without the pent-up fury, without synthetic hatred, they wouldn't put enough muscle behind their natural aggressiveness.

Both Vince and his players understood that the hatred was synthetic and that it ended as soon as the game did. "Hatred" did not lead the Packers to engage in unsportsmanlike conduct. Vince was a close friend of most of the coaches he competed against, including George Halas of the "hated" Bears. During the off-season in Chicago Willie Davis lived near the great Bears' halfback Gale Sayers. They were friends and dined together. Only on the day of the Packer-Bear game did Davis take on Sayers with determination and hostility.

In 1968 Charles Maher of the *Los Angeles Times* quizzed Vince about his views on hate. How did Vince square hatred with his Christian convictions?

"Well, maybe 'hate' was a little strong," Vince replied. "I'm not sure I know exactly what the word means. What would you say?"

"A passionate dislike," Maher suggested.

"I'd say that's what I feel for an opponent when we go out to play them," agreed Vince.

"But you think the word 'hate' is a little strong," said Maher.

"No," Vince replied. "I won't renege on that word. I'll stand by it. When I say 'hate,' I don't mean I wish anybody any physical harm. Do I mean I want to run out on the field and hit a man, or kick him, or fall on top of him and pummel him? No. I wouldn't do that. But I do have to build up an emotion before a game to do a good job. If I go out there feeling just fine about everything and everybody, I'm not going to do the job I should do." Vince added that his hatred vanished as soon as the game ended.

Maher persisted. If it was permissible to hate even for a "little" while, would it not also be permissible to steal just a "little" bit? Vince dodged the question. "I have a lot of friends who are clerics," he said, "and not one of them told me I was wrong. I'm sure I'd have heard from them if I'd gone too far."

Maher concluded that Vince's hatred was probably just make-believe. After all, real hatred was not something one could turn on and off at will. "But," Maher concluded, "if Lombardi is not teaching real hatred, shouldn't he admit it?"[35]

A famous coach who publicly sanctions hate and urges that winning is the only thing could easily be branded a moral monster, as Vince was by a few critics who knew him only from a distance. His peers, though, knew his ethics were exceptional and that he played within the rules. Vince seldom spoke on sportsmanship in football because with him it was a personal, ethical habit he communicated mostly by example, like his religious faith. Vince's own violations of the rules were infrequent and minor and were caused by spontaneous anger. On one occasion, when the officiating upset him, he pursued the officials into their dressing room to express his rage. The action violated league rules, and the officials complained to the league office. Instead of fining him, NFL Commissioner Pete Rozelle wrote him a strong letter expressing disapproval. "I said I was shocked," recalled Rozelle, "because [it] came from a man who is so personally dedicated to authority and respect for order." The letter deeply hurt Vince. He became sheepish and apologetic. "It was far more effective than if I'd fined him five thousand dollars," said Rozelle.

In general, Vince honored football with his sportsmanship, which was one reason his peers admired him. When he lost, he seldom offered excuses or alibis. He complimented the opposition and often praised his own players. Usually when a coach excelled for long in sports there were insinuations that he engaged in unsportsmanlike practices. Losers drop hints or spread suspicions. But none of his peers questioned Vince's conduct. No one said that he had been dishonorable or unethical. Moreover, for him to win any other way than fairly would take all the pleasure out of his victory. "He was a highly ethical person," Rozelle concluded. "He followed the rules."[36]

Occasionally, Vince thought he was aberrational to be so engrossed in a game. "At many a moment on many a day, I am convinced that pro football must be a game for madmen, and I must be one of them," he said in 1967. He was a religious man whose religion was based on love, yet each game required the constant conjuring of animosity. "As I talk about our opponents, I almost snarl against them." He sensed the irony of his passion for both perfection and competition. "We want to perfect ourselves so that we can win with less struggle and increasing ease, but the strange thing is that it's not the easy wins we ostensibly seek but rather the difficult struggles to which we really look forward."

Despite his passionate quest for victory, winning didn't always bring him peace of mind. At 3:15 A.M., twenty-four hours after the Packers slaughtered the Chicago Bears, 49–0, in 1962, he couldn't sleep, a problem that afflicted him after many games. "I have been asleep for three hours and, suddenly, I am awake," he mused in *Run to Daylight*. "I should be sleeping the satisfied sleep of the contented." He couldn't savor his victory because he thought it was tainted. The Bears had entered the game with injuries to key players; the slaughter embarrassed his friend George Halas; and the lopsided score might make his own players overconfident for their next encounter with the tough Detroit Lions. "Where is the elation?"

Yet his "ego" would not accept a loss. If he were "more perfectly adjusted," he could toss off defeat, "but my name is on this ball club. . . . It's a matter of my pride." His passion to win was insatiable. Success was like a "habit-forming drug," he said, that "in victory saps your elation and, in defeat, deepens your despair. Once you have sampled it you are hooked." His insight, however, never altered his philosophy or his drive. He was truly addicted.[37]

For many years Vince's hectic football schedule had absorbed him, not allowing time for reflection, and, consequently, his capacity to be abstract and philosophical mostly lay dormant. Before 1967 his speeches had focused on narrow themes, on the virtues he saw in football—spartanism, dedication, mental toughness, courage, stamina, coordinated efficiency—and on the need for schools to stress competitive athletics over physical fitness. Yet he wanted to reach more people and prove he was intelligent, sensitive, and caring, not just a football technician and a harsh taskmaster. Fortunately, his success in Green Bay led others to seek him out as an authority on issues broader than football. His first major opportunity arose after Super Bowl I, when the American Management Association invited him to speak on leadership at its convention in New York on February 8, 1967. He was overjoyed to be asked to speak before an illustrious group of business executives. "Maybe I'm not just an X's and O's guy," he told a friend. The invitation forced him to come face to face with himself, to rethink his philosophy, and to relate it to the problems of society. Moreover, the problems of society—especially the actions and values of young people—had recently captured his attention.[38]

The discord that errupted in the United States after 1965 had many manifestations, but three stand out. The interracial civil rights movement broke down, culminating in the "black power" movement and explosive social unrest, including race riots in many cities. The enormous escalation of American involvement in Vietnam led to massive antiwar activity. Finally, radical protest movements and the "counterculture" arose partly because of the divisive war and race issues and partly because of other divisions in society. Young people, especially college students, provided much of the energy behind the protests. The discord produced a generation gap, a kind of ideologicial struggle between the young and their elders.

Vince opposed racism but had neither the time nor the inclination to study closely the issues that sparked much of the protest—the Vietnam War, poverty, and continuing social and racial injustice. He neither understood nor sympathized with the critics of U.S. policy in Vietnam who complained of the deceptions used by President Lyndon Johnson to conduct the war, his abuse of power, the immorality of bombing civilians, the war's impact on America's relations with the rest of the world, and its effect on domestic reform. He agreed with conservatives who lashed the young militants as lawbreakers and self-indulgent hypocrites. His position was similar to that of House Republican leader Gerald Ford, who asked, "How long are we going to abdicate law and order—the backbone of our civilization—in favor of a soft social theory that the man who heaves a brick through your window or tosses a fire bomb into your car is simply the misunderstood and underprivileged product of a broken home?"

The new lifestyle of the young alarmed Vince. By 1967 hippiedom had become a major cultural force among youth. Hippies lived in "tribes" or "families," most visibly in New York and the Haight-Ashbury district of San Francisco, the twin capitals of the flower children. Their unkempt appearance—long hair, love beads, faded jeans, work shirts, and sandals—offended traditionalists like Vince. There were other disturbing trends. At times it appeared the entire youth culture was turning on to drugs. In 1966 LSD became a household word. Youths were "tripping," "freaking out," and "blowing their minds." Society was rejecting taboos about sex, and the sex-drenched American culture was contributing to the increase in homosexuality, lesbianism, pornography, and premarital and extramarital intercourse.[39]

The media focused on the militant extremists in the counterculture, people like Jerry Rubin and Abbie Hoffman, the self-styled leaders of the Yippies (Youth International Party). "When in doubt, BURN," Rubin advised in 1967. "Fire is the revolutionary's god. . . . Burn the flag. Burn churches. Burn. Burn. Burn." People should "farm in the morning, make music in the afternoon, and fuck wherever and whenever they want to.'' Consequently, it was easy for Vince to lump together the hippies, Yippies, and New Left radicals and perceive in them a united front against the values he cherished. They were godless and hedonistic. They broke the law and defied authority. Their revolt against work, competition, discipline—even self-discipline—seemed rampant. Logic everywhere was giving way to intuition, self-discipline to impulse. Later Vince apologized for being so slow to perceive the danger in the youth revolt. He had been "so wrapped up in the Green Bay Packers," he said, that he hadn't been attentive. "All of a sudden, there it [was] all around me. . . . I [should] have been more aware."[40]

Because of a winter blizzard, the train that took Vince from Philadelphia to New York for his AMA address arrived four and a half hours late. But more than a thousand corporate executives patiently waited. When he arrived, there was a hum of recognition that no corporate executive could hope to generate. They listened "almost spellbound" as he lectured them about the virtues of football, the need for better leadership in the world, and the desirable qualities of leadership. Above all, he spoke about character, which he saw as man's greatest need and greatest safeguard.[41]

He had been in football all his life, Vince explained, and didn't feel qualified to be part of anything else. But football was more than a great game.

> It is a symbol, I think, of what this country's best attributes are; namely, courage, stamina, and coordinated efficiency. It is a spartan game, and I mean by that, it requires spartanlike qualities in order to play it and I am speaking of the spartan qualities of sacrifice and self-denial rather than that other spartan quality of leaving the weak to die.

Great and colorful stars dotted pro football's history. They, along with thousands of high-school and college players, had brought "mental and physical relaxation" to millions. The game was "completely uninhibited by racial or social barriers." It was a team sport in which the individual's reward came from being a part of a successful whole. Like life, it taught that the price for any goal was work, sacrifice, perseverance, competitive drive, selflessness, and respect for authority.

Football also taught the proper attitude to adopt in life, Vince said.

> It's a game very much like life in that it demands that a man's personal commitment must be to an excellence and victory,

and yet complete victory can never be completely won. Yet it must be pursued, it must be wooed with all of one's might. Each week there is a new encounter, each year there is a new challenge. But all of the display, all of the noise, all of the glamor, and all of the color and excitement, they exist only in the memory. But the spirit, the will to excel, the will to win, they endure, they last forever. These are the qualities, I think, that are larger and more important than any of the events that occasion them. . . . The quality of life is a full measure of a man's personal commitment, whether it be to football, whether it be to business, or whether it be to the government.

The greatest problem plaguing contemporary American life was the growing rebellion, especially by the youth culture, against time-honored values.

In a large sense, we are engaged right now in a struggle that is far more fiercely contested than any game. It is a struggle for the hearts, for the minds, and for the souls of all of us, and it is a game in which there are no spectators, only players, and it is a struggle which will test all of our courage, all of our stamina, and all of our strength and all of our leadership ability, and only if we are physically, mentally, and spiritually ready will we win this one. We live in an age for heroes. No other time in our history has ever offered the prizes and the perils at one and the same time so great. Man must decide whether he wants to provide a full life for humanity or destroy himself with his own problems. The test of this century will be whether man mistakes the growth of wealth and power with the growth of spirit and character or like some infant playing with dangerous toys, he destroys the very house he may have inherited. . . . I think we fail miserably in our obligation unless we preserve what has always been an American zeal and that is to be first in regardless what we do and to win and to win and to win.

American freedom could be lost or succumb to "aggressive secularism and communism" unless the values underlying freedom were understood and embraced.

But before they can be understood and embraced, the values of duty and respect for authority must be embraced and we must also develop a mental discipline. I am sure you are disturbed like I am of what seems to be a complete breakdown of law and order and the moral code which is almost beyond belief. Unhappily, our youth, the most gifted segment of our population, the heirs to scientific advances and freedom's breath, the beneficiaries of their elders' sacrifices and achievements seem, in too-large numbers, to have disregard for the law's authority, for its meaning, for its indispensability to their enjoyment of the fullness of life and have conjoined with certain of their elders, who should know better, to seek a development of a new right, the right to violate the law with impunity. The prevailing sentiment seems to be if you don't like the rule, break it.

Freedom had been idealized against order. "Everything has been done to strengthen the rights of the individual and at the same time, weaken the rights of the church, weaken the rights of the state, and weaken the rights of all authority." Perhaps the battle had been won too well, he thought. "Maybe we have too much freedom."

Maybe we have so long ridiculed authority in the family and discipline in education and decency in conduct and law in the state that the freedom that we fought so hard for has brought us close to chaos and it could be that our leaders no longer understand the relationship between themselves and the people they lead. That is, while most shout to be independent, at the same time wish to be dependent and while most shout to assert themselves, at the same time wish to be told what to do.

Better leadership was necessary, but the conventional leadership was inadequate. Leadership was not just a position of command, not just the ability to direct people. It involved more than capacity and ability.

The leader must be willing to use it. His leadership is then based on truth and character. There must be truth in the purpose and willpower in the character. Leadership rests not only upon ability, but upon commitment and upon loyalty and upon pride and upon followers.

[The country needed not just engineers and scientists] but people who will keep their heads in emergencies, in other words, leaders who will meet the intricate problems with wisdom and courage. A leader is composed of not just one quality, but a blend of many and each must develop their own particular combination to their own personality. Leaders are made, they are not born. They are made by hard effort, which is the price which all of us must pay to achieve any goal that is worthwhile. In spite of what many think, none of us are really born equal, but rather unequal, and the talented have no more responsibility for their birthright than the underprivileged for theirs. The measure of each is what each does in a specific situation.

Then a passionate plea to recognize excellence and quality leadership.

It is increasingly difficult to be tolerant of a society which seems to have sympathy only for the misfits, only for the maladjusted, only for the criminal, only for the loser. Have sympathy for them, yes; help them, yes; but I think it is also time for us to cheer for, to stand up for, to stand behind the doer, the achiever, the one who recognizes a problem and does something about it, the one who looks for something to do for his country; the winner, the leader.

The leader must cultivate numerous virtues and skills. He must be "honest with himself" and must identify with and back up the group "even at the risk of displeasing his superiors." He must show approval. He must believe in "teamwork through participation." His contact with the group must be "close," "informal," and "sensitive." In return, the leader will gain the group's confidence and "possibly" its affection. Yet he ceases to be a leader if he identifies too closely with the group. "He must walk, as it were, a tightrope between the consent he must win and the control that he must exert."

The most important leadership quality, though, was mental toughness.

Mental toughness is many things. It is humility because I think a leader must remember that simplicity is the sign of true greatness and meekness is the sign of true strength. Mental toughness is spartanism with its qualities of sacrifice and self-denial, dedication, fearlessness, and love. The love I'm speaking of is not necessarily liking or the love that a man may have for his wife. The love I'm speaking of is loyalty, which is the greatest of loves. Teamwork, the love that one man has for another and that he respects the dignity of another. The love I am speaking of is charity. I am not speaking of detraction. You show me a man who belittles another and I will show you a man who is not a leader; or one who is not charitable, who has no respect for the dignity of another, is not loyal, and I will show you a man who is not a leader. I am not advocating that love which forces everyone to love the white man because he is white or the black man because he is black or the poor because he is poor or your enemy because he is your enemy, but rather of a love that one man has for another human being, any human being who happens to be white or black, rich or poor, enemy or friend. Heart power is the strength of your company. Heart power is the strength of the Green Bay Packers. Heart power is the strength of America, and hate power is the weakness of the world.

Mental toughness is also the perfectly disciplined will. The strength of the group is in the will of the leader, and the will is the character in action. The great hope of society is the character in action. We are never going to create a good society, much less a great one, until individual excellence is once more respected and encouraged. If we will create something, we must be something.

The final criteria of leadership was success, he said, but only through moral, humane methods.

No leader, however great, can long continue unless he wins battles. The battle decides all. How does one achieve success in battle? I believe it is essential to understand that battles are won primarily in the hearts of men. Men respond to leadership in a most remarkable way, and once you have won his heart, he will follow you anywhere. Leadership is based on a spiritual quality, the power to inspire, the power to inspire others to follow. This spiritual quality may be for good or for evil. In many cases in the past, this quality has been devoted toward personal ends and was partly or wholly evil. Leadership which is evil, while it may temporarily succeed, always carries within itself the seeds of its own destruction.

Vince conceded that his prescription for leadership was "dogmatic" and only briefly addressed a complex subject. Although he didn't indicate his source, his closing remarks actually urged leaders to adopt the Scholastic philosophy taught him by the Jesuits of Fordham.

The obvious difference between the group and the man who leads them is not in lack of strength, not in lack of knowledge, but rather in lack of will. The character, rather than education, is man's greatest need and man's greatest safeguard because

> character is higher than intellect. While it is true the difference between men is in energy, in the strong will, in the settled purpose, and in the invincible determination, the new leadership is in sacrifice, it is in self-denial, it is in love and loyalty, it is in fearlessness, it is in humility, and it is in the perfectly disciplined will.
>
> This, gentlemen, is the distinction between great and little men.[42]

When he finished, the audience responded with a standing ovation. Several businessmen, said *The New York Times*, "looked as if they were ready to carry him out on their shoulders." A vice-president of a small manufacturing concern remarked, "I don't know how I will feel tomorrow, but right now I feel we can take on General Motors." Vince was proud of his speech and felt deeply about the issues he raised. When his friend Ockie Krueger kidded him about the "horseradish that you put out," Vince grew indignant. "I realized [then]," observed Krueger, "that everything he was saying came from way down deep inside."[43]

Vince had tried to put the best face on his approach to football, leadership, and character. He deemphasized violence, never mentioned hate, and ignored the questionable methods he sometimes used in his coaching. Still, it was not a great speech. Occasionally it was vague, especially when he talked of the forces within society working against effective leadership. He oversimplified problems, and, to win his argument, set up straw men—aggressive secularism, communism, misfits, plus youth and "certain of their elders." Why must "victory" be the goal of one who grows, understands, and "really lives"? His extreme belief in authority could be dangerous; the communist system he attacked depended on the "respect for authority" he cherished. If not false, it is at least debatable that America's "best attributes" are courage, stamina, and coordinated efficiency; that the "most important" trait of the leader is "mental toughness"; and that "loyalty" is the chief characteristic of love. Moreover, many contemporary problems were caused by Vince's excessive desire to be first, "to win and to win and to win." Watergate, for example, was just a few years in the future. Because a leader was "willing" to use leadership, it hardly followed that his "leadership is then based on truth and character." Cruel dictators are *willing* to use leadership.

Though not an excellent speech, it had outstanding features. Candid and straightforward, Vince projected himself as a man of pure motives who, having demanded the best from his players, naturally wanted the best for society. For a respected leader to trumpet noble, traditional virtues was beneficial. He inspired with his passionate plea for personal commitment, spirit, the will to excel, and the will to win. To say society "only" had sympathy for the misfits, the maladjusted, the criminal, and the loser was gross exaggeration, but the achiever, the winner, and the leader did deserve strong support and credit. It was a commanding speech. Vince commanded attention because of his success and fame; football, society's complex problems, the reexamination of leadership, all commanded attention. His solid, concise description of leadership was the best portion of his address, and, combined with his own demonstrated ability to lead, stimulated his audience to think about the qualities of leadership—their own and their potential in others.

Vince's address struck a cord among those worried about the decline in leadership and the growing domestic turmoil and who saw the youth culture as degenerate and representative of all things godless and un-American. For the next three years he gave almost the identical speech at scores of colleges, sports banquets, and business conventions. Reporters described a peculiar "aura" surrounding his speech. The audience was always quiet, attentive, seemingly enthralled. At Hofstra College in New York, he had six hundred persons "hanging on every word." At the end of his talk, people were drawn to the dais as though by a "magnetic force." "There is no more famous football man anywhere," Gene Ward of the *New York Daily News* stated, "and his ideas are applicable to all the people and all the problems of this trouble-wracked world. He cuts to the heart of things that twist humans and nations. He deals in proven basics. He does not appeal, he challenges, and in such a way that his challenge flays your guilt and prods your intellect." Others were less effusive about the substance of Vince's remarks but no less amazed at the masterful way he conveyed his inner power, sincerity, and dedication. "Something that sounded trite or mundane if said by anyone else, he made sound like it was chiseled in stone," said the *Press-Gazette*'s Lee Remmel. Another reporter judged his speech "esoteric" but pure Lombardi. "He feels deeply, shouts loudly, compliments extravagantly, and he speaks very, very forcefully."[44]

Although Vince did not change his speech for three years, in interviews he expressed increasing alarm at the actions and values of young people. By the time he revised his address in 1970, adding shrill patriotic messages and apocalyptic warnings, he had already asserted himself into political controversy, winning plaudits from the political right and criticism from the left.

X

The Community, the Franchise, and the General Manager

IN THE 1960s THE PACKERS CAME TO SYMBOLIZE AN IDEAL OF PERFECTION analogous to the old New York Yankees, and the Packers' resurgence was one of the most interesting stories in sports. For residents of Green Bay—and to some extent all of Wisconsin—winning football was delightful fun and a matter of community pride and distinction. "You can't realize," said a Green Bay fan, "how much joy there is in this team until you know the heartaches and despair of the past." Politicians printed the Packers' schedule on their campaign literature; children scrawled "We love you, Bart Starr" at the site of the new house the quarterback was building; and pastors often cut short their sermons when the Packers played at home. "The fact that [Lombardi] represented Green Bay and Wisconsin has allowed us to bask in the glory of his image," said the *Milwaukee Sentinel*. A man in Bangor, Maine, or Pierce, South Dakota may not have been able to identify Warren Knowles (the governor) or Henry Maier (Milwaukee's mayor), said the *Sentinel*, but "if he doesn't know of Vince Lombardi, take his pulse."

The team was also a major economic asset. For the city's salesmen it often meant a wide open door wherever they called anywhere in the country. In the 1967 season Packer-related spending added $6,520,000 to the economy of the city and surrounding Brown County. Milwaukee

County, where the Packers played five games, picked up more than $2 million from the team and the fans.[1]

Noting the Packers had sold 37,700 season tickets in 1961, ranking near the top among NFL teams, Vince described Green Bay as the "sports wonder of the world." By 1967 six thousand persons were on the waiting list for season tickets. City Stadium, renamed Lambeau Field after the team's founder died in 1965, was a green and yellow monument on the edge of the city, the only stadium at that time built just for a professional football team. The field was sunk below ground level, and fans perched on bench seats had a view unobstructed by girders. Unlike some stadiums, where seats were so remote the football game was only a rumor, there were no bad seats at Lambeau Field.[2]

The Packers were the sentimental favorite wherever they played, and Vince enjoyed the role. "It's the old David vs. Goliath theme," he said. "They all want us to beat the big towns." Still, Green Bay took plenty of ribbing. Visiting sportswriters amused their readers back home with wry hyperbole about the rustic ways of Green Bay's locals. "The team got into Green Bay late because the dogsleds were running behind schedule," was a well-worn rib tickler. Another went: "You can spot the mayor of Green Bay right off—he's the one wearing the clean overalls." In late September 1966, *Los Angeles Times* columnist Jim Murray infuriated Green Bay residents with his humorous description of life in Packerland:

"Green Bay is the kind of town where, when you see someone on the street not wearing a mackinaw, you know he's a stranger. If he's wearing a necktie, you call the cops."

"It has a real nice summer—but if you sleep late you will miss it. Indian summer begins July 8. And usually ends July 8, too."

"I won't say it is square, but how many places do you find the first seven places in the Hit Parade taken up by John Philip Sousa?"

The *Green Bay Press-Gazette* answered Murray by noting that, unlike residents in Los Angeles, Green Bayites didn't have to stake their life on expressways, enjoyed clear air, and hadn't had a flood in years. "It's fun when the Yokelsville Packers defeat Los Angeles while visitors from the citadel of culture are watching," added the Green Bay newspaper. "You can identify them easily. They are the ones without mackinaws, wearing neckties and long faces." Howard Blindauer, a Packer superfan, chortled, "They can laugh at us all they want from Monday to Saturday but never on Sunday."[3]

"This team is not a Green Bay football team," Vince often pointed out, "but a Wisconsin team." He promoted the Packers throughout the state, especially in Milwaukee, where season ticket sales were sluggish when he joined the Packers. In 1959 the Packers sold twenty-eight thousand season tickets for games in Green Bay but only seventy-five hundred for those in Milwaukee. Season tickets were the lifeblood of professional football. Bad weather for games in Milwaukee would dampen attendance and ruin the team's profit for the year. Vince tried to convince Milwaukee's industry to support the Packers as it did the Milwaukee Braves baseball team, and his vigorous promotion plus the Packers' success led to significant improvement in ticket sales. Even after ticket sales increased, he continued to make many appearances in Milwaukee and to court city officials, partly to ward off the danger that the rival American Football League would locate a franchise there.[4]

"There aren't any owners here," Vince said nonchalantly in an interview in 1968; "I'm the only man who makes the decisions." Many observers assumed Vince not only made all the decisions but also exercised dictatorial control, squashing opposition from the team's governing body, the seven-member executive committee headed by President Dominic Olejniczak. Vince "ran the show," said a member of the team's board of directors; the executive committee members were mere "figureheads." Vince usually did dominate, partly because of his authoritarian instincts but primarily because his coaching success, intelligence, and sound judgment won the admiration of committee members. They willingly agreed to most of his proposals. With few exceptions his relations with them were congenial, and active discussion took place at amicable business meetings.[5]

Richard Bourguignon and Tony Canadeo, Vince's closest contacts on the committee, were also his closest friends in Green Bay. (If they didn't watch out, Vince kidded them, he would take away their "yes" vote.) Vince also respected Jerry Atkinson and the committee's treasurer, Fred N. Trowbridge, Sr., a prominent Green Bay attorney. Because committee members were busy professionals and businessmen, they were content to allow Vince to assume responsibility for most matters. "We didn't always agree with him," said Bourguignon, "but most of the time what he had to say was pretty damn solid." Vince could be persuaded. "I didn't think of that," or "That's a better idea" were his typical comments during committee deliberations. Trowbridge, who judged Vince a "dictator" by "instinct," appreciated Vince's consultation with the committee on all important issues and said that because Vince was "right" so often, members usually agreed with him. In 1965, star running backs Jim Grabowski and Donny Anderson demanded huge contracts to sign with the Packers. Since the two were also being courted by the rival American Football League, the Packers were in a poor position to deny their requests. Vince thoroughly discussed the contracts with the committee. "It made him sick" to have to dish out the money, said Canadeo; "it made us all sick."[6]

Two issues caused conflict with the committee, and Vince lost both of them. Yet neither left lasting scars. Vince often complained that he was denied membership on the Packers' board of directors, and even asked the committee to create a new position for him as executive vice-president of the Packers' corporation. "It had been very humiliating for him to have to get up and leave when they were in executive session," Marie recalled. Trowbridge vigorously opposed any increase in Vince's power because it would impede on the executive committee's freedom. Probably because of Trowbridge's objection, Vince's status remained unchanged. Whether to expand the seating capacity at the stadium also caused disagreement. After two additions, capacity in 1963 stood at 42,200. When the committee planned to expand further, Vince was adamant in his opposition. He argued that the Packers had already sold out the stadium to season ticket-holders, and expensive additions could jeopardize financial security. Moreover, the courts might void the league's practice of blacking out television broadcasts of home games in a team's home territory, leading potential ticket-buyers to remain home to watch the games on television. Committee members disagreed. Sensing they had a better perspective on the growth of the market in Green Bay and on the groundswell of fan support for the Packers, they voted for further expansion, boosting capacity in 1966 to 50,860. The decision exasperated Vince. "What the hell am I anyway around here?" he said. "I am supposed to be a general manager, and I don't even have a vote!"[7]

Vince later apologized to some members for his outburst. But he was never good at hiding his feelings. Take his attitude toward Dominic Olejniczak. The principal reason Vince appeared to view the executive committee members as figureheads was the disrespect he displayed publicly toward his boss. He never deferred to the Packers' president. Olejniczak, the mayor of Green Bay from 1945 to 1955 and the operator of a successful real-estate business, brought stability to the Packers' management and influence in the community, but these virtues were not enough to earn Vince's respect. Some stories about their relationship were embellished, but many persons witnessed Vince's abrupt—sometimes rude—behavior toward Olejniczak. When Vince concentrated on his responsibilities as coach or general manager, he resented even the slightest interference. One story alleged that shortly after Vince was hired, Olejniczak asked to speak with him, but Vince bluntly told the president to schedule an appointment. At the appointed time, Olejniczak arrived and Vince asked, "What do you want?" "I just want to talk about the organization," said Olejniczak. "I don't have time just to talk," Vince responded. End of meeting. During the 1959 training camp, in front of some players, Vince bawled out Olejniczak for asking a question and interrupting his concentration during practice. On a Monday morning after a Packer victory, as Vince met with reporters in his office, Olejniczak knocked at the door, stuck his head into the room, and said, "Nice game, Coach." Vince replied curtly, "Look, I'm busy! Sometime later!" On another occasion, when Olejniczak tried to command Vince's attention in the corridor, Vince brushed by him and said, "Not now. I have a meeting." Vince didn't say it harshly, but he didn't stop walking, either. Though often disrespectful, Vince carried on routine business with his boss and never permitted his attitude to turn into open animosity.[8]

In his annual report to stockholders, Vince outlined the increasingly bright financial picture of the Packers, but he *always* found dark clouds on the horizon. "We have to run scared in this business," he once admitted. On May 2, 1962, after explaining a large increase in profits and the huge revenues expected from the new television contract negotiated by the NFL, Vince filled the rest of his report with foreboding: competition with the American Football League, a rising player payroll, and, most worrisome, only a two-year television contract. "No one knows what TV or the sponsors will do after that time," he told the stockholders. Vince's pessimism proved groundless. He was an excellent general manager, but the NFL's lucrative television contracts made it much easier for him to balance his books.[9]

In 1957 the U.S. Supreme Court ruled that professional football was subject to federal antitrust laws, and therefore NFL teams that combined to package television rights would be in restraint of trade. NFL Commissioner Bert Bell had argued that NFL teams should negotiate as a cartel for national broadcasting rights and share the proceeds equally among league members. Teams like the New York Giants, Chicago Bears, and Los Angeles Rams, with large television markets and lucrative contracts, would have to sacrifice and share revenues. With revenues of only $105,000 in 1960, the Packers ranked last among NFL teams in money generated by television. In contrast, the New York Giants earned $340,000. If the disparity continued, competition would deteriorate as the league became dominated by a few wealthy teams, and, unable to compete, clubs like Green Bay would disappear. League cities and their congressmen lobbied for remedial action to exempt professional football from the antitrust laws. Representative John W. Byrnes of Green Bay helped shepherd the Sports Broadcasting Act through Congress in 1961, and the new legislation, plus mounting enthusiasm for pro football, opened the door for skyrocketing television contracts. In 1962 new NFL Commissioner Pete Rozelle initiated the windfall of television revenues by negotiating an annual $4.5 million contract with CBS. The turning point, though, came two years later, when CBS signed a new contract paying $14 million annually, over three times the previous contract. From $105,000 in 1960, the Packers' share of broadcasting rights soared to $1,414,000 in 1967. "What Rozelle did with television receipts probably saved football at Green Bay," commented Vince. The sharing arrangement was the major reason the Packers' after-tax net income rose from only $37,300 in 1958 to $827,400 eight years later.[10]

"What do you do in the off-season?" people often asked Vince as the hairs began rising on the back of his neck. Vince pointed out that his job required "complete absorption" year-round. The growing work load and the constant pressure increasingly bothered him; yet he thrived on work. "I'm restless, worrisome, demanding, sometimes impatient, and hot-tempered," and for these traits he thought a full schedule the best antidote. For six months, from the beginning of training camp to the end of the season, he usually worked seven days a week, often twelve to fourteen hours a day. During the off-season he maintained normal hours but concentrated almost as intently on a variety of tasks—attendance at league meetings, negotiation of players' contracts, personnel evaluation, the college draft, promotion, maintenance of the stadium and offices, plus many speeches.[11]

Vince was an organized, conscientious general manager who ran the Packers like a business. He usually delegated authority and demanded excellent performance from his staff and coaches. He didn't want to be bothered by minor problems or unthinking questioners. "Don't ask a question if you can answer it yourself!" was an injunction he delivered to several staff members. If a less important member of the staff performed his job well, Vince left him alone. "I don't know anything about photography," Vince firmly told Al Treml, his new film director; "I don't want to know anything about photography. But *you* damn well better know photography!" Fortunately, Treml knew photography, and Vince left him alone.

If Vince didn't understand a subject, he asked questions and advice. His staff seldom challenged his decisions and directives, but his personality, administrative ability, and the team's success won their confidence. "He commanded respect through fear," said Tom Miller, "and people really feared him until they got to know him. Once you did get to know

215

him, the respect remained and the fear left." Actually, for most staff members the fear never left, but the respect did grow. His outbursts caused his staff to be wary of him and more alert in their work; yet they realized his anger was mostly bluster and that he didn't hold a grudge. He was too "kindhearted" to fire anyone, said Miller.[12]

Vince often hollered at his two main assistants: Miller, his director of public relations and then assistant general manager, and Chuck Lane, Miller's successor in public relations. Initially Miller balked at his promotion to his new position because he feared that Vince would yell at him more, embarrassing him in front of the staff. When Vince promised to restrain himself, Miller took the promotion. Yet Vince continued to holler at him—"many times." Some staff members found Vince easier to live with if they aggressively challenged his angry demands. Vince liked to test their character. When Lane occasionally yelled back, he earned his boss's respect and room to breathe. After Miller reacted angrily to abuse, Vince gave him a $1,000 bonus later the same day. Occasionally Vince apologized for his angry outburst at a staff member, but his private apology did not always satisfy. In front of the players Vince chastised John Proski, the head groundskeeper, for the poor condition of the field. When Vince later apologized, Proski rebuffed him. "I'll be goddamned if I'll accept your apology!" yelled Proski. "You chew me out publicly, and I'll be goddamned if I'll have your private apology!"[13]

Vince hired ten assistant coaches during his years in Green Bay. Phil Bengtson, Red Cochran, Norb Hecker, and Bill Austin were on his original staff, and Bengtson served all nine years, Cochran eight seasons, Hecker seven, and Austin six. Tom Fears worked four years as the end coach. Ray Wietecha and Dave Hanner joined the staff in 1965, Bob Schnelker and Jerry Burns in 1966, and Tom McCormick in 1967. The assistants learned quickly that Vince ran a tight ship. "I demand the best from all of you," he told them the first year; "I'm a perfectionist, and there's absolutely no excuse for anything other than that." After an exhausting, day-long planning session studying play charts and using an overhead projector, Vince redefined the staff's goals: "We may not know any more about football than most of the other coaches in the league, but . . . we can put everything we know together so it makes good basic sense and then drill-drill-drill it into *them*."[14]

He drove all the coaches, but they seldom complained because they knew he worked just as hard or harder. The important meetings for the coaches took place all day Monday, and Tuesday afternoon and evening. They analyzed films of Sunday's game and developed plans for the next one. Wally Cruice, the chief scout, met with the coaches on Monday evening and reported on the upcoming opponent. The staff refined their strategy on Wednesday and Thursday, but Thursday was an easier workday, the first evening the coaches could plan to spend at home. Vince was calm and analytical at staff meetings; although he enjoyed an occasional joke, he was serious, organized, and methodical. Cruice prepared carefully for his scouting presentation because he knew Vince wanted a thoughtful report, not banter. "You didn't talk about anything but football," recalled Cruice; "if you didn't have the facts, he didn't want you to waste his time."

Vince and Marie graciously welcomed each new assistant and helped him and his family settle into the community. They took Tom Fears's son into their home for four months until Fears could move his family to Green Bay. After the assistant was comfortably situated, though, Vince created a gap, and their relationship thereafter became strictly business. With the exception of social functions sponsored by the Packers, Vince seldom socialized with his assistants. He was older than all of his coaches (except Bengtson), and each had his own friends. Besides, Vince believed that leaders must remain aloof from subordinates.[15]

Because Vince had spent much of his coaching career analyzing films of the opposition's defense, he had a solid understanding of defensive football. However, he never mastered the technical aspects of coaching it—the steps, drops, and angles. He directed the team overall and ran the offense; responsibility for defense he delegated to Bengtson. A tall, lean, unemotional, amiable Scandinavian, Phil Bengtson had an exceptional grasp of the technical aspects of defensive football and won the respect of his players. He was Vince's chief lieutenant, and the two had an excellent working relationship. Vince discussed defensive problems with Bengtson, but not often, and then when Bengtson asked for his opinion. Bengtson also complemented his boss's temperament; after Vince screamed at a player, Bengtson quietly encouraged the victim.

Vince tried to treat his coaches with respect and not yell at them within listening distance of the players, but he didn't always succeed. His dominating personality, natural volatility, and abrupt manner intimidated the coaches and sometimes embarrassed them. Players overheard him dress them down, and most thought the assistants—except Bengtson— were second-class citizens. "They were almost like a player," said linebacker Nelson Toburen. "They were a notch or two above us in the social strata but way below Vince, and [he] put them down sometimes in front of the players."[16]

"I couldn't get up enough nerve to call him 'Vince' to his face," said Norb Hecker, who settled on "Coach." When Vince became "absolutely

Michael O'Brien

wild" with the players, Hecker added, the coaches "felt it, too." Like sportswriters, players, and the front-office staff, the assistants tried to gauge Vince's mood when he arrived in the morning. Tom Fears observed: "You'd come in the morning sometimes and he'd say, 'How are you, Tom? How's little Patrick?' He'd be jovial. It might be the next day [that] you'd walk by and say, 'Good morning, sir,' and he'd say, 'Hummph,' like a bear. . . . You never knew where you stood with the man." During the week of Christmas 1960, as the Packers prepared for the NFL championship game with the Philadelphia Eagles, Red Cochran asked, "Coach, is there any chance of getting off before nine o'clock tonight? Maybe eight-thirty? I could do a little Christmas shopping before the stores close." Vince exploded and, pounding the table, said, "Red, you wanna be Santa Claus, or you wanna be a football coach? There's no room for both!"

If an assistant offered a suggestion, Vince rejected it immediately (though he might adopt it the next day). "We're going to do it this way," was his normal response. To circumvent him, assistants learned to plant ideas that satisfied his ego. If the idea was perceptive and the assistant strong enough in his conviction, Vince might accept it. "That's what *you* said yesterday," suggested Hecker, using his favorite strategy. Fears succeeded with a similar approach. "Maybe he never said anything like that," recalled Fears, "but if you [said] it that way he'd listen to you."

Bill Austin admired Vince, but, finding his boss's authoritarian rule too stifling, he quit the Packers in 1964 to take an assistant's job with the Los Angeles Rams. "I had been around him [for ten years] as a player and a coach. He was a domineering man," said Austin. "After a while it gets to you. . . . I just thought I had to get away . . . to see how other people operated."[17]

For the most part the assistants enjoyed working for Vince and deeply respected him. "If I were lost in the middle of nowhere with only one dime for the pay telephone and needed a doctor, a lawyer, a priest, and a friend, I'd call Vince Lombardi," said Bengtson. The coaches basked in the glory of the team's success, learned football from a master, and gained stature in their profession. Vince paid a good salary, provided annual raises, granted bonuses each year, and all the coaches received a share of the championship money. "I would've worked for him for nothing," said Hecker. "You couldn't buy an education like I was getting." In many ways Vince was easy to work for. He clearly explained responsibilities, assigned tasks, and usually didn't interfere. "If you did your job," said Bob Schnelker, "he really let you alone." He required no useless busywork. Unlike some head coaches who tolerated aimless

218

discussion, Vince ran purposeful meetings and arrived at firm decisions.[18]

Vince's role as general manager also included responsibility for player personnel and development, trades, and the draft. He was a shrewd and effective negotiator of players' contracts. Although players often argued with him in negotiations and a few—Jim Taylor and Ray Nitschke—engaged in loud, angry shouting matches, most players thought Vince was honest and fair. Partly because the team was successful and loaded with veterans, in the late 1960s the average salary of the Packers was among the highest in the NFL.

Sometimes Vince sweet-talked the player—patting him on the head and shoulder and talking optimistically about the team's future—to melt his resistance. At other times he pointed out the player's limitations and weaknesses. In the first few years he overwhelmed them with facts and statistics about their inadequacies. Soon the players arrived equally prepared, yet were still overwhelmed by their crafty boss. After the 1960 season Bart Starr was determined to be more assertive in his negotiating session. "This is what I want," Starr told Vince, "and I won't settle for anything else." Vince straightened in his chair and said, "Holy cow, I've created a monster!" They both laughed. After Gary Knafelc had an excellent year, he prepared a list outlining his accomplishments—touchdowns, pass receptions, blocking awards—to support his argument for a large raise. At his meeting with Vince he tried to appear poised, though he was actually "scared to death." Vince briefly studied the list, then crinkled it up and threw it into the wastebasket. "Gary, do you realize that all you played [was] offense?" Vince said. "Do you realize that you're not on the . . . kickoff team, and you don't do anything on extra points? All you do is play offense." His calm demeanor shattered, Knafelc settled for a moderate raise.

"He would mention all the things that you didn't do well that season," observed the often-frustrated Willie Davis, "and he would remember them all." After Davis made All-Pro, he aggressively presented his case for a large raise. "Willie," Vince said after listening to his arguments, "you forgot just one thing." "What's that, Coach?" said Davis. "Willie," Vince responded, "I made you!" From then on Davis knew he could never win a salary dispute. "When the next [contract] times came around," said Davis, "I'd just go in, have some small talk, and sign whatever he gave me."[19]

In 1966 Jim Grabowski, the All-American fullback from Illinois, was so awed in Vince's presence that he ignored his agent's insistent advice during contract negotiations. Grabowski was drafted by the Packers and the AFL's Miami Dolphins, and although he wanted to play for Green

Bay, it was to his financial advantage to prolong negotiations with the Packers. On his first trip to meet Vince, his agent repeatedly warned him not to accept Vince's first offer. "We'll wait twenty-four hours," the agent advised. Vince sent a private airplane to fly Grabowski and his agent to Green Bay, and at the Packers' offices Vince led his prized draft choice through the corridor filled with championship trophies and photographs of glorious victories. As Grabowski's agent discussed his client's contract demands, Vince listened politely. When the agent finished, Vince stared directly at Grabowski and said, "We will offer you [$400,000] spread over three years. Son, what do you think?" To his agent's astonishment, Grabowski immediately answered, "Yes."[20]

Vince's record in trades and in player development was impressive; less so his judgment of talent in the college draft. Especially in his early years, Vince negotiated brilliant trades; he was so astute and successful that other teams grew wary of dealing with him. In 1959 he acquired Bill Quinlan and Lew Carpenter from the Cleveland Browns for Billy Howton; Henry Jordan from the Browns for a fourth-round draft choice; and Fuzzy Thurston from the Baltimore Colts for Marv Matuszak. In 1960 he received Willie Davis from the Browns for A. D. Williams. Davis became a perennial All-Pro; Williams remained in obscurity. In 1964 he traded center Jim Ringo, who was approaching retirement, and reserve fullback Earl Gros to the Philadelphia Eagles for linebacker Lee Roy Caffey and a first-round draft choice. Caffey became a steller performer on the Packers' excellent defense; the draft choice turned out to be prize running back Donny Anderson. In 1965 Vince acquired Don Chandler, an excellent place kicker, from the New York Giants for a draft choice, and end Carroll Dale from the Los Angeles Rams for Dan Currie. Currie had been an All-Pro linebacker, but he retired shortly after the trade, never having fully recovered from a knee injury he suffered while still with the Packers. Dale, who enjoyed only modest success with the Rams, became an ace receiver for the Packers. "Lombardi made the deal," said Oliver Kuechle after a few fans questioned one of Vince's trades. "This is the irrefutable support for it. Lombardi doesn't make bad deals." Even when the Packers lost players through the free-agent process, the team's compensation was substantial. In payment for end Ron Kramer, who played out his option to sign with the Detroit Lions in 1964, the Packers received Detroit's first-round draft choice, which Vince later used to select Grabowski. When Jim Taylor signed with the New Orleans Saints in 1966, in compensation the Packers received the Saints' first-round draft choice, an excellent bargain since Taylor was at the end of his career. (Vince made only a few mistakes in judging a player's ability. Most noteworthy was his failure to recognize the talent of halfback Tim Brown, who after being cut from the Packers set NFL rushing records for the Philadelphia Eagles. Considering Green Bay's talent-laden running backs, however, the Packers didn't need Brown and never missed him.)[21]

One player transaction became deeply shrouded in myth, partly because Vince found the myth useful in managing his players and his budget. The trade that sent popular, seven-time All-Pro Jim Ringo to the Philadelphia Eagles is a staple of the Lombardi legend. The story alleged that in 1964 Ringo sent his agent to meet with Vince to demand a better contract. "Excuse me for a moment," Vince said, leaving the room. Five minutes later he came back and addressed the agent. "I am afraid," Vince said, "you have come to the wrong city to discuss Mr. James Ringo's contract. Mr. James Ringo is now the property of the Philadelphia Eagles."

Part of the story was true. Ringo's agent did talk to Vince, and at that time Vince resented players' agents. (Beginning about 1966, accepting the inevitable, Vince changed his mind and dealt amicably with agents.) Otherwise the story was in error in two important ways. First, the trade had been arranged before Vince met with the agent. Second, for personal reasons—known only to Ringo and to Vince—Ringo had *asked* to be traded to Philadelphia so he could be closer to his Pennsylvania home. "Vince and I were the only ones who knew why I was traded," Ringo later said. "It was more personal than it was anything, and I still had a wonderful rapport with Vince afterward."

When the mostly mythical story circulated widely, rather than dispel it, Vince actually perpetuated it. The seemingly abrupt trade, combined with the aphoristic exchange, alerted his players that no one was indispensable, and it petrified any contract bandits. In a veiled reference to the Ringo incident, Vince said publicly that he detested excessive financial demands by players, particularly players who issued ultimatums. "They both get hustled out of my office in a hurry," he said; "and the one with the ultimatum, if he does not relent, gets traded." At the same time, the story allowed Ringo to keep private his reasons for wanting to return to Pennsylvania. "It filled both our needs at the time," recalled Ringo.

Five years after the trade, with the story making excellent press copy, an interviewer grilled Vince about the incident. Did the trade actually occur over a five-minute time span? "Hell, no," Vince admitted. "That's no way to general-manage a football team." Might not the Ringo trade have been signed and sealed before Ringo's agent tapped on the general manager's door? Vince grinned. "Yeah, something like that," he said.[22]

Vince succeeded in the timely way he found replacements for retired, aging, or ineffective players. When All-Pro Bill Forester retired, Lee Roy Caffey replaced him. When Dan Currie could no longer perform effectively, Dave Robinson stepped in. Defensive tackle Ron Kostelnik was brought along slowly until Dave Hanner retired. After the Packers traded Bill Quinlan, Lionel Aldridge filled in at defensive end. Carroll Dale replaced the aging Max McGee. Seldom was there a drop-off in performance.

In the draft of college players teams selected in the reverse order of their finish the previous season, putting the Packers at a disadvantage because each year their excellent record placed them in a low drafting position. To the amazement of many observers, however, by wise management and by trading fringe players, Vince accumulated extra draft choices, including some high selections. He used many of the extra picks to draft redshirts, those players who could be drafted in their junior year despite having another year of football eligibility. Unlike weaker teams who needed players to solve immediate deficiencies, the Packers, perennially strong and loaded with veteran players, could select the redshirts for future delivery. In 1965 Vince made his most spectacular redshirt selection when in the first round he picked highly prized junior halfback Donny Anderson, who joined the team the following year. Partly because of the Packers' success in accumulating so many future selections, the league barred the drafting of redshirts until they completed their college football eligibility. Vince protested the change but in vain. "Obviously, they can't beat the Green Bay Packers on the football field," charged a sportswriter, so "they're trying to do it in the meeting room."

After the Packers signed Tom Moore, their first-round selection in 1959, Vince said, "We'll not pay a rookie more money than the veteran is getting in that position. . . . Some of those kids are talking bonuses and nonrelease contracts. Can you imagine that?" The new AFL could easily imagine such arrangements and within six years forced the Packers and other NFL teams to engage in expensive bidding wars. With the advent in 1960 of the AFL, backed by aggressive multimillionaires like Lamar Hunt, the NFL had to compete for star players, escalating salaries to astronomical dimensions. In 1965 the AFL bagged its biggest prize when the New York Jets landed talented, charismatic quarterback Joe Namath. Namath's contract, $420,000 for three years, was far in excess of any contract granted a player in pro football. The competition forced

Vince to change his policy, and near the end of the 1965 season he granted three-year contracts to grab Grabowski for $400,000 and Anderson for $600,000.

Touting his recent draft choices, Vince said in January 1968 that "The history of the Packers is in the future, as great as it has been in the past." Actually, Vince and his staff were not always astute in choosing players in the draft. His selections, argued one critic, had been "among the poorest" in the NFL, and he "willed his successor a roster depleted by retirements." In 1965 Vince lost two top picks, Larry Elkins and Alphonse Dotson, to the AFL. In the 1967 draft the Packers made nine selections in the first five rounds, yet none of the players had any long-term impact on the team. None, in fact, was even on the team four years later. Some top picks failed to live up to Vince's lavish praise and high expectations and never succeeded in professional football, including Don Horn, Dennis Claridge, Lloyd Voss, and Bob Hyland. Vince passed over many players in the draft who later became stars, and of his many redshirt selections, only Anderson and center Bill Curry eventually became successful pro players.[23]

For the most part, though, Vince was an excellent general manager—intelligent, organized, efficient, honest, and fair. He more than compensated for his weakness in drafting collegians by his extraordinary ability to motivate the players he did coach.

XI

The Media

"THE PRESS CAN BE, AND OFTEN IS, A HORROR FOR ME," VINCE ADMITTED IN A 1967 article in *Look*. Despite the mostly favorable coverage he received in the media because of the Packers' success, he was often at crossed swords with reporters. The reporter's difficult job required that he interview Vince, cull the most fascinating quotes for interesting stories from unique angles, and meet deadlines. Moreover, Vince's success and growing charisma intrigued reporters, naturally leading them to want to penetrate his wall of reserve in order to understand him. But Vince resisted. He often didn't appreciate their desires or their problems; they interfered with his single-minded goal—his own complex problem—of consistently producing winning football teams.

Vince recognized the debt sports owed to the media and accepted part of the blame for the tension. "I am shy among strangers," he explained, and for him most of the reporters were strangers. He ran "scared" because the media thrived on controversy. Repetition of the same question, altered only slightly, turned a press conference into a game of wits. "My game is pro football," he said, "not Twenty Questions." Reporters also disturbed his concentration. In *Run to Daylight* he provided an irritating example. "I'm not at my best," he said, "when I'm walking off the practice field, honestly feeling that my whole future will depend upon my discovery of some way to rearrange our blocking on our 49 Sweep to take care of some particular beast of a linebacker, and a sportswriter comes up to me and says, 'Well, Coach, what do you think today?' "

He grew increasingly sensitive about the way the media portrayed him and was painfully conscious of his reputation for explosive outbursts. When the *Chicago Tribune* wanted to do a series on him in 1960, he told the writer he was "flattered" but added, "Please be kind to me." After Howard Cosell completed a television documentary in 1964, he told Cosell he hoped the program would be "honest." "Show me as I am. Don't try to make me look good as long as you don't try to make me look bad. Just show me as I am."[1]

Vince had difficulty adjusting to the new technology that covered sports and to the swelling army of reporters who courted his attention. One of the first coaches to be exposed to large press conferences, tape recorders, and the unique demands and influence of television, he tried to accommodate, but he didn't like the changes, and he accepted them grudgingly. He realized that without the money generated by television pro football wouldn't survive, considering "all these large bonuses we've been paying," but television sometimes interfered with coaching and disrupted traditions of the game. He didn't mind the time-outs called for commercials (if they weren't at critical moments), but the "crazy starting times" and other "gimmicks" bothered him. In 1963, when a CBS interviewer went directly to the bench to interview a player during a game, he strongly objected.

The microphone encumbered and all-encompassed. It was everywhere—around his neck, in the locker room, "everyplace you turn." Aggressive, inconsiderate newsmen irritated him. "You would stick that thing in a coffin," he told a reporter who thrust a microphone into a conversation he was having with a player. Television was overanalyzing the game and saturating the market. "Football is a simple game," he argued. "Television has most of the people believing it's something complicated." He warned in 1966 that "One of these days if you don't watch out, the public won't be buying it."[2]

Vince did adapt smoothly to the thirty-minute television show he cohosted on Channel 2 in Green Bay during the season. He was gracious and charming with Al Sampson, who filmed, produced, and finally cohosted the program. Vince prepared by viewing films of the previous game, but he took no notes. On the show he was calm and controlled, having reigned tightly his emotions. He carefully avoided criticizing his players and occasionally praised them. To take the burden off Bart Starr, he accepted responsibility for poor play selection. *"We* shouldn't have called that play," he would say. The show was popular because the Packers were popular and because Vince's intelligence and exceptional concentration allowed him to analyze insightfully the thirty plays used during the program. "He had complete command of every . . . play in every game," marveled Sampson.[3]

Paul Brown once remarked that the Packers were the only team in the NFL with their own newspaper. He could just as well have said that the *Green Bay Press-Gazette* was the only newspaper in the country with its own professional football team. The relationship between the two community institutions had been mutually beneficial since the Packers were founded. In 1919, George Calhoun, sports editor of the *Press-Gazette,* assisted Lambeau in gathering players to the newspaper's dingy editorial room to organize the first Packer team. Calhoun served as the team's first manager. In 1922, Andrew Turnbull, general manager of the *Press-Gazette,* led Green Bay's businessmen in forming the team's corporation, and he served as the first president. Long before Vince arrived, Turnbull had urged fans to be loyal to the team that Turnbull's newspaper consistently promoted. Although Turnbull was sometimes privately unhappy with the coaches and the team's progress, the newspaper refused to print "damaging rumors" about the team or stories that "poisoned" the attitude of fans. In 1950 the *Press-Gazette* was first to purchase the maximum amount ($5,000) of the Packers' newly issued nonprofit stock.

Turnbull died in 1960, but not before he had impressed his philosophy on the paper's chief sportswriter, Art Daley. "It's a privilege to have a team like the Packers in Green Bay," Turnbull advised Daley in 1947, "and we want to do everything in our power to keep them here. We must promote them and boost them. If we lose the Packers, we will never get them back. There will never be another team like the Packers." Daley accepted the advice, and during the Lombardi era he provided voluminous, informative, effervescent, and almost invariably, uncritical accounts of Vince and the team.[4]

Daley respected Vince and reveled in the team's success. After many losing seasons, Daley said, "I finally had something to look forward to." Yet Vince yelled at Daley more than any other reporter, partly because Daley was around the team more than anyone. Vince seemed to take Daley's and the *Press-Gazette*'s loyalty for granted. They offered no challenge and didn't need to be cultivated. Daley doubled as the publisher of the Packers' yearbook, and his work generally won Vince's praise, until 1965. When Curly Lambeau died suddenly on June 1, 1965, Daley quickly changed the yearbook's focus to concentrate on Lambeau. On the cover he placed a photograph of Vince and Lambeau together, a photo Vince had been reluctant to pose for. When Vince learned in late July that the yearbook featured Lambeau, he was livid. "What do you mean putting me on the cover with him?" he told Daley. It was the worst yearbook he had seen, he added before he slammed down the phone. Vince's petulance arose from his jealousy and dislike of the legendary Packer hero. Vince had offered a lame excuse for missing Lambeau's funeral, and his absence was conspicuous. "He just didn't want to share the spotlight with anybody," said Daley, "much less Lambeau, who really was kind of a saint in Green Bay." Vince had a "Napoleonic complex," Daley concluded. There were rumors, though, that Lambeau's private life was anything but saintly. His divorces and reputedly dissolute lifestyle undoubtedly offended Vince's strict moral standards. For three months Vince wouldn't speak to Daley, an unusually long time for Vince to remain resentful. Finally, at a practice, Vince extended his hand and said, "You're too nice a guy. I can't go on being mad at you."[5]

Milwaukee newspapers, more emotionally and physically distant from the team, showed greater independence than the *Press-Gazette,* but they were loyal and supportive as well. They were also wary of Vince. "Don't get the guy mad," Lloyd Larson, sports editor of the *Milwaukee Sentinel,* advised his reporters. Although Bud Lea wanted to report that Jim Taylor was playing out his option and might join another team, Larson discouraged him because the touchy subject would alienate Vince.[6]

Vince expected the Wisconsin media to support the team. He made it clear to Ray Scott, the television announcer for the Packers' games, that Scott was "part of the Packer family," implying he should be loyal. The *Press-Gazette*'s Len Wagner violated Vince's loyalty code by criticizing Starr for throwing numerous interceptions in consecutive games. When Vince spotted Wagner at a press conference after the next game, his face turned red and he yelled at Wagner, "And you were a hell of a help today!" When the *Milwaukee Journal* secured a doctor's full account of Jerry Kramer's intestinal ailment in 1964, Vince attacked Chuck Johnson. "What right do you have to print Kramer's physical condition without asking me? What kind of friend are you?"[7]

Eastern reporters disparaged their Milwaukee and Green Bay counterparts for shirking their professional responsibilities, cowering before Vince's wrath, and cheering mindlessly for the team. They were "puppets for the Packer coach" said one; a "captive" press said another. Vince "used" the Wisconsin press as his own public-relations forum, Jerry Izenberg charged. "He bitched about them and was horrible to

Michael O'Brien

them, but goddamn it, he used them for what he wanted in the paper,'' said Izenberg. The critics were partly correct, but they exaggerated and misunderstood the situation. Vince never demanded that something be written or deleted and often enjoyed amiable relations with Wisconsin reporters. Critics never fully appreciated the strong emotional and historic ties the Wisconsin press had to the team and underestimated the complexity of dealing closely with a coach as intelligent, moody, and authoritarian as Vince. Besides, Vince's brilliant coaching, overall integrity, and sportsmanship left little to criticize. Some Wisconsin writers resented their distant, condescending critics. "I'd like to take . . . any of those [eastern reporters] and put them in Green Bay at the time and see how they would respond," said Bud Lea.[8]

Vince cultivated the favor of prominent sports journalists from the New York area. Among his closest friends were Red Smith, the syndicated columnist of the *New York Herald Tribune;* Arthur Daley (not to be confused with the *Press-Gazette*'s Art Daley), Pulitzer Prize-winning writer and columnist for *The New York Times;* Tim Cohane, sports editor of *Look;* Howard Cosell, reporter and commentator for ABC radio and television; W. C. Heinz, novelist and free-lance writer; and Jerry Izenberg, sportswriter for the *Newark Star Ledger.* Vince had known most of them long before he came to Green Bay. They were friendly, familiar faces. New York reporters were the most professional, he believed, and gave him national exposure. He trusted them and could relax and joke with them. Unlike the Wisconsin press, he granted them special favors and invited them to his home for parties. When he spotted Arthur Daley at the 1961 NFL championship game in Green Bay, he said, "Oh, Arthur, come on in and have a cup of coffee" as other journalists cooled their heels and ground their teeth.[9]

Vince divided the sports journalists into "us" and "them," said Izenberg, exaggerating slightly. The New York area writers were "us"; the Wisconsin writers were "them." "I was one of the faces who had been around the Giants' locker room, so that made me an 'us,' " Izenberg said. "Vince would confide in us and speak to us, and he would treat [Wisconsin writers] like dogs." The edge that New York journalists had with Vince, though, disappeared if they interrupted his practice or caught him in a surly, hypertensive mood. Both Cosell and Izenberg had angry confrontations with him, but the incidents never spoiled their special relationship.[10]

Vince established careful guidelines for dealing with the press and expected everyone within the Packers' organization to follow them. No one should say anything that disrupted the team, revealed strategy, gave an edge to an opponent, or defamed professional football. Members of the press must not disturb the team's concentration at practice or meetings. Anyone who violated his guidelines risked his wrath. "These were his Green Bay Packers," observed Lea, "and brother, you had better be careful what you said about them. Like everyone else connected with the Packers, I learned to live by his rules."

When the players and the assistant coaches granted interviews or made speeches, they enjoyed considerable leeway; the informal restrictions Vince placed on them did not unreasonably curb their freedom. Yet he expected them to be humble and dignified, to speak respectfully of opponents and teammates, and never to discuss their ailments or the team's strategy. To remind them to be careful, he placed in the locker room a sign written in large letters:

What you see here
What you say here
What you hear here
Let it stay here
When you leave here

The press occasionally interviewed Marie, but Vince issued explicit instructions to her that she not talk indelicately about the team.

He closely monitored the team's public-relations department, checking press releases as if he were correcting an English paper. Chuck Lane quickly learned Vince's guidelines for a press release. The Packers didn't "whip" the Atlanta Falcons, 56–3, in 1966; they didn't "clobber" the Atlanta Falcons, 56–3; they simply "defeated" the Atlanta Falcons, 56–3. "He didn't want to give an opponent anything that might make them play harder next time," observed Lane.[11]

Perceptive reporters soon discovered the best times to interview Vince. After reviewing the films on Monday, he granted an audience to the press. On Saturday, with game preparations completed, he was relaxed and gracious and could be approached. "On Saturday the guy was absolutely human," said Lea. The off-season and extended road trips during the season were also good occasions to interview him. A reporter, shocked at Vince's graciousness during an interview, asked him why he seemed so happy. "This is March," Vince replied, smiling. "I don't have to start worrying until June. This is my free time." When he was ready and had the time to be interviewed, he provided all the fascinating details and insight the press needed for their stories.

Vince expected reporters to attend the "five-o'clock" club, the cocktail hour that met every afternoon during training camp and every practice day on extended road trips to the West Coast. Vince wanted to relax and didn't allow formal interviews, but he was usually friendly, and the more aggressive reporters talked with him off the record. "Everyone wanted to get to know this man a little better," said one reporter.[12]

On the Monday following a game, some reporters, particularly those in Milwaukee, tried to interview him by telephone. To have a chance for success, they had to call at a prearranged time; otherwise Vince was unavailable. As the Packers became more successful, Vince received an avalanche of calls, accounting partly for his impertinence. Generally the phone interview was the worst method of getting information. Lea found them "absolutely brutal." One of Lea's interviews lasted less than a minute. To the first question, Vince answered "Yes"; to the second, "No"; to the third, "I don't know." Then, as if to rub it in, he asked with a growl, "Is that all?"[13]

Except for his closest friends in the media, Vince never allowed reporters to penetrate his reserve, or to waste his time with idle chitchat and irresponsible nostalgia. He took few reporters into his confidence, and few felt comfortable in his presence. "You couldn't have fun with him," said Art Daley. They interviewed him when he wanted to be interviewed; he answered questions he wanted to answer. When he started to look at his fingernails or out the window, the reporter knew the interview had ended. Art Daley interviewed him in his office during the off-season and purposely allowed the conversation to drift, hoping to draw Vince out for a fascinating story. The strategy was working until Daley exposed his purpose. "If I BS enough," Daley joked, "I might come out of here with a pretty good story." A cloud immediately came over Vince's face. He stood up and left the room. Daley waited, thinking he had just stepped into the men's room, but Vince didn't return.[14]

When Vince's disposition was sunny and the writer was favored by his company, he was fun and entertaining; but when he was nervous or preoccupied, there was no end to his wrath. Sometimes his mood fluctuated within minutes. Cooper Rollow of the *Chicago Tribune* was favored company on a relaxed, enjoyable, window-shopping tour in Palo Alto, California. A short time later, as Vince huddled with his coaches, Rollow asked him a question, but Vince's mood had changed. "What the hell's the idea of bothering me?" he asked with a snarl. "You know that's a silly damned question and you know I'm busy." The next morning Rollow and Vince took another stroll around the block. During training camp Chuck Johnson, who covered Vince's Packers for nine years, kept asking Vince questions all day—at breakfast; before, during and after the morning workout; at lunch; and at the afternoon workout. Sometimes Vince responded only "Yes" or "No"; sometimes he answered in almost a full sentence, or complained, "That's a stupid question," or protested, "You know I can't answer a question like that." But when Johnson walked into the "five-o'clock" club, Vince would look up, beam, and shout, "Charlie . . . Charlie Johnson." Recalled Johnson: "Then I would know that it was the first time he had really seen me that day . . . because he was concentrating on his football team. Nothing else mattered then."[15]

Stories Vince felt harmed the reputation of professional football or demeaned him or his players deeply upset him. Defensive tackle Henry Jordan aroused his ire when Jordan said to a reporter, "Show me an All-Pro offensive tackle and I'll show you a holder" and then detailed illegal holding tricks. In a 1962 article sarcastically titled the " 'Genius' at Green Bay," Dick Schaap in *The Saturday Evening Post* poked fun at Jim Taylor's intellect. "Shy and unsophisticated at twenty-seven, Taylor talks in clichés [and] thinks in circles," the article alleged. It quoted an unidentified Packer coach as saying, "Jim Taylor makes more money using less brain power than anyone else in the world." The story embarrassed Vince because it defamed Taylor and reinforced the stereotype that all football players were ignorant. Consequently, he took the unusual step of publicly defending the quality of Taylor's mind. "Taylor is one of the most intelligent backs I have ever coached," Vince stated, including "some exceptionally intelligent ones at West Point." Taylor "never" missed his blocking assignments and quickly grasped instructions.

Vince took the same approach with undignified, unprofessional photographs. After a photographer took the traditional team picture in 1962, the players asked for one with them making silly faces and gestures. When the *Press-Gazette* published the frivolous photo, Vince complained to Art Daley that it hurt the "dignity" of his team. Vince was equally sensitive of his own dignity. At a coaches' meeting at a ranch near Dallas, a photographer for *Sports Illustrated* proposed a photo scene in which coaches would hold lassos and sit on horses while Vince stood in the middle, the victim they all hoped to rope. Vince obstinately resisted the plan, and a compromise had to be arranged. "I don't ever want to be involved in a stunt like that again," he complained later.[16]

Vince's most angry outbursts occurred at postgame press conferences, or when the media interfered with his practices or exposed a serious problem on the team. On October 23, 1966, following the Packers' defeat of the Atlanta Falcons in Milwaukee, Jim Taylor told Ken Hartnett of the

Michael O'Brien

Associated Press in Milwaukee that he was playing out his option with the Packers and would be a free agent after the season. Asked if the huge bonuses paid to Donny Anderson and Jim Grabowski had affected his salary demand, Taylor answered, "Sure it does; it has a bearing both on your pride and on your performance as an individual." Two days later, when questioned about Taylor's remarks, Vince said testily, "Contract talk [is] personal business between management and the player." Privately, he was livid at Taylor and Hartnett and barred the AP reporter from the Packers' office and dressing room. The following day, under heavy pressure from the league office, he rescinded his ban. Many reporters were disturbed about Hartnett's banishment. "Hartnett's only sin is that he was showing some initiative as a newsman when he broke the story," a critic charged. "All the guy was doing was his job. He has to eat, too."[17]

Vince didn't want reporters or cameras near the practice field because they interrupted his own and the team's concentration and because he didn't want a receiver, running a pass route, to bowl over a photographer. For no obvious reason, he would suddenly pivot away from the team and with the gait and sound effects of a "phobic rhinoceros" attack the press corps. "You! You! [Bob] Schulze! Off the field! Off the goddamn field!"

When Howard Cosell and his film crew arrived in Green Bay to shoot the ABC television special about Vince, they thought Vince had agreed to the arrangements. He had, but he forgot. When Cosell's crew started filming at practice, Vince exploded. "Get the hell out of here, will ya! Get out of here with your damn people. You're all the same, give you an inch, you want a mile. Get out of here!"

"This man's crazy," Cosell fumed as his crew began packing their equipment. "I won't take that from anybody!" Moments later Vince approached again to inquire why they were packing. "What the hell's the matter with you?" he asked. "What are you doing?" Cosell expressed his anger. "What did I do?" asked Vince. When Cosell reminded him, Vince replied, "You know better. I get so absorbed, I don't even know what I'm saying. Don't leave now. Anything you want is yours, you know that." Cosell concluded that Vince was honestly sorry; practice had so absorbed his concentration he hadn't realized he offended.[18]

The atmosphere at a postgame conference was electric as reporters gauged Vince's mood. Although invariably reserved, he often provided direct, lengthy, intelligent answers. With a disposition sometimes surprisingly mellow after a defeat, he praised the opponent and answered questions with calm humility. A loss seemed to deflate him and partially took care of motivating his team for a week. Often, though, the postgame

232

meeting with reporters caught him during a period of emotional instability. Because he had painstakenly prepared his team all week and coached the game so intensely, the questions of reporters immediately after the game jarred him back to reality too quickly, like a deep-sea diver getting the bends. Consequently, many reporters felt his lash after a game. He would turn them off with an icy stare, rudely turn his back and walk out of the room, or say thunderously, "That's a stupid question!" The "stupid" question Vince resented was often asked because the interviewer needed Vince to *say* what may have been obvious. Some reporters became wary of asking him questions. "It got to be a pain in the neck," said William Wallace of *The New York Times;* "I didn't want to be beaten up." When a timid reporter neglected to ask Vince a question, a colleague teased him that he "owed" his publisher one. "I owe my kids and my insurance company more than I owe my publisher," came the reply. "Lombardi [is] not as loud as Vesuvius, but he ain't any less predictable."[19]

Sometimes Vince awaited postgame questions with simmering wrath, quiet and controlled, but ominous like a ticking bomb about to explode. On those occasions he appeared to be thinking, "All right, gentlemen, shall we arrange all of the stupid questions in any priority, or shall we take them all together?" After a loss to the Minnesota Vikings, Vince was gracious in defeat until someone commented, "Vince, at least the Packers had that long eighty-six-yard touchdown pass, which is some kind of record for—" Vince stared at the man. Fellow reporters cringed as though their colleague had blown an airhorn in a library. "Oh, for heaven's sake," Vince replied, adding thinly, "That is lovely. We will cherish that record, I'm sure."[20]

On September 26, 1965, the Packers defeated the Baltimore Colts, 20–17, in a dramatic contest in Milwaukee. With less than three minutes remaining, quarterback Zeke Bratkowski, who had replaced the injured Starr in the third quarter, threw a thirty-seven-yard touchdown pass to provide the winning margin. Fullback Jim Taylor missed the entire game with an injury, and Tom Moore replaced him. Elijah Pitts took over at halfback when Hornung left in the second quarter with a recurring neck injury. After the game the press conference dragged until Jerry Izenberg asked a question about the injuries that provoked a memorable confrontation, one relished by many reporters.

"Did you ever think you could win a game without Starr, Hornung, and Taylor in the lineup?" asked Izenberg.

"Certainly," Vince replied, careful not to undervalue the competence of Bratkowski, Pitts, and Moore.

"You mean you never had any doubts?"

"I told you, certainly!" Vince said, getting red in the face.

"Look," Izenberg persisted, "I'm not trying to badger you. Let me ask you this a different way. Did you ever think you'd have to coach a game without them?"

"That's a very stupid question, mister!" said Vince angrily.

Now Izenberg was angry, too. "I don't think you coached such a brilliant game, mister," Izenberg shot back.

"How dare you say that. You don't know a goddamn thing about football!" Vince replied.

"Agreed," said Izenberg. "And how dare you tell me my question was stupid. You don't know a goddamn thing about journalism. You stick to football and I'll stick to journalism. If you don't want to answer, don't answer."

Vince looked at Izenberg and said, "What do you want to know?"

For the rest of the press conference Vince gave explanations, though sparingly.

Wisconsin reporters particularly enjoyed the sharp exchange. "Us local yokels," recalled Lea, "we reveled in this argument because all of a sudden an outsider stood up to Lombardi and got into a screaming match with him. . . . We were just loving every second of it." The following day Vince phoned Izenberg in New Jersey and, without identifying himself, said immediately, "I was a little out of line yesterday. I just want you to know that." "I thought I was, too," replied Izenberg. "Good," said Vince. "Good," said Izenberg. And Vince hung up.[21]

Despite the blistering Vince gave to almost all reporters at some time, most admired him and many liked him. They admired his dedication, intelligence, and success, and were awed by the loyalty and affection he engendered from his players. He appreciated favorable stories about him and complimented the reporter. At times he turned on the charm and answered questions as long as reporters desired, presenting insights and explanations because he felt good at the moment or took seriously his obligation as a spokesman for professional football. Chuck Johnson "heard him answer questions at great length and answer them better than anyone." More than other coaches, he challenged the mind of the reporter. "The writers tried to think before they asked the question," said Izenberg. "I liked him," said Lea, "because he was so intelligent . . . [about] everything. When he spoke, it was not like listening to a typical football coach. His command of the English language was just amazing. His speeches were outstanding."

When he chose to indulge, he had the knack for fascinating conversation with the reporters. Those who cringed under the threat or reality of his anger were pleasantly surprised by his charm during the off-season or his "good days" during the season. Before a game in Cleveland, Vince invited reporters to dinner. Bob Schulze of Channel 5 television in Green Bay, often a victim of Vince's verbal abuse, happened to be seated next to him and was surprised by the enjoyable conversation. "He was a man of stark contrasts," Schulze concluded.[22]

For Vince to get along with the press took concentration. Putting such exceptional effort into his work to stay ahead and successful left him little energy to deal patiently with reporters. Although his coaching impressed almost everyone, many reporters never came to tolerate or understand him. Unlike Vince's friends and players, they seldom witnessed his softer qualities—his spontaneous tears, humor, fairness, and tender concern. To them he was a gruff taskmaster who made their job unnecessarily difficult, and they fostered his reputation as a single-dimensional person with a heart of stone. Others tolerated his outbursts and lauded his coaching prowess, sensitivity, intelligence, and character. For the most part, the sports media complicated Vince's life. He must have thought occasionally how wonderful it would be simply to coach his beloved game with his beloved players without meddling, burdensome reporters and only enough fans to pay the salaries.

XII

Player Relations: Teaching, Preparation, and Motivation

PREPARING HIS FOOTBALL TEAM PREOCCUPIED VINCE MOST OF HIS WAKING HOURS, particularly from July to December. Driving to work, deep in thought about the problems of his team, he often missed his exit off the highway or passed Susan's high school, forgetting to leave her off. In *Run to Daylight* he described his thoughts on a Monday morning as he stopped at a red light: "Six days a week this traffic light is the one thing that invades my consciousness as I drive to work, that consistently interrupts that single purpose of winning next Sunday's game." Five days later, with most of his workweek behind him, he finally noticed the outside world: "By Saturday, if we have not solved the problems that started accumulating on Monday, it is too late to worry about it, and so driving into town I am aware of the scenes around me for the first time in a week."[1]

To play with confidence his players had to feel everything possible was being done to prepare them fully for the game. He rarely missed practice and then only to attend an important meeting. Illness never kept him off the field. While he lay in bed with a high fever, Marie warned the doctor, "There's no way you're gonna keep him off the practice field today." The doctor replied, "I know."

It was crucial that he expertly teach, prepare, and motivate his players.

"They call it coaching," Vince said, "but it is teaching. You do not just tell them . . . you show them the reasons." Much of his success, he often said, stemmed from "my teaching ability." Better than most coaches, he taught players to understand techniques, plays, and strategy, but he pounded most lessons into them by rote. He repeated the same lessons year after year. "A coach becomes a pedagogue," he said. "So much of the teaching is repetition." On the practice field he hollered, "You gotta seal off the linebacker! You gotta seal off the linebacker! You gotta seal off the linebacker!" etching it on the players' minds. Consequently, they knew what to do, when to do it, and why they did it. He reduced complexities to essentials, making the game easier to learn. He wanted simple things done with consistent excellence rather than complicated things done poorly.[2]

Repetition posed one problem. Vince didn't believe that his players could become physically stale. Barring injury, their resilient bodies recovered from a game or a rigorous practice within twenty-four hours. But they did grow stale "mentally and psychologically." Repetition was essential for perfection; yet boredom was a constant enemy. "If I get bored coaching the same thing over and over they are going to get bored learning it," he said. Therefore, he devised various antidotes to relieve the monotony: well-planned, efficient practices, different drills spaced at short intervals, an innovative or trick play.[3]

Every Wednesday, Thursday, and Friday mornings, Vince met with his quarterbacks and refined Sunday's game plan. With them he was calm and reserved, almost clinical, yet occasionally humorous and still always a superb teacher. The meetings were casual but purposeful, more like a discussion between "father and son," said Starr, "than a lecturer and a listener." By the close of Friday's meeting the quarterbacks understood the game plan perfectly and had prepared for each contingency. Little was left to chance; no free-lancing was allowed. So thoroughly was Starr prepared that he knew—"I was positive"—that he would never face a situation he wasn't equipped to handle. Vince sold the quarterbacks on the effectiveness of the plans, thereby instilling confidence. He was "one of the finest salesmen there's ever been," said Starr. Vince conferred with his quarterback on the sideline during a game but expected the quarterback to make his own calls on the field. The quarterback could see the defensive alignment and had to call the automatic. Asked how much help he gave Starr during a game, Vince said he gave very little. "We go to school during the week," he observed. "By game time, we've got every situation covered. The only time I say anything is if [Starr] forgets," adding with a smile, but "Bart doesn't forget."[4]

To be successful the Packers had to rely on their strengths, Vince believed. Change was good, surprise had temporary value, but even surprise must be based on deception, execution, and rapid maneuver, not radical change. Coaches who made radical changes for one game were "fundamentally false," he thought, because each team expressed its own and its coach's personality, and personality did not vary from week to week. The changes he made were subtle—altered blocking assignments, different keys. All coaches borrowed from their peers, but each must add something, not merely copy. "In all my years of coaching," Vince said, "I have never been successful using somebody else's play." He also hated to repeat an old game plan because "it makes you feel that you are losing whatever creativity you may have had."[5]

Vince's strategy was not particularly creative. Seldom dazzling, his teams concentrated on vigorous, quick, synchronized execution of the fundamental elements of football. He did what everybody else did, only he did it better. "You always know what those goddamn Packers are going to do," said a rival coach, "but you still can't stop them—they never make mistakes." George Halas agreed, adding that the only way to win was to work "as hard and intelligently" as the Packers.[6]

In preparing his offense Vince's first priority was to make his system clear and simple. Before 1959 the Packers had used the outdated Shaughnessy offensive system, a superfluous and complex method of calling plays. Vince threw out the chaotic system and instituted rule blocking, allowing the linemen to make their own adjustments. He simplified the entire offense, trimming the fat and leaving a core, said Starr, that was "precise" and "beautifully designed."

Especially in Vince's early years in Green Bay, critics called him a conservative coach whose team played "dull" football, grinding out yardage in short, methodical bursts. Starr retorted that Vince's conservatism was "synonymous with what he knew would work." What worked most effectively for Vince was his running attack. He was a football traditionalist. To him the ground game was most important; not having a great and acknowledged running attack was the coach's final mortification.[7]

In 1954, his first year with the New York Giants, Vince watched films, trying to acquaint himself with professional football, and although the passing attack was impressive, he thought the running game "was like a half try." Professionals could not sustain a running game, he was told, because the defensive players were too large and too mobile. "They forgot," he observed, "that everything in football, as in physics, is relative and that the people you could put on the offense could be every bit as big and just as mobile." The passing game was also much easier to coach and safer to practice. Only two or three key players needed to be coordinated for a pass play, and passing could be practiced without contact. A running play required the split-second timing of seven or eight players and could be effectively coordinated only under the realistic condition of scrimmage, thereby greatly increasing the possibility of injury. Despite the problems, Vince concentrated on establishing an effective running attack and derived "creative satisfaction" from planning, polishing, and coordinating the seven or eight players. He built his ground game on the simple idea of "running to daylight." Except on special plays, linemen didn't have a predetermined place to take their opponent. "You just take him where he wants to go," observed Jerry Kramer. "If he wants to go inside, I'll drive him inside, and the back runs outside. If he wants to go outside, I'll drive him outside, and the back runs inside."[8]

His running attack was simple yet diversified: sweeps to the strong and weak sides with the halfback or fullback running; an off-tackle slant for the fullback; quick-hitting plays with zone blocking. The "Lombardi sweep" was effective in Green Bay partly because of Hornung's ability to block, run, or throw. The play had evolved from Vince's playing career at Fordham. Impressed with Pittsburgh's single-wing sweep, he adopted the same guard-pulling techniques and the same ballcarrier cutback feature. "There's nothing spectacular about it," Vince deadpanned. "It's just a yard-gainer." The sweep was also valuable because it set up the counter, a run inside instead of outside, using crossblocking.[9]

By the time Vince arrived in Green Bay, he had also acquired an excellent understanding of the passing game, based on the theory that players must react to the defensive situation. After coming off the line of scrimmage, the receiver was to read the defense, determine quickly if he faced zone or man-for-man coverage, and adjust his route at that moment. The quarterback also read the defense and, following a predetermined plan, hit the receiver in the cracks or seams. The Packers relied mainly on short, quick, rhythm passes, medium-distance crossing patterns, hooking and curling, and long passes to receivers streaking down the sideline or to the post. Play-action passes were effective as well because the defense had to respect the Packers' running threat. The Packers usually encountered man-for-man coverage. "We just carved up man coverage," said Starr. "They simply couldn't cover our receivers." All facets of the passing attack were carefully planned, synchronized, and practiced. Vince was the "best teacher I've ever known," said end Gary Knafelc,

239

who was taught all the tendencies of the opponent's defensive backs and all the routes of his fellow receivers. "I never went into a game in which I was not 100 percent prepared."[10]

Borrowing from Colonel Earl Blaik, Vince occasionally tried to destroy an opponent's morale by attacking its strength. "If you can bring down their best men, it's all over," he argued. He devised special maneuvers to combat Gino Marchetti, the Baltimore Colts' great defensive end, and Sam Huff, the Giants' middle linebacker, but he didn't always use the strategy, shying away, for example, from the Detroit Lions' outstanding cornerback, Night Train Lane. "You are foolish if you don't go at a team's weaknesses," said Vince. "We don't butt our heads against a stone wall," observed Starr of the Packers' usual approach. "Vince believes in doing it the easy way where possible."[11]

Vince's teaching and preparation made the Packers an exceptionally intelligent team. Before Vince arrived, said Paul Hornung, "even our quarterbacks—I was one of them—didn't know what a zone was." The quarterback called a pass on third down and "if it went incomplete, we just figured it was a bad pass. We didn't know there was a *reason* it went incomplete." But because Vince prepared them so expertly, the players responded with confidence and poise. Against the Baltimore Colts, with the Packers having the ball on third down on the left side of the field between the forty-yard lines, the players anticipated that the Colts would use a zone defense, had prepared for it, and knew exactly the most effective play to call. "Vince made us the smartest team in football," concluded Hornung.[12]

Vince's teaching, preparation, and organization influenced his players to play better, but he concentrated on stimulating them more directly. He had many talents, but he knew persuasion and motivation best of all. Because professional teams were so even in player talent, financial resources, and coaching, he realized that the degree to which players could be motivated provided the critical difference between winning and losing. To convince his players to play beyond their expectations, to push them through physical and psychological barriers, he nagged, pleaded, coaxed, threatened, charmed, inspired, and loved. He scoffed at suggestions that he was a brilliant psychologist, but the way he motivated forty players week after week, year after year, knowing whom to goad and whom to flatter, bringing them to a fever pitch at precisely the right moment yet maintaining their poise required the delicate touch of a master psychologist.[13]

Motivational strategies occupied Vince's mind much of the day, every day, from the opening of training camp to the end of the season. On a Sunday afternoon in 1962, only an hour after the Packers had defeated the Detroit Lions, 9 to 7, thanks to Herb Adderley's interception setting up a last-minute field goal, he worried that his offensive team might think it needed an interception to win the next game. He decided to simulate a situation at practice in which the opponents led, 7–6, with time running out. Giving the ball to the offense, he would make them drive eighty yards for a score. "It will be just what that offense needs," he thought, "because they're feeling now that we had to have that interception to win. . . . I've got to make them believers."

Making them believers was arduous work. "This is not easy," he reflected in *Run to Daylight,* "this effort, day after day, week after week, to keep them up, but it is essential." He scratched for every advantage. News articles that made the Packers seem invincible were detrimental. "Pack Unstoppable—Taylor," Vince read in the *Milwaukee Sentinel.* "Is this what I want?" he asked. "I don't want us strutting and spreading overconfidence." Conversely, when an opponent was quoted saying, "We'll beat the Packers," his arrogance brightened Vince's day.

Because the strength of the group depended on the strength of the leader, Vince strove to set a good example as coach and to hide his own insecurities and weaknesses. If players sensed his confusion or uncertainty, the awareness would weaken them. Many mornings, when he was worried or depressed, he gave himself a pep talk because "I am not going before that ball club without being able to exude assurance." Players sensed his assurance, bolstering their own confidence. On the Thursday before the contest with Detroit in 1962 that he described in *Run to Daylight,* he showed the team films of running plays that had succeeded against the Lions. As he taught the film lesson, he reflected, "I want them to envision [the plays] working. They must take the field with confidence." The following afternoon he showed a film of a recent Packer victory over Detroit. "We'll see no more films," he thought. "This is the picture I want to leave in their minds."[14]

Vince constantly sought the advice of others on the psychological state of his players. "Does the team look too tense, or does it need stimulation?" he asked Dr. Eugene Brusky. "Do you think they're ready?" he repeatedly inquired of Marie. Though intricate and unpredictable, his motivational strategies followed several broad patterns. He flew into a rage at least once early in the preseason—to impress the new players and to warn complacent veterans—and a few times during the season when he sensed the team needed stimulation. On the Tuesday and Wednesday after a game he was most critical. From Thursday to the start of the next game he complimented players and sold them on the new game plan because he didn't want them to brood going into the contest. "He'll cuss you early in the week," said Jerry Kramer, "and kiss you late in the week." He knew the players would be sufficiently motivated against great rivals, like the Baltimore Colts and the Chicago Bears, but for weaker teams he pressured them until "you couldn't live with him." His pep talk before the game was usually inconsequential. He delivered his primary motivational speech early in the week to stimulate them all week. He rationed his pep talks to increase their impact, yet had uncanny timing. Suddenly he would gather the players and give them a twenty-minute speech "that just knocked your eyeballs out."

After a bitter defeat he strove to restore confidence, never allowing the team to slip into a defeatist attitude. They were a "better football team" than they showed, he said; occasionally he blamed himself and the staff for poor preparation. After the Packers lost to the Bears, 13 to 10, in 1967, in reviewing the films the following Tuesday, he complimented the play of the offensive line—"Beautiful block . . . fantastic . . . great job . . . way to go." After a victory, however, even a lopsided victory, when the players seemed most content, to ward off overconfidence he would often come in on Tuesday, said Willie Davis, and "drop the bomb on you."[15]

Vince was particularly demanding of talented players. He could forgive a player for not having great ability but could not tolerate one who did not use his ability. Since the years at St. Cecilia, Marie had witnessed Vince's insistent demands on talented players. "When Vin gets one he thinks can be a real good ballplayer, I feel sorry for that boy," she said. "Vin will just open a hole in that boy's head and pour everything he knows into it, and there's no way out of it. I don't want to watch it."[16]

The satisfactions were few for a perfectionist, Vince realized, but he had never known a good coach who wasn't one. "No one is perfect," he advised the players. "But boys, making the effort to be perfect . . . is what life is all about. . . . If you'll not settle for anything less than the best, you will be amazed at what you can do with your lives." He never tolerated excuses. If the ground was muddy or frozen, the halfback shouldn't slip but adjust to the conditions; the quarterback must adjust to the wind.[17]

"He stayed on us all the time," said Ray Nitschke. Calisthenics and grass drills were designed to exhaust players at the beginning of practice, leaving their pride to carry them through the rest of the session. Henry Jordan distinguished between being in shape and being in Lombardi's shape. "Lombardi shape's when there's no sweat on your jersey in the fourth quarter when you've been in all afternoon. Shape's the guy across the line from you—the sweat dripping and the eyes glassy."

Many players found Vince's mental pressure even more taxing. Believing that perfect play execution came from repetition in practice, he ordered the same play run repeatedly until the groans of the players almost drowned out his order to run it again. "Technique, technique, technique, over and over and over, until we feel like we're going crazy," mumbled Jerry Kramer. Guard Gale Gillingham adjusted better than most to the physical regimen, but the concentration Vince demanded exhausted him. If Gillingham's foot was a few inches off line, he was chewed out. "Every detail of every single play you were under a microscope," he said. If a player jumped offside during practice, Vince berated him for losing his concentration: "Kramer! The concentration period of a college student is thirty minutes, maybe less. Of a high-school student, fifteen minutes, maybe less. In junior high, it's about five minutes, and in kindergarten, it's about one minute. You can't remember anything for even one minute! Where in the hell does that put you?"[18]

Every week during the season the assistant coaches graded the performance of each player, and on Friday Vince gathered the team to present small monetary awards at an "honors assembly." It was the old incentive plan, like the star on the report card. Players thought the coaches manipulated the grades because no matter how they performed, grading was tougher after a loss and more lenient after a victory. Some ignored the awards; others took them seriously. Players were primarily concerned about high or low grades. High grades earned the respect of peers; low grades caused embarrassment. Winning a $5 blocking award delighted Gary Knafelc—"I was twenty feet high." If Jerry Kramer rated lower than fellow guard Gale Gillingham, Kramer's pride was hurt, and he worked harder the next week.[19]

Vince's spirited explanation of his maxims also spurred the team. When he lectured on conditioning, he pointed out how fatigue made cowards. "When you're tired, you rationalize. You make excuses in your mind. You say, 'I'm too tired, I'm bushed, I can't do this, I'll loaf.' Then you're a coward." The maxims may have sounded "corny," admitted Bart Starr, but they were effective. "Physical toughness will make the opponent weaken," Vince said, "and mental toughness will make him crack." When the Packers applied intense physical pressure, Starr pointed out, the opponent *did* weaken; if the Packers didn't make mistakes, the opponent *did* crack. "The harder you work, the harder it is to surrender," Vince preached. "If you quit now, during these workouts, you'll quit in the middle of the season, during a game. Once you learn to

Michael O'Brien

quit, it becomes a habit." Jerry Kramer agreed. Often during the season, Kramer observed, "When we're in a crucial situation, we look back and we remember how hard we worked all through July and we think, 'Is that all going to be for nothing?' It really is true that the harder you work at something, the harder it is to quit."

In talking earnestly to individual players, Vince used almost the same mini-pep talk to challenge their pride. "Keep this in your mind," he told Herb Adderley, "that each time you go on the field you say to yourself, 'I want these people when they leave [the stadium] to say to themselves that they saw the best cornerback they have ever seen.' " Adderley and his teammates played games with the admonition ringing in their ears.[20]

Important games reinvigorated Vince, and players caught his infectious enthusiasm. Jolly and jovial, a gleam in his eye, he bounded about the practice field and the meeting room. "Boy, I'm getting a Bear itch," he said in a morning film session before a game with Chicago. "I'm getting ready. I don't get excited very often . . ." stopping to think a moment . . . "maybe three or four times a day. But I'm sure as hell getting excited now." At practice he nursed the players' confidence—"Tremendous . . . beautiful . . . way to go." A critical game inspired him to devise a special play—often an opening play—or a unique blocking pattern. His excitement about the innovation helped sell the players on the team's chances of victory. "I can't wait," he said gleefully. "We're going to kill 'em with this." For a game against the Bears, he arranged a new blocking scheme to assist Bob Skoronski neutralize Doug Atkins, the Bears' great defensive end. To convince Skoronski, Vince romanced the action. "We're going to kill Doug!" he bubbled. "You won't have any trouble with him!" Observed Skoronski: "It worked."[21]

Vince seldom stressed money to motivate his team because he didn't need to. Players tolerated the harsh aspects of his regime partly because they knew his overall approach would lead to substantial championship money. Thinking about the $25,000 championship prize motivated Jerry Kramer to play harder in 1967. When Vince pointed out the recognition players would achieve through the years by winning a third straight championship, Ray Nitschke hollered, "The hell with recognition through the years. Let's get the money. Let's get my car paid for."[22]

Before an important game or after a disappointing defeat, Vince used humor to ease the tension or the depression. He told a corny joke or acted uncharacteristically silly. "Okay, boys," he said a few minutes before an encounter with the Bears in 1967, "I want to tell you a little story. Did you ever hear about why Belgians are so strong?" "No," said a player.

" 'Cause they raise dumbbells." The joke comprised his entire pregame speech. "It was a silly, asinine little joke," noted Jerry Kramer, but it worked. "It took the edge off the tension." The players giggled, loosened up, and defeated the Bears, 17–13. In 1961, after losing to the Baltimore Colts, 45–21, the somber, unhappy Packers returned home on their chartered airliner. It was a funereal atmosphere until someone shouted that Vince wanted their attention. Out from a private compartment appeared Vince wearing a comical Halloween mask. He darted up and down the aisle making the players laugh. By making them loose and relaxed he helped establish the right psychological state for the next week's game, a victory over the Bears. Usually, though, Vince was so serious and his demeanor so intimidating that nobody ever laughed when he talked unless there was a joke. When he laughed, everybody laughed; when he stopped, they all stopped.[23]

"We don't ask anyone to risk permanent injury," Vince said. Still, football was violent, and for the team to be successful Vince had to motivate players to perform with "minor" injuries. Critics later indicted him for taking a dangerously callous approach to injury, alleging, said one, that his position was to "ignore it, deny it, [pretend] it doesn't exist." Although Vince's policy often was callous, it wasn't brutal or dangerous. "It must be murder to be a doctor under Vince Lombardi," observed a physician influenced by the horror stories of Vince's brutality; "it must be a constant battle with yourself." Actually, the reverse was true. Team physicians and trainers for the New York Giants and the Packers judged him more reasonable to work with than other coaches. His sound grasp of physiology allowed him to understand the physician's explanation, and he accepted bad news without complaint. "He never second-guessed the physician," said Dr. James Nellen, the Packers' orthopedic surgeon. "If you said this man was injured and couldn't play, that was it." Of all the coaches Nellen advised, he thought Vince was the most reasonable to work with.

No player ever came forward with a lawsuit or a permanent disability caused by Vince's diagnosis that a fracture was all in the mind. On occasion, though, he used poor judgment on the practice field and impulsively underestimated the seriousness of an injury, thinking the player was faking. Later, after consultation with the trainer and the physician, he accepted their diagnosis. Apparently Vince seriously underestimated an injury to end Bob Long. When Long hurt his knee in a scrimmage, Vince yelled, "Drag him off the field and let's get on with the scrimmage." Long had torn cartilage in his knee but for six weeks Vince kept playing him. "He told me that there was nothing wrong with my leg," said Long. Later the doctors operated, and Long claimed the surgeon told him the injury was the worst torn cartilage he had ever seen. The Long case was exceptional. However, Vince was ruthlessly intolerant of any player he judged a chronic malingerer. When an often-injured offensive end slipped while running a pass route and lay on the ground, Vince prevented the trainer from attending to him. "Get away from him! Leave him alone! He either stands up on his own and becomes a Green Bay Packer or he crawls off the field and out of the league." The player struggled back to his feet and resumed playing.[24]

Since he detested whiners and malingerers and admired courage and loyalty, Vince urged—sometimes insisted—that his players perform with pain. If a player had a bruised or cracked rib, a sprained ankle, a dislocated finger, or a separated shoulder, Vince expected him to play. Vince had a high threshold of pain, said Jerry Kramer; "none of our injuries hurt him at all." When Paul Hornung badly strained ligaments, Vince urged him to play—"You can't hurt them more." Hornung played. "You can't hurt a charley horse," Vince confidently informed Jim Taylor. Taylor accepted the advice. "Move!" Vince yelled at Marv Fleming, who was wincing. "Forget about that cracked rib. You don't even need it." Vince accused defensive end Lionel Aldridge of "loafing" because he hadn't begun running after having the cast removed from his broken leg less than a week earlier. Elijah Pitts played two games for Vince with a shoulder separation. "In college I wouldn't have dreamed of putting my uniform on," said Pitts. "Here, I didn't dare tell him I had it."[25]

Many times Vince didn't need to encourage his players to play with pain because their whole career had conditioned them to do so. "It wasn't that Lombardi said you [should play]; it was just the psych of the time," observed Ron Kostelnik. A player didn't want to lose his starting position or to disappoint his teammates and coach. In 1961 center Jim Ringo chose to have a pain-killer injected into his painful boils in order to play in a game against Cleveland. "How the hell could I deny [Lombardi]?" reflected Ringo; "he had done so much for us."

Vince refused to use injuries as an excuse for losing. He tended to ignore players too seriously injured to play. To dwell on a player's disabling injury, especially one to a key player, added pressure on his replacement and hurt the morale of the entire squad. When Bart Starr broke his hand in a game against the St. Louis Cardinals, Vince tried to disguise the seriousness of the injury from reporters and even ordered a photographer off the practice field for fear he would photograph Starr's cast. At the end of the season, he explained his actions: "As soon as you make a big thing out of a star player being hurt, the entire team can start to feel sorry for itself."[26]*

"He was tough and abusive and at times he was downright nasty," concluded Starr of another feature of Vince's motivational approach. Fear stimulated base human feelings, but Vince knew it could also strongly affect the performance of a player. Players feared his authority and cringed at his abuse. Fear of being criticized, fined, or burdened with extra work stimulated them to persist and to endure as well as to maintain a high level of concentration and alertness. He nurtured loyalty to the Packers, and since playing for a winning team brought fame and fortune, players feared being cut or traded. The more they feared separation, the more effectively Vince could motivate them to perform. When they saw Vince abruptly trade veteran players, his threats gained credibility.[27]

"Coach Lombardi is very fair," joked Henry Jordan. "He treats us all the same—like dogs." Joking about Vince's harsh, authoritarian rule was a luxury usually conducted in private, away from the practice field and meeting room. Players occasionally referred to him as Mussolini or Patrice Lumumba, the Congolese firebrand. One player entertained his teammates at a restaurant by repeatedly slapping an imaginary face, mimicking the day he would assert himself against his coach. That day never arrived. It was mere comic bluff. The players bowed before him.[28]

"There were two games on Sunday," said offensive lineman Norm Masters, "the game that the people were watching and the one we played on Tuesday." On Tuesday at 10:00 A.M. the players gathered for two hours to view films of Sunday's game, and the session was the most unpleasant part of their practice week. The films didn't lie. Vince expertly diagnosed their mistakes and criticized so harshly that he embarrassed individuals. Often a player's first thought after he missed an important block in a game was, "How's that going to look in the movies?" When reporters wondered why the Packers seemed blasé after defeating the Chicago Bears, Henry Jordan responded, "Sure it's a thrill, but we'll walk into the movies Tuesday morning, and we'll think we lost the game." Jerry Kramer described a Tuesday morning in which he and fellow linemen Gale Gillingham and Ken Bowman "huddled like three lambs about to be slaughtered." Perennial All-Pro tackle Forrest Gregg, the finest lineman on the team, worried constantly about Vince's reaction to his play. "When you went in to look at the film on Tuesday, you sweated blood," said Gregg. He worried himself "half to death" about

* For an explanation of Vince's view on drug abuse, see the discussion in note 26.

Michael O'Brien

whether he missed a block on a crucial play. Players came in on Tuesday with a "big scowl" on their faces, Gregg said. "You'd try to get a look at him. He would be in the coaches' office, and if he was in there with what we called that death look on his face, then we knew we were in for it." Vince often ran the same play seven consecutive times, pointing out errors. "I'm gonna make it," Boyd Dowler thought, "he's not gonna notice me." But the eighth time Vince would say, "And as for you, Dowler . . ."[29]

Vince was a "force field," Bill Curry reflected. "Some people can yell at you and you chuckle because they're ridiculous, the way they do it. But when he did it, it would go straight to your heart and your heart would go straight to your throat." His intense, booming voice and the way he pointed his exceptionally long index finger intensified the fear. "When he hollers like that," a veteran advised a young player, "the only thing to do is to sit quietly until he finishes. Five minutes after he's finished, he forgets what he was hollering about."

There were many tantrums. At halftime, too furious to talk, he kicked a wastebasket from one end of the room to the other and then kicked it back again. During another, as he passed a tableful of autographed Packer footballs, he picked one up and hollered, "You guys don't deserve to have your names on a football." He summoned equipment manager Dad Braisher: "Dad! Dad!" When Braisher arrived, he started throwing footballs at him. "Get these goddamn things out of here! It's a disgrace!" Sometimes his tantrum bordered on maniacal egotism. During a winning streak he rejoiced but let the players know who he thought was most responsible. "Don't think you're responsible for all this success," he said nastily. "Don't let it go to your heads and become impressed with yourselves, because I want you to understand that I did this. I made you guys what you are." Particularly after this kind of session, the players loathed him. He used other unlovely approaches such as arbitrary, mass punishment. Because a few players performed poorly, all were penalized with extra work. Nor would he publicly apologize for misdirecting criticism at an innocent player. "He never publicly admitted anything he did wrong," said Dave Robinson.[30]

He confused players by alternating between abuse and kindness. He screamed and hollered, making life unbearable, but then talked nicely to them, making life enjoyable again. He aimed to keep them alert and striving, yet not embittered. Players joked that he often chewed them out in front of their peers but apologized in private. "We used to say that it would be much nicer the other way around," said Starr. Still, the kind words soothed the bitterness. On a Tuesday Vince fined Max McGee for

248

violating curfew, and the two ignored each other for three days. On Friday Vince sought him out, nudged him affectionately, and told him a "horrible" joke. "I'd always accept the truce," said McGee. The day after Vince criticized Jerry Kramer for his poor performance against the Detroit Lions' great tackle Alex Karras, Vince tried to make up. "Way to go, Jerry, way to go," Vince complimented at practice. "Beautiful. That's the way to go. Attaboy." After the drill, Vince pounded on Kramer's back and complimented again. Lowering his voice, Vince added, "You know, that just breaks my heart when that guy Karras beats you like that." Kramer indicated that it broke his, too. Vince laughed. "Now we're back on speaking terms again," said Kramer.[31]

Most of Vince's tirades were spontaneous, the natural outpouring of his wrath at shoddy performance. Especially in the last few years in Green Bay, however, as he found it increasingly difficult to devise innovative ways to stimulate his team, he staged some angry performances. Usually he prepared himself in the coaches' office before he met with the team. While working himself into a frenzy, he announced to his assistants, "I'm just going to give these guys complete hell today. . . . Today is going to be one of those days." By the time he entered the meeting, he was ready, just like an actor taking the stage. Players sometimes sensed his contrived rage, but the results were the same—he overwhelmed and intimidated. He looked for little things to harp on. In 1966, with training camp running smoothly and all the players in good physical condition, the placid scene made him restless. He told Assistant Coach Dave Hanner that he needed to shake up the team. As a pretext, he used a few veteran players, who were slightly overweight, and hollered at them at a meeting. Before he finished he had chewed out most of the team. "I really gave it to them today, didn't I?" he sometimes told Vince, Jr. However, his performances taxed him physically. After fifteen minutes of shouting, he wiped the sweat off his forehead with a handkerchief, smiled, and said to an assistant, "I'm just getting too old for all of this."[32]

Some players sensed that Vince was manipulating them and felt ashamed. He yelled at Bill Curry but later placed his arm around Curry's shoulder and said, "I like the way you work. You're doing a good job, and I'm proud of you." After the rare compliment, said Curry, "I'd *die* for him!" For a long time Curry felt resentful: "He flattens me out when he wants me flat. He makes me round and bounces me when he wants to bounce me. He *makes* me." Gary Knafelc had similar experiences and feelings. Vince "saw through me," said Knafelc, who had several

Michael O'Brien

weaknesses as a player. "In the back of my mind I knew he was right, but I didn't like him telling it to everybody." Through Vince's prodding Knafelc improved significantly, but he remained angry through the transformation "because he manipulated me." He later lost his resentment and judged Vince's prodding the "greatest thing that ever happened to me. . . . He changed my life entirely."[33]

Most players hated the abuse at the time. Fuzzy Thurston and Max McGee were typical. Thurston tried to block his ears when Vince screamed at him, but the method didn't work, and he always felt miserable. "I hated him for doing it in front of everyone." McGee longed for acceptance by his coach and peers and felt like a "complete ass" when Vince bawled him out. "I couldn't stand being embarrassed in front of my teammates." Ken Bowman respected Vince's coaching prowess but never became reconciled to the abuse. During the off-season Bowman studied for his law degree, and when he made a mistake at practice, Vince often insulted him: "You're too stupid to play this game let alone become a lawyer!" The degrading criticism was "belittling" and "unnecessary," said Bowman. "In many ways he was much too harsh . . . with the players. As a man I didn't like him, but as a coach, he [was] the greatest."[34]

Mostly, Vince's hollering and abuse did succeed in motivating players. "He motivated me out of fear," said tight end Allen Brown, who worried he might be cut, traded, fined, or embarrassed. In Fuzzy Thurston's first training camp, in 1959, he was continually hurt. "Damnit, Fuzzy, if you don't play today you're going home!" Vince hollered. "You're always hurt! You're always complaining!" Thurston became furious. "I'll show that son-of-a-bitch," he said, and he tore off his bandages, played, made the squad, and eventually starred.

At a meeting Vince screamed so vociferously at his offensive guards that many players left the room, objecting. Later Henry Jordan saw the victims in their dorm room intently studying their playbooks. "Then it dawned on me," said Jordan, "that Lombardi was right. He had a message to give, and he got it across." When center Ken Iman missed a snap count at practice, Vince yelled, "You stupid son-of-a-bitch! How do you expect to play in this league if you can't remember the snap count?" Recalled Iman a few years later: "I haven't made a late snap since then." Vince bawled out some players infrequently, but one tongue-lashing or pointed comment motivated them for years. He seldom yelled at defensive tackle Ron Kostelnik, but when the five-year veteran had a "lazy" training camp, Vince walked by Kostelnik's dorm room, stuck his head in, and said simply, "Ron, maybe we're paying you too much money," and kept walking. Kostelnik immediately improved his work habits.[35]

250

"We were always trying to show him he was wrong," observed Emlen Tunnell. "That was his psych." A powerful illustration of Vince's method of group dynamics occurred late in the 1965 season. Locked in a tense duel with the Colts for the Western Conference championship, the Packers played the Rams in Los Angeles on November 28, 1965. But the last-place Rams shocked the Packers, winning, 21–10. The Packers' offense, which had bogged down much of the season, was again ineffective, gaining only twenty-two yards rushing. On the flight home defensive end Lionel Aldridge made the mistake of singing aboard the plane. Center Bill Curry later described the scene at the Tuesday meeting following the game: "It was like one of those tirades you'd see in films of Hitler going through a frenzy." Vince started by questioning "Lionel's ancestry"; then he lashed the whole team. "Goddamnit, you guys don't care if you win or lose. I'm the only one that cares. I'm the only one that puts his blood and his guts and his heart into the game! You guys show up, you listen a little bit. . . . You've got the concentration of three-year-olds. You're nothing! I'm the only guy that gives a damn if we win or lose. . . ." He hollered and screamed for what seemed an hour and a half. Suddenly there was a stirring in the back of the room, a rustle of chairs, and as Curry turned around he saw Forrest Gregg on his feet, bright red, with a player on either side holding him back by each arm. Gregg was straining forward. "Goddamnit, Coach," said Gregg, who seldom swore. "Excuse me for the profanity." Even at this moment of rage, Gregg was still respectful enough and intimidated enough to stop and apologize. " 'Scuse the language, Coach, but it makes me sick to hear you say something like that. I want to win. It tears my guts out to lose. We lay it on the line for you every Sunday. We live and die the same way you do, and it hurts." Then Bob Skoronski, the articulate cocaptain, stood up and angrily supported Gregg. "That's right," he said. "Damnit, don't you tell us that we don't care about winning. That makes me sick. Makes me want to puke. We care about it every bit as much as you do. It's our knees and our bodies out there that we're throwing around."

Curry thought Vince was dangerously close to confronting a mutinous crew. But the master psychologist triumphed again. After only a moment's hesitation, Vince said, "All right. Now, that's the kind of attitude I want to see. Who else feels that way?" At that moment Willie Davis, who had been rocking nervously on a metal chair, lost his balance and fell forward into the middle of the room. Embarrassed, Davis said sheepishly, "Yeah, me, too! I feel that way, man!" The players began echoing Davis. "Yeah, hell—me, too!" they yelled. Suddenly Vince had forty players who could lick the world. Then Vince walked up to some of them, looking each man in the face, nose to nose, demanding, "Do you want to win football games for me?" They replied, "Yes, sir," each time. The following week the Packers defeated the Vikings, 24–19. "It was the highest I've seen my team in a long time—two or three years," Vince told reporters afterward. "They were almost too high." After Vince's tirade the Packers remained undefeated during the rest of their regular-season games, knocked off the Colts in the conference playoff, and triumphed over the Browns for the NFL championship.[36]

Players tolerated Vince's verbal abuse for several reasons. They had to accept it if they wanted to stay with the Green Bay Packers, and they wanted to stay with the Packers because they admired their coach, enjoyed their success, and loved their teammates. They understood his high expectations and knew that he was usually fair and usually focused his criticism properly on their mistakes and imperfections. He seemed to find fault with everyone, thus relieving the sting. "You can't feel too bad when he gets on everybody," said Jerry Kramer. "I guess that's why he gets on everybody." Vince also bore no grudge. "You knew it was never personal," fullback Chuck Mercein thought; "he had that smile, so genuine and warm, that even after he had yelled at you and he'd smile, you forgot the yelling."[37]

Organization, preparation, demands, rewards, maxims, pep talks, enthusiasm, money, humor, and tantrums all motivated Vince's players. But there were several other remarkable features about his ability to motivate. One was his brilliant capacity to understand most of his players as individuals—their role on the team, their weaknesses and strengths—and to select the best approach to induce each of them to perform at maximum capacity. It was "maddening" to try to understand the varied natures of his players, he complained, yet the effort was crucial.[38]

Paul Hornung offered a major challenge to Vince's understanding, but the Golden Boy and his coach reached a warm understanding that rewarded both. Hornung was a handsome, charming, confident, blithe spirit who liked fun, fine restaurants, Cadillacs, and pretty girls. Together with his roommate, Max McGee, Hornung was a discipline problem who repeatedly violated Vince's rules, particularly curfew. A month into the 1959 training camp Vince caught them coming in after 11:00 P.M. and levied a $150 fine on each. In the next few years he fined them about five more times for curfew violations. (They occasionally escaped detection.) After catching them again in 1961 and fining each $500, Vince growled at his star halfback, "What do you want to be Hornung, a playboy or a football player?" Hornung replied angrily, "A playboy!"

Three years later, the evening before the Packers' game against the Bears in Chicago, Vince and his entourage entered Chicago's Red Carpet restaurant for dinner and found Hornung and his date at the bar, a flagrant violation of Vince's strict rule that his players never stand at the bar and never drink on the eve of a game. "That'll cost you five hundred dollars!" Vince shouted at him in front of the other diners. Vince subsequently reduced the fine to $300 because he discovered that Hornung had been drinking only ginger ale. "I know it was ginger ale," Vince later said, "because after he left, I tasted it."

Vince was also stern with Hornung because in practice he tended to revert to the sloppy habits he had before Vince arrived. Hornung became an important symbolic object of discipline. Vince took the team's most gifted, flamboyant athlete, one the players looked up to, and berated him and fined him in front of his teammates—and Hornung usually did not object. "If Hornung was disciplined," Ron Kramer observed perceptively, Vince "could discipline everybody else without any problem."

Because of Hornung's lifestyle and antics, plus his suspension for gambling, Vince might have gotten rid of him were it not for the fact that Hornung was also a dedicated athlete with exceptional football talents and whose confidence, poise, humor, and natural leadership contributed substantially to the team's success. Vince knew Hornung lived a fast life—"He knows I like girls," said Hornung—but Vince didn't expect him to lead the life of a monk as long as he performed. Hornung impressed Vince by running up and down the steep steps of the stadium to get his legs in shape. Hornung was bigger and stronger than Frank Gifford and just as versatile. Hornung was not fast, but he ran well, blocked exceptionally well, caught passes, threw the pass off the halfback option, and kicked field goals and extra points. In the middle of the field he was only slightly above average, Vince argued, but inside the twenty-yard line he was one of the greatest Vince had ever seen. "Any time you got down near the goal line," Vince later said, "you gave the ball to Paul, because he'd get it in there somehow. Whether there was no blocking, or whatever the hell happened, he was going to get it in there." Hornung was a "money" player who performed best in critical games. The evening after he scored nineteen points in the Packers' 1961 championship victory over the New York Giants, Hornung poured a drink for his mother at a party in Vince's home. "Look at him," Vince said in a tone of both gratitude and respect, with a big grin that wouldn't come off. "He may not be the greatest football player in the world, but the competitor never lived who came up bigger in the clutch."

Hornung could joke and tease in Vince's presence because of his style. For a game against the 49ers in San Francisco in 1961 Hornung received a weekend pass from Army reserve duty. Before the game Vince asked the players if they had anything to say. "I've got something to say," said Hornung. "I came out to San Francisco for just two reasons. I took care of the first one last night, and now let's go out and beat the 49ers."

Hornung's confidence and poise not only influenced his teammates but Vince as well. When Hornung sensed Vince's apprehension, he tried to relieve his coach's anxiety. "Coach, what are you worried about? We've got this game in the bag." Before an important game Hornung told his teammates, "Look, there's no better prepared team in the NFL than we are. We can't lose." As the Packers prepared for the 1961 championship game, observed Henry Jordan, "when Paul got that leave from the Army and walked into that locker room, you could just feel the confidence grow in that room." Vince also appreciated Hornung's subtle contributions. Hornung befriended black players, including first-year halfback Elijah Pitts, who was lonely, homesick, and worried. When Hornung accepted a speaking engagement, he often took a first-year player along and split the fee. "To the people who knew him he was a beautiful guy," observed Jerry Kramer.

In the 1966 season Hornung suffered from a chronic pinched nerve in his neck and played little. Assuming the injury and the inactivity would discourage interest in him, Vince placed his name on the list of Packers used by the New Orleans Saints to select players for their new expansion team. To Vince's surprise and anger, on February 10, 1967, the Saints picked Hornung, figuring, perhaps, that his presence would hype the sale of season tickets. It was one of the saddest days of Vince's life. After he learned the news, he met Jerry Kramer at the Packers' office. Hanging his head, Vince started to speak but couldn't; started again but the words didn't come out. Kramer asked him what was wrong. Finally Vince managed to say, "I had to put Paul . . ." he was almost stuttering. "I had to put Paul on that list and they took him." When Vince phoned Hornung and told him he was no longer a Packer, there were tears at both ends of the telephone.

Vince and his star halfback could hardly have been more different, yet Vince felt closer to Hornung than to any other player. He took pride in helping Hornung become a great performer. In part their relationship was a case of the stern father being fond of the talented, prodigal son. "He was more like a son to me," Vince admitted. Perhaps in Vince's deeply religious, Catholic mind there was a corner that in unguarded moments longed for hedonistic fantasies. Hornung was everything he was not, did everything he never dared to do. Hornung claimed Vince profoundly influenced him. "He's done more for me, on the field and off, than anybody else in my life," said the halfback. "Without his guidance, I'd hate to think what would have happened to Paul Hornung."[39]

Hornung's sidekick Max McGee was an outstanding pass receiver whose other distinctions—his wit and his many curfew violations—added spice to the team. More than Hornung, McGee's humor relieved tension for both his teammates and Vince. "I could tell when Vince really didn't want to be mean," he said, "when he wanted a way out of a situation. I gave him the way out." On a Saturday before a game against the Bears in Chicago, Vince read a long list of Chicago bars he was placing off-limits. Reading the list took so much time that he grew impatient. McGee interjected. "Jeez, Coach, you don't expect me to make all of those places in one night, do you? Next year let's come down on a Friday at least." Players often kidded Vince about his conservative dress. As he entered the team bus wearing a new suit—a "dull gray thing"—he strutted about, stuck out his chest proudly, and hollered, "How do you like this, huh? Three hundred and twenty-five bucks!" From the back of the bus McGee quipped, "I sure hope you got some change when you left the store."

Vince often caught McGee sneaking out after curfew and kept increasing his fine—from $50 to $100 to $125 to $250. Finally, after curfew, the Wisconsin State Patrol arrested McGee for speeding, and his name appeared in the newspaper. At a team meeting, Vince was so angry he shook. "Max," he bellowed, "that's five hundred bucks. I said that'll cost you five hundred bucks; if you go again, it'll cost you a thousand." The players were silent, the room hushed. Vince stopped shaking and managed a small grin. "Max ," he said softly, "if you can find anything worth sneaking out for, for a thousand bucks, hell, call me and I'll go with you." The players roared. Vince tolerated the hell-raising of McGee and Hornung as long as they absolved themselves on Sunday. They had the gall to twit him, seeing the man behind the ogre.[40]

"If Paul Hornung was Vince's pet sinner," observed Jerry Kramer, "Bart Starr was his pet saint." Starr didn't smoke or carouse, rarely drank, and was invariably polite. Before Vince arrived, Starr admitted, "I was typecast as a nice guy who couldn't win." Although he lacked exceptional physical ability, Starr possessed inner toughness; an analytic, retentive mind; and made himself a great student of the game. All year he borrowed films from the film library and studied them until he learned to probe and dissect defenses. He worked successfully to overcome his weaknesses—the long pass and his indecisiveness. Vince's system seemed perfectly suited for Starr's personality and abilities: passing that complemented the running game; a simple, disciplined attack with some sophistication and variance; and the multiple use of audibles. "I was good at [audibles]," said Starr. Players grew to respect Starr's character and effective, intelligent leadership.

With Starr, Vince was generous with praise, restrained in criticism. He didn't want to humiliate his field commander and knew Starr was sensitive. He respected Starr more than other players because he was so reliable and intelligent and seldom made mistakes. "Starr has more command of a game than any man I know," Vince said in 1967. "He makes me look like the greatest coach in the business." Of all the Packers' players, Starr came the closest to fulfilling his potential. The main reason Vince occasionally criticized him was to show the team he was so impartial he would even yell at his favorite. While chastising a group of players, Vince added, "You, too, Bart," in a tone Jerry Kramer interpreted as, "You, too, Bart, honey."

Vince helped Starr develop mental toughness. "He taught me that you must have a flaming desire to win. It's got to dominate all your waking hours. It can't ever wane." To maintain Starr at peak performance, Vince tried to keep him relaxed and confident. "You don't have to feel week after week that you're carrying the whole burden of this ball club," Vince repeatedly told him. Starr deeply appreciated Vince's guidance: "Coach Lombardi has influenced my life more than any other person."[41]

Like Starr, Forrest Gregg received less criticism than most players because Vince admired him. Poised, an exceptional, finesse blocker, Gregg loved football and studied to perfection not only his own assignments but also those for the entire offensive line. To motivate Gregg, Vince merely told him quietly that he could play better. Gregg had deep respect for his coach and desperately sought to please him. "If he thought that I was letting him down," Gregg recalled, "then I was unhappy and would try harder and do more."[42]

"I think we really got along well," reflected fullback Jim Taylor. "All he wanted from you was perfection." Taylor combined strength, fine balance, and quickness. More than any player, he took literally Vince's admonition to use "all your anger" against the opposition. "I hated them—from the opening kickoff to the final whistle." He loved to take the battle to the opponent, to smash the tackler as he struggled for extra yardage. He maintained himself in extraordinary physical condition and endured the grass drill better than anyone else. His strength came from his year-round muscle-building program, which molded his body as hard as granite. Vince appreciated Taylor's conditioning. "Attaboy, Jimmy, attaboy! Look here, everybody, here's somebody in shape," Vince yelled at practice. "Jimmy Taylor's always in shape!"

Taylor scored nineteen touchdowns in 1962, setting an NFL record, and for five consecutive seasons he rushed for over a thousand yards. Yet Vince seldom praised and often scolded him. Taylor was a "Sunday player" who had a tendency to loaf at practice. His sullen attitude and double-talk infuriated Vince. Taylor smoked cigars at team meetings and when Vince criticized his play, Taylor took a drag off his cigar, and as a large puff of smoke drifted upward, he'd grin, flick the ash off the cigar like Groucho Marx, and say sarcastically, "Guess I'm washed up, Coach."

Vince tried to motivate Taylor to overcome his complacent attitude about blocking and faking. "How to go, Jimmy!" Vince encouraged at practice (while thinking, "I have to keep him a believer when he's not carrying the ball"). "Real good move!" At a Tuesday meeting after one of Taylor's headline-grabbing rushing performances, Vince castigated him for missing his blocking assignments. "If you think you're around here just to run with the football, you've got another think coming. If you ever block like that in another game, you'll be gone from here." Despite the infrequent praise, the scolding, and the bitter contract row in 1966, which temporarily poisoned their relationship, Taylor loved Vince and benefited from his prodding. "He knew how to handle me, just like a parent handles his children," said Taylor. "I don't think I could have given more."[43]

"He's been a problem to coach," observed Vince of Ray Nitschke, the extremely rough and belligerent, 6-3, 235-pound linebacker. Nitschke was among a small group of players Vince repeatedly berated. He was Vince's "whipping dog," said one player. Nitschke joined the Packers in 1958, and serious personal problems plagued him through the early years of Vince's regime. Nitschke's father was killed when he was three, and the trauma of his mother's death ten years later caused him to become an undisciplined loner with a chip on his shoulder, "with anger seething inside me at the dirty trick life had pulled on me." At the University of Illinois and during his early years in Green Bay, a few drinks made him obnoxious. He broke furniture at bars and restaurants and brawled with patrons. "I'd say the wrong things to the wrong people," he recalled. "Stupid, immature things." Vince told a friend he feared Nitschke "might kill somebody."

Nitschke's problems also surfaced on the football field. He was "crazy as hell," said Emlen Tunnell. Frustrated at being second-string, in the locker room Nitschke would yell loudly, "Just call me the judge. Just call me the judge. 'Cause I'm always on the bench." The chant infuriated Vince. Yet he sensed that Nitschke had outstanding potential. "He *knew*," insisted Tunnell. "He handled Ray Nitschke just right."

The angriest anyone ever saw Vince was in 1960 in Santa Monica, California, where the Packers prepared for a crucial, season-ending contest against the Los Angeles Rams. The game would determine if the Packers earned the conference championship. Nitschke went to a restaurant near the team's motel, sat at the bar, and ordered a drink. When Vince and his party entered the restaurant, Vince saw Nitschke at the bar. The linebacker even welcomed him: "Hi, Coach." Vince's neck began turning red as he walked by the bar, and it got redder and redder. He brooded at his table for a while, then announced abruptly, "Let's get out of here." As he walked by Nitschke, without turning his head he said, "You're all done! You're through! Get out of town!" Because of the game's importance and the shortage of healthy linebackers, Phil Bengtson pleaded with Vince to let Nitschke play. Too proud to back down directly, Vince concocted a shrewd, face-saving solution: He would leave the decision up to a vote of the players. "We knew we had him then," recalled Norb Hecker. As expected, the players voted unanimously to allow Nitschke to play, and the Packers won the game.

Nitschke married in 1961 and credited his wife's influence for transforming his personal life. He stopped drinking, mellowed, and became a model citizen in Green Bay, actively involving himself in service and charitable work. His football fortunes improved as well. He became a stellar performer for the Packers and one of the finest middle linebackers in the history of professional football. Vince had taught him to channel his energy into football and used him as an instrument to instill fear into opponents.

Despite Nitschke's obvious talents on the field and his contributions to the Packers' success, Vince rarely complimented him and consistently used a caustic tone with him. Nitschke kept up a constant stream of chatter in practice, for example, which Vince found abrasive. "Hey, Nitschke," Vince yelled. "Yes, sir?" replied the linebacker. "Shad-dup." Nitschke infuriated Vince because he made so many mistakes. "When you would chew him out," Vince explained, "he's like a child. He's repentant and never gives you an argument, but then he turns around and does the same thing over again." Even after Nitschke's personal life improved, Vince thought criticism rolled off him until Vince wondered if it helped him at all. "You don't improve him, but happily he improves himself."

That Vince praised him less than other players hurt Nitschke—"It bothered my pride." Nonetheless, he credited Vince with improving his life. "He helped to turn me around as a person. He inspired me by his determination in what he did. He set an example I chose to follow."[44]

The trade that sent big, agile linebacker Lee Roy Caffey to Green Bay in 1964 excited Vince because he knew Caffey had extraordinary ability. It upset him, though, to discover that Caffey was also lazy and unmotivated. Observing his poor attitude at an early practice, Vince yelled, "You don't have this ball club made by a long shot! You might not be here five minutes, you big turkey!" Caffey was one of Vince's "gifted children," one who wasn't reaching his potential and needed constant attention and chastisement. "Caffey, that stinks!" Vince often yelled. When Caffey loafed during a linebacking drill, Vince tried to inspire: "Lee Roy, if you cheat on the practice field, you'll cheat in the game. If you cheat in the game, you'll cheat the rest of your life. I'll not have it." On another occasion he was direct and explicit. "Lee Roy, you may think I criticize you too much, a little unduly at times. You have the size, the strength, the speed, the mobility, everything in the world necessary to be a great football player, except one thing. YOU'RE TOO DAMN LAZY." Close observers credited Vince's constant pressure as the major reason that Caffey played excellent football for the Packers.[45]

More than any other player, Vince humiliated tight end Marv Fleming. Fleming had joined the Packers in 1963, and although blessed with excellent athletic ability, he was flighty and repeatedly missed his assignments. Vince had no suitable replacement, so he raged at him. "Look at you, stupid, you big jerk," Vince screamed in a typical tirade. "You don't have the mental capacity to retain anything for twenty-four hours." Once Vince picked up a chair, waved it at Fleming's head, and said, "I get so damned mad at Marv Fleming I'd like to beat him on the head." Some players found it painful to listen to Vince degrade Fleming. It was also painful for Fleming, yet "I never felt degraded," he said on reflection. Vince complimented Fleming privately and advised him on his personal life. Fleming was only twenty when he joined the Packers and didn't understand the meaning of hard work; Vince's prodding taught him. "I didn't know what potential I really had," Fleming observed. "He had that way of bringing the most out of people, and I'm glad he did that to Marv Fleming." A Packer assistant coach agreed: "We got the best out of Marv."[46]

Another aspect of Vince's capacity to motivate perplexed some observers. Mystified by his remarkable winning record and the loyalty he engendered from his players, they nonetheless scoffed at the notion that the seemingly hardhearted coach could arouse intense spirit and feelings of brotherhood and love and that those qualities could help account for the Packers' success. "It's the team," Vince insisted. "It's the team as a unit." "The first time you hear it," said Jerry Izenberg, a skeptic, "you say this is either corn or con. 'Come on, Vincent. This is pro football, not the Rover Boys at Harvard.' " But Izenberg heard the theme so often from Vince and his players, he began to believe. "The more you hear it, the more you wonder." Others were less resistant. "Until I saw the Packers under Lombardi," observed Tim Cohane, "I seriously doubted a pro team could match a college team in unadulterated spirit." The Dallas Cowboys, said another writer, were "only a football team; the Packers are a practicing religion."[47]

Vince's many acts of kindness earned affection from his players. After a defeat the same man who yelled at them all week would walk through the bus on the way to the airport talking gently to each player and uplifting sagging spirits. When Henry Jordan's son broke his leg, Vince phoned the hospital to inquire about the boy's health. After Jordan's mother-in-law died in an auto accident, the Packers paid Jordan's plane fare home and sent a large wreath of flowers. "I never forgot," said Jordan.

With his strong streak of sentimentality, his openly shed tears, his childlike tenderness, Vince showed his deep concern for his players. After winning an important game, he tried to express his appreciation for the players' effort, but his voice cracked, tears rolled down his cheeks, and he was unable to complete his speech. "He gets misty-eyed and he actually cries at times," said Jerry Kramer, but "no one thinks less of him for crying. He's such a man." His intolerance of his players' pain vanished when he learned of a critical injury or illness. In 1964, when Jerry Kramer suffered a mysterious intestinal ailment that appeared to be cancer, Vince became enormously distressed. He visited Kramer and told him not to worry because the Packers would pay all his medical bills and two years of his salary, even if he couldn't play. "His players are his children," said Kramer; "he nurses them when they're sick." Two years earlier, on November 18, 1962, second-year linebacker Nelson Toburen tackled John Unitas, and only Unitas rose to his feet. Toburen had broken his neck and appeared in danger of becoming a quadriplegic. When Vince walked into Toburen's hospital room and saw the body cast, he tried to speak but choked up. In the hallway outside the room, he wept profusely. Toburen recovered, but doctors advised him never to play football again.

Although under no legal obligation, Vince paid Toburen's salary for 1962 and 1963, allowing him to complete law school. "I don't think there is any question that Vince cared about us," Toburen reflected.[48]

Cutting players—especially hardworking rookies or aging veterans—upset Vince terribly. He didn't mind cutting a player who was talented but unmotivated. But when a rookie displayed desire, dedication, and courage yet was too small or too slow, when he had given maximum effort and Vince still had to tell him it wasn't good enough, "That's when you ache inside." After Vince cut a first-year defensive back, the rookie appeared on the practice field, crying, and pleaded with Vince to keep him because he wanted to play for the "greatest coach in the world." The Packers were loaded with defensive backs, Vince explained, and promised to help him find a position on another team. Afterward, drained by the emotional encounter, with tears streaming down his cheeks, Vince said, "It's guys like that who make this all worth it." After a few years, Vince could no longer bear the agony and delegated the duty of cutting rookies to Pat Peppler, his director of player personnel. Telling the bad news to a hardworking, loyal, but aging veteran was even worse. "You can't face him, you don't know how to tell him, but you do." When Emlen Tunnell finally reached the point where both he and Vince knew he was too old to continue, Vince cried.[49]

To minimize friction on the team, Vince deliberately made the players think of themselves as a unit, not as rookies and veterans, offense and defense, blacks and whites. Off the field the players congregated in different groups, with a variety of interests, but never formed cliques. The hazing of rookies and singing by the entire team bolstered spirit and fostered unity. During each dinner hour of training camp, while the veterans ate, rookies had to entertain the squad with their singing. It embarrassed them a little and relieved pressure. The veterans had many friends and instinctively resented rookies. "The first-year man may be chased out of camp," Vince observed, "because of affection for a veteran who can no longer perform as well, and the team suffers." When the veterans booed and laughed at the awkward performers, they expended some resentment, and if the rookie maintained his poise, Vince hoped, "the beginnings of new bonds start to form." On "Rookie Night," first-year men staged a show and made fun of camp, veterans, and especially their coach. Their rough caricatures portrayed Vince as a dictator and ridiculed his manner and appearance; yet Vince watched and laughed as heartily as the rest.

He expected the veterans to sing also, and a listless performance angered him. "The singing absolutely stinks. It's lousy. . . . I want to hear you. I want to see what kind of a man you are.'' After he berated them at practice, putting everyone in a foul mood, he insisted they sing after supper. Reluctantly, they began singing, first in groups, then the coaches, and then the trainers. "Finally we all sang together," said Jerry Kramer, "making a horrible racket, and the whole atmosphere changed, the whole mood of depression lifted. We were a team again."[50]

Vince didn't yell all the time, and the Packers could exist without fear and trembling over the "old man." Off the field the atmosphere was jovial and fun-loving. "We were the happiest group of people," recalled Tom Miller. Social occasions enhanced the feeling of joy and togetherness. Following each game at Thanksgiving, Vince hosted a buffet supper for the players and their families where he hugged and kissed the children and carried them around on his shoulders. "He just loved those little kids," said Bob Skoronski. After games the players and their wives or girlfriends gathered at homes and later in the evening rented a room at a restaurant for a large, joyous party. "If we all lived like we did [then]," said fullback Jim Grabowski of the close feeling at social gatherings, "it would be a fantastic world."[51]

In 1967, after Super Bowl I, a reporter asked Vince to explain the primary reason for the Packers' success. "Love," Vince answered. For the next year he took exceptional care to explain his meaning, apparently because of his baseless, slightly paranoid fear that his unqualified reply had sounded too unmasculine or—worse yet—too suggestive of homosexuality. "I have been sorry about [that] remark ever since," he told a sportswriter a few months later. "Now, you fellows know what kind of 'love' I meant." The kind he meant, he said, was loyalty, teamwork, respect for the dignity of fellow players, spartanism, "heart power, not hate power."

When he lectured to his players, Vince emphasized loyalty to teammates and respect for each man's dignity. They should "love" their teammate despite his mistakes on the field or flaws in his character or appearance. "No other coach could've used that line without getting laughed at," observed Tunnell. But Vince conveyed his message with such powerful conviction that no one laughed. Players groped awkwardly to express the intense feelings they had for each other. "It was something you couldn't explain to outsiders very well," said Nitschke. Herb Adderley described their love as a " 'we' and 'us' thing instead of 'I' and 'me.' " Linebacker Bill Forester claimed to have reached the point that he wanted his teammates to receive more credit than himself, a feeling he thought was "not natural." After the Packers traded offensive end Bob Long to the Atlanta Falcons, Long wrote Vince an emotional letter expressing how badly he missed the Packers: "I'll never forget you saying, 'We never knew how good we had it but would once we ended up in a place like Pittsburgh or Atlanta.' Well, you were right again."[52]

"They act like the brothers in an unselfish, rough family," marveled sportswriter Jimmy Cannon. Indeed, more than any other image, Vince and his players used the family to describe the teams' camaraderie. In some ways Vince was more parent than employer, more father confessor than professional coach. Although he may have been only partially conscious of it, his aim was to create a richer, more complex practice of team spirit than any corporate executive or any other leader could fully appreciate. He tried to re-create a traditional sense of family often lost in contemporary life. It was a peculiar family. Vince was an old-fashioned father who demanded that his respect and love be earned and constantly re-earned. An aging or ineffective player could be dropped from the circle at any time. Those who remained, though, found nourishment. Vince was a "parent figure" to Norm Masters, a "father image" to Gary Knafelc, a "father confessor" to others. "In one sense, we were Lombardi's family," said Nitschke; "we were his sons." For many players, fear was associated with separation from the Packer family. "The fear is simple," said Willie Davis. "It's just the plain, frightening idea that something will prevent you from remaining a part of this." Forrest Gregg feared the loss of "happiness," feared that "for some reason I would not be a part of this team and be with this man." A Catholic newspaper in Milwaukee enthusiastically praised Vince for fostering a community of Christian love: "What a world it would be if all of us respected and loved one another with the same ferocious loyalty displayed by the Packers," said the editorial. "What better practical theology could there be?"[53]

Under Vince's direction a few players tended to remain in a state of perpetual adolescence, overly dependent on his guidance and unable to function successfully on their own or later under less authoritarian and fatherly coaches. However, most players claimed to have matured under Vince's guidance, and some were profoundly influenced by him. He helped them overcome personal problems. They sensed that he strongly desired to improve their character and values, and they appreciated his efforts. "More than anything else," said Starr, "he wanted us to be great men after . . . we'd left football." They learned dedication, sacrifice, and hard work, gained confidence and poise, and overcame self-doubt. A British reporter writing a feature story on Vince for the *Sunday Times* of London, was amazed at the intense feelings the Green Bay players had for their coach. "Words like 'respect,' 'admiration,' 'pride' tumble from players when they talk about Lombardi," said the reporter.

"He's the person who made me a man," said Jim Ringo. "He made a lot of boys into men. . . . He helped me to face life. . . . You don't have many opportunities in life to come in contact with a man of such talents." Scores of players, deemphasizing the importance of Vince's verbal abuse, echoed Ringo's assessment. "He could get the best out of more people than anyone I've known," said Max McGee. John Roach, the seldom-used quarterback behind Bart Starr from 1961 to 1963, reflected that "even though it was a frivolous thing like football, he showed us a way to make ourselves better. I . . . never attained any degree of success in professional football, and yet I look back and [can] say that he probably made as big an impression on me as anybody that I ever had any contact with. . . . When you put your heart and soul into any task, if you're the lowest employee in the company . . . you're going to be a better person in everything you do and will get rewards. . . . He was a great man." Bill Curry, who initially resented Vince, changed his mind. "Later, I thought about it and now I can look back and realize that the reason I resented him was that he was making me grow up when I didn't want to. He was thinking of me." Willie Wood observed, "Very often I get into tight spots, and I refer back to some principles that Vince had said . . . like hard work, determination, will to win."[54]

Wood's praise illustrated a final, remarkable feature of Vince's relations with his players. His attempts to inculcate values and to create a spirit of love, family, and unity were best exemplified by his attitude toward black players. Unlike some NFL teams, Vince's Packers had no divisive racial problems. In the mid-1960s the St. Louis Cardinals were torn apart by a cell of white supremacists, and although the Cardinals' situation was exceptional, most professional teams experienced some racial animosity in the 1960s. But there was no friction on the Packers, no hint of racial prejudice. "I can't think of a single racial incident we have had," said Wood in 1968. "If we had any racial problems," echoed Nitschke, "I didn't know about them."[55]

With few exceptions, the NFL had rejected blacks until after World War II. By 1970 blacks comprised one third of the players, but the process of integration had often been bitter and painful. Among the real or imagined problems blacks faced in the 1960s were discrimination in pay and opportunities; stacking of blacks at certain positions (defensive backs) and exclusion from "intelligent" positions (center, quarterback); bigoted white teammates and coaches; failure to mix in dining rooms; pairing of blacks as roommates; and discrimination in the team's community.

Although Vince grew up among ethnic diversity in New York, he had little contact with black football players until he joined the New York Giants in 1954. The Giants had more blacks than most NFL teams, apparently experienced good race relations, and Vince treated his black players the same as whites. However, Roosevelt Grier, the black defensive tackle, alleged that the Giants maintained a rigid quota of black players. "We knew only six black guys would make the team no matter how good they were . . . number six. That's what it was." Black offensive tackle Jack Spinks agreed, but overall, he judged the Giants one of the "best" teams in race relations.[56]

At Green Bay Vince had the authority and the responsibility to deal with racial matters, and he responded admirably. When he arrived, the only black on the team was Nate Borden, a defensive end. Before training camp began, he acquired defensive back Emlen Tunnell from the Giants, and thereafter the number of blacks on the Packers steadily rose. In 1959 the situation in Green Bay was "bad for blacks," said Tunnell; "real bad." Housing discrimination was the major problem. Moreover, with no significant black population in Green Bay, the black player had to discipline himself more rigidly than his counterpart in New York or Chicago because he was so conspicuous if he got out of line.[57]

In a brief statement to his players at one of his first practices (repeated in subsequent years), Vince issued an injunction against bigotry: "If I ever hear [the words] 'nigger' or 'dago' or 'kike' or anything like that around here, regardless of who you are, you're through with me. You can't play for me if you have any kind of prejudice." His statement set the tone for racial attitudes for the next nine years. Sometimes he joked, "We have no other colors but green and gold and Italian." The players laughed, but they understood his message. "If you're black or white, you're a part of the family," he explained in 1968. "We make no issue over a man's color. I just won't tolerate anybody in this organization, coach or player, making it an issue. We respect every man's dignity, black or white. I won't stand for any movements or groups on our ball club. It comes down to a question of love. . . . You just have to love your fellow man, and it doesn't matter whether he is black or white. If anything is bothering any of our players—black and white alike—we settle whatever it is right away."[58]

Vince's innate sense of fairness plus the wounds of prejudice he suffered most of his life explained part of his sensitivity and understanding. So did his religious faith. Irritated by a bigoted comment about blacks that he overheard at a social event, Vince responded angrily, "How can you, as a good Christian, feel that way?" A practical reason influenced him as well. By acting against prejudice and segregation he removed a potential source of divisiveness on his team, which depended on talented black players. Good moral practice and good business practice combined to further his goal of winning. He candidly admitted that his outstanding success at Green Bay helped soothe racial tension. "When you're losing, it's easy to have discontented players—black and white."[59]

Vince did more than talk to his players about bigotry. In early September 1959, before an exhibition game against the Washington Redskins in Greensboro, North Carolina, local authorities enforced the segregation ordinance and forced the Packers' four black players to stay at an all-black college. Vince felt badly about the incident, and when a Greensboro restaurant forced the blacks to enter and leave by the back door, Vince ordered *all* his players to enter and leave by the back door. Thereafter he took greater care to book reservations where the team could eat and sleep together. Nonetheless, through the 1962 season, segregation laws continued to plague him in Jacksonville, Florida; Columbus, Georgia; and New Orleans. Frustrated and angry after losing a confrontation with local authorities over accommodations, he huddled with his black players while the rest of the squad watched silently from the bus. "I'll never—absolutely never—put you guys in this situation again," Vince told them, teary-eyed. "If it means we play no games down here, that's the way it will be." That Vince felt so strongly about the matter shocked defensive end Willie Davis and cemented his affection for his coach. "That was one of the reasons why I would do anything . . . for the man," Davis said later. Finally, Vince devised an ingenious method to circumvent the segregation. For exhibition games in Georgia in 1961 and 1962, he quartered the team at the Fort Benning Army base, where the players lived in hot, nonair-conditioned discomfort, but as a family—together.[60]

Vince also supported federal civil rights legislation and served on Green Bay's Council for Human Relations. His friends claimed that he forcefully intervened in cases of discrimination in Green Bay. When he learned of landlords, motels, restaurants, or barber shops that discriminated, he quietly urged changes, delivered a tongue-lashing to the perpetrator, or, occasionally, threatened to boycott.

Sometimes Vince needed to have racial problems pointed out. Once made aware, he acted. In 1962, when Willie Wood and a few other blacks complained about serious housing discrimination in Green Bay, Vince advised them that he would try to solve the problem. His specific action is unknown, but the following year the housing situation improved. Linebacker Dave Robinson objected to having room assignments based on race. Traditionally blacks roomed with blacks, whites with whites. Vince quietly threw out the tradition. Players could choose roommates if they desired. The rest were assigned according to a strict alphabetical system, the first (or one of the first) such system in professional football. None of the euphemisms about compatibility employed by other coaches satisfied Vince's code of ethics; any Packer should be proud to room with any other. When the players' association urged management to adopt a nondiscriminatory policy, Vince judged it unnecessary. At a meeting he told Robinson, the vice-president of the players' association, "Dave, we don't have any problems on the Packers, do we?" Robinson agreed but pointed out that other teams had racial problems and that the Packers might have them in the future. The argument swayed Vince. He changed his mind and supported a nondiscriminatory policy.[61]

Black players primarily admired Vince for the same reason whites did. "He's the best coach I've ever seen," said Wood. He criticized blacks, but no differently than whites. "It never enters my mind that I'm being chewed out because I'm a Negro," said Robinson. Vince encouraged black leaders on the team, and they, along with fair-minded, respected white players, helped create an atmosphere of racial harmony. Early leaders who bridged the gap between the races where Tunnell and Hornung. Tunnell was an experienced, respected veteran whom Vince acquired partly for his natural leadership. "Hornung knew no color," said Wood. When Hornung befriended black players and Bart Starr invited them to his home for dinner, new players joining the Packers observed their attitude. Consequently, there was only one way for them to act, no matter what they believed or where they came from. "We were all like brothers," said Bob Jeter. "We partied and socialized together."[62]

After Tunnell retired in 1962, Wood, Adderley, and Davis increasingly assumed leadership roles. Spirited, intelligent, sensible, and very ambitious, Davis urged his teammates, particularly blacks, to dedicate themselves and follow Vince's leadership. He developed a warm relationship with Vince. The two often engaged in philosophical discussions behind Vince's closed office door, discussions that focused on Vince's past and Davis's future. Vince drew parallels between his Italian-Catholic experiences and those of blacks. "Not that I can ever be black," he told Davis, "but I can understand. When you reach out, I can understand the reach." Vince reflected on the discrimination he felt trying to secure a head coaching job, and the frustration of watching friends advance in the profession ahead of him. "If you really want something," he advised Davis, "you can have it if you are willing to pay the price. And the price means that you have to work better and harder than the next guy."[63]

Vince also advised other black players or helped them in a special way. "In the three years I was in Green Bay," said Tunnell, "he picked up my hotel bill at the Northland. He didn't have to do that. . . . He did so much for me." He was like a "father" to Jeter, a "confessor" to Wood. When Wood married and didn't have enough money for a down payment on a home in Washington, D.C., Vince phoned banks in Washington and arranged financing. Marv Fleming, who claimed to have benefited from private discussions with his coach, was effusive with his praise: "When I think of Lombardi, I think of Martin Luther King. I think of Gandhi. I think of great people who led the way for freedom [and] the right way of life."[64]

Race relations in Green Bay improved in the 1960s mainly because of the understanding, tolerance, and legislation generated by the national civil rights movement. Black players on the Packers, however, also credited Vince's influence. "Vinnie turned that whole town around," said Tunnell. The Packers' racial harmony went largely unnoticed by the public until July 1968, when Jack Olsen in *Sports Illustrated* contrasted the brotherhood on the Packers with the generally dismal state of race relations in college and professional sports. Whenever racial questions were discussed by NFL players, Olsen discovered, the Packers were mentioned; in a league beset with racial confrontations, the Packers got along. Success had something to do with it, Olsen thought; a winner always found life more pleasant than a loser. "But more to the point is the attitude of the Packers' remarkable Vince Lombardi." Hundreds of coaches echoed Vince's credo, said Olsen; the difference "is that Vince means it, and he enforces his belief as only Lombardi can." Until the *Sports Illustrated* article, Vince's dignity and grace on racial matters was so natural and sincere it almost passed unnoticed.[65]

XIII

Leisure, Home, and Family

"THERE ARE SIXTY-THREE THOUSAND PEOPLE IN GREEN BAY," SAID COLUMNIST Jim Murray, "but only one of them counts." Murray meant Vince, of course, who quickly had become Green Bay's most famous and admired resident though not its most friendly or loved. Loss of privacy was the hated price Vince paid for success and fame. He shook hands with admiring fans from morning to night. "Why doesn't everyone just say hiya?" he complained. He detested the ritual of signing autographs (although he was gracious with a child's request). He cooperated, but grudgingly. He often sought a corner table at a restaurant, but some "bore" would interrupt him just as he was having his soup and drive him crazy with a pointless story. His soup cooled; he felt his face freezing, his eyes glazing. A drunken man once approached his table, knelt down on the floor, and said, "I consider you next to Jesus Christ!" As Vince stood at the urinal in the men's room of another restaurant, a man tapped him on the shoulder and asked for an autograph, explaining that he didn't want to bother Vince while the coach was eating.

One evening, as Vince and Marie dined with their friends the Ockie Kruegers, they had a corner table, but it didn't help. Vince had already autographed two menus and the back of a business card when he felt another tap on his shoulder. A plump, dark-haired man in his midthirties stood staring at him. Vince described their conversation in *Run to Daylight:*

> "Mr. Lombardi?" he says.
>
> "Yes, sir?"
>
> "I'm from Saginaw, Michigan," he says.
>
> "Very good," I say, because he has been waiting for me to say something.
>
> "I'm here to see you get beat," he says.
>
> What am I supposed to say now? I just look at him, and then at the others at our table.
>
> "But I think you've got a good team," he says.
>
> "Thank you."
>
> "Do you think you'll win?" he says.
>
> Here we go again. I should say no. I should say no, that we're just going out for the exercise and expect to be beaten.
>
> "We're going to try," I say, and this is ridiculous.
>
> "How's the weather going to be tomorrow?" he says now.
>
> "I don't know."
>
> "It'll be a better game if it doesn't rain," he says, still hanging on.
>
> "That's right."
>
> "Well," he says, "may the better team win."
>
> "That's right," I say again.
>
> "Well," he says, sticking out his hand. "Good night."
>
> "Good night," I say, shaking his hand.
>
> "Did you ever?" Doris Krueger says, after he has left. "Did you ever hear anything like that in your life?"
>
> "Yes," I say.[1]

Despite the adulation, Vince admitted, "I'm not the most popular man in this city." He did not mix as well into the community as many influential residents had hoped. Instead, he stayed close to work, home, church, friends, and Oneida Golf and Riding Club. Because he was moody, shy, and private, and because he coldly received most adult autograph hunters and acted rude to other acquaintances, he antagonized many people. He "stepped on a lot of toes," said Bud Lea. He was "probably not the most loved man in Green Bay," noted Len Wagner in the *Press-Gazette* in 1966, adding, "There are times Lombardi has displayed what appears to be a cold, impersonal attitude toward individuals."[2]

"It is very difficult for me to get close to people," Vince said. "It's just part of my personality. I find it difficult to get close to them or have them get close to me." In a crowd of strangers in a social situation, Vince was shy, retiring, and insecure. He recoiled when someone he didn't know put an arm around him, and he would avoid meeting people until a friend introduced him around the room to break the ice. Often when he met a person for the first time he gave a dead-fish handshake and avoided eye contact. Part of his shyness stemmed from his absentminded inability to remember names, a defect that offended the vanity of many acquaintances.

Paul Costello, a prominent Green Bay auto dealer, was introduced to Vince many times, but Vince regarded each occasion as the first. When they were introduced again on the first tee at Oneida, Costello was determined to drive home a point.

"What was the name?" Costello inquired after the introduction.

"Lombardi."

"And what do you do, Mr. Lombardi?" asked Costello.

"I'm a coach."

"Oh, what high school?"

After this exchange, from then on Vince was at least able to remember Costello's name.[3]

Some out-of-state journalists described Vince's Wisconsin friends as "trained seals" whose slavish devotion to his every whim brought out the worst side of his "monumental ego." His friends laughed at his corny jokes, said one cynic, "applauded his gall and called it charm, washed his golf balls and called it friendship." Vince's friends were indeed probably astonished to be buddies with a national celebrity, but actually his friendships were loyal, sincere, and enduring. Vince had exceptional capacity for close friendship. When he developed a close friend, he said, "they are friends for life. There is no way in the world anyone could break that friendship." His closest friends in Wisconsin were businessmen and executive committee members, Tony Canadeo and Richard Bourguignon; orthopedic surgeon and the Packers' physician Dr. James Nellen; insurance executive Jack Koeppler; automobile dealer Jake Stathas; and Colonel Orrin (Ockie) Krueger, former athletic director at West Point whom Vince appointed in 1961 to direct the Packers' Milwaukee operations. They and their wives enjoyed parties and fine restaurants. Most were Catholics, golfers, and, above all, successful businessmen or professionals. "Lombardi was so success-minded," observed Dr. Nellen, that "he didn't appreciate people unless they were successful . . . either professionally or financially." Vince made little effort to enlarge his circle. "You were either close to him or else you didn't have much to do with him at all," said Dr. Nellen. "There wasn't much in between." However, "when you were a friend of his, you were a *real* friend."[4]

Vince allowed only his close friends to see him with his barriers down. He seldom talked freely to outsiders about his football team, but he took his friends into his confidence about players, strategy, and recent games. He also argued politics and current events. Sometimes he purposely instigated controversy and then sat back and grinned while his friends argued. Occasionally they turned the tables, enticing him into heated argument. "He'd blow his stack," recalled Richard Bourguignon, "and all of a sudden he'd realize he had been sucked in. And we would all be laughing."

He was a good psychologist who often complimented his friends. "The doctor is real important," he said to Dr. Nellen, "and you're doing a wonderful job." Vince's circle was exceptionally affectionate. They were the "kissingest bunch," observed Vince, Jr. "They were always kissing somebody." Vince wanted his friends to know they were his friends. "You are one of my few best friends," he would say frankly, with deep sincerity. He could be demanding as well. After every home game he expected his friends to be at the party at his home, and if one didn't arrive, he phoned him to inquire why he hadn't come.[5]

Throughout the 1960s Vince continued to maintain close ties with Colonel Earl Blaik, who became chairman of the board of Avco Corporation after he retired from West Point. Both were privately involved with a group of businessmen who were seeking to purchase a professional football franchise. About once a week during the season Vince phoned Blaik to ask his mentor's advice about coaching problems. "I knew he didn't really want my advice," Blaik recalled. "He just wanted to unload to me because he knew that I understood." When Vince was coaching most brilliantly, Blaik discerned, he was also most despondent. "He was low when he was supposed to be high."[6]

Most of Vince's peers in professional football deeply respected him and enjoyed his company. He and Wellington Mara remained close friends. Vince was a "tremendous person and wonderful man," said Art Rooney, owner of the Pittsburgh Steelers. When *Fortune* magazine asked Art Modell his opinion of Vince, the owner of the Cleveland Browns was very explicit. "This is for quotation and all caps," Modell replied. "VINCE LOMBARDI IS WITHOUT A DOUBT THE GREATEST COACH IN THE HISTORY OF PROFESSIONAL FOOTBALL." "I've always liked him," said Sid Gillman. "Some coaches I never go out of my way to see. . . . But I'm always happy to see Vince." Paul Brown and George Halas were Vince's closest friends among the coaching fraternity. "He could not be anything other than honest," said Halas. "He exuded warmth." When the Packers and the Bears met, the two coaches were "enemies," but away from the game they always embraced. "That seems sort of unusual for a couple of grown men," said Halas. "Maybe it was a couple of supposedly gruff old guys seeking solace with each other."[7]

Unlike many coaches, on Friday and sometimes Saturday evening Vince was able to put aside his coaching problems, relax, dress up, and take Marie to join friends at a small party or a restaurant. "The hay is in the barn," he often said; "all the worrying won't accomplish anything." On Friday night the Lombardis and Canadeos gathered for cocktails at the Bourguignons' home, followed by a fish dinner at Proski's, a small, unpretentious restaurant in downtown Green Bay. "It was an absolute ritual," said Lois Bourguignon. On Saturday evening, the Lombardis occasionally entertained a small group of mostly out-of-town guests at their home or at a supper club.[8]

On Sunday evening after a home game, the Lombardis hosted a party at their home for about twenty-five persons. Among the guests were his close Green Bay friends, members of the Packers' executive committee, and out-of-town guests, usually friends and sports reporters from the New York area. "He was an absolutely marvelous host," said writer Bill Heinz, and Marie was a marvelous hostess. Vince effusively welcomed the guests and made certain each was comfortable and served a drink. He enjoyed seeing other people having fun. He moved quickly to solve awkward situations. When the wife of an assistant coach kicked off her shoes, embarrassing her husband, Vince interjected, "That's a good idea! Let's all take off our shoes!" and he kicked his off. At about 8:00 P.M. the party broke up, and most of the guests reassembled at Manci's Supper Club, where Vince had reserved a private room. After Manci's changed ownership in 1965, the group usually dined at Bilotti's Forvm restaurant near the stadium. After a defeat, Vince brooded for a while but quickly perked up. Meanwhile, Marie expertly counterbalanced Vince's gloom. When the Packers lost to the College All-Stars in 1963, Vince was overcome with anger and embarrassment, but afterward at a restaurant Marie visited all the guests, allowing people to smile.[9]

Assistant coaches were leery of inviting Vince to a party at their home, but on the few occasions when they did, Vince came and was congenial. When Dave Hanner invited him to a dedication party at Hanner's new home, Vince arrived an hour early, played pool and dice, and was the last to leave. Vince's excessive concern for promptness extended to all social invitations. When he and Marie were invited to a party or a dinner, Vince naïvely insisted they show up exactly at the time listed on the invitation, violating the informal social convention. "Damnit, if the invitation says six o'clock," he hollered at Marie, "then I assume they mean six!" Consequently, Vince's arrival often embarrassed the unprepared hostess. "We got tired of always being the first ones there," Marie said. They finally reached a compromise: They arrived at the time listed on the invitation, then drove around the block until someone else showed up.[10]

Vince spent most of his life in an all-male world—the seminary, St. Francis Prep, Fordham, West Point. For almost four decades he labored about bastions of masculinity—the football field and the locker room. Yet in his mostly social contacts with women, he was a charmer. Many women, hearing stories of his extreme harshness, were petrified to be seated next to him at a dinner party, but by the end of the evening Vince and the woman were usually joking and laughing together and exchanging photos of their children. The women he knew best were the wives of his close male friends, and they enjoyed him. He hugged and kissed them, complimented their appearance, and made them feel comfortable at his parties. When Ruth Canadeo, Tony's wife, badly burned her arms, Vince came to the home to express his concern. Leah Levitas, the wife of Vince's friend Bud, described him as "sweet and gentle, almost mid-Victorian in his manner. He made a woman feel like a woman." With Ruth McKloskey, his secretary, the only woman he worked closely with in Green Bay, Vince practiced old-fashioned chivalry. Unlike the male staff, she never feared him, and he didn't speak harshly to her. "He never reprimanded me," said McKloskey. "Never." He rarely swore around any women; once, when he accidentally said "hell," he immediately apologized to McKloskey. He was appreciative, kind, and sensitive with her. When her son was sent to Vietnam, Vince inquired about him, read his letters, and bought gifts for Ruth to send to the young man.[11]

Laughter kept Vince on an even keel, although humor did not come easy for him at work. "I don't think humor . . . was natural with him," observed Assistant Coach Red Cochran. His demeanor on the field was so serious some people thought he was incapable of laughing, especially at himself. "There are probably people who are surprised that Vincent Lombardi laughs," said Bob Woessner in the *Press-Gazette*. Although Vince usually had to be away from work for laughter, on those leisurely occasions his companions found him exceptionally fun and jovial. His laugh was so all-embracing it seemed to hug everyone. He guffawed; every part of his body shook. The sound resembled a deep-throated roar reverberating in a wind tunnel. *Sports Illustrated* printed it as "Ararara-rarargh!" Ockie Krueger saw him laugh so hard his "tears would just shoot out, shoot out about a foot." Lois Bourguignon never knew if she was laughing at Vince's story or his uproarious laughter. An off-color joke was so out of character for him that on the few occasions he told one, he shocked most of his listeners. ("Do you know why there aren't many fifty cent pieces anymore?" he asked. "Because they're charging more nowadays.") Most of his stories were clean and corny. He told ethnic jokes, including Italian jokes, but could be sullenly offended when others told one about his nationality because it reminded him of the blatant and subtle insults he had long endured.[12]

Vince often laughed at himself. He chuckled at a writer who began every reference to him thus: "With all his faults . . ." With friends he told and retold funny experiences. While coming home on the plane from a European vacation, he and Marie tried to fill out their Customs report. Vince sought impeccable honesty, but Marie—like many people do—had stashed a few items in her suitcase. Each time they completed the form, Marie, feeling guilty, told him something she "forgot." He had to tear up the form and start over a half-dozen times to accommodate her lapses of memory. When the pair returned from a vacation in Puerto Rico, they encountered another Customs problem. They had taken a unique rum bottle home for a decoration, but because it still contained some rum, they wrapped it in a large towel they had also taken from their vacation hotel. Customs officials, engaged in a crackdown, ordered them to open their bags, where they not only discovered the "stolen" beach towel but also intended to charge him duty on the rum. Since the officials knew he was the famous coach, Vince was mortified. "Take the goddamned stuff," he said. "I don't want it!" While retelling the two stories, said a friend, "God, how he would laugh!"[13]

He was also quick-witted. At an NFL meeting George Halas angrily chastised George Allen, his former assistant, who had bolted the team to accept Dan Reeves's offer to become head coach of the Los Angeles Rams. "George Allen is a liar!" fumed Halas. "George Allen is a cheat! George Allen is full of chicanery!" At that moment Vince turned to Reeves and said, "Dan, I think you've got yourself a winning coach." Everyone broke up laughing, including Halas. When Vince visited Dr. Anthony Pisani, his physician friend from New York, Pisani introduced him to the medical staff as "Dr. Lombardi." A curious staff member asked Vince his specialty. Stone-faced, Vince replied, "Backs."[14]

Almost every year after 1957, Vince and Marie vacationed for about ten days in the winter or early spring, often timing their trips to coincide with league meetings. They preferred warm-weather locations where Vince could golf—Miami, the Bahamas, Hawaii, Bermuda, Puerto Rico,

Arkansas, New Orleans, and two trips to Las Vegas. In May 1967 they also spent two weeks in Ireland. Their most memorable vacation, though, was a trip to Italy. Vince had often told Dr. Pisani of his strong desire to visit Italy, but every time Pisani urged him to go, Vince claimed he was too busy. After Pisani read that the Roma League of Racine had selected Vince "Italian of the Year," and that Vince had commented, "They made me Italian of the Year. Where do you figure that leaves Pope John?" Pisani used the remark to concoct a spectacular practical joke designed to nudge Vince into agreeing to a trip to Italy. Pisani arranged through papal authorities at the Vatican to have a letter written to Vince on Vatican stationery (with a copy to Pisani) demanding that Vince appear at the Vatican to explain his arrogant, sacrilegious insult to Pope John XXIII. When Vince received the letter, he phoned Pisani, laughed at the joke, and asked what he should do about the matter. "We'll have to go," insisted the doctor. Vince agreed.[15]

In January 1962, after Vince's first NFL championship, he and Marie, the Pisanis, and the Wellington Maras embarked for a five-week tour of Italy. (The Lombardis and Maras spent an additional week in Paris and London.) In Italy they toured Florence, Venice, and Rome, and on February 5 at the Vatican had a twenty-five minute private audience with Pope John. Vince was a wide-eyed tourist. From the Colosseum in Rome he sent a postcard to Tim Cohane: "Having a beer and pizza at the half. The score: Lions 8, Christians 7." He delighted in the churches, the monuments, the restaurants, and particularly the art museums. Before the trip he had prepared himself by reading Irving Stone's *The Agony and the Ecstasy*, the 1961 best-selling novel of Michelangelo's life, and kept recalling portions of the book, trying to act as the group's expert tour guide (a role performed more effectively by Pisani). Anxious to view the exceptional art, Vince often arrived at the door of the museum a half hour before it opened. Not surprisingly, considering his ambivalent feelings about his southern Italian heritage, he made no effort to explore his ancestral roots.[16]

Vince did admit to a loneliness and yearning for his American roots. He liked Green Bay, but he loved New York. About seven times a year he and Marie returned to New York City. "I'm a city man," he said. Occasionally he took a room by himself at the Waldorf-Astoria and just sat—surrounded by the city. He attended league meetings, visited his parents, went to Mass at St. Patrick's Cathedral, and golfed with friends at many area courses. "Everything was here that he liked," observed Mike Manuche, the owner of one of Vince's favorite New York restaurants, "music, arts, opera, theater, restaurants." In the evening he often dined out with his many New York friends, and afterward he loved to stay out late reminiscing, joking, and singing at an Irish tavern. Unlike Green Bay, where he shunned the adulation, he welcomed the acclaim in New York. After 1965 he couldn't walk down Fifth Avenue without scores of cabdrivers, policemen, and children yelling, "Hey, Vince!" He waved, shook hands, and signed autographs. "After I'm there for a couple of days," Vince said, "I have a tough time forcing myself to leave it. I don't think there's a city in the country to compare with what New York has to offer."[17]

Vince was an avid golfer who played often in the spring and early summer, mainly on Thursday (Men's Day) and the weekend. He scored in the low 80s, and he maintained a 9 handicap at Oneida. His game suffered from a tendency to hook and to slice, but he was a good scrambler and usually a deft putter, even under pressure. On July 21, 1965, when he played a widely publicized exhibition match at Oneida with Jack Nicklaus, Vince was delighted with his 82. (Nicklaus shot a 72.) After training camp opened in late July, Vince continued to play on Saturday, but his inability to concentrate and his infrequent play caused his score to balloon, making the round less enjoyable.[18]

Because of an unusual bye in the Packers' schedule, in the second weekend of November 1960, Jack Koeppler, Tony Canadeo, and a few other friends coaxed Vince into accompanying them on a deer-hunting weekend in northern Michigan. The expedition resembled his Canadian canoe trip in 1952—Vince knew as much about deer hunting as he did camping and canoeing. He purchased $600 worth of new gear for the outing but had never hunted and had never shot a rifle except, perhaps, on a few occasions at West Point. Yet his friends enjoyed his spirit and good-natured humor. The group rose at 4:00 A.M. on Saturday and his friends settled him in the woods, but he disliked being alone and worried that he might get lost. "Are you sure *you* know where *I* am?" he demanded of Koeppler. He carefully followed instructions, but no one thought to tell him an elementary rule of hunting. Therefore, when the cold bothered him, he built a fire in the woods, unaware that the flame and the crackling noise would scare off any nearby deer. Actually, he wasn't interested in shooting a deer; he had come along for other reasons. "He thought they were too beautiful to kill," observed Canadeo, "and didn't want to clean it. He just wanted to go for the companionship and to be able to say he went deer hunting."[19]

Vince had little free time to devote to public service and charities, but he was compassionate and generous, and he endorsed many good causes. Especially after 1965, as his income swelled from his large salary, speaking fees, and investments, Vince donated large amounts of money to charity. At Oneida Golf and Riding Club he had always been easy prey for the poor Indian caddies who gathered behind the eighteenth tee as he finished a round of golf. After inquiring how they intended to use the money, he handed out $20 bills. He once gave his brother Joe a blank check to help him through financial difficulties. "That was love," said Joe. "He had that love of his family." When a former St. Cecilia High School athlete was paralyzed in a swimming accident, Vince helped launch a fund drive for the young man. After a speech in Atlantic City, New Jersey, he stopped at a convent and turned his check over to a nun. Following a speech in New York City, he asked a friend to deliver his $2,500 fee to an official at Fordham University. He generously contributed to St. Norbert College and Fordham, once donating $5,000 to his alma mater.[20]

Vince supported an impressive list of community services, schools, and charities. He was a trustee of Fordham, special-events coordinator of the City of Hope, an unpaid adviser to the new University of Wisconsin—Green Bay's athletic and physical education programs, a member of the Council for Human Relations in Green Bay, a member of the Citizens' Committee of St. Norbert College, president of the state's Mental Health Association, chairman of the Wisconsin City of Hope Leukemia Drive, chairman of the state's Cancer Fund, director of Pop Warner Football, cochairman of the Governor's Council on Physical Fitness, and director of the World Festival in Milwaukee. He was also chairman of June Dairy Month in Wisconsin and a director of the People's Bank of Green Bay. Usually he attended a few meetings of each organization, posed for photos, and provided his personal endorsement. Occasionally his involvement was more substantial. He arranged a successful fund-raising party in Milwaukee for St. Norbert College and then helped pay the expenses for the party. "It is no secret . . . that it was A-OK only because you were behind it," Father Dennis Burke wrote him in appreciation.[21]

Shortly after they arrived in Green Bay, Vince and Marie built a comfortable, red-brick, ranch-style home at 677 Sunset Circle in Allouez, a small residential town south of the Green Bay city limits on the east side of the Fox River. They lived there for ten years, their longest stay at one location. Unlike his work, though, home and family life attracted little of Vince's attention and concern.

In late January 1966, while sparring with reporters at a press conference, Vince explained that he had to be harsh with his players because "My job is winning championships for the Green Bay Packers," emphasizing the point with a waving finger. "That comes first . . . the

Packers and winning championships . . . before everything else . . . the press, television, radio, my ffff . . . no, not my family, but everything else.'' He had almost slipped, almost admitted what was often the case: that despite a close, loving relationship with Marie, his family suffered because of his absorption with coaching.[22]

Vince often told his players, "There are three things that are important in your life: your religion, your family, and the Green Bay Packers—in that order." Actually, Vince placed Marie and the children lower on his scale of values. First came his religion, said Marie, then his football team. "I came third. I accepted that." So did the children; they had no choice.

Marie was an independent woman, but only within Vince's world, and she adjusted her life to her husband's career. She knew where she belonged, and Vince knew where she belonged. "I tried to fight it in the beginning. Then I realized I was happier doing it his way." She grew comfortable in their routine together, knowing at all times what was expected of her. Thin, always smartly dressed, with carefully coiffed hair, Marie remained strikingly handsome during the years in Green Bay. Besides attending to her husband, children, and home, she busied herself doing needlework, making Christmas decorations, planning room decors, and maintaining Vince's scrapbooks, awards, and trophies. She hunted for antiques in northern Wisconsin and shopped for current fashions. "I just hate to conform," she said of her fashion independence. "If I wear an outfit—or a hat—and we win, I'm very likely to wear it again—and again. And I really don't care who notices." Her constant companion, especially during newspaper interviews, was the gold bracelet Vince gave her carrying dozens of tiny helmets and footballs, denoting Vince's biggest triumphs, from Fordham to Green Bay. She had neither the time nor the inclination for the bowling league, the bridge groups, and theater circles she belonged to back East, but in Green Bay she did join the Antiquarian Society, the local Republican Club, assisted church groups, and served for one year as honorary chairperson of the United Cerebral Palsy telethon.[23]

Marie moved comfortably within Vince's world. She loved football and travel. She watched, rooted, and prayed at Vince's games. At the end of the 1959 season, when the Packers made their first West Coast trip, Vince became lonesome, phoned Marie, and urged her to join him. "Come on out. It's nice out here." She made the trip, and in the next ten years missed only two games; she accompanied him to many league meetings and banquets as well. "My bag is always packed," she said. She took thirty trips with Vince in 1961, and in a four-month period in

Michael O'Brien

1967 spent only twenty-two days at home. Like most of their activities, traveling settled into a routine. On airlines, they sat together in the last row of the first-class section; on chartered buses, they sat in the seat across from the driver.[24]

Marie never adjusted to Green Bay. Although she tried to hide her displeasure, she found the community too confining, isolating, and meddlesome. She missed her relatives in New Jersey, and the neon lights, the shopping, and the cosmopolitan lifestyle of metropolitan New York. When she met friends on the first trip Vince's Packers made to New York, she wept. She had the "hardest time" with Green Bay's weather. She hated every snowfall, and when she opened the door, she braced for the blast of cold air.

Except for a small circle of friends and her contacts with the players, Marie built a wall around herself in Green Bay, claiming she wanted to keep her life "uncomplicated." She couldn't permit herself to get emotionally attached to Green Bay, she said vaguely in 1961, because "it's my only protection from being crushed by a turning tide if that should ever happen." Vince took a defeat hard, she added, and didn't want to become involved in "heated exchanges" about the team's performance. "This way no one can offend him, and he can't offend anyone." Consequently, she turned down many dinner invitations, often with Vince's approval. She even resented the invitations. "Sometimes they claw at you," she said disgustedly in 1962. "Just because your husband knows how to coach football they claw at you." When the wife of John Torinus, a member of the Packers' executive committee, asked the Lombardis to dinner, Marie coldly declined. The Torinuses never asked again. "Marie wasn't pleasant to people in Green Bay at all," said one of Vince's friends.

Sometimes Marie tried to protect Vince from social events he didn't want to attend, and consequently she incurred the resentment from disgruntled callers that Vince deserved. When someone would call and ask them to dinner, Marie would repeat the name over the phone, and if Vince didn't want to accept, he would shake his head, and Marie would reject the invitation. "She took an awful lot of criticism unjustly," observed her friend Lois Bourguignon. Later, after the Lombardis moved to Washington, D.C., Marie apologized for misunderstanding "midwestern friendliness." She thought they were being nosy. "The Midwest could teach all of us a lot."[25]

People differed sharply in their assessment of Marie and her influence on Vince. "I honestly thought that she was the most wonderful woman in the world," said Vince's brother Harold. Sportswriter Chuck Johnson thought she was "tough enough to be [Vince's] wife." Her friends, house guests, and most of the players appreciated her gracious kindness. After Bart Starr threw four interceptions in a losing effort while playing with badly injured ribs, Marie called to cheer him up. When Starr's son was in the hospital, she visited the boy. "She has always struck me as a perfect partner for Coach," said Starr. Others, though, mostly Vince's friends, thought Marie was rude, emotionally unstable, an albatross around his neck. "Marie was very difficult," said one friend of Vince; "she had physical and mental problems" that "were difficult for him to understand." A West Point colleague agreed: "I have some reservations about . . . the stories . . . that Marie was the inspiration in his life." Marie did not noticeably inspire Vince, they did fight constantly, and both were difficult to live with. Yet their love for each other grew deeper each year, and their marriage was mostly fulfilling and happy.[26]

"Come football season," Marie told a friend, "I may as well kiss him good-bye." In her most widely quoted remark she explained life with Vince once the season started: "I could tell what day it was just by his mood. Monday, Tuesday, and Wednesday we didn't talk. Thursday we said hello. Friday he was civil, and Saturday he was downright pleasant. Sunday he was relaxed most of the time." They attended Mass together in the morning, and if they ate breakfast at home, Vince was quiet, "unless we had a big fight," Marie said, "which was most of the time." On his busiest days he arrived home at 5:00 P.M. and Marie served him dinner immediately to eliminate his temptation to nibble cheese and drink beer before supper. Worried about gaining weight, Vince hated to be put in the hypocritical position of being twenty pounds overweight and having to order a lineman to lose twenty pounds. After dinner he took a nap in a big chair in front of the fireplace, woke up refreshed, returned to the office at 7:00 P.M., and worked until 10:00 P.M.[27]

Vince talked little about his family life. Marie became the source for much of the information about their marriage, and since she was forthright about their life together, she inadvertently contributed to Vince's reputation as a martinet with a vitriolic temper, even within his own home. Anything could ignite his temper at home—an unpaid bill, shoddy work, or the children's poor grades and curfew violations. Like Harry Lombardi, Vince couldn't tolerate the imperfections of his wife and children nor understand why they did not adhere to his wishes or follow the letter of his rules. He probably also felt that his anger achieved his desired results. Since Marie also had a temper, they quarreled constantly for thirty years. There was always a "lot of noise in the house," said a coaching colleague at West Point. Some of Vince's friends speculated that his periodic bouts with depression stemmed partly from his conflicts with Marie.

Often they argued in public. As newlyweds in Englewood, they ate at a restaurant on Friday nights, and, according to Marie, *"We were the entertainment."* In Green Bay they quarreled in front of the other diners at the exclusive Oneida Golf and Riding Club. Vince ended one fracas there by yelling loudly, "Shut up, Marie!" At a team dinner, with Marie sitting at the head table, the only woman present, the waiter served pie for dessert. When Marie asked for ice cream as well, Vince exploded, "Goddamnit! When you're with the team, you'll eat what the team eats!" Marie was startled and turned sullen; most players heard the outburst and were embarrassed for her.[28]

While watching Susan take part in a horse show in Fond du Lac, Wisconsin, Vince and Marie debated all day whether Susan needed a new horse. On the way home, with W. C. Heinz listening sheepishly in the backseat, they continued arguing:

"What about that horse?" asked Marie.

"You're not going to get the horse; the [old] horse is fine," Vince answered.

"Thank goodness for that."

"What do you mean?"

"The horse is stabled in Madison," said Marie.

"What's wrong with the horse being stabled in Madison?" asked Vince belligerently.

"Twice a week, I'd have to drive her down to Madison for lessons," Marie pointed out.

"What's wrong with that?"

"Would you like to drive down to Madison twice a week?"

"I'm coaching a football team!"

"I've got things to do, too!" said Marie angrily. "Listen, it's your daughter, isn't it?"

"Of course."

"If your daughter needs that horse down in Madison, we'll get that horse, and *you* can go down to Madison twice a week!"

When they arrived home, Heinz congratulated Marie for her marvelous psychology.[29]

Marie usually described Vince's temper as if it were merely a lovable foible. Few people could talk back to him, but Marie could needle him in such a way that their public quarreling often turned to laughter within moments. Tex Schramm, president and general manager of the Dallas Cowboys, observed that Marie's comments "would just break you up and he'd break up, too, because she'd have him so dead to rights." "They were always fighting," agreed Wellington Mara, "but it was a nice kind of fight." While the Packers practiced in Palo Alto, California, Marie flew to Lake Tahoe for a day to visit friends. When Vince learned of her trip, he was furious. "How'd you get there?" he demanded. Now Marie was angry, too. "We flew," she said. "Over the mountains?" asked Vince. "No," Marie shouted, *"under* them, you dummy!" Their anger instantly turned to convulsive laughter. Vince's attempt at reconciliation was sincere and tender, though the resulting harmony was usually brief. After an evening argument, in church the next morning Vince would reach over and hold her hand for five minutes. That was his way of saying, "Marie, I've been hard on you. I'm sorry."[30]

Despite their stormy marriage, Vince and Marie shared many interests, valued each other's companionship, and cared deeply for each other. "Inseparable" and "very close" were the expressions most often used by friends to describe their relationship. Marie was proud of Vince's coaching ability, his character, and his capacity for public speaking. "I never wanted to be anything but married to Vin," said Marie, and Vince felt the same about her. In the last fifteen years of their marriage, they reconciled more quickly after arguments and didn't adamantly insist on the other's apology. She broadened his perspectives and stabilized his personality. "When he's looking straight down the road," she said, "I can sometimes see things from side to side that he can't see." "The great thing about Marie," Vince added, "is that she knocks me down when I'm up and she picks me up when I'm down."[31]

In some ways Vince was a model father, especially in terms of his character and moral integrity. He espoused Christian values and the virtues of family life. His children loved him and respected his dedication to his work and his coaching success. There wasn't a hint or a rumor of him being unfaithful to Marie or drinking to excess. He diligently provided for his children's material needs and encouraged them to develop in mind, body, and spirit. In his own way, he thought he loved them and cared for them. Nonetheless, he mostly failed as a parent because he was too remote, neglectful, and insensitive and was overly harsh, particularly with his son. With his children he adopted the rough, demanding, impatient qualities of his perfectionist father and disregarded most of the soft, kind virtues of both Harry and Matilda. Vince, Jr., and Susan mostly had to rely on Marie or fend for themselves. Occasionally he admitted privately to friends that he had been neglectful, but he made no sustained effort to change. Many of his friends and associates thought he was neglectful and too harsh, but they said nothing to him.[32]

Michael O'Brien

"I always felt Vince was a little too hard on the children," Marie understated, but added correctly, "I think my son had a terrible time in the father-son relationship." Vince, Jr., admired his father: "I was in awe of him. . . . My sole motivation was to please him." But until the last year of Vince's life, the two were never close. Being the son of Vince Lombardi was usually a traumatic, suffocating, unhappy experience. Vince tried to mold his son in his own image, like he tried to do with his brother Joe in Englewood, much like Harry Lombardi had tried to mold him, except Harry concentrated more on being a parent; usually Vince was too busy or too preoccupied.

Being the son of a famous coach was part of the problem. The name Vince Lombardi hung like an anchor around the son's neck. People expected great things of him, especially on the football field. He spent his childhood constantly being on guard. He couldn't get into any trouble because people would say his father could discipline football players "but he can't control his kid." As a child, young Vince could seldom command his father's attention. His father seemed to be away from home more than other fathers, and "When he was around," Vince, Jr., recalled, "sometimes he 'wasn't around.' " His father never read to him or played catch with him. Occasionally Vince took him to a movie—always a Western—but that didn't satisfy either, because Vince became restless and bored and never stayed to the end. "Enough of this," he would announce abruptly, and the two would leave the theater.[33]

Vince did not spare the rod. "Where did he hit me?" Vince, Jr., later said. "Anywhere he could catch me." Marie avoided telling her husband of even the normal misbehavior of their son for fear Vince would use physical force. She often intervened when Vince became violent. While they lived in New Jersey, Marie had to restrain him as he lunged at his son. "Get out of the way. Let me at him!" Vince yelled. "Oh, no," Marie insisted; "remember what you did to him last time." Within a few minutes Vince usually composed himself, resumed a calmer disposition, and forgot the incident.

Occasionally Vince's sensitivity and understanding surprised his son. In Vince, Jr.'s, sophomore year in high school in Fair Haven, the principal suspended him for an infraction and ordered him to bring his parents to school for a conference. He worried himself sick about his father's reaction, but Vince responded mildly, apparently realizing that his son was sufficiently remorseful and needed no additional punishment. "I wish he had been a little more nonphysical like that a little more often," said Vince, Jr.[34]

Vince adamantly insisted that his son study hard in school and achieve excellent grades. If the grades slipped, he wouldn't permit his son out of the house until the next grading period. "I had nothing to do except study," young Vince observed. Vince bruised him emotionally because he issued orders or rejected requests in such a loud, angry tone. Instead of saying, "I think it's raining. You'd better wear your boots," Vince would declare, "Get out here with your boots on!"

Vince, Jr., worked at eleven consecutive training camps, two with the Giants and nine with the Packers. Life in the man's world of his father, at the center of the football action, among famous athletes, was a wonderful fantasy world. Most of the time he worked as the assistant equipment manager. He shined shoes, changed cleats, made sure footballs were on the field—"on time"—and picked up jocks, socks, and dirty T-shirts. "He was in the shadow of his father," Wellington Mara recalled, "but when his father wasn't around, he was a bit of a cutup, with a sense of humor." Laboring under his father's watchful eye, though, was often unpleasant. When his father screamed at the players he so admired, it embarrassed him. His father also embarrassed him in front of the players. "I told you to do this!" Vince bellowed at him. "I want you to do it now!" and Vince, Jr., would slink away with his head down. Vince's attitude astonished many players. "You couldn't believe he was talking to his own son," said Bob Schnelker; "it was [embarrassing]."[35]

Fortunately, Vince never pressured his son to succeed in athletics; unfortunately, he usually didn't care either. Being the son of a prominent coach, Vince may have realized, created enough pressure on his son's athletic career, which was indeed the case. Vince, Jr., played fullback and, though not exceptionally talented, he played well enough at Premontre Catholic High School in Green Bay to earn selection on an All-State team. The pressure bothered him. "Everyone expected big things of me, including me, because I was Vince Lombardi's son. I used to feel very, very tense before games." Although he appreciated not having his father's additional pressure, it hurt that his father seldom attended his games and expressed little interest in his accomplishments. "I took it as disinterest." On a fall Saturday afternoon in Fair Haven, Vince and a friend, John Ryan, did attend Vince, Jr.'s, football game, but, said Ryan, "I'm sure he didn't see that game. He was looking out over the game, probably thinking about tomorrow's game plan."[36]

In the fall of 1960, Vince, Jr., entered St. Thomas College in St. Paul, Minnesota, but his father's regimentation continued. In his sophomore year, he and friends rented an off-campus apartment. When Vince discovered the arrangement, he angrily called the dean and said, "This is Vince Lombardi. Send my son home." The matter was settled when young Vince returned to the dormitory. Vince, Jr., had initially planned to major in physical education in the hope of becoming a football coach, but his father objected, arguing that a phys-ed major was a waste of time. Besides, Vince told his son, "You don't want to do what I'm doing." He threatened to cut off all funds for college if his son persisted. Vince had always encouraged Vince, Jr., to be a lawyer, and when his son switched to prelaw and won an academic scholarship, Vince was delighted and proud.

Rigorous academic preparation would develop his son's mind and character, Vince reasoned; arduous summer work would build his character and body. Each summer Vince arranged the jobs, and they were so dirty, so physically demanding that young Vince dreaded coming home for summer "vacation." Before training camp started, he toiled at heavy construction, loaded boxes into semitrailers, and loaded pickles into boxcars. "He made it a point never to find me an easy job," said Vince, Jr.

At St. Thomas, young Vince was a 5-11, 195-pound fullback, and though injuries dogged his career, he became a starter and the captain. A gratifying moment occurred in 1962 when his father watched the homecoming game against Gustavus-Adolphus and he scored two touchdowns and gained sixty-four yards. Afterward, in a crowded hotel room, Vince lavished praise on him. "It felt good," said the son. "I knew part of it was because I was his son, but I also knew that, within my limits, he thought I did well."[37]

Vince, Jr., graduated in June 1964. He then worked full time, married, and for four years attended night classes at William Mitchell College of Law in St. Paul. "My father and I had a [personality] conflict," he concluded of their relationship up to 1969. "My father didn't know what to make of me. [He] felt that my mother sheltered me too much, stood up for me too much, and therefore he felt he had to counteract that by being firm. . . . I saw that his philosophies at home were the same with his football team. He drove them like he tried to drive me." Though he had always feared his father's discipline and chafed under his unrealistic demands, in retrospect he thought he suffered no long-term damage. "I don't feel any worse for [it]."[38]

Susan was five years younger than Vince, Jr., and more of an extrovert than her serious brother. Vince had mellowed slightly by the time she grew up, and being a daughter saved her from physical abuse. "Obviously," said Vince, Jr., "he wasn't going to belt her around." Susan agreed. "I was the apple of his eye," she said; "Vince [Jr.] got the rough end of the deal." Susan did not have her brother's scholastic aptitude, and her father never insisted she excel at school, relieving some of the pressure. Vince took time to help her with algebra and Latin and enthusiastically encouraged her horseback riding and appearances in horse shows. They occasionally talked, and Susan most fondly remembered one piece of his advice: "You'll make a lot of mistakes in your life, Susan, but if you learn from every mistake, you really didn't make a mistake."

Vince enforced a strict curfew with Susan, but he was more lenient generally, and she knew how to circumvent him. Excellent timing and careful preparation enhanced her chances of getting her way. On Friday he was most receptive, and, in preparation, Susan stood in front of the mirror and practiced her request. If that didn't sway him, she had another method. "All I had to do was cry. If I cried, I got what I wanted."

Still, like her brother, being the daughter of Vince Lombardi was difficult. She, too, was bruised emotionally by his loud, angry demands and rejections. "We all got our feelings hurt," said Susan, "because he said it in such a powerful way." It bothered her that he remained preoccupied with coaching while at home. "He was there, but he really wasn't there. There were times when I wished he'd been there and that he wasn't Vince Lombardi—that he was just normal." Vince sensed he'd been neglectful, and, to relieve his guilt, he insisted—often against Susan's wishes—that she accompany him and Marie to games away from Green Bay.[39]

Vince mostly did not allow his family life to interfere with his work. Home was a place to recuperate for the next practice, meeting, game, or season. Beyond successful coaching, his needs were simple: cocktails and dinner with a small circle of friends, a little television, quiet time to read and reflect, plus golf and vacation in the off-season. The house, nice clothes, a large financial estate—those were mainly for Marie and the children.

Vince talked little at home, and by placing an embargo on conversation about football, he frustrated Marie because the fortunes of the Packers and her husband's work interested her. When they hosted a party or ate out with friends, Marie strained to eavesdrop on his football conversation. "That was the only way I could find out what he was thinking," she explained; "I had to find out so I would know how to handle him during the week."[40]

Vince was unwilling and unable to assist with work at home. He loved to tell friends about his house, yard, and garden but was too busy and inept to fix or maintain them. Although he pretended to know something about his bushes and trees, actually he knew little. "I would say

conservatively that he didn't know a blade of grass from a sunflower,"
said Ockie Krueger. He never turned a shovel of dirt in the yard, or
worked in the garden, or started the washing machine. Susan never saw
him fix *anything*. He was an excellent cook, but he wouldn't clean the
dishes. "That's not my department," he would say, laughing. Before
training camp, an important game, or any tense situation, he announced
abruptly that he was going to clean closets, which meant everyone had to
assist. His compulsive cleaning accomplished little. He took everything
out of a closet, piled it in the middle of the room, puzzled over his next
move, and finally pleaded with Marie, "What in hell do I do now?"
Closet cleaning did release his tension, and, added Susan, "we all
suffered along with it—we had to."[41]

"I was fool enough to be married during the football season!" said
Marie, explaining why Vince often forgot their wedding anniversary.
Marie planned a large party to celebrate their twenty-fifth anniversary on
August 31, 1965, but when she learned Vince had scheduled a team
meeting, she canceled the party. Usually Vince remembered and made
the day special with flowers, gifts, and dinner out. He tried to be secretive
about his present but lacked the subtlety. "Not that I'm going to buy you
a ring," he said once, "but what's your size?"

Holidays were the most joyous times for the family, mainly because
Vince made an extra effort to make them enjoyable. They reminded him
of his Italian roots, the virtues of family closeness, and permitted him to
express his feelings. Insisting the family join together on the holiday, he
was disappointed if arrangements failed. He particularly enjoyed Christmas and loved to give presents. In 1959 he delightfully presented Marie
with ten small boxes and one large box. She had to open the small ones
in a special order and read clues in each one, all leading to the large
box—a mink coat.[42]

Normally, though, he was too busy or preoccupied to shop early,
resulting in a bizarre, last-minute buying spree. On Christmas Eve he
would march through Prange's Department Store in Green Bay, pass a
counter, and say, "I want one of those! And one of those! And one of
those!" He bought scores of presents hurriedly and expected each to be
gift-wrapped. His selections often proved disastrous. Jerry Atkinson, a
member of the Packers' executive committee who worked at Prange's,
quickly tabbed Vince as a "desperado," Atkinson's term for the
desperate, last-minute Christmas shopper. To assist him, Atkinson made
a secret arrangement with Marie: He would call her each year before
Christmas, and she would tell him what each family member wanted.
Then Atkinson briefed store clerks so when Vince arrived on Christmas

Eve—desperate—they could steer him to the items Marie requested. From then on, each Christmas morning as he looked at the grateful faces, Vince could feel secure in the belief that he had bought wisely.[43]

In general, Vince neglected to concentrate on his family life—especially on his role as a father—because that conventional responsibility did not enthrall. Instead, he willingly, excitedly accepted responsibilities as a father in another sense. As Richard Bourguignon observed, "He'd use the word 'family' when he talked about his football team."[44]

XIV

The Dramatic Year (1967)

IN APRIL 1967, AT A SPEAKING ENGAGEMENT IN ST. PAUL, MINNESOTA, THE Dallas Cowboys' coach, Tom Landry, predicted that some team would "displace" the Packers within two years. "They are approaching an age problem," said Landry, "and other teams are improving." Landry was correct. The Packers did have an age problem and would indeed be displaced within two years. In 1967 Green Bay was the oldest team in the NFL, averaging almost five years' experience per man. Ten players were beginning at least their tenth season, and others were close to the mark. Vince, though, was determined that his team not be displaced in 1967 because he had set his sights firmly on winning the unprecedented third consecutive championship. He argued that his team blended experience with youth and had "strength, depth, and versatility at every position and a winning tradition." Yet Vince knew the third title would be exceptionally difficult. Powerhouse teams—the Rams, Colts, and Cowboys—were closing the talent gap on the Packers. He and his players must work harder. For reporters he unveiled his new motivational ploy: His players would not "defend" the title; he would insist they adopt a "positive" approach and "fight" for it.[1]

Vince fretted much of the off-season about the problem of signing again fullback Jim Taylor, who in 1966 had played out his option to become a free agent. Taylor resented the huge contracts the Packers had given star rookies Jim Grabowski and Donny Anderson, and after the 1965 season he insisted on one last, big contract—a three-year pact at about $75,000 a year. Vince was willing to pay the salary, but only for one year. Throughout 1966 he had alternated between verbal abuse and sweet talk to convince Taylor to sign but the fullback remained adamant. Because of the pounding he had taken for many years, Taylor had lost much of his fierce sting, and in both 1965 and 1966 he had averaged only 3.5 yards per carry, the lowest of his career. Aware that Taylor was in the twilight of his career, Vince had ruled out the longer pact. But with Hornung gone and Grabowski and Anderson inexperienced, Vince desperately wanted Taylor for at least one more year.

The impasse continued into the summer, fraying Vince's nerves. Since Taylor wanted to play for the New Orleans Saints, near his home, and since the Saints were willing to grant him a large salary and a multiyear contract, on July 6 Vince traded his once-great fullback to the Saints for a first-round draft choice. The failure of the drawn-out negotiations temporarily embittered Vince, leading him to throw a cruel barb at Taylor for his disloyalty. "We're going to miss Paul Hornung," he told the players early in training camp. "We're going to miss Paul a great deal. He was a leader and he added a lot of spice to professional football. . . . We will replace the other fellow."[2]

As the season began, Vince and W. C. Heinz joined forces again for two articles in September issues of *Look*. (The magazine paid Vince a total of $15,000.) Like *Run to Daylight*, the articles described Vince's thoughts on football and his players, but they were more controversial. One included Vince's endorsement of hate in professional football. Vince had seldom publicly criticized anyone in the Packers' family and deplored anyone who did, but in *Look* he embarrassed some of his players and scolded the team's fans, the players' wives, and the corporation's stockholders.

Among some players the two articles touched off a small storm. Ray Nitschke was angry that Vince mentioned the low grades he had received the previous year in the coaches' rating system. "I thought we didn't publish grades around here," Nitschke grumbled. Henry Jordan was upset with Vince's remark that Jordan tended to be "satisfied." If Bob Skoronski didn't start a game, Vince wrote, the offensive lineman underwent a "psychological relapse." Skoronski seemed hurt. Green Bay's fans had become complacent, Vince complained. Initially they had reveled in the team's victories, but after the Packers won five conference titles and four NFL championships, if the team didn't win big, "it's almost as if we have lost, and I can feel the difference in the attitude in those stands.'' Equally irritating was the ingratitude of the players' wives. After the first NFL title, Vince bought each wife a mink stole, and they overwhelmed him with expressions of gratitude. It was the same after the second title—many thank-you notes followed another major gift. After the 1965 championship, however, when Vince sent each wife a dinner ring, only half the wives responded. It was worse in 1966. A silver tea service was greeted with only a few expressions of thanks. The stockholders were also ungrateful, Vince charged. At the corporation's annual meeting, they had always given Vince a vote of thanks. Yet after the Packers showed a net profit of $827,439 in 1966, they neglected to give him a "vote of appreciation." Vince claimed, though, that he would not allow the "peripheral passiveness" to invade his ball club. "I am not satiated with success," and the only yardstick for success in pro football was winning. "Second place is meaningless. You can't always be first, but you have to believe that you should have been—that you are never beaten, time just runs out on you." If any of his players was tired of winning, Vince adamantly declared, "or tired of paying the price winning demands, he will have a one-way ticket on a plane from Green Bay, no matter who he is."

Why had Vince been so abrasive and outspoken? His frankness perplexed Jerry Kramer. "It just isn't like him to cause any controversy." The tone of the articles, Kramer concluded, seemed to confirm speculation that Vince was planning to retire after the season. Kramer was probably correct, but the articles also reflected the growing tendency among sports journalists to be more open and controversial. Heinz had urged Vince to "put the truth out," and Vince, trusting his coauthor, had obliged, releasing his pent-up resentments. He wanted to be appreciated and not have the team's success and his largess taken for granted.[3]

Unbeknownst to Vince, throughout the 1967 season he himself was under detailed scrutiny in the vivid diary Jerry Kramer kept of the season. Published the following year as *Instant Replay,* the book became a best seller. It began as an experiment. Dick Schaap, a veteran sportswriter and the project's inspiration, was seeking a pro football player who would record his actions and reactions during the long season. He selected Kramer, the Packers' right guard, because Kramer was an excellent player and unusually literate and observant. Kramer had joined the team in 1958 from the University of Idaho and had earned All-Pro honors four of his nine years with the Packers. In training camp in July 1967, he started recording his overall view of the player's world—the rituals and rewards, hate and love, boredom and exhilaration, frustrations and satisfactions of pro football. Each week he shipped his tape recordings to New York, where Schaap edited and supervised the project. Kramer's feelings and thoughts revolved largely around Vince, the diary's compelling central character. Kramer portrayed him as part foster father, part shrewd psychologist, and part tornado. He recorded his coach's violent changes in mood, tongue-lashings, roaring tirades, inspiring pep talks, and unwillingness to settle for anything less than perfection.[4]

Training camp opened in mid-July, and after two days Kramer was in agony. Vince had put the squad through seventy "up-downs" during the grass drill. "You try to block out all the pain," Kramer said, "all the gasping breaths, block it all out of your mind and function as an automaton." Vince was driving them like a "madman," Kramer said in the second week of training. "It's hard to resist hating him, his ranting, his raving, his screaming, his hollering. But, damn him, he's a great coach." Insisting on perfection and extreme effort at all times, Vince yelled at his offensive backs to run with complete abandon. "You care nothing for anybody or anything, and when you get close to the goal line, your abandon is intensified. Nothing, not a tank, not a wall, not a dozen men can stop you from getting across that goal line." He stared at them. "If I ever see one of my backs get stopped a yard from the goal line," he said, "I'll come off that bench and kick him right in the can."[5]

After a preseason victory over Pittsburgh, Vince had a few words of praise; then he harped on the five major mistakes—three fumbles and two interceptions. "We've made a living here by not making mistakes. We're a team that's noted for not making mistakes." Raising his voice a few decibels, "And we will not make mistakes." Vince kept insisting his players were too nice, too polite, but would later urge them to play hard, clean football. "Vince tells us to hate," said Kramer, "and we say, 'Yes, we hate,' and then he tells us we have to play clean, and we say, 'Yes, we'll play clean,' and we accept everything, all the contradictions. Everything that Vince Lombardi says is so, is so."

The Packers compiled a 6–0 record in their exhibition season, outscoring opponents, 157–58, but when a reporter asked if his team was ready for the regular season, Vince responded, "I don't think they're ever ready." As the season opener approached, he urged his players to appreciate the unique importance of the 1967 campaign: "Gentlemen, no team in the history of the National Football League has ever won three straight world championships. If you succeed, you will never forget this year for the rest of your lives." And as he had already told them and would retell them for the next four months, he concluded, "Gentlemen, this is the beginning of the big push."[6]

Michael O'Brien

The 1967 season was the first of a new NFL alignment. There were two conferences—Eastern and Western—and each conference was broken down into two four-team divisions. The Packers played in the Central Division of the Western Conference along with Chicago, Detroit, and Minnesota. After the Packers started weakly—a tie with Detroit and a narrow victory over the Bears—critics began to hover over the Packers' corpse. "Old age, smugness, too many victories are all dissipating the Green Bush machine," said a St. Louis sportswriter; "they're on the brink of disaster." In the *Chicago Tribune* Cooper Rollow thought the team's poor performance lent "credence to a belief held by some football men that the Packer fortress finally is starting to come unglued."[7]

A major problem had been Bart Starr, who had a total of nine passes intercepted in the two games. On October 4, Vince came to his defense, revealing that Starr had been playing with multiple injuries. "I've denied this a number of times," Vince told reporters. "I've denied it in order to protect him . . . from the opposition. He's certainly displayed a great deal of courage in playing." The day before, Vince had almost broken down when he informed the team of Starr's injuries. "I don't know if you guys know it or not," he said, "but this guy's been hurt and he's been in pain, and he's been playing hurt, and he's been . . ." He was too choked up and misty-eyed to complete the sentence. He was about ready to cry. He motioned to another coach to turn off the lights and to start the projector and was unusually quiet during the film.[8]

On October 15, the Minnesota Vikings defeated the Packers, 10–7, breaking Green Bay's seventeen-game undefeated string. The Packers were still 3–1–1, but Vince was worried or, at least, feigned worry. At the morning meeting the following Tuesday the players had expected him to explode, but he acted peculiar, confused, frustrated. He had studied the films, he said, and the situation wasn't bad. The team had blocked well and the loss wasn't a complete team breakdown. Then he called an unusual, special meeting with fourteen older veterans. "Frankly, I'm worried," he told them. "I just don't know what the hell to do." He put the responsibility on the veterans to lead the younger players. The veterans promised to do all they could, but privately they were perplexed. Vince had always known exactly what to do. "If the coach didn't know what to do," thought Ray Nitschke, "who did?" "Maybe he's trying to double-psych us," Kramer speculated.

The following day Vince was no longer confused. He was fuming. He took Fuzzy Thurston into his office and bawled him out for his poor performance against the Vikings. Then he cussed and screamed at the whole team. "I had another look at those movies, and they stink." He pointed at players, saying, "You didn't run," and "You didn't block," and "You didn't do a damn thing," and "You stink." It was the "old" Lombardi, thought Kramer. Nitschke was relieved because "things were back to normal."[9]

Following the slow start the Packers won four of their next five to stand at 5–1–1 at midseason. Vince wasn't always angry and abusive. After defeating the Cardinals, 31–23, in the seventh game, he planted a big kiss on the cheek of Ray Nitschke, who had an exceptional game, and praised safety Tom Brown, who had played the second half with a dislocated shoulder. "Some people say you're not very tough," Vince said of Brown, "but I want to tell you: You're tough enough for me."

In the eighth game, on November 5, the Packers led Baltimore, 10–0, late in the fourth quarter. The Colts scored to make it 10–6, and, on the game's crucial play, the Colts recovered an onside kick, quickly scored a touchdown, and won, 13–10. It was a sudden, shocking defeat. "Damned stupid high-school play like that," Vince fumed afterward in the coaches' room. "Damned stupid play. What in the hell were we doing? What in the hell were we waiting for?" Despite the heartbreaking loss, on the plane ride home from Baltimore Vince made his way back through the aisle, patting players on the back, roughing their hair, and talking to everyone. The next week he gave the team a new saying: "The greatest accomplishment is not in never falling, but in rising again after you fall."

The Packers suffered staggering injuries during the season. Starr, receiver Bob Long, and defensive end Lionel Aldridge all missed portions of the season, but the worst blows occurred in the loss to Baltimore. Backs Elijah Pitts and Jim Grabowski were both badly injured, and consequently inexperienced Donny Anderson, rookie Travis Williams, and aging Ben Wilson had to assume larger roles. Journeyman fullback Chuck Mercein was brought in as a stopgap. "You play with what you have," said Vince after the loss of Pitts and Grabowski. "You take the good with the bad. We've got to regroup ourselves now."[10]

The Packers were 7–2–1 as they prepared to play the Chicago Bears on November 26. A victory would clinch the Central Division championship, and Vince's pulse rate quickened in anticipation. ("I wish we could suit him up," noted Kramer.) "We've got recognition going for us, and self-preservation going for us, and twenty-five thousand dollars going for us," Vince lectured the players. "This is going to be the game of your life. I want every man to play the game of his life. . . . I want tough, hard, clean football. Tough, hard, CLEAN football."

"Boy, I'm really excited," Vince said the day before the game.

Michael O'Brien

"You're getting just like George Halas," someone commented. "Halas?" Vince said with a snort. "Halas? Hah, hah. Halas. I can whip his ass. You whip the ballplayers and I'll whip him." The Packers whipped the Bears, 17–13, but there was no wild celebration in the dressing room afterward, and some reporters thought the team's reaction was blasé. The players had sensed that the victory was only one important step in the long climb to the third championship. Still ahead were three regular-season games, the conference championship game, the NFL championship game, and the second Super Bowl game.[11]

Vince found no reason to begin celebrating either. On Tuesday following the Bear game he cussed and hollered. "If you think we're going to let down," he screamed, "you're crazy. We're going to play just as damned hard as we've ever played in our lives." At practice the following day he was still angry. When Thurston missed a block, Vince shrieked, "WHAT IN THE HELL IS GOING ON HERE? What in the hell are you thinking about? . . . I drive and I drive and I drive, and you guys don't give a damn. You've got too many restaurants, too much hunting, too many outside interests. I've had it. I'm disgusted with you guys. The hell with you. Let's go to defense. The hell with the offense. . . . You guys," he said, "can stick it in your diddy bag." None of the players had ever heard of a diddy bag (a bag sailors use to stow their gear), and Vince sounded ridiculous.

The next day, Thursday, was nearing the end of the practice week, time for Vince to change motivational strategy, time for a lighter, more optimistic, more confident tone. He was full of remorse, "genuinely sorry," thought Kramer, for having been so rough on them. He bounced around, smiled, and laughed, trying to restore good relations. He walked over to a pile of autographed footballs and started throwing them, one by one, through a door into the equipment room. He kept giggling and finally said, "That's pretty good. Ten in a row. I'm getting to be a helluva pitchout man," at which point Max McGee shouted, "Why don't you see if you can throw one in your diddy bag, Coach?" Everyone roared, including Vince. "The sun was in the sky again," noted Kramer. "Everybody was happy."[12]

In December, however, a feature story about Vince in a major magazine made Vince very unhappy. While dining out with friends, he read to his companions portions of an article in the most recent issue of *Esquire*. He was furious. "Am I like this?" he said, hurling the magazine to the floor and slamming his fist on the table. "Am I really like this?" What had aroused his ire was the most severe indictment ever written about his personality, his character, and his coaching. Len Shecter, a free-lance writer who had formerly worked on the *New York Post,* had written the story, "The Toughest Man in Pro Football." At the beginning of training camp in July 1967, Shecter had spent a week in Green Bay gathering information. Vince apparently had been accommodating and did grant him an interview. As a sportswriter Shecter possessed exceptional virtues. Indeed, his keen observations and vibrant, vivid style were among the reasons his article attracted wide attention and aroused the animosity of Vince and his admirers. Some of Shecter's observations were similar to Kramer's, only more vivid, like his description of Vince's drill-sergeant direction of the grass drill in training camp:

> "C'mon, lift those legs, lift 'em. Higher, higher." Suddenly he yells, "Front!" and the players . . . flop on their bellies and as soon as they do, even while they are falling, Lombardi shouts, "Up!" and they must leap to their feet, running, running, faster, higher. "Front!" and they are down. "Back!" and they roll over on their backs. "Up!" Run. "Front!" Down. "Up!" Over and over, always that raucous voice, nagging, urging, demanding ever more from rebelling lungs and legs. "Move those damn legs. This is the worst-looking thing I ever saw. You're supposed to be moving those legs. Front! Up! C'mon, Caffey, move your legs. Keep them moving. C'mon, Willie Davis, you told me you were in shape. Front! Up! C'mon, Crenshaw, get up. It takes you an hour to get up. Faster. Move those legs. Damnit, what the hell's the matter with you guys? You got a lot of dog in you. You're dogs, I tell you. A bunch of dogs. Let's *move.* Front! Up! For the love of Pete, Crenshaw, you're fat. Ten bucks a day for every pound you don't lose. Crenshaw! It's going to cost you ten bucks a day. *Lift those legs!*"

Shecter's graphic account of Vince's reaction to a practice injury captured Vince's impulsiveness:

> There is a pileup and out of the bottom of the pile comes a cry that has been torn out of a man's throat, a shriek of agony. It's Jerry Moore, a rookie guard, who hasn't learned he is not supposed to cry his pain. The pile untangles and Moore is left writhing on the ground, his hands grabbing at a knee which is swelling so fast that in another minute the doctor will have to cut his pants leg to get at it. "Get up!" Lombardi bawls, the thick cords on his heavy, sun-browned neck standing out with the effort. "Get up! Get up off the *ground.*" The sight has

insulted him. He is outraged. "You're not hurt. *You're not hurt.*"[13]

The strengths of Shecter's account, though, were offset by his one-sided treatment of Vince and Green Bay's players, rendering his overall interpretation unconvincing. Shecter was relentlessly hostile and sarcastic. Physically and aesthetically, he found Vince repulsive. Vince spoke in an "irritating, nasal, steel-wool-rubbing-over-grate voice." His "yellow teeth with wide spaces" made him look like an "angry jungle animal." He was overweight and walked with his "belly sucked in" and chest extended like a "pigeon's." Vince was a ruthless martinet, hotly insulting to the players—"all the time." He met news of an injury with "enmity," devised "fiendish" drills, and turned grown men with families into "groveling, sweat-soaked, foamy-mouthed animals." (The word "animal," kinds of animals, and animalistic behavior appeared frequently in Shecter's story.) Vince was "tightfisted" in negotiating players' contracts, unrelievedly hostile to the Wisconsin press, "frigidly aloof" with local townsfolk, "impolite even to his wife," and so ill-mannered he neglected to say "please" or "thank you" for social courtesies. He ran a "fiefdom" in Green Bay, and although the Packers were supposed to be municipally owned, in fact "they are an autocracy, run by Vince Lombardi." Vince's philosophy was dangerous, right-wing nonsense. His speech before the American Management Association resembled "the memoirs of some South American general." Shecter also brought forth anonymous sources to criticize. "Coach, I'm afraid," says one, "is only interested in his own image and people who can help him." Shecter quoted players who praised Vince, but within the context of the hostile story their statements seemed insipid. Shecter portrayed the Packers' players as callous, sadistic, masochistic, "crazy" monsters who in full football regalia looked like "Boris Karloff in *Frankenstein*." An accompanying article in *Esquire* labeled Green Bay's fans "raving . . . madmen."[14]

Distressed and embarrassed, Vince sought the advice and consolation of his coaching peers and friends. Shecter had portrayed him as "Mussolini" and a "Mafia man," Vince complained to Paul Brown. "I just think you ought to live with it and be yourself," Brown advised, "and the truth will eventually come out as to the kind of person you really are." Jerry Izenberg had never seen Vince so emotionally distraught. He talked quietly to Izenberg about the injustice. "If you don't talk to people, you're damned," Vince said. "If you do, you're damned. . . . I open up our place to a guy and look at what he does to me." When

Matilda Lombardi phoned to express her dismay with the article, his mother's distress refueled Vince's anger.

In a few weeks Vince had settled down. Overall he handled the problem well, marking it down as a hatchet job, refusing to issue any public statement, and letting friends handle his defense. Red Smith, Howard Cosell, and other sports reporters defended him. Shecter's onslaught did increase Vince's self-awareness, making him more conscious that he often projected himself in a rude, mean way. During the rest of the season, he was noticeably more considerate of reporters.[15]

Meanwhile, Vince kept prodding his team. When the Packers met the Rams in Los Angeles in the next-to-last regular-season game, his approach was similar to that for the Packers-Rams game of the year before. The Packers were already the Central Division champions; the Rams were 9–1–2 and in a tight race with the Colts for the Coastal Division title. Perceiving the Colts as slightly less formidable than the Rams, some Packers wanted to deny the Rams the title in order to play the Colts for the Western Conference championship two weeks later. Mostly, the Rams were fighting for their lives, and the Packers were fighting for their pride. Pride, though, was sufficient motivation for Vince.

He was hard on the players all week. In the locker room before the game he trembled; Willie Davis could see his leg shaking. "I wish I didn't have to ask you boys to go out there and do the job," he told them. "I wish I could go out and do it myself. Boy, this is one game I'd really like to be playing in. This is a game that you're playing for your pride." Davis was so aroused by the pep talk, he said later, that if Vince hadn't quickly opened the locker room door, "I was going to make a hole in it." It was an exciting game. The Packers scored in the fourth quarter to lead, 24–20, but late in the contest the Rams blocked Donny Anderson's punt, and with thirty-four seconds remaining scored on a five-yard pass to win, 27–24. Vince took the loss hard. He staggered in the hallway; one player feared he was having a heart attack. "Goddamnit, I wanted this one!" he screamed. But by the time he met with reporters he had composed himself. "Gentlemen," he said, his face suffused with pride, "I am as proud of this football team as I can be. I think it's a credit to professional football and to the National Football League when a team which clinched its division championship [two] weeks ago plays as hard as this team did today. They are men of great desire and great dedication."[16]

The game convinced many observers that Vince was a credit to pro football. Said George Allen, the Rams' coach: "Vince and the Packers played the game like champions—like it was the Super Bowl." The most extravagant praise came from *Los Angeles Times* columnist Jim Murray, who addressed himself to Vince's critics (and probably had Shecter most in mind). The Packers had gone down with "all guns firing," said Murray, an indication of their coach's dedication to excellence. America, Murray charged, increasingly had to tolerate "shiftless plumbing, downright shoddy cabinetry or carpentry, fatal assembly line work, doctors who are after yachts, not disease," but Vince was different. His team lived up to the warranty. No one asked for his money back. "His critics have said Lombardi doesn't belong in this century. And they are right. Pride in workmanship like that hasn't been seen much in this century. . . . V. T. Lombardi guarantees you are getting the original, the genuine Green Bay Packers, not a shoddy imitation. Let those who criticize him ask if THEIR product could stand that rigid inspection lately."[17]

After the Rams won the Coastal Division title, the Packers had to play them again, for the Western Conference championship, in Milwaukee on Saturday, December 23. With their record of 11–1–2 the Rams appeared to be the best team in pro football. In winning their last six games they had averaged thirty points while holding opponents to an average of only ten. In contrast, the Packers had lost their last two regular-season games, including the contest with the Rams. The Packers were too old, were slowing down, were washed up, said observers. Some players on the Rams claimed their earlier victory had broken the Packers' mystique. The Packers seemed to be a team of the past; the Rams were the team of the future.

The Rams and the prognosticators, though, had dealt Vince a pair of aces: He posted the embarrassing clippings on the team's bulletin board. At the Tuesday morning meeting with players, he began his most brilliant motivational campaign. "We may be wounded," he told the players. "We may be in trouble. Some people may be picking Los Angeles over us. But I'll tell you one thing: That damned Los Angeles better be ready to play a football game when they come in here 'cause they're going to have a battle. I'll guarantee that. This team has a history of rising to the occasion. This is it. There's no tomorrow." And, one more time, "This is really the start of the big push."

On Tuesday or Wednesday Vince read to the team the text of St. Paul's First Epistle to the Corinthians, ninth chapter, twenty-fourth verse: "Know ye not that they which run in a race run all, but one receiveth the prize. So run, that ye may obtain." For the rest of the week Vince reminded them of the biblical injunction. "Run to win," he said, burning the phrase into their minds. "I kept saying to myself," recalled Nitschke, "I'm running to win, I'm running to win." On Thursday Vince was jolly, jovial, intensified, bounding around. "It's as though he had been lying dormant for fourteen weeks," observed Kramer, "just going through the motions to get all the unimportant stuff, all those regular-season games, out of the way."[18]

His pregame speech was intense and emotional. "There are fifty thousand people out there waiting for you to come out of this dressing room. They're all your family and your friends. They didn't come here to see the Rams. They came here to see you, and any time you let a team sit in California and say how they've broken your magic and what they're going to do to you, they're challenging you, and if they get away with it, it will be something you'll have to live with the rest of your lives. It's like a guy calling you out before your family and saying, 'I'm gonna whip you.' " The week's emotional preparation and the pep talk had put the players in a frenzy. "Coach, just don't say any more!" yelled one player. "No more!" Nitschke was growling. Boyd Dowler ran to the bathroom and threw up. Bob Skoronski turned to Willie Davis and said, "I'm going to kill that [Lamar] Lundy."[19]

For over a quarter it seemed the Rams were, indeed, the team of the future. The Packers had fumbled twice and the Rams led, 7–0. But Vince was proud of his game plan. He neutralized the Rams' powerful pass rush by double-teaming Deacon Jones and Lamar Lundy on pass plays, and the Rams adjusted poorly. Early in the second quarter the tide began to change. Starr completed seventeen of twenty-three passes, Travis Williams scored two touchdowns and rushed for eighty-eight yards, and the Packers defeated the Rams, 28–7. As the Packers ran to the locker room, said Kramer, they were "laughing and shouting and absolutely floating."

In the locker room Vince could barely talk. "Magnificent. Just magnificent. I've been very proud of you guys all year long. You've overcome a great deal of adversity. You've hung in there, and when the big games came around . . ." He couldn't say any more. He knelt down, crying, and led the team in the Lord's Prayer. After the prayer, he started hugging everyone. Kramer was also misty-eyed. "I felt so proud, proud of myself and proud of my teammates and proud of my coaches. I felt like I was a part of something special. . . . It's a feeling of being together, completely together, a singleness of purpose, accomplishing something that is very difficult to accomplish, accomplishing something that a lot of people thought you couldn't accomplish." Willie Davis credited Vince for the victory. "We might have beaten them anyway but . . . I say it was the man."[20]

Eight days later, on Sunday, December 31, 1967, the Packers had to play the Dallas Cowboys for the NFL championship in Green Bay. Vince thought he had taken care of the potential problem of frigid playing conditions because earlier in the year he had purchased a gigantic electric blanket and installed it under the field. Cables laid the length of the field, six inches deep, about a foot apart, and activated by a thermostat heated the six inches of topsoil. Vince was proud of his system but had joked that if it failed, critics would call it "Lombardi's folly."[21]

On Friday Vince gave his last major pep talk for the Dallas game. "I want that third championship. AND I DESERVE IT. WE ALL DESERVE IT." Then he lowered his voice and complimented the team. "Lots of better ballplayers than you guys have gone through here. But you're the type of ballplayers I want. You've got character. You've got heart. You've got guts." He stopped abruptly. "Okay, that's it," he said. "That's my pregame speech. Let's go." At practice he remained mostly in a cheerleading mood, smacking his hands and saying, "We're ready, we're ready."

On Saturday he was happy. His electric blanket seemed to be working perfectly. Inside the stadium puffs of steam rose from the turf, like a low fog rolling across the gridiron. The ground was soft and cool but not cold. On the morning of the game, though, the frigid temperature was almost unbearable, more suited for the defense of Stalingrad or for sniping at Napoleon than for playing a football game. At kickoff it was minus thirteen degrees, with the swirling west-northwest wind bringing the wind-chill factor to between thirty and forty degrees below zero. Worried that playing the game might endanger players and spectators, some NFL officials decided to seek a doctor's advice. Vince objected. "What do you want to talk to a doctor about it for? The weather's beautiful. The sun is shining! . . . It's a great day!"

Before the game Vince was relaxed until he learned his electric blanket had failed him, conjuring up visions of "Lombardi's folly." A tarp had covered the field and heat had risen, forming moisture on the tarp. When the groundscrew pulled the tarp off, the field was soft, his system had worked perfectly, except the moisture flash-froze, quickly turning the field as hard as rock. Chuck Lane had to tell him the field had frozen. "I never heard such a bellow in my life," said Lane. Vince, Jr., was with his father when he learned the bad news. "They're gonna say that I did it on purpose," he said to his son. "They'll never believe what happened." Henry Jordan had his own explanation for the failure: "I figured Lombardi got on his knees to pray for cold weather and stayed down too long."[22]

Dallas won the pregame toss of the coin, leading a reporter to quip that the Cowboys had "elected to go home." Someone dotted the press tables with stickers shaped like a bare foot and on them inscribed, "Follow me to Miami." In the awful cold, everything was confused. On the sideline Tom Landry's communications were hampered. "You just don't play football in temperatures like that," he said later. At least three Dallas Cowboys suffered frostbite and two others had medical treatment for cold-weather problems. "I damn near froze my toes off," said Nitschke. "It was a miserable feeling." In the first half Starr threw two touchdown passes to Boyd Dowler, and the Packers led, 14–0, in the second quarter. But Dallas came back. The Dallas defense harassed Starr almost all afternoon, dumping him eight times for seventy-six yards in losses. With less than five minutes remaining in the game, Dallas led, 17–14. The Packers managed to sustain a sixty-eight-yard drive, and with thirteen seconds remaining, Starr kept the ball himself and dove one yard for the crucial touchdown. The Packers had won a thrilling 21–17 victory.[23]

Alone with the players afterward, Vince expressed his appreciation. "I can't talk anymore," he said. "I can't say any more." He tried to contain his tears as the team knelt and prayed. "Then we exploded, with shouts of joy and excitement," said Kramer, "the marks of battle, the cuts, the bruises, and the blood all forgotten." With the press Vince grinned but was unable to relax. He kept squirming in his chair, getting up and sitting down again. Asked about his decision to gamble on a touchdown when an almost sure, short field goal would have tied the game, sending it into overtime, he responded, "All the world loves a gambler . . . except when he loses." Of the failure of his prized electric blanket, he said discreetly, "It was better than it might have been but not as good as we had hoped."

Early in the season, especially during training camp, Kramer's diary had portrayed Vince as a villain, a martinet. But toward the end, the closer the Packers came to the championship—and the championship money—his comments about his coach became more sympathetic, grateful, and admiring. After the Dallas game, when he was led in front of the TV cameras, Kramer addressed himself to Shecter's criticism that Vince was cruel and vicious. "Many things have been said about Coach," he said to millions of viewers, "and he is not always understood by those who quote him. The players understand. This is one beautiful man."[24]

Tom Landry later credited the Packers' victory to the character Vince instilled in his players, which allowed them to overcome adversity. "The discipline and conditioning programs they went through, the punishment and suffering, they all tend to develop character. And once you get character, then you develop hope in all situations. That is the great thing that comes out of it. And Vince developed a lot of character in his players, character that a lot of them probably would never have had without the leadership and discipline he developed in them. Therefore, they never were out of a game. They never felt like there wasn't some hope. And that is what carried them through to that third championship," Landry concluded. "That is what beat us."[25]

During the week before the Super Bowl contest with the Oakland Raiders in Miami on January 14, 1968, Vince, who suffered a debilitating head cold, tried to prevent his team from losing its edge. He quartered the squad at the Galt Ocean Mile in Fort Lauderdale, an hour's drive from the night life of Miami, and warned them not to swim in the pool, hang around the lobby, or break curfew. He wanted them to worry about Oakland but inadvertently presented conflicting interpretations of the strength of the Raiders. It would be a "disgrace" to lose to a team in "that Mickey Mouse league," he told them, and in the same breath warned that Oakland was a "helluva good football team." He was more sentimental than usual. Players had heard the rumors that he would retire after the season, and although he didn't directly indicate his intention, they sensed the game would be his last. He tried to get riled up occasionally, but his heart wasn't in it, and his rage seemed hollow. The players were calm and confident. "We knew we would win," said Chuck Mercein. A few even seemed interested in the proper decorum in the locker room after the game. "I just can't imagine us throwing Coach Lombardi in the shower or pouring something over his head," said Marv Fleming.[26]

Unlike his rude attitude the year before, Vince was patient, gracious, and cooperative with the media at Super Bowl II. His biggest problems were behind him—the Colts, the Rams, the Cowboys. Oakland offered less to worry about. "He cooperated like crazy," said an observer, "[and] went through all kinds of interrogations." He had hellos and how-are-yous for most reporters. He was especially adept handling one awkward situation. A blind reporter grilled him relentlessly at a large press conference, but Vince was "brilliantly gracious," said Chuck Johnson, and offered to see the reporter privately at the end of the press conference. As the conference ended, the reporters gave Vince a warm ovation. "That was a first!" said Johnson.[27]

"It's very difficult for me to say anything," Vince told the team before they took the field against Oakland. "Anything I could say would be repetitious. This is our twenty-third game this year. . . . Boys, I can only say this to you: Boys, you're a good football team. You are a proud football team. You are the world champions. You are the champions of the National Football League for the third time in a row, for the first time in the history of the National Football League. That's a great thing to be proud of. But let me just say this: All the glory, everything that you've had, everything that you've won is going to be small in comparison to winning this one. This is a great thing for you. You're the only team maybe in the history of the National Football League to ever have this opportunity to win the Super Bowl twice. Boys, I tell you I'd be so proud of that I just fill up with myself. I just get bigger and bigger and bigger. It's not going to come easy. This is a club that's gonna hit you. They're gonna try to hit you and you got to take it out of them. You got to be forty tigers out there. That's all. Just hit. Just run. Just block and just tackle. If you do that, there's no question what the answer's going to be in this ball game. Keep your poise. Keep your poise. You've faced them all. There's nothing they can show you out there you haven't faced a number of times. Right? . . . Let's go. Let's go get 'em."[28]

There was no sustained drama in the game. Like Super Bowl I, it was close for the first half but no contest thereafter. The Packers led, 16–7, at halftime, but in the third quarter they scored a touchdown and a field goal, and in the fourth quarter Herb Adderley's sixty-yard interception return for a touchdown sealed the contest. The Packers won, 33–14. As Kramer and Forrest Gregg carried Vince off the field, he grinned, slapped his two linemen, and hollered, "Head for the dressing room, boys."

When he gathered the players, he said, "This has to be one of the great, great years. . . . You know everything happened to us. We lost a lot of people. . . . Boys, I'm really proud of you. We should all be very, very thankful." When Adderley expressed his congratulations, Vince gave his cornerback a big smile, a hug, and said, "Congratulations to you, too." Vince was crying. Meanwhile, hundreds of reporters had jostled and squirmed their way into the dungeons of the Orange Bowl to question him. He grinned, chuckled, and twinkled throughout the session. When the players returned to Green Bay, three thousand fans greeted them at the airport. It was a "mature" reception, not the delirious kind of some earlier championship seasons. "We're getting like the players in the locker room," said one fan. "They don't whoop it up anymore either." But, he quickly added, "We're awfully proud of this team."[29]

Vince didn't return to Green Bay with the players. He stayed in Miami to attend a league meeting and then, more importantly, to vacation for ten days in southern Florida to ponder his future. "No announcements," he had declared flatly after the game to a question about his retirement. The following day, though, he said, "I really have to sit down for some serious self-conversation and give Vince Lombardi a good, hard look. And I've got to talk to Mrs. Lombardi." Actually, for over a year he had been reflecting on retirement from his coaching duties and had almost finalized his decision.

The reason he contemplated retirement was simple: His dual roles as coach and general manager were too burdensome and growing worse, resulting in pressure so intense that he worried about his physical, mental, and emotional health. He thought the general manager's position alone was a full-time responsibility. Complex new problems were mounting. Ahead were merger meetings, the first interleague player trades, a new television contract, and negotiations with the players' union plus his normal, multifaceted responsibilities as general manager. How could he be general manager and still coach effectively at the same time? He had thought of continuing and ridding himself of some duties, but he couldn't find a way to free himself from the most burdensome coaching chores. Only he could dig out the information from game films. Only he could advise the quarterbacks. Only he could motivate the players. "I had to drive everybody—my players, my family, and myself," he said later.[30]

A year earlier, after a game in 1966, he had told Father Dennis Burke confidentially that he wanted to get away from the tensions that plagued him. "Father," he said, "I think I'm going to have to get out of this. I feel the pressure so much that I have to do something about it." A major reason he hadn't retired after the 1966 season was his concern about replacing Jim Taylor. Could young Jim Grabowski adequately fill in? There was also the overall problem of replacing aging veterans and developing younger players and the chance to win an unprecedented third straight title. "I just felt I needed [1967]," he stated.[31]

The pressure increased in 1967. The off-season was his "worst"— more league meetings, less time to golf. When he did play golf, the round was no longer relaxing. "It's not fun," he told an interviewer in May 1967. "You come in after a round and the natural thing to do is sit around, talk, and have a drink and a sandwich." But he knew he had twenty phone calls to return and telegrams that "must" be answered. "That's fun? So, I sit in the office all day long and transact business." The phone calls were driving him mad. "Many of them come from Jim Taylor, and many come in regard to Taylor. He wants to know how much we'll give him, other clubs want to know . . . his physical condition, newspapermen want to know what's new, and it goes like that day after day."[32]

After training camp started, he worked the next six months—mid-July 1967 to mid-January 1968—without a single day off. He had kept himself physically fit by doing isometrics and exercising on the Universal System, and each year he had a physical exam. In 1963, after smoking more than two packs of cigarettes a day for many years, he stopped smoking—cold turkey. Yet he increasingly worried about his physical health. Gastric pains, mild bursitis in his legs, and back spasms bothered him by 1967. Mostly he worried about dizzy spells and shortness of breath. At a press conference he suddenly stopped, shook his head, tapped his chest, and said, "Phew . . . my heart's coming right out of my shirt. I can't get my breath." He inhaled deeply, took a drink, and continued. Marie constantly worried that he might suffer a heart attack, and Vince probably did, too. Later evidence indicated that he did, indeed, have an undiagnosed heart condition, but in 1967 his specific problem was that his excitement and yelling caused him to hyperventilate. His doctors told him the problem wasn't serious, but he continued to worry.[33]

He also worried about his mental and emotional health. "Nobody will ever know the kind of pressure it was," Marie reflected. "It's too much to ask anybody to do, year in and year out." Before 1967, when he was depressed Vince occasionally said to Marie, "I'm going to quit," but he wasn't serious. In 1967 he was serious. He would come home and slump in his chair, mentally and physically exhausted. "What's the matter with the world today?" he complained to Marie. "What's the matter with people? I have to go on that field every day and whip people. It's for them, not just me, and I'm getting to be an animal."

Many noticed the pressure's damaging impact. "I noticed the change in him," recalled Landry. "The pressure that third year—for that third in a row—was tremendous on him." He shook and trembled at some team meetings. "To win you have to pay a price," observed Nitschke, "and the coach had paid more than his share." Chuck Lane seldom saw his boss relaxed. "He was blacking out," said Lane, and "had great fear for his own sanity."[34]

When he consulted Marie about his desire to quit coaching, she did not urge him to persevere. "I could have encouraged him to reconsider," she said, "but I didn't want his health on my conscience." Besides Marie, the only other person he sought out for advice was Earl Blaik. After Vince explained the burdens and the pressures, Blaik sensed the situation was serious and urged him to retire. "I told him to do it and do it quickly because he was at the end of his rope," recalled Blaik. "He needed time to recharge his batteries."[35]

Driving home in the car after the victory over Dallas, Vince informed his son he was retiring. "He told me that I had just seen him coach his next-to-last football game," said Vince, Jr. "I think I was one of the first people he told." On Friday, January 12, 1968, two days before Super Bowl II, Vince had showed up for the team meeting dressed uncharacteristically in a business suit because he later had to attend a meeting. "Okay, boys," Vince said, rubbing his hands together, thinking what to say. "This may be the last time we'll be together, so . . . uh . . ." His lips trembled, his body quivered. He was on the verge of crying. He couldn't finish the sentence. Instead he sat down, facing the movie screen, his back to the players, and ordered the team to break up. After the defensive unit left to go to its meeting, he remained with the offensive team. He turned on the projector and let it run, not saying anything, not bothering to instruct the players until late in the film. "We all had lumps in our throats," said Starr. It had been "hell" to play for Vince, thought Kramer, but he couldn't imagine playing without his coach's driving force. "I don't want to play if he's not around."[36]

In late January, after he returned from Miami, Vince informed the Packers' executive committee of his decision to retire from coaching and recommended Phil Bengtson as his replacement. Committee members desperately sought to change his mind. They offered him more money, but he wasn't moved. "Vince, is there anything we can do?" members kept pleading. "Vince, what the hell are you going to do besides open the mail?" asked Fred Trowbridge, Sr. Trowbridge urged him to postpone his decision for four months, but Vince was adamant and the executive committee had no choice but to grant his wish. On Monday, January 29, 1968, the Packers announced that Vince would hold a press conference at Oneida on Thursday evening, February 1. The unusual announcement fueled three days of speculation that he would either retire or take a position with another team.[37]

At 8:07 P.M. on Thursday, Vince rose and blinked into the lights of a dozen television cameras. One hundred twenty newsmen covered the event. To keep his emotions reined, he had written down his remarks and read them. They were typically brief and to the point. He would retire from coaching, he said, for two reasons: the complexity of directing a pro team and the requirements of coaching, a "seven-days-a-week job the whole year around." He thought it was impossible to try to do both jobs. "I must relinquish one of them." Before the press conference Len Wagner had written in the *Press-Gazette* that the "strain of coaching and general managing is taking its toll on Lombardi's health. This, I believe, is the real key factor, though Lombardi may deny it." At the press conference Vince did deny it. "I am in excellent health," he insisted, and "in good physical condition—any rumors to the contrary are false." They weren't false, of course, and Vince knew it, but for him to admit otherwise would damage his reputation. Future employers, business partners, his staff, and others might feel uneasy working with a man who had recently approached a breakdown.

At the conclusion of his statement Vince introduced the new head coach, Phil Bengtson, his "capable and loyal" assistant, whom Vince was "positive" would continue to produce "excellent" teams. After introducing Bengtson, tears trickled down Vince's cheeks, and he had to compose himself briefly in a side room. Questioned afterward by reporters, he said he had been contemplating retirement "for a year" and had mentioned it to Bengtson, but because of the "terrible blow" of losing Jim Taylor he felt it was not "fair to burden [Bengtson] with the job this year." Did his retirement mean he was committed to not coaching again? "Yes, it does," Vince replied.[38]

Vince's decision sparked widespread praise for his coaching success and his character. He was a "full-fledged genius," said Arthur Daley; a "great, great competitor," said George Halas, "and one of the great coaches in the history of football"; "a wonderful man," added Paul Brown. In the *Press-Gazette*, columnist Bob Woessner thought Vince would be remembered as a "man of excellence." In the modern world of changing values, said Woessner, it had become "cornball to be virtuous. The longhairs and the wiseguys sneer at things like loyalty and patriotism and love and devotion. But Vince Lombardi doesn't. He showed, in this world of skin-thin chrome and neon, that there is a place for the old virtues." As the torrent of praise indicated, by retiring at such a lofty plateau Vince was about to occupy a unique position—a legend in his own time.

Before his retirement, as he vacationed in Miami, Vince rested but he knew he was incapable of relaxing too long, inadvertently signaling the problem he would encounter after retirement. "This is a great life down here," he said, "but I honestly don't know how much of it I could take. If I had to stay away from work too long—well, I might not like it." After he announced his retirement some of his coaching peers questioned the wisdom of his decision. "I don't think he should have done it," said the seventy-three-year-old Halas. Paul Brown, who had been out of coaching briefly and was currently owner-coach of the Cincinnati Bengals, warned ominously, "I hope he doesn't miss coaching as much as I did."[39]

XV

The
Agony of Retirement

AFTER VINCE RETIRED, A GREEN BAY BUSINESS ASSOCIATION BEGAN PLANNING A "Vince Lombardi Day" for August 7, 1968. "This man has been the biggest single factor for putting Green Bay back on the face of the earth," explained Norman Chernick, chairman of the event. "We don't ever want Vince to feel that he has been taken for granted." Vince tried to dissuade the backers of the celebration, but they appealed to his civic pride. "If it's good for the city," he said, "I'm in favor of it. This is my home."

The day-long salute began at 7:30 A.M. mass at Resurrection Church. Vince arrived almost on Lombardi time—ten minutes early—and joked to those waiting to enter that at least "I got you all up for early Mass." A *Press-Gazette* reporter proudly delighted in some of the "corny" events during the rest of the day: baton twirlers, pompon girls, a rock 'n' roll band, hundreds of balloons, a box lunch of chicken and orangeade, plus an amateur hour. The governor proclaimed "Vince Lombardi Day" throughout the state, two downtown theaters showed Packer film highlights, and players signed autographs. Wisconsin's political leaders and the presidents of several NFL clubs attended the celebration.

On his day Vince exuded warmth, humor, and exuberance. A highlight of the festivities was the late-morning renaming of Highland Avenue to

Lombardi Avenue. On the way to the ceremony Vince asked Paul Hornung if he wanted a ride in the convertible provided Vince and Marie. "No, Coach, I wouldn't want to upstage you," Hornung responded. "You always did," Vince retorted. It was a short, familiar drive from his office to the renaming. Vince remarked to his chauffeur, his friend Jake Stathas, "Most of the [streets] have been named for dead admirals or presidents. . . . How do you tell them in your own words, this is a great honor?" Before the ceremony three Air Force Golden Hawk jets swooped low in a V formation to extend their greeting. Vince reminded the crowd that he wasn't dead yet and promised everyone present they would never get a ticket on his street. Asked if he ever dreamed as a youngster in New York that a street would be named after him, he quickly answered, "Yes, Broadway."

A capacity crowd of fifty-one hundred attended an "Evening with Vince" at the Brown County Arena. Peter Carlesimo, Fordham's athletic director and master of ceremonies, extolled Vince as a "coach for all seasons." Arthur Modell, owner of the Cleveland Browns, praised his "integrity and honesty." Vince, who had practiced swallowing the lump in his throat all day, had difficulty again at the evening event. "I do not stand alone," he said, and he thanked his staff, coaches, players, and family. He couldn't resist reminding the audience of his philosophy: "You all know what my coaching creed is, and that is to win, to win, to win." There were also light moments. Max McGee sauntered up from his seat and presented Vince with five loaves of bread and two fishes. As Vince guffawed and rose to display a fish, Carlesimo quipped to the thousands of guests, "You can pick up your portions on the way out."[1]

Unfortunately, the celebration was only a brief, joyous interlude during the most depressing, frustrating six months of Vince's life. By then he realized he had made a tragic mistake in retiring from coaching. The first five months of retirement, though, were fine. He gave speeches and accepted awards. He golfed and relaxed more than he ever had during the off-season in Green Bay. Yet his responsibilities as general manager kept him busy and interested.

NFL business occupied much of his time, particularly the ominous threat posed by the Players' Association. Compared to professional basketball and baseball players, football players had been slow to organize effectively. The NFL Players' Association was formed in 1957 but had languished until 1966. The merger of the NFL and the AFL and the subsequent decline in players' salaries, the league's highly publicized and lucrative television contracts, and reports that the Teamsters might organize the players put new life into the Players' Association. In 1968 the association drew up twenty-one demands, including increased pension benefits and a higher minimum salary. After negotiations reached an impasse, the players agreed to strike at training camps. When the owners retaliated by locking the veterans out of camp, pro football had a major crisis.

Through the spring and early summer Vince attended scores of meetings of the NFL owners' committee seeking a settlement. The challenging discussions diverted his mind from the void of not coaching. "I've been too busy . . . to miss coaching so far," he said in May. He disliked the Players' Association and supported the lockout. If there was a strike, he believed, some players would cross the picket line and create dissension. "I don't want to divide my team," he insisted. On July 14, four days after the Packers' training camp had been scheduled to open, a settlement was reached. The players' pension benefits were nearly doubled, and the minimum annual salary rose from $5,000 to $12,000.[2]

As Vince narrowed the scope of his duties, he also expanded the range of his interests. He even became an actor. In late March he appeared briefly in the United Artists' movie version of George Plimpton's book *Paper Lion*. He played himself, the Packers' coach. At 9:00 A.M. he showed up on the set and was handed the script. "As long as the lines are natural to a coach," he told the director, "everything will be all right." The scene called for Plimpton, played by Alan Alda, to ask Vince if he could work out with the Packers to write a book about his experiences. Vince was to act intrigued, but because he thought Plimpton was insane, to turn him down, firmly but sweetly. Vince was excited and grinned broadly as the props were moved and the cameras positioned. There were more people than usual on the set to watch the peerless coach, more, said an observer, "than if Cary Grant were going to make love to Raquel Welch." Stagehands hustled coffee and a soft chair for him, directors fell over one another congratulating him on his poise, and actors laughed at his quips. Rehearsal started at 9:30 A.M. Vince recited his lines stiffly but without error. Take 5 was perfect. Pleased with himself, he burst out laughing and spun around with glee. He was having fun and would make a few thousand dollars for a few hours' work. At 10:30 A.M., his acting day completed, he strolled off the set, signed autographs, and chatted with a reporter. "It's easier than coaching," he said. "You can improvise."[3]

Vince's new interests included business ventures. Marie thought her husband was a financial genius, but until he retired from coaching, Vince had no notable success with his business endeavors. By 1968, though, he was earning handsome amounts for his speeches and endorsements and during the year struck gold in two fabulously successful business enterprises. Businessmen admired him and curried his favor, not for his business acumen but for his stature as the premier exemplar of leadership, motivation, and success. After 1967 he endorsed scores of products, always linking the values he cherished in football with the product he endorsed. Along with other prominent persons, including Richard Nixon, he appeared in an advertising brochure for credit unions. "Teamwork is the primary ingredient of success," said Vince's message. "The credit union . . . is just such a team, for—like in athletics—people who work together will win, whether it be against complex football defenses, or the complex problems of modern society."

To handle some of his business activities Vince hired an agent, Frank Scott, a New Jersey resident who specialized in endorsements and personal appearances for athletes. Vince continued to arrange many of his own appearances and endorsements, but Scott arranged four: an advertisement for Nestlé's chocolate and three speeches. For each speech Vince received about $2,000. Scott later claimed he could have arranged "fifty deals" for his popular client, but Vince was selective. "He felt certain commercials weren't proper for the dignity of a coach," recalled Scott. Vince refused to endorse beer and smoking products because he thought they would adversely influence youth. When a shaving cream company offered him a $10,000 advance to endorse its product, Vince instructed Scott to reject it. "I shave with a different product," Vince told him. On this occasion and others, Scott was impressed with Vince's ethics: "Not many men would cut it that fine." Overall, in three decades of representing thousands of athletes, Scott judged Vince as the "most outstanding man that I've ever been associated with in sports." Vince was "salable," moral, and principled. As a public speaker, said Scott, "I never heard a member of the clergy or a political figure or anybody else that could be as dynamic. . . . He *moved* you."[4]

Two business ventures in 1968 succeeded beyond anything Vince could have imagined. One was the film *Second Effort,* which he made for the Dartnell Corporation. A Chicago publishing house specializing in reference books, manuals, and newsletters, Dartnell had also been a pioneer in developing sales training films. The films taught salesmen to open and close sales, make effective presentations, overcome resistance, and sell "quality." Norman Vincent Peale and Joyce Brothers had been featured in its earlier productions. When film sales began to decline, management sought an imaginative new approach. William Fetridge, Dartnell's president, had been mulling over an idea he had heard on football broadcasts—the "second effort." If the salesman could be motivated to make a second effort after being turned down, he would enjoy greater success. For over a year Fetridge sought the proper celebrity to feature in a film using his idea. Vince suddenly popped into his mind. "He's the one!" Fetridge exclaimed. He outlined his proposal in a letter, and Vince invited him to Green Bay to discuss the proposal. After a brief presentation, Vince quickly consented to act in the film. Vince's contract provided him 15 percent of the film's royalties. It was a new challenge; he had nothing to lose except a little time and work.[5]

A thirteen-man Chicago film crew produced *Second Effort* at the Packers' headquarters in only three and a half days (May 7–10, 1968). The resulting twenty-eight-minute film was awkward, stilted, and poorly acted. One reviewer's description of it as a "slogan-a-second presentation of pap, in color, which would be hysterically funny if it weren't so serious" was overly harsh but close to the mark. Ron Masak, a shy, bumbling, perspiring salesman, makes a call on Vince to sell a product. Intimidated by the famous coach, he drops his pen, fumbles his sales order, and is finally impaled by Vince's gaze. Vince asks him to call back next week, and Masak too readily agrees. Vince stops him before he leaves and asks, "Why didn't you make the second effort? Do you always give up that easily?" Vince proceeds to teach the neophyte some lessons. The same principles that apply to building a winning football team can be applied to many aspects of life, Vince explains. "For example, selling." Then the slogans start fast and furious. "Football is fierce competition, just the way selling is. . . . You can accomplish almost anything if you are willing to pay the price. . . . Success in anything in this world is 75 percent mental. . . . Winning isn't everything, but it's the only thing."

Soon Masak is calling Vince "Coach." "Suppose for a minute," Masak says, "I'm a player on the first day in this dressing room. What would you say to me?" Against a background of jubilant locker-room scenes, Vince paces up and down, punching his right fist into his left hand, mulling over his speech. He delivers a brief pep talk highlighting the importance of spartanism, confidence, perseverance, hard work, respect for authority. The two move to the film room, where Vince shows action shots of determined players. A receiver catches a pass in the end zone, bobbles the ball, then grabs it again for a touchdown. "That's what you should have done with me," Vince advises. "He made the second effort. He saw his chance to run to daylight and he took it."

Masak is overwhelmed. "This day is probably going to go down as one of the most important days of my life. . . . I've never met anybody so dedicated in my life. You really believe all this, don't you?" Vince responds, "I don't know how else to live, Ron. Unless a man believes in himself and makes a total commitment to his career and puts everything he has into it—his mind, his body, and his heart—what's life worth to him? If I were a salesman, I'd make this commitment—to my company, to the product, and most of all, to myself.''

Vince had one more lesson. In the dressing room he shows Ron his "motivators," his inspirational cards:

- "Mental toughness is essential to success." (The perfectly disciplined will; character in action; will to win.)
- "Control the ball." (If the salesman covers every point, he increases his chances of success.)
- "Fatigue makes cowards of us all." (Keep in shape.)
- "Operate on Lombardi time." (Arrive early for sales calls.)
- "Make the second effort."

At the conclusion Vince and Ron wander past the Packers' trophy case. Ron is a changed man—erect, confident, self-aware. A twenty-eight-minute transformation under the powerful, magic spell of Vince Lombardi.

As the salesman Masak was too much the overawed straight man to be convincing. Vince, Jr., kidded his father about acting in the film. His father was no Richard Burton or Paul Newman, he said. Vince laughed, but turning serious, asked his son, "Tell me what was wrong with it. Tell me." Vince's acting was as dignified as possible in the consistently awkward scenes. He was forceful and articulate, but he looked stiff, rigid, uncomfortable, self-conscious, perhaps even slightly embarrassed.[6]

Although not an artistic triumph, the film was a resounding commercial success. It relentlessly drove home the analogy between winning football games and winning sales, and for sales representatives the lessons were inspiring. Both realms did require fierce competitiveness, fundamentals, physical stamina, mental toughness, and knowledge of the opponent. Success required hard work, perseverance, self-discipline, and attention to detail. Both demanded winning—second place put "no money in your pocket." Vince sold his players on winning; the salesman must sell his customers on the product. A second effort could, indeed, make a crucial difference in both football and sales.

Dartnell was shocked by the thunderous reception the film received in the sales community. On August 27, 1968, eighty executives of midwestern corporations gathered at Oneida Golf and Riding Club in Green Bay for the world première. Afterward they surrounded Vince, eager for his autograph. Promotional literature touted the film as the finest, most stirring sales film "of all time." Many sales executives agreed. "Brings new blood into sales training and motivational area," said a representative of Bell & Howell. "Outstanding," said an executive at Miller Brewing Company. "The age bracket of our sales forces ranges from thirty-five through sixty-five years," observed a representative of another firm. "They are all professional, high-powered people with high incomes. . . . [It] takes thorough salesmanship to motivate these people, and they all stood up and applauded at the conclusion of the film. It was tremendously inspirational."

Sales and rentals were astonishing. The average *lifetime* sale of a Dartnell film was about 750 copies, but in the first *ten days* after release Dartnell sold seven hundred copies of *Second Effort*. Almost every major sales organization in the country saw the film. Dartnell eventually sold eight thousand copies and had twenty thousand rentals, making the film the largest-selling industrial film in history, the *Gone with the Wind* of training films. For three and a half days of work and a little promotion Vince's share of the royalties was $500,000. Dartnell made millions.[7]

On May 10, 1968, the same day he completed filming *Second Effort*, Vince appeared at a press conference in Milwaukee to announce that he had become chairman of the board of Public Facilities Associates, Inc. (PFA), a real-estate-development firm in Madison. His involvement with the company proved especially fortuitous, for although his investment was small and his role minimal, ten months later PFA's sudden success transformed him into a millionaire.

The responsibility for making Vince a wealthy man belonged primarily to David Carley, who along with his brother, James, had founded the company. David Carley, thirty-nine, a Ph.D. in political science, was a shrewd, industrious, dynamic businessman and a prominent Wisconsin Democrat. He headed the Wisconsin Department of Resource Development from 1958 to 1962 under Democratic Governor Gaylord Nelson, had run unsuccessfully for the Democratic nomination for governor in 1966, and currently was a member of the Democratic National Committee. After leaving state government he became president of an insurance company, but because he wanted to run for political office again and needed free time to raise funds, he quit the insurance position and in 1967 he and his brother founded PFA. David was the president and chief executive officer; James was executive vice president. The company specialized in government-subsidized public housing projects for the poor but mainly the elderly. Later it expanded into the building and financing of elementary and secondary schools as well as college and university facilities. The Carleys carefully analyzed the market, and for almost a year each drove about six thousand miles a month signing up cities for subsidized housing. By May 1968, David Carley claimed to have signed building contracts worth $60 million. Yet the Carleys had ambitious plans for expansion and sought to lure Vince into their enterprise to serve a critical role.

David Carley met Vince through a mutual friend, Jack Koeppler, an insurance associate of Carley and a golfing buddy of Vince. When Carley asked Vince to join PFA, Vince was cautious. He told Carley that the investments urged on him by friends had not succeeded. "He told me," recalled Carley, "that all the money he ever put into stock he lost." But Vince had confidence in Koeppler's judgment, and since Koeppler touted Carley, Vince set aside his reservations and agreed to join the firm. PFA also attracted him because he perceived its projects as having humanitarian and social benefits. In return for 12.5 percent of stock in PFA, Vince agreed to invest about $35,000, paid in installments. However, he ended up having to make only two installments, totaling $6,000.[8]

At the May 10 press conference Vince argued that housing for the poor and the elderly—and complex urban problems generally—must be constructively attacked by thinking people. He hoped to bring his "organizational and executive techniques" to his new role. As usual, he linked his football success with his new endeavor, saying he now had a second "team." "The game is different, the strategies must be different, the opponents are different, but make no mistake about it, we'll be looking for two championships this year." At the press conference David Carley praised Vince's business acumen and inflated the role he intended for his new partner. Vince was "very good on planning and corporate decisions," said Carley, and had enough involvement in the company "to make sure the planning is up to his standards." Vince was going to be "one of the top policymakers of our company." Carley's disingenuous statement and Vince's title—chairman of the board—left the impression Vince would play a large role in developing the company. Actually, the role projected for him, though potentially important, was strictly limited and had nothing to do with planning, policy, or corporate decisionmaking. And, ironically, events moved so swiftly that Vince never had adequate opportunity to fulfill even his limited role.

Like Dartnell Corporation, David Carley coveted Vince because of his name, his prominence, and his reputation as an exceptional leader. He wanted Vince to open the doors to investors and to attract capital to PFA. "He was a spectacular kind of person," said Carley. "He was so well respected as a person and as a leader that his name recognition on a prospectus would have been very helpful to us [in raising funds]." Vince did make a few business contacts for the firm and also appeared at dedication ceremonies for PFA projects in Marinette and Kaukauna. Overall, observed Carley, "We never really got a chance to use Vince in the way he and I first talked about it."

Vince attended board meetings and was conscientious, congenial, and occasionally decisive. But he was not involved in managing the company and did not have the time or the ability to review proposals in detail or propose analytical studies. On one occasion, when Vince argued with David Carley about the company's policy, Carley had to set him straight about who was boss. "Look, you run your football team, and I'll run the company!" he told Vince. Recalled Carley of the incident: "He was a good friend, but . . ." Usually Vince deferred to David and even called him "Coach."

The Carley brothers liked Vince and admired his coaching success, but neither was impressed with Vince's business acumen. "Contrary to comments his wife, Marie, and others made later," said David Carley, Vince "was not a great businessperson." Carley's assessment probably was correct. Vince didn't have sufficient training or adequate time to master the finer points of business, but as events the following year were to prove, he made at least one outstanding business decision: He joined a company directed by David Carley.[9]

"Political strategists in the state may be missing a real winner if they have not at least considered . . . Vince Lombardi as a potential candidate for public office," said the *Milwaukee Sentinel* in early May 1968. The *Sentinel* listed his substantial political assets: leadership, a record of success, administrative talent, a "name," and popularity that rivaled that of any public figure in Wisconsin. Vince's speech to the American Management Association had been impressive, said the newspaper. "If Hollywood movie stars can sit in the California state house [Ronald Reagan] and the United States Senate [George Murphy], what bars exist to the election of a good football coach?"

Political observers also thought politics could be Vince's next challenge. Skeptical that he could harness his energies and be content in his role as general manager, they thought politics might be the fresh interest he was seeking. Vince was indeed susceptible to a call to higher duty, did have a sense of destiny, and had demonstrated a capacity to move and influence people deeply. He said occasionally he thought there were too many "politicians" and a shortage of "statesmen," implying he would be one of the latter.[10]

Before 1967 Vince had seldom publicly expressed his political convictions, but he loved to debate them with friends. His political principles could not be conveniently pigeonholed into the easy categories of left or right, liberal or conservative. "He held mixed-up political views," observed David Carley. Increasingly, though, he became the champion of conservatives and Republicans. Vince seemed only vaguely aware of the dichotomy between his conservative public image and many of his private convictions. On domestic issues he was usually in political accord with those who scoffed at him, while many who viewed him as a political prophet held positions he probably regarded as repugnant.

On most social issues he was a liberal, believing deeply in social justice and the dignity and sanctity of human life. Capital punishment appalled him. He insisted, "We are our brother's keeper. If people can't find work, whether it's their fault or not, you've got to help them, clothe them, and house them properly and try to get rid of the conditions that have held them back." His hatred of bigotry led him to support civil rights and integration. Yet the growing black separatist movement alarmed him. Blacks could not be separate and independent; like everyone else, they were dependent on others in the larger community. "Any kind of separatism is bad," he said, "in football or anywhere else."[11]

Gun control particularly aroused his passion. The assassinations of John Kennedy and then Robert Kennedy led him to support actively the regulation of guns. In July 1968, a month after Robert Kennedy was killed, he joined eighteen pro athletes and sports celebrities in lending his name to the Emergency Committee for Gun Control, chaired by former astronaut John Glenn. The committee urged a halt to all mail-order and interstate sales of guns and favored registration of firearms and licensing of gun owners. Vince passed out petitions for the group and argued with Chuck Lane for his cause. After Vince received a hostile letter from a crank who apparently threatened to shoot him, he slammed the letter on Lane's desk and said, "See! See what your friends are trying to do to me!"

Conservatives and Republicans, though, were attracted to the philosophy he expressed in his speech to the American Management Association. His outspoken support of law, order, morality, discipline, success, authority, leadership, and patriotism and his condemnation of the youth counterculture led them to claim him as one of their own. "There has been a complete breakdown of morality," Vince repeated in speeches and interviews in 1968. The old virtues of "teamwork" and "unity" had given way to individual "license" in the guise of freedom. "There is selfishness rather than a selflessness around today. . . . Our team philosophy . . . is a selflessness. If we could get the same feeling into some of our student bodies and some of our people, we would have a better country."[12]

Until 1969 Vince was a diehard Democrat. "He could see no wrong in a Democrat," said Ockie Krueger. The origin of his party loyalty is partly a mystery. Harry Lombardi had some independent inclinations but usually voted Republican; Vince's sister Madeline was a Republican. Vince, Jr., speculated that Fordham's Jesuits, with their emphasis on social justice, strongly influenced his father. "I don't know if the Jesuits ever turn out a Republican," mused young Vince. Clearly, though, Vince's deep affection for John and Robert Kennedy cemented his loyalty to the Democrats, and when they died, the cement loosened. Vince shared Catholicism and similar social views with the Kennedys, and, like millions of people, was mesmerized by the Kennedys' mystique—their youth, energy, virility, charm, athletic ability and aggressiveness.[13]

Vince met John Kennedy outside St. Willebrord's Church while Kennedy campaigned for the April 5, 1960, Wisconsin primary election. Kennedy shrewdly cultivated Vince's affection with flattery and praise, subtly letting it be known that one of Wisconsin's most famous citizens was on his team. On February 18, fifteen hundred persons attended a reception for Kennedy at the Hotel Northland. Marie was a diehard Republican and an admirer of Richard Nixon, and it took Vince's strongest pressure to convince her to attend. "You're going!" he finally declared, and she went. They stood next to Kennedy in the receiving line, and in his speech Kennedy referred to Vince as an "old friend of mine who has moved to Green Bay and made a big success." When Kennedy defeated Nixon in the 1960 election, Vince joked to friends how nice it would be "to have someone make the sign of the cross in the White House." After Kennedy's assassination Vince's loyalty and affection turned to his brother Robert, whom Vince had also met in Green Bay during the 1960 campaign. Vince thought Robert was the "toughest, gutsiest little guy he'd ever seen." Robert admired Vince and often teased him. "My lateral motion is not quite as good, but I'm still ready to go when you need me," he wrote Vince, adding seriously, "You have been a great friend of the Kennedys and all of us appreciate it." On February 5, 1968, four days after Vince announced his retirement, Kennedy, who was about to enter the 1968 presidential campaign, cabled, "Vince, now would you please come and be my coach?" Vince had some of the peasants' awe for royalty and was always nervous in the presence of the Kennedys. At an NFL meeting at the Shoreham Hotel in Washington, D.C., he was chatting with friends when someone remarked that Bobby Kennedy had arrived. Vince immediately broke away from his group and stood on the fringe of the Kennedy circle "like an adoring schoolboy" until Kennedy spotted him and came over to talk.[14]

In 1968 Vince enjoyed the unusual distinction of having his name mentioned in the inner circles of *both* political parties for nomination to Vice President. John Mitchell, Nixon's attorney general, later told prominent Washington, D.C., attorney Edward Bennett Williams that Nixon's aides had considered Vince for the Republican vice-presidential nomination until they discovered his "political credentials were wrong." David Carley recommended to Hubert Humphrey that the Minnesota Democrat consider Vince for his running mate. Humphrey said he thought the idea "interesting" but didn't think Vince had any strength among Democratic Party regulars, and the boom for Vince was stillborn. That his name was brought up within both political parties, though, testified to his popularity and to his ambiguous political image.[15]

Most speculation about Vince's political future focused on Wisconsin. Some predicted he would challenge the reelection of incumbent U.S. Senator Gaylord Nelson, a liberal Democrat. But Vince admired Nelson, had no desire to challenge him, and during the fall campaign endorsed his reelection in television commercials. The only serious invitation came from a small group of state Democrats who asked him to consider running for lieutenant governor. Vince later admitted that he had been approached and was grateful, but he had given a "quick no." Vince was flattered by the political attention, but as reporters kept badgering him about his political plans and as the filing deadline for nomination papers neared, he finally indicated he had no plans for 1968. Like most people, he felt uncomfortable in a milieu unfamiliar to him. "I don't like that handshaking stuff," he told a friend. Although he sincerely wanted to do something for his country, he considered himself too idealistic for politics. He wasn't a compromiser, he told friends, and consequently not suited for the political "game." "They'd eat me alive in politics," he admitted to reporters.[16]

Wisconsin Republicans had suspected Vince might have political ambitions, especially after he became a business partner with David Carley. They said nothing publicly during the 1968 campaign, but later prominent Republicans admitted they had been worried. "I think people liked his somewhat autocratic way of running things," reflected Ernest Keppler, the Republican Senate majority leader from Sheboygan. "His face alone would have made him attractive. You couldn't say that he's beautiful. But that smile. It's an interesting face." Harold Froehlich,

Michael O'Brien

Appleton Republican and the Assembly Speaker, thought a contest against Vince was one no Wisconsin Republican would relish. "I thought he was a serious potential candidate," said Froehlich.[17]

Old habits died hard. As training camp approached, Vince occasionally forgot he had retired. "I'm sure ready for camp," he told a friend after a round of golf. Until mid-July Vince was enjoying himself. But on July 15, the day training camp started, his retirement turned into a nightmare of boredom, frustration, and defeat. The important league meetings were over, the players' strike averted. Now there was little for him to do. He showed up briefly to watch the first practice, staying off to the side, pretending to be aloof, but actually agonizing. "I knew right then," he later said, "that I had made a horrible mistake." Yet he completely ruled out the possibility of returning as coach of the Packers. There was no "graceful way" to do it without grievously hurting Phil Bengtson. He was trapped and spent the next six months agonizing over his predicament.

He had to force himself to stay away from practice. "What do you think I ought to do today?" he asked his secretary, Ruth McKloskey. "I don't want to go out to practice too often. I don't think it's a good idea." McKloskey would recommend golf. "You're probably right," he would say. But he felt guilty playing when everyone else was working. He needed to do something constructive to help the team. He would schedule a round of golf, then cancel it and return to the office. There he paced his office; he paced Chuck Lane's office; he paced the hallway.[18]

Vince didn't miss the tension or the horrible work schedule—up at 6:00 A.M.; home at 5:30 P.M.; back to work from 7:00 to 10:00 P.M. He claimed he didn't mind being out of the spotlight, but he did. He did miss the satisfaction of putting a game plan together and the excitement of the game, the "fire on Sunday." He yearned for the elation in winning, the resolution in losing—"two great emotions any man would want."

Mostly, he felt a void without his intense rapport with the players. "There's a great—a great *closeness* on a football team," he later said, "a rapport between the men and the coach that's like no other sport. It's a binding together, a knitting together. For me, it's like father and sons. . . . I missed players coming up to me and saying, 'Coach, I need some help because my baby's sick,' or, 'Mr. Lombardi, I want to talk to you about trouble I'm having with my wife.' " He meant nothing to the players anymore, he thought. "When I meet one of them, he says: 'Hello, Mr. Lombardi.' And that's it." Henry Jordan saw Vince on the sideline and said, "Coach, do you want to chew us out for old times' sake?" Jordan's teasing was probably more accurate than he realized.

Vince felt he wasn't needed anymore. "Vin missed the need to be needed," said Marie.[19]

Vince's personality deteriorated noticeably after mid-July. During the first half of the year, when he dined at Bilotti's Forvm restaurant, he seemed happy, joking, and teasing with the staff and the owners, Ray and Duds Bilotti. Once training camp started, however, the Bilottis noticed a dramatic change. Drained of vitality, his conversation became stilted and boring. "He was flat," said the Bilottis. "You wouldn't even enjoy [the conversation]." They tried to make him laugh, but Vince felt uncomfortable, making them uncomfortable. Occasionally Vince expressed his exasperation. How was he enjoying the season? a friend asked. "Terrible," said Vince. "The worst year I've had in my life. I made a big mistake." A major consolation was the close relationship he developed with Susan. She had married Thomas Bickham and in 1968 presented Vince with a granddaughter, Margaret Ann. Susan lived nearby and visited with her father often; she and Margaret Ann helped fill the void during the sad season.[20]

The man who now filled Vince's coaching shoes, Phil Bengtson, had been an anonymous mild man to whom few outsiders had paid much attention. He had been exceptionally loyal to Vince and the Packers, having quietly turned down offers for head coaching positions. Defensive players loved him and the rest of the team respected his dedication and his exceptional record as defensive coach. He seldom became angry at individuals. It wasn't his nature. Replacing Vince put Bengtson in an awkward position. If the Packers won, people would say it was Vince's team moving ahead on momentum; if they lost, it was Bengtson's fault. Having Vince as general manager was also awkward. Bengtson was the only person Vince could have hired and still kept his own authority. Another coach would have wanted his own system and demanded changes that Vince didn't want.

Despite many years as an assistant coach, in important ways Bengtson was unprepared for his new role. Vince had made all the team's major decisions. Vince had motivated, driven, and disciplined the entire team. Bengtson insisted that the players motivate themselves. Training camp looked like Vince's camp—the same schedule, drills, and plays—but it was more lax. Vince had required sixty to seventy up-downs during the grass drill; under Bengtson the players did fifteen. Players took water breaks or sneaked to a shaded area to rest on the ground, which Vince would never have allowed. Ron Kostelnik and Henry Jordan asked permission to run the stadium steps for a week to work their legs into shape. Given permission, they spent much of the time discussing investments in stocks and bonds. Vince never would have allowed them off the practice field.

It was impossible for Bengtson to match Vince's dynamic presence, and the players immediately sensed the void. The change from Vince's intense motivational approach was too abrupt. "We had a man driving and whipping us for nine years," said Jerry Kramer, "and when he left we were incapable of picking up the slack ourselves." Willie Davis agreed. "We spent that whole '68 season waiting for that voice to come rolling in, that 'Do this!' voice that we had come to rely on." "It was a complete difference," observed Chuck Mercein of Vince's absence, "and it showed itself in places where Lombardi always picked us up, the game plan, the midweek speech, and the pregame speech."[21]

On August 2, the Packers played the College All-Stars in Soldier Field, Chicago. Forty minutes before the game, Vince watched silently on the sideline as Bart Starr threw warm-ups. Suddenly he yelled, "Bart . . . Bart!" Starr looked puzzled and trotted over to meet him. Vince stuck out his hand in a good-luck, handshake gesture. Starr grinned and returned to the field. Vince turned, grim-faced, head down, and walked rapidly through a gate that eventually took him to his remote seat in the press box.[22]

The Packers opened the regular season in Green Bay against the Philadelphia Eagles. At 11:00 A.M. Vince toured the stadium, checking the barbed wire designed to keep out gate crashers and inspecting areas that needed paint—more mundane duties than he was used to on a Sunday in the fall. For the first time he noticed the atmosphere surrounding a home game. People in the parking lot were carrying card tables, food, and beer for tailgate parties. "Look at that guy!" said Vince. "He's bringing out a charcoal burner! There's a guy with a lawn chair! All these years and I've never noticed this before!" In the second deck of the newly constructed stadium press box, Vince watched the game in a glass-fronted, air-conditioned, soundproofed booth with a telephone and a television monitor. Despite the luxury, he didn't like his seat. He was so far removed from the game he felt in "another world." "It's murder," he admitted. "I never knew I'd miss it as much."[23]

In the fall Vince's reputation was both powerfully enhanced and severely damaged. The CBS special "Lombardi" eulogized him before a prime-time television audience, but the simultaneous publication of Jerry Kramer's *Instant Replay* earned Vince mostly hostile reviews. While consistently praising Kramer for his thoughtful, literate observations, reviewers focused on the unique love-hate relationship between the Packers and their coach. They credited Vince's softer qualities, sentimental moments, and remarkable success, but many dwelled on the negative revelations. "We see plenty of the Vince many have come to know and hate," said *Newsweek,* adding that Vince was "cold," "tyrannical," and "vicious," and his players lived in virtual "terror" of him. Some reviewers savagely indicted Vince's coaching system. *Time* said Kramer "slaves" for the Packers, a group that "barters personal freedom" to attain perfection. Led by Vince's "psychic manipulation" and "military planning," the players had become a genial bunch of "sadomasochists" whose winning attitude had to be artificially induced by "alternate whippings and strokings from an older man." Vince's only comment on the best-selling book indicated his unhappiness with the way Kramer portrayed him. "Since I was the subject," he told an interviewer, "any comment I would make probably wouldn't be fit to print."[24]

The Packers suffered a slow death during Bengtson's first season. They started with a victory and two losses, their worst start since 1958. Throughout the season they killed themselves with mistakes—penalties, fumbles, missed field goals. Some players had subpar performances, and injuries hampered the squad. On November 10, as the Packers were losing to the Minnesota Vikings at halftime, 14–3, a sportswriter gazed at the scoreboard and said, "If these were the old Packers, that score wouldn't bother them a bit. They'd come out and get about three touchdowns." A press box comedian quipped, "But these are the OLD Packers." The Vikings won, 14–10, dropping the Packers' record to 3–5–1.[25]

All season Vince fought with himself to keep from talking to the team. "I can't do it," he said, pacing his office, "but I should. I can't do it." He told friends, "I have to stay away from there." After Bengtson's invitation, he spoke once or twice to the squad to spur them on, but he didn't have the same impact as earlier. Occasionally he grumbled at the players. They had too many outside interests, he thought, and were not sufficiently dedicated to football. As evidence he noted their attempt to reflect the current styles in hair and clothes for their nonfootball activities. "Too damn many blue shirts in here," he complained, roaming the locker room after a defeat. "Too many sideburns." He was right, said Jerry Kramer: "We all had a million interests outside football."[26]

Some observers suspected Vince was secretly pleased with Bengtson's failure because it made him look better by comparison. "I could sense at times," said Max McGee, who occasionally sat with Vince in the press box, "that he did not want the Packers to win. I felt that he would have been content if the Packers had lost all fourteen games." The *Press-*

Michael O'Brien

Gazette's Lee Remmel thought Vince's occasional smile after a loss was inappropriate. "He didn't *seem* too unhappy when we lost."

Occasionally Vince slightly inhibited Bengtson's coaching, though Bengtson never complained. Throughout the season Vince prefaced his comments on the team's progress with, "It's none of my business . . . ," yet there were times when he added, "but here's what I would do. . . ." One crucial decision led insiders to believe Vince hurt Bengtson and the team. Don Chandler, the team's reliable place kicker, had a business back home that needed his attention, and he said he would continue playing in 1968 only if he could report on the Friday before Sunday's game. In 1961 Vince had allowed Hornung, Nitschke, and Dowler to play on weekends, but he refused Chandler's request and the kicker retired. Bengtson never found a suitable replacement, seriously handicapping him during the season. "[Vince] didn't help Phil nearly as much as I thought he could have," said Assistant Coach Bob Schnelker. "If Vince had [still] been coach, Chandler would have been here." However, Bengtson had agreed with Vince's decision about Chandler, and neither anticipated the Packers' place kicking would be so woefully inadequate.[27]

Vince was often enthusiastic about the team's play. Seated among a group of reporters at one game, he let out a boisterous, "Thataway!" then grinned, pulled his coat over his head, and said, "I guess I've got to be careful about that rooting up here." Overall, he understood Bengtson's awkward position, tried to be accommodating, and yet made extraordinary efforts not to interfere. He expected the same discipline from himself as he did from his players. As Red Smith had predicted, he would slash his wrist before interfering. "If I were coaching and someone else in the organization were questioning me, I couldn't take it," Vince said. "I could never do that to anyone else." Always an admirer of Vince, Bengtson remained pleased with their relationship in 1968. "Our association has been very pleasant," he said after the season. "It's comforting, rather than a discomfort, to have him in a position where he could advise."

Amazingly, after winning two games in a row, the Packers were still in contention for the Central Division title if they could defeat the San Francisco 49ers in the twelfth game. Hope abounded, but the Packers squandered a 20–7 lead and lost, 27–20. Vince stood in silence afterward, his face ashen and somber. The team finished with a 6–7–1 record, the first losing season since Vince arrived. A dynasty had died.[28]

While the Packers limped through their season, speculation had mounted about Vince's future. "The biggest fight in the league this season is over Lombardi," a sportswriter observed in late November.

"Everybody wants Lombardi," declared a team owner. Football teams had coveted Vince since 1960, and nothing darkened the skies more in Green Bay than the thought that Vince might leave. Many teams had tried to lure him away, some with exceptionally lucrative offers. Professional teams viewed him as a franchise saver who would turn chaos into an efficient, smooth-running front office, and discipline, inspire, and lead the team to championships. Late in 1962, Dan Reeves, the Los Angeles Rams' owner, tried to entice him with part ownership, $100,000 in cash, $100,000 in life insurance, and part of an oil well. Pete Rozelle commented drily, "Another club offered Vince a whole oil well." About six other teams informally had bid for Vince's services in 1962. The following year officials at the University of Notre Dame contacted him about its vacant head coaching position before hiring Ara Parseghian. In 1965 Rankin Smith, owner of the Atlanta Falcons, a new expansion team, offered him a $1 million package before Smith settled on Vince's assistant Norb Hecker. Some American Football League teams had also made pitches for Vince.[29]

Vince had decided to remain in Green Bay for several reasons. Any college position would be a step backward. He disliked some of the owners of professional teams who offered him jobs. Some of the positions didn't include equity or sufficient operating control. He disdained the AFL. "See, that's what they're going to do," he disgustedly told a friend who had witnessed an offer from an AFL official. "They're going to try to take all the people from our league." Moreover, the Packers' executive committee would have to consent to his release from his contract and might not do so. Partly to ward off raids by other teams, the executive committee had made the maximum effort to please him. They rewrote, extended, and sweetened his contract three times—in 1961, 1963, and again in 1965. Packer fans gleefully greeted each new pact he signed. "Great news," said Lloyd Larson in the *Milwaukee Sentinel* of the 1965 contract, "Yea, Vince! Yea, Packers!" By 1968 Vince earned about $115,000 a year plus generous fringe benefits. Finally, Vince felt comfortable with the Packers, had almost total control, enjoyed his success, and liked the community. He was sincerely grateful to the Packers for giving him his first head coaching position. Yet there was one crucial liability with his Green Bay position. Unlike other teams, the publicly owned Packers could not offer him equity. Vince wanted stock in a team to build an estate, feeling he had little to show financially for most of his years in sports except a heavily taxed salary and interest on a few investments.[30]

The closest Vince came to leaving the Packers stemmed from his intimate, private involvement from 1964 to 1968 with a syndicate planning to purchase a professional football team. Gene Mori, the group's principal financial backer, was the owner of Hialeah and Garden State Park racetracks, several automobile franchises, and a bank. Joseph McCrane, Jr., Mori's son-in-law and former general manager of Garden State Park, was the group's director. McCrane had played football at West Point under Red Blaik and brought his former coach into the syndicate; Blaik, in turn, brought Vince into the group. The plan was to purchase an NFL or AFL team and appoint Blaik the chairman of the board and Vince the coach and general manager. Vince would also receive stock in the new franchise. He attended a few of the syndicate's meetings and kept abreast of all its negotiations; many of the long phone conversations he had with Blaik concerned the group's delicate negotiations with team owners. It would have been an ideal situation for Vince—head coach, general manager, equity, and a close working relationship with his beloved Colonel Blaik. Apparently Vince told no one in Green Bay about his involvement. Had the syndicate succeeded in buying a team, Vince undoubtedly would have asked to be released from his contract with the Packers.[31]

McCrane first bid for the Philadelphia Eagles in 1964, but his offer of $5,105,000 was topped by Jerry Wolman's $5,500,000. Shortly after, the group toyed with the idea of starting an AFL franchise in Philadelphia—a prospect Vince probably viewed dimly—but nothing materialized. In the next few years McCrane made serious but unsuccessful efforts to purchase the Washington Redskins, the San Francisco 49ers, and the Miami Dolphins. In November 1967, he made a second attempt to purchase the Eagles, but Wolman, who owned 52 percent of the team, refused to sell. Late in 1967 or early 1968, McCrane offered about $10,000,000 to purchase the New York Jets from David A. (Sonny) Werblin. He almost succeeded, but Werblin became ill, his partners squabbled, and negotiations broke down. (Senator Robert Kennedy joined the syndicate's attempt to buy the Jets.) Vince disliked the prospect of purchasing the Jets because it would have put him in direct competition with the Giants and his friend Wellington Mara. After Wolman ran into serious financial difficulties, McCrane made his third assault on the Eagles, in December 1968, but the negotiations stalled when Wolman's tangled finances became snarled in federal bankruptcy court. (Leonard Tose later gained control of the Eagles.) All the syndicate's efforts failed because they underbid or encountered hostile or squabbling owners. "We were frustrated by owners who backed out of the deals when the chips were down," recalled Blaik.[32]

In 1968 Vince received five job offers from major corporations—all high-salaried, executive positions. He partially identified four of them: a paper company, an airline firm, an electronics company, and a transportation group. He rejected them because each would have absorbed all of his time. The most intriguing job dangled before him during the year was the top position in another sport. The commissioner of baseball, Bill Eckert, had been fired, and late in 1968 some club owners contacted Vince about his interest in the position. Vince was flattered. He loved baseball. Many thought he would be an outstanding choice. "Commissioner Lombardi?" mused Arthur Daley. "He would be a good man for baseball to grab if it could. He would be a good man to run any show, including General Motors." Vince listened, but negotiations never moved beyond the talking stage. From Vince's view there were two problems. In the past the baseball owners had been reluctant to grant power to their commissioner. They seemed to want someone they could manipulate or fire, and Vince would never place himself in that position. The job was also too similar to his general manager's role with the Packers and would keep him away from his primary love, coaching. "I wouldn't have been doing the thing I really wanted to do," he later admitted. Bowie Kuhn was subsequently selected as the commissioner.[33]

Throughout 1968 Vince was coy about his future plans, never admitting other teams had approached him. Every time a rumor circulated about his leaving Green Bay, he was deluged with phone calls. His discussions must be kept secret, he believed; otherwise the negotiations might be ruined by premature exposure. Because he couldn't be candid and didn't want to lie, he usually hedged. No one had offered him a job "yet"; he was happy in Green Bay "now"; he "doubted" he would ever go back to coaching "unless" something unforeseen developed. By mid-December rumors were flying everywhere. But little speculation focused on the Washington Redskins, whose astute president was deeply involved in a scheme some sportswriters later dubbed the great "coach-grabbing coup."[34]

Edward Bennett Williams, forty-nine, Catholic, a graduate of Georgetown University Law School, became president of the Redskins in 1965. He was one of the nation's most outstanding criminal lawyers. A staunch defender of constitutional liberty through law, he had ignored the onus of guilt by client and defended brilliantly many controversial figures, including Congressman Adam Clayton Powell, gambler Frank Costello, and Teamsters Vice President Jimmy Hoffa. In 1954 Williams assisted anti-Communist Senator Joseph McCarthy at his Senate censure; in the same year Williams defended two Hollywood writers who refused to answer congressional questions about their alleged Communist activities. A legal artist, he demolished prosecution witnesses with lethal accuracy and devastating good humor. His exceptional talent for persuasion gave him an edge over other teams vying for Vince's services.

Williams and Vince had been friends since 1961. Williams admired Vince's coaching prowess, compassion, perceptiveness, intuition, and understanding of human nature. Before Williams hired Otto Graham in 1966, he had tried to lure Vince—"You think of the greatest first," he later explained—but Vince insisted on equity in the team, and Williams couldn't offer stock. In November 1967, their friendship ruptured after Vince adopted a seldom-used procedure to pluck fullback Chuck Mercein from the Redskins' taxi squad, where he had been hidden. Williams was furious and claimed Vince had stolen Mercein. "I have lost not only a player," Williams allegedly said, "I have lost a friend." The Mercein incident caused only temporary estrangement, though, and they soon resumed their friendship.[35]

The Washington Redskins hadn't had a winning season since 1955. Williams, the fans, and many players were disenchanted with Otto Graham and his coaching staff. In three years as head coach, Graham's record progressively deteriorated: 7–7–0 in 1966; 5–6–3 in 1967; and 5–9–0 in 1968. Graham didn't work hard enough, Williams believed, and the job was too complex and difficult for him. Although Graham still had two years remaining on his contract, Williams wanted to fire him.

On Sunday, November 24, 1968, the Packers played the Redskins in Washington. At breakfast with Williams before the game, Vince looked miserable and expressed his unhappiness at being away from coaching. Williams asked him if he would be interested in replacing Graham and dangled the possibility of making stock available to him. Vince was interested, and the pair agreed to explore the matter further after the season. The meeting brightened Vince's day. He appreciated immediately the advantages of directing the Redskins. Watching the game high atop RFK Stadium, with its commanding view of the city, he exclaimed, "What a great, big, beautiful city. What a place to play in. What a place to coach in."

When Vince returned to Green Bay, he phoned Norb Hecker, his former assistant, currently unemployed. "What are your plans?" Vince asked excitedly. "Sit tight. Don't do anything till I get back in touch with you." A few weeks later he told Hecker, "I've got something going. I'm gonna get back in football, but I can't tell you any more than that now. Keep it to yourself. But I want you with me."[36]

Because Vince was under contract with the Packers and public disclosure might ruin their complicated negotiations, Vince and Williams met clandestinely in New York and Florida. At a meeting in New York before Christmas, they huddled in the back room of Joe and Rose's, a small, unpretentious Italian restaurant on Manhattan's East Side and a favorite of Lombardi's. To their astonishment, Pete Rozelle; Tex Schramm, president of the Dallas Cowboys; and a dozen other remnants of Rozelle's Christmas party walked in and spotted them. "It was like being caught with someone else's wife," recalled Williams. "Whatever secrecy we had carefully arranged was blown." Williams joked sheepishly to the unwelcome intruders that he and Vince were simply trying to settle the "Mercein deal."[37]

Yet their negotiations remained out of the public limelight, and Williams worked feverishly to secure stock for Vince. The Redskins' stock was held in five portions. Williams and Milton King, another Washington, D.C., attorney, each owned 5 percent. George Preston Marshall controlled 52 percent, but because he was physically and mentally incapacitated, Williams and King were the conservators of his stock. Jack Kent Cooke held 25 percent. Mrs. Helen DeOrsey, widow of C. Leo DeOrsey, a former Redskins' president, owned 13 percent. In complicated negotiations over two months, Williams persuaded Mrs. DeOrsey to make her stock available and prevailed on his fellow stockholders to purchase her 130 shares at $10,000 per share. Eighty shares were retired; fifty shares, worth $500,000, were made available for Vince to purchase at a low price, providing him with an immediate capital gain. The agreement they finally reached stipulated that Vince would purchase the stock, become 5 percent owner, executive vice president, and head coach at a salary of about $110,000. After consulting an accountant, Vince accepted the deal.

During their negotiations, though, Vince and Williams had overlooked two important details that later caused embarrassment—particularly to Williams—and endangered their agreement. Vince's contract with the Packers barred him from coaching another team during the life of his contract, which expired on January 31, 1974. Moreover, Williams had overlooked a league rule requiring a team seeking another team's employee to ask permission before commencing negotiations. Williams thought Vince's case was unique because as general manager of the Packers, Vince was chief executive officer. Who could Williams go to for permission but Vince? The Packers' executive committee, however, thought Williams should have asked their permission. On January 21, 1969, with the agreement almost completed, Williams denied publicly that he was even negotiating with Vince. Yes, he had recently dined with him, Williams told a reporter, but "I've had dinner with him ten times in the last year. Every time it happens somebody writes a story speculating that he is coming here. There is nothing to it."[38]

The story of Vince's decision to join the Redskins broke fitfully and clumsily over six days in a way that angered the normally placid Packers' executive committee and left traces of egg on the face of the normally meticulous Williams. Some also blamed Vince for fumbling the ball, but in public he usually remained serene and confident. On Friday evening, January 31, 1969, a Detroit sports announcer reported that Vince was heading for the Redskins. The story seemed just another rumor until weekend stories in Washington newspapers confirmed it, explained the stock arrangement, and noted Williams had suddenly begun to lose messages to return reporters' phone calls. Vince had given a speech in New York on Friday and all weekend couldn't be reached for comment.

On Sunday, February 2, reporters questioned Packers' officials about the reports. "Right now," said Richard Bourguignon, "all we know is what we've heard or read." Dominic Olejniczak, though, had keener insight. "I can read between the lines," he said. "Now it becomes serious if he has been offered stock." Vince flew back to Green Bay on Sunday evening. At 9:00 P.M. he phoned Bourguignon and asked his friend to come to his home. "I don't know if I want to come over," Bourguignon said; "I know what's coming." When Vince insisted, Bourguignon and his wife agreed to come. The two men talked privately, then came into the family room, where Vince announced his decision, put his arm around Lois Bourguignon, and cried.[39]

On Monday, February 3, sports pages throughout the country featured the story. Early in the morning, Vince drove from his Allouez home to his office, locked himself in, and refused visitors and phone calls. At 9:00 A.M. the executive committee met at Fred Trowbridge's law office in the Bellin Building in Green Bay's downtown. Vince didn't attend but had earlier given the committee notice of his desire to leave. Olejniczak announced at noon that the committee had not reached a decision and would reconvene at 3:00 P.M. in the afternoon. "This is not just an ordinary matter," he said; "there's just one Lombardi."

At about 2:30 P.M. Vince emerged from his office looking cheerful. He chatted with newsmen camped by his office before he drove to the meeting. "What's everybody doing here?" he asked, smiling. He laughed but refused to answer questions. He met with the executive committee for a half hour. When he emerged at 3:30 P.M., he held a press conference for two dozen reporters. Nervous but grinning, he began, "I might as well say it," and he confirmed the details of his plan to join the

Redskins and his request to be released from his contract with the Packers. Shortly after 4:00 P.M. he stood in the elevator on the fifth floor of the Bellin Building. He wore a heavy, tan overcoat, like the one he wore for nine years on the sideline. A band of sportswriters and sportscasters stared at him in eerie silence. As the elevator began to close to take Vince to the main floor, a reporter advised the elevator operator, "Don't take Mr. Lombardi down, ma'am. For him it's only up and up and up." Vince grinned broadly as the door clanked shut.[40]

On a day on which most Redskins' fans wanted to toss their hats in the air to celebrate the news of Vince's arrival, Williams was distressed by the quick-breaking developments. Throughout the day and the next two days, Rozelle intervened to advise Williams and the Packers' officials. When the executive committee resisted making a hasty decision, he allowed them time to deliberate and told them that if they did not recommend Vince's release, he would not approve the Redskins' agreement. The matter was "still up to serious consideration," said Olejniczak at 4:30 P.M., following the afternoon meeting with Vince. "We don't want an unhappy man, but we feel we have a stake in Lombardi, too."

The Redskins, meanwhile, had called a news conference for 1:00 P.M. (Washington time), presumably to certify Vince's hiring, but announced at 12:45 P.M. that the conference was postponed until 5:00 P.M. At about 4:55 P.M. Rozelle phoned Williams and inquired about the press conference. Williams said he intended to announce Vince's hiring. Rozelle told him firmly that he could either have the Lombardi deal eventually or the press conference, but not both. A few minutes later Williams, tight-lipped and grim, walked into the news conference and announced he had nothing to say. "I was never more humiliated," he said later.[41]

Vince had to fly to New York again on Tuesday morning, February 4, because the following evening Archbishop Terence J. Cooke was to present him with the John V. Mara Outstanding Sportsman of the Year Award at a CYO dinner at the Waldorf-Astoria. Before embarking, he talked with reporters at the airport. "It's been a great ten years," he said. He was leaving the Packers because, "Like anyone else, you always hope to own something." He also wanted the challenge of coaching again. "People say you're crazy to put your great reputation on the line," he said with a chuckle. "I say reputation, swepulation, the hell with it. I've found out the challenge in something is not maintaining it, but attaining it." By evening he was on neutral ground—New York—as two pro football teams vied for his services. He was in good spirits. "I would hope they will release me," he told reporters in New York. "If they don't, then I'll be back in Green Bay next year." Vince was actually confident the Packers would release him. After all he had done for the team and the community, how could they deny him an exceptional opportunity? Meanwhile, Otto Graham had been left in limbo, golfing in Palm Desert, California, and refusing comment. It was "sad" what happened to Graham, Vince later said, but "financially Otto is in good shape" because the Redskins would have to pay him for the rest of his contract.[42]

On Wednesday evening, February 5, the Packers' board of directors met for two hours at Bilotti's Forvm restaurant. The executive committee had called the emergency meeting, the first in ten years—since the board approved the hiring of Vince in 1959. Ironically, the meeting was held in the "Lombardi Room," dedicated only six months earlier, and as the board deliberated his fate, Vince stared at them from a huge mural on the wall. Some board members expressed outrage at the devious manner Williams had negotiated with Vince and demanded compensation from the Redskins. But calmer, more judicious voices prevailed in the end. "With deep regret," thirty board members voted unanimously to release Vince from his contract.

They also decided not to demand compensation. "I would not cheapen this deal by measuring his worth to us in dollars or a couple of players," Olejniczak said after the meeting. "I think our goodwill and stature in the league in years to come, as the result of our action tonight, will far surpass any compensation we might have received." That evening Olejniczak phoned Vince in New York and informed him of the board's decision. In Washington, Williams, who suspected the Packers had held up the deal to "embarrass" the Redskins, was finally relieved. "I haven't sweated out a jury like this in all my life." Actually, the Packers' executive committee had handled the touchy situation admirably, remaining tight-lipped and restrained. Despite the intense publicity, Olejniczak had been particularly statesmanlike, gracious, and courteous. Moreover, the Packers presented Vince with a generous financial settlement. His contract specified his pension would be fully funded in ten years—the exact number he had spent with the Packers—and for tax advantage he had stipulated that part of his salary be deferred. The pension and the deferred compensation amounted to about $225,000. Since Vince had not technically fulfilled his contract, the Packers could have quibbled, but, said John Torinus, secretary of the corporation, the Packers judged that "he had already fulfilled the terms of his contract. And it also makes us look like the good guys by doing what we did."[43]

Freed from the Packers, Vince arrived in Washington before dawn on

Thursday, February 6. He attended a 6:00 A.M. congressional prayer breakfast on Capitol Hill, leading a reporter to quip, "He's praying for help already. He's probably seen pictures of the Redskins' games." At midmorning he met with the staff at the Redskins' office at Connecticut Avenue and L Street. Williams invited him to take Williams's plush office rather than Graham's, and Vince quickly agreed, promptly took the pictures off the wall, and substituted his own. For lunch the pair walked across the street to Duke Zeibert's restaurant. When word spread that Vince was dining, patrons found excuses to walk past his table; others just stared at the "living legend."[44]

At 2:30 P.M. Williams and Vince met with the media in the Chandelier Room of the stately Sheraton-Carlton Hotel. With one hundred and twenty reporters present, the session upstaged President Richard Nixon's press conference earlier in the day. Williams, the bounce back in his stride and manner after days of looking haggard and worn, stood at a thicket of twenty-three microphones and introduced Vince. "This is the proudest moment of my life," Williams said. He looked proud—and relieved. Vince, his eyeglasses glinting against the lights, was low-keyed. He speedily disposed of the amenities. Yes, he was proud to be with the Redskins. Of course he was sad to leave Green Bay. "It is not true that I can walk across the Potomac," he joked, and, as the laughter subsided, added, "even when it is frozen." He reiterated his philosophy: "I will demand a commitment to excellence and to victory, and that is what life is all about."

He handled the questions—many of them barbed—with aplomb. Hands rose like at the President's news conference. What did he plan to do about the controversial Redskins' quarterback Sonny Jurgensen and his quoted fondness for "Scotch and broads"? Vince responded, "I will have no preconceived notions about anybody. They will be all fresh new faces to me." Williams was known to have held closed-door talks with the players—with Graham and his coaches excluded. Would Vince let Williams meet with the players? "No," Vince said, "that won't be necessary." What role would Williams play? "Well, I have been given his office," Vince said. Williams interjected in a similarly facetious vein, "I've just asked Vince if I could have my same season tickets." How had he managed to free himself from Green Bay? "They traded me for Chuck Mercein." Would he compare the Redskins and the Packers? "I think comparisons are odious." A reporter asked, "You're supposed to be a real tough guy. Are you going to put on a different face here in Washington?" Vince stared owlishly at the questioner. "I don't know if it's possible," he said innocently. "It's the same old face. Actually, I'm a pretty soft guy." The audience tittered. Finally, Vince was asked why he had returned to coaching. "Because my wife, Marie, said I was a damn fool for quitting the sidelines," Vince snapped. "And on this note, gentlemen, I thank you."

When the twenty-minute conference ended, reporters crowded around Vince to shake his hand and wish him luck. One asked for his autograph. The reporters appeared almost reverent, describing his coming as "great, fantastic, magnificent, and tremendous." On Friday, his second day in Washington, he appropriated Pat Stone as his secretary, revised the office floor plan, and analyzed the Redskins' list of draftees. Then he departed for Green Bay.[45]

Back in Green Bay, wherever fans met, they analyzed Vince's decision, often whimsically. At a coffee shop downtown a man tried to steer the subject away from Vince to the weather. "It's our last cold snap, maybe," the man told his wife. "A fine winter day—clear and chilly." "That's right," his wife replied, glancing out the window. "It's real Lombardi weather," renewing a discussion that lasted through three cups of coffee.

Most had kind words for Vince; some were critical. A few believed that he sensed the Packers were a sinking ship and was bailing out. Others assumed Marie had lobbied for the move because she hated Green Bay and longed to move back East—a contention Marie vehemently denied. (Actually, Marie was thrilled with the move to Washington.) Most frequently, critics accused him of disloyalty. They noted the irony in Vince's attempt to break his own contract for a better financial arrangement when earlier he had been livid at Ron Kramer and Jim Taylor for their "disloyalty" in using the free-agent route to achieve the same goal. In each case the Packers were handsomely compensated with a first-round draft choice, but with Vince the Packers were left with nothing but memories. If a coach or a general manager could obtain release from a five-year contract, why couldn't a player? "Vince ought to take a 10 percent pay cut," charged John Gordy, executive director of the NFL Players' Association, referring to the penalty assessed a player who sought to play out his option.[46]

Mostly, the fans and media wished Vince well and bore no grudge. As Wisconsin's most famous citizen he had contributed much to the state, both in uplifting its self-image and providing a focus for latent pride of community. After he had given Green Bay and Wisconsin the ten best years of his life, exciting teams, and unmatched national fame, it was only right that the Packers granted him his release. A cartoon reprinted in state newspapers depicted Vince carrying a giant, thumb-sucking Packer player. "Son," Vince says, "there comes a time in every man's life when he must stand on his own two feet."

Most understood that Vince's decision was in character. "I think he's a man who needed a challenge," said a twenty-year old Milwaukeean. "Now he has a challenge." In its farewell editorial, the *Milwaukee Journal* referred to him as "Mr. Lombardi" because of the "awe" with which the newspaper held him. "He gave an inspiring example of how fierce determination, fierce pride, fierce loyalty, stern self-discipline, sheer willpower, and deep faith can make a man or a team rise above limitations." Vince would give Washington a winner in due time, predicted Oliver Kuechle. "It is inevitable. It is Lombardi's way. And just a little aside to Vince himself. Thanks for the memories."[47]

Vince's last day in Green Bay, February 25, was emotionally wrenching for Vince and for those whose lives he touched. He stopped at the office to bid farewell to the secretaries, the staff, and the coaches. Ruth McKloskey had brought a cake. Bart Starr arrived to hand-deliver a personal letter. "It was damn near impossible to keep from crying," observed Tom Miller. "All the women were crying." After some emotional farewells, Vince came into McKloskey's office with tears in his eyes and said, "I can't take much more of this, Ruth." Before he left for the airport, Lee Remmel interviewed him. "A lot of people have made a contribution besides Vince Lombardi," he told Remmel. Picking up Starr's letter from his desk, he added, "Here's one young man right here, Bart Starr." Vince's jaw quivered, tears brimmed in his eyes as he said brokenly, "It's just a beautiful letter."

Susan and Margaret Ann accompanied Marie and Vince to Austin Straubel Airport. Vince had to stop off in Janesville for a speech—his last official act for the Packers—before he and Marie were off to Washington. It was an unobtrusive, almost perfunctory departure from Green Bay. Vince wanted it that way, having asked close friends not to come in order to spare him the trauma of another, final farewell.[48]

XVI

Washington Redskins

It was the "second coming of Vince Lombardi," said a Washington writer, one of many pundits who used Vince's arrival in the capital to sharpen their skill at hyperbole. Vince was the "Great Man," "His Eminence," "little Caesar," "Your Excellency," "the Savior." Humorist Art Buchwald thought Vince's hiring was the "biggest news to hit Washington since Secretary of State Seward bought Alaska for 2 cents an acre." To lure the great coach to Washington, said Buchwald, Edward Bennett Williams had promised to let him live in the White House, to move his furniture in *Air Force One*, and to finagle him the off-season job as chief justice of the Supreme Court. When Vince asked about churches, Williams told him not to worry because "We'll get Billy Graham to come to *your* house."[1]

"Everything is finally going to be all right," the *Washington Star*'s columnist John McKelway assured his readers. "Tough and talented, tireless and terrible-tempered, Lombardi is considered by many to be the greatest man alive today." Vince would not only bring a championship to the Redskins but also would complete construction of the John F. Kennedy Center for the Performing Arts, hold weekly meetings with President Nixon's Cabinet, design a freeway system, and "do something" about the post office. "So get ready," wrote McKelway. "We are on the brink of a new era, a new beginning, a virtual renaissance. Big Vince is coming! Big Vince is coming! Big Vince is coming! He's tough, man.''[2]

A reporter for *Sports Illustrated* observed that "Grown men who would not glance at Mike Mansfield and would absolutely cross the street to avoid Strom Thurmond stand in their tracks on the street as Vince Lombardi strides by, gaping in wonder and joy that the man actually exists." Vince quickly selected his favorite D.C. restaurant—Duke Zeibert's, near the Redskins' office. Zeibert, the owner, had spent fifty years in the restaurant business, had served royalty, film stars, and six Presidents, but no one galvanized his clientele like Vince. "You can hear the whole place vibrate. As soon as he walks in the door, boom!" said Zeibert. Unlike all other celebrities, Vince made Zeibert nervous. "When I saw him walk in, I used to get shook up," Zeibert recalled. "He was just so dynamic."[3]

Asked about his extravagant reception in Washington, Vince's eyes lit up, his face split into an enormous grin, and he said with a laugh that rumbled like thunder, "What the hell's a Messiah to expect?" When *Sports Illustrated* asked him to explain his success, he answered that pro coaches were approximately equal in their knowledge of football; the only difference lay in their personalities. "Now, how am I supposed to explain my own personality? What am I supposed to say? That I'm a great leader? A mental powerhouse? That I've got *charisma?*" He laughed again.[4]

Not all the reaction was favorable. Some implied that Vince's triumphs stemmed from his harsh treatment of his staff and players. "Mr. Lombardi's reputation precedes him," one commentator bluntly warned, "and it is not a reputation of benevolence or easy tolerance, kindliness or understanding. Vince Lombardi, in short, is not Albert Schweitzer."[5]

The Redskins in 1969, like the Packers when Vince arrived in Green Bay, were an old franchise with a glorious past but that had fallen on hard times. The team had been founded by George Preston Marshall, a Washington laundry owner, who in 1932 headed a syndicate that purchased an NFL franchise for Boston. Five years later he moved his Boston Redskins to Washington, D.C. From 1937 to 1945 quarterback Sammy Baugh led the team to two NFL championships, five Eastern Division titles, and a sparkling record of 68–24–5. Since 1945, however, the Redskins had had only three winning seasons, the last in 1955.[6]

Like the Packers ten years earlier, Vince was inheriting an undisciplined team demoralized by another losing season and numbed by the constant criticism of the press and public. He was expected to bring a dazzling dawn after the dreary 1968 season. The Redskins had talent in two key areas: Sonny Jurgensen, the aging but golden-armed quarterback, and brilliant receivers in Charley Taylor and Jerry Smith. In 1967 Jurgensen had completed 288 of 508 passes for 3,747 yards and 31 touchdowns, statistics far in excess of anything Starr had done at Green Bay. His receivers—Taylor at split end, Smith at tight end, and Bobby Mitchell at flanker—rated one, two, and four, respectively, in the league pass receiving race, the first time in NFL history that three members of the same team had finished so high in the standings. Overall, though, Vince had fewer resources than he had in Green Bay. In 1959 he took a young, malleable, and talented team and strengthened, molded, and maintained it. In Washington, with few exceptions, he entered a poverty pocket. The means to build a good team quickly and maintain it were missing. The Redskins were largely composed of low draft choices, free agents, and veterans acquired from other teams (sometimes at prohibitively high prices). The running backs and offensive line were mediocre, and the bench was weak. On defense the Redskins were less than adequate, ranking fourteenth of sixteen NFL teams in 1968. The defensive front four was largely unseasoned, slow in reacting, and poor in pursuit. The best linebacker—Chris Hanburger—was twenty-five pounds lighter than Green Bay's smallest linebacker. Moreover, Otto Graham's draft picks had been disastrous. Ray McDonald and Jim Smith, first-round draft choices in 1966 and 1967, respectively, had not succeeded, and prospects for the future were dim because management had traded away first-round picks in 1968 and 1969. Vince was shocked to learn his future had been traded away for crash improvement, mortgaged to past policy. He would also have difficulty trading successfully. Who would be eager to deal with him?[7]

Observers who understood the Redskins' personnel and draft predicament doubted Vince could perform a miracle. How could he make a Paul Hornung out of A. D. Whitefield, or reincarnate taxi squadder Ray McDonald into Jim Taylor? "They say he can walk on water and maybe he can," observed Francis Stann in the *Washington Star*. "But can he make the Redskins instant winners? This is doubtful." It would be a "shame," worried Oliver Kuechle, "if the image of the greatest coach pro football has ever had should be tarnished."[8]

Washington fans loved Sonny Jurgensen, the light amid the Redskins' darkness. Electricity flowed between the gregarious, personable, poised redhead and the fans in the $7 seats. A graduate of Duke University, he played for the Philadelphia Eagles for seven years until 1964, when the Redskins acquired him in a trade. A natural athlete with an uncommon instinct for football, Jurgensen was a master surgeon on the gridiron, cutting up defenses with precision. Amid the chaos of the awful Redskins' teams, Jurgensen stood out week after week, throwing passes again and again, trying desperately to score more points than the atrocious Redskins' defense would allow. In the Redskins' final game of 1967, Jurgensen completed thirty-two of fifty passes for 418 yards and three touchdowns, but Washington still lost to Cleveland, 42–37. Despite his personal success, Jurgensen was unhappy. For twelve years he had labored under poor coaches and played on consistently losing teams. "I was struggling every week," he said. "It was always second and eight. We were always disorganized. We were always making up plays in the huddle."

Some people were disturbed by Jurgensen's attitude. He loafed at practice and remained aloof from teammates. His saloonkeeper's profile—a paunch that hung over his uniform pants and wobbled like Jell-O when he dropped back to pass—hardly suggested a well-conditioned, disciplined athlete. Moreover, his talent for self-deprecating wisecracks had contributed to a public image similar to Paul Hornung's in 1958. Jurgensen had claimed a fondness for "Scotch and broads" and bragged that women were a "cinch" for him. "All the bartenders in Philadelphia wore black armbands the day I was traded to Washington," he joked to a reporter. "I can drink with my left hand," he said after injuring his right elbow. The remarks had been requoted in many stories, making him appear nonchalant and slightly disloyal to the high purpose of football.[9]

Much of Jurgensen's playboy reputation was exaggerated. "A lot of the things I said about myself were jests," he said. Linebacker Sam Huff, who roomed with him for several years, called him the "most overrated dissipater in pro football. He rarely left the room." Still, Jurgensen seemed an antidote to his new coach—as relaxed as Vince was rigid; as irreverent as Vince was proper.

Jurgensen was delighted with Vince's hiring. A few years earlier he had listened enviously as Bart Starr profusely praised Vince. Starr told Jurgensen that Vince prepared him so expertly that playing the game was "fun." For Jurgensen the game had usually been misery. After the announcement of Vince's hiring, Jurgensen asked for Paul Hornung's assessment. "Don't you worry about a thing," said Hornung. "You will love him."[10]

In the first few weeks, Vince moved quickly and decisively. He met with players, hired his coaching staff, held conferences with the media, viewed films, and planned the practice schedule and a June pretraining camp. On February 12, he met with Jurgensen for an hour of closed-door discussion. Vince's opening remarks reassured the veteran quarterback. "I've heard a lot of things about you as a person and as a player, and I'm sure you've heard a lot of things about me," Vince said. "I just ask one thing of you: I want you to be yourself. Don't emulate anyone else. Don't try to be someone you're not. Just be yourself." Jurgensen thought Vince had accepted his personality and character and didn't expect him to be Bart Starr. Vince did insist that Jurgensen shape up and lead. He warned him: "I'm going to be tougher on you than anyone else on this football team because you're the leader."[11]

Vince assembled an excellent coaching staff. He retained two able members of Graham's staff—Mike McCormack for the defensive line and Don Doll for the defensive backfield. They knew the Redskins' personnel, could answer questions and orientate Vince. George Dickson, the offensive backfield coach, was an outsider with no previous connection with Vince or the Redskins but was regarded as a savvy football coach. Four of the coaches knew Vince from his years with the Giants or served under him at Green Bay. He coaxed Sam Huff, thirty-five, out of retirement to be a player-coach. Huff, the great middle linebacker for the Giants, had retired at the close of the 1967 season after twelve years in the league, the last four with the Redskins. Huff admired Vince and needed little coaxing. "What he does to me no man has ever done," said Huff. "He excites me. Just being around Lombardi, I get very nervous. I want to play, want to hit somebody." Vince turned defensive responsibilities over to former Giant Harland Svare, and brought in Bill Austin, who had coached for him at Green Bay, to direct the offensive line, and former Packer receiver Lew Carpenter to coach the receivers. Asked why he imported his former players and coaches, Vince responded that he needed people who conformed to him. "They must bend or already be molded to your personality," he said. "I've got to have men who *bend* to me."[12]

Some veteran members of the office staff were petrified about Vince's arrival and his reaction to their work. For a few weeks Tim Temerario, director of player personnel, arrived at work at 5:30 A.M. so his new boss could observe his dedication. "I was bound and determined that . . . I would be there ahead of him," said Temerario. "I wanted to impress him." Later he judged Vince strict but friendly, polite, and an excellent manager. When Vince started, he gave his new secretary, Pat Stone, a gold necklace, immediately insuring her loyalty. Like Ruth McKloskey in Green Bay, Stone enjoyed and respected her boss. "He has a great sense of humor," she said. "I laugh a lot during the day. I've never worked for a man who works as hard as he does. He's there when I come in and he's still there when I go home." Overall, Vince managed his staff and assistants better than he had in Green Bay. He was more confident, delegated more effectively, and didn't lose his temper with them as often.[13]

At his press conference on February 12 Vince started off well with the media, displaying his best face and winning favorable reviews. In twenty minutes he gave reporters enough information, said one, to "fill a book." Vince wasn't a "bad guy," wrote Lewis Atchison in the *Washington Star*, "just a man in a hurry. . . . None of this fumbling around, wait-see, look at the films, etc. But he doesn't elaborate. If you care to pursue the subject ask another question and he'll answer it."[14]

Throughout March and April Vince and his coaches analyzed films of the Redskins. To instruct his assistants properly he showed old Packer films as well, and some brought back fond memories. As Jim Taylor broke tackles to score a touchdown, Vince jumped up from his seat next to the projector and screamed, "Look at that son-of-a-bitch run!" Vince had planned a three-week vacation in the spring, but the knotty problems forced him to cut back. "I can't spare that much time," he said, settling instead for a week in Bermuda. On June 16, 1969, he returned to the practice field for the first time in a year and a half, welcoming fifty Redskins' rookies and veterans to a four-day minicamp at Georgetown University. Despite the roar of overhead jets, his voice could be heard clearly all across the field. "Move with the ball when you catch it. . . . Two hands, Charley. . . . Let's stay awake. . . . Gimmie that ball, here's how you do it. . . . Ruuunnn off the line. . . . What's your name again?" After the opening practice he told a reporter, "It feels good to be back."[15]

On July 9 Vince opened training camp for rookies at Dickinson College in Carlisle, Pennsylvania. He had packed for all contingencies—a Catholic missal, a large volume of synonyms for lecturing the team, tape-recorded golf tips from Julius Boros, and an ample supply of the stomach soother Titralac. He even brought along a priest to conduct daily Mass for him and the team. A horde of newsmen also showed up at Carlisle. *Wide World of Sports*, CBS-TV, and *Sports Illustrated* all settled in with him.[16]

For Vince, a prisoner of his legend and his successful past, the 1969 season probably was his most difficult challenge, the most rigorous test of his combative nature. He was determined to succeed, and from the first practice on July 10 there was an unmistakable, no-nonsense flavor to training camp. He was superbly organized. The practice schedule had been mapped, and all the assistants knew their assignments. Unlike some coaches who undergo a testing period, Vince enjoyed instant respect from his players even before camp started. "Everyone was toeing the mark from the minute he stepped foot in Washington," said receiver Pat Richter. "Everyone was in awe of him," added another veteran.[17]

On the surface Otto Graham's training camp regimen appeared more rigorous than the one Vince conducted. Graham scrimmaged more often, practiced on Sunday, and occasionally worked the players for three hours. But the comparison was deceptive. Vince practiced only ninety minutes, but the session was much more intense and the level of output was maintained at a higher peak for everyone. Dressed in a baseball cap, gray flannel knickers, and a white V-neck T-shirt, Vince supervised the grass drills and wind sprints, reacting callously to the exhausted players, knowing the pain was necessary. "Hold it!" he bellowed as the first group staggered across the sprint line. "Mister," he said, addressing the group, "what did I say, sprint or walk across that finish line?" To another group he yelled, "This is a *sprint*. You *run*. You, over there—the one with the long sideburns—you run, I said. . . . You quit on me now and you'll lose a game for me in the last two minutes." After the fourth sprint of the first rookie practice, Vince had spotted an exhausted, grossly out-of-shape rookie. "Get him out of here before he gets hurt," Vince whispered to an assistant. The rookie was staked to lunch, then released as if cited as an example.[18]

Vince insisted his players perform correctly *all* the time. He wouldn't allow them to rest up for one play in order to put out on the next, to run a pass pattern correctly once but not the next, to block one time but not the next. He stood in the middle of the action, totally absorbed in instruction, exceptionally alert. Some players thought he had eyes in the back of his head. Out of the corner of his eye he caught quarterback Harry Theofiledes throw an errant pass. "Where the hell are you throwing the ball?" Vince screamed. "You throw that short and you'll get intercepted."

Most veterans judged Vince's regime the most demanding and rigorous of their career. Veteran offensive guard Vince Promuto worked harder for Vince than for his three previous pro coaches. The grass drill and the sprints at the beginning of practice were the "worst thing I've ever been through." But the conditioning accomplished its purpose. By the second week Promuto had already pushed beyond what he thought were his mental and physical limits.[19]

Vince's reputation for not tolerating injuries motivated players to perform with pain. During the nutcracker drill Pat Richter broke his nose when hit by a forearm. Although the nose had splattered over his face, he returned to his place in line because he worried about Vince's reaction.

"I probably should stay in here and take a little more," he thought, "because if I dropped out, he'd think I couldn't take much punishment." He took two more turns in the drill—and performed well—before he had the trainer attend to him. Vince admired Richter's courage, but later, sensitive to the seriousness of his injury, cautioned him to take enough time to heal. When Promuto injured his left knee, he continued to play. Later Vince asked about his condition. "I'm all right, Coach," said Promuto. "Atta way to talk," said Vince. Promuto added, "That's the name of the game; you got to play when you're hurt." Vince's face lit up as he said to his lineman, "Atta way to go, Vincent, atta way to go." Since players knew that Vince demanded they play with pain, most doctored themselves, often not even bothering to tell the trainer about their pulled muscle or sprained ankle. At a practice in late August, many players were injured but at the snap of the ball all of them scrambled to protect their jobs as if they had been playing possum.[20]

Under Otto Graham proof piled up that the players couldn't discipline themselves. At the 1968 training camp he ordered all players to arrive for breakfast at 7:30 A.M. and then seldom got up early enough for breakfast himself. Consequently, players ignored the rule and attendance was poor. Vince had the same rule but never missed breakfast himself, and the players' attendance was nearly perfect. Vince didn't issue rules against long hair, moustaches, or beards. "He didn't make a federal case out of it," said Harland Svare, approving of Vince's flexibility. Yet the players often learned quickly, though indirectly, of their coach's feelings. "How much do you weigh?" Vince asked Jerry Smith. "Oh, two-eleven or two-twelve, something like that," replied Smith. "You should be down to two-o-eight after you get your hair cut," Vince observed. Smith cut his hair. After Vince suggested to a few black players that they cut their hair, the word spread, and conservative Afros were suddenly stylish at training camp. Soon Vince had a clean-cut team, in his image.[21]

Vince was naïvely optimistic about the natural athletic ability and potential of his players until three weeks into training camp, when it clearly dawned on him that he had fewer talented athletes than he'd ever had in Green Bay. There was no Jerry Kramer and Fuzzy Thurston to lead the sweep; no Paul Hornung and Jim Taylor to run it; and no Willie Davis or Henry Jordan to crash through the line to tackle the quarterback. "We have no defense!" he exclaimed to Ed Williams. "If we had a defense," Williams shot back, "Otto Graham would still be our coach!" The prospect of acquiring new talent was also bleak. "This year's draft choices were traded away, next year's draft choices were traded away," Vince complained in August. "And everybody expects me to perform miracles.'' Vince's antidote was more effort. Once he realized the deficiencies, said Bill Austin, ''he tried to make up for it with hard work.'' Vince was often depressed. ''Why the hell did I ever come back to this?'' he told Austin after a dreary practice. By the following day, though, he usually had fortified his resolve and regained his enthusiasm.[22]

Vince endeared himself to some players with his humor. He ''loved to laugh,'' said Jurgensen, who often joked and teased with him. Vince laughed at himself. While explaining a play to the team, he tangled his words: ''And both blocks block. I mean both backs black. I mean both blacks block.'' By now Vince and the team were convulsed with laughter. The jokes Vince told were as corny as those in Green Bay, but he put so much of himself into them, was so determined they be funny, that they often were. ''He can be damn funny,'' said veteran Pat Fisher. Vince tried to inject some fun into the tedium of practice. On July 19 he announced that in lieu of calisthenics, there would be ''rooster fights.'' He seized Vince Promuto to illustrate. ''Stand on your right leg,'' he told the 245-pound Promuto. ''Now—try to knock me off balance,'' he said as he took a surprise shot at the lineman. Predictably the players were quick to scream for their boss's blood, but Vince promptly broke off the exchange, not wanting his players to enjoy the spectacle of seeing him unceremoniously dumped. ''All right,'' he said, laughing, ''now you guys do it.'' The players enjoyed themselves. On the whole, there wasn't much laughter on the Redskins in 1969, no Max McGee, Paul Hornung, or Fuzzy Thurston to break the tension. ''There may be guys on this team who have that talent for making us laugh, but they're too scared this year,'' said former Packer Bob Long; ''maybe next year.''[23]

Many Redskins were scared of Vince. ''All I want to know,'' Vince told Harland Svare, ''is how far can I push a guy.'' Some players thought he pushed too hard and feared his power and abuse. When he abruptly cut a veteran, the players got the message ''loud and clear.'' In training camp he grew increasingly frustrated with fullback Ray McDonald, who repeatedly missed assignments and wasn't adjusting to pressure. When McDonald arrived late for a team meeting, Vince screamed at him and cut him right on the spot, in front of the rest of the team. ''That really put the fear in a lot of people,'' said lineman Ray Schoenke.[24]

Vince often privately joked about his angry outbursts. ''Oh, I was mean today,'' he said with a laugh after a practice. ''I hate people to use bad language,'' he said to a staff member, ''but goddamnit, I'm awful during the football season.'' He had his favorite rebukes, his rage cresting with each word: ''I'm telling you for the last time . . . for the last goddamn time . . . don't look into that backfield.'' Or: ''You're standing around here with your fingers up your nose." His most frequent comment, "You are *really* something, *you* are, mister," was delivered in a variety of moods ranging from rage to disgust, amazement to mirth.[25]

Sometimes Vince's anger was synthetic. Assistant Lew Carpenter watched as Vince transformed himself into an angry mood. Vince arrived in the morning apparently happy. Then he went into the bathroom, looked in the mirror, and said, "Vince, you're not supposed to be so happy! You've got to get it up and get it going!" He worked himself into a rage, and a short while later marched onto the field and started hollering at the players.[26]

"He motivates through fear," one disapproving player said anonymously. "It's a terrible feeling to know you're afraid of the man you work for, terrible. . . . This is why his theory of winning has to be questioned, because of the man you become, because of the man the coaches, like Lombardi, become." Veteran Bob Brunet, one of the Redskins' best running backs before he suffered a shoulder separation, walked out of camp on September 3. "Maybe he had enough of football, or Lombardi," Vince speculated. Brunet had had enough of Lombardi. He told reporters that he didn't respond to Vince's methods. "Things that are said stay with me all day and all night," said Brunet. "He says he forgets what he says right away. But I will remember exactly things that were said to me twenty years from now."[27]

Vince justified his abusiveness. "Hell, I can't just sit around and see an error being made and not say anything about it. I like to think I've had some experience in this business, and you don't win when you're making a lot of errors. Nobody wants to be told they're making errors, not the way I tell them," he added, with the shade of a grim smile. "But they got to be told and told until they get to the point where they don't make them anymore." At times, though, it hurt Vince to be so hard on players. He would ask his coaches if they thought he had been too harsh with a player.[28]

Although Vince was tough, he was also impartial. He made the same demands on everyone, negotiated contracts fairly, and played no favorites in discipline. His graceful approach to race relations also earned praise and contributed to team loyalty. "I'm not saying I don't know who's black and who's white on the club," Vince told a writer. "I'm just saying that I have no sense of it when I'm dealing with my people." The evidence bore him out. The Redskins apparently had experienced subsurface racial strife, but after Vince arrived it dissolved into team brotherhood. Ray Schoenke, a white player, had seen racial animosity when he played for the Cleveland Browns and the Dallas Cowboys, but

Michael O'Brien

he witnessed none under Vince's Redskins. "Lombardi handled it very well," he said. In his four years in professional football, wide receiver Flea Roberts had gained a reputation as a black militant. Nonetheless, Vince signed him as a free agent. "With Lombardi," said Roberts, "my reputation . . . didn't have anything to do with whether he wanted me or not. And I really appreciate that."[29]

When Vince lectured the team, the players never took their eyes off him. He commanded their complete, undivided attention, and he won the affection and respect of many with his inspiring lectures. He tried to sell the players on the virtues of family, religion, patriotism, love, team loyalty, and hard work. "He could inspire," said Jurgensen. "He was a teacher about life itself," added Chris Hanburger. "A lot of my standards in life I developed from him."

In one speech Vince compared life to an arrow. As the arrow proceeded on its course toward a goal, Vince said, the air gathered behind it. In life the individual must also put problems behind him as he moves on to new territory, new goals. The lesson captured the imagination of defensive back Brig Owens, who said, "I'd never had a coach like that." In private conversation, Vince inspired Owens by warning him not to let the "bright lights" of pro football affect his character. "Don't ever let this game change who you are and your way of living," Vince admonished.[30]

Vince particularly focused on improving the players' professionalism. At a team meeting he held up a dictionary and asked them if they could define "professional"; then he read the definition. Pro football, he told them, was as much a profession as medicine or law, with the same demands and high standards. In some ways it was more noble because it demanded extreme sacrifice. When a doctor or a lawyer was injured, he stayed home, but a pro football player must sacrifice and play with pain. "He made us proud of our injuries," said Jurgensen. Professionalism meant high standards in dress and appearance as well. "There is no place for sideburns, turtlenecks, lavalieres, and other things that might be socially acceptable on the street," he said. "When you're traveling as a team, it's different." The standard also applied to his assistant coaches. They must wear a shirt and tie at the Redskins' office. "Gentlemen," he told the coaches, "we are coming downtown every day into the heart of the business district, among professional people in their shirts and ties. It would be a sorry thing if we came in with a bunch of cowboy clothes."[31]

For evening exhibition games on the road Vince imported a custom from Green Bay and hosted a midnight buffet for the players, their family, and their friends. He socialized with the players and their guests, leaving many flabbergasted with his warmth and charm. Like many of his coaching techniques, the buffet was supposed to build spirit, loyalty, and unity. But these qualities were easier to build in Green Bay than in Washington. The Packers had a sense of intimacy not available in the Washington environment where players were scattered, didn't socialize together, and didn't live in Washington during the off-season. "If we have a championship team," said Pat Fisher, "it won't be because of player intimacy. We'll just be a championship team."[32]

Some players reacted cynically to Vince's lectures on faith, loyalty, and love because they were frightened and insecure. They thought they were being asked to have trust and love in a brutal, impersonal sport. "How can you expect people to remain stable emotionally under such an arrangement?" observed Fisher. "You can be gone tomorrow, yet you're supposed to have this strong feeling about the Washington Redskins. . . . He's talking about very lofty, noble things, but how do you instill them when the underlying concern is insecurity?"[33]

Vince imported six players who had played for him in Green Bay— Tom Brown (defensive halfback), Bob Long (wide receiver), Chuck Mercein (running back), Leo Carroll (defensive end), Mike Bass (defensive halfback), and Dan Grimm (offensive lineman). The ex-Packers sang the praises of Vince to Washington reporters. Playing for him was the "greatest thing that ever happened" to Long; Mercein thought his coach had charisma; and Brown became misty-eyed every time he talked about Vince. Their extravagant praise led a reporter to conclude that "Playing for Lombardi must be something like being permitted to see the Holy Grail."

Bob Long was a special case. He had played four years with the Packers, including three NFL championships and two Super Bowls. Vince traded him to the Atlanta Falcons in 1968, but in the middle of the season he was badly injured in an auto crash, suffering two broken vertebrae and severe lacerations. In August 1969, Vince coaxed him out of retirement. "Coach was gentle and understanding," said Long. "It was like he knew what [the accident] was like." An additional factor explained Vince's sensitivity. "I was a part of his past," said Long. "I was a reminder of his championship years."

Some veteran Redskins resented the influx of former Packers, especially the midseason acquisitions of Mercein and Grimm. "I'd guess it's fair to say that most of the ex-Packers have not been totally accepted," said Mercein. One Redskin grumbled that "Mercein and Grimm . . . never showed anybody anything. None of the ballplayers he's brought

here from Green Bay ever had anything to do with the Packers winning.''
Having already adjusted to Vince, Long and Mercein were perceptive,
bemused observers of their befuddled Redskins' teammates who were
trying to understand their new coach. "Was he this way in Green Bay?"
players asked Mercein. Mercein concluded that the Redskins weren't
"used to [Vince] yet."[34]

Actually some players immediately understood and appreciated their
coach; others took longer; and a few never adjusted to him. Sonny
Jurgensen and Vince quickly became Washington's newest romance.
They had huddled throughout the spring and summer. Their quarterback
meetings were teaching sessions. "He was a great teacher," recalled
Jurgensen. Vince was impressed with Jurgensen's intelligence: "You
only have to tell him something once and he understands completely. He
is everything I expected." Vince tried to impress upon Jurgensen that the
Redskins were going to improve their dismal running attack. "We're
gonna run the ball some on first down and not throw it sixty times a
game," he said. Jurgensen shot back, "Coach, what are we gonna do on
second and twelve?" Vince roared.

Jurgensen arrived at training camp with his muttonchop sideburns cut
off and a flat stomach. Vince immediately encouraged his leadership.
"Take 'em down to the goalpost, Sonny," Vince said, directing him to
lead the squad in running the length of the field. Jurgensen was
respectful, referring to Vince as "Mr." "Isn't 'Mr.' his first name?"
Jurgensen joked to a reporter. Jurgensen was delighted to learn that
Vince's passing attack was as intelligent as his renowned running game.
It was the "best without question," he thought. Veteran Frank Ryan,
who joined the Redskins in mid-September as the backup quarterback,
disagreed. Tutored by Blanton Collier, the scholarly coach of the
Cleveland Browns, Ryan thought Vince's passing schemes were simplistic, lacking the large repertoire of pass plays Ryan had learned under
Collier. But for Jurgensen, who had toiled under poor coaches, Vince's
passing attack was logical, new, and exciting. Vince taught him to break
bad habits—particularly forcing the ball into a crowd of defenders—and
to read the keys of the defense. "I used to think it was just up to the
defense to react to me," said Jurgensen. "I didn't know I could react to
it." Vince closely monitored his quarterback's progress. When Jurgensen
read a complicated defense perfectly and completed a nifty sideline pass,
Vince yelled, "Sonny, I could kiss you!" Everyone roared, including
Vince, who limited his show of affection to a hearty cuff to his
quarterback's shoulder.[35]

Ray Schoenke, a 6-4, 250-pound, six-year veteran offensive guard, thought Vince was a paradox—a demented genius, an object of both loathing and admiration. Schoenke took personal pride in being a self-starter, a man with his own reasons for wanting to excel. Yet Vince drove, harassed, and badgered him. "He never lets up, never bends or gives," said Schoenke. Schoenke longed for Vince's praise. "If you did anything good, he'd tell you about it. If you did something real good, he'd make a scene about it." Early in the season Schoenke suffered a painful separation of his rib cage, and Vince's callous reaction to his physical agony shocked him. "That's a nothin' injury, Schoenke!" Vince bellowed. "If you're not ready, I'm gettin' rid of ya! You hear me? I'm gettin' rid of ya!" Although deeply and permanently resentful, Schoenke struggled to return quickly to action because "I was gonna show that son-of-a-bitch." Once healthy again, Schoenke made the greatest effort of his career, and late in the season earned Vince's praise. "Ray, you're playing outstanding football," Vince told him; "I really appreciate it." But the compliment didn't appease Schoenke. "To me it was an insult," he said.

Schoenke disagreed with those who thought Vince was warm and sensitive. "When I think of him, I don't think of warmth. I don't think of sensitivity. If he was sensitive, he certainly wouldn't have said the things he said to me." Concluded Schoenke: "As much as I hated the guy, and I did—I *hated* him!—I had tremendous respect for him. Tremendous. I played some of the best football of my life under him. . . . It is a paradox."[36]

Rookie Larry Brown, a cocky running back from Kansas State, initially bridled at Vince's methods but adjusted and played brilliantly in 1969. An eighth-round draft choice, Brown was disappointed with Vince's hiring because he understood his new coach only used big running backs. Brown was only 5-11 and 195 pounds. "And I had heard all the stories about Lombardi and his grass drills and his temper," recalled Brown. "I figured he was a madman."

In the nutcracker drill at an early practice Brown muscled his way past huge defenders, commencing an outstanding training camp that impressed Vince and earned plaudits from Washington reporters. Desperate for good running backs, Vince concentrated on developing Brown, treating him like a veteran—and criticizing him like one. Brown detested his coach's abuse, but Vince also mixed in praise. "Good play!" Vince yelled. "You're going to be a good boy!"

At one practice Brown ran a play, then quickly set the ball down. Vince rushed over and shouted, "Mister, you don't fumble in our camp!" Brown shocked his teammates by swearing at Vince and insisting he hadn't fumbled. Vince fixed him with a stare, then exploded in a tirade. "I can not only run you out of this camp," Vince hollered, "I can run you out of the whole NFL!" That Vince could cruelly blackball Brown from professional football shocked the rookie. "I hated him," said Brown. Vince had learned, though, that he couldn't push his promising rookie very far. A few days later he stopped Brown on the way to the dorm and said, smiling, "Larry, you're a hell of an athlete." Brown's resentment instantly melted. "You can get mad at me," Vince added, "you can call me anything you want to call me, but don't say it when I'm around because then you're challenging me, and I'm the head coach."

Vince noticed that Brown hesitated before darting into action at the snap of the ball. "What's the matter with you, Brown?" he said with a growl. "Are you deaf?" Brown hung his head and admitted that, indeed, he was deaf in his left ear. Vince had a special hearing aid installed inside Brown's helmet. "Can you hear me, Larry?" Vince yelled as Brown tested the new device. "Coach," said Brown with a laugh, "I never had any trouble hearing *you*."

Vince inspired Brown with the same sincere, private pep talk he gave many players. "Larry," he told him, "when you go out on that field you have to believe you're the best damn running back in the National Football League." By the end of the season Brown had become an ardent admirer of his coach. "He came strictly from the heart," said Brown appreciatively. "Nobody can duplicate that personality."[37]

On the first day of training camp Vince had instructed Joe Blair, his publicity director, to keep newsmen from disturbing the team, and when brave photographers inched onto the playing field, Vince saw them as reprehensible. "Joe Blair! Joe Blair!" he shouted. "Where are you? Get on the ball—get those people back to the running track." In the next six months Vince's relations with reporters were often tense, and he angered some. Gary Cartwright complained that after a practice he introduced himself to Vince for the "tenth time in the last five years," but Vince rudely climbed into his golf cart and drove away without a word. Vince was weary of the publicity and sought to keep reporters at a distance. "I'm sick and tired of this publicity," he exclaimed during camp. "It's gotten out of hand. I just want to be left alone to coach this football team."[38]

Yet many reporters remained awed by Vince, impressed with his intelligence, success, and coaching. He was usually quotable and informative. Jerry Izenberg thought Vince had mellowed: "You could talk to the guy more." After hollering at the *Washington Post*'s Ken

Denlinger, Vince apologized; when the *Green Bay Press-Gazette*'s Len Wagner arrived at Carlisle to research a story, Vince greeted him warmly and invited him to the "five-o'clock" club. Reporters who were patient and could tolerate his rudeness adjusted well to Vince and grew to appreciate him. At a Wednesday practice Vince walked past Bill Austin and the *Washington Star*'s Morris Siegel, ignoring their greetings. Siegel was insulted. "Who the hell does he think he is?" Accustomed to such apparent slights. Austin counseled patience. "Forget it," he told Siegel; "he's thinking of Sunday, nothing else. . . . Watch him after practice." In the dressing room thirty minutes later, Siegel discovered the "other" Lombardi—warm, gentle, and generously communicative on a variety of subjects.[39]

Vince and Ed Williams continued to enjoy mutual respect, but Vince tolerated no interference from his boss. At a Wednesday evening dinner with the coaching staff during training camp, Williams happened to mention that Jurgensen had come to talk with him. Vince immediately interjected, "Wait a minute. I want you to remember one damn thing. If you ever talk to the ballplayers or disrupt anything I'm trying to do here, you can find yourself a new coach! I'm the one who's coach. I don't want you to talk to anybody." The rebuff didn't alter Williams' intense admiration for his new coach, especially for Vince's compelling commitment to excellence. "I've craved someone to take charge," said Williams. "I want to get back to my law practice." Williams often joked about their relationship. "I have been recently referred to as a puppet president," he said at a Redskins' banquet in September. "I have been referred to by the press as a figurehead, a jackstraw executive. I resent those allegations . . . but I don't deny them. This is a unique job. I am the only president of anything who succeeds to power on the death or resignation of the vice president."[40]

"I have got to win," Vince said before the regular-season opener against the New Orleans Saints. Thinking better of his blunt, revealing, personal pronoun, he quickly corrected himself. "I mean, I hope we can win." The Redskins did win, 26–20. Yet nothing came easily for the team in 1969, and Vince looked haggard after many games, frustrated by the team's inconsistency. In the next game the Redskins came from behind to lead the powerful Cleveland Browns, 23–20, late in the fourth quarter, but the Browns scored and won, 27–23. Later in the dressing room Vince hollered at his players: "You lost this one for me. They ran through you people like you were pure air. I needed this one for the title, and you threw it away." Outside in the parking lot, there was no scramble to board the bus with Vince. Those who could, slinked toward the other bus. Gray with fatigue, Vince looked defeated. On the way to the airport he closed his eyes and fell asleep.[41]

After three games the Redskins were 1–1–1. Having trailed in all three, they had come from behind to defeat New Orleans, to pull one out and then lose to Cleveland, and to tie San Francisco. The team returned home for its first game, at RFK Stadium against the St. Louis Cardinals. The day before—Saturday, October 11—Vince was in a good mood. He had invited the players to bring their children to practice, complimented the groundskeeper, Joe Mooney, for the fine condition of the field, and had the new stereo system for the team playing "When You're Smiling."

The Redskins played one of their finest games against the Cardinals, winning, 33–17. Curt Knight hit four field goals, Jurgensen completed nineteen of thirty-four passes for 238 yards, and Larry Brown rushed for eighty-two yards. Charley Harraway, who had been picked up on waivers from Cleveland and teamed with Brown, rushed for seventy-five yards. Tom Dowling, who was writing a book on Vince's return to coaching, described the locker room as exuberant, "aglow with men strutting to the showers, sitting tall in their wooden folding chairs, ready to tell the reporters what it was like to overpower an enemy."[42]

After the St. Louis victory, the team struggled to defeat the Giants, and looked ragged in an undeserved victory over the Steelers to go 4–1–1 for the season. Some Washington fans, not used to living with success, began indulging in a new luxury—criticizing how the team won. Vince was also unhappy. "We're a team that's playing in spurts," he said. "Is it possible to keep bumbling and keep winning all the way?" a reporter asked. Lombardi gave the man a frosty glare. "They're playing with everything they got and once in a while they put it all together for a long drive," he responded. "You can't give more than the best you got. But obviously we can be outclassed. We can be overpowered. The offensive line is hurt. The defense is young, and the Steelers went to work on our rookie defensive ends. It was brutal. The Colts are going to have some pleasant game films to look at, I'll tell you." Despite the Redskins' lack of artistry, close observers detected major improvement in the team. Under Vince's direction, said Shirley Povich in the *Washington Post*, the Redskins had a "special character." In *Life*, Gary Cartwright praised the team's "mental toughness," "tenacity," and its "refusal to go down before an obviously superior opponent."[43]

In their next game the Baltimore Colts ambushed the Redskins, 41–17. It was the team's most humiliating defeat. The defense broke down on runs to the outside, the offensive line collapsed, and the team committed crucial mistakes—a blocked punt, a fumble by Harraway, interceptions, and costly penalties. Afterward Vince's hollering penetrated the thick concrete walls underneath Baltimore's stadium. When reporters interviewed him he was still angry, his eyes flecked with rage. Even his assistant coaches gave him a wide berth. "We have real good people," he said. "We just don't have enough of them." Yet he remained hopeful. "One victory doesn't make a season and neither does one defeat. . . . We're still going to battle like hell, I'll tell you that." Practice during the next week was "hell" as Vince repeatedly chewed out the team.[44]

Povich was sympathetic: "A coach who had managed a 4–1–1 record with the kind of a team he took to Baltimore must have some merit, and Lombardi may yet live up to his clippings." Sonny Jurgensen agreed and remained optimistic. "We've all got hope now," he said after the loss to the Colts. "There never was that feeling under Graham, not even at the beginning. . . . Now the people who've been pampered on this team in the past because of their exceptional ability, the people who just tried to get by—they've been forced to change. With Lombardi, cheating is out. You don't rest up for one play on the field and then put out on the next one." The problem against the Colts was that the Redskins had reverted to pre-Lombardi form, said Jurgensen. "We hadn't learned what he taught us."[45]

Vince kept pushing the team—hollering, coaxing, praising, transmitting his flaming spirit, always concentrating on getting the most out of the players. "There are obviously people I push all the time and some I don't," he said. "There are many people here it took me a longer time to find out how far I could push, don't know yet what their limit is." On a Tuesday morning Vince looked at his watch. "In another hour I'll be on them, oh, won't I just," he said with a laugh. "The films won't be much fun for anyone today. Then after I've told them what they've done wrong, I'll have to wait, wait and see what their reaction is outside. I try to shut out everything negative about them after we've seen the films."

He was asked if he liked to think of himself as a heartless man. "No," he answered. "Why would anybody? It's no damn fun being hard. I've been doing this for years and years and years. It's never been great fun. You have to drive yourself constantly. I don't enjoy it. It takes a hell of a lot out of me. And, Christ, you get kind of embarrassed with yourself sometimes. You berate somebody and you feel disgusted with yourself for doing it, for being in a job where you have to. Fortunately, I don't remember."[46]

After Tuesday's practice Vince cleverly couched his words in a positive way. Instead of saying, "We can't have any more interceptions," or "We can't have any more of this damn fumbling," or "We can't have these breakdowns in the line," Vince would say, "We've got to throw the ball just as accurately as we did in the second quarter," or "We've got to continue opening up those big holes." After Tuesday he didn't remind them of their mistakes. He sold them on winning, just as he had urged the salesman in *Second Effort.* "Each day he sells the team," said Pat Fisher. "He's leading up to the right moment to clinch the sale, and that's supposed to be on Sunday. That's the day we buy. He always tries to close the sale on Sunday. Sometimes he does and sometimes he doesn't. It's hard to sell forty men week after week." Fisher added, "I have the feeling that each day Lombardi tries to think of some little story or parable he might tell that will stick in your mind all week, make you susceptible for the Sunday sale."[47]

After a victory, two defeats, and a tie, the Redskins stood at 5–4–2. With three games remaining and no chance for the championship, Vince began focusing on a winning season. For the first time, he recalled afterward, "I didn't have much selflessness. I had never had a losing season, never coached a team that lost over a regular schedule. And suddenly, keeping that record intact became very important to me. . . . Those last three games, yes. They were important to me. Personally. And I've never felt quite that way about games, that it was a personal matter. That those games counted toward keeping Vince Lombardi's string intact. I don't say I'm proud of feeling that way. But that's the way I felt."[48]

For the most part, despite the exhausting season, the team's morale remained high. On Wednesday, December 3, the 148th day since the opening of training camp, Vince supervised wind sprints, and the players demonstrated enthusiasm down to the final one. "We have good spirit," Vince observed with pleasure. The Redskins defeated the Philadelphia Eagles, 34–29, and the New Orleans Saints, 17–14, to clinch a winning season. Vince was pleased but also tired. "It's been a long time since I've had a day off," he said before the final game against Dallas. "The season doesn't bother you much, it's just every day, every day out there. It's the constant grind, you just wear out. Every other profession you get some time off, a Sunday or something. Monday, Saturday, I don't care, but some damn day or other. Even the players are so bushed they can't keep awake, and they're just youths." The Redskins lost the final game to the Cowboys, 20–10, and finished 7–5–2.[49]

"We got no damn defense!" Vince had again exclaimed late in the season. Indeed, the defense had been the weakest link in the Redskins' team, particularly in the last portion of the season. In the opening six games the Redskins allowed seventeen points a game; in the last eight, however, the average rose to twenty-seven. The Redskins' special teams had also played poorly, mainly because at practice Vince, normally the master of detail, ignored this phase of the game. It just didn't interest him.

On the bright side, the Redskins led NFL teams in coming from behind to win after trailing at the half. They did it four times. The passing attack was excellent. Jurgensen completed 62 percent of his passes—the best mark of his career—for 3,102 yards and twenty-two touchdowns, though he was sacked twice as often as the opposing quarterbacks. Vince predicted Jurgensen would complete 70 percent of his passes the next season. Larry Brown, one of the brightest rookies in the NFL who just missed "Rookie of the Year" honors, finished as one of the league's top running backs, with 888 yards rushing.[50]

After Hank Stram's Kansas City Chiefs defeated the Minnesota Vikings in Super Bowl IV, some critics charged that Vince's offensive system was Gothic compared to Stram's multiple offense. But almost all the Redskins' players thought Vince's system was progressive, efficient, and effective, that Vince was flexible and would have modified his system and adjusted to promising modern trends, and finally that the Redskins' problems resulted from inadequate personnel, not Vince's offensive system.[51]

By the standards Vince set with the Packers, his 7–5–2 record in 1969 seemed ordinary, but it was exhilarating for Redskins' fans because the team hadn't been over .500 for fourteen years. "He did a fantastic job," said Williams. "He may have done his greatest coaching job in 1969. If there were some way to measure what one can do with the material at hand, I think we could demonstrate he did his greatest job here."[52]

Vince won intense loyalty, affection, and respect from his coaches. He stimulated Harland Svare. "He stimulates everybody," said Svare. "If you could select your own father, you would want him to be like Vince," said Sam Huff. "He is the most dedicated, hardworking, motivating man I've ever seen. I loved every minute I spent with him." George Dickson agreed. The year he spent with Vince was the "most enjoyable" in his thirty-six years of coaching. It was also the easiest because Vince let him coach and didn't interfere. Dickson thought Vince was a great leader: "Leadership always starts with morality, integrity, and character. These qualities he had to a marked degree."[53]

Some veteran players hated Vince at first, said Bob Long. "But as the season progressed, they stopped bitching and started praising him. By the end of the year, they all loved him—every single one of them." Long exaggerated—a few players never forgave Vince for his verbal abuse—

but the large majority intensely admired him, and many deeply appreciated his influence on their lives. "He's molded the team already, taught us three years' worth of football in one," said Pat Fisher. Brig Owens was "thankful the good Lord allowed him to come my way in life. He made you reach within your own soul." "Until I played for him," said Vince Promuto, "I thought I was a man with strong self-discipline. I was wrong. As high as I set my own goals, Lombardi kept raising them for me. I thought I was pushing myself to the limit, but he pushed me even further. . . . He taught me a lot about myself." Flea Roberts had played on winning and losing teams, under all breeds of coaches, but Vince was special: "There's an average coach who just has knowledge, and then there's a good coach who has knowledge and can get it across; then there's an excellent coach—aw, hell, a great coach—who has the knowledge, the ability to get it across, and the fire to make a group of people go into their beyondness, to make them play above their level, and there's no doubt Lombardi has that quality." Even Bob Brunet, who had rebelled from Vince's abuse and left training camp, changed his mind after the season. In February 1970 he nervously phoned Vince, hoping to be allowed back on the team. "Let us let bygones be bygones," Vince told him and accepted him back. "He treated me like a father," said the delighted Brunet.

Vince himself seemed to doubt that he had captured the team's heart. "Once you win a team's heart they'll follow you anywhere, they'll do anything for you," he said after the season. "I haven't won this team's heart yet, maybe. But it's not for lack of trying. And I'll keep trying."[54]

While Vince was preparing his Redskins for the 1969 season, his business partner David Carley was making him a rich man. In early March 1969, while Vince watched films with his coaches, he was interrupted by a long-distance phone call from Carley. "Yeh! My God! Oh, my God!," Vince declared. "That's great! Great!" After he hung up, he told Bill Austin, "I just made a million dollars!" Actually, Vince had just made almost $2 million.

Two months earlier, seeking additional capital and a public stockholder base for Public Facilities Associates, David Carley had opened negotiations with Scholz Homes, Inc., of Toledo, Ohio, a publicly held company that designed and sold custom homes and apartment complexes. Scholz's executives were impressed with the potential of Carley's company. (PFA's earnings rose from $35,179 in fiscal year 1968 to $792,665 in 1969.) On March 14, 1969, Scholz announced it had agreed in principle to acquire PFA. The Carleys and Vince were to become members of the board of Scholz, and, most important, PFA investors would receive stock in Scholz. The stock transfer made the Carleys multimillionaires and brought Vince stock worth $1.8 million.[55]

The agreement needed final approval at the Scholz stockholders' meeting in Chicago on August 15, 1969. The Carleys had made careful preparations for the event and practically ordered Vince to attend. They anticipated the largest crowd of stockholders in Scholz's history—plus reporters and stock analysts—mainly because Vince was expected to be there. But Vince hated to leave Carlisle in the middle of training camp. He could help finalize an agreement that would make him a millionaire, but he was more concerned with the Redskins' passing schemes, running attack, and the exhibition season. It took the Carleys' most determined efforts to convince him to leave his team. They arranged for a private plane to fly him from Carlisle to Chicago, but the flight arrived ninety minutes late, further aggravating Vince's foul mood. On the drive from the airport he yelled and swore at James Carley, complaining he had "work" to do back in training camp. He was so upset that James worried he wouldn't be able to memorize the speech the Carleys had prepared for him.

A standing-room-only crowd of 150 persons—three times more than usual—attended the meeting. Vince quickly composed himself, read over his speech, and delivered it flawlessly. "We now can make a serious approach to the national market, offering expertise in all areas," he said. "We are the pros, and the big season is ahead of us." After the meeting Vince was relaxed and happy. He now officially owned a significant estate—$1.8 million in stock in a publicly held company. Late that evening he returned to Carlisle in a far better mood than he arrived.

David Carley still wasn't finished. A few weeks after the Scholz stockholders' meeting he opened negotiations with Inland Steel Corporation of Chicago, hoping the giant company would be interested in acquiring Scholz. Fortunately, Inland did want to diversify, particularly into the housing field, and on September 29, 1969, agreed to acquire Scholz. At first Vince objected, not fully appreciating the advantages of the new agreement, but when David Carley explained that the deal involved another exchange of stock with greater market value, Vince concurred. The agreement allowed him to exchange his stock in Scholz for Inland's stock, a high-yield class of preferred stock.[56]

A month after Vince took the Redskins' job, he and Marie paid $125,000 for a new four-bedroom brick home on Stanmore Drive in Potomac Falls, Maryland, ironically just down the road from Otto Graham. Potomac Falls was noted for its elegant homes, rustic post-and-rail fences, built-in bridle paths, and assortment of wealthy residents. The home met Vince's only two requirements: plenty of space and a short drive to a Catholic church. Located on a two-acre lot, the home featured a master bedroom suite overlooking a stream and picturesque woodland, a large living room with marble-fronted fireplace, and a large paneled recreation room.

Each morning Vince rose at 6:00 A.M. and attended Mass, usually at 7:00 A.M. at nearby Our Lady of Mercy Catholic Church, or, after the thirty-minute drive to his Redskins' office, the 7:30 A.M. Mass at St. Matthew's Cathedral near the office. At home Vince renewed his strength for the next day's coaching, happy to read the newspaper quietly or putter outside with his golf clubs. He didn't maintain the home, leaving that chore to his friend Ockie Krueger, whom Vince lured from the Packers to become the Redskins' business manager. Krueger arranged all the lawn and home maintenance. "I took care of his household chores," he said.[57]

In Washington Vince grew closer to his son. In June 1969, Vince, Jr., received his law degree from William Mitchell College of Law in St. Paul, Minnesota, and the following October passed his bar examination. Married with children, young Vince had worked during the day and attended classes in the evening. Vince had always wanted his son to be a lawyer, and Vince, Jr.'s, sacrifice and hard work earned his respect. He proudly introduced young Vince to his friends as "My son the lawyer." When Vince, Jr., trained as a stockbroker in New York, he and his father often visited, and their relationship improved. "We were pretty close," said Vince, Jr., "probably for the first time." Vince enjoyed his grandchildren, but he scared Vince, Jr.'s, oldest son by playfully sneaking up behind the child and yelling, "Hey!" frightening the boy. For a while the youngster refused to go near his grandfather until Vince smoothed over their relationship.[58]

In early February 1969, Marie told a Washington reporter that her husband could be a "real fun guy," but because of the challenge of rebuilding the Redskins, "he won't relax now for two years." Marie exaggerated. Vince worked exceptionally hard throughout 1969, yet he had always appreciated his leisure, and he found time for it in Washington, especially after the 1969 season. He often golfed and held memberships in three golf courses: the Winged Foot Golf Club in Mamaroneck, New York; the Congressional Country Club in Washington, D.C.; and the Indian Creek Golf Club in Miami Beach.[59]

The Lombardis hosted a cocktail party on Sunday evening after almost every game and were in great demand on the party circuit. They often attended parties at Ed Williams's home, where they met Robert Kennedy's widow, Ethel Kennedy, and Art Buchwald. At social functions

Vince's reputation and demeanor often intimidated new acquaintances, especially women. Rene Carpenter, wife of astronaut Scott Carpenter, thought she was chicly dressed until she took her turn to meet Vince at a party. "Then I felt like my skirt was too short and that my back was too bare. All of a sudden it was the worst dress. We were all reduced to feeling like children." As the publisher of the *Washington Post,* Katharine Graham had met many famous and powerful persons, but when seated next to Vince at an exclusive social affair, she grew self-conscious and tongue-tied. "I am sorry, Mr. Lombardi," she said, "I have wanted to talk to you all evening, but to tell the truth, I have been petrified at the idea." Vince laughed. Invariably, though, his charm won over his nervous table companion. Ethel Kennedy had "that sinking feeling" when she learned she'd been assigned to sit next to Vince at a dinner party. But she found him warm and sympathetic. "The coach was so relaxed," she later wrote Marie, "he was a million laughs and he spellbound our table describing the various players in that terse, succinct, clipped manner which made you conscious all at once of his toughness, his kindness, his superior intellect, his understanding of human foibles, his ability to make you better than you are and—most amazing of all for a Georgetown dinner—his closeness to God."[60]

In early February 1970, Vince and Marie attended the glittering opening of Art Buchwald's comedy *Sheep on the Runway* at Broadway's Helen Hayes Theater. Vince enjoyed the play but not the party afterward with Buchwald's three hundred celebrity friends at Sardi's West. Fawned over by pretentious people, he smiled grimly, ill at ease. Finally he tugged at a friend and insisted they "get the hell out of here. These are not my people." He led a small group to the back room of a Third Avenue saloon, loosened his tie, and relaxed. Later he directed his contingent to a "fun spot," an Irish pub, where he accompanied the band as a soloist for several Irish and Italian songs. He even danced with *Washington Post*'s reporter Myra MacPherson. "I've never seen you like this," marveled a friend. "This is the off-season," Vince replied.[61]

When Max McGee and Paul Hornung visited Washington, they joined Vince and Marie for dinner. When they excused themselves early to meet some "people," Vince flashed his grin and said, "You guys haven't changed at all. Every senator in this town, every congressman, and half the President's cabinet would give anything to spend time with me, and you guys are still running out on me at eleven o'clock!"[62]

Vince continued to win honors. The National Council of the Boy Scouts of America granted him the Silver Buffalo Award for his service to boyhood, and St. Peter's College, a Jesuit institution in Jersey City,

New Jersey, awarded him an honorary Doctor of Laws degree. He assisted an impressive list of civic concerns and supported numerous charities. He appeared in newspaper advertisements endorsing the District of Columbia police department's recruitment drive, and he devoted time to the police boys' clubs. He was also on the advisory board of the National Capital Area Council of the Boy Scouts of America; a member of the board of trustees of the District of Columbia Division, American Cancer Society; on the committee for Children's Hospital of the District of Columbia; and honorary chairman of the Washington Kidney Foundation drive for 1970. The $5,000 he received for a speech he donated to a scholarship fund. After he appeared in an advertisement for artificial turf, he instructed the manufacturer to forward his check to the American Cancer Society. When the son of Leroy Washington, Vince's chauffeur, was killed in Vietnam, Vince gave Washington $1,000.[63]

"Nobody asks me any questions about football anymore," Vince said after returning from a speech in Chicago. "All they wanted to hear [were] my views on the country's problems." Since Vince's address to the American Management Association in 1967, the violence and division that ravaged American society had escalated dramatically and so had Vince's concern. On April 4, 1968, civil rights leader Martin Luther King was killed on the balcony of a Memphis motel, sparking outraged blacks to rampage through ghettos in Chicago, Washington, and other American cities. On June 4, after the California primary election, Vince's beloved Robert Kennedy was also assassinated. Between January 1 and June 15, 1968, there were 221 major demonstrations involving thirty-nine thousand students, on 101 campuses. Radicals dynamited buildings, roughed up college administrators, painted obscenities on walls, and shouted at policemen. At the Democratic National Convention in Chicago in the summer of 1968, left-wing protesters provoked confrontations, and authorities responded with a "police riot."

The most striking manifestations of social conflict occurred after 1968. Supporters of law and order had good reasons for concern. "In New York City," noted historian James Patterson, "bomb threats averaged 1,000 a month in 1969–70. Within fifteen months 368 bombs actually exploded. In 1970 the FBI reported 35,202 assaults on policemen, four times the number in 1960." In April 1970, when President Nixon sent American troops into Cambodia, the reaction on campuses surpassed all previous disruptions. On May 4 Ohio National Guard troops killed four students at Kent State University. The Cambodian invasion and the Kent State deaths caused such a torrent of protests on campuses that 250 universities had to close down by the end of the semester.

Much of the turmoil took place in Washington. In mid-November 1969, 250,000 demonstrators engaged in three days of protests, and on May 9, 1970, a hundred thousand persons stormed Washington, transforming the White House into an armed camp. Vince watched some of the capital demonstrations from his office window, outraged at the appearance and actions of the young marchers, particularly at their desecration of the American flag.[64]

By 1969 the growing youth rebellion had reinforced Vince's love for his country, turning him into a fierce patriot. The American flag became a sacred symbol for him. Each morning he proudly raised his flag up a white pole at his home. At a party he handed out small flags. "Stand up and be proud of your country," he earnestly instructed each friend. "You wear this forever." During the National Anthem he sang the words out loud, his shoulders back and stomach in, standing at rigid attention, like a Marine honor guard.[65]

On Sunday, November 9, at the halftime of the Eagles-Redskins game at RFK Stadium, Vince put on the "Flag Story," a huge patriotic spectacle to commemorate Veterans' Day. He had imported the custom from Green Bay, but the spirit behind it seemed more pugnacious in the nation's capital a few days before the beginning of the November antiwar demonstrations. Each spectator received an American flag, the U.S. Army Band played martial tunes, color guards were on hand, the crowd sang "America the Beautiful," and a Medal of Honor winner in Korea recited the Pledge of Allegiance. A critic described the occasion as "jingoism, not patriotism, and spleen, not homage," and Vince seemed to confirm that judgment when he asserted afterward, "That's our answer to whatever the hell they're going to have on Wednesday or Thursday." Most of the response was favorable. "Lombardi, and apparently thousands of others," said Bob Addie in the *Washington Post,* "devoutly believe it does not violate the Constitution to show you love your country." President Nixon wrote to congratulate him for his "thrilling presentation," adding, "You have always demonstrated on the field and off the qualities of faith and determination which are at the heart of true patriotism."

A week later, at the Redskins-Dallas game, Vince put on another patriotic display, inviting a Marine drum and bugle corps, a silent drill platoon, a flag platoon, and three other platoons. Earlier in the week, when three busloads of Marines arrived at practice to go through their paces, Vince greeted them rapturously, the only time, said Tom Dowling, "I had ever seen him overjoyed at the arrival of strangers at practice."

Conservatives helped transform Vince from a football coach into a national hero. The Nixon Administration and its supporters thought America needed a deeper faith in itself, firmer hope in the future, and a rededication to winning as the supreme virtue. America had never lost a war and would not lose in Vietnam. Consequently, Vince was asked to join prominent conservative Republicans in sponsoring advertisements endorsing two of President Nixon's most controversial policies, the antiballistic missile system (ABM) and the Vietnam War. Vince was encouraged to join by William O'Hara, secretary of the group and a Fordham classmate. Among those sponsoring the ads were William J. Casey, Robert Abplanalp, Clare Boothe Luce, and John Bricker. "None of them were liberals," O'Hara pointed out. "We were for America first. We were wholeheartedly aiding the President and his policies." Vince's political philosophy, O'Hara judged, was "very much to the right."[66]

Vince and ten others helped solicit endorsements from 350 persons for full-page newspaper advertisements supporting Nixon's ABM system. "Here! Sign here!" he ordered Ed Williams. But Williams rebuffed him. "Not me! I'm not going to sign that. I don't think you know what you're signing." Vince, however, remained confident his cause was righteous. "He was rather naïve politically," Williams later said.

The ABM ad, which appeared in the *Washington Post* on June 30, 1969, stressed that "84 percent of all Americans support an ABM system"; only a "noisy 10 percent" opposed it. Without the ABM the Soviets had the capability to "annihilate" the United States with "nuclear missiles." Trust President Nixon, the ad urged; with the nation's "military, scientific, and intelligence skills at his disposal," he was in the best position to "evaluate the need for this protection."[67]

On December 7, 1969, calling themselves the "Tell It to Hanoi Committee," Vince and his conservative associates sponsored a strident, full-page ad endorsing President Nixon's Vietnam policy. The ad patronizingly referred to the "young participants" in the Vietnam moratoriums as "sincere," "well-meaning," and "idealistic," but criticized their methods and "youthful impatience." The war pitted "proponents of two completely different systems of government." The North Vietnamese had a "communist, totalitarian system" and engaged in "brutal and indiscriminate murder"; the South Vietnamese offered the "promise of political freedom as we know it." Americans were advised to support President Nixon's policies or else pave the way for "a communist victory."[68]

On June 24, 1970, Vince announced he would serve as honorary vice chairman of Honor America Day, scheduled for July 4, 1970. J. Willard Marriot, chairman of the Marriot Corporation, started the event. Vince had promptly accepted his invitation and was the first leader to appear on television to promote the affair. "This is not a demonstration but a celebration," he explained. President Nixon supported the program and was grateful for Vince's participation, but Vince, not wanting to appear partisan, pointed out that former Presidents Lyndon Johnson and Harry Truman also endorsed the event. Vince argued that the program was not pro-Nixon or prowar, "just pro-America." "Dissent is good," he added. "It is a form of articulation, but destruction is anarchy. Problems cannot be solved by waving the American flag, but neither can they be solved by tearing down the American flag and waving the Vietcong flag and breaking windows and kicking in doors."[69]

Vince often seemed oblivious to the concerns and goals of the young rebels. "I don't know what the devil they're dissatisfied about." At other times he conceded that their cause had a few virtues. "I know this country has a serious racial problem," he said, but the problem must be solved "sensibly." Young people were more intelligent than previous generations, he said. "I would call it the why generation. . . . They're raising some questions that aren't being answered." Vince also claimed that while he favored law and order and deplored permissiveness, "I'm not for any repression." Still, Vince never identified the "intelligent" questions, and his concessions to youth drowned amid his intense, wide-ranging condemnation of their values.[70]

It wasn't just counterculture youths who aggravated Vince; the new attitude among athletes bothered him as well, particularly the problem star Joe Namath, the quarterback of the New York Jets, winners of Super Bowl III. Vince admired Namath's athletic ability—"Joe Namath," he said, "is an almost perfect passer"—but he deplored Namath's attitude and lifestyle. "I Like My Girls Blond and My Johnny Walker Red," a chapter title in Namath's 1969 book, celebrated Scotch and sex. Moreover, Namath briefly retired from football in the summer of 1969 rather than obey Commissioner Pete Rozelle's edict that he sell his share in Bachelors III, an East Side, New York, bistro allegedly frequented by known gamblers. Vince sided firmly with Rozelle and almost developed a phobia about Namath. "Namath has set back the image of football twenty years," Vince told an interviewer. "My father ranted a lot about Namath," recalled Vince, Jr., "and talked about getting the police after him." Vince seldom had nightmares, but he had them about the Jets' quarterback, waking up one time yelling, "Joe Namath, you're not bigger than football! Remember that!"[71]

A few days into the 1969 training camp, three rookies—the fifth, seventh, and fourteenth draft choices—quit the squad. Since all three had received bonus money, Vince was furious, and he cited them as symbols of the immorality of college youth. None of the three had distinguished himself at camp, nor had they been special targets of abuse. "I did what my heart told me to do," one of the rookies apparently told his coach. "My heart tells me to lie down and take a rest," Vince shot back, "but I don't do it. I keep going from early in the morning until late at night." Vince assumed the three had come to camp only to collect their bonus money and leave. "They are examples of the moral code today about honoring contracts," he told reporters. "This is what they are teaching in the colleges."[72]

Vince constantly called for better leadership and bemoaned the death of "heroes." "We need another Kennedy," he told his executive assistant Dave Slattery. "You've got to win the hearts of the people that you lead," he said in an interview. "The personality of the individual has to do it—the incandescence. . . . There's no hereditary strata in leading. They're not born; they're made. There has to be an inclination, a commitment, a willingness to command."

Some thought Vince himself was an ideal political leader. "Vince Lombardi for President?" said the teaser caption for an article on Democratic Party politics in the *Chicago Daily News* on June 10, 1970. The story reported the advice Democrats had recently received for winning the November election—start acting like a "liberal" Vince Lombardi. Ted Van Dyk, a former associate of Hubert H. Humphrey, cited Vince as an example of the "personal strength and toughness" Democratic liberals must project. The majority of voters, argued Van Dyk, were most troubled by campus and ghetto disturbances and crime, but they also wanted to be fair to blacks and the poor and would pay higher taxes to do it. Democrats, however, could not expect to win elections by making legalized marijuana and abortion their central campaign issues. Van Dyk cited Robert Kennedy and Iowa's Democratic Senator Harold Hughes as persons who, like Vince, knew the formula of conveying strength and toughness.[73]

When Vince left his Redskins' office he often headed for the airport rather than home. He handled more public-speaking engagements than most politicians. He continued to talk about crisis and creed, self-discipline and dedication, and spartanism and success. By 1970 he had nearly doubled the length of his speech, adding some humor, anecdotes, patriotic messages, and apocalyptic warnings about the dangerous youth culture. He joked about his reputation, retelling stories first told by the Packers' Henry Jordan. "I have picked up a reputation for being tough or for being hard," he said to a business group in Dayton, Ohio, and I admit I have some mixed emotions about that reputation, particularly when one of my former players was asked, "What is it like to work with Vince Lombardi?" and his answer was, "Well, I'll tell you in a nutshell. When Lombardi turns to us in the locker room and tells us to sit down, I don't even look for a chair."

Most of the new material in his speech stressed the breakdown of law and order and the dangerous, un-American values pervading the country. Until recently, he said, it had always been the "American zeal" to be first in everything and "to win and to win and to win." Not anymore:

> Today we have a new ideology—that is to be homogeneous, no letter grades, no classification. The only line that some of our people seem to want today is a line between passing and failing. There is no hunt for excellence, in other words. And you and I both know that this is the easy way. The prevailing idea today is to take the easy way—and that effort and that work are unnecessary.

The young radicals were disregarding law and authority, Vince said. When they didn't like the rule, they broke it. There was a tendency to "distrust or discredit anything of traditional value." Not only was there a "complete breakdown of law and order" but also a "complete breakdown of our moral code." His partial explanation for both breakdowns was communist subversion, and his evidence could have been lifted from a manual of the John Birch Society. "I'd like to read you something," he told the audience:

> I won't tell you where this came from until I am through. It says, "Corrupt the young people. Get them interested in sex, make them superficial, and destroy their ruggedness. Get people's minds off their government by focusing their attention on sex, plays, and immoral movies. Divide the people into hostile groups, destroy the people's faith in their natural leaders by holding the latter up to contempt and ridicule, preach true democracy but seize power as fast and as ruthlessly as possible, encourage them in extravagance, produce fear of inflation with rising prices and general discontent. Incite unnecessary strikes in vital industries, encourage civil disorders, and force a lenient and soft attitude on the part of government toward disorders. Cause a breakdown of the overall virtues of honesty, sobriety, self-respect, faith in the

pledged word, and ruggedness." That's not something I extracted from the *Washington Post* or from *The New York Times* last week. This was printed in 1919 at Dusseldorf, Germany, and is the Communist Rules of Revolution—it was fifty years ago. It is of widespread concern. I want to say that—right now!

Vince usually spoke to business groups who loved to hear the successful coach impart his football philosophy as a philosophy of life. Most of his mail praised his speeches. His message did attract some critics. Gary Cartwright, writing in *Life,* described his address as "an *America: Love it or leave it!* speech that ought to be reprinted on the head of a pin." Vince claimed the criticism didn't bother him. "I expect I will get criticized. I don't care, because I think I am doing the right thing."[74]

In private Vince was even more conservative and less tolerant of the youth culture. Ed Williams thought he had acquired simplistic views, arrived at without great study. "He was very, very conservative, very right-wing, and very hard-line . . . nationally, internationally, and ecclesiastically," said Williams. Vince now believed that Pope John XXIII had been a "disaster" for the Catholic Church because he had softened many Church doctrines. "He was very impatient and intolerant of the kids and their revolutionary ideas," added Williams. "He really felt a certain hostility to the tremendous forces of change. . . . He saw everything as black and white. He saw a dichotomy between right and wrong; he didn't see twilight areas."[75]

XVII

Illness and Death

NOSTALGIA AND SENTIMENT DOMINATED MAY 1970. ON THE MORNING OF THE twelfth at the Pfister Hotel in Milwaukee, Vince addressed the convention of the Independent Insurance Agents of Wisconsin. It was his first visit to the state since leaving Green Bay fifteen months earlier, and he was apprehensive, worried he might be returning "too soon." But his warm reception delighted him. After his speech, he met with reporters. Asked if any team would dominate pro football like the Packers had in the 1960s, Vince rubbed his huge Packer Super Bowl ring, grinned, and replied, "I hope someday the Redskins will." Some questions focused on the antiwar movement and the unrest on college campuses. Vince's call for "law and order and discipline" drew much applause from several dozen conventioners who had drifted into the press conference and clapped approvingly at frequent intervals.[1]

By late afternoon he was with friends on the Oneida Golf Course. He stayed in Green Bay for three days—the guest of the Richard Bourguignons—and golfed, visited friends, and met with reporters. "It's a pleasure to be back," he said. "I made so many great friends here in ten years—you just don't forget them in a hurry." Seven weeks earlier Susan had given birth to twins—Marie and Paul—and Vince beamed as he told everyone. He took a nostalgic drive past his former home on Sunset

Circle. Somebody asked him, "Vince, why don't you come back to Green Bay? This is more like a home to you." Tears welled in his eyes as he responded, "I would like to, but . . . ." Although he was actually content in Washington, his sentimental trip led him to tell friends privately that leaving Green Bay was the "worst mistake he ever made." When the staff at the Packers' office learned Vince would visit, the tempo of work picked up noticeably. Although Vince couldn't yell at him anymore, Chuck Lane still cleaned off his desk. "The whole efficiency of the place picked up," observed Lane. Vince had undergone a thorough physical examination in early May and boasted to friends, "I'm the greatest fifty-six-year-old specimen you ever saw. I feel wonderful." His Wisconsin friends agreed. He looked in robust health.[2]

On May 15 Vince flew from Green Bay to New York to accept another award, from Fordham. He remained for a few days visiting friends and family. Vince and Marie, Joe Lombardi and his wife, Betty, and Vince, Jr., and his wife, Jill, went out on the town in New York. Vince was more emotional than usual about his family, talking with pride about Susan's twins, and Vince, Jr.'s, family and law degree. "He was beaming," said Joe. "It was probably the most relaxed evening I'd ever spent with him." Added Betty: "He's never looked better."[3]

On June 15 Vince greeted sixty-two mostly rookies and free agents at a four-day pretraining camp at Georgetown University. He watched in amusement as the players attempted to impress him, managing an "Oh, well, it's only June" look as receivers stumbled untouched, punts were dropped, and quarterbacks sailed passes twenty feet over intended targets. During the camp, though, Vince suddenly felt ill and fatigued. He first sensed something was wrong during his usual exercise regimen. While running up and down the slope of the hill by his home, he grew unexplainably tired and couldn't finish. On about June 17 he became so weak and faint at a party he almost toppled over and had to ask Dave Slattery for assistance. "I'm so damn tired I cannot stand up," he said.[4]

During the next week he suffered severe constipation even though he had a continuous urge to defecate. On June 22, he fulfilled a commitment and spoke to a business convention in Dayton, Ohio. The Dayton newspaper noted he was ill. The following day he visited Dr. George Resta, the Redskins' team physician. Suspecting the ailment might be cancer, Dr. Resta referred him to Dr. Robert Coffey, an experienced cancer surgeon at Georgetown University Hospital. On June 24 Vince entered the hospital, the first time he had ever been a hospital patient. The following day Dr. Coffey performed a sigmoidoscopy, and a biopsy revealed cancer of the colon. After the tests Vince overheard Marie discussing the results outside his hospital room. "Don't stand out there in the hall and talk!" he yelled. "C'mon in here. I know what you're talking about." The bad news saddened him, and he immediately did what he had done all his life—he prayed. On the morning of June 27, Dr. Coffey operated on Vince for over two hours, removing a two-foot section of his colon, including a three-centimeter tumor. The postoperative pathology report was ominous—evidence of metastasis to the regional lymph nodes.[5]

Vince was among seventy-five thousand Americans who in 1970 developed colon cancer, one of the most common forms of major malignancy. Failures in colon cancer operations had come to dramatic public attention with the deaths of notable figures such as Secretary of State John Foster Dulles and the great athlete Babe Didrikson Zaharias. Vince's family history was apparently not a contributing factor. His friends later speculated that his refusal to allow the uncomfortable rectal procedure during physical examinations was crucial in not detecting his tumor, but Dr. Coffey dissented. A rectal exam would not have come near the region of his tumor; Dr. Coffey explained that the tumor was too far away for the doctor's hand to feel. He had symptoms for only a week; and his cancer was exceptionally virulent. "This was not the ordinary cancer," reflected Dr. Coffey. "It was vicious."[6]

Marie understood immediately the seriousness of the disease, knew he might die, and was initially distraught. She insisted that the nature of his illness not be made public. "I had shared him for years," she later explained. "This is one thing I'm not going to share." After the operation, therefore, the hospital refused to comment on Vince's tests for cancer, usually indicating only that he was "recuperating satisfactorily." Despite the vague medical bulletins, rumors circulated widely that he was seriously ill. The news blackout frustrated reporters such as Bob Addie of the *Washington Post,* who said, "People don't want to pry. They are genuinely interested in how Lombardi is getting along."

Despite the grim prognosis, Vince's postoperative condition was uneventful, allowing him to recover some of his optimism. He was determined to "lick it," he said. "Lombardi will want to get to camp quickly," speculated Williams after the operation. "Our biggest problem will be trying to restrain him." On July 10 Vince left the hospital to recuperate at home.[7]

Meanwhile, NFL owners were heatedly negotiating with the Players' Association over pension rights. An impasse had ensued, and it appeared the season would be seriously disrupted. When Vince learned the owners were meeting in New York on July 21, he told a friend, "I must go to that meeting. I must go." When he told Dr. Coffey his intentions, the doctor was incredulous. "We would have questioned whether he ought to go out in the hall in a wheelchair at that point," he recalled. It would be "absurd" and "harmful" to attend, he told Vince, but Vince was adamant. "No one is going to stop me," he said. "I've got to meet with the owners to put some steel in their backs."[8]

The trip to New York was his first public appearance since his operation, and while his presence was dramatic, the effort tragically exposed his precarious health. Marie put him in a wheelchair, ordered a chauffeured limousine to take them both to the airport, and Vince arrived in New York for the afternoon session. Looking pale and gaunt but with the old fire still blazing within him, he spoke forcefully as the firm voice of management. "These are a bunch of twenty-year-old kids," he told the silent, attentive owners. "We can't turn over to them what so many have built and sweated for."

The flight back to Washington was a nightmare. When he and Marie had traveled in recent years, they had received VIP treatment—a limousine to the runway, a fancy, private lounge—but after the New York meeting, exhausted and most in need of special treatment, he didn't receive any. They waited in a long line at LaGuardia Airport, and to the ticket attendant Lombardi was just another name. After Marie finally maneuvered him aboard the plane ahead of others, the stewardesses ignored them. By the time Marie struggled to settle him in his seat, she was crying. On the flight Vince was ashen gray. When the plane landed, Marie struggled to get him to his feet. They wrestled with their suitcases until assistance finally arrived. "Can I help you, Coach?" said a young man, and Vince Lombardi, who ordinarily never needed help, answered desperately, "Yes, please help me!"[9]

The following day Vince felt strong enough to watch the Redskins veterans practice informally at Georgetown University. He shook hands with many of the players, and, later, while they did the grass drill, players heard him in the distance saying, "Down. Down." On July 26 he insisted on attending the rookie scrimmage in Baltimore between the Redskins and the Colts. He looked terrible—pale, weak, thin—but despite the obvious strain, he later spoke to the Redskins' rookies in the locker room. It was his last public appearance.[10]

While recuperating at home, Vince began experiencing abdominal pain and constipation that grew progressively worse. On July 27 Dr. Coffey readmitted him to Georgetown University Hospital, where tests disclosed a large tumor in the colon with widespread peritoneal seeding and multiple metastases throughout both lobes of the liver. Dr. Coffey was shocked by the quick-spreading cancer. "I've done thousands of cases of colon cancer," he said, "and I've never seen one this virulent. His number was up the day the first cell started to change." He performed a colostomy on the twenty-seventh and instituted chemotherapy and cobalt therapy, but Vince's condition worsened. "Every day you could see him getting weaker and going downhill," recalled the doctor. The day after the operation the Redskins announced Vince would not resume his coaching duties. Bill Austin, who had been filling in for him, assumed the head coaching position.[11]

Vince fought his illness with courage and stubbornness, and mostly with a lack of self-pity. He had little physical pain but much mental anguish. As Marie observed, "How could Vince Lombardi accept something he couldn't lick?" He told Father Tim Moore that he wasn't afraid to die: "I'm not afraid to meet my God now. But what I do regret is that there is so damn much left to be done on earth." He often prayed, and when Bishop Aloysius Wycislo visited and asked if he had gone to confession, Vince was reassuring. "Last night about two A.M. I didn't feel well," Vince replied, "so I called the chaplain. I'm all straightened out. Don't worry about me."[12]

On August 8 he watched on television the first half of the Redskins' exhibition game against the Cincinnati Bengals. When the Redskins made mistakes, his swearing blistered the ears of the nurses. President Nixon phoned three days later to thank him for his contributions to his country, especially to its youth. "You are very kind," Vince replied. "What you have said is very flattering." On August 13 the House of Representatives honored him as "one of the great Americans."[13]

Marie continued to keep reporters and photographers—plus healers and "hippies" who wanted to pray over him—away from his bed. Family and friends, though, kept a close vigil. For a while, Marie had disguised the seriousness of the illness from Vince's parents and Susan, not wanting to upset them. As his condition deteriorated, the hospital offered Marie a room across the hall, allowing her to remain nearby twenty-four hours a day. "She was at his beck and call," observed Dr. Coffey, impressed by her devotion. "When she wasn't in his room, she was sitting in a chair outside his room." Wellington Mara phoned every day at 3:00 P.M. If the call came a little late, Vince grew impatient. "It's after three. Where the hell is Well?"[14]

The hospital visits by friends and former players were emotionally distressing; many left his room feeling they had said their last good-bye. Marie warned guests not to be surprised by his condition, but most insisted on seeing him anyway to raise his spirits or to express their

Michael O'Brien

gratitude. Despite Marie's warning, Vince's weight loss, sunken cheeks, and gray color often shocked them. Vince was embarrassed by his appearance. "I hate to have you see me this way," he told Bob Skoronski. When Willie Davis learned the seriousness of Vince's condition, he flew from San Diego to Washington for a visit. "Coach, if you'll come back to Green Bay and coach again," he teased, "I'll come out of retirement." Vince smiled, tears welled in his eyes, and he said, "Willie, you're a hell of a man." Vince started to cry. "Get out of here," he ordered Davis. The visit lasted only a minute and a half. Afterward Davis stood for a half hour in the hospital corridor, his head against the wall.[15]

Edward Bennett Williams visited the hospital each morning, but Vince was usually heavily sedated and incoherent, frustrating Williams's attempt to communicate with him. One morning Williams arrived while Vince was lucid. Thinking he might never again have the opportunity for a perfectly clear dialogue, Williams took advantage of the occasion. "I was driven to say to him something I never said to another man," recalled Williams. "Vince," he said, "I love you as my friend for what you've done for . . . my life, for the lives of my children—who have been so influenced by you and love you so much—for my family, for my city, and for this country. I want you to know that." Vince cried. It was the last conversation Williams had with him.[16]

By August 20 Vince was experiencing periods of disorientation. Five days later he was semiconscious most of the time. On August 30, his thirtieth wedding anniversary, he was markedly jaundiced and the medical staff had difficulty maintaining his blood pressure. Yet he briefly opened his eyes and said to Marie, "Happy anniversary. Remember, I love you." On September 2, with Vince in a deep coma, Marie allowed the hospital to break the two-month blackout of information and announce Vince's grim condition. He died at 7:20 A.M. on September 3, 1970. The autopsy report discovered extensive metastases in the brain, lungs, liver, spleen—everywhere. It also showed that although he had no symptoms, he suffered from coronary sclerosis that, left untreated, probably would have caused a heart attack.[17]

Poignant reactions to Vince's death flowed from former players and peers. "It was like losing a father," said Bart Starr. "All the things a man searches for all his life I found in Coach Lombardi," said the Redskins' Jerry Smith. Assistant Coach George Dickson thought he was the "epitome of what manliness is all about, the greatest man that ever walked the sidelines." Bill Sullivan, president of the Boston Patriots, labeled Vince "pro football's proudest boast."[18]

Too tactful to debunk at the moment of death, Vince's critics were mostly silent. They would raise their voices later. Some commentators expressed bewilderment that a person as ill-tempered as Vince could engender such fierce loyalty from his players. *Newsweek* called it "magic"; *Time* thought he had "elevated coaching to the level of mysticism." As if they anticipated later criticism, Vince's friends in the media defended him from "inaccurate" portraits. Red Smith conceded that Vince's explosive temper, intolerance for shoddy work, and impatience with gadfly reporters had contributed to his image as an "ogre." But Smith disagreed: "If there is a sports figure around today who resembles his public image less than Vince Lombardi did, he's got to be in some field like professional wrestling, where they're all fictional characters." Shirley Povich agreed, noting that Vince was "plagued" by the prevailing image of him as the curmudgeon autocrat of the practice field. "That picture of Lombardi as an insensitive slave driver was a wildly inaccurate one. An instant after his quick anger, the kindly emotions ran deep with him."[19]

Most observers praised Vince's integrity, values, leadership, indomitable will, and commitment to excellence. They lauded him for inspiring zeal and loyalty in his players. Some of the reaction took a political slant. "For a while," observed the *Washington Post*, "we were traveling first class, which doesn't happen all that often, let's face it, in this city of second-class citizens, built around the industry of politics, which is itself essentially a game of compromise. With Lombardi, there was no such word as compromise." Claiming him as one of their own, conservatives touted Vince's traditional values—sacrifice, patriotism, discipline, morality—and bemoaned their absence among radical youths in the 1960s. He "loved his country," said the *Washington Star*, and "believed it right more often than wrong. His was a simpler faith, bred in a simpler era, but it had a basic strength and purity to it which spoke to all of us. Not fashionable, not trendy, but right."[20]

At a White House dinner President Nixon called Vince a "man who in a time when so many seem to be turning away from religion was devoutly religious and devoted to his Church; at a time when the moral fabric of the country seems to be coming apart, he was a man who was deeply devoted to his family; at a time when it seems rather square to be patriotic, he was deeply and unashamedly patriotic; at a time when permissiveness is the order of the day in many circles, he was a man who insisted on discipline . . . discipline and strength."[21]

Vince's body lay in a closed casket at the Joseph Gawler's Sons funeral home in Washington, D.C., on September 4, and for the next two days

Michael O'Brien

at The Abbey funeral home in New York. In Green Bay on Sunday evening, September 6, two thousand persons attended an ecumenical service at the Veterans' Memorial Arena. Taking issue with Vince's disclaimer that he was not a legend, Methodist minister Roger Bourland declared in his homily that "Vince Lombardi was a legend, whether he liked it or not. He was no saint but he strove for excellence with a vengeance that is impressive in this modern age of mediocrity. That's what legends are all about."[22]

On September 7, three thousand persons attended Vince's funeral Mass in the shadowy gloom of St. Patrick's Cathedral in New York. An equal number pressed against police barricades outside, on Fifth Avenue. It was the largest funeral at St. Patrick's since Robert Kennedy's in 1968. (In Washington, President Nixon joined another thousand mourners at a noon memorial Mass at St. Matthew's Church.) In his homily Archbishop Terence Cooke frequently quoted St. Paul, who often used athletic terms to describe the mysteries of life and death. To the world of the first century St. Paul had preached the virtues of the athlete—a strong sense of responsibility and integrity, dedication and teamwork, exemplary conduct and good example. The virtues of the athlete were still important, insisted Cooke. "I have fought the good fight to the end," Cooke quoted St. Paul. "I have run the race to the finish; I have kept the faith." Vince had fought the "good fight," said Cooke. "He has finished the course; he has kept the faith."[23]

After the Mass a procession of forty limousines drove straight down the middle of Fifth Avenue through a city deserted during the Labor Day holiday. But clusters of people gathered at the roadside in every small community in New Jersey as the procession made the forty-five-mile journey to Mount Olivet Cemetery outside Red Bank. After a brief cemetery service, Vince was buried on a gentle slope near a crabapple tree. Within five minutes from the time the casket was lowered, the canopy was down, the metal poles removed, and a mobile crane with grappling hooks had been rolled up to lift the heavy bronze lid on top of the vault. "You know," mused a man reacting to the abrupt efficiency of the action, "it's almost as if Vince himself, in one of his hurry-up, no-nonsense moods, had directed this part of it."[24]

Epilogue

After Vince died, a turnpike restaurant in New Jersey and schools in Green Bay and New York were dedicated to him. Charity golf tournaments raised funds in his name, and Georgetown University established the Vincent T. Lombardi Cancer Research Center. Naturally, football came forth with prominent symbols to honor him. The sterling-silver trophy awarded to the winner of the Super Bowl, and the annual award dinner honoring college football's outstanding lineman were both named for him. Former players and friends lavished praise on Vince in books, interviews, and speeches, and two television specials treated him affectionately.[1]

In the early 1970s Vince's coaching philosophy continued to win praise from conservatives who viewed football as a healthy antidote to the breakdown of law and order and to the destructive behavior of the counterculture. The Nixon administration often aligned football with politics and with cherished American values. President Nixon phoned victorious teams, granted plaques symbolizing national championships, surrounded himself with coaches and ex-coaches, and dabbled in quarterback decisions prior to important games. On July 30, 1971, when he spoke in Canton, Ohio, at the induction of Vince into the Pro Football Hall of Fame, he said, "Let's always try to be number one. In the spirit of American football at its best, let's be for our team. Let's be for our country."

Epilogue

Vice President Spiro Agnew aggressively championed Vince's approach to sports. "I . . . would not want to live in a society that did not include winning in its philosophy; that would have us live our lives as identical lemmings, never trying to best anybody at anything, all headed in the same direction," said Agnew in 1972. Vince was a "devout believer in the American competitive ethic," the Vice President continued. "So long as there is an America . . . we are going to stay in the competitive race. And we are going to run *to win.*"[2]

Paralleling the honors and tributes Vince received, however, were highly critical appraisals of his techniques, his values, his slogans, and particularly the example he set for coaches of youth and amateur sports. Taken together, the harsh indictments muddied Vince's reputation. Only three years after his death a writer for *Harper's Bazaar* dismissed him as an example of "authority figures" who were now "outdated." The social critic and writer Murray Kempton suggested that Vince's and Earl Blaik's "obsessions" to win had led to the "pressures" on West Point's student athletes and the 1951 cribbing scandal. Kempton also dismissed the praise Vince received from his former players because they celebrated Vince's "callous and brutal" acts "as proof of virtue."[3]

Numerous observers found widespread abuses in sports, and since Vince was so prominent and recently successful, critics used him as an example of much that was wrong not only with sports, but with all of American society. Vince had used tyrannical methods, some charged. "Lombardi's special skill in developing men," said Kempton, "appears to have been for keeping them high-school boys." "Hating" opponents and preaching that "winning is the only thing" were poor standards for anyone to live by, critics said. It was difficult to appreciate the beauty and the virtues of football, said George Sauer, the New York Jets' great receiver, "when you have a Vince Lombardi type of coach hollering at you to hate the other guy, who's really just like you in a different-colored uniform." Because coaches were in a cutthroat business, constantly under siege to produce, Vince's stress on winning put a terrible strain on sportsmanship. Some conceded that winning was a self-evident truth in professional football, but objected to the way Vince's slogan was transformed into high principle. "To make America the Green Bay Packers and the NFL the planet Earth, is fascist rhetoric," said sportswriter Robert Lipsyte. (The words "fascist" and "fascism" appeared surprisingly often in criticism of Vince and his philosophy.)

A few of Vince's former players also objected to his methods and approach. A former Washington Redskin thought Vince had left "many scars" on his players. "I've used fear. I've intimidated people," he

378

reflected. "I've also brought some of those [scars] home. My children have been affected." Henry Jordan mostly admired Vince, but criticized his philosophy of life. "I want to relax and enjoy life," said Jordan. "That's my idea of happiness. To Lombardi, happiness was only one thing: lying exhausted in victory."[4]

Because football was violent, often spoken of in military metaphor and touted by the Nixon administration, liberal and radical antiwar activists and proponents of the counterculture linked football to the U.S. intervention in Vietnam. Only a superaggressive, dehumanized nation addicted to football could pursue such an immoral, brutal war, they said. The Watergate revelations helped to expose the sordid aspects of the sports mentality that underlay the thinking in Nixon's White House. When Watergate burglar James McCord showed signs of independence, he was chastized for not following the "game plan." Other conspirators were told to be "team players." In the 1972 Nixon campaign, in the secret room used by the Committee to Re-Elect the President (CREEP), Jeb Magruder and his Watergate accomplices planned spying operations and dirty tricks. On the wall hung a sign with the legend WINNING IN POLITICS ISN'T EVERYTHING, IT'S THE ONLY THING. What the White House needed, suggested one political observer, was "less Vince Lombardi and more Abraham Lincoln."[5]

Several prominent observers joined the critical chorus. In his widely used psychology textbook, the respected social psychologist Elliot Aronson criticized our culture's "staggering cultural obsession with victory," and cited Vince's "winning" slogan as a prime example. "What is frightening about the acceptance of [Lombardi's] philosophy," said Aronson, "is that it implies that the goal of victory justifies whatever means we use to win, even if it's only a football game—which, after all, was first conceived as a recreational activity."

In his sober, intelligent book *Sports in America* (1976), James Michener criticized Vince's methods and his winning philosophy. The prominent novelist liked Vince's dedication to accomplishment and his doctrine that when you engaged an opponent, you did so to win, but Michener charged that Vince had "kept mature athletes in a state of juvenile dependence, making grown men tremble when he frowned, or rejoice when he deigned to smile upon them." Losing a game was not equivalent to death, said Michener. "Failing to be numero uno does not make me a lesser human being." Fortunately, Michener added, there seemed to be a general rejection of the "reign of terror" Vince had inspired. "The rejection of his methods was by no means universal, and it was shamefully late in coming, but it was substantial."[6]

Epilogue

When usurped and abused by neurotic coaches of youthful amateurs, critics contended, the Lombardi legacy was exceptionally dangerous. Vince's approach became the norm for some coaches in colleges, high schools, and Little League. "Many deaths and injuries, physical and psychic, are caused by pseudo-Lombardis," charged Lipsyte. When Michener researched his chapter on children for his book, he heard the same complaint from a score of resentful parents: "Our Little League coach thinks he is obligated to behave like Vince Lombardi."

A few coaches adopted a grotesque understanding of Vince's winning philosophy. In Santa Ana, California, the coach of a youth football team called the Packers handed out mimeographed rules to an eight-year-old player. The "Rules for a Successful Packer to Live By" stated:

> Become an all-out runner: Dig for more yards!
> Punish the tackler! Put fear in his eyes! Bruise his body!
> Break his spirit! Bust his butt! Make him pay a price for tackling you!
> Dig for more yards!
> Become a competitor! A competitor never quits. Be hostile!
> Be angry! Be violent! Be mean! Be aggressive! Be physical!
> Remember always—loosing [sic] is nothing! Winning is everything![7]

Vince's critics were partly correct. He was often rude, inconsiderate, impatient, egotistical, and terrible-tempered. He never seemed to appreciate that the values he cherished in sports could just as often be gained through other intense endeavors. His coaching methods, his emphasis on winning, and his careless endorsement of hate were, indeed, easily abused by others.

Yet even Vince's harshest critics conceded that Vince himself would have had the presence of mind to condemn excesses done in his name. Lipsyte admitted that Vince "would have spotted [neurotic coaches]" and have judged them "emotionally insecure and mentally unprepared." Another critic of Vince's winning slogan noted that the "motto has been taken as a justification for methods Lombardi would never have approved." Some found fault with Vince no matter what he said. When he let it be known that he taught his players to "hate" an opponent for a week, he was condemned for desecrating a biblical injunction; when he credited the "love" the Packers had for each other as a reason for the team's greatness, he was accused of being corny.[8]

The way Vince's winning slogan has been interpreted by critics has infuriated Vince's family and admirers. Vince wouldn't have "sold his mother to win a football game," stated Marie in exasperation. "I think some of my liberal friends have used it to downgrade Vince's character," said Wellington Mara. "I can feel the hair on the back of my neck stand up when I hear people speaking disparagingly of [his] creed because they don't know what they are talking about." Willie Davis insisted that "if you knew the man, you knew it was the pursuit [of winning]. I hope we never reach the point where we're planning to lose, and that's all Lombardi meant."[9]

"Winning is the only thing" can indeed be a model standard when understood as an attitude, a desire, a spirit. Winning does provide evidence of excellence, perfection, and proper preparation. It need not mean that one must win at all cost, fair or foul, or that losing is without dignity. Vince's Packers lost occasionally. Yet they had so much elan and professional integrity that even in defeat they played with distinction— and lost with dignity.[10]

In general, the critical appraisal of Vince created a shallow, one-dimensional portrait. It unfairly misrepresented his methods and philosophy, blamed him for the neurotic actions of others, ignored his considerable virtues, and dismissed the tributes of the persons who knew him best. Vince's "hate" for opponents was clearly synthetic and temporary. True, he was obsessed with winning, but those who observed him closely knew that his ethics were exceptional and that he honored football with his sportsmanship. Few of his former players seemed to have absorbed dangerous or unhealthy lessons from him. Some may have remained in a state of perpetual adolescence; a few suffered tragically from family problems, alcoholism, mental illness, bankruptcy, and unemployment. Yet only a tiny fraction of those who suffered problems blamed Vince for contributing in any way to their personal or professional misfortunes.

Although Vince's approach to sports harbored serious potential dangers, it was hard to argue with a man and a philosophy demanding the best from everyone. In *Coming Apart,* his social history of the 1960s, historian William O'Neill praised Vince and observed that "in an age marked by fakery, hedonism, and contempt for work, sport was one of the few areas in which hard work and ability were still pre-eminent and unmistakable." Vince's teams exemplified those traits and created a modern metaphor for collective excellence. When Vince spoke out for old-fashioned standards and victory properly arrived at he was praised by people nostalgic for lost values. "There was something pathetic about all this," said O'Neill, because Vince's crusade showed the bankruptcy of a tradition once championed by Theodore Roosevelt and John Kennedy. "Sport used to seem a metaphor for such virtues as drive, ambition, respect for standards, and individual excellence," O'Neill concluded. "Now many thought it their last resort."[11]

Although the manipulative, abusive, and dictatorial features of Vince's coaching are obviously poor models for any leader, in other ways Vince was a sterling model for leadership. He was intelligent and organized, persevering and enthusiastic, dedicated and dramatic, apologetic and forgiving, civic-minded and charitable. His character and integrity were exceptional; his dignity and grace in racial matters exemplary. He had uncanny ability to understand his players as individuals and to select the best approach to induce each to perform at maximum capacity. An outstanding teacher, he inspired his players, insisted on professionalism, and instilled values.

Since Vince's death, the overwhelming majority of his players, assistants, staff, peers, and friends have expressed their admiration and affection.

"I am here to be close to the memory of a man that I revere," Howard Cosell told a Milwaukee sports banquet. "I am here because I love Vince Lombardi."

"I want my kids to grow up to be like Vince," said Frank Gifford, "to be as honest and [as] dedicated."

"I was proud to be called an extension of him," Bart Starr reflected. "I owe my life to that man."

"I have a special pantheon of heroes formed from thirty years in sport," said W. C. Heinz. "Vince is not only on it, he's the leader."

After his football career, defensive end Lionel Aldridge suffered for over a decade as a paranoid-schizophrenic, finally diagnosed as caused by a chemical imbalance in his brain. He is now recovering. "Coach Lombardi . . . once said that the greatest success was not in never falling but in rising every time you fell," Aldridge said recently. "That became very meaningful to me."

Willie Davis earned a master's degree in business administration from the University of Chicago and became a millionaire through investments in several businesses, including ownership of a major wine and beer distributorship in Los Angeles. "I jog in the morning," Davis told W. C. Heinz, "and there are days when I wake up and I don't feel like getting up and crawling into the office. I say to myself that I own the Willie Davis Distributing Company, and today I'm going to exercise my prerogative and not go in. Then I think, 'What would Lombardi do?' I get up and out of bed. It's six o'clock, and I throw on my sweats and drive here and I jog."

Herb Adderley ran a construction company in Philadelphia. He said he worked hard at his business partly because he remembered Vince's advice: "The harder you work, the harder it is to surrender." "Do you think of him often?" Jerry Kramer asked Adderley. "Every day," Adderley replied. "And I love my father, who is also deceased, but I don't think about my father every day."

"So many people have a misconception about Lombardi," Tom Brown said. "They act crazy with kids and then use Lombardi as an excuse. . . . I hate it when people misuse him."

Jerry Kramer recalled Vince's slogan *"You don't do things right once in a while. You do them right all the time."* Said Kramer, "Of all the lessons I learned from Lombardi, from all his sermons on commitment and integrity and the work ethic, that one hit home the hardest. I've found in business that only fifteen or twenty percent of the people do things right all the time. The other eighty or eighty-five percent are taking short cuts, looking for the easy way, either stealing from others or cheating themselves. I've got an edge, because whenever I'm tempted to screw off, to cut corners, I hear that raspy voice saying, 'This is the right way to do it. Which way are you going to do it, mister?' "[12]

Notes

INTRODUCTION

1. *Washington Post,* September 13, 1968.
2. *Green Bay Press-Gazette,* August 4, 1968.
3. *The New York Times,* September 11, 1968; *Washington Post,* September 13, 1968.
4. *Green Bay Press-Gazette,* September 12 and 15, 1968; *The New York Times,* September 15, 1968; *Philadelphia Daily News,* September 13, 1968.
5. *Milwaukee Journal,* September 16, 1968; *Philadelphia Bulletin,* September 15, 1968.
6. Clipping, unprocessed Susan (Lombardi) Bickham Papers, Plantation, Fla.; *Green Bay Press-Gazette,* September 12 and 15, 1968.
7. *Green Bay Press-Gazette,* September 15, 1968; *Washington Post,* September 13, 1968.
8. Bill Ward to Vince Lombardi, September 16, 1968, Bickham Papers; *The New York Times,* September 15, 1968; *Washington Post,* September 13, 1968.
9. *Green Bay Press-Gazette,* September 17, 1968; *New York Post,* September 12, 1968; *Philadelphia Bulletin,* September 15, 1968; *Philadelphia Daily News,* September 13, 1968; *Philadelphia Inquirer,* September 15, 1968.

10. *Ibid.*
11. *The New York Times,* September 11, 1968.

CHAPTER ONE

1. Alexander DeConde, *Half Bitter, Half Sweet: An Excursion into Italian-American History* (New York: Charles Scribner's Sons, 1971), pp. 79, 381; Nathan Glazer and Daniel Moynihan, *Beyond the Melting Pot* (Cambridge, Mass.: The M.I.T. Press, 1963), pp. 183–184; Luciano Iorizzo and Salvatore Mondello, *The Italian Americans* (Boston: Twayne, 1980), pp. 20, 60.
2. Samuel Baily, "The Adjustment of Italian Immigrants in Buenos Aires and New York, 1870–1914," *The American Historical Review* 88:2 (April 1983): 299, 301; Herbert Klein, "The Integration of Italian Immigrants into the United States and Argentina: A Comparative Analysis," *The American Historical Review* 88:2 (April 1983): 324, 326, 327; George Pozzetta, "The Italians of New York City, 1890–1914" (Ph.D. dissertation, University of North Carolina at Chapel Hill, 1971), pp. 94, 104; DeConde, *Half Bitter, Half Sweet,* pp. 77–109; Glazer and Moynihan, *Melting Pot,* p. 184; Silvano Tomasi, *Piety and Power: the Role of the Italian Parishes in the New York Metropolitan Area, 1880–1930* (New York: Center for Migration Studies, 1975), pp. 22, 26, 27.
3. DeConde, *Half Bitter, Half Sweet,* pp. 98, 101, 102, 119; Patrick Gallo, *Old Bread, New Wine: A Portrait of the Italian-American* (Chicago: Nelson-Hall, 1981), p. 238; Glazer and Moynihan, *Melting Pot,* p. 207; James Patterson, *America in the Twentieth Century, A History,* 2nd Ed. (New York: Harcourt Brace Jovanovich, Inc., 1983), p. 175.
4. DeConde, *Half Bitter, Half Sweet,* pp. 85, 88; Gallo, *Old Bread,* pp. 45, 47, 152; Glazer and Moynihan, *Melting Pot,* pp. 197, 207; Jerry Della Femina and Charles Sopkin, *An Italian Grows in Brooklyn* (Boston: Little, Brown and Co., 1978), pp. 7–11; Tomasi, *Piety and Power,* p. 31; Ralph Weld, *Brooklyn Is America* (New York: Columbia University Press, 1950), pp. 141–142.
5. Erik Amfitheatrof, *The Children of Columbus* (Boston: Little, Brown and Co., 1973), pp. 165–167; Robert Foerster, *The Italian Emigration of Our Times* (New York: Arno Press and the New York Times, 1969), p. 383; Gallo, *Old Bread,* pp. 48–49; interviews, Peter Izzo, Madeline Werner.
6. Interviews, Peter Izzo, Madeline Werner.

7. J. P. Cole, *Italy: An Introductory Geography* (New York: Frederick A. Praeger, 1966), pp. 224–225; interviews, Buddy Izzo, Peter Izzo, Clara Parvin, Madeline Werner.

8. Interviews, Dorothy Pennell, Madeline Werner.

9. *New York Herald Tribune,* June 7, 1964; Ruth Lines, "The Story of Sheepshead Bay, Manhattan Beach, and the Sheepshead Bay Library" (unpublished typescript, Brooklyn Public Library, n.d.), pp. 1–4; Joseph Milgram, "An Informal History of Sheepshead Bay" (Brooklyn: Brooklyn Public Library, n.d.), pp. 4, 7, 8, 19.

10. George Flynn, *The Vince Lombardi Scrapbook* (New York: Grosset and Dunlap, 1976), pp. 33–34; Robert Wells, *Lombardi: His Life and Times* (Madison: Wisconsin House, LTD, 1971), p. 23; interviews, Buddy Izzo, Peter Izzo, Clara Parvin, Madeline Werner.

11. *Green Bay Press-Gazette,* September 6, 1970: *Milwaukee Journal,* January 7, 1973; Vince Lombardi (with W. C. Heinz), *Run to Daylight* (New York: Grosset and Dunlap, 1963), pp. 114–115; Wells, *Lombardi,* pp. 23–26; interviews, Peter Izzo, Patrick Joyce, William Joyce, Joe Lombardi.

12. Wells, *Lombardi,* p. 24; interviews, Peter Izzo, Harold Lombardi, Joe Lombardi, Madeline Werner.

13. Jerry Kramer (ed.), *Lombardi: Winning Is the Only Thing* (New York: World Publishing Co., 1970), p. 10; interview, Madeline Werner.

14. Gallo, *Old Bread,* p. 262; Will Irwin, *Highlights of Manhattan,* rev. ed. (New York: D. Appleton-Century Company, 1937), p. 291; Fremont Rider, *Rider's New York City* (New York: The Macmillan Company, 1924), p. 198; interviews, Vince Lombardi, Jr., Madeline Werner.

15. *Milwaukee Sentinel,* September 7, 1970; *New York Daily News,* September 6, 1970; interviews, Joe Goettisheim, Dorothy Pennell, Madeline Werner.

16. *Milwaukee Sentinel,* September 7, 1970; interviews, Joe Goettisheim, Peter Izzo, Madeline Werner.

17. Lines, "Story of Sheepshead Bay," pp. 43–44; Milgram, "History of Sheepshead Bay," p. 7; interviews, Joe Goettisheim, Leo Paquin, Madeline Werner.

18. *New York Daily News,* September 6, 1970; interviews, Joe Goettisheim, Madeline Werner.

19. Leonard Shecter, "The Toughest Man in Pro Football," *Esquire,* January 1968, p. 145; interview, Madeline Werner.

20. *Cathedral Annual,* 1930–32; interviews, John Crane, Joe Goettisheim.
21. *Cathedral Annual,* 1930.
22. *Ibid.,* 1931–1932; interviews, John Crane, Patrick Joyce.
23. Interview, John Crane.
24. Shecter, "Toughest Man," p. 145; *Time,* December 21, 1962; interview, Madeline Werner.
25. Interview, Ruth McKloskey.
26. *SFP 1858–1983,* St. Francis Preparatory School—150-year anniversary booklet (Fresh Meadows, New York, 1983); Brother Becket Ryan to author, January 17, 1983; interviews, James Duggan, Brother Edmund Holmes, Dan Kern, Salvator Maggio.
27. Interviews, Brother Edmund Holmes, Dan Kern, Salvator Maggio.
28. *Ibid;* Gene Schoor, *Football's Greatest Coach: Vince Lombardi* (Garden City, N.Y.: Doubleday, 1974), pp. 17–18.
29. *Sanfran,* 1933 (Yearbook of St. Francis Preparatory School); Schoor, *Greatest Coach,* pp. 17–18; interviews, Patrick Joyce, William Joyce, Salvator Maggio.
30. Schoor, *Greatest Coach,* p. 18; interviews, Patrick Joyce, Salvator Maggio.
31. *The New York Times,* September 25, October 9, 16, 23, and 30, November 6, 1932; interviews, Patrick Joyce, Salvator Maggio.
32. Newspaper clipping, unprocessed Roger Fay Papers, Bergenfield, N.J.; *Sanfran,* 1933; interviews, Joe Goettisheim, Dan Kern, Patrick Joyce, Dorothy Pennell, Madeline Werner.
33. *Sanfran,* 1933; interview, Brother Edmund Holmes.
34. Lombardi's Fordham College and Law transcripts, Fordham University Papers, N.Y.; interviews, Brother Edmund Holmes, Dan Kern.
35. Interview, Dan Kern.

CHAPTER TWO

1. *The Story of Fordham* (New York, 1941), pp. 18, 21; *Commonweal,* September 19, 1941, p. 526.
2. *Green Bay Press-Gazette,* February 4, 1968; *New Haven Register,* July 27, 1969; interview, Jim Lawlor.
3. Robert Wells, *Lombardi: His Life and Times* (Madison: Wisconsin House, LTD, 1971), pp. 35–36; interviews, Jim Lawlor, George Mulrey, Leo Paquin.
4. Interview, Jim Lawlor.

5. *Fordham Ram,* October 16 and 23 and December 11, 1936; *Maroon* (Fordham yearbook), 1936, 1937; Richard Whittingham, *What a Game They Played* (New York: Harper & Row, 1984), p. 157; interviews, Al Bart, Michael Kochel, Jim Lawlor, George Mulrey, Leo Paquin.

6. *Fordham University Bulletin of Information, Catalogue 1936–37* (New York: Fordham University, 1937), p. 31; Gilbert Highet, *The Art of Teaching* (New York: Alfred A. Knopf, 1966), pp. 200–224; interviews, Jim Lawlor, George Mulrey, Leo Paquin.

7. Vincent T. Lombardi's Fordham College and Fordham Law School transcripts, Fordham University Papers, Fordham University, New York; *Washington Star,* September 4, 1970; *Fordham University Bulletins,* 1934–37.

8. *Army Football Programs,* 1949–53, Special Collections, United States Military Academy Papers, West Point, N.Y.

9. Speech, "Leadership in Management," 1968, Ruth McKloskey Papers, Green Bay, Wis.

10. George Flynn (ed.), *The Vince Lombardi Scrapbook* (New York: Grosset & Dunlap, 1976), p. 53; Jerry Kramer (ed.), *Lombardi: Winning Is the Only Thing* (New York: World Publishing Company, 1970), p. 19; interviews, Jim Lawlor, Wellington Mara, Leo Paquin.

11. Dagobert Runes (ed.), *Dictionary of Philosophy,* 15th ed., rev. (Paterson, N.J.: Littlefield, Adams and Co., 1964), pp. 280–81; Samuel Enoch Stumpf, *Socrates to Sartre: A History of Philosophy,* 3rd ed. (New York: McGraw-Hill, 1982), pp. 168–69, 181–82, 479.

12. *Fordham University Bulletin, 1936–37,* pp. 43–47; interviews, Wellington Mara, Leo Paquin, Joseph Rickert, Neal Roche.

13. *Fordham University Bulletin, 1936–37,* pp. 26–28; *Fordham Ram,* October 2, 1936.

14. Flynn, *Lombardi Scrapbook,* p. 53; interviews, Wellington Mara, Leo Paquin, Joseph Rickert.

15. Ignatius Cox, *Liberty: Its Use and Abuse,* 2nd ed. (New York: Fordham University Press, 1939); *America,* March 13, 1937, p. 550; *Catholic World,* October 1937, p. 125; T. V. Smith, *American Journal of Sociology* 43 (November 1937): 496–97.

16. *Milwaukee Journal,* January 12, 1964; Tim Cohane, *Bypaths of Glory* (New York: Harper & Row, 1963), pp. 62–63.

17. Clipping, Football Scrapbook, Vol. 1, 1934, Fordham University Papers, Archives, Fordham University, New York; Jack Newcombe, "Nothing-to-Nothing: Fordham vs. Pitt was Football's Finest Hour," Robert Smith (ed.), *The Grantland Rice Award Prize Sports*

Stories (Garden City, N.Y.: Doubleday & Company, 1962), p. 251;
interviews, Hugh Devore, John Druze, Leo Paquin.

18. Cohane, *Bypaths of Glory*, pp. 64–69; Kramer, *Lombardi: Winning*,
p. 23; Vince Lombardi (with W. C. Heinz), *Run to Daylight* (New
York: Grosset & Dunlap, 1963), pp. 57–58.

19. *Ibid.*; Wells, *Lombardi*, p. 32; interviews, Michael Kochel, George
Mulrey, Leo Paquin.

20. Newcombe, "Fordham vs. Pitt," *Grantland Rice Award*, p. 250;
Arch Ward, *Frank Leahy and The Fighting Irish: The Story of Notre
Dame Football* (New York: G. P. Putnam's Sons, 1944), p. 129;
interviews, Al Bart, John Druze, Ed Franco, Leo Paquin.

21. Newcombe, "Fordham vs. Pitt," *Grantland Rice Award*, p. 246.

22. Clipping, Roger Fay Papers, Bergenfield, N.J.; clipping, Susan
(Lombardi) Bickham Papers, Plantation, Fla.; Al Silverman (ed.),
Lombardi (New York: Macfadden-Bartell Corp., 1970), p. 22;
interviews, Jim Crowley, George Mulrey.

23. Kramer, *Lombardi: Winning*, p. 18; interviews, Jim Crowley,
Michael Kochel, George Mulrey, Leo Paquin.

24. *The New York Times*, September 5, 1934; clippings, Football
Scrapbooks, Vol. 2, 1934, and Vol. 2, 1935, Fordham University
Papers; *Fordham Ram*, September 28, October 5, 11, and 19, and
November 10, 1933; *ibid.*, May 3, October 4, December 13, 1934;
interview, Jim Lawlor.

25. Clippings, Football Scrapbooks, Vols. 1–5, 1935, Fordham University Papers; *Fordham Ram*, March 28 and October 11, 1935.

26. Lombardi, *Run to Daylight*, p. 9; interview, Pat Joyce.

27. *The New York Times*, September 10, 1936; clippings, Football
Scrapbooks, Vols. 1–4, 1936, Fordham University Papers.

28. *Washington Post*, May 17, 1970; Kramer, *Lombardi: Winning*, p.
19; Wells, *Lombardi*, p. 33; interviews, George Mulrey, Leo
Paquin.

29. *Time*, December 21, 1962, p. 58; Newcombe, "Fordham vs. Pitt,"
Grantland Rice Award, pp. 247, 258, 264; interview, Ed Franco.

30. *New York Sun*, November 5, 1936; *New York Post*, November 18,
1936; Lombardi, *Run to Daylight*, p. 115; *Time*, December 21,
1962, p. 58.

31. *New York Post*, November 18, 1936.

32. *Washington Post*, February 9, 1969, and May 17, 1970; Cohane,
Bypaths of Glory, pp. 71–72; interview, Tim Cohane.

33. Clippings, Football Scrapbooks, Vols. 4 and 5, 1936, Fordham
University Papers.

34. Silverman, *Lombardi*, p. 22.
35. *Fordham Ram*, April 23, 1937; interviews, Jim Lawlor, William McGettrick, George Mulrey, Leo Paquin.
36. John Wiebusch (ed.), *Lombardi* (Chicago: Follett Publishing Company, 1971), pp. 66–67; interview, Jim Lawlor.
37. Interview, Jim Lawlor.
38. Kramer, *Lombardi: Winning*, pp. 22–23; interviews, Tim Cohane, Leo Paquin.
39. Wiebusch, *Lombardi*, p. 67; interview, Jim Lawlor.
40. *Milwaukee Journal*, February 1, 1959.
41. Kramer, *Lombardi: Winning*, p. 24; interview, Leo Paquin.
42. Lombardi's Fordham College and Fordham Law School transcripts, Fordham University Papers; *New York Daily News*, September 10, 1970; Wiebusch, *Lombardi*, p. 67.
43. *Evening Journal* (Wilmington, Del.), February 16, 1968; *Green Bay Press-Gazette*, February 9, 1960; *The New York Times*, October 6, 1938; Lombardi, *Run to Daylight*, p. 112; interview, Leo Paquin.
44. *Maroon*, 1936, 1937; interviews, Jim Lawlor, Leo Paquin.
45. Silverman, *Lombardi*, p. 22; interviews, Jim Lawlor, Leo Paquin.
46. *Time*, December 21, 1962, p. 58; interview, Leo Paquin.
47. Interviews, Jim Lawlor, Joe Lombardi.
48. Lombardi's Fordham College and Fordham Law School transcripts, Fordham University Papers.

CHAPTER THREE

1. *Englewood Press*, September 7, 1939; newspaper clipping (probably August 1939) in the unprocessed Roger Fay Papers, Bergenfield, N.J.
2. George Flynn (ed.), *The Vince Lombardi Scrapbook* (New York: Grosset & Dunlap, 1976), p. 19; interview, Andy Palau.
3. *Englewood: A Community Handbook* (Englewood, N.J.: The League of Women Voters, 1977), pp. 1–10; interview, Andy Palau.
4. Interviews, Timothy Moore, Elizabeth Vanderbeek, Andy Palau.
5. *Englewood Press*, September 21, 1939; Vince Lombardi (with W. C. Heinz), *Run to Daylight* (New York: Grosset & Dunlap, 1963), p. 74; interviews, Roger Fay, Merv Hyman, Andy Palau.
6. Lombardi, *Run to Daylight*, pp. 74–75; Jerry Kramer (ed.), *Lombardi: Winning Is the Only Thing* (New York: World Publishing Company, 1970), p. 29; interview, Merv Hyman.
7. Interviews, Timothy Moore, Elizabeth Vanderbeek, Andy Palau.

8. *Englewood Press,* December 12, 1940, and December 25, 1941.
9. *Englewood Press,* August 29 and September 5, 1940; interviews, John DeGasperis, Francis Garrity, Merv Hyman, Timothy Moore, Al Quilici, Madeline Werner.
10. Kramer, *Lombardi,* pp. 30–31; interview, Merv Hyman.
11. Kramer, *Lombardi,* p. 29; interviews, William Corcoran, Francis Garrity, Merv Hyman, Timothy Moore, Andy Palau.
12. Vincent Lombardi (with W. C. Heinz), "A Game for Madmen," *Look,* September 5, 1967, p. 86; interview, Francis Garrity.
13. *Arcade* (St. Cecilia School newspaper), October 9, 1942; John Wiebusch (ed.), *Lombardi* (Chicago: Follett Publishing Company, 1971), p. 68.
14. Interviews, Francis Garrity, Timothy Moore.
15. Interview, Andy Palau.
16. Interviews, Charles Bollinger, Richard Doheny, Francis Garrity, Timothy Moore, Andy Palau.
17. Interviews, William Corcoran, Donald Crane. The critical assessment was made by a confidential source.
18. *Englewood Press,* February 26, 1942 and March 22, 1945; *Bergen Evening Record,* March 19, 1945; interviews, Charles Bollinger, John DeGasperis, Francis Garrity, Merv Hyman, Richard Stahlberger.
19. John Moon to author, March 22, 1983; interview, William Corcoran.
20. *Englewood Press,* February 13, 1941 and March 15, 1945; interview, Charles Bollinger.
21. *Silverian* (St. Cecilia School annual), 1939–47; Lombardi, *Run to Daylight,* pp. 73–74; interview, Larry Higgins.
22. *Englewood Press,* May 17, 1945; *New York Journal-American,* December 31, 1961; interviews, Neal Roche, Elizabeth Vanderbeek.
23. Interviews, Dorothy Bachmann, Kenneth Clare, William Corcoran, Martin Fay, Neal Roche.
24. Kramer, *Lombardi: Winning,* p. 14; *Silverian,* 1945; interviews, Dorothy Bachmann, Martin Fay, Roger Fay, Timothy Moore, Neal Roche.
25. Interviews, Charles Bollinger, Joseph McPartland, Al Quilici, Neal Roche.
26. *Englewood Press,* July 9, 1942; *Bergen Evening Record,* August 1, 1941.
27. *Englewood Press,* September 17, 1942; *Bergen Evening Record,* July 30, 1942.

Notes

28. Interviews, Joseph McPartland, Timothy Moore.
29. *Arcade,* October 23, 1942; interviews, Francis Garrity, Neal Roche.
30. Newspaper clipping, Roger Fay Papers; Kramer, *Lombardi: Winning,* p. 17; interview, Al Quilici.
31. Flynn, *Lombardi Scrapbook,* p. 46; interview, Al Quilici.
32. Flynn, *Lombardi Scrapbook,* p. 45; interviews, John DeGasperis, Joseph McPartland, Richard Stahlberger.
33. Flynn, *Lombardi Scrapbook,* p. 46; interview, Joseph McPartland.
34. *Bergen Evening Record,* December 2 and 4, 1943.
35. Interviews, John DeGasperis, Al Quilici.
36. Interviews, Kenneth Clare, Richard Doheny.
37. Kramer, *Lombardi: Winning,* pp. 12–13; interviews, Francis Garrity, Al Quilici.
38. *Englewood Press,* October 12, 1944; Kramer, *Lombardi: Winning,* p. 14; interview, Tom Morgan.
39. *Englewood Press,* August 26, 1943 and August 31, 1944; *Bergen Evening Record,* September 9, 1943; interview, Francis Garrity.
40. *Englewood Press,* August 26, September 2 and 9, 1943; interviews, Patrick Best, John DeGasperis, Richard Doheny, Roger Fay, Joe Lombardi, Timothy Moore, Al Quilici.
41. Dave Condon, Chet Grant, and Bob Best, *Notre Dame Football: The Golden Tradition* (South Bend, Ind.: Icarus Press, 1982), p. 45; Allison Danzig, *The History of American Football* (Englewood Cliffs, N.J.: Prentice-Hall, 1956), pp. 359–60; Arch Ward, *Frank Leahy and the Fighting Irish: The Story of Notre Dame Football* (New York: G. P. Putnam's Sons, 1944), pp. 178–79.
42. Frank Leahy, *Notre Dame Football: The T Formation* (New York: Prentice-Hall, 1949), pp. 14–17.
43. Newspaper clipping, unprocessed Timothy Moore Papers, Englewood, N.J.; interviews, Kenneth Clare, Richard Doheny, John Druze, Francis Garrity, Joseph McPartland, Leo Paquin.
44. Interview, Thomas Della Torre.
45. Donald William Rominger, Jr., "The Impact of the United States Government's Sports and Physical Training Policy on Organized Athletics During World War II," Ph.D. dissertation, Oklahoma State University, 1976, pp. 4, 5, 129, 130, 227, 287.
46. *Ibid.,* pp. 28, 43; *Bergen Evening Record,* September 8, 1943.
47. Flynn, *Lombardi Scrapbook,* p. 46; Wiebusch, *Lombardi,* p. 68; interview, Vince Lombardi, Jr.
48. Kramer, *Lombardi: Winning,* p. 30; interviews, John DeGasperis, Joseph McPartland.

49. Kramer, *Lombardi: Winning,* pp. 11, 15; interview, Joe Lombardi.
50. Flynn, *Lombardi Scrapbook,* pp. 30, 45; interviews, John DeGasperis, Joe Lombardi, Al Quilici.
51. Kramer, *Lombardi: Winning,* pp. 11–12; interview, Joe Lombardi.
52. Flynn, *Lombardi Scrapbook,* pp. 31, 42, 43; interview, Joe Lombardi.
53. Kramer, *Lombardi: Winning,* pp. 9, 15; interview, Joe Lombardi.
54. Interview, Joseph McPartland.
55. Kramer, *Lombardi: Winning,* p. 13.
56. *Ibid.;* interview, Neal Roche.
57. *Ibid.; Arcade,* May 26, 1944; interview, Joseph McPartland.
58. Flynn, *Lombardi Scrapbook,* pp. 46–47; interviews, Kenneth Clare, William Corcoran, John DeGasperis, Joseph McPartland, Al Quilici.
59. Interviews, John DeGasperis, Joseph McPartland.
60. Kramer, *Lombardi: Winning,* pp. 13–14; Joe Donnelly, "Whip-cracker of the Packers," *Sport,* January 1962, p. 25; interview, John DeGasperis.
61. Newspaper clippings, Timothy Moore Papers; *Englewood Press,* December 9, 1943 and November 30, 1944; *Bergen Evening Record,* November 29, 1944; Donnelly, "Whipcracker," p. 25.
62. Newspaper clipping, Roger Fay Papers; Al Silverman (ed.), *Lombardi* (New York: Macfadden-Bartell Corp., 1970), p. 66.
63. Lombardi and Heinz, "A Game for Madmen," *Look,* September 5, 1967, p. 87; Flynn, *Lombardi Scrapbook,* p. 29; *Englewood Press,* December 2, 1943, October 19, 1944, and October 3, 1946; *Silverian,* 1943; interviews, Dorothy Bachmann, John DeGasperis, Roger Fay, Timothy Moore.
64. *Englewood Press,* May 25, 1944, May 17, 1945, and January 30, 1947; Kramer, *Lombardi: Winning,* p. 29; Vince Lombardi (with Tim Cohane), "Why the Pros Play Better Football," *Look,* October 24, 1961, p. 109; interview, Merv Hyman.
65. *Bergen Evening Record,* May 15, 1945; interview, Timothy Moore.
66. *Ibid.; New York Daily News,* September 7, 1970; interviews, John DeGasperis, Al Quilici, Richard Stahlberger.
67. *Ibid.; Englewood Press,* May 31, 1945.
68. *Bergen Evening Record,* June 7, 1945; *Englewood Press,* June 14, 1945; interview, Timothy Moore.
69. *Bergen Evening Record,* April 11, 1947.

CHAPTER FOUR

1. *Bergen Evening Record,* April 12, 1947.
2. Robert I. Gannon, *Up to the Present: The Story of Fordham* (Garden City, N.Y.: Doubleday & Company, 1967), pp. 253–54; interview, Tim Cohane.
3. Newspaper clippings, Football Scrapbook, 1946–47, Volume I, Fordham University Papers, Archives, New York; *The New York Times,* October 19, 1947; Gannon, *Up to the Present,* pp. 253–54.
4. *New York Daily News,* February 21, 1946; *New York Journal-American,* November 15, 1946; interview, Edward Danowski.
5. *Fordham Ram,* October 3, 1947; *The New York Times,* December 2, 1954; interviews, Tim Cohane, Edward Danowski, Jim Lansing, Joe Ososki, Leo Paquin, and others.
6. Interviews, Edward Danowski, Jim Lansing, Leo Paquin.
7. George Flynn (ed.), *The Vince Lombardi Scrapbook* (New York: Grosset & Dunlap, 1976), p. 31; interviews, Edward Danowski, Joe Lombardi, Andrew Lukac, Leo Paquin.
8. Newspaper clippings, Football Scrapbook, 1946–47, Volume I, Fordham University Papers; interviews, Larry Higgins, William Landmark, Herbert Seidell.
9. Newspaper clippings, Football Scrapbook, 1946–47, Volume I, Fordham University Papers; *Fordham Ram,* November 26 and December 12, 1947; interviews, Richard Doheny, Herbert Seidell.
10. Newspaper clippings, Football Scrapbook, 1947, Fordham University Papers.
11. Jerry Kramer (ed.), *Lombardi: Winning Is the Only Thing* (New York: World Publishing Company, 1970), p. 33; interviews, Timothy Moore, Daniel Murphy. There have been three different reports on the salary Vince was offered to join Brewster—either $15,000, $40,000, or $50,000. The $15,000 figure seems the most realistic. For accounts of the different figures note Kramer, *Lombardi: Winning,* p. 33; newspaper article by Harry J. Nicolay in *The Courier,* July 31, 1969 in the unprocessed Timothy Moore Papers, St. Cecilia High School, Englewood, N.J.; interview, Timothy Moore.
12. Newspaper clippings, Football Scrapbook, 1947–49, Fordham University Papers; interviews, Larry Higgins, Herbert Seidell.
13. Kramer, *Lombardi: Winning,* p. 51; clipping, *Bergen Evening Record* [July 1948] in Susan (Lombardi) Bickham Papers, Plantation, Fla.; *Bergen Evening Record,* October 2, 1947.

14. Tim Cohane, *Bypaths of Glory* (New York: Harper & Row, 1963), p. 6; interviews, Edward Danowski, Lou DeFilippo, Larry Higgins, William Landmark, James Lansing, Andrew Lukac, Herbert Seidell.
15. Newspaper clippings, Football Scrapbook, 1947–48, and Football Scrapbook, 1947–49, Fordham University Papers; *Fordham Ram,* December 9, 1948.
16. *Ibid.*
17. *Ibid.;* interviews, Richard Doheny, Larry Higgins, William Landmark, Andrew Lukac, Herbert Seidell.
18. Newspaper clipping, Football Scrapbook, 1947–49, Fordham University Papers; interview, Leo Paquin.
19. Interviews, Richard Doheny, Leo Paquin.
20. Newspaper clippings, Football Scrapbook, 1947–48, and Football Scrapbook, 1947–49, Fordham University Papers; *The New York Times,* December 7, 1948; interview, Edward Danowski.
21. Interview, Ed Franco.
22. *Englewood Press,* January 6, 1949; interviews, Herbert Seidell, Langdon Viracola.

CHAPTER FIVE

1. Earl Blaik, *The Red Blaik Story* (New Rochelle, N.Y.: Arlington House, 1974), p. 436; Tim Cohane, *Bypaths of Glory* (New York: Harper & Row, 1963), p. 6; George Flynn (ed.), *The Vince Lombardi Scrapbook* (New York: Grosset & Dunlap, 1976), p. 58; Jerry Kramer (ed.), *Lombardi: Winning Is the Only Thing* (New York: World Publishing Company, 1970), pp. 36–37; interviews, Earl Blaik, Tim Cohane.
2. Interviews, Paul Amen, Earl Blaik, Murray Warmath.
3. Earl Blaik (with Tim Cohane), *You Have to Pay the Price* (New York: Holt, Rinehart & Winston, 1960), p. 28; Thomas J. Fleming, *West Point* (New York: William Morrow & Company, 1969), pp. 330–31; Al Silverman (ed.), *Lombardi* (New York: Macfadden-Bartell Corporation, 1970), pp. 25–26.
4. Blaik, *Pay the Price,* pp. 274–75; Fleming, *West Point,* pp. 330–31; Stephen E. Ambrose, *Duty, Honor, Country: A History of West Point* (Baltimore: The Johns Hopkins Press, 1966), p. 316; Donald William Rominger, Jr., "The Impact of the United States Government's Sports and Physical Training Policy on Organized Athletics During World War II," Ph.D. dissertation, Oklahoma State University, 1976, p. 264.

5. Clipping, Administrative Historical File, United States Military Academy Papers, Archives, West Point, N.Y.; Joe Dineen, "A Tribute to Colonel Earl 'Red' Blaik," *Army Football Program,* September 30, 1978, p. 27; Howard Cosell, *Cosell* (Chicago: Playboy Press, 1973), p. 97; interview, Murray Warmath.

6. Blaik, *Pay the Price,* pp. 175–76; Cohane, *Bypaths of Glory,* pp. 217–18; *The Sporting News,* November 15, 1969; interviews, Russell Reeder, John Sauer, Murray Warmath.

7. Clipping, Sports Clippings, 1952–53, Public Information Office File, USMA Papers.

8. Blaik, *Pay the Price,* p. 64; Kramer, *Lombardi: Winning,* pp. 37–38; interview, Murray Warmath.

9. Blaik, *Pay the Price,* pp. 64, 174, 301, 302, 312; clipping, Sports Clippings, 1952–53, Public Information Office File, USMA Papers.

10. Blaik, *Pay the Price,* p. 177.

11. Fleming, *West Point,* p. 334; interview, John Sauer.

12. Blaik, *Red Blaik Story,* p. 436; Flynn, *Lombardi Scrapbook,* pp. 58–59; Kramer, *Lombardi: Winning,* pp. 37, 40; John Wiebusch (ed.), *Lombardi* (Chicago: Follett Publishing Company, 1971), p. 20; interview, Earl Blaik.

13. Gene Ward, "Memories of Vince Lombardi," *Army Football Program,* October 28, 1978; Kramer, *Lombardi: Winning,* pp. 48–49; interviews, Earl Blaik, Robert Guidera, Ted Hodge, Russell Reeder, John Sauer, Joel Stephens; one confidential source.

14. Interviews, Paul Dietzel, Murray Warmath.

15. Interviews, Robert Haas, Harry Loehlein.

16. Kramer, *Lombardi: Winning,* p. 39; Stanley Woodward, "Football's Greatest Father and Son Act" in Gene Schoor (ed.), *The Army-Navy Game: A Treasury of the Football Classic* (New York: Dodd, Mead & Company, 1967, pp. 248–54; interview, Robert Blaik.

17. *New York Daily Mirror,* November 20, 1952; Blaik, *Pay the Price,* p. 176; Fleming, *West Point,* pp. 334–35; Vince Lombardi (with W. C. Heinz), *Run to Daylight* (New York: Grosset & Dunlap, 1963), pp. 47–48; Silverman, *Lombardi,* pp. 25–26; Wiebusch, *Lombardi,* p. 68; interviews, John Sauer, Murray Warmath.

18. John F. Bart, "The Blaik System," *The Pointer,* September 29, 1950; Blaik, *Pay the Price,* p. 265; Flynn, *Lombardi Scrapbook,* p. 15; Kramer, *Lombardi: Winning,* p. 38; Lombardi, *Run to Daylight,* pp. 8–9, 48; Silverman, *Lombardi,* pp. 25–26; interviews, Paul Amen, Doug Kenna, Murray Warmath.

19. Lombardi, *Run to Daylight*, p. 104; George Flynn (ed.), *Vince Lombardi on Football*, Vol. 1 (Greenwich, Conn.: New York Graphic Society Ltd. and Wallynn, Inc., 1973), p. 100; interviews, Paul Dietzel, Robert Haas, Russell Reeder.

20. Interviews, Paul Amen, Earl Blaik, Paul Dietzel.

21. Interview, Russell Reeder.

22. Interviews, Doug Kenna, Murray Warmath.

23. Clipping, Sports Clippings, 1952–53, Public Information Office File, USMA Papers; interviews, Paul Amen, Doug Kenna, Joel Stephens.

24. Kramer, *Lombardi: Winning*, pp. 39, 46; interviews, Paul Amen, Paul Dietzel, Doug Kenna, Orrin Krueger, Vince Lombardi, Jr., John Sauer, Joe Steffy, Murray Warmath.

25. Kramer, *Lombardi: Winning*, p. 40; interviews, Paul Amen, Doug Kenna.

26. Blaik, *Pay the Price*, pp. 262–64; Cohane, *Bypaths of Glory*, pp. 216, 217, 220, 223–26; interviews, Paul Amen, Russell Reeder, Murray Warmath.

27. Russell Reeder to Tim Cohane, July 4, 1974, in unprocessed Tim Cohane Papers, Watertown, Mass.; Russell Reeder to author, March 14, 1983.

28. *New York Herald Tribune*, January 26, 1952; Blaik, *Pay the Price*, p. 266; Fleming, *West Point*, p. 335; interviews, Robert Haas, Harry Loehlein.

29. *The New York Times*, August 4 and September 6, 1951; Ambrose, *Duty, Honor, Country*, p. 318; Blaik, *Pay the Price*, pp. 279–89; Fleming, *West Point*, pp. 235–37; interview, Robert Blaik.

30. *The New York Times*, August 4, 5, September 6, 7, and October 9, 1951; clipping, Administrative Historical File, USMA; Ambrose, *Duty, Honor, Country*, pp. 319–20; Fleming, *West Point*, p. 336.

31. *New York Herald Tribune*, January 26, 1952; clipping, Administrative Historical File, USMA; Ambrose, *Duty, Honor, Country*, pp. 319–20; Fleming, *West Point*, p. 337.

32. *Detroit Free Press*, January 16, 1952; *New York Herald Tribune*, January 26, 1952; Blaik, *Pay the Price*, pp. 299–300.

33. *The New York Times*, August 8, 1951; Blaik, *Pay the Price*, pp. 315, 326, 331; Blaik, *Red Blaik Story*, pp. 437–38; Kramer, *Lombardi: Winning*, p. 39.

34. Clipping, unprocessed Susan (Lombardi) Bickham Papers, Plantation, Fla.; Ambrose, *Duty, Honor, Country*, p. 321; Blaik, *Red Blaik Story*, pp. 437–38.

35. Clipping, Bickham Papers; *Philadelphia Inquirer*, December 22, 1960; Tom Dowling, "The Legend of St. Vincent," *Washingtonian*, August 1969, p. 28; Cohane, *Bypaths of Glory*, p. 217; Flynn, *Lombardi Scrapbook*, p. 59; Wiebusch, *Lombardi*, p. 69; interviews, Paul Amen, Earl Blaik, Robert Guidera, Murray Warmath.
36. *New York World-Telegram and Sun*, December 28, 1953; *The New York Times*, December 29, 1953; *New York Daily News*, December 29, 1953; Kramer, *Lombardi: Winning*, p. 40; Wiebusch, *Lombardi*, p. 70; Barry Gottehrer, *The Giants of New York* (New York: G. P. Putnam's Sons, 1963), p. 233; interviews, Earl Blaik, Jim Lee Howell.
37. Blaik, *Red Blaik Story*, p. 431; Kramer, *Lombardi: Winning*, pp. 40–41; Silverman, *Lombardi*, pp. 25–26.

CHAPTER SIX

1. Eliot Asinof, *Seven Days to Sunday* (New York: Simon & Schuster, 1968), p. 131; Benjamin G. Rader, *American Sports: From the Age of Folk Games to the Age of Spectators* (Englewood Cliffs, N.Y.: Prentice-Hall, 1983), pp. 251–52; Harold Rosenthal, *Fifty Faces of Football* (New York: Atheneum, 1981), pp. 154–55; Jim Terzian, *New York Giants* (New York: Macmillan Publishing Company, 1973), pp. 7, 12; William N. Wallace, *Frank Gifford: The Golden Year 1956* (Englewood Cliffs, N.J.: Prentice-Hall, 1969), pp. 12–13; interview, Wellington Mara.
2. *The New York Times*, December 14, 1955 and December 31, 1956; Gerald Eskenazi, *There Were Giants in Those Days* (New York: Grosset & Dunlap, 1976), pp. 2, 35, 134; George Flynn (ed.), *The Vince Lombardi Scrapbook* (New York: Grosset & Dunlap, 1976), p. 164; Barry Gottehrer, *The Giants of New York: The History of Professional Football's Most Fabulous Dynasty* (New York: G. P. Putnam's Sons, 1963), p. 232; Terzian, *Giants*, pp. 8, 111; Wallace, *Gifford*, pp. 13–14; interview, William Wallace.
3. Clippings, unprocessed Roger Fay Papers, Bergenfield, N.J.; Eskenazi, *There Were Giants*, p. 37; Gottehrer, *Giants of New York*, p. 235; Terzian, *Giants*, p. 112.
4. Charles Moritz (ed.), *Current Biography: Yearbook 1972* (New York: H. W. Wilson Company, 1972), p. 270; Wallace, *Gifford*, p. 14.

5. *Ibid.*; Eskenazi, *There Were Giants,* pp. 116–17; Bob St. John, *The Man Inside Landry* (New York: Avon Books, 1979), pp 77–78.

6. Eskenazi, *There Were Giants,* pp. 37, 119, 120; Mickey Herskowitz, *The Golden Age of Pro Football: A Remembrance of Pro Football in the 1950s* (New York: Macmillan Publishing Company, 1974), pp 133–34; St. John, *Landry,* p. 78; Wallace, *Gifford,* pp. 14–15.

7. Vince Lombardi (with W. C. Heinz), *Run to Daylight* (New York: Grosset & Dunlap, 1963), pp. 41, 97.

8. Charles Moritz (ed.), *Current Biography: Yearbook 1965* (New York: H. W. Wilson Company, 1965), pp. 350–51.

9. Perian Conerly, *Backseat Quarterback* (Garden City, N.Y.: Doubleday & Company, 1963), p. 152; Frank Gifford, *Gifford on Courage* (New York: M. Evans & Company, Inc., 1976), pp. 109, 110, 114, 142; Lombardi, *Run to Daylight,* p. 97; interview, Bob Schnelker.

10. Eskenazi, *There Were Giants,* pp. 46, 47, 100; Gifford, *Courage,* p. 122; Wallace, *Gifford,* p. 15; interview, Frank Gifford.

11. *Time,* December 21, 1962; Gifford, *Courage,* p. 119; Gottehrer, *Giants of New York,* p. 235; Jerry Kramer (ed.), *Lombardi: Winning Is the Only Thing* (New York: World Publishing Company, 1970), pp. 54–55; John Wiebusch (ed.), *Lombardi* (Chicago: Follett Publishing Company, 1971), p. 70; interviews, Frank Gifford, Kyle Rote, Jack Stroud.

12. Kramer, *Lombardi,* p. 153; interviews, Bill Austin, Donald Heinrich.

13. Flynn, *Lombardi Scrapbook,* p. 64; Gifford, *Courage,* pp. 118–21; interviews, Charlie Conerly, Jack Stroud.

14. Flynn, *Lombardi Scrapbook,* p. 63; Gifford, *Courage,* pp. 118–19; Kramer, *Lombardi: Winning,* pp. 55–56; Wiebusch, *Lombardi,* p. 71; interviews, Charlie Conerly, Kyle Rote.

15. Eskenazi, *There Were Giants,* pp. 42–44.

16. Lombardi, *Run to Daylight,* p. 98; interviews, Jim Lee Howell, Kyle Rote, Jack Stroud.

17. Earl Blaik, *The Red Blaik Story* (New Rochelle, N.Y.: Arlington House, 1974), pp. 438–39; interviews, Earl Blaik, Ray Walsh.

18. Gottehrer, *Giants of New York,* p. 234; Herskowitz, *Golden Age,* p. 134.

19. Eskenazi, *There Were Giants,* p. 66; Gottehrer, *Giants of New York,* pp. 240–41; Don Smith, *New York Giants* (New York: Coward-McCann, 1960), p. 144; Wallace, *Gifford,* pp. 19–20.

20. Asinof, *Seven Days*, p. 132; Eskenazi, *There Were Giants*, pp. 60–61; Gottehrer, *Giants of New York*, p. 246; St. John, *Landry*, p. 67; Terzian, *Giants*, p. 13; Wallace, *Gifford*, pp. 8–9, 63, 66; interview, Sid Moret.
21. Gifford, *Courage*, pp. 128–29; Gottehrer, *Giants of New York*, p. 249; Kramer, *Lombardi: Winning*, p. 61; Wiebusch, *Lombardi*, p. 71.
22. Clipping, unprocessed Susan (Lombardi) Bickham Papers, Plantation, Fla.; *Long Island Star-Journal*, November 11, 1958; *New York Sunday News*, November 25, 1956; Eskenazi, *There Were Giants*, p. 44; interview, Wellington Mara, Bob Schnelker.
23. Gifford, *Courage*, p. 119–20; interviews, Robert Epps, Frank Gifford, Bob Schnelker, Jack Stroud.
24. Gifford, *Courage*, pp. 121–22; interviews, Jack Stroud, Ray Wietecha.
25. *Green Bay Press-Gazette*, January 30, 1959; *New York Sunday News*, November 25, 1956; Eskenazi, *There Were Giants*, p. 131; Gifford, *Courage*, p. 128; Wallace, *Gifford*, pp. 74–75.
26. Clipping, unprocessed Timothy Moore Papers, Englewood, N.J.; *Green Bay Press-Gazette*, January 30, February 5, 1959; *New York Sunday News*, November 25, 1956; Wallace, *Gifford*, pp. 73–74.
27. Gifford, *Courage*, p. 126.
28. Eskenazi, *There Were Giants*, p. 37; Kramer, *Lombardi: Winning*, p. 56; interviews, Robert Epps, Frank Gifford, Ken Kavanaugh, Sid Moret.
29. Gifford, *Courage*, pp. 124–25; Kramer, *Lombardi: Winning*, pp. 57–58, 128–29; interviews, Robert Epps, Frank Gifford, Don Heinrich, Jack Stroud.
30. Kramer, *Lombardi: Winning*, pp. 47–48; interview, Don Heinrich.
31. Kramer, *Lombardi: Winning*, pp. 58, 67; Lombardi, *Run to Daylight*, p. 97; Wiebusch, *Lombardi*, p. 70; interviews, Charlie Conerly, Jack Stroud, Alex Webster, Ray Wietecha.
32. Eskenazi, *There Were Giants*, p. 100; Flynn, *Lombardi Scrapbook*, p. 66; Kramer, *Lombardi: Winning*, pp. 58–60; interview, Frank Gifford.
33. Clipping, Bickham Papers; Rosenthal, *Fifty Faces*, pp. 153, 155–56; Flynn, *Lombardi Scrapbook*, p. 164; interview, Jerry Izenberg.
34, *Green Bay Press-Gazette*, January 30, 1959.
35. Eskenazi, *There Were Giants*, pp. 116–17; Flynn, *Lombardi*

Scrapbook, p. 64; St. John, *Landry,* p. 77; Wiebusch, *Lombardi,* p. 15; interviews, Jim Lee Howell, Wellington Mara.

36. *The New York Times,* December 31, 1958; Eskenazi, *There Were Giants,* p. 36; interviews, Tim Cohane, Jim Lee Howell, Wellington Mara.

37. *The New York Times,* February 12, 1955, March 1 and December 18, 1956, and January 22, 1957; *Time,* November 17, 1958, and December 21, 1962; Tim Cohane, *Bypaths of Glory* (New York: Harper & Row, 1963), pp 2–4; Vincent Lombardi (with W. C. Heinz), "A Game for Madmen," *Look,* September 5, 1967; interviews, Tim Cohane, Jim Lee Howell.

38. *Milwaukee Journal,* January 2, 1972; *New York Daily News,* September 8, 1970; *The New York Times,* January 12, 1958; Wiebusch, *Lombardi,* p. 70; interviews, Wellington Mara, Vince McNally.

39. *The New York Times,* December 30, 1958; Asinof, *Seven Days,* p. 132; Gottehrer, *Giants of New York,* p. 263; St. John, *Landry,* p. 90.

40. Clipping, Fay Papers; *Green Bay Press-Gazette,* February 11, 1959; *Long Branch Daily Record,* December 4, 1956; *New York Sunday News,* November 25, 1956; Wiebusch, *Lombardi,* p. 73; interviews, Susan (Lombardi) Bickham, Edward Breslin, Nick Egidio, Roger Fay, Vincent Lombardi, Jr., Anthony Pisani, John Ryan.

41. Clippings, Fay Papers; *New York Daily News,* January 21, 1959; *New York Herald Tribune,* February 1, 1959; Vince Lombardi and Tim Cohane, "Why the Pros Play Better Football," *Look,* October 24, 1961; interview, Anthony Pisani.

CHAPTER SEVEN

1. *Milwaukee Journal,* November 3, 1958; Chuck Johnson, *The Green Bay Packers* (New York: Thomas Nelson & Sons, 1961), pp. 41, 42, 46, 64, 84, 88–94, 109.

2. *The National Observer,* November 19, 1962; Richard Schickel, "On Pro Football," *Commentary,* January 1969, p. 68; Herbert Warren Wind, "The Sporting Scene: Packerland," *The New Yorker,* December 8, 1962, p. 213; William Furlong, "Small Town Smack in the Big Time," *The New York Times Magazine,* October 14, 1962, pp. 26, 27, 90; Johnson, *Packers,* pp. 139–43.

Notes

3. Johnson, *Packers,* p. 140; Harold Meyers, "That Profitable Non-profit in Green Bay," *Fortune,* November, 1968, pp. 143, 183–84.

4. *Green Bay Press-Gazette,* September 26, November 4, December 16, 1958; *Milwaukee Journal,* November 7, 1958, January 1, 1967; Paul Hornung (with Tim Cohane), "How Winning Improved My Image," *Look,* November 20, 1962, pp. 124–26; Jerry Kramer and Dick Schaap, *Jerry Kramer's Farewell to Football* (New York: Bantam Books, 1969), pp. 108, 113, 114; Robert Wells, *Mean on Sunday: The Autobiography of Ray Nitschke* (Garden City, N.Y.: Doubleday & Company, 1973), pp. 48, 53; interviews, Walter Cruice, Gary Knafelc, Don McIlhenny, Jim Ringo.

5. *Green Bay Press-Gazette,* October 6, 1958; Hornung and Cohane, "Image," *Look,* pp. 124–26.

6. *Milwaukee Journal,* December 3, 1958; George Flynn (ed.), *The Vince Lombardi Scrapbook* (New York: Grosset & Dunlap, 1976), p. 69.

7. *Milwaukee Journal,* December 10, 1958 and December 18, 1962; Jerry Kramer (ed.), *Lombardi: Winning Is the Only Thing* (New York: World Publishing Company, 1970), p. 79; Vince Lombardi (with W. C. Heinz), *Run to Daylight* (New York: Grosset & Dunlap, 1963), p. 95; interview, Jim Ringo.

8. Clipping, unprocessed Susan (Lombardi) Bickham Papers, Plantation, Fla.; *Green Bay Press-Gazette,* December 16, 17, 1958, and January 20, April 19, 1959; *Milwaukee Journal,* November 25, 1958; Meyers, "Profitable Nonprofit," p. 186; Johnson, *Packers,* p. 111.

9. Clipping, Bickham Papers; Johnson, *Packers,* p. 112; John Torinus, *The Packer Legend: An Inside Look* (Neshkoro, Wis.: Laranmark Press, 1982), p. 112; interviews, Jerry Atkinson, Wellington Mara.

10. Clipping, Bickham Papers; *Green Bay Press-Gazette,* January 29, 1959; Paul Brown (with Jack Clary), *PB: The Paul Brown Story* (New York: Atheneum, 1979), p. 255; John Wiebusch (ed.), *Lombardi* (Chicago: Follett Publishing Company, 1971), p. 77, 83; interviews, Jerry Atkinson, Tony Canadeo.

11. Wiebusch, *Lombardi,* p. 78; interview, Wellington Mara.

12. *Green Bay Press-Gazette,* January 29 and 30, 1959; interview, John Torinus.

13. Wiebusch, *Lombardi,* p. 78; interview, Tony Canadeo.

14. Clipping, Bickham Papers; *Bergen Evening Record,* January 30, 1959; *Green Bay Press-Gazette,* January 30, 1959; Wiebusch, *Lombardi,* p. 78; interview, Wellington Mara.

15. *Green Bay Press-Gazette,* February 3 and 4, 1959; *Milwaukee Journal,* February 3, 4, and 8, 1959; *The New York Times,* December 27, 1961; interviews, Ruth McKloskey, John Torinus.
16. Wiebusch, *Lombardi,* p. 78; interviews, Susan (Lombardi) Bickham, Vince Lombardi, Jr.
17. *Green Bay Press-Gazette,* March 3 and 11, April 14, May 14, 1959; *Milwaukee Journal,* February 8, 1959.
18. *Green Bay Press-Gazette,* April 1, May 14, July 10 and 22, 1959; and July 18, 1976; *Milwaukee Journal,* February 4, 1959; Johnson, *Packers,* pp. 23–24; interview, John (Red) Cochran.
19. *Green Bay Press-Gazette,* April 25, May 23, and June 27, 1959; *Milwaukee Sentinel,* January 19, 1982; Vince Lombardi (with Tim Cohane), "Why the Pros Play Better Football," *Look,* October 24, 1961, p. 109; Flynn, *Lombardi Scrapbook,* p. 71; interview, Art Daley.
20. Kramer, *Lombardi: Winning,* pp. 70, 71, 90; Marshall Smith, "The Miracle Maker of Green Bay, Wis.," *Life,* December 7, 1962, p. 50; *Time,* December 21, 1962, p. 59; Emlen Tunnell (with Bill Gleason), *Footsteps of a Giant* (Garden City, N.Y.: Doubleday & Company, 1966), pp. 184, 187; interview, Jim Ringo.
21. *Green Bay Press-Gazette,* April 3, 1959; *New York Journal-American,* December 31, 1961; Paul Hornung (with Al Silverman), *Football and the Single Man* (Garden City, N.Y.: Doubleday & Company 1965), pp. 159–60; interview, John (Red) Cochran.
22. Kramer, *Lombardi: Winning,* pp. 132–33.
23. Clipping, unprocessed Vince Lombardi, Jr., Papers, Bloomfield Hills, Mich.; Hornung, *Football and the Single Man,* pp. 158–59; Kramer, *Lombardi: Winning,* p. 133; Bart Starr and John Wiebusch, *A Perspective on Victory* (Chicago: Follett Publishing Company, 1972), p. 58; Wiebusch, *Lombardi,* p. 80; interviews, Robert Skoronski, Bart Starr.
24. *Green Bay Press-Gazette,* July 31, 1959 and December 16, 1966; *Milwaukee Journal,* August 11, 1959; Smith, "Miracle Maker," pp. 51–52; William Johnson, "ARARARARARARGH!," *Sports Illustrated,* March 3, 1969, p. 30; Art Daley and Jack Yuenger (eds.), *The Lombardi Era of the Green Bay Packers* (Milwaukee: Inland Press, 1968), p. 63; Hornung, *Football and the Single Man,* p. 159; Johnson, *Packers,* pp. 20–21; Jerry Kramer, *Instant Replay* (New York: The New American Library, 1968), p. 28; Tunnell, *Footsteps,* pp. 188–90; interview, Jim Ringo.
25. *Milwaukee Journal,* August 11, 1959; *Time,* December 21, 1962, p.

60; Hornung, *Football and the Single Man*, pp. 160–61; Kramer, *Farewell to Football*, p. 123; interview, Lamar McHan.

26. Clipping, Bickham Papers; *Green Bay Press-Gazette*, July 25, August 1, 1959; *Milwaukee Journal*, July 26, October 29, 1959; Daley and Yuenger, *Lombardi Era*, p. 63; Hornung, *Football and the Single Man*, pp. 160–61; Kramer, *Farewell to Football*, p. 123.

27. *Milwaukee Journal*, July 26, 1959; Kramer, *Instant Replay*, pp. 26, 33; interview, Jim Ringo.

28. *Milwaukee Journal*, July 26, August 2, 1959; Smith, "Miracle Maker," pp. 51–52; Daley and Yuenger, *Lombardi Era*, p. 63; Wells, *Mean on Sunday*, p. 59; interviews, Dave Hanner, Jim Temp.

29. *Milwaukee Journal*, August 11, 1959; Kramer, *Instant Replay*, pp. 71–72, 77–78; interview, Don McIlhenny.

30. Clippings, Bickham Papers; *Milwaukee Journal*, July 30, August 7 and 11, 1959.

31. *Green Bay Press-Gazette*, August 13, 1959; *Milwaukee Journal*, August 25, 1959; Lombardi, *Run to Daylight*, p. 149; interview, Jim Temp.

32. *Green Bay Press-Gazette*, September 11, 1959; Vincent Lombardi (with W. C. Heinz), "Secrets of Winning Football," *Look*, September 19, 1967, p. 70; Bart Starr, "Vince Lombardi: The Man Who Made Me," *Sport*, October 1970, p. 62; Johnson, *Packers*, p. 127; Kramer, *Farewell to Football*, pp. 122–23; Starr and Wiebusch, *Perspective on Victory*, p. 12; interview, Bart Starr.

33. *Green Bay Press-Gazette*, September 21, December 2 and 22, 1959; *Milwaukee Journal*, August 31 and September 9, 1959.

34. *Green Bay Press-Gazette*, September 25, November 27 and 28, 1959; Wiebusch, *Lombardi*, p. 113.

35. Clipping, Bickham Papers; *Milwaukee Journal*, October 29, November 10 and 16; Hornung, *Football and the Single Man*, p. 164; interview, Don McIlhenny.

36. *The New York Times*, December 27, 1961; Starr and Wiebusch, *Perspective on Victory*, p. 61.

37. *Green Bay Press-Gazette*, November 27 and December 7, 1959.

38. *Green Bay Press-Gazette*, December 14 and 15, 1959; *Milwaukee Journal*, December 14, 1959.

39. *Milwaukee Journal*, October 11, 1959; Smith, "Miracle Worker," p. 52; Daley and Yuenger, *Lombardi Era*, p. 63; interviews, Gary Knafelc, Lamar McHan, Bart Starr.

40. *Green Bay Press-Gazette*, December 15, 1959.

41. Wiebusch, *Lombardi*, p. 83; interviews, Jerry Atkinson, Wellington Mara.
42. Clipping, Bickham Papers; *Green Bay Press-Gazette*, December 22, 1959.

CHAPTER EIGHT

1. Tom Dowling, *Coach: A Season with Lombardi* (New York: W. W. Norton & Company, 1970), p. 8; Benjamin G. Rader, *American Sports: From the Age of Folk Games to the Age of Spectators* (Englewood Cliffs, N.J.: Prentice-Hall, 1983), pp. 242, 263.
2. Dowling, *Coach*, p. 101; Rader, *American Sports*, pp. 242, 243, 245.
3. *Milwaukee Journal*, January 1, 1967.
4. *Green Bay Press-Gazette*, July 15, 21, and 26, 1960.
5. *Ibid.*, July 26, August 11, 19, and September 19, 1960; Art Daley and Jack Yuenger (eds.), *The Lombardi Era of the Green Bay Packers* (Milwaukee: Inland Press, 1968), pp. 5, 20; Bart Starr and John Wiebusch, *A Perspective on Victory* (Chicago: Follett Publishing Company, 1972), p. 61.
6. *Green Bay Press-Gazette*, November 25, December 8 and 12, 1960; *New York Herald Tribune*, December 12, 1960; Paul Hornung (with Al Silverman), *Football and the Single Man* (Garden City, N.Y.: Doubleday & Company, 1965), p. 172.
7. *Green Bay Press-Gazette*, December 18 and 19, 1960; *Time*, December 19, 1960, p. 43; Chuck Johnson, *The Green Bay Packers* (New York: Thomas Nelson & Sons, 1961), pp. 39–40.
8. *Green Bay Press-Gazette*, December 27 and 28, 1960; Johnson, *Packers*, p. 150; Vince Lombardi (with W. C. Heinz), *Run to Daylight* (New York: Grosset & Dunlap, 1963), p. 151; Starr and Wiebusch, *Perspective on Victory*, p. 76; Emlen Tunnell (with Bill Gleason), *Footsteps of a Giant* (Garden City, N.Y.: Doubleday & Company, 1966), p. 195; John Wiebusch (ed.), *Lombardi* (Chicago: Follett Publishing Company, 1971), p. 114.
9. *Green Bay Press-Gazette*, March 30 and December 27, 1960, and January 9, 1961; *Milwaukee Journal*, December 1, 27, and 28, 1960; *The New York Times*, December 13, 1960; interview, Wellington Mara.
10. *Green Bay Press-Gazette*, April 6 and 7, 1961.

Notes

11. *Ibid.*, March 21, 1961; *Milwaukee Journal,* March 16, 1961; Johnson, *Pakers,* p. 150.

12. *Green Bay Press-Gazette,* October 26 and 28, 1961; William Furlong, "Small Town Smack in the Big Time," *The New York Times Magazine,* October 14, 1962, p. 90; Harold Claassen, *The History of Professional Football* (Englewood Cliffs, N.J.: Prentice-Hall, 1963), pp. 179–80; one confidential interview.

13. *Green Bay Press-Gazette,* December 6, 18, and 21, 1961; *Milwaukee Journal,* December 5, 1961.

14. *Green Bay Press-Gazette,* December 29, 1961; Hornung, *Football and the Single Man,* p. 178; Wiebusch, *Lombardi,* p. 117; one confidential interview.

15. Wiebusch, *Lombardi,* pp. 116–17; interviews, Wellington Mara, Anthony Pisani.

16. *Green Bay Press-Gazette,* January 1 and 3, 1962; *Sports Illustrated,* January 8, 1962, pp. 14–15; Hornung, *Football and the Single Man,* pp. 193–98; Wiebusch, *Lombardi,* p. 116.

17. Clippings, unprocessed Susan (Lombardi) Bickham Papers, Plantation, Fla.; Jerry Kramer (ed.), *Lombardi: Winning Is the Only Thing* (New York: World Publishing Company, 1970), p. 100.

18. *Green Bay Press-Gazette,* May 1, 1962; *Milwaukee Journal,* May 1, 1962.

19. *Green Bay Press-Gazette,* January 25, July 15 and 22, August 12 and 22, September 9 and 17, November 12, 1962; Robert Wells, *Mean on Sunday: The Autobiography of Ray Nitschke* (Garden City, N.Y.: Doubleday & Company, 1973), p. 89.

20. *Green Bay Press-Gazette,* January 25, August 26, October 11, December 30, 1962; *Milwaukee Journal,* December 18, 1962.

21. Kramer, *Lombardi: Winning,* pp. 144–45; Wiebusch, *Lombardi,* p. 120.

22. *Green Bay Press-Gazette,* December 20, 1962, April 7 and 8, 1963; Daley and Yuenger, *Lombardi Era,* p. 24.

23. *Green Bay Press-Gazette,* December 31, 1962 and January 6, 1963; *Milwaukee Sentinel,* January 1, 1963; Wiebusch, *Lombardi,* pp. 122–24; interview, Earl Blaik.

24. *Green Bay Press-Gazette,* December 31, 1962; Wiebusch, *Lombardi,* p. 125.

25. W. C. Heinz to author, May 2, 1984; clippings, unprocessed W. C. Heinz Papers, Dorset, Vt.; interviews, George Flynn, W. C. Heinz.

26. W. C. Heinz, *Once They Heard the Cheers* (Garden City, N.Y.:

Doubleday & Company, 1979), pp. 276–77; interview, W. C. Heinz.

27. Heinz, *Heard the Cheers*, pp. 276–79; George Flynn (ed.), *The Vince Lombardi Scrapbook* (New York: Grosset & Dunlap, 1976), pp. 133–35; interview, W. C. Heinz.

28. Clippings, Heinz Papers; clippings, Bickham Papers; *Chicago Tribune*, September 29, 1963; *Green Bay Press-Gazette*, September 22, 1963; *Milwaukee Journal*, September 29, 1963; interview, W. C. Heinz.

29. Heinz to author, May 2, 1984; Vince Lombardi to Tim Cohane, March 6, 1968, unprocessed Tim Cohane Papers, Watertown, Mass.; "Publication agreement," March 15, 1962, Heinz Papers; *Green Bay Press-Gazette*, December 6, 1963; interview, George Flynn.

30. *Green Bay Press-Gazette*, January 8, 1963; interview, James Nellen.

31. *Green Bay Press-Gazette*, January 8, 20, April 17, 18, May 7, and June 4, 1963; Hornung, *Football and the Single Man*, p. 27; Wiebusch, *Lombardi*, p. 163; interviews, Orrin Krueger, James Nellen.

32. *Green Bay Press-Gazette*, June 4, July 10, August 19, November 18, December 8 and 16, 1963.

33. *Milwaukee Journal*, December 17, 1963; Flynn, *Lombarai Scrapbook*, p. 19.

34. *Green Bay Press-Gazette*, September 10, 21, October 19, 26, and 27, 1964.

35. *Green Bay Press-Gazette*, December 15, 31, 1964, January 4, 1965.

36. *Green Bay Press-Gazette*, July 20, August 7, and 11, 1965; *Milwaukee Journal*, July 13, 1965.

37. *Appleton Post-Crescent*, September 15, 1982; *Green Bay Press-Gazette*, October 18, 1965; George Plimpton, *One More July: A Football Dialogue with Bill Curry* (New York: Harper & Row, 1977), pp. 131–32; Starr and Wiebusch, *Perspective on Victory*, p. 100.

38. *Green Bay Press-Gazette*, January 9, 1966; *Milwaukee Journal*, December 30, 1965, and January 4, 1966.

39. *Green Bay Press-Gazette*, October 25, November 1 and 15, 1965.

40. *Green Bay Press-Gazette*, December 20 and 27, 1965, January 3 and 9, 1966; *The New York Times*, January 3, 1966; Wiebusch, *Lombardi*, p. 129.

41. *The Detroit News*, December 24, 1965; *Green Bay Press-Gazette*, January 9, 1966; *Milwaukee Journal*, December 30, 1965; *The New York Times*, January 3, 1966.

42. *Ibid.; Milwaukee Journal,* January 4, 1966.
43. *Green Bay Press-Gazette,* July 12 and December 12, 1966.
44. *Green Bay Press-Gazette,* December 17, 1966; *Milwaukee Journal,* December 15, 1966; *Milwaukee Sentinel,* December 19, 1966; *Sport,* October, 1970, p. 92; *Time,* December 30, 1966, p. 44; interview, Phil VanderSea.
45. *Green Bay Press-Gazette,* December 11, 1966.
46. *Green Bay Press-Gazette,* December 27, 28, and 29, 1966; *Milwaukee Sentinel,* December 29, 1966 and January 4, 1967; Starr and Wiebusch, *Perspective on Victory,* p. 118.
47. Vincent Lombardi and W. C. Heinz, "A Game for Madmen," *Look,* September 5, 1967, p. 87; *Sports Illustrated,* January 16, 1967, pp. 11–13; Flynn, *Lombardi Scrapbook,* pp. 170–71; Starr and Wiebusch, *Perspective on Victory,* p. 124; Wiebusch, *Lombardi,* pp. 136, 138; interviews, Zeke Bratkowski, Ron Kostelnik.
48. *Green Bay Press-Gazette,* January 16, 1967; *Los Angeles Times,* December 8, 1967; Lombardi and Heinz, "Game for Madmen," p. 87; Wiebusch, *Lombardi,* pp. 136, 139.
49. *Dallas Times-Herald,* December 28, 1966; *Green Bay Press-Gazette,* December 29, 31, 1966; *Milwaukee Journal,* December 29, 1966 and January 1, 1967.

CHAPTER NINE

1. Clipping, unprocessed Vince Lombardi, Jr., Papers, Bloomfield Hills, Mich.; *The New York Times,* May 12, 1967; Jerry Kramer, *Instant Replay* (New York: World Publishing Company, 1968), p. 49.
2. *Sunday Times* of London, November 14, 1968; Herbert Warren Wind, "The Sporting Scene: Packerland," *The New Yorker,* December 8, 1962, p. 227; Robert Lipsyte, *SportsWorld: An American Dreamland* (New York: Quadrangle/*The New York Times* Book Company, 1975), p. 56.
3. Vince Lombardi to Tim Cohane, June 7, 1966, unprocessed Tim Cohane Papers, Watertown, Mass.; *Washington Post,* August 9, 1969; interviews, Vince Lombardi, Jr., Ruth McKloskey, Aloysius Wycislo.
4. *Chicago Tribune,* October 4, 1970; Jerry Kramer (ed.), *Lombardi: Winning Is the Only Thing* (New York: World Publishing Company, 1970), p. 139; John Wiebusch (ed.), *Lombardi* (Chicago: Follett

Publishing Company, 1971), p. 97; interviews, David Carley, Bill Gleason, Chuck Lane.

5. Clipping, unprocessed *Green Bay Press-Gazette* Papers, Green Bay, Wis.; *The Bergen County Record*, February 6, 1968; Wiebusch, *Lombardi*, pp. 65, 103; interviews, Bob Schulze, William Wallace, Aloysius Wycislo.

6. *Green Bay Press-Gazette*, September 3, 1970; William Johnson, "ARARARARARARGH!," *Sports Illustrated*, March 3, 1969, p. 30; Michael Novak, *The Joy of Sports* (New York: Basic Books, 1976), p. 230; Wiebusch, *Lombardi*, p. 15.

7. *The Miami Herald*, April 3, 1979; Vince Lombardi and W. C. Heinz, "Secrets of Winning Football," *Look*, September 19, 1967, p. 71; Novak, *Joy of Sports*, p. 221.

8. Interviews, Jim Manci, Cooper Rollow.

9. *The Catholic Commentator*, June 2, 1967; *Milwaukee Journal*, December 26, 1963; *Time*, December 21, 1962; Tom Dowling, *Coach: A Season with Lombardi* (New York: W. W. Norton & Company, 1970), p. 195.

10. *Green Bay Press-Gazette*, September 3, 1970; George Flynn (ed.), *The Vince Lombardi Scrapbook* (New York: Grosset & Dunlap, 1976), p. 51.

11. Clipping, *Green Bay Press-Gazette* Papers; *Green Bay Press-Gazette*, September 3, 1970; *Janesville Gazette*, September 4, 1970; *Los Angeles Herald-Examiner*, February 5, 1968; Richard Schickel, "On Pro Football," *Commentary*, January 1969, p. 67; Dan Harman, *Carroll Dale Scores Again!* (Anderson, Ind.: Warner Press, 1969), p. vi.

12. Reverend Dennis Burke, speech "The Vince I Knew!" in the unprocessed Reverend Dennis Burke Papers, De Pere, Wis.; *The Green Bay Catholic Compass*, November 20, 1982; *Green Bay Press-Gazette*, May 16, 1968; *Miami Herald*, September 9, 1973; Wiebusch, *Lombardi*, p. 194; interviews, Susan (Lombardi) Bickham, Dennis Burke, Vince Lombardi, Jr., Ruth McKloskey, Robert Parins.

13. *The Green Bay Catholic Compass*, November 20, 1982.

14. Tom Dowling, "The Legend of St. Vincent," *Washingtonian*, August 1969, p. 53; *Guideposts*, January 1968, p. 6; Robert Wells, *Mean on Sunday: The Autobiography of Ray Nitschke* (Garden City, N.Y.: Doubleday & Company, 1973), p. 151; interviews, Tom Fears, Vince Lombardi, Jr., Kenneth Moore.

15. Burke, "Vince I Knew!," Burke Papers; Dowling, "Legend of St.

Vincent," pp. 55–56; interviews, Ruth McKloskey, Bob Schulze, Aloysius Wycislo.

16. Clipping, Vince Lombardi, Jr., Papers; interviews, Vince Lombardi, Jr., Aloysius Wycislo.

17. Burke, "Vince I Knew!," Burke Papers; clipping, Vince Lombardi, Jr., Papers; *Green Bay Press-Gazette*, September 3, 1970; *Miami Herald*, September 9, 1973; John Torinus, *The Packer Legend: An Inside Look* (Neshkoro, Wis.: Laranmark Press, 1982), p. 162; interviews, Susan (Lombardi) Bickham, Jack Koeppler, Vince Lombardi, Jr., John Torinus.

18. Joseph Epstein, "Obsessed with Sport" in D. Stanley Eitzen (ed.), *Sport in Contemporary Society: An Anthology* (New York: St. Martin's Press, 1979), pp. 13–17; Guy Lewis, "Sport, Youth Culture, and Conventionality 1920–70," *Journal of Sport History*, Vol. 4, No. 2, Summer 1977, pp. 129–39; Paul Weiss, *Sport: A Philosophic Inquiry* (Carbondale, Ill.: Southern Illinois University Press, 1969), p. 84.

19. John D. Massengale, "Coaching as an Occupational Subculture" in Eitzen, *Sport in Contemporary Society*, pp. 204–7; Schickel, "Pro Football," p. 66; Jay J. Coakley, *Sport in Society: Issues and Controversies* (St. Louis: C. V. Mosby Company, 1978), pp. 220–21, 225; Allen Guttman, *From Ritual to Record: The Nature of Modern Sports* (New York: Columbia University Press, 1978), pp. 121–22; James Michener, *Sports in America* (New York: Random House, 1976), pp. 254–55.

20. *The National Observer*, November 19, 1962; William Phillips, "A Season in the Stands," *Commentary*, July 1969, p. 66; Phil Bengtson and Todd Hunt, *Packer Dynasty* (Garden City, N.Y.: Doubleday & Company, 1969), pp. 207–8; Kramer, *Lombardi: Winning*, p. 100; Guttman, *Ritual to Record*, pp. 121–22; Novak, *Joy of Sports*, pp. 84, 88.

21. *Green Bay Press-Gazette*, September 3, 1970; *Milwaukee Sentinel*, August 17, 1976; *Washington Star*, June 15, 1969; Harman, *Carroll Dale*, p. 21; Kramer, *Lombardi: Winning*, p. 143; Wiebusch, *Lombardi*, pp. 37, 99; interviews, Bob Skoronski, Phil VanderSea.

22. Lipsyte, *SportsWorld*, p. 67; Vince Lombardi (with W. C. Heinz), *Run to Daylight* (New York: Grosset & Dunlap, 1963), p. 13; Weiss, *Sport*, pp. 11, 19.

23. *Washington Star*, February 6, 1969 and September 6, 1970; Harold Meyers, "That Profitable Nonprofit in Green Bay," *Fortune*,

November 1968, p. 142; Kramer, *Lombardi: Winning,* pp. 116–17; interview, Duke Zeibert.

24. *Green Bay Press-Gazette,* September 3, 1970; Bengtson, *Packer Dynasty,* p. 227; Lipsyte, *SportsWorld,* pp. 57, 67; Leverett Smith, *The American Dream and the National Game* (Bowling Green, Ohio: Bowling Green University Popular Press, 1975), pp. 245–51; Wiebusch, *Lombardi,* p. 92; interview, Nelson Toburen.

25. *Green Bay Press-Gazette,* July 31, 1966; *Detroit News,* December 24, 1965; Flynn, *Lombardi Scrapbook,* pp. 23–24; Phil Pepe, *Winners Never Quit* (Englewood Cliffs, N.J.: Prentice-Hall, 1968), pp. xiii, xv; interview, Tom Fears.

26. Novak, *Joy of Sports,* p. 140; William N. Wallace, *Frank Gifford: The Golden Year 1956* (Englewood Cliffs, N.J.: Prentice-Hall 1969), p. vi; Weiss, *Sport,* pp. 67, 70.

27. Flynn, *Lombardi Scrapbook,* p. 24; Lombardi, *Run to Daylight,* p. 11.

28. *Green Bay Press-Gazette,* March 15, 1962; *Time,* December 21, 1962, p. 58; William Bennett, "In Defense of Sports," *Commentary,* February 1976, pp. 69–70; Howard Cosell, *Cosell* (Chicago: Playboy Press, 1973), p. 106; Michener, *Sports in America,* pp. 425–27; Robert Osterhoudt (ed.), *The Philosophy of Sport* (Springfield, Ill.: Charles C Thomas, 1973), pp. 157–58, 165.

29. Flynn, *Lombardi Scrapbook,* p. 134; Wiebusch, *Lombardi,* p. 18; interviews, Eugene Brusky, W. C. Heinz, Jerry Izenberg.

30. *Green Bay Press-Gazette,* July 25, 1961.

31. Guttman, *Ritual to Record,* pp. 36, 47–55; Howard S. Slusher, *Man, Sport, and Existence* (Philadelphia: Lea & Febiger, 1967), p. 148; Thomas Tutko and William Bruns, *Winning Is Everything and Other American Myths* (New York: Macmillan, 1976), pp. 7–8.

32. *Milwaukee Journal,* April 9, 1962; Andrew Hamilton and John Jackson, *UCLA on the Move* (Los Angeles: Ward Ritchie, 1969), p. 179; Tutko and Bruns, *Winning,* p. 4.

33. Kate Giles, "Mrs. Vince Lombardi: The Life of a Wife of a Legend," *Harper's Bazaar,* January 1973, p. 88; Lipsyte, *SportsWorld,* pp. 56–57; Michener, *Sports in America,* p. 432; interviews, Dominic Gentile, Jerry Izenberg, Jim Lawlor.

34. Vincent Lombardi and W. C. Heinz, "A Game for Madmen," *Look,* September 5, 1967, p. 88; Kramer, *Instant Replay,* pp. 65, 92.

35. Clipping, *Green Bay Press-Gazette* Papers; *Los Angeles Times,* December 8, 1967; Lombardi and Heinz, "Game for Madmen," pp. 85–86; Bengtson, *Packer Dynasty,* p. 204; W. C. Heinz, *Once They*

Heard the Cheers (Garden City, N.Y.: Doubleday & Company, 1979), p. 292; Novak, *Joy of Sports*, pp. 90–91; Weiss, *Sport*, p. 33; interview, Bob Schnelker.

36. Clipping, unprocessed Susan (Lombardi) Bickham Papers, Plantation, Fla.; *Green Bay Press-Gazette*, October 1, 1961; Vince Lombardi (with Tim Cohane), "Why the Pros Play Better Football," *Look*, October 24, 1961, p. 109; Wiebusch, *Lombardi*, p. 59.

37. Lombardi and Heinz, "Game for Madmen," pp. 85–86; Lombardi, *Run to Daylight*, pp. 7–9, 89, 149.

38. *Green Bay Press-Gazette*, March 15, 1962; *Milwaukee Journal*, April 9, 1962; Cosell, *Cosell*, p. 114; Wiebusch, *Lombardi*, p. 195.

39. William Manchester, *The Glory and the Dream* (Boston: Little, Brown and Co., 1973), pp. 1109–13; William L. O'Neill, *Coming Apart* (Chicago: Quadrangle Books, 1971), pp. 233, 245, 253, 254, 265; James T. Patterson, *America in the Twentieth Century: A History*, 2nd ed. (New York: Harcourt Brace Jovanovich, 1983), pp. 407, 411–24; Irwin Unger, *The Movement: A History of the American New Left: 1959–72* (New York: Dodd, Mead & Company, 1974), pp. vi, 132–33.

40. *Milwaukee Journal*, May 31, 1970; O'Neill, *Coming Apart*, pp. 254, 265, 270–71; Patterson, *America: A History*, pp. 426–27.

41. *Green Bay Press-Gazette*, February 9, 1967; *The New York Times*, February 9, 1967.

42. Vince Lombardi, speech, "Leadership in Management" (1968), in the unprocessed Ruth McKloskey Papers, Green Bay, Wis. A copy of the exact text of Vince's speech to the AMA has not survived. I have used a copy of the speech he delivered in 1968. However, judging by newspaper descriptions of his speeches, Vince delivered almost exactly the same address from 1967–1969.

43. *The New York Times*, February 9, 1967; Wiebusch, *Lombardi*, p. 99; interview, Orrin Krueger.

44. *Milwaukee Journal*, August 4, 1968; *New York Daily News*, November 27, 1968; interviews, Lee Remmel, Len Wagner.

CHAPTER TEN

1. *Green Bay Press-Gazette*, February 12, 1967; *Milwaukee Sentinel*, February 3, 1968; William Furlong, "Small Town Smack in the Big Time," *The New York Times Magazine*, October 14, 1962, p. 90; Harold Meyers, "That Profitable Nonprofit in Green Bay," *Fortune*, November 1968, pp. 141, 143; Richard Schickel, "On Pro Foot-

ball,'' *Commentary,* January 1969, p. 66; Herbert Warren Wind, "The Sporting Scene: Packerland,'' *The New Yorker,* December 8, 1962, p. 213.

2. *Green Bay Press-Gazette,* July 25, 1961, December 25, 1966, and February 12, 1967; *The National Observer,* November 19, 1962.

3. *Green Bay Press-Gazette,* July 25, 1961, December 30, 1962, October 3 and 4 and December 25, 1966, and December 28, 1967; *Los Angeles Times,* September 28, 1966.

4. *Green Bay Press-Gazette,* February 9 and May 12, 1960, and March 16, 1961; *Milwaukee Journal,* February 9, 1960.

5. Meyers, "Profitable Nonprofit,'' pp. 143, 186; John Wiebusch (ed.), *Lombardi* (Chicago: Follett Publishing Company 1971), p. 83; interviews, Chuck Lane, James Nellen.

6. George Flynn (ed.), *The Vince Lombardi Scrapbook* (New York: Grosset & Dunlap, 1976), p. 83; Wiebusch, *Lombardi,* pp. 92, 94; interviews, Orrin Krueger, Chuck Lane, Thomas Miller, Fred Trowbridge, Sr.

7. *Milwaukee Sentinel,* January 26, 1981; John Torinus, *The Packer Legend: An Inside Look* (Neshkoro, Wis.: Laranmark Press, 1982), pp. 97, 157; interviews, Lois Bourguignon, John Torinus, Fred Trowbridge, Sr., one confidential source.

8. *New York Daily News,* September 9, 1970; *Washington Post,* September 4, 1970; Joe Donnelly, "Whipcracker of the Packers,'' *Sport,* January, 1962, p. 81; Wiebusch, *Lombardi,* p. 44; interview, Bud Lea.

9. *Green Bay Press-Gazette,* May 3, 1962 and May 5, 1965.

10. Meyers, "Profitable Nonprofit,'' p. 183; Roger Noll (ed.), *Government and the Sports Business* (Washington, D.C.: The Brookings Institution, 1974), pp. 44, 283, 290, 292; Benjamin G. Rader, *American Sports: From the Age of Folk Games to the Age of Spectators* (Englewood Cliffs, N.J.: Prentice-Hall, 1983), p. 256; Torinus, *Packer Legend,* p. 87.

11. Vince Lombardi (with Tim Cohane), "Why the Pros Play Better Football,'' *Look,* October 24, 1961, p. 110; Vincent Lombardi and W. C. Heinz, "A Game for Madmen,'' *Look,* September 5, 1967, p. 88.

12. Flynn, *Lombardi Scrapbook,* p. 70; interviews, Dominic Gentile, Orrin Krueger, Chuck Lane, Paul Mazzoleni, Thomas Miller, Al Treml.

13. Flynn, *Lombardi Scrapbook,* pp. 77, 142; Wiebusch, *Lombardi,* p. 21; interview, Thomas Miller.

Notes

14. Phil Bengtson and Todd Hunt, *Packer Dynasty* (Garden City, N.Y.: Doubleday & Company, 1969), p. 18; Art Daley and Jack Yuenger (eds.), *The Lombardi Era of the Green Bay Packers* (Milwaukee: Inland Press, 1968), p. 49; Jerry Kramer (ed.), *Lombardi: Winning Is the Only Thing* (New York: World Publishing Company, 1970), pp. 96–97.

15. Bengtson, *Packer Dynasty*, p. 114; Kramer, *Lombardi: Winning*, p. 155; Wiebusch, *Lombardi*, pp. 78, 80; interviews, Phil Bengtson, Wally Cruice, Tom Fears.

16. *Green Bay Press-Gazette*, February 7, 1969; Kramer, *Lombardi: Winning*, pp. 96, 98; George Plimpton, *One More July: A Football Dialogue with Bill Curry* (New York: Harper & Row, 1977), p. 24; Wiebusch, *Lombardi*, p. 45; interviews, Phil Bengtson, Ken Bowman, Bill Forester, Chuck Lane, Gary Knafelc, John Roach, Nelson Toburen.

17. Kramer, *Lombardi: Winning*, pp. 97–99, 155; Wiebusch, *Lombardi*, p. 50; interviews, Bill Austin, Tom Fears, Bob Skoronski.

18. Kramer, *Lombardi: Winning*, pp. 95–98; Al Silverman (ed.), *Lombardi* (New York: Macfadden-Bartell Corporation, 1970), p. 15; interviews, Red Cochran, Dave Hanner, Bob Schnelker.

19. Lombardi and Heinz, "Game for Madmen," p. 90; Flynn, *Lombardi Scrapbook*, p. 113; Noll, *Government and Sports*, p. 197; Bart Starr and John Wiebusch, *A Perspective on Victory* (Chicago: Follett Publishing Company, 1972), p. 62; interviews, Gary Knafelc, Bob Skoronski.

20. Interview, Jim Grabowski.

21. Clipping, unprocessed, *Green Bay Press-Gazette* Papers, Green Bay, Wis.; *Milwaukee Journal*, April 28, 1966; Vincent Lombardi and W. C. Heinz, "Secrets of Winning Football," *Look*, September 19, 1967, p. 72; Daley and Yuenger, *Lombardi Era*, pp. 10–13.

22. Lombardi and Heinz, "Game for Madmen," p. 90; Tom Dowling, *Coach: A Season with Lombardi* (New York: W. W. Norton & Company, 1970), pp. 21–22; interview, Jim Ringo.

23. Clippings, unprocessed, Susan (Lombardi) Bickham Papers, Plantation, Fla.; *Green Bay Press-Gazette*, January 8, 1960 and March 16, 1967; *Milwaukee Journal*, January 2, 1966; *Milwaukee Sentinel*, April 24, 1981; Pete Rozelle, "Professional Sports: The View of the Owners" in Stanley Eitzen (ed.), *Sport in Contemporary Society: An Anthology* (New York: St. Martin's Press, 1979), p. 306; William Bralick, *Will the Real Vince Lombardi Please Stand Up?*, pamphlet, State Historical Society of Wisconsin, Madison, Wis.; Daley and

Yuenger, *Lombardi Era*, pp. 10–13; James Michener, *Sports in America* (New York: Random House, 1976), pp. 389–90; Rader, *American Sports*, p. 257.

CHAPTER ELEVEN

1. *Chicago Tribune*, October 26, 1960; Vince Lombardi and W. C. Heinz, "A Game for Madmen," *Look*, September 5, 1967, p. 87; Howard Cosell, *Cosell* (Chicago: Playboy Press, 1973), p. 105; Vince Lombardi (with W. C. Heinz), *Run to Daylight* (New York: Grosset & Dunlap, 1963), p. 16.

2. Clipping, unprocessed *Green Bay Press-Gazette* Papers, Green Bay, Wis.; *Green Bay Press-Gazette*, June 28, 1964 and December 16, 1966; John Wiebusch (ed.), *Lombardi* (Chicago: Follett Publishing Company, 1971), p. 84; Paul Zimmerman, *A Thinking Man's Guide to Pro Football* (New York: E. P. Dutton & Company 1970), p. 330.

3. Interview, Al Sampson.

4. *Green Bay Press-Gazette*, October 22, 1960; interviews, Art Daley, Len Wagner.

5. *Green Bay Press-Gazette*, January 14, 1968; Wiebusch, *Lombardi*, p. 88; interviews, Art Daley, W. C. Heinz, Chuck Lane, Cooper Rollow, William Wallace.

6. Interview, Bud Lea.

7. George Flynn (ed.), *The Vince Lombardi Scrapbook* (New York: Grosset & Dunlap, 1976), p. 151; Wiebusch, *Lombardi*, pp. 54–55; interviews, Chuck Johnson, Len Wagner.

8. Clipping, unprocessed Susan (Lombardi) Bickham Papers, Plantation, Fla.; Flynn, *Lombardi Scrapbook*, pp. 138, 167–68; interview, Bud Lea.

9. Flynn, *Lombardi Scrapbook*, pp. 159, 168; Harold Rosenthal, *Fifty Faces of Football* (New York: Atheneum, 1981), p. 159; interviews, Bill Gleason, Cooper Rollow, William Wallace.

10. Flynn, *Lombardi Scrapbook*, pp. 165–66; interview, Jerry Izenberg.

11. *Milwaukee Journal*, November 19, 1967; *Milwaukee Sentinel*, September 4, 1970; Kate Giles, "Mrs. Vince Lombardi: The Life of a Wife of a Legend," *Harper's Bazaar*, January 1973, p. 105; Wiebusch, *Lombardi*, pp. 49, 91–92; interviews, Dominic Gentile, Chuck Lane, Thomas Miller, Robert Skoronski.

12. Clipping, unprocessed Vince Lombardi, Jr., Papers, Bloomfield Hills, Mich.; *Milwaukee Journal*, January 12, 1964; Joe Don-

nelly, "Whipcracker of the Packers," *Sport*, January 1962, pp. 80–81; Wiebusch, *Lombardi*, p. 39; interviews, Bud Lea, Bob Schulze.

13. *Milwaukee Sentinel*, September 4, 1970; Wiebusch, *Lombardi*, p. 39; interview, Bud Lea.

14. *New York Daily News*, September 10, 1970; Flynn, *Lombardi Scrapbook*, p. 166; Wiebusch, *Lombardi*, p. 50; interviews, Art Daley, William Wallace.

15. *Chicago Tribune*, September 4, 1970; *Milwaukee Journal*, September 3, 1970; interview, Cooper Rollow.

16. *Green Bay Press-Gazette*, November 6, 1962; *Milwaukee Journal*, November 19, 1967; Dick Schaap, " 'Genius' at Green Bay," *The Saturday Evening Post*, November 3, 1962, Wiebusch, *Lombardi*, p. 92; interview, Art Daley.

17. Clipping, Bickham Papers; *Green Bay Press-Gazette*, October 24, 25, and 27, 1966.

18. Heywood Hale Broun, *Tumultuous Merriment* (New York: Richard Marek Publishers, 1979), p. 103; Cosell, *Cosell*, pp. 99–103; Wiebusch, *Lombardi*, p. 44; interviews, Chuck Lane, Bob Schulze.

19. Clipping, unprocessed Ruth McKloskey Papers, Green Bay, Wis., *Milwaukee Sentinel*, September 4, 1970; Tom Dowling, "The Legend of St. Vincent," *Washingtonian*, August 1969, p. 57; *New York Daily News*, September 10, 1970; Flynn, *Lombardi Scrapbook*, p. 166; Wiebusch, *Lombardi*, p. 60; interviews, Jerry Izenberg, Bob Schulze, Len Wagner, William Wallace.

20. Clipping, McKloskey Papers; clipping, Vince Lombardi, Jr., Papers.

21. *Milwaukee Journal*, September 27, 1965; Flynn, *Lombardi Scrapbook*, pp. 166–67; interviews, Bud Lea, Jerry Izenberg.

22. *Milwaukee Journal*, November 19, 1967; *The Sporting News*, August 24, 1968; Flynn, *Lombardi Scrapbook*, p. 168; interviews, Chuck Johnson, Bud Lea, Lee Remmel, Cooper Rollow, Bob Schulze.

CHAPTER TWELVE

1. Vince Lombardi (with W. C. Heinz), *Run to Daylight* (New York: Grosset & Dunlap, 1963), pp. 12, 36, 137; interview, Vince Lombardi, Jr.

2. *New York Journal-American*, December 31, 1961; William Furlong,

"Small Town Smack in the Big Time," *The New York Times Magazine,* October 14, 1962, p. 86; Richard Schickel, "On Pro Football," *Commentary,* January 1969, pp. 66–67; Chuck Johnson, *The Green Bay Packers* (New York: Thomas Nelson & Sons, 1961), p. 120; Lombardi, *Run to Daylight,* p. 146; John Wiebusch (ed.), *Lombardi* (Chicago: Follett Publishing Company 1971), pp. 39, 49, 50.

3. Lombardi, *Run to Daylight,* p. 102.
4. *Green Bay Press-Gazette,* January 3, 1967; Jerry Kramer, ed., *Lombardi: Winning Is the Only Thing* (New York: World Publishing Company, 1970), pp. 90–92; Johnson, *Packers,* p. 120; Wiebusch, *Lombardi,* pp. 45, 47; interviews, Zeke Bratkowski, John Roach, Bart Starr.
5. Lombardi, *Run to Daylight,* pp. 54, 83, 84; Wiebusch, *Lombardi,* p. 45.
6. *Time,* December 30, 1966, p. 44; Kramer, *Lombardi: Winning,* p. 51; Bart Starr and John Wiebusch, *A Perspective on Victory* (Chicago: Follett Publishing Company, 1972), pp. 58–59; Wiebusch, *Lombardi,* p. 60.
7. Tom Dowling, *Coach: A Season with Lombardi* (New York: W. W. Norton & Company, 1970), p. 151; Robert Lipsyte, *SportsWorld: An American Dreamland* (New York: Quadrangle/*The New York Times* Book Company, 1975), p. 56; Starr and Wiebusch, *Perspective on Victory,* pp. 58–59, 134; interview, Bart Starr.
8. Vince Lombardi and Tim Cohane, "Why the Pros Play Better Football," *Look,* October 24, 1961, p. 108; Jerry Kramer, *Instant Replay* (New York: World Publishing Company 1968), p. 79; Lombardi, *Run to Daylight,* pp. 52–53.
9. Lombardi, *Run to Daylight,* pp. 70–72; Wiebusch, *Lombardi,* p. 84; interview, Bart Starr.
10. Dan Harman, *Carroll Dale Scores Again!* (Anderson, Ind.: The Warner Press, 1969), p. 20; Wiebusch, *Lombardi,* p. 45; Pau Zimmerman, *A Thinking Man's Guide to Pro Football* (New York: E. P. Dutton & Company, 1970), p. 197; interviews, Tom Fears, Gary Knafelc, Bart Starr.
11. *Green Bay Press-Gazette,* January 12, 1967; *Time,* December 1962, p. 57; Vincent Lombardi and W. C. Heinz, "Secrets of Winning Football," *Look,* September 19, 1967, p. 75; Johnson, *Packers,* p. 118; Lombardi, *Run to Daylight,* p. 54; Wiebusch, *Lombardi,* p. 119.

12. George Flynn (ed.), *The Vince Lombardi Scrapbook* (New York: Grosset & Dunlap, 1976), p. 74; Kramer, *Lombardi: Winning,* pp. 79–80.
13. *Milwaukee Journal,* November 19, 1967; Phil Bengtson and Todd Hunt, *Packer Dynasty* (Garden City, N.Y.: Doubleday & Company, 1969), p. 224; Al Silverman (ed.), *Lombardi* (New York: Macfadden-Bartell Corporation, 1970), p. 63; Zimmerman, *Thinking Man's Guide,* p. 202.
14. Lombardi and Heinz, "Winning Football," pp. 74–75; Lombardi, *Run to Daylight,* pp. 37, 38, 61, 102, 103, 111, 186; interview, Bob Skoronski.
15. *Green Bay Press-Gazette,* December 29, 1961; *The Sunday Register* (Schrewsburg, N. J.), February 8, 1981; Bart Starr, "Confidence Is Contagious," *Guideposts,* January, 1968, pp. 4–5; Kramer, *Instant Replay,* pp. 120, 161; Kramer, *Lombardi: Winning,* pp. 111–12; interviews, Eugene Brusky, Red Cochran, Tom Fears, Dave Robinson.
16. Lombardi and Heinz, "Winning Football," p.73
17. *Ibid.,* p. 75; Lombardi, *Run to Daylight,* p. 29; Wiebusch, *Lombardi,* pp. 49, 54.
18. Tom Dowling, "The Legend of St. Vincent," *Washingtonian,* August 1969, p. 50; Flynn, *Lombardi Scrapbook,* pp. 72, 99; Kramer, *Instant Replay,* pp. 49, 159, 160; Robert Wells, *Mean on Sunday: The Autobiography of Ray Nitschke* (Garden City, N.Y.: Doubleday & Company, 1973), p. 76; Steve Wright, *I'd Rather Be Wright* (Englewood Cliffs, N.J.: Prentice-Hall, 1974), p. 47; interview, Gale Gillingham.
19. Kramer, *Instant Replay,* p. 64; Lombardi, *Run to Daylight,* pp. 131–32; interviews, Art Daley, Gary Knafelc, Bob Skoronski.
20. Kramer, *Instant Replay,* pp. 31, 38; Starr and Wiebusch, *Perspective on Victory,* p. 64; Wiebusch, *Lombardi,* p. 178; interview, Dave Robinson.
21. Kramer, *Instant Replay,* pp. 192–93; interview, Bob Skoronski.
22. Kramer, *Instant Replay,* p. 204; interview, Red Cochran.
23. Kramer, *Instant Replay,* p. 173; Gene Schoor, *Football's Greatest Coach: Vince Lombardi* (Garden City, N.Y.: Doubleday & Company, 1974), pp. 173–74; Wiebusch, *Lombardi,* pp. 22, 25; interviews, Zeke Bratkowski, John Roach.
24. Lombardi and Heinz, "Winning Football," p. 74; Kramer, *Lombardi: Winning,* p. 159; Lipsyte, *SportsWorld,* p. 58; Zimmerman,

Thinking Man's Guide, pp. 247–48; interviews, Eugene Brusky, Dominic Gentile, James Nellen, Anthony Pisani.

25. Lombardi and Heinz, "Winning Football," p. 74; Kramer, *Lombardi: Winning,* p. 149; Wiebusch, *Lombardi,* pp. 55, 176.

26. Lombardi and Heinz, "Winning Football," p. 74; Flynn, *Lombardi Scrapbook,* pp. 152–53; George Plimpton, *One More July: A Football Dialogue with Bill Curry* (New York: Harper & Row, 1977), pp. 36–37; Wiebusch, *Lombardi,* p. 87; interviews, Art Daley, Ron Kostelnik, Jim Ringo, Bob Schnelker. In Green Bay Vince did not focus his attention on the problem of drug abuse because he didn't perceive drugs as a major problem. From 1959 to 1961, some Green Bay players did abuse dangerous drugs, particularly amphetamines and pep pills. In approximately 1962 the NFL commissioner apparently warned the coaches to ban the drugs. Consequently Vince enforced strict guidelines, and the dangerous drugs disappeared from the locker room. Kramer, *Instant Replay,* p. 160; interviews, Eugene Brusky, Jim Temp.

In his recent book *Distant Replay,* Jerry Kramer described drug use during Vince's years in Green Bay: "Early in my NFL career, we did take amphetamines, pep pills, most of us, even Coach Lombardi once in a while. We didn't know too much about them. They were the kind of things the wives were taking for dieting. Initially, our trainer carried a bottle of the pills, and you could go to him and get whatever you wanted. One of our guys always took too much of anything. He got so up before games, he had to take a big black felt-tipped pen and write numbers on his left hand and his right hand, so that he'd know which way to block on which plays. One of the wives used to take a pep pill at halftime so that she'd be ready to keep up with her husband at the parties after the game. At first, we had no knowledge of the downside effects of the drugs. Then, when the dangers became known, when society became concerned, the pills disappeared from the trainer's kit. Players still got them, if they wanted them badly enough, but not so easily, not so abundantly. We were much more into Novocain, and codeine, pain-killers, something to soothe our bumps and bruises, sprains and abrasions. We didn't have to feel high. We just didn't want to feel hurt." Jerry Kramer (with Dick Schaap), *Distant Replay* (New York: G. P. Putnam's Sons, 1985), p. 98.

27. Bill Hammer, "A Brief Look at Motivation in Coaching" in Craig A. Fisher (ed.), *Psychology of Sport* (Palo Alto, Calif.: Mayfield

Publishing Company, 1976), pp. 186–87; Wiebusch, *Lombardi*, p. 22.

28. *Green Bay Press-Gazette*, September 3, 1970; *Milwaukee Journal*, November 19, 1967; interview, Gary Knafelc.

29. Kramer, *Instant Replay*, pp. 112, 174; Wiebusch, *Lombardi*, pp. 40–42; interviews, Forrest Gregg, Norm Masters.

30. *Milwaukee Journal*, June 24, 1971; *New York Journal-American*, December 31, 1961; Plimpton, *One More July*, pp. 29, 31; Wiebusch, *Lombardi*, p. 41; interviews, Dave Robinson, Bob Skoronski, Willie Wood.

31. Bart Starr, "Vince Lombardi, The Man Who Made Me," *Sport*, October 1970, p. 92; Kramer, *Instant Replay*, pp. 115, 116, 133; Wiebusch, *Lombardi*, p. 166.

32. Wiebusch, *Lombardi*, p. 41; interviews, Dave Hanner, Chuck Lane, Vince Lombardi, Jr.

33. Plimpton, *One More July*, p. 16; interview, Gary Knafelc.

34. *Milwaukee Journal*, June 25, 1971; Kramer, *Lombardi: Winning*, pp. 119, 120, 133, 134, 144; Lombardi, *Run to Daylight*, pp. 48, 69; interview, Ken Bowman.

35. Wiebusch, *Lombardi*, pp. 41, 42, 54, 55, 176; interviews, Allen Brown, Ron Kostelnik.

36. *Green Bay Press-Gazette*, November 29 and December 6, 1965; Kramer, *Lombardi: Winning*, p. 73; Plimpton, *One More July*, pp. 23–25; interview, Forrest Gregg, Bob Skoronski. There is some confusion about the date of Vince's tirade. I've chosen the Tuesday meeting after the November 28 game against the Rams because Bill Curry's account is very explicit. However, some players recalled the incident taking place two weeks earlier, during the week following the November 14 game in Milwaukee against the Rams.

37. Flynn, *Lombardi Scrapbook*, p. 192; Kramer, *Instant Replay*, p. 92; interviews, Willie Davis, Norm Masters, Bob Schnelker.

38. Vincent Lombardi and W. C. Heinz, "A Game for Madmen," *Look*, September 5, 1967, p. 90.

39. *Chicago Sun-Times*, August 4, 1967; *Green Bay Press-Gazette*, April 21, 1967; *Milwaukee Journal*, February 2, 1968; Lombardi and Heinz, "Game for Madmen," p. 90; Howard Cosell, *Cosell* (Chicago: Playboy Press, 1973), p. 104; Dowling, *Coach*, pp. 312–13; Paul Hornung (with Al Silverman), *Football and the Single Man* (Garden City, N.Y.: Doubleday & Company, 1965), p. 13; Kramer, *Instant Replay*, pp. 19, 20, 205; Kramer, *Lombardi:*

Winning, pp. 79, 81; Lombardi, *Run to Daylight,* pp. 17, 19; John Torinus, *The Packer Legend: An Inside Look* (Neshkoro, Wis.: Laranmark Press, 1982), p. 127; Wiebusch, *Lombardi,* pp. 163, 179; Wright, *Wright,* p. 52; interviews, Red Cochran, Jerry Izenberg, Ron Kramer.

40. *Chicago Tribune,* October 4, 1970; Kramer, *Instant Replay,* pp. 28–30; Kramer, *Lombardi: Winning,* pp. 132, 136, 137; Wiebusch, *Lombardi,* pp. 50, 166.

41. *Green Bay Press-Gazette,* August 25, 1963 and April 14, 1967; Lombardi and Heinz, "Winning Football," pp. 70–71; Kramer, *Instant Replay,* pp. 99, 160; Kramer, *Lombardi: Winning,* pp. 87–89, 92–93; Lombardi, *Run to Daylight,* pp. 24–25; Starr and Wiebusch, *Perspective on Victory,* pp. 12–13, 37, 51; interviews, Red Cochran, Bart Starr.

42. *Milwaukee Sentinel,* January 15, 1982; Flynn, *Lombardi Scrapbook,* p. 96; Wiebusch, *Lombardi,* p. 176; interview, Forrest Gregg.

43. Kramer, *Lombardi: Winning,* pp. 147–48; Lombardi, *Run to Daylight,* p. 106; Plimpton, *One More July,* pp. 13–14; Wells, *Mean on Sunday,* pp. 61–62; Wiebusch, *Lombardi,* p. 171; Wright, *Wright,* pp. 68–69; interviews, Eugene Brusky, John Roach, Jim Taylor.

44. Lombardi and Heinz, "Winning Football," p. 71; Kramer, *Lombardi: Winning,* pp. 102–3; Lombardi, *Run to Daylight,* p. 68; Plimpton, *One More July,* p. 170; Wells, *Mean on Sunday,* pp. 4–33, 46, 60, 70–72, 87, 227; Wiebusch, *Lombardi,* p. 171; interviews, Jim Manci, Ray Nitschke.

45. Kramer, *Instant Replay,* pp. 26, 77; Wiebusch, *Lombardi,* p. 178; interview, Chuck Johnson.

46. Kramer, *Instant Replay,* pp. 141, 179; interviews, Marvin Fleming, Jim Grabowski, Bob Schnelker.

47. Tim Cohane, *Bypaths of Glory* (New York: Harper & Row, 1963), p. 10; Silverman, *Lombardi,* p. 58; Wells, *Mean on Sunday,* p. 181.

48. *Green Bay Press-Gazette,* November 20, 1962; Cosell, *Cosell,* p. 104; Kramer, *Instant Replay,* pp. 20, 49–50, 199; Kramer, *Lombardi: Winning,* p. 121; Silverman, *Lombardi,* pp. 15, 63; interviews, Ron Kostelnik, Nelson Toburen.

49. Lombardi and Heinz, "Madmen," pp. 85–90; Cosell, *Cosell,* pp. 104–5; Kramer, *Lombardi: Winning,* p. 76; Wiebusch, *Lombardi,* p. 42; interview, Cooper Rollow.

50. Cosell, *Cosell,* p. 101; Kramer, *Instant Replay,* pp. 53–54, 65–66, 75, 83; Kramer, *Lombardi: Winning,* p. 68; Lombardi, *Run to Daylight,* p. 123; Wiebusch, *Lombardi,* p. 31.

51. Flynn, *Lombardi Scrapbook,* p. 74; interviews, Jim Grabowski, Bob Jeter, Bob Skoronski.

52. Bob Long to Vince Lombardi, November 26, 1968, unprocessed Susan (Lombardi) Bickham Papers, Plantation, Fla.; *Green Bay Press-Gazette,* May 9, 1967; *Milwaukee Sentinel,* January 15, 1971; Kramer, *Lombardi: Winning,* pp. 73–74; Wells, *Mean on Sunday,* pp. 226–27; Wright, *Wright,* pp. 58–59; interview, Bob Skoronski.

53. *Los Angeles Herald-Examiner,* February 5, 1968; Schickel, "On Pro Football," p. 67; Leverett Smith, *The American Dream and the National Game* (Bowling Green, O.: Bowling Green University Popular Press, 1975), pp. 236–37, 253; Silverman, *Lombardi,* p. 58; Wells, *Mean on Sunday,* pp. 181, 187; interviews, Gary Knafelc, Norm Masters, Jim Ringo.

54. *Chicago Today,* September 6, 1970; *Sunday Times* of London, November 14, 1968; *Washington Post,* September 7, 1970; *Washington Star,* January 10, 1971; Kramer, *Lombardi: Winning,* p. 92; Wiebusch, *Lombardi,* pp. 161, 178, 195; interviews, Thomas Miller, Jim Ringo, John Roach, Willie Wood.

55. Jack Olsen, "The Anguish of a Team Divided," *Sports Illustrated,* July 29, 1968, pp. 20–24, 29–35; Jack Olsen, *The Black Athlete: A Shameful Story* (New York: Time-Life Books, 1968), p. 189; Wells, *Mean on Sunday,* p. 63.

56. Gerald Eskenazi, *There Were Giants in Those Days* (New York: Grosset & Dunlap, 1976), p. 57; Olsen, *Black Athlete,* pp. 169–79; interview, Jack Spinks.

57. Olsen, *Black Athlete,* pp. 188–89; Emlen Tunnell, *Footsteps of a Giant* (Garden City, N.Y.: Doubleday & Company, 1966), p. 205; Wiebusch, *Lombardi,* p. 81.

58. Jack Olsen, "In the Back of the Bus," *Sports Illustrated,* July 22, 1968, p. 41; Wiebusch, *Lombardi,* p. 81; interviews, Dominic Gentile, Marv Fleming.

59. *The Monday Paper* (Manalapan, Fla.), August 9, 1976; Terry Bledsoe, "Black Dominance of Sports: Strictly from Hunger" in Stanley Eitzen (ed.), *Sport in Contemporary Society: An Anthology* (New York: St. Martin's Press, 1979), p. 361; Kramer, *Lombardi: Winning,* p. 32; interview, Willie Davis.

60. *Green Bay Press-Gazette,* September 11, 1961 and August 18, 1962;

Kramer, *Instant Replay,* p. 39; interviews, Willie Davis, Nelson Toburen.

61. Bledsoe, "Black Dominance," p. 361; Heywood Hale Broun, *Tumultuous Merriment* (New York: Richard Marek, 1979), p. 105; Wiebusch, *Lombardi,* p. 81; interviews, Dennis Burke, David Carley, Dave Robinson, Bob Schulze, Willie Wood.

62. *Green Bay Press-Gazette,* May 13, 1962; Olsen, *Black Athlete,* p. 189; interviews, Red Cochran, Bob Jeter.

63. W. C. Heinz, *Once They Heard the Cheers* (Garden City, N.Y.: Doubleday & Company, 1979), p. 286; Plimpton, *One More July,* p. 123; Wiebusch, *Lombardi,* p. 171; interviews, Red Cochran, Willie Davis.

64. Wiebusch, *Lombardi,* p. 173; interviews, Marv Fleming, Willie Wood.

65. *Green Bay Press-Gazette,* August 3, 1968; Olsen, "Back of the Bus," p. 41; Flynn, *Lombardi Scrapbook,* p. 111; Kramer, *Lombardi: Winning,* p. 72; Olsen, *Black Athlete,* pp. 188–89; Wiebusch, *Lombardi,* pp. 81, 171.

CHAPTER THIRTEEN

1. Clipping, unprocessed Susan (Lombardi) Bickham Papers, Plantation, Fla.; *Los Angeles Times,* September 28, 1966; Vince Lombardi (with W. C. Heinz), *Run to Daylight* (New York: Grosset & Dunlap, 1963), p. 148; John Wiebusch (ed.), *Lombardi* (Chicago: Follett Publishing Company 1971), pp. 20, 28, 31; interview, Jim Lawlor.

2. *Green Bay Press-Gazette,* October 25, 1966; *Washington Star,* September 6, 1970; Harold Meyers, "That Profitable Nonprofit in Green Bay," *Fortune,* November 1968, p. 195.

3. *Green Bay Press-Gazette,* February 26, 1969; Meyers, "That Profitable Nonprofit," p. 195; Wiebusch, *Lombardi,* pp. 15, 20, 193; interviews, Thomas Miller, James Nellen, Robert Parins, Lee Remmel.

4. *Green Bay Press-Gazette,* February 26, 1969; Tom Dowling, "The Legend of St. Vincent," *Washingtonian,* August 1969, pp. 53–54; interviews, Eugene Brusky, Vince Lombardi, Jr., James Nellen.

5. Wiebusch, *Lombardi,* pp. 20, 22, 85; interviews, Eugene Brusky, James Nellen.

6. *Washington Star,* September 6, 1970; Earl Blaik, *The Red Blaik*

Story (New Rochelle, N.Y.: Arlington House Publishers, 1974), p. 439; interviews, Earl Blaik, Thomas Miller.

7. *Chicago Today,* September 4, 1970; *Washington Star,* February 27, 1969; Meyers, "That Profitable Nonprofit," p. 142; Jerry Kramer (ed.) *Lombardi: Winning Is the Only Thing* (New York: World Publishing Company 1970), pp. 51–52; Wiebusch, *Lombardi,* p. 28.

8. Interviews, Lois Bourguignon, Ruth Canadeo, Tony Canadeo, Cooper Rollow, William Wallace.

9. George Flynn (ed.), *The Vince Lombardi Scrapbook* (New York: Grosset & Dunlap, 1976), p. 135; Wiebusch, *Lombardi,* p. 186; interviews, Jerry Atkinson, Lois Bourguignon, Ruth Canadeo, Tony Canadeo, Ruth McKloskey, Cooper Rollow.

10 Wiebusch, *Lombardi,* p. 188; interviews, Red Cochran, Dave Hanner.

11. *Green Bay Press-Gazette,* September 4, 1970 and July 18, 1976; Wiebusch, *Lombardi,* p. 31; interviews, Ruth Canadeo, Mike Manuche, Ruth McKloskey.

12. *Green Bay Press-Gazette,* August 4, 1968; *Milwaukee Journal,* September 8, 1967 and September 3, 1970; Wiebusch, *Lombardi,* pp. 25–27; interviews, Lois Bourguignon, Red Cochran, Jack Koeppler, Len Wagner.

13. *Milwaukee Journal,* September 3, 1970; Wiebusch, *Lombardi,* p. 22.

14. Wiebusch, *Lombardi,* pp. 26–27.

15. *Green Bay Press-Gazette,* February 4, 1968; interviews, Jack Koeppler, Wellington Mara, William O'Hara, Anthony Pisani.

16. Tim Cohane, *Bypaths of Glory* (New York: Harper & Row, 1963), p. 4; interviews, Wellington Mara, Anthony Pisani.

17. Clipping, unprocessed *Green Bay Press-Gazette* Papers, Green Bay, Wis.; *Time,* December 21, 1962; Wiebusch, *Lombardi,* p. 30; interviews, Edward Breslin, Tim Cohane, Mike Manuche, William Wallace.

18 *Green Bay Press-Gazette,* July 22, 1965; interviews, Eugene Brusky, Tony Canadeo, Jack Koeppler.

19. Flynn, *Lombardi Scrapbook,* p. 86; interviews, Tony Canadeo, Jack Koeppler.

20. *Bergen County Record,* September 3, 1970; Flynn, *Lombardi Scrapbook,* p. 36; interviews, Edward Breslin, Dennis Burke, Tom Della Torre, Jack Koeppler, Kenneth Moore.

21. Dennis Burke to Vince Lombardi, September 9, 1965, unprocessed Dennis Burke Papers, De Pere, Wis.; *Green Bay Press-Gazette,* June

1, 1962, November 4, 1965, and December 7, 1966; *Newsday*, September 4, 1970; interview, Dennis Burke.

22. *Green Bay Press-Gazette*, February 5, 1966; George Plimpton, *One More July: A Football Dialogue with Bill Curry* (New York: Harper & Row, 1977), p. 20.

23. *Green Bay Press-Gazette*, October 1, 1961, August 30, 1964, December 19, 1965, January 23, 1966, and February 4, 1968; *Miami Herald*, September 9, 1973; *Milwaukee Journal*, January 2, 1972; *Milwaukee Sentinel*, November 1, 1960; *Washington Post*, February 7, 1969; Kate Giles, "Mrs. Vince Lombardi: The Life of a Wife of a Legend," *Harper's Bazaar*, January 1973, p. 88; interview, Gary Knafelc.

24. *Green Bay Press-Gazette*, October 1, 1961, December 19, 1965, and February 4, 1968; *The New York Times*, April 20, 1982.

25. *Green Bay Press-Gazette*, October 1, 1961 and April 18, 1982; *Milwaukee Sentinel*, November 1, 1960 and February 8, 1969; *Washington Star*, February 7, 1969; Lombardi, *Run to Daylight*, p 11; interviews, Lois Bourguignon, John Torinus, one confidential source.

26. Al Silverman (ed.), *Lombardi* (New York: Macfadden-Bartell Corporation, 1970), p. 66; interviews, Chuck Johnson, Harold Lombardi; four confidential sources.

27. *Miami Herald*, September 9, 1973; *Milwaukee Journal*, October 22, 1976; *Washington Star*, February 7, 1969; *Washington Post*, February 7, 1969; Vincent H. Lombardi, "Vince Lombardi, Father and Coach," *TWA Ambassador*, June 1974, p. 13; Silverman, *Lombardi*, p. 67; Wiebusch, *Lombardi*, p. 186; interview, Anthony Pisani.

28. *Washington Post*, February 7, 1969; interviews, W. C. Heinz, Ron Kostelnik, Vince Lombardi, Jr., John Sauer, Robert Skoronski, one confidential source.

29. Interview, W. C. Heinz.

30. *Milwaukee Journal*, April 18, 1982; *The New York Times*, April 20, 1982; Wiebusch, *Lombardi*, p. 185.

31. *Green Bay Press-Gazette*, December 19, 1965 and November 17, 1972; *Miami Herald*, September 9, 1973; *The New York Times*, April 20, 1982; *Washington Post*, February 7, 1969; Wiebusch, *Lombardi*, p. 185; interview, Tom Miller.

32. Wiebusch, *Lombardi*, p. 20; four confidential sources.

33. Clipping, unprocessed Roger Fay Papers, Bergenfield, N.J.; *The Monday Paper* (Manalapan, Fla.), August 9, 1976; *Washington*

Post, February 7, 1969; Lombardi, Jr., "Father and Coach," p. 13; Wiebusch, *Lombardi,* pp. 186–87; interview, Vince Lombardi, Jr.

34. *Milwaukee Journal,* January 7 1973; Lombardi, Jr., "Father and Coach," p. 13; Wiebusch, *Lombardi,* p. 21; interview, Vince Lombardi, Jr.

35. *Milwaukee Journal,* January 7, 1973 and April 4, 1975; *The New York Times,* March 30, 1982; *Washington Post,* February 7, 1969; Wiebusch, *Lombardi,* p. 21; interviews, Ken Bowman, Gary Knafelc, Bob Schnelker, Robert Skoronski.

36. Clipping, Fay Papers; *Milwaukee Journal,* January 7, 1973; Wiebusch, *Lombardi,* p. 187.

37. *Green Bay Press-Gazette,* October 19, 1962 and November 10, 1963; *Milwaukee Journal,* November 27, 1961 and January 7, 1973; *The New York Times,* March 30, 1982; Lombardi, Jr., "Father and Coach," p. 14; Wiebusch, *Lombardi,* p. 187; interview, Vince Lombardi, Jr.

38. Clipping, Fay Papers; *Milwaukee Journal,* January 7, 1973; Lombardi, Jr., "Father and Coach," p. 13; interview, Vince Lombardi, Jr.

39. *Green Bay Press-Gazette,* February 4, 1968; *Milwaukee Journal,* June 5, 1964; Lombardi, Jr., "Father and Coach," p. 13; interview, Susan (Lombardi) Bickham.

40. *The Miami Herald,* September 9, 1973; *Milwaukee Journal,* October 22, 1976; *The Monday Paper,* August 9, 1976; interview, Susan (Lombardi) Bickham.

41. Wiebusch, *Lombardi,* p. 186; interview, Susan (Lombardi) Bickham.

42. *Green Bay Press-Gazette,* December 19, 1965; *Washington Star,* September 18, 1969; Lombardi, Jr., "Father and Coach," pp. 13–14; Wiebusch, *Lombardi,* p. 188.

43. Interview, Jerry Atkinson.

44. Wiebusch, *Lombardi,* p. 161.

CHAPTER FOURTEEN

1. *Green Bay Press-Gazette,* April 21 and 27, July 11, and August 1, 1967; *Newsweek,* January 29, 1968.

2. *Green Bay Press-Gazette,* April 29 and May 11, 1967; *Milwaukee Sentinel,* May 3, 1967; Jerry Kramer, *Instant Replay* (New York: New American Library, 1968), p. 32; Jerry Kramer (ed.), *Lombardi:*

Winning Is the Only Thing (New York: World Publishing Company, 1970), pp. 147, 149; interview, Jim Taylor.

3. *Green Bay Press-Gazette*, August 22, 1967; Vincent Lombardi and W. C. Heinz, "A Game for Madmen," *Look*, September 5, 1967, pp. 85–90; Vincent Lombardi and W. C. Heinz, "Secrets of Winning Football," *Look*, September 19, 1967, pp. 70–75; Kramer, *Instant Replay*, pp. 84–85, 99; interview, W. C. Heinz.

4. *The New York Times*, September 14 and 15, 1968; Kramer, *Instant Replay*, p. xii.

5. Kramer, *Instant Replay*, pp. 33, 49, 53.

6. *Green Bay Press-Gazette*, September 10, 1967; Kramer, *Instant Replay*, pp. 72, 87, 107.

7. *Green Bay Press-Gazette*, September 29, 1967.

8. *Green Bay Press-Gazette*, October 5, 1967; Kramer, *Instant Replay*, p. 126.

9. Kramer, *Instant Replay*, pp. 139–41; Robert W. Wells, *Mean on Sunday: The Autobiography of Ray Nitschke* (Garden City, N.Y.: Doubleday & Company 1973), pp. 153–54.

10. *Green Bay Press-Gazette*, November 6 and December 15, 1967; Kramer, *Instant Replay*, pp. 151, 156, 159.

11. Kramer, *Instant Replay*, pp. 171–72.

12. Kramer, *Instant Replay*, pp. 174–76.

13. *Green Bay Press-Gazette*, July 21, 1967; Leonard Shecter, "The Toughest Man in Pro Football," *Esquire*, January 1968, pp. 68–71, 138, 140, 144–46; John Wiebusch (ed.), *Lombardi* (Chicago: Follett Publishing Company, 1971), p. 97; interview, Cooper Rollow.

14. Shecter, "Toughest Man," pp. 68–71, 138, 140, 144–46.

15. George Flynn, *Vince Lombardi Scrapbook* (New York: Grosset & Dunlap, 1976), p. 173; Wiebusch, *Lombardi*, p. 94; interviews, Jerry Izenberg, Cooper Rollow.

16. *Green Bay Press-Gazette*, December 10, 1967; Kramer, *Instant Replay*, pp. 181–82; Kramer, *Lombardi: Winning*, pp. 110–11; interview, Allen Brown.

17. *Los Angeles Times*, December 12, 1967.

18. *Green Bay Press-Gazette*, December 23, 1967; Dan Harman, *Carroll Dale Scores Again!* (Anderson, Ind.: The Warner Press, 1969), pp. 79–80; W. C. Heinz, *Once They Heard the Cheers* (Garden City, N.Y.: Doubleday & Company 1979), pp. 296–97; Kramer, *Instant Replay*, pp. 191, 196; Bart Starr and John Wiebusch, *A Perspective*

on Victory (Chicago: Follett Publishing Company, 1972), p. 130; Wells, *Mean on Sunday*, pp. 159–61; Wiebusch, *Lombardi*, p. 144. The recollections of players differ widely concerning which day of the week Vince gave his biblical quotation. The most likely day was Tuesday or Wednesday.

19. Kramer, *Instant Replay*, pp. 193–94; Heinz, *Heard the Cheers*, pp. 296–97; Starr and Wiebusch, *Perspective on Victory*, p. 130; Wiebusch, *Lombardi*, p. 144; interview, Ron Kostelnik.
20. Kramer, *Instant Replay*, p. 199; Heinz, *Heard the Cheers*, p. 297; Starr and Wiebusch, *Perspective on Victory*, p. 130; Wiebusch, *Lombardi*, pp. 144–47.
21. *Green Bay Press-Gazette*, February 13, 1967; *Milwaukee Journal*, July 11, 1967.
22. *Green Bay Press-Gazette*, December 31, 1967 and January 2, 1968; Kramer, *Instant Replay*, pp. 209–10; Starr and Wiebusch, *Perspective on Victory*, p. 134; Bob St. John, *The Man Inside Landry* (New York: Avon Books, 1979), p. 131; Wiebusch, *Lombardi*, p. 150; interview, Vince Lombardi, Jr.
23. Sam Blair, *Dallas Cowboys: Pro or Con?* (Garden City, N.Y.: Doubleday & Company, 1970), p. 273; Art Daley and Jack Yuenger (eds.), *The Lombardi Era of the Green Bay Packers* (Milwaukee: Inland Press, 1968), p. 46; St. John, *Landry*, pp. 132, 134; Wiebusch, *Lombardi*, p. 154.
24. *Green Bay Press-Gazette*, January 2, 1968; Kramer, *Instant Replay*, pp. 217–18.
25. Wiebusch, *Lombardi*, p. 153.
26. *Milwaukee Journal*, January 23, 1981; *The New York Times*, January 15, 1968; Flynn, *Lombardi Scrapbook*, pp. 194–95; Kramer, *Instant Replay*, p. 223; Wiebusch, *Lombardi*, p. 157.
27. *Green Bay Press-Gazette*, January 9, 1968; Flynn, *Lombardi Scrapbook*, p. 172; Wiebusch, *Lombardi*, pp. 156–57; interview, Chuck Johnson.
28. Kramer, *Instant Replay*, pp. 230–31.
29. *Green Bay Press-Gazette*, January 15, 1968; *The New York Times*, January 15, 1968; Kramer, *Instant Replay*, p. 232; Wiebusch, *Lombardi*, pp. 156–57.
30. *Green Bay Press-Gazette*, January 15 and 16 and March 22, 1968; W. C. Heinz, "I Miss the Fire on Sunday," *Life*, September 27, 1968, p. 122.
31. Dennis Burke, "The Vince I Knew," unprocessed Dennis Burke

Papers, De Pere, Wis.; *Green Bay Press-Gazette,* March 22, 1968; interview, Dennis Burke.

32. Clipping, unprocessed Susan (Lombardi) Bickham Papers, Plantation, Fla.

33. Clippings, Bickham Papers; interviews, Eugene Brusky, Chuck Lane, Vince Lombardi, Jr., James Nellen.

34. Heinz, "Fire on Sunday," p. 121; Flynn, *Lombardi Scrapbook,* p. 143; Wells, *Mean on Sunday,* pp. 202–3; Wiebusch, *Lombardi,* p. 149.

35. *Green Bay Press-Gazette,* February 16, 1969; interview, Earl Blaik.

36. Kramer, *Instant Replay,* pp. 227–28; Starr and Wiebusch, *Perspective on Victory,* p. 142; Wiebusch, *Lombardi,* p. 154; interview, Vince Lombardi, Jr.

37. *Green Bay Press-Gazette,* January 29 and February 1, 1968; *Milwaukee Journal,* February 2, 1968; interview, John Torinus.

38. "Lombardi's Resignation Statement," unprocessed *Green Bay Press-Gazette* Papers, Green Bay, Wis.; *Green Bay Press-Gazette,* January 29 and 30 and February 2, 1968; *Milwaukee Journal,* February 2, 1968; *The New York Times,* February 2, 1968.

39. *Green Bay Press-Gazette,* January 16 and February 2, 3, and 4, 1968; *The New York Times,* February 2, 1968.

CHAPTER FIFTEEN

1. *Green Bay Press-Gazette,* May 23, August 4, 5, 7, 8, 1968; *Milwaukee Journal,* August 4, 1968; *Milwaukee Sentinel,* August 6, 8, 1968; *The Sporting News,* August 24, 1968.

2. *Green Bay Press-Gazette,* June 29, 1968; *Milwaukee Sentinel,* May 16, 1968; *Sports Illustrated,* March 3, 1969; Benjamin Rader, *American Sports: From the Age of Folk Games to the Age of Spectators* (Englewood Cliffs, N.J.: Prentice-Hall, 1983), pp. 349–50; interview, Dave Robinson.

3. Clipping, unprocessed Dennis Burke Papers, De Pere, Wis.; *Green Bay Press-Gazette,* May 12, 1968; *New York Post,* March 28, 1968; *The Sporting News,* August 24, 1968.

4. Pamphlet, "Timeless Tributes to Credit Unions," Cuna Mutual Insurance Society, 1970, unprocessed Susan (Lombardi) Bickham Papers, Plantation, Fla.; Frank Scott to Mrs. Vince Lombardi,

Notes

September 22, 1970, unprocessed Vince Lombardi, Jr., Papers, Bloomfield Hills, Mich; interview, Frank Scott.

5. William Fetridge, *With Warm Regards: A Reminiscence* (Chicago: Dartnell Corporation, 1976), pp. 186–87; interview, William Fetridge.

6. Videotape, *Second Effort* (Chicago: Dartnell Corporation, 1968); *Boston Herald,* November 19, 1968; *Green Bay Press-Gazette,* May 12 and August 28, 1968; Bob Sales, "The Lombardi Pitch" in Irving Marsh and Edward Ehre (eds.), *Best Sports Stories, 1969 Edition* (New York: E. P. Dutton & Company, 1969), pp. 146–48; John Wiebusch (ed.), *Lombardi* (Chicago: Follett Publishing Company, 1971), p. 99.

7. William Fetridge to author, September 21, 1984; advertising brochure for *Second Effort,* Bickham Papers; "Dartnell Training Film Catalog," Dartnell Corporation, Chicago, Ill.; Fetridge, *Warm Regards,* p. 188; interviews, William Fetridge, Frank Scott.

8. *Green Bay Press-Gazette,* February 14, 1969; *Milwaukee Sentinel,* May 11, 1968; interviews, David Carley, James Carley.

9. *Green Bay Press-Gazette,* May 11, 1968, and February 14, 1969; *Milwaukee Journal,* May 11, 1968; interviews, David Carley, James Carley, Jack Koeppler.

10. *Milwaukee Sentinel,* May 6, 1968; *The Sporting News,* August 24, 1968; Tom Dowling, "The Legend of St. Vincent," *Washingtonian,* August 1969, p. 56.

11. Dowling, "St. Vincent," p. 58; interviews, David Carley, Mike Manuche.

12. *Green Bay Press-Gazette,* July 13 and 20 and August 4, 1968; *Milwaukee Sentinel,* July 16, 1968; Wiebusch, *Lombardi,* p. 197; interviews, Jack Koeppler, Chuck Lane.

13. Thomas Domer, "Sport in Cold War America, 1953–63: The Diplomatic and Political Use of Sport in the Eisenhower and Kennedy Administrations" (Ph.D. dissertation, Marquette University, 1976), pp. 208–9; Jay Coakley, *Sport in Society: Issues and Controversies* (St. Louis: The C. V. Mosby Company, 1978), p. 22; interviews, Jack Koeppler, Orrin Krueger, Vince Lombardi, Jr., Madeline Werner.

14. Robert Kennedy to Vince Lombardi (n.d.), Bickham Papers; Robert Kennedy to Vince Lombardi, February 5, 1968, Vince Lombardi, Jr., Papers; *Green Bay Press-Gazette,* February 19, 1960; *Washington Post,* September 4, 1970; Wiebusch, *Lombardi,* p. 197;

interviews, David Carley, John Cochran, Art Daley, Ruth McKloskey, James Nellen.

15. Wiebusch, *Lombardi,* p. 105; interviews, David Carley, Edward Bennett Williams.

16. *Green Bay Press-Gazette,* August 7, 1968 and February 6, 1969; *Milwaukee Sentinel,* August 3, 1968; *The Sporting News,* August 24, 1968; Dowling, "St. Vincent," p. 56; Wiebusch, *Lombardi,* pp. 98, 105; interview, Ruth McKloskey.

17. *Green Bay Press-Gazette,* February 6, 1969.

18. *Green Bay Press-Gazette,* September 4, 1970; *Milwaukee Sentinel,* March 22, 1969; W. C. Heinz, "I Miss the Fire on Sunday," *Life,* September 27, 1968, p. 121; *Sports Illustrated,* March 3, 1969, p. 33: Wiebusch, *Lombardi,* p. 101; interviews, Orrin Krueger, Chuck Lane, Ruth McKloskey, Thomas Miller.

19. *Washington Post,* February 7, 1969; Heinz, "Fire on Sunday," p. 121; *Sports Illustrated,* March 3, 1969, p. 33; Wiebusch, *Lombardi,* p. 101.

20. Clipping, Bickham Papers; George Flynn (ed.), *The Vince Lombardi Scrapbook* (New York: Grosset & Dunlap, 1976), p. 120; Jerry Kramer (ed.), *Lombardi: Winning Is the Only Thing* (New York: The World Publishing Company, 1970), p. 32; interview, Susan (Lombardi) Bickham.

21. *Milwaukee Journal,* December 23, 1970; *Milwaukee Sentinel,* February 6, 1969; *Newsday,* July 30, 1968; *The New York Times,* February 3, 1968; Flynn, *Lombardi Scrapbook,* p. 196; Jerry Kramer and Dick Schaap, *Jerry Kramer's Farewell to Football* (New York: Bantam Books, 1969), pp. 18–20; Wiebusch, *Lombardi,* p. 101; interviews, Ken Bowman, Ron Kostelnik.

22. *Green Bay Press-Gazette,* August 3, 1968.

23. Heinz, "Fire on Sunday," pp. 121–22.

24. *Janesville Gazette,* February 26, 1969; *Newsweek,* September 26, 1968; *Time,* November 22, 1968.

25. *Green Bay Press-Gazette,* September 30 and November 11, 1968.

26. Kramer and Schaap, *Farewell to Football,* p. 20; Wiebusch, *Lombardi,* p. 102; interview, James Nellen.

27. *Green Bay Press-Gazette,* February 6, 1969; Kramer, *Lombardi: Winning,* p. 139; John Torinus, *The Packer Legend: An Inside Look* (Neshkoro, Wis.: Laranmark Press, 1982), p. 178; interviews, Phil Bengtson, Lee Remmel, Bob Schnelker.

28. *Green Bay Press-Gazette,* July 9, November 2, and December 5,

1968; *Milwaukee Journal,* February 16, 1969; *Milwaukee Sentinel,* July 16, 1969; Kramer and Schaap, *Farewell to Football,* p. 34; interview, Phil Bengtson.

29. *Green Bay Press-Gazette,* December 13, 1962, January 2, December 14 and 26, 1963, November 4, 1965, November 29, 1968; *Milwaukee Journal,* December 22, 1968; *The New York Times,* March 23, 1968; Harold Meyers, "That Profitable Nonprofit in Green Bay," *Fortune,* November 1968, p. 195; *Time,* December 21, 1962; interviews, Hugh Devore, one confidential source.

30. *Green Bay Press-Gazette,* August 8, 1961, December 13, 1962; *Milwaukee Sentinel,* November 5, 1965; *Washington Post,* February 6, 1969; interviews, Anthony Pisani, John Torinus.

31. Clipping, Sports Scrapbook, Vol. 61, United States Military Academy Papers, West Point, N.Y.; *Green Bay Press-Gazette,* June 4, 1965; *The New York Times,* November 17, 1967; Earl Blaik, *The Red Blaik Story* (New Rochelle, N.Y.: Arlington House, 1974), p. 440; interviews, Earl Blaik, Joseph McCrane.

32. *Ibid.;* clipping, Vince Lombardi, Jr., Papers; *Green Bay Press-Gazette,* October 26, 1968, January 11, 1969.

33. *Green Bay Press-Gazette,* August 4, 1968, February 11, 1969; *Milwaukee Journal,* January 20, 1969; *Milwaukee Sentinel,* January 18, February 10, and March 22, 1969; *The New York Times,* January 15, 1969.

34. *Green Bay Press-Gazette,* February 5, 1969; *Milwaukee Journal,* December 22, 1968, February 4, 1969; *Milwaukee Sentinel,* November 13, 1968.

35. *Milwaukee Journal,* October 3, 1968, February 12, 1969; Charles Moritz (ed.), *Current Biography: 1965 Yearbook* (New York: H. W. Wilson Company 1965), pp. 456–58; interview, Edward Bennett Williams.

36. *Washington Star,* February 1 and 2, 1969; *Washington Post,* February 2 and 7, 1969; Kramer, *Lombardi: Winning,* pp. 104–6; interviews, Morris Siegel, Edward Bennett Williams.

37. *Milwaukee Journal,* February 12, 1969; *Milwaukee Sentinel,* February 5, 1969; interview, Edward Bennett Williams.

38. *Milwaukee Journal,* February 5 and 13, 1969; *Milwaukee Sentinel,* January 22, 1969; *The New York Times,* February 4, 1969; *The Sporting News,* February 22, 1969.

39. *Green Bay Press-Gazette,* February 2, 1969; *Milwaukee Sentinel,* February 3, 1969; *The New York Times,* February 5, 1969; *The Sporting News,* February 22, 1969; interview, Lois Bourguignon.

40. *Green Bay Press-Gazette,* February 3 and 4, 1969; *Milwaukee Sentinel,* February 4, 1969; *Washington Post,* February 4, 1969.

41. *Milwaukee Journal,* February 5, 1969; *Milwaukee Sentinel,* February 4 and 6, 1969; *Washington Star,* February 4 and 5, 1969; *Washington Post,* February 4, 1969.

42. *Green Bay Press-Gazette,* February 4 and 5, 1969; *Janesville Gazette,* February 26, 1969; *The New York Times,* February 5, 1969.

43. *Green Bay Press-Gazette,* February 5, 6, 8, and 16, 1969; *Milwaukee Journal,* February 18, 1969; *Milwaukee Sentinel,* February 6, 1969; *Washington Star,* February 6, 1969; interview, Edward Bennett Williams.

44. *Washington Evening Star,* February 6 and 7, 1969; *Washington Post,* February 7, 1969.

45. *Milwaukee Journal,* February 7, 1969; *Milwaukee Sentinel,* February 7, 1969; *The Sporting News,* February 22, 1969; *Washington Star,* February 7, 1969; *Washington Post,* February 7 and 8, 1969.

46. *Milwaukee Journal,* February 4, 5, and 9, 1969; *Washington Post,* February 5, 1969; interview, Paul Mazzoleni.

47. *Green Bay Press-Gazette,* February 7, 1969; *Milwaukee Journal,* February 5 and 6, 1969; *Milwaukee Sentinel,* February 4, 1969.

48. *Green Bay Press-Gazette,* February 26, 1969 and September 4, 1970; Flynn, *Lombardi Scrapbook,* p. 76; interview, Ruth McKloskey.

CHAPTER SIXTEEN

1. *Green Bay Press-Gazette,* February 9, 1969; *Washington Post,* February 7 and 11, 1969; *Washington Star,* February 7, 1969.

2. *Washington Star,* February 5, 1969.

3. *Washington Post,* October 12, 1969; William Johnson, "ARARA-RARARARGH!," *Sports Illustrated,* March 3, 1969, p. 29; interview, Duke Zeibert.

4. Johnson, "ARAR . . .!," pp. 29–30.

5. *Milwaukee Journal,* February 6, 1969.

6. Tom Dowling, *Coach: A Season with Lombardi* (New York: W. W. Norton & Company, 1970), pp. 77–79.

7. Brochure, *Redskins Remember Lombardi,* May 11 and 12, 1973, in the unprocessed Vince Lombardi, Jr., Papers, Bloomfield Hills,

Notes

Mich.; Dowling, *Coach,* pp. 34, 61–63; *Milwaukee Journal,* February 4, 1969; *Milwaukee Sentinel,* February 8, 1969; *Pro Football Weekly,* October 2, 1969; *Washington Post,* September 10, 1969 and January 29, 1970; *Washington Star,* February 18, 1969.

8. *Milwaukee Journal,* February 16, 1969; *Washington Star,* February 6, 1969.

9. John Underwood, "We're Going to Win—You Better Believe It," *Sports Illustrated,* July 28, 1969, p. 20; Ken Denlinger and Paul Attner, *Redskin Country: From Baugh to the Super Bowl* (New York: Leisure Press, 1983), pp. 86, 97–101; Dowling, *Coach,* p. 40; interviews, Gerry Allen, Sonny Jurgensen.

10. Underwood, "We're Going to Win," pp. 20, 23; Denlinger, *Redskin Country,* pp. 100–101; Dowling, *Coach,* p. 215; *Washington Post,* October 17, 1969; interview, Sonny Jurgensen.

11. *Washington Star,* February 13, 1969 and September 6, 1970; Dowling, *Coach,* p. 215; Jerry Kramer (ed.), *Lombardi: Winning Is the Only Thing* (New York: World Publishing Company, 1970), p. 168; interview, Sonny Jurgensen.

12. *Redskins Remember Lombardi,* Vince Lombardi, Jr., Papers; *Washington Post,* September 6, 1969; Dowling, *Coach,* pp. 42–43; Johnson, "ARAR . . .!," p. 30.

13. *Washington Post,* October 12, 1969; interview, Tim Temerario.

14. *Washington Star,* February 13, 1969.

15. *Milwaukee Sentinel,* June 17, 1969; *Washington Post,* March 16 and June 16 and 17, 1969; Kramer, *Lombardi: Winning,* p. 165.

16. *Washington Post,* July 6 and 10, 1969; Underwood, "We're Going to Win," pp. 19–20.

17. Dowling, *Coach,* pp. viii, 7; interviews, Gerry Allen, Pat Richter.

18. *Washington Post,* July 11 and 27, 1969; *Washington Star,* September 6, 1970; Larry Brown (with William Gildea), *I'll Always Get Up* (New York: Simon & Schuster, 1973), pp. 115–16; Dowling, *Coach,* pp. 46–47.

19. *Washington Post,* July 18 and October 30, 1969; Dowling, *Coach,* p. 218; George Flynn (ed), *The Vince Lombardi Scrapbook* (New York: Grosset & Dunlap, 1976), pp. 207–8.

20. *Washington Post,* August 27, 1969; Dowling, *Coach,* p. 64; interview, Pat Richter.

21. Gerry Allen, "The Summer of '69: Vince Lombardi," p. 1, unpublished article given to the author by Gerry Allen, New York, N.Y.; *Washington Post,* July 13, 1969; Underwood, "We're Going

to Win," p. 19; Dowling, *Coach,* pp. 89–90; interviews, Lew Carpenter, Harland Svare.

22. *Washington Post,* August 14, 1969; Dowling, *Coach,* p. 50; Kramer *Lombardi: Winning,* p. 156; interview, Bill Austin.
23. *Washington Post,* July 20, 1969; Dowling, *Coach,* pp. 136, 137, 286; Kramer, *Lombardi: Winning,* p. 170; interviews, Sonny Jurgensen, Pat Richter.
24. Interviews, Brig Owens, Ray Schoenke, Harland Svare.
25. Gary Cartwright, "The Unlikely Vincification of Sonny Jurgensen," *Life,* October 24, 1969, pp. 48–51; Brown, *I'll Always Get Up,* pp. 126–27; Dowling, *Coach,* p. 37; John Wiebusch (ed.), *Lombardi* (Chicago: Follett Publishing Company, 1971), p. 42; interview, Dave Slattery.
26. Interview, Lew Carpenter.
27. *Washington Post,* September 5, 1969; Dowling, *Coach,* p. 65.
28. Dowling, *Coach,* pp. 274, 286; interview, Harland Svare.
29. *Washington Post,* September 4, 1970; Brown, *I'll Always Get Up,* pp. 113–14; Dowling, *Coach,* pp. 232, 314, 315; interviews, George Dickson, Pat Richter, Ray Schoenke, Harland Svare.
30. Kramer, *Lombardi: Winning,* p. 169; interviews, Chris Hanburger, Sonny Jurgensen, Brig Owens, Frank Ryan.
31. *Janesville Gazette,* February 26, 1969; Brown, *I'll Always Get Up,* p. 12; Kramer, *Lombardi: Winning,* p. 171; interview, George Dickson.
32. *Washington Post,* August 25, 1969; Dowling, *Coach,* p. 287.
33. Dowling, *Coach,* pp. 236, 285.
34. *Washington Post,* April 19, 1969; Dowling, *Coach,* pp. 136, 241, 276, 290; Kramer, *Lombardi: Winning,* pp. 158, 160; Wiebusch, *Lombardi,* p. 105.
35. *Washington Post,* March 16, June 19, and August 22, 1969; Underwood, "We're Going to Win," p. 23; Denlinger, *Redskin Country,* p. 102; Kramer, *Lombardi: Winning,* p. 169; interviews, Lew Carpenter, Sonny Jurgensen, Frank Ryan.
36. Dowling, *Coach,* p. 214; interview, Ray Schoenke.
37. *Redskins Remember Lombardi,* Vince Lombardi, Jr., Papers; *Milwaukee Journal,* November 15, 1970; *Washington Post,* July 13, 1969; Brown, *I'll Always Get Up,* pp. 16, 106, 118, 127; Denlinger, *Redskin Country,* pp. 146–47; interview, Brig Owens.
38. *Washington Post,* July 11 and 15, and September 30, 1969; Cartwright, "Unlikely Vincification," p. 50; Dowling, *Coach,* pp. 35, 60; interview, Dave Slattery.

39. *Green Bay Press-Gazette,* September 8, 1970; *Washington Star,* September 4, 1970; Flynn, *Lombardi Scrapbook,* p. 174; interviews, Kenneth Denlinger, Dave Slattery.

40. *Milwaukee Journal,* February 12, 1969; *Washington Post,* September 13, 1969; interviews, Lew Carpenter, Shirley Povich, Edward Bennett Williams.

41. Dowling, *Coach,* pp. 94, 121–22.

42. *Washington Post,* October 12, 1969; Dowling, *Coach,* pp. 141, 155–59.

43. *Washington Post,* September 24 and October 28, 1969; Cartwright, "Unlikely Vincification," p. 51; Dowling, *Coach,* p. 188.

44. *Washington Post,* November 3 and 4, 1969; Brown, *I'll Always Get Up,* p. 136; Dowling, *Coach,* p. 199.

45. *Washington Post,* November 4, 1969; Dowling, *Coach,* p. 218.

46. Dowling, *Coach,* pp. 313–14.

47. Dowling, *Coach,* p. 130.

48. Dowling, *Coach,* p. 269.

49. *Washington Post,* December 4, 1969; Dowling, *Coach,* p. 320.

50. *Washington Post,* January 4, 1970; Dowling, *Coach,* p. 199; interviews, Sonny Jurgensen, Frank Ryan.

51. *Washington Post,* February 21 and July 21, 1970; Cartwright, "Unlikely Vincification," p. 51; interviews, Gerry Allen, Sonny Jurgensen, Pat Richter.

52. Denlinger, *Redskin Country,* p. 116; Wiebusch, *Lombardi,* p. 105; interview, Edward Bennett Williams.

53. Kramer, *Lombardi: Winning,* pp. 164–65; interviews, Lew Carpenter, George Dickson, Harland Svare.

54. Clipping, unprocessed Timothy Moore Papers, Englewood, N.J.; *Washington Post,* March 10, 1970; Dowling, *Coach,* pp. 286–87, 328–30; Kramer, *Lombardi: Winning,* p. 162; interview, Brig Owens.

55. *Green Bay Press-Gazette,* March 15, 1969; *Milwaukee Sentinel,* August 16, 1969; *The New York Times,* March 15, 1969; interviews, Bill Austin, James Carley.

56. *Milwaukee Sentinel,* September 4, 1970; *Washington Post,* August 20, 1969; interviews, David Carley, James Carley.

57. Clipping, Vince Lombardi, Jr., Papers; *Milwaukee Journal,* February 27, 1969; *New Haven Register,* July 27, 1969; *Washington Star,* February 26, 1969; interviews, George Dickson, Orrin Krueger

58. *Milwaukee Sentinel,* June 10, 1969; *Washington Post,* October 7, 1969; Vincent H. Lombardi, "Vince Lombardi, Father and Coach,"

TWA Ambassador, June 1974, pp. 13–14; Wiebusch, *Lombardi,* pp. 188, 189; interview, Vince Lombardi, Jr.

59. Series of letters written by Orrin Krueger in 1970, after Vince's death, canceling Vince's memberships in clubs and organizations, Vince Lombardi, Jr., Papers; *Washington Post,* February 7, 1969.

60. Ethel Kennedy to Marie Lombardi (1970), unprocessed Susan (Lombardi) Bickham Papers, Plantation, Fla.; *Washington Post,* October 12, 1969, September 4, 1970; *Washington Star,* September 4, 1970; Wiebusch, *Lombardi,* p. 16; interviews, Jackie Anderson, Lewis Anderson, Edward Bennett Williams.

61. *Milwaukee Journal,* February 2, 1970; *Washington Star,* September 4, 1970; Wiebusch, *Lombardi,* p. 20; interview, Morris Siegel.

62. Kramer, *Lombardi: Winning,* p. 85.

63. *Green Bay Press-Gazette,* May 22, 1969; *The New York Times,* June 16, 1969; *Washington Post,* March 4, May 2, and September 5, 1970; interviews, Zenon Hansen, Shirley Povich.

64. *Washington Post,* June 25, 1970; William Manchester, *The Glory and the Dream* (Boston: Little, Brown and Co., 1973), pp. 1131, 1174, 1175, 1211; James T. Patterson, *America in the Twentieth Century: A History,* 2nd ed. (New York: Harcourt Brace Jovanovich, 1983), pp. 431–33, 443, 448, 449; interview, George Dickson.

65. *Milwaukee Journal,* January 2, 1972; *Washington Star,* September 4, 1970; Wiebusch, *Lombardi,* p. 195.

66. Richard Nixon to Vince Lombardi, November 14, 1969, Bickham Papers; *Newsday,* September 8, 1970; *Washington Post,* November 8, 10, 12, and 15, 1969; Dowling, *Coach,* pp. 220–21, 242; interview, William O'Hara.

67. *Washington Post,* June 30, 1969; Wiebusch, *Lombardi,* p. 197.

68. *Washington Post,* December 7, 1969.

69. *Washington Post,* June 25 and September 4, 1970.

70. *Milwaukee Sentinel,* March 12, 1969; *Washington Post,* June 25, 1970; Dowling, *Coach,* p. 193.

71. *Janesville Gazette,* February 26, 1969; *Washington Post,* September 4, 1970; Dave Anderson (ed.), *The Red Smith Reader* (New York: Random House, 1982), pp. 66, 71; Joe Willie Namath (with Dick Schaap), *I Can't Wait Until Tomorrow . . . 'Cause I Get Better-Looking Every Day* (New York: Random House, 1969); Wiebusch, *Lombardi,* pp. 196, 203.

72. *Washington Post,* July 16 and September 7, 1969.

73. *Chicago Daily News,* June 10, 1970; *Milwaukee Journal,* May 31, 1970; interview, Dave Slattery.
74. Clipping, Vince Lombardi, Jr., Papers; pamphlet, *Vince Lombardi Speech,* June 22, 1970, Dayton, O. (Dayton: Mead Papers Publishers, 1970), a copy of which was given to the author by Kenneth Moore, Norwood, N.J.; *Washington Post,* June 25, 1970; Cartwright, "Unlikely Vincification," pp. 50–51.
75. Wiebusch, *Lombardi,* pp. 196–97; interview, Edward Bennett Williams.

CHAPTER SEVENTEEN

1. *Green Bay Press-Gazette,* May 13, 1970; *Milwaukee Journal,* May 12, 1970; *Milwaukee Sentinel,* May 13, 1970.
2. *Green Bay Press-Gazette,* May 13 and September 3, 1970; *Milwaukee Sentinel,* September 4 and 7, 1970; John Wiebusch (ed.), *Lombardi* (Chicago: Follett Publishing Company, 1971), p. 106; interviews, Art Daley, Edward Breslin, Chuck Lane.
3. Jerry Kramer (ed.), *Lombardi: Winning Is the Only Thing* (New York: World Publishing Company, 1970), p. 16.
4. *Milwaukee Journal,* January 2, 1972; *Washington Daily News,* June 16, 1970; interview, Dave Slattery.
5. Robert Coffey, "A Case of Highly Anaplastic and Virulent Carcinoma of the Sigmoid Colon—The Terminal Illness of Vincent T. Lombardi," *Georgetown Medical Bulletin,* Vol. 31, No. 1, August 1977, p. 4; *Dayton Daily News,* June 23, 1970; *Washington Star,* September 4, 1970; *Washington Post,* June 28, 1970; interviews, Jackie Anderson, Lewis Anderson, Robert Coffey.
6. *Milwaukee Journal,* August 1, 1970; interview, Robert Coffey.
7. *Washington Post,* June 28 and July 2 and 3, 1970; interviews, Jackie Anderson, Lewis Anderson, Robert Coffey.
8. *Washington Post,* July 22, 1970; Wiebusch, *Lombardi,* pp. 202–3; interview, Robert Coffey.
9. *Miami Herald,* September 9, 1973; *The New York Times,* September 4, 1970; *Washington Post,* September 2, 1970; Wiebusch, *Lombardi,* pp. 202–3.
10. *Washington Post,* September 4, 1970.
11. Coffey, "Terminal Illness," p. 4; interview, Robert Coffey.
12. *Milwaukee Journal,* June 23, 1972; Wiebusch, *Lombardi,* p. 204; interview, Aloysius Wycislo.
13. *Washington Post,* August 14 and September 2, 1970.

14. *Miami Herald*, September 9, 1973; *The New York Times*, September 3, 1970; George Flynn (ed.),*Vince Lombardi Scrapbook* (New York: Grosset & Dunlap, 1976), pp. 40–41; Wiebusch, *Lombardi*, p. 203; interviews, Susan (Lombardi) Bickham, Robert Coffey.

15. *Milwaukee Journal*, August 26, 1970; Wiebusch, *Lombardi*, p. 203; interviews, Willie Davis, Bob Skoronski.

16. Interview, Edward Bennett Williams.

17. "Vince Lombardi's Medical Records," unprocessed Robert Coffey Papers, Washington, D.C.; *Palm Beach Post-Times*, October 18, 1975; *Washington Post*, September 3, 1970; interview, Robert Coffey.

18. *Washington Post*, September 4, 1970.

19. *Milwaukee Journal*, September 3, 1970; *Newsweek*, September 14, 1970; *Time*, September 14, 1970; *Washington Post*, September 4, 1970.

20. *Green Bay Press-Gazette*, September 3, 1970; *Milwaukee Journal*, September 3, 1970; *Milwaukee Sentinel*, September 4, 1970; *National Review*, September 22, 1970; *The New York Times*, September 4, 1970; *Washington Post*, September 4, 1970; *Washington Star*, September 3, 1970.

21. *Green Bay Press-Gazette*, September 8, 1970.

22. *Green Bay Press-Gazette*, September 8, 1970; *The New York Times*, September 4 and 6, 1970.

23. *The New York Times*, September 8, 1970; *Washington Post*, September 8, 1970.

24. *Green Bay Press-Gazette*, September 8, 1970; *Milwaukee Sentinel*, September 8, 1970; *Washington Star*, September 8, 1970; *Washington Post*, September 8, 1970.

EPILOGUE

1. *Green Bay Press-Gazette*, December 16, 1970, January 17, 1971, and December 13, 1973; *Milwaukee Journal*, March 1 and May 28, 1971; December 4, 1972; and March 5, 1973; *Milwaukee Sentinel*, December 13, 1973, and February 25, 1974; Red Smith, *To Absent Friends from Red Smith* (New York: Atheneum, 1982), pp. 67–68.

2. *Milwaukee Journal*, July 31, 1971; *National Review*, September 22, 1970; Spiro T. Agnew, "In Defense of Sport," in Stanley D. Eitzen (ed.), *Sport in Contemporary Society: An Anthology*, (New York: St. Martin's Press, 1979), pp. 257–58; James Michener, *Sports in America* (New York: Random House, 1976), p. 380; Benjamin G.

Rader, *American Sports: From the Age of Folk Games to the Age of Spectators* (Englewood Cliffs, N.J.: Prentice-Hall, 1983), pp. 262–63.

3. *Harper's Bazaar*, January, 1973; Murray Kempton, "Jock-Sniffing," *The New York Review of Books*, February 11, 1971, p. 35.

4. Kempton, "Jock-Sniffing," p. 34; Jerry Kramer (ed.), *Lombardi: Winning Is the Only Thing* (New York: World Publishing Company, 1970), p. 122; Robert Lipsyte, *SportsWorld: An American Dreamland* (New York: Quadrangle/The New York Times Book Co., 1975), pp. 56–57; Michael Novak, *The Joy of Sports* (New York: Basic Books, Inc., 1976), p. 90; John Underwood, *The Death of an American Game* (Boston: Little, Brown and Co., 1979), p. 58; one confidential interview.

5. Michener, *Sports in America*, p. 380; Novak, *Joy of Sports*, pp. 84–89; Rader, *American Sports*, pp. 262–63; Theodore H. White, *Breach of Faith: The Fall of Richard Nixon* (New York: Dell Publishing Co., 1975), pp. 199–200.

6. Elliot Aronson, *The Social Animal*, 2nd ed. (San Francisco: W. H. Freeman and Co., 1976), pp. 153–54; Michener, *Sports in America*, pp. 421–23, 440.

7. Lipsyte, *SportsWorld*, p. 54; Michener, *Sports in America*, p. 440; Underwood, *Death of an American Game*, pp. 68–69.

8. Phil Bengtson and Todd Hunt, *Packer Dynasty* (Garden City, N.Y.: Doubleday & Company, 1969), p. 202; Neil D. Isaacs, *Jock Culture U.S.A.* (New York: W. W. Norton & Company, 1978), p. 108; Lipsyte, *SportsWorld*, p. 54.

9. *Milwaukee Sentinel*, December 23, 1972; W. C. Heinz, *Once They Heard the Cheers* (Garden City, N.Y.: Doubleday & Company, 1979), p. 292; interview, Wellington Mara.

10. Novak, *Joy of Sports*, p. 31.

11. Gary Cartwright, "The Unlikely Vincification of Sonny Jurgensen," *Life*, October 24, 1969, p. 48; William O'Neill, *Coming Apart: An Informal History of America in the 1960's* (Chicago: Quadrangle, 1971), p. 230.

12. *Green Bay Press-Gazette*, January 17, 1971; *Milwaukee Journal*, March 1, 1971; Dick Schaap, "How Lionel Aldridge Defeated Mental Illness," *Parade Magazine*, March 1, 1987, pp. 8, 9; Heinz, *Once They Heard the Cheers*, p. 291; Kramer, *Lombardi: Winning*, p. 63; Jerry Kramer (with Dick Schaap), *Distant Replay* (New York: G. P. Putnam's Sons, 1985), pp. 40, 72, 166, 170, 232.

Sources

MANUSCRIPTS

My primary research goal was to locate and use all important manuscript materials related to Lombardi. The goal was only partially achieved since most of Lombardi's correspondence appears to have been lost. This deficiency is not crippling, however, because he was not a man of letters, and there are indications that his correspondence was not of great significance to a biographer.

All the manuscript collections I used were unprocessed or only partially processed. Most valuable were the family's papers held by Marie Lombardi. After her death in 1981, her children, Vince, Jr., and Susan, divided the collection. I studied the Vince Lombardi, Jr., Papers at Vince, Jr.'s, home in Bloomfield Hills, Michigan, and the Susan (Lombardi) Bickham Papers at her home in Plantation, Florida. Another valuable collection, the Fordham University Papers (New York), contain important newspaper clipping files and Vince's educational records. The United States Military Academy Papers (West Point, New York) shed light on the five years Vince coached at West Point. The Reverend Timothy Moore Papers (Englewood, New Jersey) were valuable for all aspects of Vince's life, particularly the years he worked at St. Cecilia High School.

Sources

Some important information was found in the Reverend Dennis Burke Papers (De Pere, Wisconsin); Cathedral Preparatory Seminary Papers (Brooklyn, New York); Robert Coffey Papers (Washington, D.C.); Tim Cohane Papers (Watertown, Massachusetts); Roger Fay Papers (Bergenfield, New Jersey); *Green Bay Press-Gazette* Papers (Green Bay, Wisconsin); W. C. Heinz Papers (Dorset, Vermont); Ruth McKloskey Papers (Green Bay, Wisconsin); Joe McPartland Papers (Norwood, New Jersey); Russell Reeder Papers (Garrison, New York); and the Saint Francis Preparatory School Papers (Fresh Meadows, New York). Several individuals sent me their collections for photocopying.

BOOKS AND ARTICLES

I studied 150 books and articles for this biography, including works on Italians, New York, politics, sports, football, specific football teams, reminiscences of friends, coaches, and players, plus Vince's own published thoughts. There is no need to mention them all here. Readers should consult footnote citations for the specific sources used. What follows are the most significant and relevant sources about Vince.

Two books of memoirs with Lombardi as a primary focus are especially rewarding. Both were critically acclaimed and popular best sellers. Vince Lombardi (with W. C. Heinz), *Run to Daylight* (New York: Grosset & Dunlap, 1963), provided unique insight into the way Lombardi prepared his players for a game. The best portions are Lombardi's analysis of his players—their strengths and weaknesses as human beings. Jerry Kramer, *Instant Replay* (New York: The New American Library, 1968), furnished an original behind-the-scenes glimpse of pro football. Kramer, the right guard for Lombardi's Green Bay Packers, kept a diary of the 1967 season and recorded his feelings as his coach bullied, maligned, mothered, inspired, and loved the players.

No major biography of Vince exists. A brief, early one is Robert Wells, *Lombardi: His Life and Times* (Madison: Wisconsin House, LTD, 1971). Three similar books provide important, edited excerpts of interviews with persons who knew Lombardi. They are George Flynn (ed.), *The Vince Lombardi Scrapbook* (New York: Grosset & Dunlap, 1976); Jerry Kramer (ed.), *Lombardi: Winning Is the Only Thing* (New York: World Publishing Company, 1970); and John Wiebusch (ed.), *Lombardi* (Chicago: Follett Publishing Co., 1971).

Scores of former players described their careers under Vince. The most useful reminiscences are Larry Brown (with William Gildea), *I'll Always*

Get Up (New York: Simon and Schuster, 1973); Paul Hornung (with Al Silverman), *Football and the Single Man* (Garden City, N.Y.: Doubleday & Company, 1965); Ray Nitschke (as told to Robert Wells), *Mean on Sunday: The Autobiography of Ray Nitschke* (Garden City, N.Y.: Doubleday & Company, 1973); and Bart Starr and John Wiebusch, *A Perspective on Victory* (Chicago: Follett Publishing Co., 1972).

Phil Bengtson and Todd Hunt, *Packer Dynasty* (Garden City, N.Y.: Doubleday & Company, 1969), describes Bengtson's view of his boss. Howard Cosell, *Cosell* (Chicago: Playboy Press, 1973), devotes an insightful chapter to Vince. Tim Cohane, *Bypaths of Glory* (New York: Harper and Row, 1963), contains important information from Vince's long-time friend. Art Daley and Jack Yuenger (eds.), *The Lombardi Era of the Green Bay Packers* (Milwaukee: Inland Press, 1968), is a good, brief survey of Vince's career with the Packers. Tom Dowling, *Coach: A Season with Lombardi* (New York: W. W. Norton, 1970), is a sprightly written, detailed account of Vince's 1969 season with the Washington Redskins. Gerald Eskenazi, *There Were Giants in Those Days* (New York: Grosset & Dunlap, 1976), is the best study of the New York Giants. George Flynn (ed.), *Vince Lombardi on Football*, 2 vols. (Greenwich, Conn.: New York Graphic Society Ltd. and Wallynn, Inc., 1973), explains some of Vince's specific coaching methods. Chuck Johnson, *The Green Bay Packers* (New York: Thomas Nelson and Sons, 1961), covers the history of the Packers and Vince's early years with the team. Jerry Kramer (with Dick Schaap), *Jerry Kramer's Farewell to Football* (New York: Bantam Books, 1969), is autobiographical but not nearly as insightful as *Instant Replay*. Jerry Kramer (with Dick Schaap), *Distant Replay* (New York: G. P. Putnam's Sons, 1985), takes an endearing, nostalgic look at Vince and updates the lives of some of the Packers who played for him. George Plimpton, *One More July: A Football Dialogue with Bill Curry* (New York: Harper and Row, 1977), has a mostly critical section about Vince from the view of a former player. Al Silverman (ed.), *Lombardi* (New York: Macfadden-Bartell Corp., 1970), surveys Vince's life. John Torinus, *The Packer Legend: An Inside Look* (Neshkoro, Wis.: Laranmark Press, 1982), views Vince and the Packers from the vantage point of a veteran member of the Packers' executive committee.

Important articles on Vince include Joe Donnelly, "Whipcracker of the Packers," *Sport* (January 1962); W. C. Heinz, "I Miss the Fire on Sunday," *Life* (September 27, 1968); Richard Schickel, "On Pro Football," *Commentary* (January 1969); and Leonard Shecter, "The Toughest Man in Pro Football," *Esquire* (January 1968). Vince Lom-

Sources

bardi (with Tim Cohane), "Why the Pros Play Better Football," *Look* (October 24, 1961), presents some of Vince's views on football. Two articles in *Look* in 1967 update *Run to Daylight:* Vincent Lombardi and W. C. Heinz, "A Game for Madmen," *Look* (September 5, 1967) and "Secrets of Winning Football," *Look* (September 19, 1967).

NEWSPAPERS AND PERIODICALS

Research into newspapers proved exceptionally time-consuming, but the results were indispensable. Those newspapers studied comprehensively were *Arcade* (St. Cecilia High School student newspaper, 1941–44), *Bergen Evening Record* (1939–47), *Cathedral Annual* (Cathedral Preparatory Seminary yearbook, 1930–32), *Englewood Press* (1939–47), *Fordham Ram* (Fordham University student newspaper, 1933–37, 1947–49), *Green Bay Press-Gazette* (1958–70), *Maroon* (Fordham University yearbook, 1934–37, 1947–49), *Milwaukee Journal* (1958–70), *Milwaukee Sentinel* (1962–70), *The New York Times* 1932, 1937–41, 1951, 1954–56, 1962–70), *The Pointer* (USMA student newspaper, 1949–53), *Sanfran* (Saint Francis Preparatory School, yearbook 1933), *Silverian* (St. Cecilia High School yearbook, 1940–47), *Washington Post* (1969–70), and the *Washington Star* (1969–70).

I also discovered useful information through selective research into many other newspapers. (Sometimes the information was located in the various clipping files I studied). Among them were the *Appleton Post Crescent* (1980, 1983), *Chicago Daily News* (1970), *Chicago Sun-Times* (1968), *Chicago Today* (1970), *Chicago Tribune* (1970), *Dallas Times-Herald* (1966), *Dayton [Ohio] Daily News* (1970), *Detroit Free Press* (1952), *The Detroit News* (1965), *The Football News* (1970), *The Green Bay Catholic Compass* (1982), *Janesville Gazette* (1966, 1969–70), *The [London] Sunday Times* (1968), *Long Island Star Journal* (1958), *Los Angeles Times* (1967), *Miami Herald* (1973), *The National Observer* (1962), *Newark Evening News* (1956), *New Haven Register* (1969), *The [New] Jersey Journal* (1966), *Newsday* (1968–70), *New York Daily News* (1959, 1970), *New York Herald Tribune* (1952, 1959, 1960, 1964), *New York Journal-American* (1961), *New York Mirror* (1958), *New York Post* (1968), *New York Sunday News* (1956), *New York World-Telegram and Sun* (1958), *Philadelphia Bulletin* (1967, 1968), *Philadelphia Daily News* (1968), *Philadelphia Inquirer* (1968), *The Sporting News* (1950, 1969), and *The Wall Street Journal* (1968).

I also found significant material in the national periodicals *Commentary, Esquire, Fortune, Life, Look, Newsweek, The New Yorker Sport, Sports Illustrated,* and *Time.*

INTERVIEWS

Valuable, intimate material on Vince's life was gathered in interviews with 204 persons. One quarter of them were personal interviews; three quarters were telephone interviews. A few interviews were brief; some persons were interviewed at length or more than once. Almost all the interviews were tape-recorded. All the taped interviews are in my possession, and, at some future date, I intend to donate them to an historical depository. I interviewed the following persons:

Allen, Gerry	Carley, David
Amen, Paul	Carley, James
Anderson, Jackie	Carpenter, Lew
Anderson, Lewis	Clare, Kenneth
Atkinson, Jerry	Cochran, John
Austin, Bill	Coffey, Robert
Bachmann, Dorothy	Cohane, Tim
Bart (formerly Babartsky), Al	Conerly, Charlie
Bengtson, Phil	Corcoran, William
Best, Patrick	Cowles, Frank
Bickham, Susan (Lombardi)	Crane, Donald
Bilotti, Ray	Crane, John
Blaik, Earl	Crowley, Jim
Blaik, Robert	Cruice, Walter
Blindauer, Howard	Daley, Art
Bollinger, Charles	Danowski, Ed
Bourguignon, Lois	Davis, Willie
Bowman, Ken	DeFilippo, Lou
Bratkowski, Zeke	DeGasperis, John
Breslin, Ed	Della Torre, Tom
Breslin, William	Denlinger, Kenneth
Brown, Allen	Devore, Hugh
Brusky, Eugene	Dickson, George
Burke, Dennis	Dietzel, Paul
Canadeo, Ruth	Doheny, Richard
Canadeo, Tony	Druze, John

Sources

Duggan, James
Egidio, Nick
Epps, Robert
Fay, Martin
Fay, Roger
Fears, Tom
Fetridge, William
Fleming, Marv
Flynn, George
Forester, Bill
Franco, Ed
Freyermuth, Larry
Garrity, Francis
Gentile, Dominic
Gifford, Frank
Gillingham, Gale
Gleason, William
Goettisheim, Joe
Grabowski, Jim
Gregg, Forrest
Guidera, Robert
Haas, Robert
Hanburger, Chris
Hanner, Dave
Hansen, Zenon
Heinrich, Donald
Heinz, W. C.
Higgins, Lawrence
Hodge, Ted
Holmes, Edmund
Howell, Jim Lee
Hyman, Merv
Izenberg, Jerry
Izzo, Buddy
Izzo, Peter
Jeter, Robert
Job, Joe
Johnson, Chuck
Joyce, Pat
Joyce, William
Jurgensen, Sonny

Kavanaugh, Ken
Kenna, Doug
Kern, Daniel
Knafelc, Gary
Kochel, Michael
Koeppler, Jack
Kolman, Ed
Kostelnik, Ron
Kramer, Ron
Krueger, Orrin
Landmark, William
Lane, Chuck
Langan, John
Lansing, James
Lawlor, James
Lea, Bud
Loehlein, Harry
Lombardi, Harold
Lombardi, Jill
Lombardi, Joe
Lombardi, Marie
Lombardi, Vincent, Jr.
Lukac, Andrew
Maggio, Salvator
Manci, Jim
Manuchi, Mike
Mara, Wellington
Martinkovic, John
Masters, Norm
Mazzoleni, Paul
McCrane, Joseph
McGettrick, William
McHan, Lamar
McIlhenny, Don
McKloskey, Ruth
McNally, Vince
McPartland, Joseph
Meilinger, Steve
Miller, Thomas
Moon, John
Moore, Kenneth

Moore, Timothy
Moret, Sid
Morgan, Tom
Mulrey, George
Murphy, Dan
Nellen, James
Nitschke, Ray
O'Hara, William
Olejniczak, Dominic
Ososki, Joseph
Owens, Brig
Palau, Andy
Paquin, Leo
Parins, Robert
Parvin, Clara
Parvin, Edward
Pennell, Dorothy
Pisani, Anthony
Povich, Shirley
Quilici, Al
Reeder, Russell
Remmel, Lee
Richter, Pat
Rickert, Joseph
Ringo, Jim
Roach, John
Robinson, Dave
Roche, Neal
Rollow, Cooper
Rote, Kyle
Ryan, Frank
Ryan, John
Sampson, Al
Sauer, John
Schnelker, Bob
Schoenke, Ray

Schulze, Bob
Scott, Frank
Seidell, Herbert
Siegel, Morris
Skoronski, Robert
Slattery, Dave
Spinks, Jack
Stahlberger, Dick
Starr, Bart
Steffy, Joe
Stephens, Joel
Stroud, Jack
Svare, Harland
Taylor, Jim
Temerario, Tim
Temp, Jim
Toburen, Nelson
Torinus, John
Treml, Al
Trowbridge, Fred, Sr.
Vanderbeek, Elizabeth
VanderSea, Phil
Viracola, Langdon
Wagner, Len
Wallace, William
Walsh, Ray
Warmath, Murray
Webster, Alex
Werner, Madeline (Lombardi)
Wides, Robert
Wietecha, Ray
Williams, Edward Bennett
Wood, Willie
Wycislo, Aloysius
Zeibert, Duke

A final note. As usual in such an enterprise, despite extensive effort, I failed to secure interviews with a few important persons, most notably, Paul Hornung and Pete Rozelle. In each case I compensated by gathering

Sources

their views from books, articles, and previously published interviews. Early in my research, I briefly interviewed Marie Lombardi. I planned to interview her again at length, but she became ill and died in 1981. Fortunately, I discovered a dozen interviews she had earlier granted, usually to newspaper reporters.

I also gathered some important information from personal correspondence with six persons:

Fetridge, William   Moon, John
Heinz, W. C.   Pennell, Dorothy
Kern, Daniel   Ryan, Becket

Index

ABC, 232
Adderley, Herb, 241, 244, 262, 267, 305, 383
Addie, Bob, 363, 371
Agnew, Spiro, 378
Aldridge, Lionel, 222, 246, 251, 295, 382
Allen, George, 275, 299
Ambrose, Stephen, 101
Amen, Paul, 90, 96, 104
American Football Association, 48, 107, 130
American Football League, 212, 213, 219, 222, 327
American Management Association, 201, 203, 298, 318, 319, 362
Anabasis, 32
Anderson, Donny, 15, 176, 212, 220, 222, 223, 236, 291, 295, 299
Aquinas, Saint Thomas, 38
Aronson, Elliot, 379
Atchison, Lewis, 343
Atkinson, Jerry, 135, 212, 288

Atlanta Falcons, 229, 327
Austin, Bill, 116, 117, 140, 216, 218, 342, 346, 353, 358, 373

Babartsky, Al, 43, 46
Baltimore Colts, 126–127, 129, 132, 155, 171, 174, 176, 233, 240, 245, 295, 354–355
Bass, Mike, 349
Baugh, Sammy, 140, 339
Bednarik, Chuck, 156, 162
Bell, Bert, 136, 137, 141, 214
Bengtson, Phil, 15, 140, 146, 172, 182–183, 191, 216, 218, 258, 308, 309; description of, 217; as head coach of Packers, 322–326
Bergen Evening Record, 58, 63, 67, 76
Bettis, Tom, 146, 151
Bickham, Susan. *See* Lombardi, Susan
Bilotti, Duds, 323
Bilotti, Ray, 323
Bilotti's Forvm, 273, 323, 334
Blackbourn, Lisle, 131

Index

Blaik, Earl, 14, 108, 115–116, 128, 136, 161, 163, 181, 188, 193, 194, 197, 240, 272, 307, 328, 378; and coaching at West Point, 86–106; and cribbing incident, 100–103; description of, 88–90; and Lombardi, 191
Blaik, Robert, 100; and Lombardi, 93
Blair, Joe, 352
Blanchard, Felix, 88
Blindauer, Howard, 211
Bollinger, Charles, 59
Borden, Nate, 265
Boston College, 41, 67, 83, 84
Bourguignon, Lois, 273, 275, 280, 332
Bourguignon, Richard, 137–138, 169, 212, 271, 272, 289, 332
Bourland, Roger, 376
Bowman, Ken, 171, 173, 247, 250
Braisher, Dad, 248
Bratkowski, Zeke, 177–178, 179, 233
Breslin, Edward, 128
Brewster Construction Company, 81, 394
Brooklyn Eagles, 48
Brooklyn Prep, 28, 29, 70
Brown, Allen, 250
Brown, Larry, 351–352, 354, 357
Brown, Paul, 108, 135, 136, 137, 141, 196, 226, 272, 298, 309
Brown, Tim, 220–221
Brown, Tom, 295, 349, 383
Brunet, Bob, 347, 358
Brusky, Eugene, 241
Buchwald, Art, 338, 360, 361
Bull Pond, 98
Burke, Dennis, 187, 188, 189, 278, 306
Burns, Jerry, 216

Caffey, Lee Roy, 15, 220, 222; and Lombardi, 259
Cahill, Joe, 87
Canadeo, Ruth, 274
Canadeo, Tony, 137, 196, 212, 213, 271, 277
Cannon, Jimmy, 263
Carlesimo, Peter, 311
Carley, David, 183, 316–318, 319, 321, 358–359
Carley, James, 316, 359
Carpenter, Lew, 141, 220, 342, 347
Carpenter, Rene, 361
Carroll, Gerry, 45

Carroll, Leo, 349
Cartwright, Gary, 110, 352, 368
Cathedral Prep, 26–28, 56
Catholic Church, 20, 22, 36, 93
Cavanaugh, Frank, 40
CBS, 117, 215, 225, 343
Chandler, Don, 15, 172, 174, 220, 326
Chernick, Norman, 310
Chicago Bears, 31, 66, 118, 120, 148, 154, 170–171, 174, 199, 201, 214, 242, 244, 295–296
Chicago Cardinals, 107, 131, 140
Chicago Daily News, 366
Chicago Tribune, 162, 185, 225, 230, 294
Clare, Ken, 64
Claridge, Dennis, 223
Cleveland Browns, 108, 118, 135, 141, 174, 353
Cochran, John, 140, 216, 218, 274
Coffey, Jack, 33, 52, 82, 83, 84, 104
Coffey, Robert, 370–373
Cohane, Tim, 45, 82, 87, 98, 104, 125, 164, 169, 228, 260, 276
Collier, Blanton, 135, 136, 350
Collins, J. Lawton, 101
Coming Apart, 381
Conerly, Charlie, 113–116, 119, 120–122, 147; description of, 111
Cooke, Terence, 333, 376
Cosell, Howard, 195, 225, 228, 232, 299, 382
Costello, Paul, 271
Cox, Ignatius, 39–40, 188
Crane, John, 27, 28
Crowley, Jim, 51, 53, 70, 78, 79, 194, 197; and coaching Fordham, 40–45; description of, 40–41
Cruice, Wally, 216, 217
Currie, Dan, 151, 220, 222
Curry, Bill, 223, 248, 249, 251, 264

Dale, Carroll, 172, 220, 222
Daley, Art, 132, 139, 145, 162, 175, 176, 226–227, 228, 230, 231
Daley, Arthur, 84, 126, 127, 175, 228, 309, 329
Dallas Cowboys, 173, 178, 260, 290, 301–303, 356
Dallas Times-Herald, 180
Danowski, Ed, 74, 77–85, 86; description of, 79
Dartnell Corporation, 313, 315, 316

David, Brother, 32
Davis, Glenn, 88, 89
Davis, Willie, 163, 176, 199, 219, 220, 242, 251, 252, 263, 266, 267, 299, 301, 324, 374, 381, 382; description of, 167
DeFilippo, Lou, 82
DeGasperis, John, 71
Del Greco, Al, 57–58, 61, 63
Democratic party, 316, 320, 321
Denissen, Roman, 155
Denlinger, Ken, 352–353
DeOrsey, C. Leo, 331
DeOrsey, Helen, 331
Detroit Lions, 140, 149, 150, 158, 162–163, 168, 199, 201, 241
Devore, Hugh, 41, 125, 126
Dickson, George, 342, 357, 374
Dietzel, Paul, 90, 92, 95, 96, 97, 104
Doheny, Richard, 64
Doherty, Eddie, 67
Doll, Don, 342
Dowler, Boyd, 158, 159, 179, 248, 301, 303
Dowling, Tom, 354, 363
Draper, Philip, 98
Druze, John, 46

Ed Sullivan Show, The, 13
Eichelberger, Robert, 88
Englewood High School, 55, 61, 64, 70, 73
Englewood Press, 53, 54, 57, 64, 65, 75
Epps, Bobby, 116, 119
Esquire, 296–299
Evashevski, Forrest, 135, 136

Fay, Roger, 53
Fears, Tom, 216, 217, 218
Ferguson, Howard, 142
Fetridge, William, 313–314
Fisher, Pat, 349, 356, 358
Fleming, Marv, 246, 268, 304; and Lombardi, 259
Fordham University, 14, 32, 33, 37, 49, 52, 56, 60, 62, 68, 70, 74, 86, 87, 94, 104, 124, 137, 183, 195, 207, 239, 278; and football, 40–46; founding of, 34; and Lombardi as assistant coach, 77–85
Fordham University Law School, 49–50

Forester, Bill, 143, 146, 149, 164, 222, 262
Four Horsemen, 40
Francis, Joe, 129, 147, 150
Franco, Ed, 43, 44, 45, 85
Froehlich, Harold, 321–322

Galiffa, Arnold, 92, 93
Gannon, Robert, 39, 78, 82, 83, 84
Garrity, Francis, 55, 56, 62
Georgetown University, 370, 372, 377
Gifford, Frank, 110–122, 142, 179, 194, 253, 382; description of, 111, 122–123
Gillingham, Gale, 243, 247
Gillman, Sid, 81, 86, 95, 104, 120, 272
Goettisheim, Joe, 25, 26, 31, 54
Goldberg, Marshall, 44
Grabowski, Jim, 176, 177, 212, 219–220, 232, 262, 291, 295, 306
Graham, Katharine, 361
Graham, Otto, 135, 330, 334, 335, 340, 342, 344, 345
Green, John, 90, 104
Green Bay, Wisconsin, 96, 159; description of, 129–130, 131; and Packers, 210–211
Green Bay Packers, 40, 107–108, 128; finances of, 214–215; history of, 129–132; Lombardi as coach of, 135–152; 1959 season of, 148–150; 1960 season of, 154–157; 1961 season of, 158–161; 1962 season of, 161–164; 1963 season of, 170–171; 1964 season of, 171–172; 1965 season of, 172–175; 1966 season of, 175–180; 1967 season of, 290–305; 1968 season of, 325–326
Green Bay Press-Gazette, 13, 132, 133, 137, 148, 150, 154, 155, 156, 158, 162, 175, 180, 209, 211, 227, 231, 270, 274, 308, 309, 310, 325, 326, 353; and the Packers, 226
Gregg, Forrest, 146, 159, 171, 176, 179, 247, 248, 251, 263, 305; description of, 167; and Lombardi, 256
Grier, Roosevelt, 116, 265
Grimm, Dan, 349
Gross, Milton, 175
Gustafson, Andy, 104

Index

Haas, Robert, 93
Hackensack High School, 74, 75
Halas, George, 66, 107, 136, 137, 147, 170, 178, 199, 201, 238, 272, 273, 275, 296, 309
Hall, Dale, 128, 161
Hanburger, Chris, 340, 348
Hanner, Dave, 15, 146, 154, 216, 222, 249, 273
Harper's Bazaar, 378
Harraway, Charley, 355
Hartnett, Ken, 175, 231–232
Hebel, Everett, 58
Hecker, Norb, 140, 216, 217, 218, 258, 327, 330
Heinrich, Don, 116, 122
Heinz, W. C., 228, 273, 282, 291, 292, 382; and *Run to Daylight*, 165–169
Higgins, Larry, 82
Holmes, Brother Edmund, 32
Horn, Don, 223
Hornung, Paul, 14, 140, 145, 149, 150, 155, 156, 158, 159, 160, 162, 171, 172, 173, 174, 175, 177, 233, 239, 240, 246, 267, 291, 311, 341, 361; description of, 133–134, 167; and Lombardi, 142, 252–255; and suspension for gambling, 169–170
Howell, Jim Lee, 105, 110, 111, 115, 116, 117, 118, 121, 124, 125, 136, 138, 151, 152, 157, 193; description of, 108–109
Howton, Billy, 141, 220
Huff, Sam, 164, 240, 341, 342, 357
Hughes, Charles Evans, 22
Hughes, John, 34
Hutson, Don, 130, 141
Hyland, Bob, 223
Hyman, Merv, 53, 54, 55, 57, 59, 61, 64, 68, 73, 75, 76

Iman, Ken, 250
Inland Steel Corporation, 359
Instant Replay, 14, 292–293; and Lombardi, 324–325
Irving, Frederick, 101, 102, 103
Italian immigrants, 19–22, 24–25
Izenberg, Jerry, 109, 123, 168, 197, 227, 228, 233–234, 260, 298, 352
Izzo, Anthony, 21
Izzo, Dorothy, 31
Izzo, Frank, 21

Izzo, Loretta, 21
Izzo, Matilda. *See* Lombardi, Matilda

Jerome, Brother, 29, 32
Jesuits, 36–37, 137, 207, 320
Jeter, Bob, 267, 268
Johnson, Chuck, 139, 147, 227, 230–231, 234, 280, 281, 304
John XXIII, Pope, 276, 368
Jordan, Henry, 141, 185–186, 220, ~~i~~, 242, 247, 250, 254, 260, 291, 302, 322, 323, 366; description of, 167; humor of, 193
Joyce, Pat, 30, 31, 43, 44
Jurgensen, Sonny, 335, 348, 353, 355, 357; description of, 340–341; and Lombardi, 341–342, 350

Kane, Harry, 29, 30, 40, 197
Kansas City Chiefs, 178, 179, 180, 357
Karras, Alex, 169, 173, 249
Kavanaugh, Ken, 121
Kempton, Murray, 378
Kenna, Doug, 90, 96, 97
Kennedy, Ethel, 360–361
Kennedy, John F., 158, 159, 160, 161, 319, 320, 382
Kennedy, Robert, 319, 320, 321, 328, 362, 366
Kensil, Jim, 178
Keppler, Ernest, 321
Kern, Dan, 32–33
King, Joe, 123–124
King, Milton, 331
Knafelc, Gary, 146, 150, 219, 239, 240, 243, 249–250, 263
Knight, Curt, 354
Kochel, Michael, 42
Koeppler, Jack, 271, 277, 317
Kolman, Ed, 116
Korean War, 96–97
Kostelnik, Ron, 222, 246, 250, 323
Kramer, Jerry, 14, 133, 146, 147, 158, 171, 173, 181, 227, 239–262, 294, 295, 296, 301, 303, 305, 324, 383; description of, 167; and *Instant Replay*, 292–293, 324–325
Kramer, Ron, 193, 220, 253, 336
Krueger, Doris, 270
Krueger, Orrin, 208, 271, 274, 288, 320, 360
Kuechle, Oliver, 134, 135, 137, 147,

149, 150, 159, 162, 168, 185, 220, 337, 340

Lambeau, Earl, 40, 131, 135, 226–227; description of, 130–131
Lambeau Field, 211
Landmark, William, 80
Landry, Tom, 109–110, 112, 124, 127, 136, 290, 303–304
Lane, Chuck, 182–183, 216, 229, 302, 307, 319, 322, 370
Langan, John, 82
Lansing, Jim, 79
Larson, Lloyd, 227, 327
Lawlor, Jim, 34, 35, 36, 47, 49, 197
Lea, Bud, 227, 228, 229, 230, 234, 270
Leahy, Frank, 41, 42, 47, 62, 63, 66 81, 194, 197
Leone, Gene, 87, 98
Levitas, Leah, 274
Life, 368
Lipsyte, Robert, 378, 380
Loehlein, Harry, 93
Lombardi, Claire (sister), 22
Lombardi, Eddie (uncle), 21
Lombardi, Enrico. *See* Lombardi, Harry
Lombardi, Harold (brother), 22, 24, 280
Lombardi, Harry (father), 22, 25, 26, 45, 52, 54, 65, 68, 73, 188, 193, 281, 283, 320; description of, 23–24; early life of, 20, 21
Lombardi, Jill (daughter-in-law), 370
Lombardi, Joe (brother), 22, 62, 65, 278, 370; and Vince Lombardi, 68–69
Lombardi, Madeline (sister), 22, 23, 24, 26, 28, 31
Lombardi, Marie (wife), 14, 43, 47, 52, 55, 73, 125–127, 138, 139, 146, 157, 165, 166, 181–186, 189, 193, 213, 217, 229, 236, 241, 242, 273–275, 278, 284, 287–289, 298, 307, 320, 323, 336, 337, 359–361, 370, 372, 381; description of, 34–35, 279–281; and Vince Lombardi, 54, 278–283, 373, 374
Lombardi, Matilda (mother), 22, 26, 68, 72, 283, 299; description of, 24; early life of, 21–22
Lombardi, Susan (daughter), 54, 127,

139, 186, 187, 189, 236, 288, 33 369, 373; and Vince Lombardi, 286–287, 323
Lombardi, Vincent (grandfather), 20, 21
Lombardi, Vincent T. (Vince): beliefs and values of, 185–209, 348, 362–368; birth of, 22; and black players, 264–268, 347–348; and canoe trip, 98–99; and David Carley, 316–318, 358–359; and Catholic religion, 25, 36, 186–189, 368; and coaching at Fordham, 76, 77–85; and coaching New York Giants, 105, 108–127; and coaching at West Point, 86–106; and college, 33, 34–48; criticism of, 16, 175, 177, 198, 296–299, 325, 336, 378–380; death of, 374; and drug abuse, 247, 419; early life of, 24–26; father's influence on, 23–24; friends and social life of, 54–55, 137–138, 269, 271–277, 287, 360–361; funeral of, 375–376; as general manager, 212–223, 342–343; and golf, 93, 94, 97–98, 196, 277, 306; health of, 306–309; and high school, 29–33; home life of, 278, 287–288, 359–360; illness of, 370–374; and Italian heritage, 24–25, 47, 49, 104, 152, 183–184, 288; and law school, 49–50; and Joe Lombardi, 68–69; and Marie Lombardi, 34–35, 54, 278–283, 373–374; and Susan Lombardi, 286–287, 323; and Vince Lombardi, Jr., 284–286, 360; and media, 123–124, 153–154, 173–174, 178, 214–215, 224–235, 338–339, 352–353; and 1959 season (first year) with Green Bay Packers, 135–152; and 1960 season, 154–157; and 1961 season, 158–161; and 1962 season, 161–164; and 1963 season, 170–171; and 1964 season, 171–172; and 1965 season, 172–175; and 1966 season, 175–180; and 1967 season, 290–305; and 1968 television show, 13–17; personality and character of, 15, 47–48, 71, 91–92, 96, 103, 112–113, 120–121, 122–124, 126, 163, 181–185, 193, 244–245, 269–271, 274–275, 339, 346, 380, 381; and Philadelphia Eagles, 125–126; and

Index

Lombardi, Vincent T. (Vince) (*cont.*)
player preparation and motivation,
70–72, 236–268, 345, 348–349, 357;
and politics, 318–322, 366; praise of,
16, 122, 161, 175, 299–300, 303,
309, 337–339, 375, 376, 377–378,
381–383; and public service and
charity, 277–278, 361–362; and relations with individual players,
113–114, 142, 252–259, 344–352;
retirement of, 14, 305–309, 322–326;
and *Run to Daylight,* 164–169; and
St. Cecilia High School, 51–76; and
Second Effort, 313–316; and
speeches, 53, 139, 143, 195, 196,
201–209, 313, 362, 366–368; and
study for priesthood, 26–28; and
teaching, 59–60, 118–119, 144–145,
237; and trade of Jim Ringo,
221–222; and Vince Lombardi Day,
310–311; and Washington Redskins,
329–358; and women, 274; and youth
culture of 1960s, 201–209, 362–368
Lombardi, Vincent (Vince), Jr. (son),
54, 98, 127, 138, 139, 187, 188,
189, 249, 272, 302, 307–308, 315,
320, 370; and Vince Lombardi,
284–286, 360
Lombardi (film), 13
Long, Bob, 245–246, 262–263, 295,
346, 349, 350, 357
Look, 87, 198, 224, 228, 291
Los Angeles Rams, 15, 120, 149, 150,
155, 163, 173, 174, 176, 177, 214,
251, 299–301, 327, 420
Los Angeles Times, 199, 211, 299
Luckman, Sid, 31, 66

MacAfee, Ken, 116, 117
MacArthur, Douglas, 88, 103, 139, 191
McCarthy, Daniel, 25, 26
McCormack, Mike, 342
McCormack, Tom, 216
McCrane, Joseph, 328
McDonald, Ray, 340, 346
McGee, Max, 142, 143, 175, 179, 182,
222, 248, 249, 250, 252, 264, 296,
311, 325, 361; and Lombardi, 255
McHan, Lamar, 141, 145, 147, 148,
150, 155
McIlhenny, Don, 150
McKelway, John, 338–339
McKloskey, Ruth, 140, 274, 322, 337

McLean, Ray, 131, 132, 134, 135
McNally, Vince, 125–126
McNamee, Frank, 125
McPartland, Frank, 63
McPartland, Guy, 71
MacPherson, Myra, 361
Maggio, Salvator, 29, 30, 31
Maher, Charles, 199–200
Manci, Jim, 184
Manci's Supper Club, 273
Mantell, Roger, 51
Manuche, Mike, 276
Mara, Jack, 105, 108
Mara, Tim, 108
Mara, Wellington, 38, 39, 48, 82, 83,
105, 108, 110, 115–117, 120,
124–127, 135–138, 151–152, 157,
160, 184, 272, 276, 283, 285, 328,
373, 381
Marriot, J. Willard, 364
Marshall, George Preston, 331, 339
Masak, Ron, 314–315
Masters, Norm, 247, 263
Matisi, Tony, 44, 45
Mercein, Chuck, 252, 295, 304, 324,
330, 335, 349, 350
Michener, James, 379
Miller, Tom, 134, 149, 215, 216, 262,
337
Milwaukee Journal, 134, 138, 139,
168, 185, 227, 337
Milwaukee Sentinel, 210, 227, 241,
318, 327
Minnesota Vikings, 294
Mischak, Robert, 122
Mitchell, Bobby, 340
Modell, Art, 272, 311
Modzelewski, Dick, 116
Molenda, Bo, 26
Moody, Lady Deborah, 22
Moore, Ray, 81
Moore, Timothy, 55, 56, 57, 60, 61,
65, 72, 74, 75, 81, 188, 373
Moore, Tom, 171, 222, 233
Morgan, Tom, 64
Mori, Gene, 328
Morris, Paul, 25
Mullin, Willard, 98
Mulqueen, Harold, 35–36
Mulrey, George, 46
Murphy, Jimmy, 83
Murray, Jim, 159, 211, 269, 299–
300

Namath, Joe, 222, 365
Nellen, James, 169, 245, 271, 272
Nelson, Gaylord, 316, 321
Newark Star Ledger, 168, 228
New Orleans Saints, 254, 353, 356
Newsweek, 325, 375
New York Daily News, 83, 105, 209
New York Giants, 15, 26, 48, 74, 79,
    81, 151–152, 157, 159, 160, 163,
    164, 172, 199, 214, 265; Lombardi
    as coach of, 105, 108–127, 238–
    239
New York Herald Tribune, 98, 123,
    228
New York Jets, 222, 328, 365
New York Post, 45, 175, 297
New York Sun, 45, 165
New York Times, The, 67, 84, 101,
    126, 175, 208, 228, 233
New York University, 46, 80, 83, 84
New York World-Telegram, 83
New York World-Telegram and Sun, 98,
    105
NFL (National Football League), 48,
    120, 130, 214–215, 294, 371–372;
    history of, 107–108
NFL Films, 14
NFL Players Association, 311–312
Nicklaus, Jack, 277
Nitschke, Ray, 158, 159, 160, 174,
    219, 291, 294, 295, 300, 301, 307;
    and Lombardi, 257–259
Nixon, Richard, 320, 321, 335, 362,
    364, 365, 375, 376, 377, 379
Notre Dame, University of. *See* Univer-
    sity of Notre Dame

Oakland Raiders, 304–305
O'Brien, Kevin, 82, 83, 84
O'Hara, William, 364
Olejniczak, Dominic, 134, 135, 136,
    137, 139, 151, 152, 212, 213–214,
    332–334
Olsen, Jack, 268
Oneida Golf and Riding Club, 196,
    277, 278, 282, 308, 315, 369
O'Neill, William, 381, 382
Owen, Steve, 105, 108, 111, 112
Owens, Brig, 348

Palau, Andy, 51, 52, 53, 55, 56, 57,
    60, 61; description of, 52; and rela-
    tionship with Lombardi, 52–53

Paper Lion, 312
Paquin, Leo, 38, 39, 45, 47, 66, 84;
    and assessment of Lombardi, 48
Parilli, Babe, 129, 148
Parthenian Sodality, 36
Peppler, Pat, 261
Pfeifer, Rudy, 51
Philadelphia Eagles, 120, 125, 137,
    155–156, 162, 220–221, 328, 356
Pierce, Nat, 43, 45, 46, 51
Pisani, Anthony, 128, 160, 275, 276
Pitts, Elijah, 177, 233, 246, 254, 295
Pittsburgh, University of. *See* Univer-
    sity of Pittsburgh
Pittsburgh Steelers, 154
Planitz, Arthur, 34
Planitz, Marie. *See* Lombardi, Marie
Povich, Shirley, 354, 355, 375
Prentice-Hall, 164, 169
Price, Eddie, 113, 121
Promuto, Vince, 344, 345, 346, 358
Proski, John, 216
Public Facilities Associates, 316–318,
    358

Quilici, Al, 71
Quinlan, Bill, 141, 142, 220, 222
Quinn, Brother, 46

Reeder, Russell, 96, 98, 99
Reeder, Russell, III, 98–99
Reeves, Dan, 275, 327
Remmel, Lee, 154, 209, 326, 337
Resta, George, 370
Resurrection Church, 186–187, 310
Rice, Grantland, 40, 196
Richter, Pat, 344–345
Riger, Robert, 168, 169
Ringo, Jim, 134, 141, 142, 171, 220,
    246, 264; trade of, 221–222
Roach, John, 264
Roberts, Flea, 348, 358
Robinson, Dave, 222, 248, 266, 267
Robustelli, Andy, 116
Roche, Neal, 59–60, 62
Rockne, Knute, 40, 130
Rollow, Cooper, 162, 185, 230, 294
Ronzani, Gene, 131
Rooney, Art, 272
Rosenthal, Harold, 123
Rote, Kyle, 110, 112, 114, 115, 116,
    119, 122; description of, 111
Rote, Tobin, 148

Index

Rozelle, Pete, 14, 169, 170, 193, 200, 215, 327, 331, 333, 365
Run to Daylight, 164–169, 183, 201, 224, 236, 241, 291
Ryan, Frank, 350
Ryan, John, 127–128, 285

Sabol, Ed, 14, 16
St. Cecilia High School, 15, 50, 80, 82, 94, 137, 166, 278; and Lombardi, 51–76
St. Francis Prep, 29–32, 40, 56
St. Louis Cardinals, 172, 246, 354
St. Mark's Church, 25; school, 26
St. Mary's College, 40, 43, 45, 47, 70
St. Norbert College, 142, 186, 187, 278
St. Thomas College, 285, 286
St. Willebrord's Church, 186
Sampson, Al, 225–226
Sanders, Henry, 197
Sanfran, 31, 32
San Francisco, University of. *See* University of San Francisco
San Francisco 49ers, 140, 149, 155, 174, 326
Saturday Evening Post, The, 231
Sauer, George, 378
Sauer, John, 90, 91, 92, 104
Sayers, Gale, 177, 199
Schaap, Dick, 231, 292, 293
Schnelker, Bob, 116, 118, 216, 218, 285, 326
Schoenke, Ray, 346, 347, 350–351
Scholasticism, 38–40, 188, 207–208
Scholz Homes, 358–359
Schramm, Tex, 282, 331
Schulze, Bob, 187–188, 232, 235
Scott, Frank, 313
Scott, Ray, 227
Second Effort, 313–316, 356
Seidell, Herbert, 82, 85
Seven Blocks of Granite (Fordham line), 45–46, 51, 52, 87, 99
Shaughnessy, Clark, 66
Shecter, Len; and criticism of Lombardi, 296–299, 300, 303
Sheepshead Bay, Brooklyn, 21–22, 24, 25
Sherman, Allie, 105, 157
Siegel, Morris, 353
Skoronski, Bob, 143, 171, 244, 262, 291, 301, 374

Slattery, Dave, 366, 370
Smith, Jerry, 340, 345, 374
Smith, Rankin, 327
Smith, Red, 78, 89, 102, 132, 154, 155, 156, 164, 175, 180, 299, 326, 375
Spalding, William, 187
Spinks, Jack, 265
Sports Broadcasting Act, 214–215
Sports Illustrated, 117, 161, 183, 231, 268, 274, 339, 343, 379
Stann, Francis, 340
Starr, Bart, 14, 129, 142, 143, 146, 150, 154, 155, 160, 163, 171–177, 191, 210, 219, 225, 233, 237–240, 243, 246–248, 263, 264, 267, 281, 294, 301, 303, 308, 324, 337, 342, 374, 382; description of, 147–148, 166–167; and Lombardi, 255–256
Stathas, Jake, 271, 311
Stone, Pat, 336, 342
Stram, Hank, 357
Stroud, Jack, 116, 119, 121, 122, 124
Sullivan, Bill, 374
Super Bowl I, 178–180
Super Bowl II, 304–305
Super Bowl IV, 357
Svare, Harland, 116, 342, 345, 346, 357
Swiacki, Bill, 115

Taylor, Charley, 340
Taylor, Jim, 144, 156, 163–164, 172–175, 177, 219, 220, 227, 231–233, 246, 290–291, 306, 309, 336, 343; description of, 167; and Lombardi, 256–257
Temerario, Tim, 342
Temp, Jim, 147
Theofiledes, Harry, 344
Thurston, Fred, 141, 163, 171, 173, 220, 250, 294
Time, 156, 162, 177, 325, 375
Toburen, Nelson, 217, 260–261
Toomey, Bill, 195
Torinus, John, 280, 334
Treml, Al, 215
Triplett, Mel, 116, 117, 119, 121–122
Trowbridge, Fred, Sr., 136, 151, 212, 213, 308
Tunnell, Emlen, 115, 116, 141, 144, 150, 154, 251, 258, 261, 262, 265, 268
Turnbull, Andrew, 226

Unitas, John, 127, 177, 260
University of Notre Dame, 40, 41, 63, 66, 90, 91, 124, 130, 327
University of Pittsburgh, 44, 45, 74
University of San Francisco, 74

Vainisi, Jack, 133, 135
Van Brocklin, Norm, 126, 156
Van Dyk, Ted, 366
Vietnam War, 364, 379
Vince Lombardi Day, 310–311
Vincent T. Lombardi Cancer Research Center, 377
Viracola, Langdon, 83, 84, 85
Voss, Lloyd, 223

Wagner, Len, 162, 180, 227, 270, 309, 353
Wallace, William, 120, 233
Walsh, Lawrence, 82
Walsh, Ray, 115
Ward, Gene, 209
Warmath, Murray, 86, 89, 90, 92, 94, 95, 97, 104
Washington, Leroy, 362
Washington Post, 352, 354, 361, 363, 364, 371, 375
Washington Redskins, 48, 66, 147, 150, 330–336, 372–373; history of, 339

Washington Star, 340, 343, 353, 375
Watergate scandal, 379
Webster, Alex, 116, 117, 122
Werblin, David, 328
West Point, 15, 37, 38, 81, 85, 110, 112, 118, 124, 128, 161; and cribbing incident, 100–103; Lombardi's coaching at, 86–106, 115–116
Whitefield, A. D., 340
Whittenton, Jesse, 160
Wietecha, Ray, 116, 119, 122, 216
Williams, Edward Bennett, 321, 329–335, 338, 345, 353, 357, 360, 364, 368, 371, 374
Williams, Joe, 83
Williams, Travis, 15, 295, 301
Wilmington, Delaware, Clippers, 48
Wilson, Ben, 295
Woessner, Bob, 274, 309
Wojciechowicz, Alex, 44, 46
Wolman, Jerry, 328
Wood, Willie, 264, 266, 267, 268
Woodward, Stanley, 98
Wright, Steve, 198
Wycislo, Aloysius, 188, 373

Xenophon, 32

Zeibert, Duke, 335, 339